THE SECRET POLICE AND THE SOVIET SYSTEM

PITT SERIES IN RUSSIAN AND EAST EUROPEAN STUDIES
JONATHAN HARRIS, EDITOR

KRITIKA HISTORICAL STUDIES

THE SECRET POLICE & THE SOVIET SYSTEM

NEW ARCHIVAL INVESTIGATIONS

EDITED BY MICHAEL DAVID-FOX

UNIVERSITY OF PITTSBURGH PRESS

Published by the University of Pittsburgh Press, Pittsburgh, Pa., 15260
Manufactured in the United States of America
Printed on acid-free paper
10 9 8 7 6 5 4 3 2 1

Cataloging-in-Publication data is available from the Library of Congress

ISBN 13: 978-0-8229-4802-5
ISBN 10: 0-8229-4802-8

Cover design: Joel W. Coggins

Contents

List of Abbreviations

AK—Home Army
AKhChU—Association of Artists of Red Ukraine
AKhRR—Association of Artists of Revolutionary Russia
ARMU—Association of Revolutionary Art of Ukraine
ASSR—Associated Soviet Socialist Republic
CC—Central Committee
CDU—Christian Democratic Party (Germany)
Cheka, VChK—All-Russian Extraordinary Commission to Combat Counterrevolution and Sabotage, origin of the term "chekist," which refers to any officer of the secret police
CIA—Central Intelligence Agency
CPSU—Communist Party of the Soviet Union (1952–1991)
DIA—Defense Intelligence Agency
DON—cases of operative surveillance
DOP—cases of operative verification
EC(b)P—Estonian Communist Party (Bolshevik), later ECP
ESSR—Estonian Soviet Socialist Republic
FSB—Federal Security Service
GDR—German Democratic Republic
GKO—State Committee on Defense
GPU, OGPU—State Political Administration/Unified State Political Administration
Gulag (GULag)—Main Administration of Corrective Labor Camps and Colonies
GUMIMZ—Main Administration for Soviet Property Abroad
ITK—corrective labor colony
KGB, MGB—Committee for State Security, Ministry of State Security
Komsomol—Communist Youth Organization
KPD—Communist Party of Germany
KSČ—Communist Party of Czechoslovakia
KSPO—Red Banner Western Border District

LEF—Left Front of the Arts
LSSR MGB—Ministry of State Security, Lithuanian Soviet Socialist
    Republic
MBP—Ministry of Public Security (Poland)
MOSKh—Moscow Regional Union of Artists, Moscow Artists' Union
MVSU—Ministry of Internal Affairs of Ukraine
narsud—people's court
NEP—New Economic Policy
NKIu—People's Commissariat of Justice
NKVD, MVD—People's Commissariat of Internal Affairs, Ministry of Inter-
    nal Affairs
OCHO—Secret Police Detachment
OITK—Department of Corrective Labor Camps and Colonies
OSMU—Association of Contemporary Masters of Ukraine
PZPR—Polish United Workers' Party
RABIS—Professional Union of Art Workers
RKP(b)—Russian Communist Party (Bolshevik) (1918–1925)
RSFSR—Russian Soviet Federated Socialist Republic
SANO—medical-sanitation departments (of the Gulag)
SBU—Security Service of Ukraine
SED—Socialist Unity Party (Germany)
SMERSH—Smert' shpionam (Death to Spies)
Sovnarkom—Council of People's Commissars
SPD—Social Democratic Party (Germany)
spetsposelentsy—special settlers
StB—State Security (Czechoslovakia)
SVR—Foreign Intelligence Service
SVU—Union for the Liberation of Ukraine
TSC—Tallinn State Conservatory
TsIK SSSR—Central Executive Committee of the USSR
UC—Union of Composers
UITLK—Administration for Corrective Labor Camps and Colonies
ULLP—Administration of Forestry Camps
URO-OURZ—allocation-distribution departments (of the Gulag)
VKP(b)—All-Union Communist Party (Bolshevik) (1925–1952)
VTsIK—All-Russian/All-Union Central Executive Committee
zek—prisoner

Place names ending in *-lag* (Astrakhanlag, Dmitlag, Siblag, etc.) refer to indi-
    vidual camps within the Gulag system.

THE SECRET POLICE AND THE SOVIET SYSTEM

Into and Beyond the Stalinist Model of Secret Policing

Michael David-Fox

ON 20 DECEMBER 1917, FELIKS DZERZHINSKII WAS APPOINTED TO THE ALL-Russian Extraordinary Commission to Combat Counterrevolution and Sabotage (VChK). On 19 August 1991, a state of emergency was declared after Vladimir Kriuchkov, chairman of the Committee for State Security (KGB), convened other leaders of the abortive August coup in a KGB guesthouse in Moscow. The first date is connected to the birth of the new Soviet regime in 1917, the second to its collapse in 1991, pointing to the outsized role the secret police played in the history of communism at home and abroad. The institution's well-known acronyms—Cheka or VChK, GPU, OGPU, NKVD, NKGB, MGB, MVD, KGB—changed regularly. Its notoriety did not. Over the decades, historians, journalists, and citizens collected a wealth of detailed knowledge and documentation. Windows into its secretive and classified world have been opened in several bodies of literature that have achieved empirical depth and, in a number of cases, conceptual sophistication. At the same time, the state of our knowledge remains highly uneven.

The greatest depth has been concentrated in a group of topics that coincided with the more general "archival revolution" in the decade and a half after 1991 and that built on older literatures. The topics that commanded by far the most intense historical and political scrutiny involved the role of the secret police in Bolshevik political violence and the crimes of Stalinism. Along the way, we have gained a strong overall grasp of the secret police's institutional reorganizations and the biographies of its leading personnel.[1] One strand of inquiry focused on the Cheka in the red terror starting in 1918.[2] Another was connected to the creation circa 1930 of the empire of forced labor that became known as the Gulag archipelago.[3] The greatest number of investigations concerned the NKVD's role as Iosif Stalin's tool during collectivization, the Great Terror, and other repressive operations throughout the Soviet period.[4] Less voluminous, yet important as prisms into the crucial function of the secret police in information gathering, have been the literatures on domestic surveillance and, more recently, on disinformation and late Soviet "active measures."[5] It should also be noted that numerous annotated collections of documents declassified after 1991 have been published on topics that command broad political and public interest, such as the KGB files on Sakharov and Solzhenitsyn.[6]

From today's perspective, we can perceive that the first post-1991 archival-historiographical "opening" in the study of the Soviet secret police was not only partial in its focus but largely domestic or national in its preoccupations, as opposed to international, comparative, or transnational.[7] As all-Union Moscow-centrism was supplemented by new national historiographies in the Baltics, Ukraine, and other newly independent states, scholarly fragmentation followed geopolitical division. Speaking more broadly about the communist "second world," there have certainly been studies in several languages about, for example, cooperation among Soviet and East European security services. But East European archival openings, in particular the intensive study of the East German Stasi, followed different dynamics and directions from the archival revolution in Russia, Ukraine, the Baltics, and other post-Soviet countries. They appear to have experienced cross-fertilization with Soviet studies less in terms of broadly conceptual or comparative interactions than in the footnotes of specialized investigations.[8]

In terms of the secret police on the international stage, quite a lot has been published over the years on Soviet espionage. Works on this topic include frequently cited memoirs and much-discussed documents smuggled out by émigré defectors.[9] Collections of online documents have been made available by the National Security Archive, the Cold War International History Project, and, for example, online portals with documents from former KGB archives in Lithuania and Ukraine. The literature on espionage and intelligence is also rife with works of mixed scholarly value or outright sensationalism. As with the study of Soviet foreign policy in general but even more so, the study of intelligence and espionage proceeded without the extensive archival access that became the norm for other parts of the party-state.[10] The revival of the Soviet public cult of state security in Putin's Russia and the memory wars across Eastern Europe have also led to large-scale publication of genuine yet selectively arranged documentary collections that, because of their slant, represent erudite or quasi-scholarly outposts of information warfare.[11] Even so, documentary publications from the Lubianka archive have included genuinely valuable materials, even as they remain silent about selection criteria and what remains unpublished.[12]

In comparative terms, however, the great deal we learned about the security organs in the wake of the Soviet collapse amounts to relatively little, given the depth of what we know about the Party and the state. The secret police was from 1922 de jure subordinate to the Communist Party, and in the Stalin period it was de facto subordinate to the general secretary.[13] It was important enough at the center and at every level of the power hierarchy, however, that alongside the Party and the state it can be considered as one of the major institutional pillars of Soviet power. Its centrality to the consolidation of the new regime after 1917 and to Stalinism and its role in terror and forced labor were part of "extraordinary measures" later condemned as "excesses." But even though it crystallized in revolution and civil war and represented the tip of the spear in Stalin's "second revolution," the secret police was never just "extraordinary," in the sense of carrying out emergency measures, suspensions of legality, or "states of exception." It also formed a constituent part of the regular, peacetime penal, penitentiary, and policing systems.[14] The secret police commanded its own economic empire spanning forced labor and sensitive, high-priority sectors of the economy. It was deeply invested in the informational ecosystem, media, and information technology not only for policing but to influence political decision making and "social engineering." It had its own elite security and border troops and special role within the military. Its local, regional, and republican-level branches connected it to every level of the continental, multinational state, and its extensive international operations made it a key part of foreign policy and international relations. Finally, given its formidable and intensively cultivated public image and mass networks of informers, it had a profound cultural and social impact. In sum, as one sprawling pillar of Soviet power, the activities and operations of the secret police should be seen not in terms of a small handful of areas connected to repression and espionage but as ranging widely across state and society, politics and culture, information and economics, art and ideology.

In this sense, the secret police clearly remains the branch of the power structure that we know by far the least about. Indeed, how central has it been to practitioners and those training to enter the field? It is fair to say that most mainstream historians working in those areas of twentieth-century Russian and Soviet history at the center of the field's attention in the decades surrounding 1991 did not delve into the history of the secret police as an instructive or crucial frontier for their own research.

If the 1990s marked the beginning of the first major phase in the archival study of the secret police, a cardinally new situation emerged after 2015, when the second phase in the study of the Soviet secret police archives began. On 9 April of that year, as part of a package of legislation on history and memory billed as decommunization, the Ukrainian parliament passed a law opening the country's Soviet-era secret police archives. In small but steady numbers, scholars began traveling to Kyiv. The Ukrainian materials, which contain runs of all-Union documentation from the "center" as well as from a key union republic, could then be added to ongoing work in repositories in the Baltics, where Soviet-era materials date to 1939, and, inter alia, to those in Georgia, where the bulk of the former KGB archive was destroyed by fire and flood in 1991–1992.[15] Students of these materials had the possibility of connecting to growing bodies of scholarship based in the secret police archives of the former Eastern bloc. But the pioneering, often younger scholars who saw the potential of these repositories and joined the stream of scholars gathering material for their own research were not necessarily historians of intelligence history or secret policing per se. Bringing them together to paint a picture of what the new investigations added up to was the motivation behind the 2020 international conference sponsored by the Jacques Rossi Memorial Fund for Gulag Research at Georgetown University that formed the basis for this book.[16]

The second archival period between the 2010s and the Russian invasion of Ukraine in 2022 in certain respects was reminiscent of an earlier time in other parts of Russian/Soviet history when the "archival revolution" in the 1990s began to transform the field. Or, put another way, the opening of these repositories could well be seen as a new phase of that archival revolution, which began in the late 1980s in Moscow and the Russian Soviet Federative Socialist Republic (RSFSR) but by the 2010s had shifted to former union republics that became independent states.

It is characteristic of the present moment that even as new archival sources have opened up because they align with political-historical agendas and archival policies in not so newly independent states, others have been closed down as memory wars and the politicization of history continue apace. Mikhail Nakonechnyi, who used local Gulag archives in his study, has dubbed this an archival counterrevolution. Such reversals, decreasing access, or reclassifications are phenomena present not only in the Russian Federation. For example, the archive of the biggest forced labor camp outside of Russia proper—the once available Karlag archive in Karaganda, Kazakhstan—is now closed.[17]

In that earlier era of archival openings, Russian and Eurasian historians debated the extent to which new perspectives derive from open archives or whether such openings only reinforce preconceived categories of analysis. As scholars justified or modified old positions or forged careers in renamed, newly accessible repositories, the unconventional and skeptical voices at first seemed to have the upper hand. They convincingly argued that the often uninterrogated purpose and structure of the archival repositories themselves, the search for revelations their opening engenders, and the way fields use them to pour old wine into new bottles make the knowledge they create less than revelatory.[18]

These warning voices from the 1990s remain relevant. A significant infusion of new primary sources in and of itself is not sufficient to produce new analysis. If it is a truism that what we make of archives always depends on how we approach and analyze them, however, it is equally the case that in historical scholarship, evidence and interpretation are intertwined in intricate ways. With the hindsight of over three decades of Soviet history in the archival era, it has become clearer that the availability and allure of new sources have served as a potential, often even necessary impetus to widen and refocus our vision.[19]

The details, nuance, and texture that significant in-depth access provides do add up; quantity eventually turns into quality. Along the way, unexpected finds provoke reassessments and unexpected explorations. This volume demonstrates the sheer breadth and scope of the investigations—ranging across politics and ideology, culture and technology, institutions and practices, as well as domestic, transnational, and international history—that talented scholars began to produce once the series of previously classified secret police archives became relatively accessible. The chapters of this book showcase research conducted in former KGB archives in Ukraine, Georgia, Estonia, Latvia, and Lithuania, as well as other secret police archives in Germany, Romania, Poland, Bulgaria, and the Czech Republic. They were produced by a remarkably international cast of scholars, from newly minted PhDs to senior professors from almost a dozen countries.

This introduction explores four areas in which the book's chapters make contributions that are at once empirical and conceptual in the study of the history of the secret police. The first is the internal institutional history of the secret police, about which we still have much to learn, and the long arc of its evolution across the Soviet century. The second, closely related to the first, is the practices of secret policing—methods, operations, approaches, and technologies—that evolved dramatically as the institution changed with the times and the Soviet system itself. A third area has to do with the role of the secret police in the realm of culture—including art, film, photography, information, print media, and technology, all as they intersect with ideology. Along the way, several chapters include transnational and international dimensions, especially in the Soviet Union's "outer empire" in Eastern Europe, suggesting the many benefits in this field of wide-angle, cross-border approaches that do not segregate the domestic and the international in secret police history. Finally, after exploring these innovations, we turn to a well-worn topic crucial to any student of the twentieth century: perpetrators and victims. It will be, however, to suggest that in this case there is some new wine to be poured into an old bottle. Many of the chapters make contributions to more than one of these four areas, and the goal is neither to produce an exhaustive catalogue nor to treat each author's work comprehensively. Rather, I illuminate the synergy running through this curated slice of exciting new archival research, suggesting how in my reading the whole appears greater than the sum of its parts.

INTERNAL EVOLUTION AND INSTITUTIONAL ARC

The creation in 1922 of the little-known, multiagency Special Assembly (Osoboe soveshchanie) explored by Marc Junge, Andrei Savin, and Aleksei Tepliakov is suggestive of consequential institutional twists and turns in the history of the secret police. The Cheka's powers of summary justice and its network of concentration camps in the period of War Communism had been curtailed and partially dismantled. The turn to the New Economic Policy (NEP) involved a partial retreat—economic-social concessions such as the tax in kind and an emphasis on "socialist legality," rerouting Bolshevik agendas into state building and political centralization. Stymied in outright socialist offensive, the Party turned to the "third front" of culture and the pursuit of ideological hegemony. The Special Assembly that came to be dominated by the secret police skirted the legal system not through rough-and-ready summary justice or revolutionary tribunals but rather via the administrative measures of an interagency bureaucracy. Its creation was linked to Vladimir Lenin and Lev Trotsky's determination in 1922 to deport ideologically dissident members of the intelligentsia. But the authors' research into local Ukrainian militia as well as secret police archives shows that in practice the Special Assembly targeted "socially dangerous elements" such as prostitutes, "hooligans," and petty criminals. This extralegal, well-funded bureaucratic body operating under the radar of the legal code, in the authors' interpretation, morphed into a panoply of other special bodies taking "extraordinary measures" administratively during the dislocations of collectivization and the Stalinist 1930s. The authors argue that we must view this lineage as the most important origin of the NKVD's mass operations during the Great Terror, as opposed to a concern circa 1937 with a fifth column in the event of war.[20]

Readers can judge for themselves whether the chapter's argument amplifies as opposed to revises existing interpretations of the Terror.[21] Regardless, it does directly spotlight the institutional interactions between policing and secret policing, judicial and extrajudicial forms of penality. After all, the Commissariat of Justice was also represented on the Special Assembly, and in the reorganization of 1934 the secret police took over the regular militia.

As the chapters of the book provide successive snapshots over the entire life cycle of the Russian Revolution from youth to old age, a duality in the institutional history of the secret police comes into focus. On the one hand, many chapters add to the initial picture painted by Junge, Savin, and Tepliakov: the secret police was deeply embedded in the multiagency party-state. It was one of the most powerful of the octopoid arms of a leviathan organism that was evolving within its broader ecosystem across the very different subperiods of Stalinism and after. On the other hand, the secret police also stood in terrible isolation. Starting in the 1920s, it was empowered at key moments to stand over the Party and the state, and in the late 1930s this became the key institutional mechanism of the Great Terror.

As in any complex bureaucracy, the secret police feuded and fought with rivals; many chapters here show how it also engaged in internal infighting. Mikhail Nakonechnyi's deductions about Gulag mortality statistics were themselves made possible by "poorly researched bureaucratic feuds on the local level of the camp system," as well as the ever-present gulf between top-level officialdom in Moscow and the recipients of its decrees in the far-flung localities. Timothy Blauvelt and David Jishkariani's chapter on Stalinist perpetrators in Georgia during the Great Terror highlights the internal divisiveness and upheaval resulting from Lavrentii Beria's patronage network stretching from Moscow to Tbilisi. The zealous mid-level cadres in Beria's network played a key role in radicalizing the Georgian NKVD and normalizing the use of torture, then became targets in the public prosecution of Beria's group after the secret police chief's ouster and execution in 1953. Molly Pucci's study of the NKVD's role in the Stalinization of the security services of the Eastern bloc centers on a "generational revolution"—the rise of a new cohort with a worldview shaped by the Terror and the fight against fascism—in the export of the institutional culture of the NKVD to Eastern Europe. But this Stalinist model of secret policing could not last, and not only because of the events of 1953 and 1956. It has been argued that the NKVD's much-practiced organizational, indeed professional expertise in efficiently carrying out mass repressions such as the rapid deportation of entire national groups made it the "cutting edge of Soviet high modernism."[22] But despite this gruesome expertise and the all-powerful reputation of the "organs," the Stalinist model was failing dramatically in many key respects.

Emilia Koustova's study of Sovietization and late Stalinism in Lithuania highlights a shift in institutional focus from 1930s-style mass operations, "the traditional model of mass Stalinist repression," toward new yet partial postwar "trends toward more targeted, individual, judicialized repression based on more sophisticated surveillance and information management." The late Stalinist MGB, far from its all-powerful image, was challenged by severe understaffing, wracked by purges and reorganizations, and drowning in paperwork created by an unsustainable mass network of unreliable informers. It is against this backdrop that we should understand the subsequent, post-Stalinist evolution in the KGB's institutional focus and ethos as it struggled to move beyond the Stalinist paradigm. We get insight into this from Edward Cohn's chapter on *profilaktika,* the method of warning potential transgressors as individuals (as opposed to repressing entire categories as groups), in late Soviet Lithuania. This was one key part of a Thaw-era reorientation after the end of mass terror that, as the chapter shows, itself became routinized in the Brezhnev era. An especially illuminating window into the late Soviet KGB is Joshua Sanborn's chapter on the KGB's troubled lurch toward computerization. Sanborn's comparison of computerization under Iurii Andropov's KGB with J. Edgar Hoover's FBI suggests that "the stumbles of the Second Main Directorate were not the result of backwardness in terms of national computer technologies but derived from the special challenges of creating a counterintelligence computer database." As one of the most successful examples of comparative history in the book, Sanborn's material suggests the potential of targeted comparisons in future research.

When we add up all the chapters, what comes into focus is a long institutional arc that, not unlike the Soviet system itself, can be understood as a trajectory to and from the pathologies of Stalinist mass terror.

PRACTICES OF SECRET POLICING

This decades-long institutional evolution to and from the Stalinist model of secret policing, as these chapters also clearly show, was intimately intertwined with the practices of Soviet and Soviet-style secret policing. That was because the Stalinist model crystallized in the period between forced collectivization and mass terror, and it was defined by practices. These were, most notoriously, the sanction of torture during the Great Terror (explored by Blauvelt and Jishkariani) and linking caloric intake and medical treatment to productivity in the Gulag system of slave labor (Nakonechnyi). But there was a panoply of other discrete practices of secret policing associated with the mass repression of entire categories of the population (Junge, Savin, and Tepliakov) via the fabrication of anti-Soviet conspiracies that linked internal and external enemies. That internal-external linkage is such a ubiquitous theme that it is discussed in well over half the chapters ranging across the Soviet period, from Tatiana Vagramenko's exploration of interwar antireligious operations to Douglas Selvage's treatment of active measures against dissidents in the late Soviet years.

While the practices associated with mass repression left a profound impact on the chekist tradition, some of them had roots in the tsarist period or dated to 1918, not 1930 or 1937. Those practices, moreover, hardly shaped all aspects of policing during the entire period between 1929 and 1953. Indeed, a key conceptual difficulty in defining Stalinism is that in many ways it cannot be neatly extracted from Sovietism, and in many ways it was not a coherent phenomenon. Many crucial features of the Stalin period emerged before 1929, and the fundamental structures set up in the 1930s and 1940s survived the death of the *vozhd'*. There were great divergences, moreover, between early and late Stalinism and the different cycles of "socialist offensive" and retrenchment that punctuated and transcended the Stalin period. Even more, in the realm of culture and ideology, there was a major split between the heyday of class-war collectivism in Stalin's "second revolution" and the hierarchical, revolutionary-conservative hybrid of the mature Stalinism that emerged after the mid- to late 1930s.[23] In addition to being lashed to this systemic and evolutionary dynamic, the secret police was a pillar of a regime that intently observed its great-power rivals, represented one distinctive outpost within the international circulation of modern practices, and was itself defined by changing techniques and technologies. Twentieth-century methods of surveillance, organizing and classifying information, managing and centralizing authority and bureaucratic routines, and, of course, contemporary policing were developing rapidly across the decades even as they may have been domesticated in the USSR in distinctive ways.[24]

One set of practices illuminated here might be dubbed "statistical-bureaucratic." Mikhail Nakonechnyi's detective work on "double accounting" in Gulag mortality rates works to establish that Gulag camps and labor colonies released (physically but also "on paper") sick and frequently starving inmates so as to under-report the death rate. His work appears as the opposite of the "gold rush" manner of cherry-picking sensations from the central archives. Rather, Nakonechnyi mined local records, including those of camp procurators and medical files of regional camp administrations, in an effort to recalculate central statistics in light of the "release-to-die" strategy. In his separately published debate with Stephen Wheatcroft and Golfo Alexopoulos about how regular these practices were beyond the worst crisis periods of cuts in provisions and medicine, particularly in 1942–1943, Nakonechnyi confirmed that his approach relied not only on deciphering statistics and improvised, handwritten abbreviations on local paperwork. He was also guided by more general insights into local authorities in the pressure cooker of the Stalinist bureaucracy.[25] They scrambled at once to conform to and to evade Moscow decrees from on high—such as the central NKVD's Order no. 0033 from January 1943, signed by Beria himself, to "conserve and improve the physical capability" of zeks. The documents on death statistics, in Nakonechnyi's words, "reveal an intricate web of conflicting power relations surrounding the mortality of former prisoners at all levels of the bureaucratic ladder," exemplifying "how the Soviet penal bureaucracy operated as a specific stratum within the Stalinist state apparatus."

A range of other practices illuminated in several chapters can be termed "informational-analytical." They have to do not with statistics or paperwork per se but with practices related to classifying enemies and categorizing crimes, both for groups and for individuals. Much of Koustova's chapter on the hunt for "state criminals" in postwar Lithuania, for example, deals with the workings of secret police profiling in the wake of the Sovietization of the Baltics. This brings out the complexity of all the elements that went into profiling enemies: the discussion ranges across surveillance, relations with informers, categories of suspicion and criminality, and construction of the "police identity" of targeted individuals in the files and dossiers. Even as postwar methodologies became more refined in comparison with the mass repressions of the 1930s, Koustova points out, ideological obsessions rampant in the public sphere ran through these clandestine procedures: "A 'hierarchy of enemies' emerged, dominated by parachutists—the most fantasized figure in the police imagination in these western territories, where the reality of conflict" with postwar armed insurgencies "was mixed with phobias and suspicions forged in the pure Stalinist tradition."

Other chapters give insight into interrogations and their role in the compilation of secret police dossiers over many years. Angelina Lucento's chapter on the Ukrainian school of modernist monumental artists known as the Boichukisty shows that the artists' NKVD interrogator in 1936, Solomon Gol'dman, had started to collect compromising evidence against Mykhailo Boichuk and his school a half-decade before, when the Boichukisty reached the height of their influence over the Ukrainization of visual art. Not at all untypically, there was a time lag between the gathering of compromising materials and the persecution of the interrogated. Depositions and interrogations collected over the 1931–1935 period shaped the fabricated case prosecuted in 1936–1937, but that took place in the decidedly different era of the Terror. This phenomenon informs how Lucento reads the case files: it brings into stark relief how the latter round of interrogations took a "surprising and unprecedented turn" in terms of secret police interest in Socialist Realism and the ideology behind the art.

Insight into the gathering and presentation of evidence in a range of other chapters suggests how crucial the linguistic, visual, and technological dimensions of these practices could become. Pucci pays close attention to the language of conspiracy, which had to be translated from the Russian during the Stalinization of East European secret police work. Vagramenko and Cristina Vatulescu, both discussed below, pursue a pioneering angle in decoding the visual language of secret police photography and film. Indeed, even as those chapters highlight practices that also shed light on both secret police record keeping and agents in the field, the techniques they highlight surrounding the injection of political meanings into crime scene photographs and filmic "mug shots" might be classified separately as "aesthetico-representational."

In his chapter on KGB cybernetics, Sanborn shows how computerization was first pushed in the analysis wing of the KGB under Andropov's leadership at the very end of the 1960s. In its first phase, this was mainly to create a more efficient and quickly accessible form of electronic database storage than paper files or superpositional punch cards. But it was also part of Andropov's effort to modernize and bolster the low status and priority placed on "informational-analytical" work. The personnel in newly created, understaffed subdivisions around the country was often female, as opposed to the chekist "field agents who dominated the self-image of the organization."

In terms of those field agents, a final set of practices illuminated in these chapters could be labeled "agent-operational." Erik Scott's chapter, drawing on oversight materials in Kyiv and criminal cases from the Georgian KGB, gives us much insight into the operations of the KGB's Soviet Border Troops along the Black Sea coast. These outsiders—their leadership was overwhelmingly Slavic rather than Transcaucasian, and the rank and file were drafted from the Soviet interior—patrolled and criminalized movement in forbidden border zones separating the Soviet Union from NATO and extending into the waters of the Black Sea. They launched counterintelligence operations in port cities like Batumi and Odessa, seized contraband, put foreigners and especially foreign sailors under surveillance, and monitored their Soviet contacts and sexual misbehavior on shore. Intelligence officers capitalized on the global connections of the bustling ports and international resorts such as Yalta to recruit assets and gather intelligence. The dual nature of these operational practices—involving both perceived dangers and opportunities that either shut down or took advantage of cross-border movement—underpins Scott's overall argument about the Black Sea coast as a unified intelligence landscape encompassing bridges and borders, openings and enclosures.

Cohn's chapter on the KGB's tactic of "prophylaxis" gives insight into the methods and reports of agents who conducted warning conversations with recidivists, dissidents, and other targeted members of the population. The KGB pinned great hopes on the approach as an effective post-Stalinist "pedagogical" measure, and its boosters even invested it with the transformative potential to redeem those engaging in antisocial and anti-Soviet behavior. But in practice, Cohn's examination of the warning chats and post-*profilaktika* surveillance suggests that "KGB officers lacked a strong incentive to provide detailed evidence that offenders had changed their ways." Hopes for a form of secret police-led social engineering more targeted, individualized, and effective than the Stalinist model foundered not only on perfunctory implementation but on many of the targets' late Soviet imperviousness to rehabilitation. The reactions of dissidents, religious believers, and women involved with foreigners, Cohn concludes, "cast doubt on the idea that profilaktika could change the attitudes and worldview of KGB targets whose actions were driven by strong beliefs."

THE SECRET POLICE AS CULTURAL
AND IDEOLOGICAL ACTOR

So-called agent-operational measures involving secret cameras, photographs of crime scenes, and displays of confiscated imagery figure in Vagramenko's chapter on secret police photography from the 1920s to the 1950s. As she discusses, they complemented standard photo lab procedures such as mug shots and preparation of judicial evidence "first developed in Europe in the late nineteenth century and then elaborated in detail in Soviet police manuals." Looking at the use of photographs in Soviet antireligious operations against primarily rural Orthodox religious movements from 1930 to 1952, Vagramenko's chapter brings across how the professionalization of criminalistics developed hand in hand with the "manipulative and instrumental" use of visual imagery to present scattered peasant underground religious communities as links in a vast counterrevolutionary conspiracy. In Vagramenko's material, one finds a complex overlap between regular "police standards of signaletic photography and crime scene photographic inventories" and politically driven practices of "retouching, photomontage, collage, [and] cropping."

The widespread use of secret police photography in antireligious propaganda, as this chapter suggests, was deeply grounded in the use of photography in standard Soviet criminal and courtroom procedure. Internal, classified, or top-secret methods had numerous interconnections with the saturation coverage of mass propaganda. The implications of this are important for Vagramenko's chapter, and they extend well beyond the history of photography. The issue she highlights goes beyond the secret police violating procedure or manipulating evidence. It goes beyond even the question of the degree to which propagandists may or may not believe their own propaganda. Rather, it shows the secret police as a major player in cultural and ideological production. Vagramenko depicts the secret police as standing at the heart of the Soviet "iconographic tradition of visualizing the religious enemy." Precisely in that overlapping space between internal methodologies and public presentation, it was a core actor in the creation of a new "regime of truth." Vagramenko calls this criminalization of religion the "production of a new kind of knowledge," but it could be seen as a key part of ideology—if we conceive the many faces of ideology to include not only codified doctrine but also discourse and worldview.[26]

In Lucento's chapter, "The NKVD and the Political Origins of Socialist Realism," Kyiv NKVD Captain Solomon Gol'dman and his colleagues criminalized the previously celebrated modernist monumental artists' interest in Ukrainian folk motifs as "national fascist" and, significantly, anti-Russian. These secret policemen may have understood little about art, but, in Lucento's words, they "knew plenty about the power and bureaucratic significance of visual propaganda." Boichuk and his left-leaning followers had risen to fame in one era of the socialist Ukrainization of culture, championing a brand of internationalism that celebrated aesthetic elements present in Ukraine but also, as Boichuk saw it, in all national forms. They met their downfall during the political-ideological frenzy of the Great Terror, which also coincided with a new era in Soviet nationalities policy and the adoption of Socialist Realism as an official style by the central and regional unions of visual artists around the USSR.

The origins of Socialist Realism, the key doctrine in all the arts in the Soviet Union from the 1930s to the 1950s, has been explored in a large and wide-ranging literature.[27] It has also been portrayed as central far beyond the artistic realm. It can be seen as a core component part of Stalin-era ideology if, again, that is broadly conceived not as doctrine but as worldview. Sheila Fitzpatrick first drew attention to this notion by showing the sheer prevalence in the Stalinist 1930s of approaching life not as it was, but as it was becoming and should be.[28] But "police aesthetics," as developed in literature and film representing the secret police and unmasking enemies that were often created or influenced by the secret police itself, reached beyond a future-oriented lens. Police aesthetics taught how vigilantly to penetrate beneath the surface of an ostensibly benevolent reality. This was a mode of representation that unmasked the ideologically true, conspiratorial political essence and thus, in Vatulescu's words, saw "past the foreground, past the misleading surface of reality, and into its deepest recesses."[29] It is in this light that we can read a quotation from NKVD Senior Lieutenant Aleksandr Khazan, a Beria client in Tbilisi during the Great Terror, in the chapter by Blauvelt and Jishkariani. At his trial, Khazan attempted to explain the atrocities he had committed: "An extreme suspiciousness developed in me. Any material coming in compelled me to seek out deeper roots."

Yet the role that the secret police played specifically in the emergence of Socialist Realism, either in the visual arts or as part of this broader ideological construct, has never been explored. As Socialist Realism in the visual arts was defined in Soviet Ukraine, Lucento emphasizes, the Boichukisty themselves were prosecuted and condemned alongside the specific "Ukrainizing forms" in their works. Accordingly, the state that had commissioned their artwork did not only execute the artists but also burned, shredded, or disappeared their works. Of course, as Lucento concludes, the secret police was far from the only player in the construction of Socialist Realism. But to fully grasp how it was established, we must consider the messages sent by this simultaneous physical, material, and ideological execution.

At first glance, Vatulescu's chapter on secret police aesthetics, focusing on a 1959 feature-length filmic reenactment of a bank heist carried out jointly by the Romanian Securitate and the Documentary Film Studio Sahia, might seem to have only tangential connections with Selvage's densely documented history of how Andropov's KGB persecuted human and civil rights activists between 1967 and 1980. Vatulescu draws on film theory and studies in visual culture and communist ideology; Selvage closely reconstructs a chronological narrative of the KGB's Operation Wedge, so-called active measures against Soviet human-rights activists between 1976 and 1980. Yet the two chapters have much to say to one another.

Vatulescu's reading of the 1960 film *Reconstituirea* (Reenactment) is informed by her immersion in a twenty-seven-volume case file about this aesthetico-political collaboration in the Securitate archives. Vatulescu argues that the film was the most elaborate example of a much broader phenomenon—a secret police "visual pedagogy" that sought to teach a "way of looking," vigilance—that was grounded in concrete visual and filmic instan-tiations of the Stalinist cultural-ideological obsession with masking and unmasking. Selvage documents how Operation Wedge was constructed by KGB counterintelligence officers as a conspiracy narrative, one that linked dissidents to foreign journalists or internal and external enemies in the wake of the Helsinki Final Act of 1975. Much of that narrative was constructed by placing KGB disinformation in *Literaturnaia gazeta*, the most important cul-tural journal since the Thaw and a go-to venue for KGB disinformation.

The two chapters demonstrate that the secret police was far from only repressing and suppressing, "arresting" or destroying works of culture. Rather, they show the extent to which it was also a significant player in the cultural realm and in the media, standing at the intersection of cultural production and ideology. For Vatulescu, *Reenactment* was "carefully constructed as a secret police *ars cinematica*, deliberately laying out and putting into practice cinema's potential uses for policing." Using this insight, one might infer that the exten-sive KGB relationship with mass media that Selvage documents displayed a crude literary pedagogy. If so, "active measures" were about more than cre-ating narratives beneficial to the KGB; they were one part of promoting a "way of reading" the news. Selvage's chapter shows how the deep-seated secret police involvement with the press formed one piece of an entire range of other operational activities in "active measures," including surveillance, infiltration, entrapment, and espionage. Both chapters stand out for their in-depth atten-tion to the nitty-gritty details of the means and manner by which the secret police acted, in the cultural sphere and otherwise. But how did the audience react? Vatulescu reports that audience response to the filmic reenactment was carefully monitored. But it would require a spoiler alert before I could reveal how the audience affected the film's "ending."

PERPETRATORS AND VICTIMS

A final area these chapters illuminate is one about which students of the twen-tieth century have written libraries: the study of perpetrators and victims. No matter how much has been written, this is a topic that retains urgency for us to understand today. How does new archival evidence in this realm intertwine with the advance of new interpretations?

The chapter on "ordinary perpetrators" by Blauvelt and Jishkariani builds on recent studies of NKVD personnel in Ukraine, which came out of the remarkable trial evidence from the "purge of the purgers" at the end of the Great Terror. Shifting the focus to Tbilisi involves a shift to a different source base: the trials against Beria's clients conducted by the USSR procurator gen-eral after the secret police chief's ouster and execution in 1953. Focusing on three mid-level Beria clients at the epicenter of the use of torture in Tbilisi during the Terror, the chapter probes the thorny question of perpetrator motivations. Piecing together trial and other evidence in this chapter explicitly aims to elucidate the interplay among the institutional, national, and biographical contexts in which the perpetrators acted.

Aleksandr Khazan was Jewish and born in Odessa; Nikita Krimian was an ethnic Armenian born in Kars; and Konstantin Savitskii was an ethnic Russian born in Tashkent. All were outsiders not only in national terms but in terms of their lack of "social capital" with the Georgian Bolsheviks, intellectuals, and professionals they purged. "A most dangerous imbalance of authority and esteem may have obtained," the chapter observes, "when the NKVD investigators found themselves in a position of unrestrained power over arrestees who until very recently had considered themselves to be the investigators' social betters." The radicals' sense of empowerment was reinforced within the Georgian NKVD by their membership in Beria's patronage network.[30]

Strikingly, however, each zealous perpetrator also stood under a sword of Damocles, compromised, alongside so many other Soviets, by biography and potential guilt by association. Khazan had had ties with Trotsky supporters and relatives abroad. By social origin Savitskii was a minor noble, and his émigré father apparently fought for the Whites. Krimian had been implicated in embezzlement, and his mentor within the NKVD, a virtual father figure, was arrested in 1937. By concealing these dangerous elements of their lives and reinventing themselves as the most zealous perpetrators, the chapter argues, they were at once enacting a very typical Soviet form of imposture and routing out the enemy within themselves, a fundamental aspect of Soviet subjectivity during this period. Even as their outsider status and vulnerability within the concrete context of the NKVD prompted a selective self-presentation, the violence they committed gave them every incentive to internalize the ideology that justified rooting out counterrevolutionaries. The chapter concludes that Stalinist subjectivity, often posited as true belief, and imposture—often conceived as its opposite, contrived conformity—went hand in hand. It was these commonalities with broader Stalinist society that made Khazan, Savitskii, and Krimian at once extraordinary perpetrators and "ordinary" men.

Aigi Rahi-Tamm's chapter takes us from the interrogation rooms of the secret police in Estonia to the halls of the Tallinn State Conservatory. Walking into that building, which as late as 1948 lacked Soviet-style portraits and slogans, Jaak Ottender, a party member from Moscow arriving as the new chair in Marxism-Leninism, perceived it as completely "not Soviet" even in outward appearance: "It felt as if I had entered some bourgeois institution." In explaining just how quickly that changed after 1948 both in that key cultural institution and Estonia itself, Rahi-Tamm's treatment is notable for situating secret police interrogations and arrests in a far broader, long-term context. This includes three phases of the Sovietization of Estonia: 1940–1941, 1946–1948, and the most repressive phase of 1949–1951. It also involves placing the actions of the secret police within the cultural-ideological campaigns of the Zhdanovshchina and the anticosmopolitan campaign. At the center of her discussion is not the mere fact of interrogations, arrests, and deportations. It is the breakdown of "networks of trust" as the crucible of the Stalinist campaigns put into place the rituals and norms of a new political culture. "The way in which people trust or distrust each other," Geoffrey Hosking has observed, "is part of the deep grammar of any society." Because the "wildfire spread of generalized social distrust" was both mechanism and consequence of Stalinist terror, the secret police and its operations are a key locus for discussing how networks of trust are broken down—and how difficult they are to rebuild even decades later.[31]

Rahi-Tamm focuses on three prominent musicians and conductors who had been honored in 1947 during the Estonian Song Festival. This was a choral institution dating from 1869 that became a major part of the Estonian national awakening in the nineteenth century and expressions of Estonian national identity in the twentieth. Tuudur Vettik, Riho Päts, and Alfred Karindi were honored as Folk Artists of the Estonian SSR after organizing the festival in 1947; they were arrested in 1950 on its eve. In between lay the heyday of criticism/self-criticism, purging, and institutional reorientation. The interrogations and arrests carried out by the secret police are described as one key piece of a mosaic that involved the party organization of the Tallinn State Conservatory, the Estonian Union of Composers, and the press. The opposite of collegial trust and the old intelligentsia's professional and personal networks was suspicion and conflict, fueled by interpersonal rifts and survival tactics.

Rahi-Tamm's treatment is notable for its attention to the long tail of that secret police repression, combined as it was with trauma and ruined friendships. Its aftereffects were felt long after the secret police reopened old files during the rehabilitations of de-Stalinization, which itself emerged as a complex and divisive process. The secret police's role in this long-term saga appears outwardly successful in spearheading the establishment of elaborate, multilayered levers of control over cultural institutions and the intelligentsia. Even so, reading Rahi-Tamm's conclusion, it was also marked by failure: "Although Soviet authorities hoped to 'domesticate' the song festival for Soviet purposes, they were never able to make the song festival theirs."

The chapters of this book work together in evidence and interpretation to connect the secret police more closely than ever to the dynamics of Soviet history at home and abroad. How will they fit into the post-Soviet archival study of the secret police? As this volume goes to press in June 2022, Russian forces have retreated from Kyiv but renewed assaults on eastern Ukraine. The future of archival and historical research in our field, along with the entire international order upended by the invasion, is clouded. In these dark days, it seems certain that we have entered a new and very different era, but it is difficult to predict how things will unfold. However, the director of the SBU Archive in Kyiv, reached in Lviv, confirmed that digital records of secret police material made by his agency in recent years were secure and redoubled efforts at preservation are ongoing.[32]

NOTES

1. For example, documentary collections include A. I. Kokurin and N. V. Petrov, *Lubianka: Organy VChK-OGPU-NKVD-NKGB-MGB-MVD-KGB, 1917–1991. Spravochnik* (Moscow: ROSSPEN, 2003); and David Shearer and Vladimir Khaustov, *Stalin and the Lubianka: A Documentary History of the Political Police and Security Organs in the Soviet Union, 1922–1953* (New Haven: Yale University Press, 2015), based on a more extensive series of documentary volumes in Russian. Landmark monographs encompassing institutional history include George Leggett, *The Cheka: Lenin's Political Police. The All-Russian Extraordinary Commission for Combating Counter-Revolution and Sabotage (December 1917 to February 1922)* (New York: Oxford University Press, 1981); David R. Shearer, *Policing Stalin's Socialism: Repression and Social Order in the Soviet Union, 1924–1953* (New Haven: Yale University Press, 2009); and Amy W. Knight, *The KGB: Police and Politics in the Soviet Union* (Boston: Unwin Hyman, 1988). Noteworthy studies of leaders and personnel include Marc Jansen and Nikita Petrov, *Stalin's Loyal Executioner: People's Commissar Nikolai Ezhov, 1895–1940* (Stanford, CA: Hoover Institution Press, 2002); and Alexander Vatlin, *Agents of Terror: Ordinary Men and Extraordinary Violence in Stalin's Secret Police*, ed. and trans. Seth Bernstein (Madison: University of Wisconsin Press, 2016).

2. Documentary collections include V. Vinogradov et al., eds., *Arkhiv VChK: Sbornik dokumentov* (Moscow: Kuchkovo pole, 2007). Secondary studies include I. S. Ratkovskii, *Krasnyi terror i deiatel'nost' VChK v 1918 godu* (St. Petersburg: Izdatel'stvo Sankt-Peterburgskogo universiteta, 2006); and Aleksei Litvin, *Krasnyi i belyi terror v Rossii 1918–1922 gg.* (Moscow: Iauza-EKSMO, 2004).

3. The indispensable collection of documents on the Gulag is Aleksandr Bezborodov et al., eds., *Istoriia stalinskogo GULAGa: Konets 1920-kh–pervaia polovina 1950-kh godov. Sobranie dokumentov*, 7 vols. (Moscow: ROSSPEN, 2004–2005). One of several other landmark documentary collections is Oleg Khlevniuk, V. A. Kozlov, and S. V. Mironenko, eds., *Zakliuchennye na stroikakh kommunizma: GULAG i ob"ekty energetiki v SSSR. Sobranie dokumentov* (Moscow: ROSSPEN, 2008). Noteworthy studies include Michael Jakobson, *Origins of the GULAG: The Soviet Prison Camp System, 1917–1934* (Lexington: University Press of Kentucky, 1993); Oleg Khlevniuk, *The History of the Gulag: From Collectivization to the Great Terror* (New Haven: Yale University Press, 2004); Viktor Berdinskikh, *Istoriia odnogo lageria (Viatlag)* (Moscow: AGRAF, 2001); V. N. Zemskov, *Spetsposelentsy v SSSR, 1930–1960 gg.* (Moscow: Nauka, 2003); Lynne Viola, *The Unknown Gulag: The Lost World of Stalin's Special Settlements* (New York: Oxford University Press, 2007); Wilson T. Bell, *Stalin's Gulag at War: Forced Labor, Mass Death, and Soviet Victory in the Second World War* (Toronto: University of Toronto Press, 2018);

and Alan Barenberg, *Gulag Town, Company Town: Forced Labor and Its Legacy in Vorkuta* (New Haven: Yale University Press, 2014).

4. Documentary collections include Viktor Danilov, Roberta Manning, and Linn [Lynne] Viola, eds., *Tragediia sovetskoi derevni: Kollektivizatsiia i raskulachivanie. Dokumenty i materialy*, 5 vols. (Moscow: ROSSPEN, 1999); Viola, Mark Iunge [Marc Junge], and Dzheffri Rossman [Jeffrey Rossman], eds., *Ekho bol'shogo terrora: Sbornik dokumentov*, 3 vols. (Moscow: Probel, 2017–2018); N. F. Bugai, ed., *L. Beria—I. Stalinu: "Soglasno Vashemu ukazaniiu . . ."* (Moscow: AIRO-XX, 1995); and A. A. Makarov et al., eds., *Vlast' i dissidenty: Iz dokumentov KGB i TsK KPSS* (Moscow: Moskovskaia Khel'sinskaia gruppa, 2006). Monographs include Paul R. Gregory, *Terror by Quota: State Security from Lenin to Stalin (An Archival Study)* (New Haven: Yale University Press, 2009); Pavel Chinsky, *Micro-histoire de la Grande Terreur: La fabrique de culpabilité à l'ère stalinienne* (Paris: Denoël, 2005); Nicolas Werth, *L'ivrogne et la marchande de fleurs: Autopsie d'un meurtre de masse, 1937–1938* (Paris: Tallandier, 2009); Iunge and Rolf Binner, *Kak terror stal bol'shim: Sekretnyi prikaz no. 00447 i tekhnologiia ego ispolneniia* (Moscow: AIRO-XX, 2003); and Viola, *Stalinist Perpetrators on Trial: Scenes from the Great Terror in Soviet Ukraine* (New York: Oxford University Press, 2017).

5. Documentary collections include Andrei Artuzov and Oleg Naumov, eds., *Vlast' i khudozhestvennaia intelligentsiia: Dokumenty TsK RKP(b)-VKP(b), VChK-OGPU-NKVD o kul'turnoi politike, 1917–1935* (Moscow: Mezhdunarodnyi fond "Demokratiia," 1999); and Nicolas Werth and Gaël Moullec, eds., *Rapports secrets soviétiques: La société russe dans les rapports confidentiels, 1921–1991* (Paris: Gallimard, 1995). Secondary works include Vladlen Izmozik, *Glaza i ushi rezhima: Gosudarstvennyi politicheskii kontrol' za naseleniem sovetskoi Rossii v 1918–1928 godakh* (St. Petersburg: Izdatel'stvo Sankt-Peterburgskogo universiteta ekonomiki i finansov, 1995); Peter Holquist, "'Information Is the Alpha and Omega of Our Work': Bolshevik Surveillance in Its Pan-European Context," *Journal of Modern History* 69, no. 3 (1997): 415–50; James Harris, "Intelligence and Threat Perception: Defending the Revolution, 1917–1937," in *Anatomy of Terror: Political Violence under Stalin*, ed. Harris (Oxford: Oxford University Press, 2013); and Thomas Rid, *Active Measures: The Secret History of Disinformation and Political Warfare* (New York: Farrar, Straus, and Giroux, 2020).

6. Joshua Rubenstein and Alexander Gribanov, eds., *The KGB File of Andrei Sakharov*, trans. Ella Shmulevich et al. (New Haven: Yale University Press, 2005); Michael Scammel, ed., *The Solzhenitsyn Files* (Chicago: Edition q, 1995).

7. A kind of historiographical *summa* of this first archival wave can be found in "La police politique en Union soviétique, 1918–1953," special issue of *Cahiers du monde russe* 42, no. 2–4 (2001).

8. This is now changing: see Molly Pucci, *Security Empire: The Secret Police in Communist Eastern Europe* (New Haven: Yale University Press, 2020).

9. Perhaps the best known is the collection of the former KGB archivist Vasilii Mitrokhin, now housed at the Archives Centre, Churchill College, Cambridge. See Christopher M. Andrew and Vasili Mitrokhin, *The Sword and the Shield: The Mitrokhin Archive and the Secret History of the KGB* (New York: Basic Books, 1999); and https://www.chu.cam.ac.uk/archives/collections/papers-vasiliy-mitrokhin-1922-2004/.

10. For an overview, see Jonathan Haslam, *Near and Distant Neighbors: A New History of Soviet Intelligence* (New York: Farrar, Straus, and Giroux, 2015).

11. Julie Fedor, *Russia and the Cult of State Security: The Chekist Tradition from Lenin to Putin* (London: Routledge, 2011); Paula Chan, "Documents Accuse: The Post-Soviet Memory Politics of Genocide," *Journal of Illiberalism Studies* 1, no. 2 (2021): 39–57.

12. For example, see V. S. Khristoforov, ed., *Organy gosbezopasnosti SSSR v 1941–1945 gg.* (Moscow: Glavnoe arkhivnoe upravlenie goroda Moskvy, 2011), one of over seventy documentary collections edited by a military and intelligence historian who is both a lieutenant general in the Federal Security Service (FSB) and, since 2016, a corresponding member of the Russian Academy of Sciences.

13. Vladimir N. Khaustov, "Razvitie sovetskikh organov gosudarstvennoi bezopasnosti," *Cahiers du monde russe* 42, no. 2–4 (2001): 357–74.

14. See the discussion in Wilson T. Bell, "Forced Labor on the Home Front: The Gulag and Total War in Western Siberia, 1940–1945," in *The Soviet Gulag: Evidence, Interpretation, and Comparison*, ed. Michael David-Fox (Pittsburgh: University of Pittsburgh Press, 2016), 114–35; the phrase comes from Giorgio Agamben, *State of Exception*, trans. Kevin Artell (Chicago: University of Chicago Press, 2005).

15. See Archive of the Ministry of Internal Affairs of Georgia, http://archive.security.gov.ge/fond_6 .html.

16. Michael David-Fox, "Conferences, Coronavirus, and the KGB: The Webinar Series on 'The Political Police and the Soviet System: Insights from Newly Opened KGB Archives in the Former Soviet States,'" *NewsNet* [ASEEES] (June 2020): 2–6.

17. Mikhail Nakonechnyi, "'Archival Counterrevolution': Why are GULAG Regional Archives so Important?," *Peripheral Histories*, 6 July 2018, https://www.peripheralhistories.co.uk/post/archival -counterrevolution-why-are-gulag-regional-archives-so-important.

18. Mark von Hagen, "The Archival Gold Rush and Historical Agendas in the Post-Soviet Era," *Slavic Review* 52, no. 1 (1993): 96–100; Stephen Kotkin, "The State—Is It Us? Memoirs, Archives, and Kremlinologists," *Russian Review* 61, no. 1 (2002): 35–51.

19. Here see Oleg Budnitskii, "A Harvard Project in Reverse: Materials of the Commission of the USSR Academy of Sciences on the History of the Great Patriotic War—Publications and Interpretations," *Kritika: Explorations in Russian and Eurasian History* 19, no. 1 (2018): 175–202; and Michael David-Fox, "Re-Reading Fainsod in Smolensk," *Kritika: Explorations in Russian and Eurasian History* 22, no. 4 (2021): 811–38.

20. The "fifth column" as a trigger of the Great Terror has been emphasized most prominently by Oleg Khlevniuk. See, for example, Khlevniuk, *Master of the House: Stalin and His Inner Circle,* trans. Nora Favorov (New Haven: Yale University Press, 2009).

21. In emphasis and argument, the chapter overlaps with Shearer, *Policing Stalin's Socialism*. See also Paul Hagenloh, "'Chekist in Essence, Chekist in Spirit': Regular and Political Police in the 1930s," *Cahiers du monde russe* 42, no. 2–4 (2001): 447–76.

22. Mark Levene, *The Crisis of Genocide*, vol. 2: *Annihilation: The European Rimlands, 1939–1953* (Oxford: Oxford University Press, 2013), 316.

23. For my take on these issues, see "Razmyshleniia o stalinizme, voine i nasilii," in *SSSR vo Vtoroi mirovoi voine: Okkupatsiia. Kholokost. Stalinizm*, ed. Oleg Budnitskii and Liudmila Novikova (Moscow: ROSSPEN, 2014), 176–95.

24. There is a massive literature on these topics, but in this context see esp. Yves Cohen, *Le siècle des chefs: Une histoire transnationale du commandement et de l'autorité (1890–1940)* (Paris: Éditions Amsterdam, 2013); Cohen, "Circulatory Localities: The Example of Stalinism in the 1930s," *Kritika: Explorations in Russian and Eurasian History* 11, no. 1 (2010): 11–45; and Paul Hagenloh, *Stalin's Police: Public Order and Mass Repression in the USSR, 1926–1941* (Baltimore: Johns Hopkins University Press, 2009).

25. Nakonechnyi's exchange with Stephen Wheatcroft and Golfo Alexopoulos's commentary are in "Forum: How Deadly Was the Gulag?," *Kritika: Explorations in Russian and Eurasian History* 23, no. 4 (2022).

26. Michael David-Fox, "The Blind Men and the Elephant: Six Faces of Ideology in the Soviet Context," *Crossing Borders: Modernity, Ideology, and Culture in Russia and the Soviet Union* (Pittsburgh: University of Pittsburgh Press, 2015): 75–103.

27. The single most wide-ranging compilation on the topic is Gans Giunter [Hans Günther] and Evgenii Dobrenko, eds., *Sotsrealisticheskii kanon* (St. Petersburg: Akademicheskii proekt, 2000).

28. Sheila Fitzpatrick, "Becoming Cultured: Socialist Realism and the Representation of Privilege and Taste," in *The Cultural Front: Power and Culture in Revolutionary Russia* (Ithaca, NY: Cornell University Press, 1992), 216–37. This mode of representation had a key international dimension: it was foreshadowed by 1920s practices of presenting the Soviet Union to foreigners that informed Maksim Gor'kii's influential writings after his return in 1928. See Michael David-Fox, *Showcasing*

the *Great Experiment: Cultural Diplomacy and Western Visitors to the Soviet Union, 1921–1941* (New York: Oxford University Press, 2011), 55, 114, 144–74.

29. Cristina Vatulescu, *Police Aesthetics: Literature, Film, and the Secret Police in Soviet Times* (Stanford, CA: Stanford University Press, 2010), 112.

30. For more on Beria's network, see Timothy K. Blauvelt, "March of the Chekists: Beria's Secret Police Patronage Network and Soviet Crypto-Politics," *Communist and Post-Communist Studies* 44, no. 1 (2011): 73–88.

31. Geoffrey Hosking, "Trust and Distrust in the USSR: An Overview," *Slavonic and East European Review* 91, no. 1 (2013): 1–25.

32. Correspondence with Andriy Kohut, director, Haluzevyi derzhavnyi arkhiv Sluzhba bezpeky Ukraïni (HDASBU), 6 March 2022; "A Conversation with Andriy Kohut from Lviv," discussion at Georgetown University (via Zoom), 29 March 2022.

The Origins of Stalin's Mass Operations

The Extrajudicial Special Assembly, 1922–1953

Marc Junge, Andrei Savin, and Aleksei Tepliakov

Translated by Caroline Cormier and Daniel Mülle

The machine of the Special Assembly—two handles, one bike.

> —Varlam Shalamov

He who is not with me is against me, and he who does not gather with me scatters.

> —Matthew 12:30

MOST RESEARCHERS HAVE ARGUED THAT EXTERNAL DANGER, SPECIFICALLY the threat of war, is the key to explaining the Great Terror in the Soviet Union between 1936 and 1938.[1] The danger presented by Japan in the Far East and by Nazi Germany in the West generated fears that a "fifth column" would emerge within the Soviet Union.[2] Many scholars regard this fear as the main factor driving the "larger political strategy of the purges."[3] In our previous research, however, we have argued that the threat of war was only one of many reasons for the Great Terror. Imposing collectivization, supporting industrialization, and combating epidemic social problems played a greater role. Domestic conflict was at least as important at this time—perhaps even more important, because Stalin and his comrades underestimated the threat of war.[4] They thought they wielded enough power with sufficient scope to continue the great project of socialist transformation and to discipline society. We suggest that it was not until the summer of 1938 that the regime understood that war was imminent and, as a result, immediately ended the Great Terror.[5]

There is more to the discussion, however. Stephen Kotkin, in his biography of Stalin, calls into question the theory that terror in the Soviet Union grew out of the experience of the Spanish Civil War and the idea that fighting a fifth column could prevent trouble in the event of a war.[6] Kotkin writes, "Spain was convenient but unnecessary for Stalin's terror."[7] Later he adds: "There was no 'dynamic' forcing him to do so [i.e., forcing Stalin to launch the mass operations in the summer of 1937], no 'factional' fighting, no heightened threat abroad. . . . He just decided, himself, to approve quota-driven eradication of entire categories of people."[8] Kotkin argues that Stalin used the fifth column threat only as the main public justification for the Terror. He contends that invocations of a fifth column were a story line aimed at the public, rather than the real motivation behind the Terror. Moreover, Stalin himself introduced this cover story at the March 1937 plenum to justify the devastating purges, which greatly undermined the USSR's readiness for war.[9]

Kotkin believes that Stalin primarily focused on competing currents within the Party—Trotskyists, Zinov'evites, and Bukharinites. At the same time, however, he notes that Soviet society had astonishingly little overt political opposition of any kind.[10] He also rejects the attribution of the Great Terror to Stalin alone, attributing the murderous episode of 1937 to the chronic dysfunction of the political system and, most importantly, the nature of communism as a conspiracy to seize and hold power.[11] In sum, Kotkin rejects situational and structural arguments and prefers to focus on the regime's ideological character.

Unlike Kotkin, David Shearer in "Stalin at War" does not distance himself from the dominant view on the causes of the Great Terror but substantantially expands the line of argument to include the importance of the threat of war and the fifth column.[12] What Shearer's work has in common with Kotkin's is that they both focus strongly on Stalin and the Moscow center. Shearer's new approach to the subject is evident in his method. His stated aim is to use a broad historical perspective, spanning the period from 1918 to 1953, "to connect the cyclical patterns of violence perpetrated under Stalin with the waxing and waning of fears about invasion."[13] To this end, he weaves together the fragmented secondary literature on foreign policy, internal mobilization, and state violence into a cohesive narrative whose common thread is the threat of war. A number of sources from the central archives on Stalin's role in 1918–1920 and on Stalin's subsequent comments on foreign and domestic policy underpin Shearer's approach. His main thesis is that the mass persecutions of both the early 1930s and the Great Terror, as well as those perpetrated during the Great Patriotic War of 1941–1945, were all "linked to Stalin's expectation of war and invasion, and they followed a pattern established during the dictator's experience as a military commander in the Russian revolutionary and Civil Wars, from 1918 to 1920."[14] According to Shearer, the revolution and civil war shaped the perceptions of Stalin—and many others—in such a way that the external danger became the all-important factor in the survival of the Soviet system. As a result, domestic policy also appears to have been largely shaped by the threat of war.

From Stalin's assumption of power until the end of the Five-Year Plan in 1932, domestic policy was structured in practice by the threat of Poland, with Great Britain in the background, and Japan already appearing on the horizon. During the Terror of 1936–1939, first Japan and then Germany moved to the center of attention as factors shaping domestic policy. Only during the Great Patriotic War were Germany and Japan clearly in the foreground. Finally, in the period from 1946 until 1953, the Cold War with the United States became a structuring element for domestic policy, still viewed against the backdrop of Stalin's Civil War experience. Each of these situations, in combination with this pattern of behavior, gave rise to "massive internal repression tied to urgent economic and social mobilization, and intense diplomatic maneuvering."[15] As Shearer explains in his detailed analysis, the timing of each set of repressive measures, their intensity, the selection of target groups, and even the time of their implementation were linked "to the change from a policy of containment of 'anti-soviet elements' to a policy of extermination of what were perceived as potentially insurgent social groups."[16]

Shearer's narrative takes the persecution of several target groups as his main examples. For instance, he attributes perceptions of the threat posed by Poland to several specific events: the assassination of the Soviet ambassador Petr Voikov in Warsaw in June 1927; the shooting of twelve aristocrats on 10 June 1927; the screening of twenty thousand individuals, which led to nine thousand arrests shortly after the assassination and would have been mostly confined to the border regions of Ukraine and the North Caucasus, which were a stronghold of the Mensheviks; the Shakhty trial of industrial engineers in 1928; the prosecution of the Industrial Party; and the Menshevik trials in late 1930 and early 1931.[17] The domestic war against the peasants during collectivization also set up the Soviet Union for a possible war with Poland and/or Japan.[18] The outside threat also drove the Moscow show trials of 1936 against Trotskyists, Bukharinites, Zinov'evites, and military leaders, as well as the crackdown on local party structures and the functional elite. Last but not least, in this view, the threat of war had a decisive influence on the mass operations of the Great Terror, especially those aimed at nationalities but also those orchestrated against "socially harmful elements." In particular, it affected the motivation for and radicalization of these campaigns.

A side effect, and certainly not one intended by Shearer, of the view in which the threat of war eclipses the importance of ideology, social utopia, and the unconditional will to power is an apologetic undertone. In this respect, Shearer's explanation exhibits two problematic tendencies. First, despite the broader historical perspective and the clever reorganization of research, there is a danger of supporting a strategy used by former Politburo members such as Viacheslav Molotov and Lazar' Kaganovich, which by overemphasizing the reactive and situational element of the persecution—more commonly referred to as "repression"—makes excessive state violence appear objectively meaningful or necessary for survival.[19] Second, it raises the question of whether the distorted perceptions of Stalin and many of his comrades in response to the Civil War, a phenomenon well substantiated by Shearer, is sufficient to declare external danger to be the main determinant of domestic policy, especially since this approach involves a considerable psychological dimension and is therefore difficult to verify. It is also striking that the distortion of perception caused by the Civil War is a response not to the war itself but to the imperialist intervention. Stalinist perceptions of the Civil War in the 1930s have not been adequately analyzed, although authoritative historical-political journalism such as the publication of *The History of the Civil War*, initiated by Maksim Gor'kii in 1929, and later work by instructors of the Central Committee could certainly shed light on this.[20] Ultimately, however, the concepts of repression and distortion come back to the classic revisionist position of the weak and driven dictator who was permanently on the defensive and motivated by fear.[21]

In juxtaposition to Kotkin and Shearer, Lynne Viola prefers a multifunctional approach. She maintains that a solid explanation for the Great Terror leaves room for multiple causes, including preventive or preemptive measures rooted in the fear or expectation of war.[22] Accordingly, her *Stalinist Perpetrators on Trial* underscores that the fear of war remained on equal footing with the Civil War ethos. The first sentence of the chapter "The Incomplete Civil War and the Great Terror" reads, "The Soviet Union was in the grip of a never-ending civil war in the years from the Revolution of 1917 to the Great Terror, and perhaps beyond." She goes on: "It was a contrived civil war, mainly one-sided, periodically revived and manipulated by the Stalinist regime during phases of radical and violent transformation."[23] In relation to a central theme of the book—namely, what role the Chekists played in the Great Terror—Viola addresses the idea that certain NKVD torturers thought they were prosecuting a civil war and not just following orders: "Fleishman in particular certainly believed there were enemies. He not only believed, he knew there were enemies. He had fought in the civil war and knew it still cut a swath through

Soviet territory. And he knew, or thought he knew, or lied that he knew who the enemies were." In addition, there were "fears of a generation of NKVD officials, like Fleishman, who had fought in the civil war and understood enmity. Their fears were not just based on the civil war . . . but also on their actions in the years following the civil war. Many of these NKVD officials and policemen had served in the violent collectivization and dekulakization campaigns. . . . Guilt and memory may have consolidated their fears, thereby helping to shape their actions during the Great Terror."[24] According to Viola, the general psychology of the Civil War also determined the mass operations of the Great Terror: "Stalin and the NKVD leadership also believed in the enemy. . . . The logic of the mass operations was such that it did not matter what former enemies had done in the interval between the end of the civil war and the start of mass operations."[25] She concludes that "the Russian civil war determined the terror's field of enemies as well as its dominant rhetoric. . . . The goal of the Great Terror was to complete the civil war with the final elimination of all remaining members of the old prerevolutionary elites, members of prerevolutionary political parties and movements, the kulak (again), recidivist criminals, and foreign elements who could possibly engage in espionage."[26] Viola agrees with Shearer in finally realizing that the threat of war and the activization of a fifth column were "the chief animating factor in determining the terror's urgency, speed, and compression."[27] She concludes: "apocalyptic thinking and a conspiratorial view of the world growing out of war, revolution, and civil war likely played a more important role than Marxist ideology per se in the atmosphere of the times. The Communist Party and the NKVD saw themselves as locked in an endless and inevitable war with internal and external enemies."[28]

Viola's argument about how the Great Terror came about is structured in the following way: the civil war ethos of the elites—kept alive, manipulated, and controlled by the regime—shaped the identification and treatment of enemies. The pinnacle of the state and of political use of the civil war ethos was the merciless treatment of the opponents of collectivization and industrialization. In contrast, she attributes the deadly escalation of mass terror in 1937–1938 to the interaction between the civil war ethos and the threat of war.

Viola's strength is that she addresses vulnerabilities in her own thinking. She notes that the enemies of the Civil War were no longer the same as those of the dekulakization and industrialization campaigns or the Great Terror. She also keeps in mind the absence of any organized social and political competition within and outside the Party from at least the mid-1930s. In this context, it would be interesting to discuss the term "civil war ethos" or Viola's metaphor of an "incomplete civil war." Does the term encompass only an inevitable and persistent distortion of the chekist psyche—indeed, that of the political and state elite as a whole—in response to specific conditions, which subsequently led to the constant production of real and imagined enemies? It is possible that during the Civil War, active use was made of situational factors and politically shaped guidelines, as well as the application of revolutionary means—such as the newly designed penal system, which did not dispense with extrajudicial organs until 1953—to subjugate, control, and transform society. The latter interpretation would, for example, open up more options for explaining the apparently stark change in target groups from social and political "enemies" of the system and "disloyal" members of the Soviet elite to hundreds of thousands of ordinary people outside the regular judicial system. This shift in focus to the mass search for "enemies" at a very low level of social influence would become more apparent over time.[29] It therefore became obvious that, confusingly, the designation of "enemies" remained largely the same, but the group of people affected changed and expanded considerably. In this sense, new wine was poured into old wineskins.

By mass operations we mean the campaigns against so-called kulaks and "counterrevolutionary elements"; against Germans, Poles, Iranians, and other nationalities; and against "socially harmful elements," including beggars, prostitutes, criminals, and the unemployed. The victims were the ordinary, nonprivileged, or disgraced members of the Soviet population.[30] Moreover, unlike the punitive actions of the Cheka and the revolutionary tribunals during the Civil War, these campaigns were carried out in peacetime. In formal terms, the mass operations were characterized by a high degree of bureaucratization and control by the Moscow center. From a purely legal standpoint, most of the criminal files created during the mass operations were nonadmissible cases, or cases that were classified as such for a variety of reasons. In total, these operations affected about 1.6 million people. In 1937–1938, the mass operations transformed the Terror of previous years into the Great Terror.[31] We would also describe as mass operations, in both qualitative and quantitative terms, the work of the troikas during collectivization from January 1930 onward, as well as the activity of the Special Assembly between 1922 and 1953, because these actions also meet the listed criteria.

In this sense, the unstructured mass repression conducted by the secret police with the help of troikas and revolutionary tribunals between 1917 and 1922, which were only minimally regulated by decrees and ordinances, are not mass operations by our definition.[32] The same applies to the prosecution of the (Soviet) elite and organized gangs by the extrajudicial Justice Council

(Sudebnaia kollegiia) under the OGPU Collegium and by the "normal" judiciary from 1922 to 1953, including the revolutionary tribunals in the transport sector left over from the revolutionary period and Civil War in the 1920s.[33]

FROM THE WHY TO THE HOW

Here we are deep in the morass of subjective considerations, including perceptions of threat and the motives of Stalin, the Chekists, and the regime. To develop a new perspective on the Great Terror, especially on mass operations, we—as David Shearer suggests and did—are looking closely at the 1920s, drawing not on Stalin but on Lenin and, especially, on archival materials from Ukraine. In particular, we examine the archives of the militia, which open a new perspective on the situation.[34] With these sources, it is possible to take a closer look at the main characteristic of the Great Terror: namely, that it was carried out with the help of *extrajudicial* bodies. The focus is thus shifted from the motives behind the Great Terror to the question of why the regime was *able* to carry out such mammoth and inhuman actions. Our working hypothesis is that the Great Terror was not exceptional in its treatment of or reaction to external and internal problems. Instead, the Great Terror of 1937–1938 can be seen as the cumulative consequence and peak of a specifically Soviet system of administrative punishment and social discipline that acted proactively, in the sense of political and social engineering and control, below the judicial system.[35]

The birth of this system occurred on 8 June 1922, when the Politburo of the Central Committee of the Russian Communist Party (Bolshevik) (CC RKP[b]) instructed the highest state legislative regulatory body of the Soviet Republic, the All-Russian Central Executive Committee (VTsIK), to form the Special Assembly (Osoboe soveshchanie). This Special Assembly, to be directed by the People's Commissariat of Foreign Affairs and the People's Commissariat of Justice, would have the right "in cases where there is the possibility, to avoid a more severe punishment, to replace the penalty with deportation abroad or with deportation to certain places in the RSFSR."[36] The Soviet regime therefore pretended to stretch its leeway to impose lenient sentences to the maximum. Prison sentences were to be dispensed with, and resettlement was to appear to be an act of compassion, especially since there was still no discussion of sending convicts to labor camps.

This new body was to be controlled by a separate commission consisting of representatives of the secret police, the judiciary, and a member of the Politburo. The political mandate to set up the Special Assembly was embedded in a broader package of measures aimed at controlling the educational system and public organizations.

Two months after the decisive Politburo meeting, VTsIK was instructed to produce a decree on the Special Assembly. The content of this decree corresponded exactly with the spirit of the Politburo decision made in June 1922. According to the decree, the maximum duration of isolation was set at three years. In one important area, however, the decree deviated from the Politburo decision: it removed the People's Commissariat of Foreign Affairs from the list of institutions charged with supervising the Special Assembly. Instead, the secret police (OGPU) played a prominent role in the Special Assembly, and the chairmanship went to the People's Commissariat of Internal Affairs (NKVD). In reality, the secret police took over the Special Assembly, because its head, Feliks Dzerzhinskii, was also people's commissar of internal affairs. The participation of representatives from the People's Commissariat of Justice in the Special Assembly remained unchanged; there was no longer talk of a separate control commission. Due to the prominence of the secret police, the control commission had been merged with the Special Assembly. Only a member of the Politburo was missing. The decree was published in the government newspaper, *Izvestiia*, on 18 August 1922.[37]

The initiative to establish the Special Assembly can be traced back to V. I. Lenin.[38] In a confidential letter written in mid-May 1922 to Dzerzhinskii, Lenin had, not for the first time, insisted on discussing the deportation of writers and professors who were "playing into the hands of the counterrevolution."[39] In subsequent meetings, also held in mid-May 1922, the focus was on authors of noncommunist journals. Lenin himself had written reviews of books and magazines, and he felt it was urgent to commission other communist writers to share their opinions. Lenin, who was already seriously ill and barely mobile at that time, recommended that the members of the Politburo should spend two to three hours a week dealing with various print media. He requested written reports and demanded that all noncommunist editions be sent to Moscow, without exception. "The secret police should be instructed," Lenin continued, "to collect systematic information on the political activity, field of work, and literary activity of professors and writers."[40]

The secret police took up Lenin's suggestions, but broadened the rationale for the measures. It was explicitly linked to the introduction of the New Economic Policy (NEP) and the associated revival of social activity.[41] The argumentation was based on the fact that the planned measures were intended to avoid possible "political turbulence."[42] But responsibility for this step lay not only with Lenin; Lev Trotsky also made his contribution. In a notorious commentary, he publicly sold the action against the intelligentsia and their resettlement as a humanitarian act: "We expelled these people because there was no reason to shoot them, but it was impossible to bear them."[43]

POLITICAL LOYALTY

Previous research has concentrated on the measures by which the Bolsheviks prevented deviant political and social activity and, by extension, created good behavior. The sources used to support this claim include the world press, memoirs, investigation files—especially those associated with members of the elite—and documents about the leadership. The main finding is that leaders and followers who openly or covertly criticized the measures of the Soviet regime were punished for having a "nonjudicial conviction of attitude," even when these allegations could not be proven.[44] This process is quite rightly linked to the introduction of the New Economic Policy, repeating the well-known view that economic freedom had to be paid for with the dismantling of social and political freedoms.[45]

To test the central argument of "nonjudicial convictions of attitude," we will use the promised new source material—specifically, the criminal files from the Ukrainian militia archives.[46] The criminal files make it possible, on the one hand, to determine more precisely who was actually sentenced by this extrajudicial body and, on the other hand, to understand how the mechanism of sentencing worked. These files also provide an opportunity to recapitulate the history of the creation of the extrajudicial bodies at this time.

Even a cursory review of the criminal files reveals cracks in the argument that the convictions handed down by the Special Assembly were "nonjudicial convictions of attitude." The files show that the Special Assembly was also used to combat minor social deviance involving small-time criminals, prostitutes, hooligans, and others. The disciplining of the intelligentsia was therefore only the occasion for forming the Special Assembly, not its actual goal. Rather, the core task of this extrajudicial body was to combat the social milieu in which social and political deviation, including resistance, could arise.[47]

The mechanism of sentencing illustrated in the criminal files also draws attention to the history of the extrajudicial bodies. The founding of the Special Assembly on 10 August 1922 coincided with a period of reorganization of the entire existing extrajudicial repressive apparatus. The apparatus was centralized and brought under greater control by a hierarchical bureaucratic system. At the governmental and republican levels, the Cheka Collegium, which had been established in 1919, lost its right both to pass judgments against political opponents and members of gangs and to carry out the judgments after consultation with the executive committees of the soviets. This right was transferred to the OGPU Collegium in Moscow. The subordinate bodies had to send a request to Moscow, enclosing the delinquent's file, and receive permission to sentence the named person to the penalty listed in the request.

The so-called Justice Council under the OGPU Collegium in Moscow—which, despite its misleading label, was an extrajudicial body of OGPU executives—then took the case, examined it, and reached a verdict, which the subordinate bodies then implemented.[48]

But what was the situation at the Special Assembly of the Collegium of the State Political Administration (GPU) of the Ukrainian SSR, the body we are talking about? In the 1920s and early 1930s, the decision to move a particular case to the Special Assembly was made within the jurisdiction in which the alleged crime occurred. In the case of ordinary criminals, hooligans, prostitutes, and other social deviants, this could be the city, provincial, or republic level of the militia. Cases that involved border violations, however, went to the GPU's departments for border security.[49] Suspected cases of espionage were transferred to the Counterintelligence Department of the GPU of the Ukrainian SSR.[50] Depending on the nature of the crime, cases were handed over to other GPU departments at different levels. Here is an example.

On 21 October 1925, an investigator from the Odesa (Odessa) City Investigation Department, a militia-led and -staffed subdivision of the Administrative Department of the Executive Committee of the City Soviet, arrested Fedor Vladimirovich Fedin.[51] That same day, Fedin was handed over to the inspector on duty. In the inspector's follow-up report, the term "administrative" already catches the eye. Thus the commissioner pointed out that Fedin should be marked for administrative resettlement.[52] Three days later, the employee of the Odesa City Investigation Department of the Odesa City Soviet filled out a "Form for an Administrative Deportation" about Fedin. Personal information was requested, such as his name, marital status, place of residence, occupation, and origin.[53]

The next day, the procedure continued, with the assistant to the head of the Odesa City Investigation Department of the Odesa City Soviet using another form. In the form, the material basis and the decisions outlining why the delinquent was to be administratively deported were recorded. Three convictions for theft by people's courts and one by the Odesa provincial court were listed. The highest sentence was for a duration of one year. After that, the militia employee listed six more arrests for burglary and horse theft. The form then offered the standardized wording that Fedin was to be classified as a "socially dangerous element" and that, on the basis of the VTsIK decision of 6 December 1922 "on the fight against criminal banditry and smuggling" and a decision of the TsIK of the USSR of 24 March 1924, a request would be made to remove him administratively.[54]

The Fedin file was sent to the Administrative Affairs Department of the Odesa District Executive Committee—a civil government body—on 27

October. Another form records the results of the committee's examination. The list of prior convictions and arrests was copied onto this form on 28 October without additional investigation. The decision was preformulated and individualized only by the entry of the name "Fedin" on the form, implying that, based on the already mentioned decisions of the VTsIK and TsIK, Fedin was a "socially dangerous element" and a request should be made to the Special Assembly of the GPU of the Ukrainian SSR to deport him administratively.[55]

As is also clear from the district executive committee's form, however, this request could not be sent directly to the secret police structure of the Ukrainian SSR but had to first pass over the desk of the public procurator's office of the Odesa District with Fedin's file attached. Based solely on this file, the procurator agreed to ask the Special Assembly of the Collegium of the GPU of the Ukrainian SSR to deport the twenty-eight-year-old married carpenter to Arkhangel'sk Province for three years.[56]

Having secured formal permission to forward Fedin's case to Kharkiv, the Ukrainian capital, the militia or its Investigation Department engaged in more detailed research. They requested the verdicts of the people's courts and of the provincial court. They discovered, for example, that on 17 September 1921 the People's Court of Odesa's Ninth District had sentenced Fedin to six months imprisonment under section 180 of the Criminal Code of the Ukrainian Soviet Socialist Republic for stealing large quantities of flour—a total of three poods, or almost fifty kilograms. He had, however, been released later that year due to overcrowding in the prison.[57]

Finally, in early February 1926, the request for permission to sentence Fedin administratively, together with his growing file and a completed registration card, was sent, via the militia and the Investigation Department of the Odesa District, to the Special Assembly at the Collegium of the GPU of the Ukrainian SSR in Kharkiv. These efforts, however, were ultimately in vain, because on 9 February 1926 the Special Assembly rejected the request. The evidence was not substantive enough for this body of the republic-level secret police and the procurator of the Ukrainian SSR. The immediate release of Fedin was ordered.[58] Because of its refusal, the Ukrainian Special Assembly did not refer the request to the Special Assembly under the OGPU Collegium in Moscow, which would have had the final word on deporting Fedin.[59]

In another case, the Ukrainian Special Assembly did forward a request to its all-Union counterpart in Moscow. Ivan Dmitrievich Zhigulev, allegedly a thief with repeated offenses, was sent to a labor camp for three years by the USSR Special Assembly on 15 January 1926 as a "socially harmful element."[60] On 10 December 1925, the head of the Registration and Information Department of the Ukrainian GPU in Kharkiv—which acted as a transit point between the Ukrainian and Soviet special assemblies—had handed Zhigulev over to the USSR Special Assembly.[61] However, in its decision of 24 November 1925, the Special Assembly of the Ukraine had actually recommended that the twenty-one-year-old repeat offender be deported to Arkhangel'sk for two years, a sentence that the Special Assembly in Moscow then revised by sending him to a labor camp and adding a third year. There was also no longer an exact place where he was to be imprisoned.[62]

To wind up in the coils of the Special Assembly, however, a person need not, as in the cases of Fedin and Zhigulev, have several previous arrests carried out by the GPU and leading to conviction. Efforts to curb smuggling or the black market trade were sufficient.[63] For example, on 15 July 1926, in response to a request from the Odesa District GPU, the Special Assembly of Ukraine recommended that the Special Assembly in Moscow exile Konstantin Dmitrievich Stefatis to Siberia for three years because he was a "malicious trader in foreign currency and a socially dangerous element."[64] Extracts from the GPU "black market" file and investigation files of the Odesa District GPU compiled by the Economics Section of the Odesa District GPU had been sufficient to refer his case to the Ukrainian Special Assembly—that is, to condemn him administratively.[65] The corresponding memorandum contained only statements provided by secret police agents and denunciations of Stefatis given by arrested dealers or buyers of foreign currency. It is worth noting that Stefatis had not been arrested several times; he did not even have a criminal record.

ADMINISTRATIVE PUNISHMENT

The key term in all cases is "administrative." It is the very heart of the Special Assembly system. The delinquents were selected and screened with the help of a sophisticated bureaucratic administrative act, and after sentencing the Special Assembly either deported them abroad, usually for three years, placed them in a labor camp in distant or isolated areas of the RSFSR, or "only" banished them to a faraway place under the supervision of the secret police. The administrative act was characterized by the fact that various state organs at all levels of the hierarchy were involved: the militia, the Investigation Department of the Soviet Executive Committee, the Executive Committee itself, the secret police, and the judiciary in the person of the public procurator. The participation of numerous authorities and institutions served as a means of mutual control, and the system as a whole was strictly tiered. The secret police held a key position at almost all levels. Furthermore, the position of the public procurator's office with its right of veto was also significant. The militia had a great deal of responsibility at the lower and middle levels with regard to social deviance.

When the cases were elaborated, a file was created. From time to time, paragraphs from the Criminal Code were listed, and in the end a kind of punishment was imposed. Nevertheless, the basis for the whole procedure was not the Criminal Code but decisions and orders of VTsIK and the Council of People's Commissars (Sovnarkom). Only in exceptional cases did the investigative file contain delinquents' interrogation protocols, and then very brief ones.[66] In contrast, the corresponding provision required that the "prior clarification of the reasons for resettlement must be accompanied by a personal summons and questioning of the person to be resettled."[67] However, there were no regulations on how detailed and how many questionings should take place. Witness records were made irregularly, and when they were documented, they were not very detailed.[68] All this meant that when the file was compiled, the focus was rather on materials *about* a person, such as agent reports, detailed descriptions of investigators, and documents about raids, fingerprints, past arrests, and court convictions. When the case was finally heard before the Special Assembly, first in Kharkiv and then in Moscow, the delinquent was not present. There were no defense attorneys.

In justifying the administrative deportation or sentencing of a person to a labor camp, the public procurator, militia, and secret police regularly referred to the Decree on the Rights of the OGPU in the Area of Administrative Resettlement and Admission to a Labor Camp, issued by VTsIK on 24 March 1924.[69] This decree laid out not only the structure described above—the composition of personnel, the level of penalties, the type of involvement of the public procurator's office, and the competencies of the Special Assembly—but also the target groups of the Special Assembly, which was of central importance for the ongoing proceedings. A dichotomy should be noted here. Article 4 covers crimes of political and state relevance, and article 6 addresses social deviance, including organized crime.[70] The naming of target groups is further characterized by the fact that the scope for action was high in the case of political deviation and low in the case of state and socially significant deviation. For the latter groups, very specific information was provided:

Article 4 . . .

(a) [persons] involved in counterrevolutionary activity, espionage, and other state crimes under sections 57–73 of the Criminal Code of the RSFSR;

(b) those suspected of smuggling goods or crossing the border without proper authorization or of encouraging such crossing;

(c) [persons] suspected of manufacturing counterfeit money and state identity documents . . .;

(d) who trade in gold coins, foreign currency, precious metals, and crude platinum and whose activities are associated with foreign organizations without being [officially sanctioned] trade; . . . [persons] who are suspected of being involved in the manufacture of counterfeit money and government identification documents . . .; . . . [persons] who are suspected of being involved in the manufacture of counterfeit money and government identification documents without being [officially sanctioned] trade; . . . [persons] who are suspected of being involved in the manufacture of counterfeit money and government identification documents.

Article 6 . . .

(a) [persons] who are suspected of committing robbery [or] robbery and looting and their supporters and confidants . . .;

(b) [persons] who are unemployed and not engaged in productive work, in particular: (1) professional gamblers at games of chance and persons who bet money on horse races and gamblers in gambling salons; (2) cheats and swindlers; (3) operators of any kind of dives and brothels; (4) dealers in cocaine, morphine, santonine, alcohol, and other alcoholic substances without proper permission; (5) speculators on the black market, against whom there is information about their particular malice or contacts with the social-criminal milieu; [and] (6) persons who are socially dangerous because of their past behavior, in particular who have had no less than two convictions in the past or four arrests on suspicion of theft of property or attacks on a person and his or her dignity (hooliganism, involvement in prostitution, procuring, etc.).[71]

Beyond the procedure and the definition of target groups, the ordinance also regulated the further treatment of the delinquents after their sentencing: not only did the resettled persons lose the right to stay in their places of origin for up to three years, but they also lost the right to stay in certain places that were listed by the OGPU. Even the treatment of the condemned in exile was an issue. Therefore, it was determined that if the condemned were not immediately imprisoned in a labor camp, they would have to live under the constant supervision of the local GPU and "during the resettlement, they lost the right to vote and to stand for election and the right to be a member of public organizations, as well as the right to freedom of movement in the district of their exile."[72]

BELOW THE RADAR

The Special Assembly system was characterized by the use of a special language that referred directly to the institution's broader goals. The delinquents were regularly labeled as "socially harmful elements" or "socially dangerous elements" as soon as the proceedings began. This was a shift away from a concrete act to an abstract conception of danger—a step toward the protection of the working class and its regime from undesirable influences and threats. Accordingly, in the administrative proceedings of the Special Assembly, the concrete act was secondary, even if it justified the arrest. The basis for assessing and defining a person was the overall impression of how well someone fell into line with the new society, both in the present *and* the past. Arrests could even be made purely on the basis of records. Convictions already served counted. The actual act receded into the background to such an extent that, strictly speaking, one cannot speak of "conviction," "sentence," or "punishment" by the Special Assembly, especially since these terms rarely appear in the files. One obvious sign was that escape from a camp was to be expressly prosecuted but a "conviction" by the Special Assembly did not initially appear on a person's criminal record. The fixation on the overall impression was also reflected in the conduct of the proceedings. The guiding principle was not, as in court, to prove and substantiate the suspicion of a concrete act. The proceedings, by bringing forward the threshold for intervention, began with suspicion—that is, at the moment of general suspicion, long before the evidence was presented. The procedure then bypassed impartial evidence altogether and, finally, with the sending abroad—to either a labor camp or a distant area—resulted in a preventive-educational measure for the social adaptation and, in the long run, reintegration of the individual. Consequently, the goal was not an appropriate punishment for a deviant individual so much as justification for a generalized, didactic instruction for action. Against this backdrop, the typical three-year deportation abroad or to distant regions, which appears excessive from a criminal law perspective, also makes sense. It again points to the decoupling of power and the nature of the state's criminal reaction from the proven individual guilt of a delinquent.

The Special Assembly system, aptly called "administrative," served not only to control and paralyze potentially deviant attitudes and to prevent the self-organization of society. A review of the penal practice of the Special Assembly reveals that the core task of this extrajudicial body was to combat deviance of any kind in its social milieu and social structure. The body did record and punish soft forms of political deviance—as has long been known—but it also curbed, as the examined criminal files from the Ukrainian militia archives show, less severe but persistent social deviance. The widely visible disciplining of the intelligentsia and the prevention of "autochthonous political-social initiative" (to quote Manfred Hildermeier), which was visible on the surface, was thus the reason given for but by no means the main intention behind the establishment of the Special Assembly. The objective was to combat less significant political and social deviation as well. This included social networks and communalization beyond state and party in the pre-political, noninstitution-alized space and the parallel social worlds of nonorganized crime—including contacts with the criminal milieu, hooliganism, begging, drifting, the world of the unemployed and unlicensed, moonlighting, smuggling, border violations, and other minor social deviations. For this reason alone, it is absurd to invoke comparisons to the similarly named Special Assembly of the tsarist empire, which concentrated on deviations from the system.[73]

The goal of using the USSR Special Assembly to combat all forms of devi-ance within the social milieu was not a development that resulted from crimi-nal practice. The combination was either planned from the very beginning or, at least, introduced in 1924.[74] This is evident in the Decree on the Rights of the OGPU in the Field of Administrative Resettlement and Admission to a Labor Camp, which referred to political and social deviants as "socially dangerous" and meticulously listed them as target groups of the Special Assembly.[75] In the Ukrainian SSR, in contrast, penal practices were precisely what led to both political and social deviance being dealt with primarily at the highest level. As a result, at least in Ukraine, the possibility laid down in the decree of 24 March 1924—that social deviance, in contrast to political deviance, could be handled at the republican level, not only by the USSR Special Assembly in Moscow—was implemented only sporadically. Such punishments were per-mitted, however, only if the plans called for targets to be exiled within the republic. In Ukraine, which may have been an exception, few social dissenters were exiled within the republic, and the OGPU's Special Assembly in Mos-cow took over the handling of social dissent almost in its entirety.[76] The USSR Special Assembly was also unable to fill the position left vacant by the revo-lutionary tribunals, which were abolished as soon as they were established. The jurisdiction of the revolutionary tribunals was instead transferred to the Justice Council under the OGPU Collegium.

Did the establishment of the Special Assembly relieve the people's and other courts? In fact, the task of the Special Assembly was to take over cases in which the people's and provincial courts had proven to be ineffective. While only a side effect, and not one of the reasons for establishing the Special Assembly, it was also true that it relieved overcrowding in prisons. Nor did the new form of comprehensive discipline of the social milieu via the Special Assembly serve to supplement the legal codes of the socialist state, which were revised in June 1922 or to circumvent them at the same level. It was instead an instrument designed to operate *below* the radar of the legal code. A specific extrajudicial state agency was born. By comparison, the tsarist Special Assem-bly, on the basis of emergency and special legislation, circumvented "normal" law or acted without its limitations.[77]

REVOLUTIONARY JUSTICE

With the creation of the Special Assembly, the Bolsheviks sought new forms of social discipline and social defense (*défense sociale*) beyond the law, trials, sentences, and punishment. Above all, we can conclude from criminal practice that the institution was intended to issue an objective ruling on the isolation of a deviant individual, in the literal sense of the word, based on a hierarchically, bureaucratically structured process of investigation, far from the scene of the event and relying only on the files, but under the supervision and with the participation of a lawyer. With a great deal of goodwill, even the idea of resocialization can be discovered by interpreting the sending abroad or to distant areas of the RSFSR as a humanitarian and legitimate act: the individual was taken out of his harmful social milieu by the Soviet state and was able to come to his senses abroad or, under the supervision of the secret police, at home, in a labor camp, or in exile.

The end does not justify the means. Focusing on the actions of the administration makes it clear that the founding of the Special Assembly meant the intermingling of the executive and the judiciary. The executive was even placed above the judiciary, with the secret police clearly dominating the Special Assembly. Not only was the separation of powers abolished, but it was also possible to impose penalties officially sanctioned by the state without a regular court having proven the delinquent's guilt. A safeguard was built in so that lawyers sat in the Special Assembly and, therefore, had to be involved in the decision making. The body was also controlled by a strictly hierarchical, bureaucratic confirmation procedure in which civilian state bodies also participated.

We should emphasize that this new, extrajudicial state body was politically initiated and officially set up by the government. The press wrote about it. It did not supplement the legal code or circumvent it, but instead operated below its radar. With the formation of the Special Assembly, the illegal but common practice of the secret police of harassing and disciplining society in areas not relevant to criminal law was officially given a state-bureaucratic foundation, tightly controlled, and provided with a proper budget. The special powers that had allowed the Cheka to intimidate the population without criminal legitimation, which had previously only been tolerated, were thus not abolished. Instead of disappearing altogether, these powers were removed to some extent from the Cheka's jurisdiction but given greater state and political weight as the fight was organized more effectively and on a broader scale.

A fundamental problem with the administrative procedure is that the Special Assembly did not seek a (milder) alternative to social discipline in the codification of socialist legality. The focus on milieu and structural control below the radar of the legal code was not intended to moderate power or to protect or supplement the newly codified socialist legal system. On the contrary, in the name of social defense and loyalty building, it brought about a systematic expansion of state intervention beyond the areas of criminal law through a purely administrative act, one characterized by the principle of "in case of doubt, rule against the accused." The primacy of complete and generally comprehensible evidence to establish the truth and make it possible to assess a punishment that would be fair for the individual—and thus the ability to legitimize the state before society—was nullified. Contrary to the rhetoric that the threat from outside left the state with no choice but to apply administrative, extrajudicial punishment, the question was rather about a new technology of punishment that could prevent any tendencies to establish "traitors" who would strike their blows from within society. The generation of loyalty, not the fight against illegitimacy, was in the foreground. Rather than to administer justice, the state aimed to create a set of tools with which it could build up sovereign power over an area of society that had never before been penetrated to this extent and in this form.[78] Prophylaxis advanced to become a means of power.

Seen from the perspective of milieu and structural control, the idea that the economic freedom of the New Economic Policy had to be paid for with the dismantling of social and political freedoms appears to be an artificial link that resonates with a certain interpretation of the increase in political and social controls. The one had less to do with the other, however, than previously thought. The dismantling of political and social freedoms can be described less as a situational accompaniment and ad hoc reaction designed to regulate the economic crisis than as a proactive overall package aimed at disciplining politics and society. This package included the hand-picked preselection of candidates for the "democratic" election of soviets, the elimination of socialist competitors, the ban on factions within the party, and the reorganization of the extrajudicial system of punishment and social discipline, to name only four central points. It is undeniable that Lenin, in particular, effectively used conditional withdrawal in the economic sphere to push through these radical systemic changes. In retrospect, the stakes were set and would, in the long run, contribute decisively to the distortion of the social system, including the socialist economic system.

In conclusion, with the introduction of the Special Assembly, the Bolsheviks paid unprecedented attention to the social milieu and structural control of potentially politically resistant and socially deviant sections of the population below the radar of the legal code. In 1934, the Special Assembly was given the right to impose up to five years of banishment or imprisonment in a camp. From 1937 on, an additional five to eight years of political imprisonment were possible for political cases. Starting in 1941, the Special Assembly could even impose the death penalty in all cases.[79] A special, broad-based extrajudicial system developed as a result. With the beginning of collectivization and again in the Great Terror, other special bodies with extended or limited powers were grouped around the Special Assembly, depending on need, situation, and politics. This category includes the various troikas of 1929–1933 and the so-called kulak troikas (Order no. 00447), national troikas, police troikas, and dvoikas of 1937–1938.[80] In this sense, the formation of the Special Assembly in 1922 was the nucleus of the Great Terror in 1937–1938 and anticipated Stalin's mass repression. The Special Assembly was the starting point and a tool, then the center of force and escalation, in the social purge and restructuring of Soviet society.

This extrajudicial system was, in the spirit of Lenin, the decisive lever to manage the NEP, collectivization, industrialization, the threat of war, and the Great Terror. In this context, the Great Terror can be seen more as a combination of long-lasting systemic changes that occurred at the level of the penal system and the culmination of ruthless political, social, and economic engineering. In 1937, it became increasingly deadly, because the regime wanted to enforce its main goals once and for all. These goals included collectivization, rapid industrialization, and high investments in the defense and heavy industries in preparation for war.

According to this interpretation, the threat of war was not the trigger but an important motivation for the mass purge of society, as well as the party-state and the army. Most importantly, the argument regarding the threat of war as the defining element for the radicalization of social cleansing and, simultaneously, as the motivation to institute the Great Terror requires contextualization. The common thread between 1922 and 1953 is rather an indisputably intertwined and specifically Soviet interplay between a simultaneously proactive and reactive domestic war and an anticipated foreign one, with the Great Terror and the Great Patriotic War as the respective climaxes of these two cumulative drives.

NOTES

Many thanks to Peter Solomon, Benno Ennker, David Shearer, Carmen Scheide, Gábor Rittersporn, Lynne Viola, and the two anonymous peer reviewers for their comments on our chapter. Our research is supported by the German Science Foundation (Deutsche Forschungsgemeinschaft).

1. See, e.g., Geoffrey Roberts's formulation "No fascist threat, no terror" ("The Fascist Threat and Soviet Politics in the 1930s," in *Russia in the Age of Wars, 1914–45*, ed. Silvio Pons and Andrea Romano [Milan: Feltrinelli, 2000], 158).

2. The term "fifth column" originated with a 1936 radio address by Emilio Mola, a Nationalist general during the 1936–1939 Spanish Civil War. As his army approached Madrid, a message was broadcast that the four columns of his forces outside the city would be supported by a fifth column of his supporters inside the city, intent on undermining the Republican government from within.

3. Our in-depth exploration and broader discussion of the pre-2016 historical literature about the controversial motives that induced the Soviet leadership to extend the Terror in the summer of 1937 from members of the elite to the population at large via mass operations, thereby transforming "terror" into the Great Terror, can be found in Marc Junge, *Stalin's Mass Repression and the Cold War Paradigm*, Kindle ed. (New York: Marc Junge, 2016), 27–51, page nos. from the PDF available at https://www.research gate.net/publication/307013676_Stalin's_Mass_Repression_and_the_Cold_War_Paradigm.

4. Junge, *Stalin's Mass Repression*, 47–51.

5. Junge, *Stalin's Mass Repression*.

6. Stephen Kotkin, *Stalin*, vol. 2: *Waiting for Hitler, 1929–1941* (New York: Penguin, 2017), 307, 368, 374–75, 377, 428–35.

7. Kotkin, *Stalin*, 2:429.

8. Kotkin, *Stalin*, 2:433.

9. Kotkin, *Stalin*, 2:435; Oleg Khlevniuk, "Reasons for the Great Terror: The Foreign Political Aspect," in *Russia in the Age of Wars*, 159–69. Many thanks to Michael David-Fox and David Shearer for strengthening our review of Stephen Kotkin's work.

10. Kotkin, *Stalin*, 2:307, 368, 374–75, 377, 428–33.

11. Kotkin, *Stalin*, 2:307–8, 378, 439. Kotkin also discusses the reasons for the Great Terror in the historiography. See his chapter "Terror as Statecraft," in *Stalin*.

12. David Shearer, "Stalin at War, 1918–1953: Patterns of Violence and Foreign Threat," *Jahrbücher für Geschichte Osteuropas* 66, no. 2 (2018): 188–217. Our review obscures the contributions of Shearer's book, which, in conjunction with Paul Hagenloh's *Stalin's Police: Public Order and Mass Repression in the USSR, 1926–1941* (Baltimore: Johns Hopkins University Press, 2009), brought out the whole idea of the purges of the socially harmful, the practices of mass operations. On Shearer's and Hagenloh's works, see Junge, *Stalin's Mass Repression*, 27–51.

13. Shearer, "Stalin at War," 189.

14. Shearer, "Stalin at War," 188.

15. Shearer, "Stalin at War," 213.

16. Shearer, "Stalin at War," 190, 191–212.

17. Shearer, "Stalin at War," 192–93.

18. Shearer, "Stalin at War," 195–201.

19. With respect to the Politburo members Viacheslav Molotov and Lazar Kaganovich, held up in the literature as the chief witnesses attesting to the central significance of the threat of war, we ask whether their after-the-fact appeals—their statements originate in the 1960s and 1970s—are but ex post facto justifications utilizing World War II, which unexpectedly targeted the leadership, as an explanation for the mass operations. See David Shearer, *Policing Stalin's Socialism: Repression and Social Order in the Soviet Union, 1924–1953* (New Haven: Yale University Press, 2009), 16–17; and Junge, *Stalin's Mass Repression*, 27–51.

20. Ol'ga Bystrova, "Izdatel'skii proekt M. Gor'kogo 'Istoriia grazhdanskoi voiny': Po materialam arkhiva Gor'kogo (IMLI RAN) i RGASPI," *Studia Litterarum*, no. 4 (2017): 378–93, http://studlit.ru /images/2017-2-4/Bystrova.pdf.

21. Many thanks to Benno Ennker for strengthening our review of David Shearer's work.

22. Discussion with Lynne Viola on 22 November 2020.

23. Lynne Viola, *Stalinist Perpetrators on Trial: Scenes from the Great Terror in Soviet Ukraine* (New York:

Oxford University Press, 2017), 10. Our thematic review of Viola's book was inspired by Michael David Fox, "Review of Lynne Viola, *Stalinist Perpetrators on Trial*," *Russian Review* 77, no. 4 (2018): 668–69; and Heather J. Coleman, Alan Barenberg, Wendy Z. Goldman, Tanja Penter, and Lynne Viola, "A Roundtable on Lynne Viola's *Stalinist Perpetrators on Trial*," *Canadian Slavonic Papers*, published online 15 Apr 2019, https://doi.org/10.1080/00085006.2019.1594490.

24. Viola, *Stalinist Perpetrators on Trial*, 87–88.

25. Viola, *Stalinist Perpetrators on Trial*, 88.

26. Viola, *Stalinist Perpetrators on Trial*, 172.

27. Viola, *Stalinist Perpetrators on Trial*, 172.

28. Viola, *Stalinist Perpetrators on Trial*, 173.

29. In that sense, Viola clairvoyantly "places little emphasis on the Kirov murder in precipitating the terror." See "Comment by Wendy Z. Goldman," in Coleman et al., "Roundtable," 7.

30. Vladimir Khaustov and Lennard Samuel'son, *Stalin, NKVD i repressii 1936–1938 g.* (Moscow: ROSSPEN, 2009), 281, 286, 328.

31. About the various extrajudicial boards of the mass repression, see Junge, *Stalin's Mass Repression*, 10–13.

32. It is indisputable that even during the Civil War the Cheka showed a tendency toward the mass registration of unreliable population groups in order to persecute them in the future. An example of this is the registration of the so-called White officers, but also the systematic and mass registration of "kulaks"—for example, in Tiumen. See V. Shishkin, "Sekretnaia operatsiia tiumenskoi GUBChEKa po uchetu kulatskogo elementa, iiul' 1920–aprel' 1921," in *Sibirskaia derevnia: Problemy istorii. Sbornik nauchnykh trudov*, ed. V. A. Lamin (Novosibirsk: Institut istorii RAN, 2004), 107–13.

33. Matthew Rendle, "Revolutionary Tribunals and the Origins of Terror in Soviet Russia," *Historical Research* 84, no. 226 (2011): 693–721.

34. Our research is based on 6,155 investigation files from the police archives of Odesa (Odessa), Mykolaiv (Nikolaev), and Kyiv (Kiev), all dating from 1920 to 1948. See Haluzevyi derzhavnyi arkhiv Ministerstva vnutrishnikh sprav Ukraïny (HDA MVSU), Kyiv f. 32, op. 1; Odesa, ff. 3–4; and Mykolaiv f. 1, op. 1. Additionally, we analyzed 1,125 Special Assembly protocols of the Ukrainian Republic from 1926 to 1934 in the police and secret police archives. See "Protokoly Osobogo soveshchaniia pri OGPU-NKVD SSSR," nos. 77–128/1225 (16 November 1926–5 July 1934); HDA MVSU, Kyiv f. 42, op. 1; and Haluzevyi derzhavnyi arkhiv Sluzhby bezpeky Ukraïni (HDASBU), Kyiv f. 6, spr. 4. We examined the protocols of the Ukrainian Republic troika and the various troikas of the Odesa, Mykolaiv, and Kyiv regions from 1929 to 1938 in the secret police and police archives in Kyiv and in the police archive in Odesa (HDASBU, Kyiv f. 6, op. 4; HDA MVSU, Kyiv f. 42, op. 1; HDA MVSU, Odesa f. 6). Many thanks to Volodymyr Mel'nyk (HDA MVSU, Kyiv), and Serhii Kokin, Maria Panova, and Andrii Kohut (HDASBU, Kyiv).

35. "Soviet state violence was not simply repressive. It was employed as a tool for fashioning an idealized image of a better, purer society. It was employed as a tool for fashioning an idealized image of a better, purer society" (Peter Holquist, "State Violence as Technique: The Logic of Violence in Soviet Totalitarianism," in *Stalinism: The Essential Readings*, ed. David L. Hoffmann [New York: Wiley, 2003], 134); "The content of this specific totalitarian terror is never simply negative—for example the defeat of the enemies of the regime—but rather serves positively the realization of the given totalitarian fiction—construction of a classless society or a community of people or a race-based society" (Hannah Arendt, *Elemente und Ursprünge totaler Herrschaft* [Frankfurt am Main: Piper, 1955], 666–67). All quotations indicate the political force, the will, etc. that was behind the instrumentalized institutions.

36. "Postanovlenie Politbiuro TsK RKP(b) po dokladnoi zapiske GPU 'Ob antisovetskikh gruppirovkakh sredi intelligentsii,'" 8 June 1922, Arkhiv Prezidenta Rossiiskoi Federatsii (AP RF) f. 3, op. 58, d. 175, ll. 6–6 ob., https://www.alexanderyakovlev.org/almanah/inside/almanah-doc/56017.

37. "Vypiska iz protokola no. 53 zasedaniia Prezidiuma VTsIK po voprosu ob utverzhenii dekreta 'Ob administrativnoi vysylke,'" 10 August 1922, AP RF f. 3, op. 58, d. 175, l. 71, https://www.alexander yakovlev.org/almanah/inside/almanah-doc/56069. The Decree on Administrative Deportation was not drawn up by the People's Commissariat for Justice, as the Politburo decision indicated, but by the GPU apparatus.

38. From 1922 to 1924, the Special Assembly was known as the Special Commission of the NKVD of the RSFSR; it later became the Special Assembly under the OGPU Collegium of the SSSR.

39. "Pis'mo V. I. Lenina F. E. Dzerzhinskomu [o vysylke pisatelei i professorov za granitsu]," 19 May 1922, in Lenin, *Polnoe sobranie sochinenii*, 5th ed., 55 vols. (Moscow: Institut marksizma i leninizma, 1958–1965), 54:265–66.

40. "Pis'mo V. I. Lenina F. E. Dzerzhinskomu."

41. "Dokladnaia zapiska GPU v Politbiuro TsK RKP(b) 'Ob antisovetskikh gruppirovkakh sredi intelligentsii," 31 May 1922, AP RF f. 3, op. 58, d. 175, ll. 8–12, https://www.alexanderyakovlev.org/almanah/inside/almanah-doc/56015.

42. "Dokladnaia zapiska GPU v Politbiuro TsK RKP(b)."

43. M. A. Osorgin, "Kak nas uekhali," in his *Vremena* (Paris: ALON, 1955), 180–85; L. D. Trotskii, "Diktatura, gde tvoi khlyst?," *Pravda* 121 (1922); draft at https://bessmertnybarak.ru/article/diktatura_gde_tvoy_khlyst/.

44. Oleg Mozokhin, *Osoboe soveshchanie v Rossii i SSSR, 1881–1953*, http://www.observer.materik.ru/observer/N3-4_02/3-4_14.htm.

45. Andrei Nikolaevich Artizov, "'Ochistim Rossiiu nadolgo': K istorii vysylki intelligentsii v 1922 g.," *Otechestvennye arkhivy* 1 (2003): 65–96, http://portal.rusarchives.ru/publication/deportation.shtml.

46. The militia archives are currently not accessible in Russia or in any of the other Soviet Union's successor states.

47. *Social milieu*: the people, physical, and social conditions and events that provide the environment in which someone acts or lives.

48. "Delo Davida Lazarevicha Cherkaskogo," 1924, HDA MVSU, Odesa f. 3, spr. 8221.

49. "Delo Sergeia Fedotovicha Kardasheva," 1924, HDA MVSU, Odesa f. 3, spr. 10197.

50. "Delo Vladimira Lvovicha Slonina," 1924, HDA MVSU, Odesa f. 3, spr. 8219.

51. "Protokol obyska F. V. Fedina," 21 October 1925, HDA MVSU, Odesa f. 3, spr. 10179, ark. 8; "Postanovlenie no. 1066 Odesskogo gubernskogo upravleniia militsii i ugolovnogo rozyska o F. V. Fedine," 22 October 1925, HDA MVSU, Odesa f. 3, spr. 10179, ark. 1.

52. "Raport upolnomochennogo 2 ranga ugolovnogo stola Odesskoi gorodskoi militsii," 21 October 1925, HDA MVSU, Odesa f. 3, ark. 7.

53. "Anketa administrativno vysylaemogo F. V. Fedina," 24 October 1925, HDA MVSU, Odesa f. 3, ark. 11.

54. The document erroneously states the date as 22 March 1924, but the correct date is given in "Polozhenie o pravakh OGPU v chasti administrativnykh vysylok, ssylok i zakliucheniia v kontsentratsionnyi lager, 24.03.1924," in *Lubianka: VChK-OGPU-NKVD-NKGB-MGB-MVD-KGB, 1917–1960. Spravochnik*, ed. Aleksandr Kokurin, N. V. Petrov, and R. G. Pikhoia (Moscow: Mezhdunarodnyi fond "Demokratiia," 1997), 179–81. For the request to remove him, see "Postanovlenie pomoshchnika nachal'nika Odesskoi militsii i ugolovnogo rozyska S. Rakoshits o F. V. Fedine," 25 October 1925, HDA MVSU, Odesa f. 3, spr. 10179, ark. 12.

55. "Postanovlenie Rakoshits o Fedine," 25 October 1925, HDA MVSU, Odesa f. 3, spr. 10179, ark. 12.

56. "Postanovlenie starshego pomoshchnika prokurora po adminnadzoru Moskvin o F. V. Fedine," 4 November 1925, HDA MVSU, Odesa f. 3, spr. 10179, ark. 4.

57. "Postanovlenie Rakoshits o Fedine," 25 October 1925, HDA MVSU, Odesa f. 3, spr. 10179, ark. 12; "Protokol doprosa F. V. Fedina," 21 December 1925, HDA MVSU, Odesa f. 3, spr. 10179, ark. 14; "Spravka o F. V. Fedine," 14 November 1925, HDA MVSU, Odesa f. 3, spr. 10179, ark. 2.

58. "Vypiska iz protokola no. 44 Osobogo soveshchaniia pri Kollegii GPU USSR," 9 February 1926, HDA MVSU, Odesa f. 3, spr. 10179, ark. 26; "Vypiska iz protokola Osobogo soveshchaniia pri Kollegii OGPU SSSR," 15 January 1926, HDA MVSU, Odesa f. 3, spr. 8230, ark. 32.

59. Another case was tried and convicted by the Special Assembly under the OGPU Collegium of the SSSR in Moscow: that of Ivan Dmitrievich Zhigulev. On 15 January 1926, this committee sent him to a labor camp for three years as a "socially hostile element" ("Delo Ivana Dmitrievicha Zhiguleva," 1925–1926, HDA MVSU, Odesa f. 3, spr. 8230).

60. "Vypiska iz protokola Osobogo soveshchaniia," 15 January 1926, HDA MVSU, Odesa f. 3, spr. 8230, ark. 32.

61. "Nachal'nik uchetno-osveditel'nogo upravleniia GPU USSR v Osoboe soveshchanie pri Kollegii OGPU SSSR ob administrativnoi vysylke I. D. Zhiguleva," 10 December 1925, HDA MVSU, Odesa f. 3, spr. 8230, ark. 1.

62. "Vypiska iz protokola no. 38 Osobogo soveshchaniia pri Kollegii GPU USSR," 24 November 1925, HDA MVSU, Odesa f. 3, spr. 8230, ark. 2.

63. "Delo Iakova Venikhovicha Fraymana," started 15 June 1926, HDA MVSU, Odesa f. 3, spr. 8256.

64. "Vypiska iz protokola no. 57 Osobogo soveshchaniia pri Kollegii GPU USSR," 15 June 1926, HDA MVSU, Odesa f. 3, spr. 8243, ark. 53.

65. "Memorandum Ekonomicheskogo otdeleniia Odesskogo okruzhnogo otdela GPU o K. D. Stefatise," 13 May 1926, HDA MVSU, Odesa f. 3, spr. 8243, ark. 34–36.

66. Article 9, "Polozhenie o pravakh OGPU," 180–81. Articles 4 and 6, "Polozhenie o pravakh OGPU," 179–80.

67. "Delo Fedora Savel'evicha Moskalenko," HDA MVSU, Odesa f. 3, spr. 10047.

68. "Delo Feraponta Trafimovicha Tserniavskogo," HDA MVSU, Odesa f. 3, spr. 10079.

69. "Polozhenie o pravakh OGPU," 179–81.

70. Articles 4 and 6, "Polozhenie o pravakh OGPU," 179–80.

71. "Polozhenie o pravakh OGPU," 179–80.

72. Article 10, "Polozhenie o pravakh OGPU," 180.

73. Mozokhin, *Osoboe soveshchanie v Rossii*.

74. Documentary evidence shows that starting from 16 October 1922, which was a good two months after the founding of the Special Assembly, social deviants could also be administratively sentenced via this extrajudicial body. Those sentenced were repeat offenders who had been convicted twice for nonpolitical offenses and, based on the paragraphs listed in the document, were to be categorized as social deviants. See "Dekret VTsIK no. 427/c o dopolnenii k postanovleniiam 'O Gosudarstvennom politicheskom upravlenii' i 'Ob administrativnoi vysylke,'" 16 October 1922, in *Ostrakizm po-bol'shevistski: Presledovaniia politicheskikh opponentov v 1921–1924 gg.*, ed. V. G. Makarov and V. S. Khristoforov (Moscow: Russkii put', 2010), 29.

75. "Polozhenie o pravakh OGPU," 179–81.

76. Article 6, "Polozhenie o pravakh OGPU," 180.

77. The assessments of the tsarist Special Assembly are based primarily on the work of Vadim Ermakov ("Formirovanie rezhima iskliuchitel'nogo upravleniia v Rossiiskoi imperii," *Vestnik Moskovskogo universiteta*, ser. 21: *Upravlenie (gosudarstvo i obshchestvo)*, no. 4 (2009): 127–45.

78. Our theoretical and practical assessment of the formation of the Special Assembly draws on Michel Foucault, *In Verteidigung der Gesellschaft: Vorlesungen am Collège de France 1975/1976* (Frankfurt am Main: Suhrkamp, 1999), 161–64; Foucault, *Discipline and Punish: The Birth of the Prison*, trans. Alan Sheridan (New York: Random House, 1977); Marc Ancel, *Die neue Sozialverteidigung* (Stuttgart: Ferdinand Enke, 1970); Michael Baumann, *Zweckrationalität und Strafrecht: Argumente für ein tatbezogenes Maßnahmenrecht* (Opladen: Ulrich Beck, 1987); Susanne Krasmann, "Von der Disziplin zur Sicherheit: Foucault und die Kriminologie," in *Foucaults Machtanalytik und Soziale Arbeit: Eine kritische Einführung und Bestandsaufnahme*, ed. Roland Anhorn, Frank Bettinger, and Johannes Stehr (Wiesbaden: Springer, 2007), 155–68, esp. 164–65; Norbert Püttner, Wolf Dieter Narr, and Heiner

Busch, "Bekämpfungsrecht und Rechtsstaat: Vorwärtsverrechtlichung in gebremsten Bahnen?," *Bürgerrechte und Polizei* 82, no. 3 (2005): 6–15; Foucault, "Brief an einige Führer der Linken," in his *Schriften in vier Bänden*, vol. 3: *1976–1979* (Frankfurt am Main: Suhrkamp, 2003), 502–4; and Michael Hardt and Antonio Negri, *Empire: Die neue Weltordnung* (New York: Campus, 2002), 28, 52.

79. "Postanovlenie Politbiuro TsK VKP(b) ob utverzhdenii proekta postanovleniia TsIK SSSR 'Ob obra-zovanii obshchesoiuznogo Narodnogo komissariata vnutrennikh del,'" 15 July 1934," in *Lubianka: Stalin i VChK-GPU-OGPU-NKVD, ianvar' 1922–dekabr' 1936*, ed. V. N. Khaustov, V. P. Naumov, and N. S. Plotnikova (Moscow: Materik, 2003), 543–44; "Postanovlenie Politbiuro TsK VKP(b) ob utver-zhdenii polozheniia ob Osobom soveshchanii," 8 April 1937, in *Lubianka: Stalin i Glavnoe upravlenie gosbezopasnosti NKVD, 1937–1938*, ed. Khaustov, Naumov, and Plotnikova (Moscow: Materik, 2004), 126–27; "Postanovlenie Gosudarstvennogo komiteta oborony no. GKO-903ss.," 17 November 1941, http://www.soldat.ru/doc/gko/text/0903.html.

80. *Kulak troika and national troika*: committees of three formed in the capital and in all large adminis-trative units of the USSR, presided over by the corresponding head of the secret police, the NKVD. Members were procurators and party secretaries at the appropriate levels. The chairman of the police troika was usually the local, regional, or federal head of the NKVD or his representative, the other members being the state procurator and the leader of the administration of the civil police (*militsiia*), as well as the leader of the respective police departments. *Dvoika*: a commission of two, composed of the federal, regional, or local state procurator and the current head of the NKVD.

The NKVD and the Political Origins of Socialist Realism

The Persecution of the Boichukisty in Ukraine

Angelina Lucento

ON 17 DECEMBER 1936, AN NKVD COMMITTEE LED BY THE SPECIALIST SOL-
omon Gol'dman (fig. 2.1) interrogated the recently arrested painter Mykhailo
Boichuk (fig. 2.2) in a Kyiv prison cell. It seems likely that Boichuk's captors
had beaten or otherwise tortured him just before Gol'dman's interrogation to
force the artist into confessing to having been a Ukrainian nationalist. After
all, until the moment of his arrest, Boichuk had been the leader of the most
influential school of Ukrainian monumental artists known as the Boichukisty
(fig. 2.3), and the NKVD was especially interested in the Ukrainian character
of the group's projects. They asked Boichuk, "As part of your practical work,
what did you do?"[1] The "detrimental old Ukrainian art, ancient painting, and
the achievements of the bourgeois formal schools," he replied. "I sent youth
down that pathway of specialist training, tearing them consciously away from
the pathway to Socialist Realism, and in so doing, tore them away from their
participation in the building of socialism."[2]

Despite the content of his "confession," Boichuk did not in fact promote
bourgeois nationalism or work to undermine the building of socialism. In

Работники НКВД, награжденные орденами

Figure 2.1. NKVD Specialist Solomon Gol'dman (second from left). Photographic portraits by E. Komma for the newspaper *Sotsialisticheskii Donbass*, published 23 December 1937.

fact, Gol'dman's officers probably prefabricated this particular deposition statement, for as Lynne Viola has shown, the NKVD in Soviet Ukraine generally aimed to carry out quick and simple interrogations "with an eye to establishing the 'criminal connections' of those arrested."[3] Nevertheless, Boichuk's case file, like the files of his students, contains several pages of interrogation protocols about his views on national self-expression and Socialist Realism, testifying to a lengthy and sophisticated exchange on the topic before his eventual conviction and execution in 1937.[4] Despite its falsifications and fabrications, the semantic content of the discourse between the Boichukisty and their captors offers significant insight into the relationship between the secret police and the development of Socialist Realism in early Soviet Ukraine.

While art and cultural historians have long debated the relationship between visual art and the Soviet state, to date no scholar has studied the connection between the secret police and the development of Socialist Realism in the visual arts.[5] This omission is especially interesting, given that the central and regional unions of visual artists adopted Socialist Realism as their official style during the Great Terror. Instead, scholars have focused on party directives and specific internal debates among members of the artists' unions and other regulating institutions. Igor Golomstock, for example, based the sections about Soviet visual art and Socialist Realism in *Totalitarian Art* on an assessment of articles from the Soviet press, published party declarations, and formal comparisons of the heroes of Soviet Socialist Realist art to the superhuman and idealized figures that proliferate in works by Nazi artists and propagandists of Italian Fascism. From this Golomstock concluded that

Figure 2.2. Portrait of Mykhailo Boichuk, late 1920s.

Socialist Realism became the dominant style because the Bolshevik government representatives regulating the visual arts began to deny commissions, materials, and exhibition space to those who failed to conform to Socialist Realism's prescribed forms.[6]

Based on analyses of archival documents, however, scholars such as Christina Kiaer and Susan Reid have since shown that the central party bureaucracy was not solely responsible for the development and implementation of Socialist Realism in the visual arts. Kiaer demonstrates specifically that the diverse group of Soviet artists that constituted the membership of the Moscow Regional Union of Artists (Moscow Artists' Union, MOSKh) supported the turn to Socialist Realism. They viewed the style as an opportunity to produce a socialist aesthetic that would help build the collective by finally and fully "undermining the coordinates of capitalist exploitation."[7] Reid further shows that even as definitions of what constituted Socialist Realism in all realms of culture became more concrete in the late 1930s, conflicting political, administrative, and aesthetic imperatives drove the style's evolution in the visual arts.[8] In contrast to Golomstock's assertion, Reid demonstrates that there was no single party line directing Socialist Realism's implementation in painting from the top down; the Stalinist visual arts bureaucracy was too unstable for that.[9] While this new research reveals the history of Socialist Realism's complex origins and evolution within the visual arts, it does not explain the style's relationship to the broader political questions driving the development of Soviet cultural policy in the 1930s, which focused primarily on the meaning of national form and its role in socialist culture.

Through its analyses of the discourse of the NKVD interrogations of the Boichukisty from the Ukrainian Security Service's archive and works produced by the artists, this article demonstrates that the Ukrainian NKVD played a critical role in the style's evolution. During the Great Terror, specialists like Gol'dman pursued artists and intellectuals whose activities they considered a

Figure 2.3. Group portrait of the Boichukisty on Vynohradna Hill near the Mezhyhirya Ceramics School. Left to right: Oksana Pavlenko, unidentified, Mariia Pleskivska, Ivan Padalka, Onufrii Biziukov, Vasyl Sedliar, and Volodymyr Tsyndria, c. 1926. Central State Archive-Museum of Literature and Art of Ukraine, Kyiv

threat to the Soviet state. Through its analysis of NKVD deposition discourse and the Boichukisty's work, this chapter shows that Gol'dman and his officers succeeded in turning the artists and the particular agricultural motifs and folk patterns that they favored into examples of what Socialist Realism in the Ukrainian Republic should not be. It further shows that the NKVD's purge of the Boichukisty and their works, most of which were either destroyed outright or locked away in museum storage units (*spetsfondy*), led to the redefinition of national form in Socialist Realist art in the Ukrainian Republic, and discusses the implications of such a redefinition for the broader evolution of the official style of Soviet visual art.

THE BOICHUKISTY:
AN AESTHETIC FOR A SOCIALIST UKRAINE

To understand why Gol'dman and his team targeted the Boichukisty and their works, it is first necessary to consider the history of the Boichukisty as socialist artists and the popular appeal of their approach to art both in the Ukrainian Republic and among artists and officials in Moscow. In 1917, Boichuk developed the practical and philosophical aspects of his aesthetic theory for socialism while working as the head of the mosaic, fresco, and icon section of the

Ukrainian Academy of Arts in Kyiv, an organization he helped establish.[10] The
city had been a hotbed for artistic experimentation since the beginning of the
twentieth century, and students traveled great distances to work with worldly
yet distinctive modernists like Boichuk and Alexandra Exter.[11] Unsurprisingly, those young, left-leaning Ukrainian artists who were interested in figurative painting and the forms and crafts associated with peasant life flocked to
Boichuk's studio.[12] As Michael F. Hamm has shown, when Ukraine went from
an independent to a contested political territory in 1918–1921/22, Kyivans
eagerly threw off the symbolic vestiges of the Russian Empire and began to
explore all the elements of national language and culture, including the visual
and material traditions of agrarian life, that had been banned under tsarist
rule.[13] Boichuk and his students began to think of these elements as the basis
of postrevolutionary socialist life.

In 1922, during the course of these debates, Boichuk gave a series of public
As a working group, the Boichukisty first gained a foothold in Kyiv's postrevolutionary visual arts scene in the early 1920s. At that time, early Soviet
Ukrainian artists' groups, like all other artists' groups across the USSR, were
debating what socialist art should look like. The groups' platforms were broad
and diverse. There seemed to be advocates for every style and every moment,
from traditional forms of academic realism to avant-garde abstraction. Boichuk and his students, however, stood out from the rest. Instead of making
arguments about the pros and cons of easel painting, they emphasized the
importance of monumental frescoes, traditional Ukrainian patterns, and figurative images of peasant life above all else.[14]

In 1922, during the course of these debates, Boichuk gave a series of public
presentations wherein he provided a detailed explanation of his school's position on the role of visual art in the socialist context.[15] He stressed above all that
for art to transform culture through its creativity, it needed to proliferate and
enter into every aspect of culture. "When art flourishes," Boichuk explained,
"it penetrates and saturates all popular creativity, from architecture to dress
(sewing, embroidery, etc.), and food (gingerbread, Easter eggs, etc.); from
poetry (words) to music it is present in popular celebrations (processions) and
daily entertainments."[16] To ensure that socialist visual art "flourished" and
began to saturate every aspect of postrevolutionary culture, Boichuk, a maxi-
malist in his theory of creative production, emphasized that above all it must
draw on works from different epochs and world regions, as well as the best
global traditions of art making that had preceded it.[17] Socialist artists would
be able to achieve this in practice only by learning collectively to produce
"analytic" sketches—deconstructed copies of works by master artists who had
preceded them.[18] This strategy, Boichuk explained, would allow socialist artists to master the practice of painterly composition, to learn how to best fill

in the work's surface details, and most importantly, to understand how to draw the human figure in a way that relies on the forms found in nature.[19] In Boichuk's view, once socialist artists had attained this skill set and could apply it to renderings of their contemporary and local content, they would be able to produce works that would penetrate all aspects of both world and Soviet culture.

An astute aesthetic thinker with a deep interest in Ukrainian history and folk culture, Boichuk spent much of his time as an artist and teacher working to understand which forms and types of figurative content could most effectively penetrate local Ukrainian culture.[20] "I think," Boichuk explained during another debate presentation on 22 March 1922, "that we have no reason to fear history . . . our task is to reveal, decipher, and understand history."[21] Although the artist does not offer specific instructions on how to "reveal, decipher, and understand history," his constant emphasis on the need to critically analyze and deconstruct all forms of masterful local art, including folk art, suggests that socialist artists would be able to expose the history of their local context in a way that would influence its development only when they learned to use the tools of art making to represent the forms and content specific to particular ethnic groups and places within Ukraine.

In practice, Boichuk encouraged his students to use the skills they had gained from the rigorous practice of analytic sketching to masterfully depict scenes from life around Ukraine, with an emphasis on the agrarian experience. The Boichukisty's renderings of Byzantine-like figures engaged in all aspects of peasant life and labor came to define their art. The artist also described the presence of regular patterns, particularly as they appear in Ukrainian folk art, as critical components of any and every artwork in history that managed to influence its surrounding culture. "Regulated patterns," he explained, "give creativity its power, constancy, and definition. Any unregulated pattern is temporary, short-lived, and shallow in its mass significance."[22] In addition to their emphasis on scenes from agrarian life, which in itself was not an uncommon motif in early Soviet Ukrainian art, the Boichukisty's consistent and strategic inclusion of the abstract decorative patterns found in Ukrainian folk art distinguished their work from that of the many other Ukrainian artists involved in the debates about the definition of socialist visual art.

Just as he never fully elucidates what it means for a work to "reveal history," Boichuk also does not explicitly explain how a work of art, once it contains the local content and ethnic patterns it needs to have an impact, will contribute to the development of socialism in Ukraine. He does, however, consistently underscore that every "high achievement," including the production of world-altering "Great Art," comes "from collective endeavor."[23] Boichuk spent the first half of his adult life traveling and studying art in different European cities, including Lviv, Kraków, Vienna, Munich, and Paris, where he established his first art school in 1908.[24] He grew up, however, in a peasant family in Romanivka, Austria-Hungary, which is now part of contemporary Ukraine's Ternopil region. Boichuk's emphasis on collective work, agrarian content, and folkloric patterns suggests that he viewed Ukraine's precapitalist, collectivist agricultural societies as the ideal models for its new and modern socialist system.[25] The historically familiar content and forms of his work and that of his students would "penetrate" contemporary culture by reminding Soviet Ukrainian viewers of the egalitarian, collectivist past their ancestors had all been part of until the twin evils of capitalism and imperialism remade the social order. Most of the Boichukisty also came from agrarian backgrounds, and by extending art education to other Ukrainian peasants, Boichuk also aimed to help his students become active participants in the development of the new socialist world by teaching them to harness their own creativity to skillfully produce art objects that could penetrate and encourage the redevelopment of ancient, Ukrainian collectivist culture.

Boichuk's 1920 poster *Shevchenko Day* (fig. 2.4) provides an example of how the artist imagined his particular aesthetic theory would be integrated into the broader postrevolutionary political project in the Ukrainian Republic. Here he depicts Taras Shevchenko dressed as a Cossack, a reference to the claim that the beloved national poet descended from members of the Zaporizhian Host. Boichuk shows Shevchenko leaning into the dark mane of his spotted tiger horse. As the animal gallops ahead at full speed, the poet carries a red banner bearing a verse from his 1845 poem "Testament." "Oh bury me and rise ye up," the banner reads. "And break your heavy chains. And water with the tyrants' blood the freedom you have gained."[26]

On the one hand, Boichuk's decision to apply Shevchenko's call to revolutionary action to the poster's bright red banner suggests that he supported Lenin's ongoing commitment as Bolshevik leader to quash the vestiges of empire and capitalism across Ukraine.[27] On the other hand, the particular application of a regulated pattern of national form to Shevchenko's hat and coat indicates that the artist imagined that Ukrainian socialism would develop not based on verbal directives from Moscow but on the republic's own national aesthetic.[28] Boichuk emphasizes that the naturally occurring dots on Shevchenko's fur hat, his collar, and the right cuff of his fur-trimmed coat have been shaped into a pattern by the Ukrainian craftspeople who made the national costume for the Cossack poet. Shevchenko's dynamic image, with its emphasis on patterned national craft, combines with the banner's call to

Figure 2.4. Mykhailo Boichuk, *Shevchenko Day* poster, 1920

revolution in an effort to awaken ideas and feelings about national freedom and unity against imperial tyranny.

By drawing the figure of Shevchenko holding his dotted right cuff against the spotted mane of his tiger horse, Boichuk also links a Ukrainian craft-work pattern to what he described in his presentations as an international artistic aesthetic. While spotted tiger horses were not terribly common in early twentieth-century Ukraine, they do feature in the Paleolithic paintings found in the Altamira Cave in Spain, which were discovered and written about publicly in the late nineteenth century. Ancient artisans used the cave's naturally occurring patterns—such as the element-derived chips in its stone walls, which created small areas of negative space resembling patterns of dots—to indicate the spots on the horses' coats. By linking the material pattern of Ukrainian national form to the material body of the horse, Boichuk asks potential international spectators to recognize the connection between the aesthetics of their own collectivist, precapitalist past and the aesthetics of a precapitalist, collectivist Ukraine.

Under their professor's guidance, the Boichukisty—who included left-leaning avant-garde artists such as Vasyl Sedliar, Ivan Padalka, and Oksana Pavlenko (fig. 2.3)—spent hours in the studio painstakingly acquiring the skills necessary to install figurative realist frescoes in socialist public space.[29] Boichuk believed that frescoes and other forms of monumental art had the greatest potential to influence the spectator, because they worked together with architectural forms to shape the public's experience of its environment. "Everything has to be subordinated," Boichuk explained, "to the place and position of a given architectural whole, to its character, its content, and the goal for which it is intended."[30]

As Boichuk's students honed their fresco installation skills, they also developed their own unique interpretations of the Boichukist approach. They then established the Mezhyhirya Artistic-Ceramic Technical School in the fall of 1921. The group appointed Sedliar, one of Boichuk's most productive and politically engaged students, as its director.[31] Located in the village of Mezhyhirya, just outside Kyiv, the school aimed to fulfill Boichuk's mission of making artistic education accessible to the peasant masses so that they might harness their creative potential and begin producing practical objects that could foster the development of an egalitarian agrarian collective. Classes were organized into workshops to promote collective work and the development of comradely relationships among students and faculty. As the 1927 advertisement for the school (fig. 2.5) shows, Pavlenko, Sedliar, and the other Boichukisty emphasized the production of traditional folk crafts, everyday pottery

Figure 2.5. Advertisement for the Mezhyhirya Artistic-Ceramic Technical School, 1927. Oksana Pavlenko is pictured in the center, together with Vasyl Sedliar, Ivan Padalka, and others

decorated with Ukrainian folk patterns, and the development of educational puppet shows about pre- and postrevolutionary agrarian life.

Although Boichuk's own views on Marxism-Leninism remained elusive, the core members of the Boichukisty—Sedliar, Padalka, and Pavlenko—embraced the philosophy in their own way. They led political discussions among the Mezhyhirya students about the value of Marxism-Leninism. And as Ukrainian debates about what constituted the most effective visual aesthetic for socialism intensified, both Boichuk and his students helped establish the Association of Revolutionary Art of Ukraine (ARMU) in late 1925.[32] As I. I. Vrona explained in the group's manifesto *Art of the Revolution and ARMU*, the organization's goal was to work "according to a sociopolitical line and to ensure that the works of artists and art as a whole are guided by issues of social class."[33] ARMU's platform, with its sincere and clearly stated commitment to social and class issues, further legitimized the Boichukisty's platform within the context of the early Soviet visual arts debates. It also provided them with an institutional structure that effectively promoted their monumental folk aesthetic as the best aesthetic for Ukrainian socialism within a system that encouraged the various artists' platforms to compete for both visibility and state funding.[34]

During the mid- to late 1920s, ARMU's most prominent competitors consisted of the Association of Contemporary Masters of Ukraine (OSMU) and the Association of Artists of Red Ukraine (AKhChU). Like the Boichukisty's ARMU, each had its own approach to the problem that the influential Moscow-based critic Iakov Tugendkhol'd described as the move from prerevolutionary "bourgeois-nationalist" art to "national-revolutionary art" in the Ukrainian Republic.[35] OSMU drew on West European modernisms, while AKhChU, as an affiliate of the Moscow-based Association of Artists of Revolutionary Russia (AKhRR), relied on a figurative realist style inspired by the nineteenth-century Russian Wanderers.[36] Despite intense and unrelenting public criticism of the ARMU artists' work by AKhChU's most prominent spokesperson, Fedir Krichevskii, ARMU's socialist platform, the popularity of Boichukism within the academy, and students' eagerness to attend their school at Mezhyhirya helped ensure that the Boichukisty became increasingly influential within the realm of the visual arts in early Soviet Ukraine.[37]

However, these were not the only factors that contributed to their rise. The prominent and very vocal Moscow-based critic and art historian Aleksei Fedorov-Davydov visited the Technical School at Mezhyhirya on several occasions. Impressed, he declared in a 1927 letter that the school's atmosphere was in fact "ideal," suggesting that the Boichukisty's achievements in the realm of socialist arts education exceeded those of the other early Soviet art schools, including the Higher Artistic and Technical Studios (VKhUTEMAS) in Moscow.[38] Fedorov-Davydov was especially enthusiastic about Oksana Pavlenko's work, so much so that he recommended her to Soviet Commissar of Enlightenment Anatolii Lunacharskii, who in 1929 invited Pavlenko to contribute to an exhibit of "Russian" art that was to be held at the Luxembourg Museum in Paris.[39] Lunacharskii's invitation not only helped Pavlenko gain a reputation as a talented Soviet Ukrainian artist. His recognition of the significance of her Boichukist aesthetic, with its emphasis on textile patterns and village life (fig. 2.6, *Female Delegates*, 1925), further elevated the status of the Boichukisty both within Moscow's visual arts circles and in the Ukrainian Soviet Republic.

The Boichukisty's influence as socialist artists devoted to Ukrainian themes and forms increased even further in the period from 1927 to 1929. Mykola Skrypnyk, a Bolshevik Party member and the then commissar of enlightenment of Soviet Ukraine, emphasized the need to expand the drive for Ukrainization—a cultural

Figure 2.6. Oksana Pavlenko, *Female Delegates*, 1925. Picture postcard printed by Sovetskii khudozhnik in 1976

program that emphasized the propagation of all aspects of Ukrainian culture, especially language, without "deviating" into nationalism.[40] Ukrainization was initiated in 1923, shortly after the Twelfth Party Congress decreed that it would adopt an "indigenization" (*korenizatsiia*) policy in the republics.[41] As a result, ethnic Ukrainians were recruited into the party-controlled institutions in the republic and the promotion of Ukrainian culture was officially endorsed.[42] The process was slow; the shift to Ukrainian language education in schools only reached its peak in 1930–1932, and even then large areas of the country in the east and south remained underserved.[43]

Following Skrypnyk's initiative, however, the work of the Boichukisty helped ensure that visual art made efficient and significant progress toward Ukrainization. By 1930, their folk patterns and scenes from agrarian and, to a lesser extent, industrial life had made them the most influential and powerful artists in Soviet Ukraine. As a result, the Boichukisty won multiple commissions to install frescoes in new public buildings that would soon have thousands of visitors. One such commission involved the installation of frescoes in the worker's club of the State Political Administration (GPU) in Odessa (fig. 2.7, c. 1930). That the Boichukisty won this commission to decorate a regional

Figure 2.7. Boichukisty. Fresco installed in the workers' club of the State Political Administration in Odessa. Photograph from a glass negative, c. 1930. National Art Museum of Ukraine, Kyiv

unit of the State Political Administration is itself a testament to both their prominence and the scope of their influence. The Odessa fresco focuses largely on the need for international workers, from the Ukrainian miner in the right foreground to the stream of Mexican peasants in national costume who appear to march toward him from behind, to unite in the struggle for socialism. However, the Boichukisty's clever superimposition of a disproportionately large loaf of bread over the hammer and sickle in the top right corner serves as a reminder to the Ukrainian viewer that the republic's path to socialism will depend on a return to the most basic precapitalist, collectivist peasant traditions, such as harvesting and grinding wheat to bake the bread that for centuries has fed families and villages.

Ironically, just as the Boichukisty's influence over the Ukrainization of visual art had reached something of a fever pitch, the Ukrainian GPU (reorganized under the name People's Commissariat for Internal Affairs [NKVD] in July 1934) first took serious notice of the group's activities.[44] On the one hand, the Ukrainization efforts of both central and local representatives of the Party depended on members of the cultural intelligentsia such as Boichuk and his students, because their knowledge of Ukrainian language, ethnic forms, and agrarian life had enormous potential to engage and unify the "peasant masses" under the aegis of the socialist project as stipulated by the First Five-Year Plan. On the other hand, as Matthew Pauly has demonstrated, both local party representatives and the GPU feared the ethnic Ukrainian intelligentsia, worrying constantly that its influence over the peasant-proletarian population would eventually outpace the Party's.[45] This anxiety reached its initial peak in March–April 1930 with the show trial against the Union for the Liberation of Ukraine (SVU). The SVU, however, was not a real entity. The party leaders, together with the GPU, fabricated it so that they might have a reason to arrest and prosecute "anti-Soviet" Ukrainian "nationalists" in an effort to ease their fears about losing control of the republic.[46] Pedagogical workers teaching in Ukrainian as part of the party-dictated Ukrainization effort constituted the majority of those targeted.[47] In the wake of the SVU show trial, Boichuk and the Boichukisty—as intellectuals, teachers, and artists—were not spared GPU scrutiny. Although none were arrested, the Ukrainian GPU's 1931 investigation into their activities laid the groundwork for the ultimate demise of the Boichukisty and their particular style of painting just as it began to define Socialist Realism in Soviet Ukraine.

SOCIALIST IN CONTENT, MUTED IN FORM

The NKVD file on Ivan Padalka (1894–1937) shows that Gol'dman started to collect materials that would eventually allow him to build a fabricated case against the Boichukisty while they were working on the Odessa frescoes.[48] Padalka's file includes a handful of informant depositions (*pokazaniia*), which consistently describe the artists—especially Boichuk, Padalka, and Sedliar—as chauvinists and anti-Soviet nationalists. The most significant depositions in the collection came from two "informants"—A. I. Popov and N. F. Sulima—two members of the Ukrainian intelligentsia who had been falsely convicted as being part of the SVU. Both informants offered "proof" of the Boichukisty's Ukrainian nationalism by describing them as eager to join in the SVU's purportedly anti-Soviet activities. It is unclear from the depositions whether Popov and Sulima were imprisoned at the time they submitted these signed statements, or if they had been re-detained by Gol'dman specifically for the sake of establishing false evidence against the artists. Either way, the GPU almost certainly used physical and/or psychological intimidation to coerce both men into making incriminating statements about the Boichukisty, just as they had during the lead-up to the SVU show trial, when they forced those identified as members of the organization to denounce other "members" in order to build their fabricated case.[49] Popov's and Sulima's depositions are also filled with statements about not knowing the details of the group's work and never having met one or more of its key members. Such frequent remarks about absent information not only underscore the falsity of the depositions' content; they suggest that Popov and Sulima may not have actually known the Boichukisty very well.

In his 15 April 1931 deposition, for example, Popov limited his accusations to the "Kyiv chauvinists" Padalka and Sedliar, claiming that he got to know these "students of Boichuk" in 1924. He went on to write that the artists' "active, anti-Soviet mood, which was based on Ukrainian nationalism, had an especially strong influence on discussions [about art and culture]."[50] Popov also commented that Boichuk, Padalka, and Sedliar greatly influenced their own students at the Kyiv Art Institute and at Mezhyhirya, "training them in a pointedly chauvinistic and anti-Soviet spirit."[51] He fails, however, to provide any concrete information about the nature of their involvement in the SVU. Popov first explains that in 1925 a third party with the surname Doroshkevich informed him of the Boichukisty's interest in joining the Kyiv section of the SVU. "Exactly what kind of work they did there," he writes, "I don't know."[52] He then remarks that he met Sedliar a few times in the summer of 1927, but once again cannot provide any specific details of their nationalist practices. "He told me," Popov explains, "that they (Boichuk, Padalka, Sedliar) truly belong to our organization and are part of the cell within the Kyiv Art Institute, which is led by Boichuk. Regarding the details of their work, I don't remember exactly what he said."[53]

Sulima begins his 4 July 1931 deposition a bit differently. First, he describes Sedliar as an antisemite, claiming that in 1927 the artist told him he got into a fight with a Jewish man over a seat on a steamboat and hurled ethnic slurs at him.[54] Sulima then comments that Sedliar visited Popov in Kharkiv and maintained a professional relationship with him.[55] "A.I. Popov," Sulima wrote, in a further attempt to confirm the artists' link to the SVU, "called Sedliar 'our man,' meaning a nationalist. But I do not have any concrete knowledge of Sedliar's counterrevolutionary work."[56] Having failed to specifically incriminate Sedliar, the author moved on to Padalka but failed there, too. "Padalka. Popov also characterized that artist as our man," Sulima wrote, "but I personally did not have close professional relations or nationalistic conversations with Padalka."[57] As part of a last-ditch effort to provide the GPU with the proof it sought, Sulima moved on to Boichuk. Once again he offers a secondhand description, writing that Popov always referred to Boichuk as a "Ukrainian talent" before commenting that he had no information about the artist "other than what was in the press" and that he never knew him personally.[58] Popov, Sulima concludes, always recommended that he act grateful toward those associated with the theater and film director Les Kurbas and the Boichukisty, "as representatives of Ukraine and Ukrainian nationalism in the arts, and I understood this to mean that cadres of Ukrainian nationalists clustered around Kurbas and Boichuk."[59]

Popov's and Sulima's pathological inability to offer any concrete information about the Boichukisty's SVU activities reveals that no matter how much Gol'dman tried to force them to provide fabricated evidence for a case against the "nationalist" artists, they simply could not write accounts of events that never actually happened.[60] In this impossible context, Sulima's accusation of antisemitism against Sedliar also reads less like fact and more like an effort to provide incriminating information that he hoped might temporarily satisfy Gol'dman's team.[61] Moreover, the informants' frequent references to the Boichukisty's chauvinism and nationalism, and in particular Sulima's implication that Popov's reference to Boichuk as a "Ukrainian talent" automatically indicated the artist's involvement in the SVU reflect Gol'dman's team's Ukrainophobia and desire to discredit Ukrainization.[62] That is, Popov and Sulima, irrespective of their own views or experiences with the Boichukisty, knew that these were the key phrases the GPU wanted to hear added to their narratives. In providing them, the pair, despite serious information gaps, gave Gol'dman exactly what he wanted—the beginnings of an incriminating case against the Boichukisty, which might justify their arrest and prosecution.

Having finished with Popov and Sulima, the GPU officer remained undeterred in his pursuit of the group and continued to collect incriminating "evidence" against the Boichukisty throughout the early 1930s. The content of these additional depositions, which are included in Boichuk's NKVD file, strongly resemble Popov's and Sulima's accounts in their lack of specific detail about nationalistic activities among the Boichukisty and their false claims about the group members being part of counterrevolutionary organizations. For example, one N. F. Khristovyi claims that ARMU "represented a vibrantly expressive nationalistic organization" and used the GPU-generated term "bourgeois-nationalist" to describe Boichukism.[63] As usual, however, the informant provides no details about ARMU's supposedly nationalistic activities, nor does he explain what exactly makes Boichukism bourgeois-nationalist.

After 1933, the nature of the accusations against Boichuk and the Boichukisty changed slightly to reflect the Ukrainian GPU's new priority: the rising external threat of Nazi Germany. Within the context of this new imperative, those interrogated by Gol'dman and his team began to accuse the Boichukisty of the most incriminating act they could fathom: of sympathizing and/or aligning themselves with Nazi fascism, a claim that could not have been farther from the truth. During a 15 February 1935 interrogation, for example, Hryhorii Epik, a Ukrainian-language poet who had been a member of the avant-garde writers' group Free Academy of Proletarian Literature (VAPLITE), denounced his "close friend" Ivan Padalka as a "fascist, an active supporter of Hitler's [political] orientation, who has demanded and led the struggle for Ukraine's immediate separation from Russia."[64] Epik and the other members of VAPLITE had been targeted as part of the GPU's ongoing anti-Ukrainization campaign and, like Sulima and Popov, would have been under severe pressure to confirm the incriminating evidence Gol'dman's team sought to compile against the Boichukisty.[65]

Despite the tenacity of his pursuit, Gol'dman did not arrest any of the Boichukisty between 1931 and 1935. The Ukrainization campaign, however embattled, remained in effect during this period. The Boichukisty continued to win commissions to produce highly visible monumental frescoes whose socialist themes appealed to Ukraine's peasant and proletarian masses, because theirs was exactly the type of work the Party sought. Meeting the needs of Ukrainization, even while under intense GPU surveillance, made it possible for the Boichukisty not only to enter into the debates about Socialist Realism in the visual arts but also to influence early definitions of the official style within and beyond the Ukrainian Republic.

The first major debates about the definition of Socialist Realism in Soviet visual art began at MOSKh in 1933. Most of the union's members agreed, without any external pressure from the Party, that they needed to formulate a unifying style of artistic representation that could contribute to socialist construction by producing works that actively created that reality.[66] As a Ukrainian representative and contributor to the Moscow union's affairs, Pavlenko emphasized this point in a 1933 letter to a fellow union member, the Hungarian émigré artist and theorist Béla Uitz. "Socialist Realism," she explained, "is not a theoretical system. It creates wall paintings. It is our living life and is manifold like our socialist reality."[67] Artists in the Ukrainian Republic and especially the members of the Ukrainian section of the all-Soviet Professional Union of Art Workers (RABIS) faced the same challenge as their Moscow colleagues; they needed to determine exactly what Socialist Realism should look like. Which forms and what content would best define it? No scholar has yet assessed the critical role that negotiations among the members of the Ukrainian section of RABIS, individual artists, and the Soviet state organs responsible for buying and commissioning works (e.g., museums and the central and local sections of the Commissariat of Enlightenment) played in changing definitions of Socialist Realism in the visual arts in early Soviet Ukraine.[68] We do know, however, based on commissions received and Sedliar's appointment as secretary of the organizing committee for the development of the Soviet Ukrainian Artists' Union, that the Boichukisty's influence over the visual artists in the republic, including discussions of definitions of Socialist Realism, continued to escalate until their arrest in the autumn of 1936.[69] From their perspective, Socialist Realism in Ukrainian visual art should be defined by the presence of ethnic folk patterns, especially as rendered on clothing, and scenes from agrarian life. Such form and content should not be confined to the canvas; it should, as Pavlenko explained to Uitz, create "wall paintings."

Boichuk's final preparatory sketch for *Harvest Holiday* (fig. 2.8), a fresco depicting a collective farm that he contributed to the group's commission to decorate the Red Industrial Plant Theater in Kharkiv, offers visual insight into the group's particular definition of Socialist Realism.[70] As in his earlier works, Boichuk relies on figurative realism to ensure that the picture as a work of art will be universally recognizable to both Soviet and international viewers.

Figure 2.8. Mykhailo Boichuk, *Harvest Holiday*. Final sketch for the fresco installed at the Red Industrial Plant Theater in Kharkiv, c. 1935

Unlike the laconically drawn, flat figure in his *Shevchenko Day* poster (fig. 2.4), the peasants in *Harvest Holiday* (fig. 2.8) appear solid and three-dimensional, with muscular curves and detailed facial features that seem to belong more to a photograph than to a sketch for a painting. The modern tractor steered by a skilled female driver, which makes its way diagonally through the center of the picture, divides the scene into two. The adult agricultural workers to the left of the tractor are dressed simply, in the traditional costumes worn by peasants in Ukraine. Some of the textiles in the painting, such as the embroidered blouse on the man holding the watermelon in the lower left corner, contain the traditional decorative patterns so critical to the Boichukisty's style. The tight-knit peasant group moves forward with the procession bearing the fruits of its labor. Boichuk highlights the importance of collective labor by placing two women working together to bear a heavy sheaf of wheat at the center of the peasant group and the two young boys sharing the burden of a full basket of apples in the picture's main foreground.[71] Here the artist underscores yet again that continuous contact with the forms of the past (clothing, decorative patterns) and with one another through agricultural practices will continue to serve as the basis for the development of an egalitarian, collective society.

Boichuk's depiction of the modernized crowd to the right side of the tractor contrasts sharply with his rendering of the peasantry. The figures to the
right of the band appear as ideal products of postrevolutionary Soviet modernity: male collective-farm bureaucrats in workers' caps, a tall sailor, a woman
in a white coat who might be the farm's hygiene specialist or medical worker,
and a row of tidy Pioneer children in the right foreground who look like they
are well on their way to being accepted into the Komsomol. Two traditionally dressed peasant women with very young children stand at the edge of
the crowd, closer to the painting's central foreground. Unlike the modern
Soviet crowd, they appear indifferent and even doubtful. The peasant mother
in the picture's right corner, for example, pulls her son and daughter close
to her body as they gaze and point excitedly at the tractor. This protective
gesture betrays her uncertainty about whether the tractor—a symbol of state-
initiated, industrialized collectivization—really will improve the lives of peasants in Ukraine.

This final sketch for *Harvest Holiday* reveals that in 1935 Boichuk defined
Socialist Realism as a specific type of monumental painting identifiable by its
reliance on three-dimensional, fleshed-out figures that, whether modern or
traditional, exhibit robust health. He also defined it as a style that emphasized
the importance of folk designs and agricultural traditions to the development
of a socialist collective, just as he and his students had done in their pre-
Socialist Realist pictures. What is striking, however, about Boichuk's Socialist
Realism is the dialogue he creates between traditional peasant collectivity and
the Soviet government's modern, machine-based collectivization initiative.
Despite his central emphasis on the impressive steel-bodied tractor designed
to complete in hours tasks that once took days, Boichuk distributes the majority of the fruits of the harvest among the traditionally dressed, traditionally
collectivized peasants and places a skeptical and protective peasant mother
in the picture's foreground. Socialist Realism, he suggests, must be critical
and question whether industrial collectivization, which produces orderly and
hygienic modern citizens like those shown on the right side of the frame,
can alone maintain the USSR's agricultural collectives. In Boichuk's Socialist
Realism, traditional forms and content expressing the "ancient" agricultural
experience are rendered as vital dialogical components of the march forward
toward the establishment of true socialist collectivity among the peasant
masses in Soviet Ukraine.[72]

In addition to their own tireless efforts, the Boichukisty's close ties to
Béla Uitz, Pavlenko's close friend and colleague in Moscow, helped them
maintain their status as authorities on Socialist Realism in monumental art
despite continued criticism from the AKhChU-Krichevskii circle and GPU

surveillance. In 1933, Uitz, who was not only a MOSKh member but also a cultural policy maker at the Communist Academy, initiated his own campaign for the inclusion of traditional ethnic forms, with a particular emphasis on their material textures (*faktura*), in Soviet Socialist Realism more broadly. As I have shown elsewhere, some of Uitz's own ideas about the importance of traditional, national forms in the development of a true, anti-imperial socialist collective emerged from his dialogue with the Boichukisty and their work.[73] Uitz in turn defended Boichuk against accusations of nationalism and separatism when some of his works were shown without his permission in a Berlin exhibition devoted to Ukrainian "anti-Soviet" artists. "Boichuk," Uitz wrote in a presentation delivered at either MOSKh or the Communist Academy, "as far as I know has never had any conflicts with the Soviet authorities and to this day has worked uninterruptedly for Soviet power."[74] Such unflagging support from Uitz together with the Boichukisty's ongoing dialogue with him about the role of traditional, ethnic forms in Socialist Realism helped ensure their continued influence in the Ukrainian visual arts until 1936.

As Hennadii Yefimenko has shown, after the peasant revolt against forced, industrialized collectivization in 1929–1933, Stalin's own view of Ukrainization became increasingly negative, even though he continued to recognize its importance as a means of communicating and carrying out party objectives.[75] By 1936–1937, those members of the Party pushing the anti-*korenizatsiia* hard line—who like Stalin, viewed Ukrainization as a potential catalyst for a counterrevolutionary, anti-Soviet insurgency—triumphed over those continuing to support the campaign.[76] Ukrainizing projects like the Boichukisty's were now considered a threat to the Soviet state, and Stalin began to put additional pressure on state security and other Bolshevik organizations to purge Ukraine of "bourgeois national" cultural elements once and for all.[77] This, plus the fact that after Kirov's assassination in 1934 Soviet law had become, as Lynne Viola demonstrates, increasingly "enabled for terror," created the perfect opportunity for Gol'dman to finally arrest the Boichukisty.[78] Hryhorii Epik's (forced) 1935 denunciation of Padalka as a "fascist, an active supporter of Hitler's [political] orientation, who has demanded and led the struggle for Ukraine's immediate separation from Russia" served as the first concrete catalyst to the artists' ultimate demise.

By asserting that Padalka was somehow aligned with Hitler *and* leading a campaign for Ukraine's separation from Russia/the USSR, Epik effectively declared the artist a saboteur working against the Soviet state on not one but two fronts. In the wake of Kirov's death, Soviet law had granted the GPU-turned-NKVD a simplified procedure for the pursuit and conviction of those considered terrorists and saboteurs.[79] The Party's emphasis on the liquidation of such elements and the new, simplified procedure for their capture and conviction made it possible for Gol'dman and his team to arrest Padalka on 30 September 1936. The first question one Lieutenant Grushevskii asked Padalka was, "Are you going to continue to deny the charge that you are a member of a counterrevolutionary, Ukrainian national fascist organization?"[80] This accusation referred directly to Epik's 1935 description of the artist as an affiliate of Hitler and a Ukrainian separatist. The phrase "are you going to continue to deny" suggests that Padalka, who had never been a member of such an organization, had tried to tell the truth for some time and had gravely disappointed Gol'dman's team. Under immense psychological pressure and probably also physical torture he responded that he would no longer deny this "fact." The artist then proceeded, or rather was forced, to denounce both Boichuk and Sedliar as the creators of the "national fascist group" to which he belonged.[81] The group, he went on to explain, constituted an "integral part of the counterrevolutionary underground."[82]

Now Gol'dman had what he needed, "evidence" that Boichuk, Sedliar, and their group posed a direct threat to the Soviet state. Gol'dman's team arrested both Boichuk and Sedliar on 23 November 1936. In the order for his arrest, Boichuk was described as "one of the leaders of a national fascist terrorist organization," who if he remained free would be "socially dangerous."[83] Sedliar was also said to be an active "participant in a terrorist organization."[84] This official designation of the two most prominent members of the Boichukisty as terrorists made it possible under post-Kirov Soviet law for Gol'dman to quickly prepare an express, straight-to-conviction case not only against Padalka, Boichuk, and Sedliar but also against other group members and any additional Ukrainizing "elements" that they could force the three men to name during interrogations.[85] The other Boichukisty—with the exception of Pavlenko, who was in Frunze working on a monumental commission with Uitz, and a few students with loose ties to the circle—were arrested shortly after Boichuk and Sedliar.

Like Padalka, Boichuk and Sedliar quickly gave the NKVD the confessions they wanted to hear. Under pressure from one of Gol'dman's officers to describe his crime according to his "own admission," Sedliar replied that was "guilty of actively participating in a Ukrainian nationalist movement on the territory of the Ukrainian SSR. I became part of Boichuk's counterrevolutionary, national fascist group, occupying one of its central positions."[86] During his first recorded interrogation, Boichuk also "confessed" that he had aimed to carry out an "organized struggle against Soviet power" and had created a counterrevolutionary group for the sake of such a struggle between 1933 and 1934.[87] When the officer in charge of the protocol asked Boichuk to name the participants of his *"Ukrainian* counterrevolutionary *national fascist* organization," the artist responded with a list of names after parroting back *"Ukrainian* counterrevolutionary *national fascist* organization" exactly as the interrogator set it out for him, exposing what seems to be a clear instance of an NKVD officer prompting him to further incriminate himself and his friends and students for the sake of an expedient mass conviction.[88]

While the 1931–1935 GPU depositions and interrogations focus on the group's pedagogical activities and their influence on students in the context of their alleged connection to SVU members and other nationalist, counterrevolutionary groups, Boichuk's, Padalka's, and Sedliar's 1936–1937 NKVD documents, while chock full of references to the group's purportedly terrorist and anti-Soviet activities and the names of so-called terrorist elements, at times take a surprising and unprecedented turn. During several interrogation sessions, Gol'dman's officers asked for specific details about the practical aspects of the Boichukisty's work. They specifically wanted to know about the ideology behind their art and pressed for details about the particular forms and content that the Boichukisty used in their distinctive Socialist Realist frescoes. During the interrogation that took place on 17 December 1936, Khaet, an NKVD officer and one of Gol'dman's men, pressured Boichuk to divulge more names from the "cadres of student-nationalists" that he had selected and prepared for anti-Soviet work.[89] After being forced to produce yet another list of group members, Boichuk then added, "While working with these individuals, I asked them to focus primarily on the nationalistic forms of art, on the nationalistic traditions of Ukrainian artists, creating single-minded specialists in nationalist doctrine."[90]

Given that Boichuk consistently described himself and his monumental paintings as internationalist, it would be absurd to read this description of his pedagogy as nationalistic as a sincere statement. The protocol fragment reads instead like the work of Gol'dman's team, who had been trying since 1931 to convict Boichuk as a devoted Ukrainian nationalist. However, rather than focusing on describing a particular nationalist ideology, the NKVD forced Boichuk to describe the traditional ethnic patterns and forms on which he did in fact ask his students to focus their attention as "nationalistic forms" and "nationalistic traditions." The agency's Ukrainophobia seems to have suddenly expanded from Boichuk as a teacher to the forms of art he asked his students to integrate into their works. For the NKVD agents, material forms in pictures seemed to pose as much of a threat to the USSR as potentially counterrevolutionary Ukrainian artists. That is, they sought to convict not only the Boichukisty but also the particular Ukrainizing forms visible in these artists' work.

As I pointed out in the introduction to this chapter, when Boichuk was asked to describe the particular nature of his work, he replied that it was the "detrimental old Ukrainian art, ancient painting, and the achievements of the bourgeois formal schools. I sent youth down that pathway of specialist training, tearing them consciously away from the pathway to Socialist Realism, and in so doing, tore them away from their participation in the building of socialism."[91] Once again the forms of the "detrimental old Ukrainian art" are as guilty as Boichuk, if not more so, in tearing the students "consciously away from the pathway to Socialist Realism." After all, he only drew their attention to these and other harmful "bourgeois" forms. The visual and material properties of traditional Ukrainian art turned the Boichukisty into nationalist painters rather than Socialist Realist artists.

Similarly, in an interrogation protocol from 11 January 1937, Khaet asked Sedliar to describe "concretely the type of counterrevolutionary work" the participants in the "counterrevolutionary" Boichukist organization carried out "in their practical work."[92] According to the interrogation protocol Sedliar responded:

> In our practical work, all of us participants in the counterrevolutionary
> organization carried out harmful [vreditel'skaia] work. The work of our group
> organization was harmful, because we consciously included counterrevolu-
> tionary, nationalistic content in our creative installations. This content was,
> of course, not in the themes of the work, which were almost always Soviet.
> It had to do with questions of style, the foundation of which was inoculated
> [privivanie] with the customs and traditions of Ukrainian national art, on the
> one hand, and, on the other, with the traditions of world art. These were used
> to strengthen the Ukrainian-separatist nationalistic positions with respect
> to the question of style against all of Russian artistic culture and the tasks of
> Socialist Realism.[93]

While Sedliar's response to Khaet is somewhat more nuanced than Boichuk's, his statement that the Boichukisty included the "traditions of world art" in their work to strengthen the style's "Ukrainian-separatist" position comes across just like Boichuk's statement that his pedagogical aims were nationalistic. The Boichukisty included forms of world art to strengthen the *internationalist* position of their paintings, which again suggests that Khaet forced Sedliar to twist whatever he may have wanted to say into an incriminating statement. Furthermore, his strange remark that the artists "inoculated" the Soviet themes in their monumental pictures with the "customs and traditions of Ukrainian national art" to shore up their works' nationalistic position "against the tasks of Socialist Realism" stands out as another attempt

by the NKVD to vilify Sedliar and the Boichukisty while once again condemning traditional Ukrainian forms, such as the decorative patterns and
peasant costumes in Boichuk's *Harvest Holiday*, as physical toxins capable of
introducing an anti-Socialist Realist, separatist disease into a work of Soviet
monumental art.

The NKVD's sudden introduction of the idea into Sedliar's January 1937
protocol that inoculating Soviet monumental art with traditional Ukrainian
forms strengthens its nationalistic position not only against Socialist Realism
but also against "all of Russian artistic culture" indicates a desire to bring
yet another incriminating charge against the group. In 1937, the Party began
to promote Russocentrism in Soviet culture, which as David Brandenberger
demonstrates, privileged Russian national form and Russian identity over
the national forms and identities of all the other citizens of the USSR.[94] The
party emphasized Russian identity based on the logic that since Russians had
been the instigators of the October Revolution, they had earned their place
at the top of the Soviet hierarchy. According to Russocentric logic, Russians
had demonstrated heroic actions not only during the modern, revolutionary
period but throughout history.[95] The Party promoted Russocentrism while
the officers of the NKVD, including Gol'dman's team, continued to carry out
their antiterrorist purges. By suggesting that the visual forms that Sedliar and
the Boichukisty included in their Socialist Realist frescoes posed a specific
threat to Russian culture established grounds for an expedient conviction and
sentencing of both artists on three basic counts, each construed as a type
of anti-Soviet terrorism: nationalist-separatism, fascist sabotage, and anti-
Russian actions. By including the "evidence" they had gathered from 1931 to
1935 into each artist's file, Gol'dman's team "demonstrated" that the Boichukisty had been working toward their "terrorist" goals since the early 1930s.
It was more than enough for the procurator. Padalka, Boichuk, and Sedliar
were all convicted, sentenced to death, and executed on 13 July 1937. They are
assumed to have been buried in a mass grave near the village of Bykivnia, on
the outskirts of Kyiv. By 1939, the NKVD had executed all the other Boichukisty they had arrested at the height of the Terror in Ukraine.

And what about the particular forms that defined their Socialist Realist
style, which the NKVD implied should be understood as a type of biological
weapon? It is my argument that the NKVD convicted and executed Boichukist Socialist Realism, with its traditional Ukrainian forms and scenes from
premodern village life rendered visually in Soviet-themed monumental paintings, when it convicted and executed the artists who created that style. This
execution of the style had both material and ideological consequences. Many
of the artists' works were torn to shreds, burned, or in the case of the frescoes,

Figure 2.9. Vladimir Shatalov, *Bridesmaids*, 1940.

covered over. Others were, as previously mentioned, locked away in special closed museum and archival repositories. The NKVD's case against the Boichukisty and their style, and especially the dramatic disappearance en masse of the artists and their pictures, played an important role in the further development of Socialist Realism in the early Soviet Ukrainian visual arts.

Before discussing the nature of the NKVD's influence, it is necessary to emphasize that Gol'dman and his officers were not art experts, critics, or art historians. As the Boichukisty's interrogation protocols make clear, the officers relied on the artists' descriptions of how they combined the traditional forms from Ukrainian art with elements from world art to create a popular and distinctive style of Socialist Realism. The NKVD agents made sure, however, that the Boichukisty used the most incriminating terms possible—"nationalistic," "national fascist," "counterrevolutionary," "bourgeois," and so on—to describe their style. Although they may have known little about art,

Figure 2.10. Tatiana Yablonska, *Bread*, 1950. Oil on canvas, State Tret'iakov Gallery, Moscow

Gol'dman's men knew plenty about the power and bureaucratic significance of visual propaganda, a category that included monumental painting.[96] Their own Ukrainophobia, together with the Party's drive to liquidate "nationalistic" Ukrainizing elements and insistence on the continued push for mechanized collectivization, gave them license to designate the Boichukisty's traditional decorative patterns and emphasis on premodern forms of agrarian collectivity as toxic, biological threats capable of inciting terror or stimulating a separatist revolt. The NKVD's execution of the works alongside their creators sent a strong message to all the other visual artists involved in the development of Socialist Realism in early Soviet Ukraine. They should not repeat the Boichukisty's mistakes and should refrain from combining traditional folk patterns with images of premodern collectivism among the peasantry.[97]

Traces of the NKVD's contribution to Socialist Realism in Stalinist Ukraine can be seen in both Vladimir Shatalov's *Bridesmaids* (fig. 2.9) and Tatiana Yablonska's *Bread* (fig. 2.10). Shatalov's painting offers a portrait of two young peasant bridesmaids admiring themselves and their national costumes in front of a hand mirror. Despite the recent liquidation of threatening Ukrainizing elements, the Party maintained a somewhat contradictory policy, which emphasized that images of the USSR should emphasize its status as a multicultural, multinational socialist state to ensure, at least in part, that Ukrainians and members of other national groups felt connected to each other within the broader Soviet project.[98] Shatalov's emphasis on the women's traditional celebratory hair ribbons, their floral crowns, and especially the embroidery on their blouses (*vyshyvanki*) certainly constitutes a contribution to this policy. Indeed, the picture appears to be positively overflowing with traditional Ukrainian forms. A closer inspection, however, reveals that Shatalov has gone to great lengths, with the help of impressionistic brushstrokes, to mute and obscure the exact details of the patterns on the women's *vyshyvanki*. This perhaps suggests anxiety over just how much of the products of Ukraine's premodern, collective agrarian past he can safely show. The artist's decision to paint the peasant women seated in an empty domestic interior also totally abstracts them from their agricultural context, perhaps as compensation for rendering the embroidered patterns in as much material detail as he did. While the women do share a close tactile bond, in contrast to Boichuk's *Harvest Holiday* (fig. 2.8), there is nothing in Shatalov's painting to suggest that these women formed their bond by participating in ancient forms of agrarian labor that might provide a viable socialist alternative to mechanized collectivization. Here Shatalov defines Ukrainian Socialist Realism as a depiction of peasants with only the vaguest link to their collectivist past through costumes and obscured folk patterns, who exist not in the active socialist present but in the timeless vacuum of a blank interior.

In *Bread* (fig. 2.10) Yablonska, by contrast, depicts Ukrainian peasant women as gathers of a bountiful grain harvest on an industrialized collective farm. While the women in the painting are clad in traditional peasant skirts, blouses, and headscarves, their clothing is mostly bereft of traditional folk patterns. When Yablonska does endow the women's blouses with folk decorations, she, like Shatalov, makes it difficult for the spectator to discern details. Steering clear of Boichuk's open criticism of mechanical collectivization in *Harvest Holiday*, Yablonska defines Ukrainian Socialist Realism as a celebration of industrial agriculture, which is defined by machine achievement, not by close, tactile bonds developed through traditional physical labor. This is most evident in her depiction of the female figure in the central foreground, who gestures excitedly at the mechanical grain harvester in the picture's right corner as the source of Soviet Ukraine's bountiful and joyful collectivity.

My aim in describing the politics of Boichukism, its contribution to Socialist Realism in Soviet Ukraine, and its demise at the hands of the NKVD has been to demonstrate the role that the secret police played in the evolution of official visual art in the Ukrainian Republic and to emphasize the human tragedy that came with it. While the NKVD should not be understood as the only organ that contributed to the negotiated development of Socialist Realism in early Soviet Ukraine, it is clear that we cannot develop a comprehensive knowledge of the style's evolution without considering the role of the secret police.

NOTES

This article would not have been possible without financial, intellectual, and moral support from the institutions and individuals who assisted me as I researched and wrote. A Getty/ACLS Postdoctoral Fellowship in the History of Art from the American Council of Learned Societies, generously supported by the Getty Foundation and funds from the Higher School of Economics (HSE) University Basic Research Program allowed me to conduct research in Ukraine. I could have never seen this article through to fruition without the feedback I received from the following colleagues: David Brandenberger, Susan Grunewald, Tracy McDonald, Erina Megowan, and Jessica Zychowicz.

1. "Protokol doprosa obviniaemogo Boichuka Mikhaila L'vovicha," 17 December 1936 (Haluzevyi derzhavnyi arkhiv Sluzhby bezpeki Ukraïni [HDASBU] f. 6, op. 1, d. 46293, l. 32).

2. HDASBU f. 6, op. 1, d. 46293, l. 33.

3. Lynne Viola, *Stalinist Perpetrators on Trial: Scenes from the Great Terror in Soviet Ukraine* (Oxford: Oxford University Press, 2017), 14.

4. As Myroslav Shkandrij demonstrates in his work on Boichuk's aesthetic, the artist's view of art never "became in any way myopically nationalist or exclusionary." Indeed, Boichuk supported the development of internationalism through the recognition of universal aesthetic elements that he argued were present in all national forms. See his "Modernism, the Avant-Garde, and Myhailo Boichuk's Aesthetic," *Journal of Ukrainian Studies* 19, no. 2 (1994): 54. Regarding NKVD protocols, it is worth noting that each document is a transcript of several interrogations, not a real-time stenographic account of an individual interview.

5. While he does not study Socialist Realism in the visual arts, Serhii Bilokin' did rely on NKVD interrogations when he constructed his history of the Boichuk School. See his *Boichuk: Ta yoho shkola* (Kyiv: Mystetsvo, 2017).

6. Igor Golomstok, *Totalitarnoe iskusstvo* (Moscow: Galart, 1994), 95.

7. Christina Kiaer, "Was Socialist Realism Forced Labor? The Case of Aleksandr Deineka," *Oxford Art Journal* 28, no. 3 (2005): 336–37.

8. Susan Reid, "Socialist Realism in the Stalinist Terror: The *Industry of Socialism* Art Exhibition, 1935–41," *Russian Review* 60, no. 2 (2001): 183.

9. Reid, "Socialist Realism in the Stalinist Terror," 183–84.

10. Sokoliuk, "Shkola ukrains'koho monumentalizmu Mykhaila Boichuka," in *Boichukizm*, ed. Valentyna Klymenko (Kyiv: Mystetskyi arsenal, 2018), 14.

11. For a detailed discussion of experimental modernisms in Kyiv and their relationship to visual art in both Moscow and the West, see Irena R. Makaryk, "Introduction: Reconnecting Modernisms," in *Modernism in Kyiv: Jubilant Experimentation*, ed. Irena R. Makaryk and Virlana Tkacz (Toronto: University of Toronto Press, 2010), 3–4.

12. Boichuk was far from being the only modernist painter in Kyiv interested in the decorative patterns of Ukrainian folk art. As Dmytro Horbachov has shown, the abstract painter, theorist, and pedagogue Alexandra Exter also integrated folk patterns into her paintings and even worked closely with the peasant craft artist Hanna Sobachko. The difference, however, between Exter, whose abstract methods influenced the development of Suprematism, and Boichuk is that the former had no interest in figurative realism or in conveying specific scenes from peasant life. She drew on folk patterns for the vibrancy and rhythm of their color schemes, whereas Boichuk and his students relied on them for their connection to history. See Horbachov, "In the Epicentre of Abstraction: Kyiv during the time of Kurbas," in *Modernism in Kyiv*, 172, 174.

13. Michael F. Hamm, "'Special and Bewildering': A Portrait of Late Imperial and Early Soviet Kyiv," in *Modernism in Kyiv*, 62–63.

14. Boichuk had established his position as a promoter of monumental art and Ukrainian national form well before the Bolsheviks took control of Kyiv in 1918. In 1910, he opened an art school in Lviv

devoted to the techniques of monumental art, in particular the Byzantine Revival style. The school remained operational until 1914. See Hamm, "'Special and Bewildering,'" 13.

15. Boichuk's responses in his presentations to the mistakes of and criticisms from LEF, the avant-garde artists' group behind Vladimir Mayakovsky's journal *Left Front of the Arts* (*LEF*), indicates his own deep involvement in the Soviet debates about the definition of socialist art. While LEF advocated for a turn away from "bourgeois" realist easel painting to an aesthetic based on industrial production, groups like AKhRR in Moscow and the Boichukisty in Kyiv argued that figurative realist painting was not obsolete but indeed critical to the establishment of a socialist aesthetic in the visual arts. See Myhailo Boichuk, "Myhailo Boichuk's Lectures on Monumental Art," 1922, trans. Myroslav Shkandrij, in *Journal of Ukrainian Studies* 19, no. 2 (1994): 63.

16. Boichuk, "Myhailo Boichuk's Lectures," 59.

17. "Contemporary artists," Boichuk explained, "will be creators of the Great Future when they fuse with the extratemporal in world art through the many sided practice of studying artistic cultures" ("Myhailo Boichuk's Lectures," 64).

18. Boichuk, "Myhailo Boichuk's Lectures," 61.

19. "Every form has to be worked from nature," Boichuk explained. "It is particularly important that the figure whose composition is being elaborated be thought through to the end; ideally that it be seen and confirmed in nature, and not invented, in order to avoid creating nonsense" ("Myhailo Boichuk's Lectures," 65).

20. I agree with Myroslav Shkandrij in that Boichuk's emphasis on the significance of embroidery, Easter eggs, gingerbread, and popular processions in his passage on the role of a "flourishing" art in everyday culture also constitutes a valorization of folk creativity as "an assertion of peasant-national identity." See Shkandrij, "Modernism, the Avant-Garde, and Myhailo Boichuk's Aesthetic," 54.

21. Boichuk, "Myhailo Boichuk's Lectures," 66.

22. Boichuk, "Myhailo Boichuk's Lectures," 65.

23. Boichuk, "Myhailo Boichuk's Lectures," 60–61.

24. For a detailed discussion of Boichuk's training, travels, and early pedagogical work, see Shkandrij, "Modernism, the Avant-Garde, and Myhailo Boichuk's Aesthetic," 43–44.

25. In the contested period between 1917 and 1921–1922 when the Bolsheviks, the White Army (under Denikin), and the Ukrainian People's Army all vied for control of the country, many leftist, Kyiv-based politicians and intellectuals developed and promoted their own particular definitions of socialism. Within this context it is unsurprising that Boichuk formulated his own understanding of the concept based on an idealization of precapitalist, preimperial collective agrarian life. Nor is it surprising that he continued to promote this perspective in the 1920s, as the Bolshevik's policy of Ukrainization took hold. For an overview of diverse socialist perspectives in postrevolutionary Ukraine, see Hamm, "'Special and Bewildering,'" 64.

26. Taras Shevchenko, "Zapovit," trans. John Weir, Toronto, 1961. Made publicly available by the Taras Shevchenko Museum, Toronto, Ontario, http://www.infoukes.com/shevchenkomuseum/poetry .htm#link3.

27. For an alternative reading of the image as politically ambiguous, see Myroslav Shkandrij, *Avant-Garde Art in Ukraine, 1910–1930: Contested Memory* (Boston: Academic Studies Press, 2019), 41.

28. As Serhy Yekelchyk has shown, Soviet statehood provided Ukrainians with the administrative and cultural structures they needed to form a modern (Soviet) national identity. It is clear from Boichuk's image of Shevchenko that he, like many others, took advantage of a Bolshevik-provided, mass-produced agitational medium to begin building a platform for his theory for the development of an agrarian socialist collective in Ukraine based on a combination of international and national aesthetics and creativity. See Serhy Yekelchyk, *Ukraine: Birth of a Modern Nation* (New York: Oxford University Press, 2007), 95.

29. Several of the Boichukisty, including Sedliar and Padalka, also worked in the graphic arts, producing in their prints what Myroslava M. Mudrak has described as "precise contouring and expressive linear values." See her "The Graphic Arts: From Page Design to Theatre," in *Modernism in Kyiv*, 432.

30. Boichuk, "Myhailo Boichuk's Lectures," 60.

31. Anatolii Zaika, *Na tli Mezhyhirs'kikh kruch: Zabuti storinki istorii Kiievo-Mezhyhirya* (Kyiv: A+C, 2016), 296.

32. L. L. Savitskaia, "ARMU (Assotsiatsiia revoliutsionnogo iskusstva Ukrainy, Asotsiatsiia revoliutsiionoho mystetstva Ukrainu), 1925–1932," in *Entsiklopediia russkogo avangarda*, http://rusavangard.ru/online/history/armu/.

33. I. I. Vrona, *Mystetstvo revoliutsii i ARMU* (Kyiv: Ts.B.A.R.M.U, 1926), 6.

34. In 1926, for example, ARMU carried out what Mudrak describes as a "series of programmatic exhibitions" that promoted Boichukism as the most politically effective aesthetic in early Soviet Ukraine ("Graphic Arts," 431).

35. Iakov Tugendkhol'd, "Izobrazitel'noe iskusstvo narodov SSSR," in *Iskusstvo narodov SSSR* (Moscow and Leningrad: Gosudarstvennoe izdatel'stvo, 1930), 43.

36. Tugendkhol'd, "Izobrazitel'noe iskusstvo narodov SSSR," 4, 46.

37. In her letter to Valentine Marcadé, Alla Ioganson, one of Boichuk's younger students who managed to survive the purges, described Krichevskii as the "spokesman for the campaign against Boichuk at the Kyiv Art Institute." See Valentine Marcadé, "Mikhail Boichuk," *Experiment/Eksperiment*, no. 1 (1995): 330.

38. Tsentral'nyi derzhavnyi arkhiv-muzei literaturi i mystetstva Ukraïny (TsDAMLMU) f. 356 (Personal Papers of O. T. Pavlenko), op. 1, d. 303, l. 2 (letter to O. T. Pavlenko from A. A. Fedorov-Davydov, 1927).

39. "Pis'mo O. T. Pavlenko ot Narkoma prosveshcheniia A. V. Lunacharskogo," 1929 (TsDAMLMU f. 356, op. 1, d. 332, ll. 16–17).

40. Yekelchyk, *Ukraine*, 103, 105. Matthew Pauly notes that Stalin also recognized the need to step up Ukrainization efforts among the proletariat in 1926. While he opposed forced Ukrainization, he emphasized that the Party needed to make a more active effort to promote Ukrainian culture ("Tending to the 'Native' Word: Teachers and the Soviet Campaign for Ukrainian Language Schooling, 1923–30," *Nationalities Papers* 37, no. 3 [2009]: 263).

41. Pauly, "Tending to the 'Native' Word," 103–4.

42. Pauly, "Tending to the 'Native' Word," 104.

43. Pauly, "Tending to the 'Native' Word," 269.

44. The first Soviet secret police organization, the Cheka, had once been interested in Boichuk, but only briefly. They arrested him in 1920, probably because they feared that as an ethnic Ukrainian from Austro-Hungarian territory he would undermine the Bolsheviks' efforts to take the country. They swiftly released him, however, without charges. Gol'dman's officers seem to have made no effort to dig up anything about the first arrest as part of their effort to bolster their case. Boichuk's interrogation protocol reads only that he was "not convicted of anything" after his 1920 arrest. See HDASBU f. 6 (NKVD File on Mykhailo Boichuk), op. 1, d. 46293, l. 21 (Mykhailo Boichuk: Interrogation protocol, 1 December 1936).

45. Pauly, "Tending to the 'Native' Word," 264, 266.

46. Pauly, "Tending to the 'Native' Word," 264.

47. Pauly, "Tending to the 'Native' Word," 265.

48. Gol'dman, who was from a Jewish family in Chernihiv, had worked for the Bolshevik secret police since 1920. When he initiated the chase against the Boichukisty in 1936, he was a Kyiv NKVD captain. During the final months of the investigation he was promoted to head of the Fourth Section of the Ukrainian NKVD for the Donetsk region, where he was in charge of the region's purges. For his efforts against the Boichukisty and the purges in Donetsk, Gol'dman was promoted to deputy head

of the Fourth Section of the Ukrainian NKVD. Ultimately, however, he too was purged. Arrested in 1941, Gol'dman died in a Siberian camp the following year. See "Memorial: Members of the Cadres of the Organs of State Security, 1935–1939," https://nkvd.memo.ru/index.php.

49. As Yuri Shapoval demonstrates, in building the SVU case, the GPU did not always use physical pressure to generate "evidence" from detainees. At times, the officers relied instead on "bespoke methods of blackmail." See Shapoval, "The 'Union for the Liberation of Ukraine' ('SVU') Trial: Fabrication, Mechanisms, Consequences," in *Political and Transitional Justice in Germany, Poland, and the Soviet Union from the 1930s to the 1950s*, ed. Magnus Brechtken, Władysław Bułhak, and Jürgen Zarusky (Göttingen: Wallstein, 2019), 45.

50. "Vypiska iz pokazanii A. I. Popova," 15 April 1931 (HDASBU f. 6, op. 1, d. 76506, l. 56).

51. HDASBU f. 6, op. 1, d. 76506, l. 56.

52. HDASBU f. 6, op. 1, d. 76506, l. 56.

53. HDASBU f. 6, op. 1, d. 76506, l. 56.

54. "Vypiska iz pokazanii N. F. Sulimy," 4 July 1931 (HDASBU f. 6, op. 1, d. 76506, l. 60).

55. HDASBU f. 6, op. 1, d. 76506, l. 60.

56. HDASBU f. 6, op. 1, d. 76506, l. 60.

57. HDASBU f. 6, op. 1, d. 76506, l. 60.

58. HDASBU f. 6, op. 1, d. 76506, l. 60.

59. HDASBU f. 6, op. 1, d. 76506, l. 60. For a detailed analysis of Les Kurbas's work and his relationship to the Soviet state, see Mayhill C. Fowler, *Beau Monde on Empire's Edge: State and Stage in Soviet Ukraine* (Toronto: University of Toronto Press, 2017), 127–67.

60. Shapoval, in his analysis of the GPU's surveillance reports on the imprisoned Sergii Efremov, the academic they had designated as "leader" of the SVU, demonstrates that the GPU's repeated attempts to force Efremov to provide incriminating evidence of events that never happened, together with their repeated insistence that he *must* have knowledge of these mythical happenings, did not result in the prisoner producing the desired narratives. Instead, the impossibility of the task only led Efremov to voice his desire for immediate execution, a fate he considered more humane than trying to fulfill the GPU's impossible request for nonexistent information. Popov's and Sulima's inability to provide information about the Boichukisty's nonexistent SVU activities indicates that they too were caught in the maddening cycle of being asked to write what had not actually occurred. See Shapoval, "'Union for the Liberation of Ukraine,'" 46.

61. As Mayhill C. Fowler has shown, accusations of antisemitism appear frequently in GPU/NKVD documents and were often falsely applied. It is, of course, possible that such an incident did occur. However, given that no traces of antisemitic behavior have come to light in Sedliar's personal history, the internationalism of the Boichukisty's platform, and the fact that Boichuk welcomed Jewish students to his courses, the incident is most likely a Sulima fabrication. See Fowler, *Beau Monde on Empire's Edge*, 179.

62. Shapoval demonstrates, through his analysis of GPU documents from late 1929, that texts relating to the SVU, with their frequent references to "chauvinism" and "nationalism" and the negative implications associated with anything Ukrainian, reveal the secret police's "absolute Ukrainophobia" and with it, its desire to discredit Ukrainization. That the same sorts of references appear through the 1931 documents "linking" the Boichukisty to the SVU indicates that the GPU's Ukrainophobia and desire to discredit Ukrainization lasted much longer than the SVU case itself. See Shapoval, "'Union for the Liberation of Ukraine,'" 49.

63. "Vypiska iz protokola doprosa Khristovogo N. F.," 6 September 1933 (HDASBU f. 6, op. 1, t. 1, d. 46293, l. 88).

64. "Vypiska iz protokola doprosa Epika," 15 February 1935 (HDASBU f. 6, op. 1, t. 1, d. 46293, l. 89).

65. For a detailed discussion of the GPU's actions against VAPLITE, see Olena Palko, *Making Ukraine Soviet: Literature and Cultural Politics under Lenin and Stalin* (London: Bloomsbury Academic, 2020), 132.

66. Kiaer, "Was Socialist Realism Forced Labor?," 336–37.

67. "Letter from O. T. Pavlenko to Béla Uitz," Kharkiv, 1933 (TsDAMLMU f. 356, op. 1, d. 142, l. 3).

68. Such negotiations were no doubt at least as critical to the development of Socialist Realist visual art in the Ukrainian Republic as the NKVD's intervention into the style. For a broader discussion of the importance of these negotiations to the development of the arts in the Soviet regions, see Serhy Yekelchyk, "Diktat and Dialogue in Stalinist Culture: Staging Patriotic Historical Opera in Soviet Ukraine, 1936–1954," *Slavic Review* 59, no. 3 (2000): 599.

69. Although an organizing committee for its establishment was formed in Kharkiv in 1933, the Ukrainian Artists' Union, originally called the Union of Soviet Artists of Ukraine, was only officially established in 1938, two years after the core members of the Boichukisty were arrested.

70. This sketch, like all the others Boichuk made for the fresco, was no doubt as much a product of negotiations with the authorities commissioning the picture and the other Boichukisty working on the theater, as it was of Boichuk's individual artistic process. Future research may seek to uncover any remaining archival documents that yield insight into these negotiations.

71. In a more finished version of the fresco, Boichuk added a flower rope weighed down by fruit to the peasant section. The three Pioneer children behind the drummer in the left foreground were shown bearing it together. It is impossible to know, however, what the finished picture looked like, because the Boichukisty's frescoes were painted over. No photographs of the finished installation remain. See Bilokin', *Boichuk*, 62–63.

72. The fact that the painting was created two years after the Holodomor makes Boichuk's idea that Socialist Realism should critically assess industrial collectivization all the more interesting and poignant.

73. Uitz found Padalka's and Pavlenko's emphasis on the *faktura* of national decorative patterns in textiles particularly inspiring. See Angelina Lucento, "Painting against Empire: Béla Uitz and the Birth and Fate of Internationalist Socialist Realism," *Russian Review* 79, no. 4 (2020): 588.

74. The text, "Fascist Culture: Smoke, Slander, Forgery, and Lies," offered a broad description of the state of art in Hitler's Germany in 1933. See Private Archive (Personal Papers of Béla Uitz), "Fashistiskaia kul'tura: Dym, klevetka, podlog i lozh'," 1933, n.p.

75. Hennadii Yefimenko, "The Soviet Nationalities Policy Change of 1933, or Why 'Ukrainian Nationalism' Became the Main Threat to Stalin in Ukraine," *Holodomor Studies* 1, no. 1 (2009): 37.

76. See Yefimenko, "Soviet Nationalities Policy Change," 37; and Terry Martin, *The Affirmative Action Empire: Nations and Nationalism in the Soviet Union, 1923–1939* (Ithaca, NY: Cornell University Press, 2001), 225.

77. Yefimenko, "Soviet Nationalities Policy Change of 1933," 39.

78. Viola, *Stalinist Perpetrators on Trial*, 16.

79. Viola, *Stalinist Perpetrators on Trial*, 16.

80. "Protokol doprosa obviniaemogo PADALKI Ivana Ivanovicha," 10 October 1936 (HDASBU f. 6, op. 1, d. 76506, l. 20).

81. HDASBU f. 6, op. 1, d. 76506, l. 20.

82. HDASBU f. 6, op. 1, d. 76506, l. 20.

83. "Postanovlenie," 23 November 1936 (HDASBU f. 6, op. 1, t. 1, d. 46293, l. 2).

84. "Postanovlenie ob areste," 23 November 1936 (HDASBU f. 6, op. 1, t. 1, d. 75840, l. 3).

85. Viola, *Stalinist Perpetrators on Trial*, 16–17. Boichuk's interrogations are especially interesting in this regard, because unlike the others he was frequently asked about his travels abroad and his connections to the Ukrainian Greek Catholic Church, all in an effort to force him to divulge more and more names. See "Protokol doprosa obv. Boichuka Mikhaila L'vovicha," 4 December 1936 (HDASBU f. 6, op. 1, d. 46293, l. 15).

86. "Pokazaniia obv. Seldiara Vasiliia Feofanovicha," 4 December 1936 (HDASBU f. 6, op. 1, d. 75840, l. 17.)

87. HDASBU f. 6, op. 1, d. 46293, l. 21.

88. HDASBU f. 6, op. 1, d. 46293, l. 21.

89. HDASBU f. 6, op. 1, d. 46293, l. 30.

90. HDASBU f. 6, op. 1, d. 46293, l. 31.

91. HDASBU f. 6, op. 1, d. 46293, l. 33.

92. "Protokol doprosa obviniaemogo Sedliara Vasiliia Feofanovicha," 11 January 1937 (HDASBU f. 6, op. 1, d. 75840, l. 37).

93. HDASBU f. 6, op. 1, d. 75840, l. 37.

94. David Brandenberger, *National Bolshevism: Stalinist Mass Culture and the Formation of Modern Russian National Identity, 1931–1956* (Cambridge, MA: Harvard University Press, 2002), 55.

95. Brandenberger, *National Bolshevism,* 61.

96. In Moscow at least, NKVD RSFSR (1917–1930) officers were known to have attended exhibitions together with artists and arts officials so that they might collectively assess, for example, the work of artists' groups and artists' brigades. See "Stenogramma ekstrennogo obshchego sobraniia ob"edineniia khudozhnikov-realistov sovmesto s komissiei NKVD po obsledovaniiu khudozhestvennykh obshchestv i rabochei brigadov," 14 March 1930 (Rossiiskii gosudarstvennyi arkhiv literatury i iskusstva [RGALI] f. 645, op. 1, d. 453, l. 1).

97. As Matthew Pauly demonstrates, a similar phenomenon existed within the educational system after the SVU trial, in that "terror and policy adjustments shaped what Ukrainian teachers chose *not* to do" (emphasis in original). See Pauly, "Tending to the 'Native' Word," 271.

98. For a detailed discussion of how national art was used to forge bonds between fellow citizens of the Soviet national republics, see Isabelle R. Kaplan, "The Art of Nation-Building: National Culture and Soviet Politics in Stalin-Era Azerbaijan and Other Minority Republics" (PhD diss., Georgetown University, 2017), 28.

KGB Photography Experimentation

Turning Religion into Organized Crime

Tatiana Vagramenko

To photograph is to appropriate the thing photographed. It means putting oneself into a certain relation to the world that feels like knowledge—and, therefore, like power.

—Susan Sontag, *On Photography*

THE SOVIET SECRET POLICE MADE A HABIT OF PHOTOGRAPHING THEIR TAR-gets and visually capturing what was meant to be evidence of their crimes. "The improvement of photography opens up a diversity of new opportunities for its use in criminal investigation, both for the fixation of a crime scene and for undertaking the most complicated investigation, otherwise impossible to realize by other means," states a 1935 textbook on Soviet criminalistics.[1] Soviet police manuals carefully elaborated the use of photography in crime investigation, instructing how to produce photographs of criminals and how to capture scenes and traces of crime: murdered body, arson, firearm traces, blood, sperm, footprints, cigarette butts, and so on. Police photo labs produced mug shots of suspects in custody, while field officers took photos of crime scenes and criminal evidence in addition to relevant shots in Committee for State Security (KGB) prisons and courts.[2] The KGB also used photography in "agent-operational measures," deploying concealed cameras to conduct surveillance and to document intercepted or confiscated materials. In doing all this, KGB photographers were formally abiding by the standard procedures of judicial or investigative photography first developed in Europe in the late nineteenth century and then elaborated in detail in Soviet police manuals.[3] Whereas criminalistics manuals and KGB internal instructions claimed the pursuit of justice, professionalism, and objectivity, *political* crimes were far more difficult to capture in photos, thus leaving secret police officers room for creativity and manipulation.

Photographs were often subject to manipulation through techniques such as montage, cropping, overlapping, retouching, or collaging. Confiscated images, art, manuscripts, and personal photographs were also redeployed for the organs' own documentary purposes, such as when the KGB cropped and pasted images of this sort into its own photo albums and collages or reprinted them in its instructional media or propaganda publications. Regardless of where they came from, all the varied visual materials that found their way into KGB hands were forced to bend to a single dominant interpretation.[4] Their purpose was to advance the cause of Soviet justice by exposing criminality, proving guilt, and keeping watch on suspected offenders.

KGB photography, however, was much more than just a tool of crime work. Unlike classic forensic and judicial photography, photographs produced by the KGB were often far from reflecting or upholding the principles of accuracy or objectivity. Whereas Soviet official documentation advocated the triumphal revelation of the truth, the images located in the former KGB archives show how intentional photography manipulation generated different photographic meanings and concealed the inherent violence. In that sense, the statement "what you can't see, you can't photograph" has little relevance when it comes to the work of the Soviet secret police. But does this mean that the images of suspects and manipulation of police photography that we see below were mere falsification? The distinction between the KGB photograph and Soviet reality was more complicated and awkward than a yes or no answer can capture. Inscribed with ideological presumptions, the Soviet secret police photograph was neither an objective documentation of the truth nor a simple falsification, but rather an instrument designed to produce and transmit a discourse of truth—or what John Tagg calls, following Foucault, "the régime of photographic truth," whose aim was not merely to advance the KGB's case but to shape the image of the class or national enemy.[5] As Tagg continues, discussing the institutional use of photography as evidence in nineteenth-century Western Europe, "here, the knowledge and truth of which photography became the guardian were inseparable from the power and control that they engendered."[6] In this regard, KGB photography appeared as a material "force field" that was at the same time the product of the state machine and an element in the technologies of knowledge production—the technologies that, according to Ann Stoler, reproduced the state itself.[7] What Roland Barthes has called the "evidential force" of the photograph became repurposed as the instrument of a new disciplinary and repressive regime.[8] Thus KGB photography evolved both as a means for producing new evidence regarding the state's enemies and as a justification for their continued repression. This is all the more important as the constructed imagery of the enemy provided an opportunity to enhance the secret police's own authority and to create new forms of state power. By and large, the image of the enemy—a giant counterrevolutionary conspiratorial foe—was the *capital* that allowed the secret police to establish itself as an immense power and to form a vision of the chekist as a Soviet superman.

This chapter examines the history of Soviet secret police photographic practices, arguing that the agency's rich array of visual methodologies helped create a lasting image of the "people's enemy" in the Soviet socialist imagination. Using photographic sources relating to a key area of KGB work, I expose how the knowledge/power nexus embedded in institutional photographs contributed to the establishment of the new Soviet social order and power and in this way became inseparable from the social and material practices of state authority. In the process, I combine the analysis of two important yet often disconnected factors in the relationship between photography and power: one is the instrumentality of state security photographs—that is, the way that photographic images were deployed to serve state goals; and the other is the reality of photographs as physical objects in keeping with what Elizabeth Edward and Janice Hart have referred to as the materiality of the photograph.[9] Photographs are produced, exchanged, confiscated, or intercepted, as well as altered, published, republished, or destroyed. Their nature as physical objects is thus inseparable from their semantic and practical function. In what follows, I focus on the social function of a range of KGB-curated photographs and the social conditions of their production and use, what James Hevia calls "the photography complex," which involves a network of actors and a set of relationships: all of which in turn allows me to examine not only the institutions and individuals who took the photos but also the people, practices, and meanings that the photographs were intended to expose.[10]

The materials in this research come from the recently declassified Security Service of Ukraine (SBU, former KGB) archives in Ukraine. The provenance of documentation stored there, however, is diverse and encompasses not only the former Ukrainian Soviet Socialist Republic but also other parts of the Soviet Union. Some documents and images analyzed below were produced by the Unified State Political Administration (OGPU, as the Soviet secret police was known until 1934) branches in Voronezh, Belgorod, Samara, Ivanovo-Voznesensk, and, of course, Moscow. One of the schematic images below was signed by Evgenii Tuchkov, the head of the Sixth (later Third) Sector of the OGPU Secret-Political Department responsible for all-Soviet antireligious campaigns between 1922 and 1939. All these reports and model penal files circulated up and down the regional police hierarchy. Similarly, files and images produced by regional OGPU (and after 1934, People's Commissariat of Internal Affairs [NKVD]) officers in Ukraine were oftentimes part of all-Union special operations, hence reported up the hierarchy crowned by the Kremlin and Lubianka. As a result, although the sources for this research come from the Ukrainian archives, the origins of the documentation are not always clear, and it is safe to assume that we are dealing with standardized and centralized photographic practices and documentation genres.

"THE ECCLESIASTIC-MONARCHIST UNDERGROUND"

The Soviet state had numerous enemies that its officials were expected to hunt down and bring to justice. My focus here is on religious dissent or what became known as the religious underground—that is, religious groups outlawed by the Soviet state. Though religion was repressed in the Soviet Union, it was not entirely prohibited, and indeed some types of religious activity remained legal throughout the Soviet period. At the same time, certain religious groups were considered unacceptable and banned as "harmful to the state by the very fact of their existence."[11] Followers of the catacomb True Orthodox movement, Jehovah's Witnesses, Reformed Seventh Day Adventists, Pentecostals, and a number of other believers fell within this category. Whereas mainstream religious institutions that enjoyed legal or semilegal status (like the Russian Orthodox Church or registered Evangelical Christian-Baptists, for instance) fell under the control of the Council for Religious Affairs established under the Council of People's Commissars (later Council of Ministers), banned minority religious groups fell under the secret jurisdiction of the secret police.[12] A section on the "religious underground" regularly appeared in annual and monthly official reports and surveys at every level of the police hierarchy.

The photographs below come from group penal cases (including what I call model penal cases and model indictments) against peasant nonconformist underground Orthodox communities that in secret police files were commonly referred to as the True Orthodox Church.[13] Starting in the late 1920s, underground Orthodox movements scattered from Western Siberia to the North Caucus and Ukraine were under the gaze of the secret police. The first all-Union "liquidation campaigns" against popular religious movements were launched on the wave of the state's struggle against mass peasant resistance to forced collectivization and dekulakization. By then, popular resistance was imbued with religious symbolism of the coming apocalypse; and priests and monastics often became vocal actors in local acts of disobedience.[14] By the early 1930s, the majority of churches in the Soviet Union were closed and monasteries disbanded. Thousands of disenfranchised priests with their families, and displaced monks and nuns, were left homeless, banned from living in particular cities, or subject to immediate resettlement from areas of collectivization. They wandered from village to village, begging or doing some casual day labor, clandestinely performing rituals and preaching about the arrival of the apocalyptic Red Dragon and the Antichrist. These "vagrant clergymen" brought to life numerous popular prophets and saints, *iurodivye* (holy fools), *klikushi* (shriekers), *startsy* (elders), *prozorlivye* (foreseers), and *bogoroditsy* (mothers of God).[15] The phenomenon of popular prophetism proliferated, developing new forms, like *boliashchie* (holy invalids) or *spiashchie* (holy sleepers). Some yelled on the streets that the Communists were putting the stamp of Antichrist on the foreheads of those entering kolkhozes or participating in elections or the census; that men in kolkhozes would share wives, and everybody would sleep under a common blanket; that children would be taken away from their parents; that aged people "would be recycled for soap production"; and "human hair, instead of wool, would be exchanged for American tractors."[16] Mushrooming "wild parishes" (*dikie prikhody*) or "hut groups" (*khatnicheskie gruppy*, from Ukrainian *khata*, peasant hut) were spontaneous and uncontrollable—they were as difficult to control as they were difficult to define.

As I argue elsewhere, Soviet record keeping, particularly the documentation created by the secret police, played a specific role in the formation of the image of the True Orthodox Church as an organized, networked, and politically subversive organizational structure. When followers of these faiths were arrested, they were charged not for their beliefs but rather for their actions as would-be members of the "insurgent counterrevolutionary ecclesiastic-monarchist underground" or a "red-dragon-type [*krasnodrakonovskii tip*] organization."[17] As Lynne Viola posits, the Stalinist state did not merely create much of the political environment for resistance through its repressive politics but also "generated the lens and language of resistance" and "set the parameters of resistant behaviors, acts, and even intent"; it furthermore "produced most of our sources on resistance."[18] In this chapter, I further develop this point by focusing on how the Soviet system framed popular religious traditions as political resistance and counterrevolutionary conspiracy in visual terms, a process in which the secret police too played an important role.

In making their case against these groups, the Soviet organs frequently accumulated massive evidentiary files, including data from criminal records, samples of indictments and closing arguments, reports, circulars, surveys, and articles on religious dissent from internal publications. In all this, visual material played a critical role as photographs, graphics of various sorts, photo collages and photomontages of confiscated images became drummed into service to bolster the argument that organized political subversion lurked behind the mask of religion. The role of the photograph in the cause (along with the support of a wide range of other materials included in the case file) was to establish the typology of religious dissident as a deserving target of state repression, a figure who could be comfortably placed in a rogue's gallery alongside other stereotypical foes: the counterrevolutionary, the courier, the spy, or the terrorist.[19] In the process, the photo of the religious dissenter came to serve as a kind of "ideological blueprint," the first rendering of the criminal to be enhanced, as needed, with the help of additional visual techniques, the purpose of which was not just to expose the enemy within but to give him or her recognizable physical form.

The file stories and the photographs discussed in this chapter date from 1930 to 1952 and cover various Stalinist antireligious operations in the Russian and Ukrainian countryside. First, they were part of major reforms in the village during the ambitious First Five-Year Plan. This was also the time when the Soviet secret police consolidated its vast power and began to rise as an empire within a state. Hence the need to think and act with the lavish scale: to create a giant conspiracy (like the ecclesiastic-monarchist underground or the terrorist counterrevolutionary organization) to fight against; to create new paradigms, new concepts and models. The religious network schemes and collages featured here belong to this period when the secret police had unlimited opportunities to enhance its power. Symptomatically these images of a networked conspiratorial enemy mimicked the very structures and hierarchies of Soviet institutions, including the secret police themselves.

Another group of images from the postwar period reflects the refining of antireligious policies and offers a glimpse of different strategies to control proliferating postwar popular religiosity. Once the power paradigm had been set and the rogue's gallery of stereotypical foes was in place, the secret police carried out surgical-strike operations against grassroots religious communities. Each case was thoroughly sorted according to existing categories, and images were adjusted (manipulated if needed) to make them fit into the respective "box" of enemies. This is when we start seeing the faces and hearing the voices of individual believers and their silenced stories, all hugely distorted. To delve into the logic of secret police photography, I approach these images in a chronologically reversed order: we begin with individual stories and images of repressed believers from the postwar period in order to understand how they were transformed into giant faceless schemes on the eve of the Great Terror. Finally, and this unites them all, the photographs below reveal the twofold rationale of the Soviet secret police: to control all types of political and cultural dissent but also to build its own immense power and state capacity through the construction of the image of a religious, conspiratorial counterrevolution—the enemy the police forcefully fought and who may never have existed.

THE SOCIAL BIOGRAPHIES OF TOP-SECRET PHOTOGRAPHS

Secret police photography functioned as an extension of the textual narrative. Images in the KGB archives are not catalogued separately. Rather, all the various types of images—mug shots of arrestees, surveillance photographs, photocopies of confiscated materials—appear as inserts within standard text files and are frequently described in detail in the file itself. Photographs were thus very much part of the story, underscoring or buttressing the textual claims. Being narrativized in this simple and straightforward way, KGB photographs represent a revealing example of a historical source that bears the mark of the mechanism of knowledge production. Hence comes our opportunity to read the image as text, studying the meanings and (photographic) ideologies that were invested in it while also reading the often conflicting textual interpretations of the image given in the accompanying file story. As John Tagg puts it, "every text—including the photographic text—is an activity of production of meaning which is carried on within a certain *régime of sense*."[20]

But the importance of the photograph as a historical source is not just a question of content—that is, who or what it shows, the specific story it tells or mood it conveys. As Edwards and Hart argue, "Photographs are both images *and* physical objects that exist in time and space and thus in social and cultural experience."[21] While the file was in active use, photos tended to be pasted or glued between typed sheets of paper or enclosed in an inserted envelope, where they might be marked, numbered, and cropped. Prior to being sent to the archive, certain photos might then be reproduced to assist with other investigations or recycled for other purposes within the organization. In this way, photographs produced or acquired by the security services found themselves inevitably bound up as material forms in various modes of handling and presentation, all of which affected their social and historical meanings. This is what Edwards and Hart have in mind when they underscore the value of investigating the "social biographies" of photographs as material objects.[22]

Of course, given that KGB photographs were top-secret documents whose circulation was limited to a small circle of agency personnel, one might wonder whether the question of a social life even applies. Still, despite their obvious distinctiveness compared to other types of photos, secret police photographs indeed had social lives.

To begin with, the term "secret" in the phrase "top secret," as Cristina Vatulescu has noted in building on observations by Hannah Arendt, is misleading with regard to the Soviet security services, as most of the Soviet population was fully aware of the existence of the secret police and their secret files and was in fact fascinated by the possibility of learning what these files contained. Thus it was not true secrecy but rather the "spectacle of secrecy" that made things seem secret and ultimately allowed for "the uncovering of (fabricated) anti-Stalinist plots." Vatulescu compares the social effects of the secret police file with Soviet propaganda, the largest area of state textual production, and concludes that "the file won the battle over propaganda in the fascination it exerted on the public."[23] Yet the secret police file's relation to state propaganda was more material and pragmatic than the metaphoric battle over which form appeared more fascinating to the public. This is because the secret file literally extended and expanded its social life *through* propaganda as materials and images seized or produced by the KGB were recycled for propaganda purposes. Photos of crime scenes, individuals under arrest, and confiscated manuscripts and artwork featured regularly in show trials, propaganda films, and media campaigns, thus becoming seamlessly interwoven within the state's propaganda design.

As for inside the secret police institutions, here, too, the photos had their own distinct social life as they circulated between case files and different offices as part of internal KGB communications and information exchange. Photographs were collaged into illustrations for primers and reprinted in sample case files or internal secret police periodicals. They might appear in manuals for KGB officers to browse in the chekist library or in exhibits on the history of the Soviet security organs such as *The Chekist's Office* (Chekistskii kabinet).[24] A given photograph could take on additional meaning whenever a KGB officer scribbled a note or a date across the front of it or wrote a brief summary about it on the back. Photos also changed meaning—that is, took on new social lives—when they were transplanted from one case file to another or purposefully altered. One could say that their social life even continued in cases when they "disappeared" and continued to exist only as an item listed as "missing" or "destroyed."

Following the opening of the secret police archives after 1989 and in Russia (for a period) after 1991, the life of these secret materials then embarked on an entirely new journey. Retrieved from institutional obscurity in their dusty files, KGB documents began to travel through the public sphere through exposure in museum exhibits, popular histories, and media reports.[25] Today they circulate more widely still on various social media platforms, where one often finds them completely removed from any sense of their original context and pasted into new narratives. Within these new interpretive frameworks, the documents—including photographs—not surprisingly acquire new meaning and new agency as witnesses for the prosecution, this time not for the dictatorial regime but against it. As such, the once secret documents contribute to the generation of new memories and new discourses about life under socialism, allowing postsocialist publics both to reexperience past traumas and to reconnect broken historical threads. While the response to these declassified materials varies between Russia, former Soviet republics, and different states in Eastern Europe, these basic registers appear to be at work virtually everywhere, effectively shaping the way that scholars and members of the public have learned to read KGB materials in the present moment.

In his study of visual materials related to religious minorities from the secret police archives of Moldova, Romania, and Hungary, James Kapaló organizes the evidence according to the type of image in question: crime scene photos; photographs taken during surveillance operations (often with the assistance of hidden cameras); reenactments or restagings of events when real surveillance photography could not be obtained; photos of arrestees; and confiscated or intercepted photos.[26] For the purposes of this study, I divide these various photographic genres into two main categories: photos taken prior to the moment of arrest and those taken after. As Vatulescu argues, the moment of arrest was a critical turning point both in the arrestee's life and in the dynamic of power being deployed against them.[27] Upon arrest, the individual ceased to be the subject of an investigation and became instead the target of a more assertive exercise of state authority. It follows that this was also when the KGB's diverse arsenal of photographic types and techniques could be applied to their fullest and the arrestee—an otherwise ordinary person staring back at the police camera—could be turned into a tool for the construction of socialist knowledge about the enemy. Once in custody, suspects could be photographed for their police file—the mug shot. They could also be shot at the supposed crime scene and/or in reenactments or restagings of their criminal activity. In one fashion or another, arrest thus marked the beginning of the turn toward using photography as a means to possess the body of the criminal, disciplining him or her through images, while at the same time redefining them as an enemy type. In what follows, I focus on these post-arrest photographs, paying particular attention to how they were made to serve the goal of defining the enemy and justifying his or her condemnation and punishment.

FRAMING GUILT

After the Great Patriotic War, the Ukrainian NKVD was busy with a general postwar "cleanup" of the formerly occupied territories in Ukraine, searching for former Nazi collaborators and those who presumably benefited from the occupation regime. The relative religious freedom provided by the Reichskommissariat Ukraine in the occupied territories led to reopening of Orthodox churches and an overall rise of popular religious movements—things the Soviets sought to bring back under control. In the mid-1940s, the NKVD discovered a network of True Orthodox underground churches and monasteries in the Kharkiv region led by a catacomb priest and hieromonk by the name of Serafim (birth name: Shevtsov). The spaces of worship attended by the group were housed underground, either in caves or in cellars built beneath huts in the countryside. Between 1945 and 1955, the authorities destroyed more than fifteen such subterranean places, including a monastery in the town of Chuhuiv near Kharkiv, which the police uncovered in July 1945. At the time of the raid, the police found some thirty people worshipping at the underground site, most of whom were monks and nuns who lived on the premises—that is, they lived underground—including Father Serafim. The police took a series of photos of the space and confiscated items that were later added to Serafim's file. Given that the monastery was eventually destroyed, these photos are the only remaining visual record we have of the site. They show an entrance hidden behind a wooden structure within the wall of a vault. Once inside, an archway gallery opened into a series of separate chambers, including a spacious subterranean church replete with a full altar and iconostasis.[28]

The images follow standard police photography principles and at first glance seem to be no more than a set of inventory shots that routinely capture the crime and the perpetrator. In line with Kapaló's categorization of crime scene photographs, one can see here an "environment photo" of a rural house beneath which the monastery was discovered; "overview photos" that provide a general view of the scene by depicting the hidden entrance stairs, a ladder leading to the underground monastery, and means of concealment such as the wooden structure hiding the entrance; "central photos" that illustrate key features of the crime—an underground altar and iconostasis; and "detail photos" of confiscated icons and other valuables, a subterranean stove, and a mill.[29] In one photo (fig. 3.1), we see Serafim seated on a chair surrounded by religious vestments, utensils, and icons.[30] It was a common practice to produce staged photographs with suspects seated amid evidence of the crime. As in Serafim's case, such photographs were usually set up and shot after the arrest of a suspect.

Figure 3.1. Father Serafim seated amid religious items taken from the catacomb monastery

All the objects here were confiscated during the raid. The photo thus neatly places Serafim at the scene of the crime and, like all such staged crime scene photographs, aims to underscore a direct link between the would-be offender and the site of his offense to lock in evidence against the accused. The crime here is not in question. Its reality is simply assumed, cemented into place by the photograph, which captures both the criminal and the location of his crime along with numerous objects that appear to reinforce the commission of the crime and that would all, of course, later be used as material evidence (*veshchdok*) at trial. Serafim sits quite literally in the midst of his guilt, surrounded by the tools of his transgression.

The production of knowledge about the crime begins right here, in this photograph, with what might be called the grammar of the image, which restructures the elements of the scene according to a new semantic register. The most important restructuring is the most obvious and therefore most potentially overlooked: the invitation to see a religious person—in this case, a priest—as a criminal. Nothing here is faked: Serafim is pictured with the icons, crucifixes, and vestments of his religious community. The meaning of his *relationship* to these objects has been profoundly altered, however. One sees this clearly by comparing this crime scene photo with the only pre-arrest image of Serafim that I have found in which we see him sitting with the same crosses and icons that appear in the secret police photo (fig. 3.2).[31]

In this image, he wears his monastic clothing along with a monk's skullcap (*skufiia*). In the background, icons hang above a homemade altar. In his right hand he holds a cross, a religious symbol of martyrdom; in his left, the Gospels. The scene evokes the image of a martyr saint. The crime scene photo, by contrast, utterly negates the religious meaning of the pictured objects by changing their semantic order. In the pre-arrest image, Serafim appears in his original

Figure 3.2. Father Serafim in his priestly vestments before his arrest

cultural frame—that is, a frame in which he functions as priest, prophet, and religious leader. In the police image, however, the icons in view are no longer arranged as an iconostasis but instead heaped together or nailed to the wall, while the vestments that Serafim would have worn hang on a bare cord, and a set of consecrated altar cloths (antimins) appears draped over a kind of cart. The altering of the authentic order of things represses their original religious meaning, thus moving them into the semantic field of criminal evidence. In the same way, Serafim himself is no longer a man of the cloth but instead appears in the typical garb of an elderly peasant man, his hands resting helplessly on his knees. Though he remains close to the center of the image, with the attributes of his faith all around him, his relationship to the objects has been completely redefined. Once a monk, he is now a criminal, and his churchly objects and clothing are now proof of his stance against the state.

DISCIPLINING THE BODY

The decontextualization of the body represented a further step in the KGB's recasting of religious dissidents as criminals. The most obvious form this took was the criminal identification portrait, commonly known as the mug shot, which in police organizations the world over effectively defined the individual as a criminal.[32] In part, this identification occurred as an effect of the very genre of the photo. Rigid rules and guidelines applied to the taking of mug shot photos across Europe and the United States, tsarist Russia and the USSR included. According to Soviet criminalistics practice, "signaletic photography" had a standardized two-shot form, one full frontal facial view paired with a view from the side, almost always shot against a light background, free of distractions that might obscure the contour of the face and with only the inscription of the arrestee's name and date of birth or the date the photograph was taken marked across the bottom.[33] The semiotic tensions we can see on Serafim's crime scene photograph have been resolved by stripping away or minimizing every other material indicator of who the individual might be,

Figure 3.3. Mug shot of Father Serafim taken shortly after his arrest

effectively erasing his or her noncriminal social identity.[34] As such, the mug shot obscured traces of history.

In Serafim's case, his mug shot was taken shortly after the raid on the underground monastery (fig. 3.3).[35] In the photo, however, he is not identified as Serafim—the name he assumed on ordination as a monk—but rather by his birth name, Daniil Shevtsov. Alongside the image one finds a description of his features, including the shape of his nose and ears, the color of his eyes, and the presence of scars and other distinguishing features. Capturing this combination of the visual and the textual, the inventor of the mug shot, the French policeman-criminologist Alphonse Bertillon, referred to these photos aptly as "spoken portraits" (*portraits parlés*).[36] Bertillon's system (*bertillonage*) was adopted in Soviet police practice too.

Arrest photographs are perhaps the most striking of the visual materials one finds in Soviet-era penal files and dossiers. They stare back at you from the opening page of nearly every penal file, and they are clearly not meant as portraits in the traditional sense but rather as "accusatory images" whose role is to identify the criminal body or even a criminal type.[37] The "signaletic photograph" expresses nothing: its artless power dehumanizes the body, stripping the individual of his or her identity, agency, and history and recasting him or her effectively as a nonperson shorn of any identifiable social experience.

Tellingly, as I show below, in those cases when the police could not take an arrest photograph, they would occasionally resort to using a confiscated pre-arrest image of the accused, which they would then shade and alter to make it appear more like a mug shot, removing any evidence of the individual's social identity.

Yet for all that the arrest photographs were purposefully decontextualized, they were never neutral. The generic "look" of the mug shot contained its own coded representation, which ultimately did more than simply represent the criminal. As Tagg suggests, the point of this photographic form is to offer "a portrait of the product of the disciplinary method: the body made object; divided and studied . . . subjected and made subject. When accumulated, such images amount to a new representation of society."[38]

In the depersonalized image of the mug shot, what we are witnessing in effect is the state's assertion of absolute power over its insubordinate subject, which in this case amounts to the disciplining of the offender's body and the reduction of his or her likeness to conform to that of a homogenized, anonymized, and generic enemy—a portrait of the dissenter captured and defeated. The mug shot betrays no violence or struggle but instead communicates a kind of eerie stillness, which is itself a critical aspect of what makes the whole composition so dehumanizing. Yet in truth these photos often were implicated with enormous violence, carefully concealed behind the mask of their form. The whole point of the mug shot was to edit out the violence. Sometimes, however, the police could not fit the moment to the form, and the violence spilled out.

"GOD KNOWS": RESISTANCE BY IMAGE

They never stopped singing and praying. They kept at it when the police came for them, as their arrest photographs were being taken, during the interrogations that preceded their trial, even during the court hearing. In May 1952, a group of twenty-three believers was arrested in eight villages in the Kiev region. No one knew much about them. Their co-villagers described them as Stundists or Baptists and could say nothing more than that they never went to an Orthodox church and did not consult with the local priests even though they displayed Orthodox icons, crosses, and church books in their homes. The members of the group never discussed their faith except to repeat the phrase "God knows" (Bog znaet). All we know about them now is that they were poor peasants who gathered for prayer in secret in their homes, sometimes traveling between villages to pray together. Statements taken from forty-eight witnesses (all of them recorded nearly a month before the group's arrest) confirmed that the believers refused to enroll in local collective farms or to work at other state enterprises, never paid taxes or registered for other Soviet documents, and never used money ("the mark of the dragon") or sent their kids to public school.[39] They farmed their individual plots and occasionally worked on the side in exchange for food and clothes. Some had been arrested before and had spent time in prison. Others had had their kids forcefully taken from them and had never seen them again.

The Ministry of State Security (MGB, as the Soviet security services were known at the time) predictably charged the group with conducting anti-Soviet activity and propaganda as members of the "ecclesiastical-monarchist organization 'the True Orthodox Church.'" Their arrest and trial were anything but ordinary, however. Based on the description of events that appears in the case file, the believers resisted being taken away when the authorities came for them, barricading themselves in their houses, tearing off their clothes, falling to the floor, and crying and singing out loud. Their pretrial review was brief: a mere three days of interrogations followed by a night of twenty-two orchestrated confrontations between the arrestees and witnesses. During the review, the believers refused to answer questions, responding to everything by saying simply "God knows" or "I will only answer to the Judgment of God." They offered no denunciations or confessions, and they continued praying and singing hymns throughout, even while in court. Following their arrest, a number of the believers went on hunger strikes and were forcibly fed, as a result of which possibly as many as five of them died just a few days after sentencing. They also refused to walk, talk, or even to sleep on their beds while in prison, which meant that they had to be carried everywhere, the interrogation rooms and the courtroom included. In the end, they were sentenced to between ten and twenty-five years in the camps, although most had their sentences reduced in 1955 and then commuted altogether in 1956 as a result of the amnesty following Stalin's death. Some were rearrested in 1957, however, and sentenced to new ten-year terms.

Despite repeated pressures, all of which are described in the four-volume case file, the believers never broke. There were no confessions, no triumphal unmasking of the crime. In figure 3.4 we see two versions of the arrest photographs taken by the MGB officers.[40] As the photos were being taken, the believers intentionally closed their eyes, turned their heads away, or sang while the officers tried to restrain them, their hands and gloves clearly visible (fig. 3.4). Police officers later tried to correct these "tainted" photographs by removing the evidence of their violent intervention from the images, which one can see in the spruced-up copies with the hands of the policemen shaded

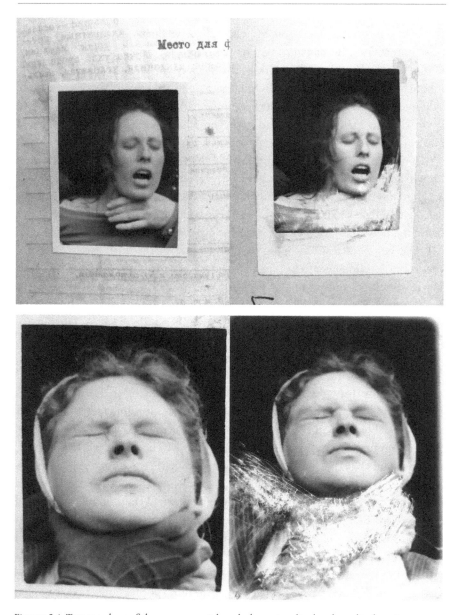

Figures 3.4. Two members of the group on trial, each shown in edited and unedited versions

out. The handless photos were used in the formal documentation of the case, while the smaller-size, original photos with the hands were appended to the back of the arrest questionnaires.

Prisoners' resistance to being photographed was not necessarily uncommon. In the broader European context, one finds instances of police attempting to photograph reluctant arrestees, such as Irish Fenians refusing to sit for their mug shots and laughing at the camera or a female suspect contorting her face for the photographer.[41] Such candid photos reveal the hidden reality that lurks behind police photography in general—that is, as Christian Phéline describes it in *L'image accusatrice* (The Accusatory Image), the exercise of political power on the body and image of the suspect in which the camera itself operates as an extension of the law and the embodiment of the disciplinary mechanism.[42]

The fact that the Kiev police photo laboratory, at a time of technological scarcity and shortages of photographic paper and chemical developer, did not proceed with producing a correct set of mug shots, as required by criminalistics standards, presents us with a rare opportunity to not only to look behind the veil to see the story and violence that the MGB tried to conceal; it also allows us to see the technical approach of an officer to a photograph and the logic behind it. What could actually spoil a mug shot: the things outlined in internal manuals, such as suspects' closed eyes or grimacing faces, or aspects that could not be found in manuals, such as the hands of policemen violently restraining an arrestee? The somewhat crude editing of the images shown above—replete with shaded-out gloves and hands—tells us something of the techniques used by the police in their photographic work and reveals a further struggle in the domain of photography. These physical alterations, or what Edwards and Hunt would refer to as "material intervention in the narrative" of the photograph, have the power to fundamentally alter the meaning and content of the image.[43] Thus in addition to exposing the usually hidden coercion that was inherent to the arrest process, this set of MGB photos also reveals how the language of the photograph itself was prone to reinstrumentalization.[44]

THE PHOTO COLLAGE AS COMPOSITE NARRATIVE

In the photographic practices of the secret police, arrest photographs were not simply a form of criminal identification. They also constituted part of a specific Soviet process used to create the appearance of networks. According to Soviet law, citizens could not be persecuted for their religious beliefs. The infamous article 58-10 of the Soviet Penal Code, the so-called "political" article that served as the basis for charges in most religious dissent cases, said nothing about religious belief but rather proscribed "anti-Soviet and counterrevolutionary propaganda and agitation." Religious dissenters were thus tried as political subversives acting under the guise of their religious beliefs. As a result, prophets, monastics, and priests found themselves transformed into anti-Soviet agents, spies, and counterrevolutionaries—all of whom, along with their conspiracies and deceptive practices, needed to be exposed as a kind of giant pseudoreligious enemy whose true nature was that of an organized and centralized political organization hiding behind the mask of religion. Constructions like the ecclesiastic-monarchist underground, the counterrevolutionary religious organization, or "insurgent counterrevolutionary ecclesiastic-monarchist red-dragon-type organization," most of which were completely made up by the authorities, were the product of this kind of thinking. Groups like the widely distributed True Orthodox believers, many of whom practiced their faith in subterranean caverns, fit perfectly into this state scenario of the giant hidden enemy. Such representations of religious dissenters as part of a coordinated and centralized political underground were common in secret police documents and in numerous forms of Soviet antireligious propaganda going back to the early post-1917 period.[45]

But how was one to put an image to this kind of enemy? How did one give form to a networked, octopus-like foe? The secret police's answer to this question was to reassemble the materials at hand—in the first order, mug shots and various confiscated photographs—in photo collages that, by grouping various photos together within a single image, helped underscore the would-be reality of a centralized yet interconnected antistate network. The logic behind it was similar to that of the massive propaganda portrait galleries of Communist Party leaders or the Council of People's Commissars that appeared in official textbooks or printed in newspapers. It visualized the organizational structure and hierarchies—regardless of whether they were real or constructed—and reinforced state-sponsored hegemonic narratives.

Figure 3.5 shows a photo collage appended to the indictment made against a group of thirty-eight True Orthodox believers allegedly overseen by a certain Bishop Aleksii of Voronezh Diocese (top row, fourth from the left).[46] This model indictment was published as a brochure by the OGPU in Voronezh in 1930. Several tens of copies of the brochure were later sent to other OGPU offices, including the one in Kiev, where it was supposed to serve as a manual for local officers. The individuals on trial were Russian and Ukrainian peasants as well as a handful of priests and monks, all of whom were arrested in 1929–1931 and charged with belonging to the "counterrevolutionary ecclesiastical-monarchist organization of the Buevtsy." (Bishop Aleksii's birth name was Semion Bui, hence the name Buevtsy or Buevshchina that the secret police gave to the case.) In the indictment, Bishop Aleksii was accused of heading up an organization of believers across some forty districts (*raiony*) in southern Russia and Ukraine. A show trial in every sense, the court case against Aleksii and thirty-seven other believers was meant to expose both their individual crimes and their collective participation in a secret illegal network, all of which was neatly captured in the collage—which, being physically attached

Figure 3.5. Collage of True Orthodox believers arranged to depict a counterrevolutionary group
    dubbed the Buevtsy

to the indictment, appeared to offer unassailable visual confirmation of their
guilt.

As a rule, the secret police used arrest photographs for collages of this sort,
but confiscated photos also occasionally appeared, even though police manuals counseled against making use of nonstandard civilian photos. For example,
several images in Figure 3.5 (top row, last right; third row first left; bottom
row first left) seem to have been taken from a pool of such confiscated images.
To make these nonpolice photos fit alongside the mug shots, police technicians
simply spruced them up a little, shading out the background that would have
identified them as ordinary portrait shots.

Another collage (fig. 3.6) presented a more complicated narrative, visualizing a hierarchical network of former monks and nuns (most of those pictured
are monastics) clandestinely united around their religious leaders.[47] The collage was included alongside the text of a model indictment against the "insurgent counterrevolutionary monarchic red-dragon-type organization" of the
Samosviatsy and the Ioannites that was published as an internal OGPU (of the
Central Black Earth Region) brochure in Belgorod in 1930.[48] Large-size photos
in the center identify the heads of the organization, while the smaller photos represent the various believers organized like followers around them. To

Figure 3.6. Collage designed by the secret police to suggest a hierarchy of monks and nuns allied
for counterrevolutionary purposes

underscore the idea of a hierarchy of political subversion, the collage makers
have mixed generic mug shot photos with pre-arrest photos confiscated from
the suspects that revealed something of their background and general social
identities (for example, religious clothing). The largest of the photographs
located at center top is of Hieromonk Feognost (Pilipenko) who appears in his
monk's cassock and wearing a cross. Ekaterina Titova (central column, second

top), a nun and a prophetess who headed one of the underground monasteries, also appears in religious dress, while Andrei the Sickly (*Boliashchii*), a local charismatic figure, is pictured half-reclining and surrounded by flowers. These photographs clearly were not mug shots but rather photos from the subjects' pre-arrest life that underscored their religious affiliations. While creating the composite image of the organized enemy, the security services used the materials at hand—arrest photographs and confiscated images—to create, as Cristina Vatulescu eloquently puts it, "a disturbing collage of found objects still pregnant with untold stories."[49]

As these images suggest, the photo collages produced by the secret police were not intended simply to document criminals as they might appear in a more ordinary kind of printed rogue's gallery or criminal lineup. With its bricolage-like technique of cutting and pasting images of different aspect, shape, size, and provenance to create a composite narrative, the secret police collage repurposed individual photographs to make them serve the cause of visualizing a collective enemy, an enemy whose individual foot soldiers were linked together through hidden and dangerous threads. This technique included one additional step.

META-DISCIPLINING: THE KGB PANOPTIC DIAGRAM

If photo collages combined images of individual enemies into a collective picture, the ultimate next step was the complete stripping away of this individual element. Individual enemies have faces and names. They can be identified, touched, known. Abstract enemies, by contrast, are by definition untouchable, unable to be seen, all of which makes them even more insidious and fearful. Thus as the secret police further elaborated their image of the collective enemy, they inclined toward representing him or her (more appropriately, it) as an abstract form with no human features at all, an enemy without a social identity or any individual marker, in effect, the enemy as a dot, or rather as a series of dots connected to each other within an integrated enemy network. This vision of the enemy as an abstract network drew on a long-standing KGB habit of representing criminal activity in terms of social connections. A suspect would be identified, and his or her various connections—friends, family, lovers, colleagues—would then be drawn into a schema that linked the group, with this web then becoming no less important for understanding the crime than the criminal him- or herself. Such schemas of social relations are found in abundance in the secret police archives in Eastern Europe.[50] Moreover, this paradigm of personality as a repository of social relations laid the foundation for the entire Soviet system. As Katherine Verdery has suggested, social connections rather than individuals form "the basic unit of [socialist] society."[51]

In a context in which the individual is simply a "composite of all [of his or her] social relations," then to know the social network is in effect to know the truth.[52] The danger posed by the socialist enemy therefore was not that of the individual dissenter so much as the danger of the social networks they formed and operated.

Not surprisingly then, one of the tasks of the secret police was to create visual diagrams of the religious underground, all the more so because such diagrams were a common means of picturing the connections that under-pinned religious communities. Sharing the same foundational logic and even a similar design, religious network schemes resembled diagrams and charts mapping relationships within a particular Soviet structure that widely cir-culated as illustrative material in textbooks and official media, such as orga-nizational schemes of the Communist Party, diagrams of prerevolutionary Bolshevik party organizations, or even organizational diagrams of the security service branches themselves.[53]

These police diagrams, which invariably presented religious groups as cen-tralized, subversive political organizations, could vary in their quality. Many were quite carefully drawn, some to the point of extreme precision, and were printed using high-quality techniques. Others, by contrast, were just hand-drawn sketches. As a rule, these schemas tended to be included as inserts in official reports, manuals, or other internal top-secret police documents, and usually represented religious communities as vertical networks built accord-ing to a hierarchy of ascending importance in which all the links and dots of the network converged toward either the top or the center. At the bottom of the diagram one found so-called local cells—that is, religious groups located in villages or small towns, sometimes with the number of arrestees/followers in the locale indicated in the middle of the dot, circle, or rectangle that repre-sented the cell. These "local cells" were then connected to each other by small lines to form larger sets of regional cells, which were in turn subordinated to the top or center, which invariably represented a command group located in an administrative capital or housed within a foreign-based, and therefore a priori anti-Soviet, political or religious organization.

The network diagram of the True Orthodox Church (fig. 3.7), for exam-ple, which dates to 1931, purports to reveal a series of branches and cells located across the USSR, with larger outlined circles identifying those cells and branches that were known to carry out supposedly significant subversive operations.[54] The diagram indicates two degrees or types of social connection: a direct link between cells, rendered as a full line, and an indirect link, indi-cated by a dotted line. It is unclear what an indirect link means in this instance, but the inclusion of such a link at least allowed the diagram's designers to

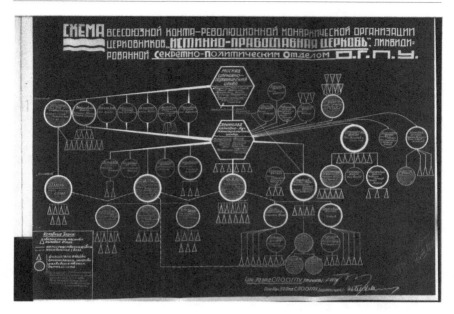

Figure 3.7. Network diagram of the True Orthodox Church

suggest that every group, branch, and cell in the entire country enjoyed some form of interconnection, while at the same time being subordinated to the various regional and central nodes above them, with the two oversized hexagons of Moscow and Leningrad crowning the scene at the center.

A 1930 brochure-indictment covering the case of an "ecclesiastic-monarchist counterrevolutionary organization" from Ivanovo-Voznesensk enclosed a more ambitious diagram (fig. 3.8).[55] The group on trial was the community of the Holy-Cross Church (*Krestovozdvizhenskaia obshchina*) that fell under the canonical jurisdiction of Bishop Augustin (Beliaev). In 1926 Bishop Augustin was repressed (and executed in 1937), and the church was soon closed down and demolished. Although the group of fifty-two believers on trial was a parish community that was mainly charged with having church gatherings and organizing an "anti-Soviet church sisterhood" and other youth groups, the diagram enclosed in the brochure pictured a giant web. It interlinked various alleged groups (of youth, former members of the "monarchist party," traders, and pogrom activists) and different parishes in Ivanovo, which it expanded by including "counterrevolutionary elements" in exile and in emigration.

Much like Foucault's panopticon as a metaphor for the modern disciplinary society, the KGB network diagram offers a laconic yet highly efficient rendering of a form of omnipresent surveillance that renders all social and individual relations visible while disguising the gaze itself, in effect hiding it from view. The diagram thus visualizes the effects of power. We see the enemy,

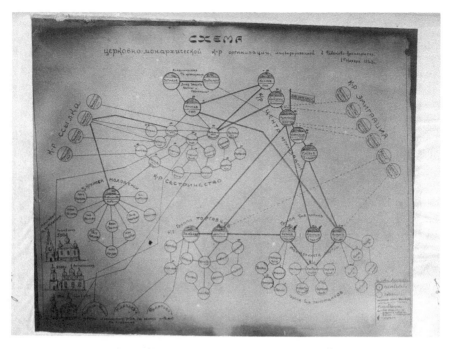

Figure 3.8. Network diagram of the "ecclesiastic-monarchist counterrevolutionary organization" from Ivanovo-Voznesensk

its subversive organization, and the many links that hold it together, all of which can now be disciplined because it can be seen. Visibility thus emerges as a guarantee of order.[56] The value of the panopticon lay in its power to expose not just the individual offender but everything that surrounded him or her, the entire network of otherwise unseen and therefore unknowable relations. To strip away the individuality of the dissenter and transform him or her into a dot or node within the KGB's panopticon-like diagram was a means of disciplining him or her and at the same time of exercising power over dissent itself. In the world of the diagram, offenders are grouped together, given a number, and the connections between them subjected to permanent surveillance. The KGB's panopticon even envisions social connections that may not exist (viz. the indirect links that we see in fig. 3.7), thus allowing the police to anticipate and intervene even before a "crime" is committed.[57] This habit of police diagramming—in this case, the elaboration of diagrams that underscore the apparent omnipresence of enemies and the need to keep them under constant surveillance—is a small yet telling indication of the disciplinary mechanisms that ultimately came to deeply penetrate Soviet society.

The Soviet regime developed its own iconographic tradition of visualizing the religious enemy. Antireligious campaigns were visually rich: a wide range of propaganda publications, posters, caricatures, films, newsreels, and public exhibitions was mass-produced and distributed to every corner of the country. Institutional practices of representation and visualization of the criminals required rigid standardization, although many repressed believers were barely literate peasants who left no name for their faiths nor rich material traces of their subversive practices—such as religious art, manuscripts, books, or anything that could be used as visual incriminating evidence in both court and propaganda. As I argue, the Soviet secret police was at the core of this process—an institution that produced, sanctioned, and controlled the distribution of what became an iconic imagery of a dangerous and harmful, organized and deceitful enemy hidden behind the mask of a religious believer. KGB documentation—increasingly available in recent years due to the opening of state archives in Ukraine, Georgia, Latvia, and other postsocialist countries—provides new insights into the origin and mechanisms of the production of knowledge and imagery of the enemy.

The photographs shown here were not propagandistic stills, although they could appear in propaganda publications. Some of them followed Soviet police standards of signaletic photography and crime scene photographic inventories, but many also indicate a manipulative and instrumental use of KGB photography. Retouching, photomontage, collage, cropping—these techniques were either formally prohibited in police practice or were not clearly specified. As I suggest, they were not as simple as open violations of police procedure or conscious manipulation of police photography for malevolent ends. Nor were they a mere embodiment of a disciplinary technique. As I have attempted to show in this chapter, the use of photography by the Soviet secret police assisted the production of a new kind of knowledge. Through the repurposing of photographs into new functions by collaging or pasting them into albums or shading elements that were considered to be out of place, the secret police created new objects of knowledge and reinforced the regime of truth that laid the foundation of a new social order. Yet whether we describe this process as knowledge production or simply distortion, the making of the micropatterns of a new Soviet reality or merely fabrication, what secret police photography discloses is the internal mechanisms of the creation of an apparatus of totalitarian control and state violence. The attribution of enormous power (and hence disproportionate attention) to marginal religious dissent of hardly any political threat to Soviet power and the dissidents' representation as subversive, extremist, even terrorist organizations allowed the state and its secret police to accumulate their own power and to legalize new forms of domination. In the panoptic religious network schemes shown above, we see the reflection of the Soviet paradigm of social control and the very structure of the totalitarian system.

But the KGB photography is not only about the exercise of power; it also reveals the fear of failure that characterized the totalitarian system. It was this fear that led police officers to compile their files, (mal)adjust their documentation to suit Soviet standards and codes, and report their findings up the chain of command. "This was an audience existing in dangerously thin air," as Viola puts it.[58] The images from 1952—shaded hands placed on crying women—reveal more about the fear on the part of the secret police of breaking the code of silence surrounding the use of violence and of disclosing what might be seen as a failed case of enemy unmasking. To say that the Stalinist regime was utterly and openly violent is to project our knowledge, with all the sources that we have today, onto the past. Back then, the Stalinist constitution nominally granted all basic rights and freedoms, including religious freedom, and represented itself as protecting human rights; hence everyday state violence and terror needed to be concealed from public and international spheres. It needed to be erased from secret police records too.[59] The manipulation of both internally produced as well as confiscated photographs, presented alongside other types of documents, allows us to glimpse the internal conflict and the weakness of the Soviet system. While trying to "unmask" ordinary believers by the means of violent repression, the totalitarian regime often stumbled in its efforts to expose the ultimate "victory" over the enemy. As a result, even today the religious beliefs of these victims of Soviet power remain obscure and hard for us to see.

NOTES

The research conducted in this publication was funded by the Irish Research Council (award no. 21/PATH-A/9310) and COST Action 16213. The chapter is the result of my collaboration with the team of researchers in the Hidden Galleries Project (ERC project no. 677355). I am particularly grateful to James Kapaló for his enormous support throughout my research on the KGB archives. An earlier version of the chapter benefited from vivid discussions during my stay at the Woodrow Wilson International Center for Scholars in the winter of 2019–2020, as well as critical comments from David Brandenberger and *Kritika*'s anonymous reviewers.

1. A. Ia. Vyshinskii, ed., *Kriminalistika*, vol. 1: *Tekhnika i taktika rassledovaniia prestuplenii* (Moscow: Sovetskoe zakonodatel'stvo, 1935).

2. I use here the anachronistic term "KGB" to refer to the Soviet secret police and intelligence agencies that underwent a series of restructuring reforms and different names (VChK-OGPU-NKVD-NKGB-MGB-MVD-KGB) throughout the Soviet period. When talking about particular historical cases, I use the name corresponding to a given period.

3. Jens Jäger, "Photography: A Means of Surveillance? Judicial Photography, 1850 to 1900," *Crime, History, and Societies* 5, no. 1 (2001): 27–51; Sandra S. Phillips, Mark Haworth-Booth, and Carol

Squiers, *Police Pictures: The Photograph as Evidence* (San Francisco: Chronicle Books, 1997); Edgar J. Hoover, "Photography in Crime Detection," *Scientific American* 162, no. 2 (1940): 71–74.

4. Katherine Verdery, *Secrets and Truth: Ethnography in the Archive of Romania's Secret Police* (New York: Central European University Press, 2014), 51–52.

5. John Tagg, *The Burden of Representation: Essays on Photographies and Histories* (Minneapolis: University of Minnesota Press, [1988] 1993), 94–95.

6. Tagg, *Burden of Representation*, 80.

7. Ann Laura Stoler, *Along the Archival Grain: Epistemic Anxieties and Colonial Common Sense* (Princeton, NJ: Princeton University Press, 2009), 22–28.

8. Roland Barthes, *Camera Lucida: Reflections on Photography*, trans. Richard Howard (New York: Hill and Wang, [1980] 2010), 89; John Tagg, *The Disciplinary Frame: Photographic Truths and the Capture of Meaning* (Minneapolis: University of Minnesota Press, 2009), xxviii.

9. On the first point, see Tagg, *Burden of Representation*; and Suren Lalvani, *Photography, Vision, and the Production of Modern Bodies* (Albany: State University of New York Press, 1996). On the second, see James R. Ryan, *Picturing Empire: Photography and the Visualization of the British Empire* (Chicago: University of Chicago Press, 1997); and Elizabeth Edwards and Janice Hart, "Introduction: Photographs as Objects," in *Photographs, Objects, Histories: On the Materiality of Images*, ed. Elizabeth Edwards and Janice Hart (New York: Routledge, 2004), 1–15.

10. James L. Hevia, "The Photography Complex: Exposing Boxer-Era China (1900–1901), Making Civilization," in *Photographies East: The Camera and Its Histories in East and Southeast Asia*, ed. Rosalind C. Morris (Durham, NC: Duke University Press, 2009), 81; Elizabeth Edwards, "Objects of Affect: Photography beyond the Image," *Annual Review of Anthropology* 41 (2012): 223.

11. Haluzevyi derzhavnyi arkhiv Sluzhby bezpeky Ukraïni (HDASBU) f. 3, op. 1, spr. 331, ark. 206.

12. The list of registered religious groups varied in different periods of Soviet religious politics. In 1946 there were established two government bodies: the Council for the Affairs of the Russian Orthodox Church and the Council for the Affairs of Religious Cults, which oversaw religious organizations other than the Russian Orthodox Church.

13. The term referred to the then-underground communities who did not accept the Declaration of Loyalty to Soviet Power signed by Metropolitan Sergii in 1927 and consequently broke up with the official church. The movement, however, was far more heterogeneous and many, even those loyal to the Moscow Patriarchy, chose (or were forced into) an illegal underground position simply because it was impossible to comply with newly created registration procedures and requirements for religious groups. In the context of the mass closure of churches and oftentimes the absence of official clergymen, grassroots religious communities had no choice but to take care of their religious needs on their own, creatively adapting religious practices to changing circumstance. See Aleksei Beglov, *V poiskakh "bezgreshnykh katakomb": Tserkovnoe podpol'e v SSSR* (Moscow: Arefa, 2008); and D. V. Pospielovskii, *Russkaia pravoslavnaia tserkov' v XX veke* (Moscow: Respublika, 1995), 174–75.

14. Lynne Viola, "The Peasant Nightmare: Visions of Apocalypse in the Soviet Countryside," *Journal of Modern History* 62, no. 4 (1990): 747–70; Tracy Mcdonald, "A Peasant Rebellion in Stalin's Russia: The Pitelinskii Uprising, Riazan, 1930," in *Contending with Stalinism: Soviet Power and Popular Resistance in the 1930s*, ed. Lynne Viola (Ithaca, NY: Cornell University Press, 2002), 89.

15. HDASBU f. 16, op. 1, spr. 206, ark. 184.

16. A. I. Demianov, *Istinno-pravoslavnoe khristianstvo: Kritika ideologii i deiatel'nosti* (Voronezh: Izdatel'stvo Voronezhskogo universiteta, 1977), 25; HDASBU f. 16, op. 1. spr. 206, ark. 16–17; spr. 45, ark. 73–74.

17. Tatiana Vagramenko, "Visualizing Invisible Dissent: Red-Dragonists, Conspiracy and the Soviet Security Police," in *The Religious Underground and the Secret Police in Communist and Post-communist Central and Eastern Europe*, ed. J. Kapaló and K. Povedák (New York: Routledge, 2021), 60–82.

18. Lynne Viola, "Introduction," in *Contending with Stalinism*, 9–13.

19. Cristina Vatulescu, *Police Aesthetics: Literature, Film, and the Secret Police in Soviet Times* (Stanford, CA: Stanford University Press, 2010), 38; Verdery, *Secrets and Truths*, 56.

20. Tagg, *Burden of Representation*, 98–99.

21. Edwards and Hart, "Introduction," 1.

22. Edwards and Hart, "Introduction," 4; Edwards, "Objects of Affect," 224.

23. Vatulescu, *Police Aesthetics*, 2–6.

24. Although the term "chekist" at large was ambiguous in Soviet society, it was (and still is) used as a positive self-designation for members of the KGB (and nowadays of the Federal Security Service).

25. Many photographs published in this chapter were displayed in a series of public exhibitions of the Hidden Galleries Project in Romania, Hungary, Ireland, and Republic of Moldova in 2019–2021 (http://hiddengalleries.eu).

26. James A. Kapaló, "The Appearance of Saints: Photographic Evidence and Religious Minorities in the Secret Police Archives in Eastern Europe," *Material Religion: The Journal of Objects, Art, and Belief* 15, no. 1 (2019): 82–109.

27. Vatulescu, *Police Aesthetics*, 36.

28. For more on this case, see Tatiana Vagramenko, "True Orthodox Underground Monastery," in *Hidden Galleries: Material Religion in the Secret Police Archives in Central and Eastern Europe*, ed. James Kapaló and Tatiana Vagramenko (Münster: Lit, 2020), 16–17.

29. For Kapaló's categorization, see his "Appearance of Saints," 91–94. His observations are based on Hungarian criminology manuals, which, however, adopted the KGB standards.

30. HDASBU f. 6-fp, vol. 2, spr. 75976. A similar type of photograph can be found in Anca M. Şincan, "The Typewriter," in *Hidden Galleries*, 44–45; and Ágnes Hesz, "Forbidden Materials," in *Hidden Galleries*, 41.

31. "Ieromonakh Serafim (Shevtsov)," http://true-orthodox.narod.ru/harkov/stu/Serafim4.html.

32. Jäger, "Photography," 46.

33. Vyshinskii, *Kriminalistika*, 52–54.

34. Tom Gunning, "Tracing the Individual Body: Photography, Detective, and Early Cinema," in *Cinema and the Invention of Modern Life*, ed. Leo Charney and Vanessa R. Schwartz (Berkeley: University of California Press, 1995), 29–31; Phillips, Booth, and Squiers, *Police Pictures*, 19–21.

35. HDASBU f. 6-fp, spr. 75976, vol. 1, ark. 17.

36. Robert A. Sobieszek, *Ghost in the Shell: Photography and the Human Soul, 1850–2000* (Cambridge, MA: MIT Press, 1999), 113–15; Phillips, Booth, and Squiers, *Police Pictures*, 20. On the use of "spoken portraits" in Soviet criminalistics, see Vyshinskii, *Kriminalistika*, 45–51.

37. Ernest Lacan, quoted in Sobieszek, *Ghost in the Shell*, 113; Allan Sekula, "The Body and the Archive," *October* 39 (Winter 1986): 18–19.

38. Tagg, *Burden of Representation*, 76; Breandán Mac Suibhne and Amy Martin, "Fenians in the Frame: Photographing Irish Political Prisoners, 1865–68," *Field Day Review* 1 (2005): 102.

39. Quoted phrase from HDASBU f. 6-fp, spr. 69346, vol. 4, ark. 71 rev.

40. HDASBU f. 6-fp, vol. 1, spr. 69346, ark. 185, 192rev, 242, 249 rev.

41. Suibhne and Martin, "Fenians in the Frame," 107; Gunning, "Tracing the Individual Body," 27–29; Tagg, *Disciplinary Frame*, xxv.

42. Quoted in Gunning, "Tracing the Individual Body," 27.

43. Edwards and Hunt, "Introduction," 13.

44. Tagg, *Disciplinary Frame*, xxvi.

45. Vagramenko, "Visualizing Invisible Dissent."

46. HDASBU f. 13, op. 1, spr. 390, ark. 1; see also Tatiana Vagramenko, "Photo-Collage of Members of the True Orthodox Church," in *Hidden Galleries*, 38–39.

47. HDASBU f. 13, op. 1, spr. 388, ark. 1 rev.

48. The *Samosviatsy* (deriving from the term for "self-consecration") were part of the catacomb True Orthodox movement. The Ioannites were followers of John of Kronstadt (an archpriest from a town

near St. Petersburg [1829–1908]), who worshipped him as a saint and a prophet. For more details, see Vagramenko, "Visualizing Invisible Dissent."

49. Cristina Vatulescu, "Arresting Biographies: The Secret Police File in the Soviet Union and Romania," *Comparative Literature* 56, no. 3 (2004): 243.

50. Similar religious network diagrams are found in Romanian and Hungarian secret police archives. See Ágnes Hesz, "Jehovah's Witness Network Scheme," in *Hidden Galleries*, 37; and Ágnes Hesz, "Network Scheme of Hungarian Catholic Underground Cells," http://hiddengalleries. eu/digitalarchive/s/en/item/423.

51. Katherine Verdery, *My Life as a Spy: Investigations in a Secret Police File* (Durham, NC: Duke University Press, 2018), 244.

52. Verdery, *Secrets and Truths*, 187.

53. See, e.g., NKVD internal troop schemes from the Russian State Military Archives, http://rgvarchive. ru/dokumenty-chast-2.shtml-0. David Brandenberger has suggested the comparison with charts published in the 1930s that mapped the relationships between economic institutions during the First Five-Year Plan.

54. HDASBU f. 13, op. 1, spr. 388, ark. 49. See also Tatiana Vagramenko, "Model Network Schemes of the True Orthodox Church," in *Hidden Galleries*, 35–36.

55. HDASBU f. 13, op. 1, spr. 391, ark. 76.

56. Michel Foucault, *Discipline and Punish: The Birth of the Prison*, trans. Alan Sheridan (New York: Random House, [1975] 1995), 200.

57. Compare with Foucault, *Discipline and Punish*, 206.

58. Viola, "Popular Resistance in the Stalinist 1930s: Soliloquy of a Devil's Advocate," in *Contending with Stalinism*, 27.

59. Besides, the memory of the 1939 purges within the NKVD was still alive. In that case, several thousand lower-ranking local chekists were scapegoated for "violation of socialist legality," which included the use of violence and torture during the Great Terror. See M. Iunge [Marc Junge], L. [Lynne] Viola, and Dzh. [Jeffrey] Rossman, eds., *Ekho bol'shogo terrora: Sbornik dokumentov*, 3 vols. (Moscow: Probel-2000, 2017–2019).

4

The Gulag's "Dead Souls"

Mortality of Released Invalids in the Camps, 1930–1955

Mikhail Nakonechnyi

> Before historians begin to use historical statistical data, they should attempt
> to discover how the data was collected and calculated and by whom these
> operations were carried out. They should attempt to see whether there are
> any reasons for doubting the reliability of these data. Where doubts do arise
> as to their reliability, they should attempt to make an assessment of the pos-
> sible scale of the inaccuracy. It is extremely dangerous to accept figures on
> trust without understanding their origin and history.
> —Stephen Wheatcroft and Robert Davies

HOW VERACIOUS ARE THE OFFICIAL MORTALITY STATISTICS OF THE GULAG,
an odious system of Soviet forced labor camps?[1] For decades, this seemingly
perennial question elicited considerable controversy in historical circles,
both in Russia and in the West. As of 2021, the answer remains inconclusive,
intensely politicized, and vociferously contested. This chapter contributes to
the ongoing debate on the subject. Broadly, it is devoted to the critical quantitative reassessment of official death rates in several Gulag localities. The first
scholarly recalculations of this kind, they reveal that the actual mortality in a
random sample of camps and colonies appears to be significantly higher than
the official data indicate. As its principal empirical contribution, the present
chapter establishes a novel methodological algorithm for the quantitative revision of camp death rates. It identifies new sources and methods one can use to
factor in previously omitted fatalities of ex-inmates, released from the Gulag
on medical grounds (the so-called *aktirovannye* invalids). This chapter for the

first time demonstrably proves that ex-prisoners' mortality constituted not a unique coincidence, typical of a single deadly locality, but a consistent demographic pattern that repeated itself on an as yet unknown but broad temporal and spatial scale.

More broadly, the chapter adds to the institutional history of Stalinist criminal justice. It sheds new light on paradoxes surrounding the registration of prisoner mortality data in the Gulag. By doing so, the chapter reveals the understudied idiosyncrasies and contradictions of the Soviet state apparatus's operation. To properly articulate the chapter's research questions, however, I begin with a succinct overview of the historical literature.

"MAFIOSI INTERNAL RECORDS" VERSUS "RELEASE TO DIE"

The Soviet Union never published prisoner mortality data. Only after the partial opening of the archives in 1989–1991 did scholars finally obtain the once top secret internal statistics of the Gulag. The declassified data were extracted from summary reports of the system's central administration in Moscow. They contained the empirical discovery that Steven Barnes presciently called "the most important archival-based revelation" concerning the Gulag—the numbers of prisoner deaths and releases between 1930 and 1953.[2] Out of roughly 18 million people who entered the system in these years, "only" 1.7 million died. These internal archival figures appeared to be dramatically less than anticipated by "traditionalist" pre-archival scholarship, which relied on extrapolations and prisoners' memoirs (e.g., Robert Conquest). The latter also claimed that liberations from the Gulag were exceptionally rare and very few prisoners survived their sentence.[3] To the surprise of many scholars, however, the Gulag possessed an unexpected "revolving door."[4] Central records indicated that 90 percent of prisoners purportedly survived their incarceration and were listed as released.[5] In fact, between 1934 and 1953, the camps liberated from 20 percent to 40 percent of its population annually, "many times more than died in the same year."[6]

Over the years, historians have expressed radically divergent views on the putative veracity of these archival data. Viktor Zemskov considered the data, including mortality statistics, to be "exemplary" or even "absolutely precise" due to the alleged "rigorous order" of the NKVD's internal accounting.[7] Some of his Western colleagues tended to be more critical but still considered the figures to be if not ideal, then generally reliable.[8] For example, as Stephen Wheatcroft notes, "it would be rash to presume these data were in any absolute way perfect, but there seem to be no intrinsic grounds for presuming that these indicators are greatly falsified."[9] To counter Conquest's dubious supposition that all Gulag records could be totally fabricated, he argued that "camp officials were made responsible for the prisoners that had been entrusted to them, and there was conscientious reporting of this. I stand by the statement . . . that 'there is a satisfactory degree of reliability in accounting.'"[10] In 2009, Wheatcroft remarked more confidently about penal accounting agencies, "their data was secret at the time, but there is no reason to doubt the ability, honesty and reliability of their calculations."[11]

In 1999, John Keep warned scholars not to be mesmerized by the newly available central figures and underscored that the Soviet penal system was, after all, a "criminal body" and therefore its records are as reliable as "the average Mafioso's tax return." Wheatcroft famously retaliated by comparing Mafioso tax returns to Potemkin publications in *Pravda*, whereas classified Gulag data (including mortality statistics) were more like internal (and therefore scrupulously accurate) records of the Mafia.[12] Wheatcroft prudently emphasized the provisional nature of our knowledge, however, and urged scholars to assess the available archival data critically. According to Simon Ertz, penal mortality statistics were not only top secret but also functional, because Gulag leadership required objective information from the localities for rational decision making.[13] Wheatcroft supported this sentiment: "Their health departments needed to know how many were dying."[14] Even many years after the partial opening of the Soviet archives, no convincing critique of these rationalizations had appeared. Zemskov, meanwhile, began to argue that no substantial additions to the statistics that he published were possible, and his figures were definitive.[15] As a result, the data on death and mass releases precipitated a major reconceptualization of the Gulag. Increasingly, it came to be viewed as a far more "survivable" system than it had been deemed before 1989–1991.

Since then, however, a group of scholars has drawn attention to the alleged policy of "release-to-die," completely ignored by Zemskov and others.[16] Terminally ill invalids, discharged on medical grounds by a court decision via articles 457 and 458 of the RSFSR Criminal Procedural Code, died soon after release, but camp doctors deliberately excluded these fatalities from medical registries and vitiated registered mortality. The impetus behind these statistical shenanigans was to cut costs, produce "convenient" indicators in the reports to placate superiors, and avoid prosecution for high mortality rates from inspectors.[17]

However, almost none of these historians looked into this argument on a deeper empirical level. They provided valuable single documents and narrative sources but never elaborated the "release-to-die" argument in detail, with the sole exception of Golfo Alexopoulos.[18] In her groundbreaking monograph, she used a considerably broader source base than her predecessors and trenchantly asserted that "Stalin's Gulag eliminated much of its death rate . . . by moving dying prisoners out of the system."[19]

Although important and useful, the evidentiary base of the release-to-die argument manifests a few limitations. The first of these is the overconcentration on the Gulag central archive (kept in Moscow). The second is the absence of critical comparison of local and central mortality data.[20] The third combines an excessive focus on a single bureaucracy (the NKVD) with neglect of other agencies responsible for administering medical discharges, notably the camp procuracy (which provided oversight) and the Ministry of Justice (which issued the final verdict in each case).[21]

The most important gap, however, constitutes the lack of statistical evidence of ex-inmates' mortality or any detailed information about what happened to invalids immediately after discharge.[22] They are only presumed to be dying en masse, based on circumstantial evidence. For instance, Alexopoulos states that "many died shortly after their release," but presents only four cases of ex-prisoners' fatalities drawn from secondary literature and eyewitness testimonies.[23]

Moreover, some scholars have conceded that it is impossible to revise and recalculate official mortality because allegedly no recordkeeping of deaths after release existed (e.g., Anna Tsepkalova).[24] According to Alexopoulos, "given the high degree of deception and false accounting," no exact mortality figure will ever be produced.[25] Oleg Khlevniuk contends that released invalids' deaths "no longer affected camp reports" and "it is impossible to count all such victims of the GULAG."[26] Given this conviction, none has provided the "smoking gun" quantitative proof that central Moscow statistics contained any understatement of deaths due to medical release. No scholar has yet adduced direct statistical evidence of mortality distortion using evidence of mortality distortion via medical release for even a single locality.

This chapter at least partly amends the abovementioned "blank spots." That said, the present author is intellectually indebted to and builds on the significant achievements of the previous scholarship.

CONTRIBUTION, METHODOLOGY, AND SOURCES

The present chapter strengthens the release-to-die argument with new quantitative data on ex-inmates' mortality. Its central thesis runs like this. A more complete picture of Gulag death statistics can be achieved only via assiduous cross-referencing of previously overlooked data, extracted from local archives of individual camps, courts, and procurators' offices and added to the published summary central reports of the Gulag.

The aims of this chapter are twofold. First, I seek to use statistical evidence to empirically prove the reality of the released invalids' mortality as a historical phenomenon. I reveal the previously unexplored registration process of these fatalities and demonstrate their wide temporal and spatial proliferation. Second, I elucidate how medical releases reduced death rates by using concrete quantitative examples. I recalculate death indexes for several camps and periods to expose the degree of underreporting in the central statistics. The analysis discloses how camp medics accounted for "dead souls" at the local level but purposely excluded them from the central summary registries. In the longer-term perspective, other Gulag scholars can use this new method as a heuristic and analytical tool for further systematic recalculation of the data, as more evidence from yet inaccessible camp archives becomes available.

In addition, I argue that the mortality of ex-inmates was quantitatively and practically significant during the most extreme phases of the Gulag's existence. These encompassed the famine of 1932–1933, the war of 1941–1945, and the famine of 1946–1947. In nonfamine periods (1934–1936, 1939–1941, 1948–1955) the incidence of death among those released was lower. Furthermore, there was a pronounced regional and institutional variation during both famine and nonwar and nonfamine phases—notably between camps of various production profiles, the camps' position in the supply chain, and the type of incarceration (colonies versus camps).[27]

In historiographical terms, this chapter challenges both the "Mafioso internal records" analogy, advanced by Wheatcroft, and the pessimistic presupposition about the impossibility of mortality recalculations, espoused by some proponents of the release-to-die argument. On the one hand, Wheatcroft and Ertz are right to claim that Gulag internal data were not a total fabrication. Khlevniuk and Alexopoulos are equally correct to argue that it is unlikely that we can enumerate all fatalities among medically released ex-inmates. However, by factoring in overlooked deaths found at the local level, the present chapter bridges the divide between those seemingly juxtaposed interpretations. It adumbrates an underrated methodological algorithm to arrive at a more accurate approximation of official mortality data than previously thought possible—at a minimum, for some peripheral camps and periods. To be sure, given the biases and imprecisions of the regional quantitative sources, discussed below, the ideal "real" accuracy remains tentative and unattainable.

Nonetheless, I still make a case for the usefulness of local death statistics of released ex-inmates. First, these data, however imperfect, help us to pinpoint more confidently the yet unknown incidence, as well as the temporal and spatial spread of these deaths. This new knowledge is instrumental to counter potential and so far unaddressed counterarguments about the isolated nature of deaths after release. Second, quantitative recalculations supplement the available qualitative evidence, underpinning the release-to-die contention. It makes the whole argument even more persuasive—notwithstanding the limitations of local statistics, discussed below.

To play devil's advocate, let us assume that local statistics can understate the case (which they indeed seem to do). If we add these incomplete regional figures to the central statistics and discover the degree of underreporting to be significant (say, 25 percent or even higher), this result will irrefutably prove the egregious inadequacy of the Gulag central reports using direct evidence, at least for some camps and periods. These concrete quantitative proportions, in my opinion, are more convincing than the general claim that medical releases skewed the data of this or that camp to some unknown extent. Although not definitive, the recalculations bring us one step closer to a more complete picture of Gulag-induced deaths.

In terms of sources, I strongly emphasize the archives of local camp health services. In my view, a key to solving the seemingly intractable riddle of mortality recalculations lies in these rarely mined primary medical files of regional camp administrations. In addition to central Moscow records, this chapter is based on archives in Samara, Tambov, Arkhangel'sk, and Cheliabinsk. It also uses material from local document collections (Kemerovo and Novosibirsk provinces). To supplement the Gulag records, I extensively draw on the reports of so-called camp procurators and judges to get a fresh, multi-institutional perspective on the issue of mortality recordkeeping. This approach reveals poorly researched bureaucratic feuds at the local level of the camp system (e.g., tensions between a few intransigent procurators and Gulag officials). They are interesting in themselves and facilitate a more sophisticated, multifaceted understanding of the Stalinist state apparatus's operation.

To make these arguments, I first dissect the labyrinthine registration process of ex-inmates' deaths. Next I provide a set of recalculation cases, accompanied by an analysis of diagnoses assigned to candidates for release. I finish up with a broad sweep of the quantitative data to demonstrate the wide dissemination of the phenomenon across time and space.

"CHAOS AND CLANDESTINE AGENDAS": REGISTRATION OF RELEASED INVALIDS' MORTALITY

Any scholar who decides to quantify the mortality of released invalids immediately faces a methodological perplexity that seems, at the first glance, practically insuperable. How is it possible to get *statistical* evidence of deaths that officials intentionally kept ostensibly hidden and unrecorded? The answer lies in the bureaucratic paradoxes surrounding the registration of invalids' mortality. To reveal these "unseen fatalities," I utilize two approaches: comparisons of local camp records with central Gulag data (for recalculation of mortality in the camps) and institutional triangulation.

THE "CENTRAL-LOCAL" APPROACH AND ITS CHALLENGES

The Soviet Union sought to control every potentially problematic demographic process within the purview of its apparatuses.[28] A catastrophic surge of deaths among the registered penal population in 1941–1943 is a well-known fact.[29] What remains obscure is that the surge correlated with an unprecedented exodus of debilitated ex-inmates from the localities in three successive and, in some instances, overlapping "waves" in 1941, 1942–1943, and 1944. Many of the freed ex-prisoners could not be transported from their places of confinement due to their extreme emaciation and the severe logistical collapse of the railroad network. These ex-prisoners, released on medical grounds, began to die at an alarming rate in the camp hospitals and barracks, leaving rank-and-file personnel at a loss as to how to record these fatalities.[30] Local camp administrations inundated Moscow with a flurry of inquiries on how to proceed with this ambiguous and rapidly deteriorating situation. The Gulag top command responded on 2 April 1943 with Secret Directive no. 42/232546, signed by Gulag Director Viktor Grigor'evich Nasedkin himself, which hinted at the importance of the problem.[31] It read: "Several localities sent inquiries about how to account for released prisoners who died in the camps and colonies. The Gulag clarifies that data on the freed prisoners who died in the camps and colonies right after their discharge should be recorded on a separate explanatory accounting sheet alongside the general medical report. Peripheral locations should not include these dead former prisoners in mortality reports on civilian camp personnel or prisoners per se."[32]

Six months later, on 7 September 1943, an additional directive, no. 42/233211, emanated from another influential figure in the Gulag machinery—David Maksimovich Loidin, head of the central Medical-Sanitation Department (SANO), an embedded penal health service. The chief Gulag doctor demanded that 116 local SANO heads report on "the number of the released dead prisoners who remained in the camps due to the impossibility of their transportation beyond the camp limits" since the beginning of the mass release campaign (September 1942). He also enjoined camp administrators to report such fatalities in a "separate memo" on a monthly basis.[33]

These two directives initiated a radical change in the technique of mortality registration in the Gulag. In my view, it almost openly sanctioned top officials' data manipulation at the ground level. But why was such forthright authorization given precisely in the spring of 1943? In short, an exceptionally desperate situation catalyzed exceptional honesty. To understand the

Table 4.1. Mortality in the Gulag NKVD USSR (January–December 1943)

Month	Mortality (absolute)	Month	Mortality (absolute)
January	34,800	July	22,383
February	30,845	August	22,019
March	31,156	September	16,275
April	29,414	October	11,588
May	27,439	November	9,428
June	23,309	December	9,162

Source: GARF f. R-9414, op. 1, d. 1181, l. 31.

bureaucratic deliberations behind the top-level decision to hide released invalids' deaths, we need to look at the historical context.

In January 1943, the central NKVD issued Order no. 0033 to "conserve and improve the physical capability" of prisoners.[34] Pragmatic high-level demands to enhance the productivity of forced labor by lowering sickness and mortality rates appeared regularly between 1941 and 1945.[35] What distinguished Order no. 0033 is that it bore the signature of Lavrentii Beria himself. It also imposed the highest level of accountability on the NKVD chain of command. The minister of internal affairs warned all camp commanders that they would be held personally responsible for successful "decrease of sickness rates." These were no idle threats. The failure to present "positive statistical dynamics" (in the typical Stalinist managerial manner—the sooner the better) was dangerous not only to the usual scapegoats, such as rank-and file medics, but also for the top managers of the system.[36]

The paradox was that the political leadership at the time, in Barnes's words, "mouthed . . . concern without providing any real assistance in ameliorating conditions."[37] The Gulag suffered the worst cuts in food and medical provision in its history during 1942 and 1943.[38] All resources were diverted to the war effort. The penal system's top command was regularly briefed about the objective situation on the ground and found itself in an odd predicament. It had to allay a crisis of eschatological magnitude with hardly any supplies.[39] The goal was unattainable by the "legal" or "conventional" means at their disposal. Therefore, I would argue that NKVD Order no. 0033 was impractical without centrally approved, system-wide statistical subterfuge. By issuing Directive no. 42/232546, the Gulag director offered his subordinates "an emergency tool" to save the "honor of the uniform" and themselves. It allowed officials of all ranks to cast themselves as efficacious crisis managers. They fulfilled Beria's Order no. 0033 and delivered a tangible result—on paper.[40] This result was backed up by the "positive" downward trend of registered monthly deaths in 1943–1944 in camps and colonies of the Gulag (table 4.1).

The absolute figures of the dead plummeted from roughly thirty thousand per month in the winter of 1942–1943 to less than ten thousand in the winter of 1943–1944 (see table 4.1). Usually, the literature rationalizes this decline by quoting the self-aggrandizing statements of Gulag doctors.[41] The camp medics understandably lionized their professionalism and conventional efforts to improve prisoners' health.[42] To give just one example of this institutional self-aggrandizement, Colonel Loidin, head of the central SANO, in his 1944 report eulogized "major organizational activities" that Gulag medics had conducted since 1941 to decrease sickness and mortality rates. He lauded the "purposefulness" of Gulag NKVD USSR in "ensuring adequate sanitary conditions" and the implementation of fastidious "wide health-improvement measures" for the inmates. However, these measures were not as effective as the chief Gulag doctor depicted them to be. As Alexopoulos shrewdly argued, "the precipitous drop in mortality beginning in 1943 can be partly explained by the large releases of sick prisoners in 1943."[43] We will see how this played out at the ground level.

As the war ended, Loidin ingratiatingly praised Beria's Order no. 0033 as one of the main causes for the dramatic reduction of morbidity and mortality rates under his purview.[44] In his reports, though, Loidin omitted any mention of the exceptionally massive releases of dying invalids that he himself had condoned and sanctioned in 1943. The camp health service did not submit mortality data of the discharged to the NKVD top command. It remained in the internal Gulag document flow.

This practice gives rise to a second question: does the change in mortality registration indicate that prior to April 1943 these "additional deaths" were included in the regular counts, or were they not recorded at all? A provisional answer can be found in the primary accounts of the Gulag's local camp SANO and allocation-distribution (URO-OURZ) departments.[45] For instance, the record of ex-inmates' mortality can be tracked in the local URO records in Arkhangel'sk regional labor colonies as early as 30 March 1943.[46] The physicians of Bezymianlag in Kuibyshev oblast also employed a specific accounting technique for these "problematic" deaths before March–April 1943. They used fractions and handwritten footnotes to indicate them. To illustrate this, in the monthly report for November 1942 on the distribution of deaths based on age, length of detention, ethnicity, category of labor, and length of hospitalization, the acting director of the camp SANO, Doctor Bernshtein, presented the data in table 4.2.

At the bottom of the page, there are several laconic handwritten remarks. One of them reads, "eleven people died among those freed who could not travel home."[47] The way the data are presented is peculiar—invalids' fatalities

Table 4.2. Number and distribution of deaths in Bezymianlag camp, November 1942

| DIAGNOSIS | LABOR CATEGORIES | | | | |
	light	medium	heavy	invalids	total
Dysentery	5	3	1	6/2	
Pellagra	24	10	2	37/7	
Respiratory diseases	4	1	–	3	
Lobar pneumonia	9	6	–	–	
Tuberculosis of the lungs	4	5	4	4/1	
Diseases of the circulatory system	5	1	–	–	
Other	8	5	1	1/1	
TOTAL	59	31	8	51/11	149

Source: Report fragment from Gosudarstvennyi arkhiv Samarskoi oblasti (GASO) f. R-2064, op. 2, d. 47, l. 106.

are shown as fractions. The meaning behind them can be deduced from an analogous report for October 1942, which includes similar fractions in totals for the invalids' category—79/15. The doctor who compiled the document also explained these fractions in a note: "the denominator includes those who were eligible for release according to a court decision."[48] In my opinion, the data for both months can be interpreted as a clarification of death distribution among invalids. However, it is uncertain whether these numbers were sent to the central SANO (and hence included in the regular mortality report) or compiled for the purposes of camp doctors, remaining at the local level. Although more research regarding the particularities of pre-1943 registration is required, these examples are noteworthy. They show that at least one local SANO and one OURZ decided to record these fatalities even before Nasedkin's directive of April 1943 urged them to do so retroactively.

Finding local responses to both Loidin's and Nasedkin's directives is, however, a challenge. They are not available at the system's central archive in Moscow. It seems likely that they were not declassified or were destroyed. But luckily for historians, Gulag administrative practice required local officials to retain copies of all reports in the camps' own archives. The Bezymianlag medics' response to Loidin's directive was located in its SANO archive.[49] This response made it possible to recalculate death rates for this particular camp. Most other local archives are, unfortunately, unreachable as of 2022.

In sum, Nasedkin's and Loidin's directives are crucial in three ways. First, they confirm that the very pinnacle of the Gulag hierarchy, both administrative and medical, sanctioned statistical mendacity. Nasedkin is crystal clear that these "dead souls" should be excluded from regular mortality records. Loidin also insisted on their separation from "ordinary accounting." It is obvious that the Gulag's top administrators not only were perfectly cognizant of the released invalids' deaths but also consciously legitimized their omission from the summary central data.[50] Therefore, the omission was not a local *tufta* aimed at deluding Moscow (a far better-known phenomenon) but a system-wide *tufta* directly sanctioned by the central Gulag authorities.[51] Second, the Gulag leaders attempted to monitor the process via idiosyncratic "parallel" accounting. The documents reveal that URO began systematic registration of "concealed" deaths in the spring of 1943 that was backed up by retrospective SANO accounting from the autumn of the same year. Third, and most importantly, the existence of these data offers an heretofore-underappreciated methodological opportunity to recalculate death rates for each penal establishment and the entire system (at least from 1943) by adding these "hidden" figures to the central summary reports. The vast majority of answers to Directives no. 42/232546 and no. 42/233211, however, are kept in inaccessible archives. This represents the main challenge of the "central-local" approach.

THE MULTI-INSTITUTIONAL APPROACH AND ITS CHALLENGES

To circumvent the problem of data availability, I developed a second approach—institutional triangulation. This approach highlights the empirical discovery that every one of the agencies involved in medical releases did register "hidden" mortality during the 1930–1955 period—each for different reasons and under varying circumstances. Materials of the camp procuracy and camp courts, in addition to those of the Gulag, reveal valuable statistical evidence that otherwise would have remained concealed. However, this approach has its own set of obstacles. Agencies often engaged in competition and were embroiled in outright institutional war with one another. Additionally, there was a curious antagonism within formally unified bureaucracies. These inexorable conflicts, in some instances, generated statistical data on ex-inmates' mortality, but they often dissuaded officials from honest reporting.

The main obstacle to research is the sensitive political nature of released prisoners' deaths. In some respects, these deaths were even more contentious than the mortality of prisoners who remained in the camps, because the releases became entangled with the partisan interests of numerous competing bureaucratic actors on horizontal and vertical levels. These interests were often mutually exclusive. On the one hand, medical releases were, in a sense, spurious. It made no practical sense for bureaucrats to register deaths that they were trying to hide. This consideration applied both to low-level tiers and the Gulag top command in interactions with their respective superiors. A similar reticence also sometimes emerged in "pocket" camp procurators or judges under the sway of the NKVD.[52]

On the other hand, a countervailing imperative existed to monitor and register "hidden" mortality. Pressure came simultaneously from within the Gulag central administration (e.g., through the creation of the bizarre "parallel" accounting in 1943) and from outside NKVD structures via the penitentiary system's bureaucratic rivals (the regional and, in rare instances, camp procuracy, the Ministry of Justice, or other civilian ministries). For instance, independently minded camp procurators exposed and prosecuted camp officials for falsifying mortality statistics. Materials of their inspections, as shown below, are invaluable in uncovering concrete examples of accounting fraud.

The overall result of this Gordian knot of contradictions is the somewhat arbitrary nature of available statistical evidence, extracted from all involved agencies. The most salient issues can be subdivided into three main categories: ambiguities in the recorded data, underreporting of deaths, and the outright concealment of deaths. It is fruitful to analyze them in turn.

Uncertainties about the recorded figures pose the first impediment. Although the Gulag appears to be an assiduously regulated and structured institution, this image holds only if we look at the system exclusively through the prism of instructions from the center. As local materials reaffirm, their actual implementation morphed into a chaotic ocean of irregularities in its lower tiers, especially during crises. One can discern inconsistency in the techniques of tracing released invalids' deaths even after Nasedkin and Loidin initiated their systematic registration. To elaborate, record-keeping forms standardized in Moscow were altered on the ground and became incongruent with one another. For instance, the Ponyshlag (Molotov oblast) SANO included an additional column for mortality among the *aktirovannye* (freed) in their 1(3) form on sickness and mortality for the first quarter of 1944.[53] In another report, in addition to twenty-eight "regular" deaths, Ponyshlag medics openly listed twelve additional fatalities among the released under the specially printed subheading.[54] By contrast, the supposedly identical 1(3) form used by the Bezymianlag physicians for roughly the same period (March 1943) did not have this printed column with a subheading for released invalids, listing only "regular" mortality.[55] But from alternative sources compiled by the same Bezymianlag medics, we know that discharged inmates died as "free citizens" in Bezymianlag hospitals in exactly the same month. Thus, in addition to 290 regularly registered inmate deaths in March 1943, a special "parallel" report (created in response to Loidin's Directive no. 42/233211) listed 83 deaths among "released invalids" for the same month.[56]

To complicate things even more, Bezymianlag doctors used a third data collection form (the so-called analysis of mortality), where they did have a column for the "released" subcategory, next to the "invalids" column. But this column was left intentionally blank because the camp SANO apparently complied with Nasedkin's Directive no. 42/232546 to exclude these fatalities from "regular accounting."[57] This blank column for those released remained in the monthly reports until it disappeared entirely in June 1943. This example (as well as the analysis of pre-1943 registration above) demonstrates that there was no universal blueprint for the recording of data. Only scrupulous cross-referencing of variegated sources reveals these "inconvenient" fatalities. The record keeping seems to be dependent more on the discretion of the individual functionary and the unique circumstances (time and place) of the document's creation.

The underreporting of deaths (both intentional and unintentional) poses another subtle conundrum. This conundrum can be illuminated with a multiperspective analysis of intra- and interbureaucratic conflicts. Thus in a report from 14 April 1942, Shul'ga, the procurator of Iargrinlag (Arkhangel'sk oblast), misinformed his superiors that only thirty-four released invalids passed away on their way home in the winter of 1941 in Niandoma and Konosha.[58] But the competing Arkhangel'sk regional procurator, Chicherin, exposed in his report that, in fact, seventy-six ex-prisoners perished.[59] This discrepancy is an exemplary indication of the division lines that ran within the Procuracy, pitting different divisions of a single bureaucracy against each other. In another instance of underreporting, Sergei Stepanovich Sofronov, the Kargopol'lag procurator, reported 590 ex-inmates' deaths during 1943 and January 1944, whereas the Kargopol'lag SANO recorded 1,059 fatalities in the same time frame.[60]

The procurator of Ponyshlag, a small camp, informed Moscow that twelve invalids died after release during the first half of 1944. But comparison with the local Ponyshlag SANO records for the same period discloses that thirty-two ex-inmates died in the camp.[61] Top bureaucrats in the Procuracy also tried to whitewash the actual situation in their overviews of medical release campaigns. Anatolii Antonovich Volin, procurator of the RSFSR, in his almost anodyne report from April 1943 to his superior, Viktor Mikhailovich Bochkov, procurator of the USSR, noted just two deaths among the released.[62] However, from alternative sources we know that this was a very significant understatement. Occasionally it was not procurators but camp physicians who underreported data. For example, Doctor Bernshtein, the head of the Bezymianlag SANO, reported thirty-nine deaths among the released in May 1943 in response to Loidin's Directive no. 42/233211. Meanwhile, an alternative report suggested that the real number was almost three times higher (103 deaths).[63]

Concealment of deaths is the most difficult problem to unravel. In nonfamine periods, there was a strong propensity to evade direct mention of this type of mortality even in classified internal memoranda. Only when the penal system started to crumble and disintegrate (1942–1943) did officials became more candid. Even then, many tried to eschew blunt directness. As soon as the tide of war turned in the Soviet Union's favor, officials deftly occluded the mortality of the released in enigmatic equivocation and Aesopian language. The head of the Kargopol'lag SANO used the cryptic abbreviation "M.R." to obfuscate these fatalities in his statistical retrospective return from 1944.[64] Bernshtein of Bezymianlag failed to include mortality figures of the released for October and November 1942 in his retrospective response to Loidin's inquiry, even though his superior explicitly demanded numbers from the beginning of the campaign (September 1942).[65] Only analysis of the alternative SANO primary raw figures for the end of 1942 helps expose this understatement.

However, this phenomenon can be glimpsed by the application of a rarely used method—the analysis of handwritten markings and crossed-out original text in the documents' drafts. To illustrate, the chairman of the camp court of Tatarskaia SSR Ibatulin in his 1949 report mentioned that 59 cases of medical release were processed by the republican Administration for Corrective Labor Camps and Colonies (UITLK) judiciary, two former prisoners died and 57 invalids were released early during the third quarter of 1949. Then the author obviously decided not to report the fatalities to the Ministry of Justice headquarters and blurred over the text containing the fact of invalids' deaths.[66]

Nor were mid-level physicians and local commanders in the NKVD–MVD exceptions in terms of clandestine behavior. In August 1943, Popov, the commander of the Tambov Department for Corrective Labor Colonies (OITK), and Chernyshova, the head of its medical-sanitation department, initially informed the central SANO in Moscow that thirty-seven prisoners had died in July of that year.[67] At first, they explicitly noted that among them three invalids passed away immediately after the expiration of their sentence. Then, local officials, probably in the interests of decreasing mortality in their zone of responsibility, crossed out the initial confession and corrected the number "37" to "34." This revision artificially lowered the registered and reported monthly figure by 8 percent. This may seem to be an insignificant alteration. But for small penal establishments with a low daily average number of prisoners (and Tambov OITK was tiny by Gulag standards) it made a difference.[68] As a rule, it was easier to fudge mortality figures for small colonies than for the bigger forced-labor camps, because even the concealment of several deaths per month guaranteed a considerable decrease of the relative death rate. We should always bear in mind that inspectors evaluated camp medics' performance in their "fight" against mortality based on relative coefficients, not absolute values.[69]

The highest echelons of the NKVD bureaucratic ladder were not exempt from this predilection to avoid direct mention of invalids' deaths, even in internal communications, whenever possible. In February 1942, Nasedkin, the Gulag director, issued a top-secret circular to all camp and colony commanders.[70] Using typical NKVD technocratic vocabulary, it advised how to "avoid the mistakes of the previous year" pertaining to the largest medical release campaign in the history of Soviet camps. Nasedkin's initial draft listed two main drawbacks that had to be avoided this time: "excessive delays of contingents who were supposed to be released" and their "sickness and mortality during transportation due to disorganized logistics." Then the author obscured all indications of deaths and morbidity of former prisoners and presented a new, final variant that read, "to avoid . . . excessive delays . . . and disorganization pertaining to transportation of the released."[71] This document, among other things, confirms that Nasedkin was well aware that invalids died in the camps after release in each of the consecutive years 1941, 1942, and 1943 but was purposely taciturn about these deaths when he had the opportunity.

In sum, the problems of this subsection have implications that go beyond methodology or source study. They reveal an intricate web of conflicting power relations surrounding the mortality of former prisoners at all levels of bureaucratic ladder. These contradictions may seem byzantine or even abstruse, but they exemplify how the Soviet penal bureaucracy operated as a specific stratum within the Stalinist state apparatus. Conceptually, this overview significantly extends our knowledge of the interlinked issues of multilayered Gulag secrecy, bureaucratic self-representation, and strategies of appearing effective in the Stalinist administrative paradigm by using, altering, or hiding ex-prisoners' mortality data. Next I briefly analyze the health of discharged invalids on release as a major factor leading to their death in large numbers almost immediately after release.

HEALTH CONDITION OF THE RELEASED

Most of the invalids released during "extreme" stages of the Gulag's operation (war, famine) were in extremely poor health. To prove this point and to estimate ex-prisoners' chances of survival, I analyzed numerous data samples of the diagnoses stated in the case files as grounds for medical release. The resulting conclusion is that roughly half and, more often than not, the majority of those released during turbulent periods (1932–1933, 1941–1945, 1946–1947) were set free with second- or third-grade "nutritional dystrophy," a Soviet medical euphemism for starvation disease.[72]

Table 4.3. Distribution of diagnoses among medically released invalids from Sverdlovsk regional labor colonies, first quarter of 1945

DIAGNOSES	Absolute	Relative (%)
Third-grade dystrophy	203	40.6
Second-grade dystrophy	276	55.2
Tuberculosis	14	2.8
Others (pleurisy)	7	1.4
TOTAL	500	100.0

Source: GARF f. R-8131, op. 37, d. 2498, l. 63.

For a glimpse of the pertinent data, I offer the diagnoses distribution among invalids released by the Sverdlovsk UITLK in the relatively "survivable" year 1945 (table 4.3).

The data sample indicates that 95.8 percent of those discharged by the Sverdlovsk UITLK had second- or third-degree dystrophy, the latter being a terminal condition. This state of health made the death of a substantial proportion of the released inevitable. Now let us look at a set of recalculation cases that substantiate this claim.

THE CONCEALMENT OF "DEAD SOULS" RELEASED FROM THE CAMPS

CASE STUDY: SUKHOLOZHSKAIA COLONY NO. 15

In the summer of 1945, Perevozchikov, the procurator for the Sverdlovsk regional labor camps launched a deep investigation into a corruption scandal around Gulag Colony (ITK) no. 15. All its officials—including its commander, Junior Lieutenant Emul Davidovich Zelenyi; his deputy Ragulin; and the head of its SANO, Doctor Zil'berg—found themselves charged with a plethora of fraudulent activities. Among these offenses were, to quote the procurator, "eyewash [ochkovtiratel'stvo] in medical practice and concealment of prisoner mortality."[73]

Crucially, the procuratorial ruling began with an overt mention of Beria's Order no. 0033 from January 1943 as a catalyst for the data distortion. As mentioned above, with this order Beria pressured local Gulag camps to reduce prisoners' sickness and mortality rates at all costs. Doctor Zil'berg, with the full approval of Zelenyi and Ragulin, began, as the procurators put it, "to artificially deflate the number of the dead via various 'combinations'" to fulfill Beria's categorical demands. According to the procurator, the Gulag officials chose medical discharge under articles 461 and 462 of the Criminal

Procedural Code as their main device for statistical falsification. Zil'berg "released" already dead prisoners "on paper" and falsely listed them as "medically released." Then he sent the cases of "dead souls" to the local people's court (*narsud*) to obtain a formal release ruling and consciously omitted these fatalities in his reports to the central SANO.

For example, on 7 May 1945 colony administrators identified for medical release a certain gravely ill prisoner Korsukov, sentenced to two years of deprivation of liberty. The penal colony's physicians transferred his case to the Leninskii district court of Sverdlovsk on 31 May 1945 for a release ruling. Meanwhile, Korsukov died on 12 June 1945 in the colony hospital. The local SANO properly registered his passing. However, the doctors did not send Korsukov's death certificate to the statistical OURZ of the colony, as internal instructions required. To avoid listing Korsukov under the "dead in the colony" heading in the data collection form, Doctor Zil'berg sent two telegrams to the court to expedite the ruling on Korsukov's release, although he was already dead. He was removed from the colony's statistical records eighteen days after his passing. In another instance of data falsification, the prisoner Zasorin, sentenced to two years of deprivation of liberty, died on 2 February 1945. To hide the man's death, Doctor Zil'berg visited the court in person on the very same day to receive a ruling on release of the "actually deceased" Zasorin.[74]

In the end, Zil'berg's machinations were exposed due to interpersonal conflict. When another prisoner, Andrei Ivanovich Potapov (sentenced to one year of deprivation of liberty), passed away in the colony hospital on 25 June 1945, Zil'berg once again appeared in the local court the next day to receive a court ruling on Potapov's release. Afterwards he approached Shisterov, the head of the colony's Registration and Distribution Department and main statistician-registrar, with an offer "to write off Potapov as not dead but released." For some unspecified reason, Shisterov declined. Zil'berg decided to use his connections with the colony command and invited Ragulin, the deputy commandant, to make the obstinate Shisterov more compliant. Ragulin gave a direct order to count Potapov as "released." Shisterov continued to resist, and later the procurators prosecuted the colony administration.[75]

The officials distorted mortality data in Colony no. 15 for at least six months. During the first half of 1945, Doctor Zil'berg managed to conceal sixteen deaths via medical release with the approval of and acting on the order of the colony administrators.[76] The doctor reported only thirty fatalities to the central SANO in January–June 1945, while the real number of dead was forty-six. As in the case of the Tambovsk OITK, it was easy for small labor colonies (Sukholozhskaia Colony no. 15 had 389 prisoners, on average) to tweak their

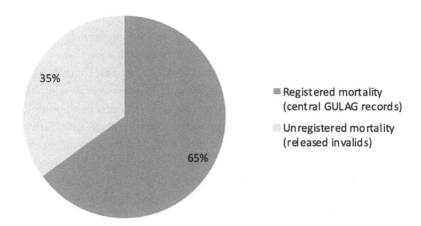

Figure 4.1. Relative mortality undercount in Sukholozhskaia Colony no. 15, January–June 1945.
    Source: GARF f. R-8131, op. 37, d. 2498, l. 148.

mortality rates by hiding even two to four deaths per month.[77] Although the undercount was comparatively low in absolute figures, all that mattered to the local physicians was the reduction of the reported coefficient, the principal metric of their qualifications in the eyes of their superiors. In this case, we can calculate a practically significant relative understatement of almost 35 percent (fig. 4.1). These data show that every third prisoner who died in the colony during the first half of 1945 was not counted in the system's central statistics.

An incredulous skeptic can always object that one should avoid jumping to conclusions based on a single example. Hypothetically, falsifications in this one colony may have been singular and isolated. But we have evidence for various years and regions where camp officials "released" on medical grounds already dead prisoners and internees.[78] It proves that this specific variety of subterfuge was not uniquely characteristic to Sukholozhskaia Colony but represented a sustained, duplicitous practice of Gulag medicine.

CASE STUDY: SEROVSKAIA COLONY NO. 17

In the summer of 1945, the Procuracy of the Sverdlovsk UITLK initiated an inquiry into another Gulag establishment, Serovskaia Colony no. 17. It attracted the inspectors' attention because of its high mortality rate (thirty-five prisoners died in May 1945 alone) and massive number of medical releases. During the second quarter of 1945, this tiny colony released 195 prisoners on medical grounds. A significant proportion of its population suffered from "nutritional dystrophy." Deputy Procurator Somov found all the detainees to be emaciated. One hundred sixty-five of them lay forsaken in the crude hospital, without any care or supervision.

According to the Procuracy's statement, one of the doctors, a certain Fidel'man, refused to treat the sick, officials stole the prisoners' food, hospital wards were dirty, and doctors carelessly provided unboiled water to inmates afflicted with dysentery. More importantly, Doctor Fidel'man falsified mortality statistics. She registered and reported only fifteen deaths, hiding an additional twenty.[79] The procurator arrested the doctor, but Somov's inspection precipitated a thorough investigation of the colony administration's operations. It revealed systematic distortion of mortality data, just as in the case of the Sukholozhskaia colony, with full approval and under the direction of the colony's top officers from at least December 1944.

Junior Lieutenant Nikita Ivanovich Vostrikov, the commandant of the colony, along with senior medical personnel, was charged with negligence that led to elevated mortality and the "degradation" of his administrative apparatus. The procuratorial investigation discovered that around November–December 1944 Vostrikov—together with Doctor Kanevskaia, the head of the colony's SANO—gave a special order to concentrate all the weakened and sick prisoners in the colony's central hospital. Because of this transfer, two hundred emaciated inmates were squeezed into a ward designed for eighty people. The resulting extreme overcrowding had forced physicians to sew blankets together to cover seven or eight patients at once and to lay them down together on solid bunks.[80] The heating was irregular, the air became putrid, lice infested prisoners, and bedbugs filled the ward. There was even a shortage of boiled water, which was given out at long intervals. The cook habitually stole the rations, depriving prisoners of their daily meals. Low temperatures in the barracks provoked cases of pneumonia—even among healthier inmates such as Ryskov and Petelin—or other diseases (Starikov). All three were denied hospitalization until they were discovered by the procurator but died soon after.[81]

Inevitably, the prisoners' health deteriorated into "second- and third-grade dystrophy" and they began to die en masse from hunger. From 1 December 1944 to 1 June 1945, more than a hundred inmates passed away, the majority of them petty offenders sentenced to very short terms. Deaths had become so mundane and regular that they fomented the complete disregard of professional ethics among medical personnel, even in its Soviet "non-Hippocratic" iteration. The attitudes of the colony's physicians toward dead bodies had become nihilistic to the point that it startled even the UITLK procurator. Instead of quickly burying the corpses, Doctor Kanevskaia ordered the nurse to remove them to an ordinary storehouse of the hospital. The procurator found that the eyes, fingers, and ears of the dead had been gnawed by rats.

To quote the Procuracy report, "to hide his own criminal neglect, Vostrikov ordered Kanevskaia, the chief doctor, to conceal the real mortality from the

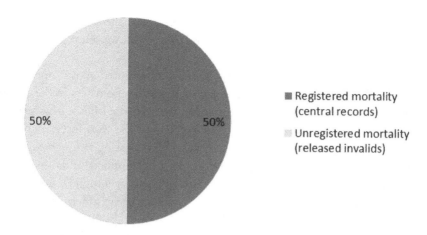

Figure 4.2. Relative mortality undercount in Serovskaia Colony no. 17, December 1944–May 1945. *Source:* GARF f. R-8131, op. 37, d. 2498, ll. 122–23.

central SANO and to resort to various contrivances." What were those "contrivances"? As in ITK no. 15, they included the deceitful use of medical releases, but on a truly egregious scale. When death rates started to balloon, Vostrikov ordered the colony doctors—in the procurators' words—"to avoid mortality" not by improving "medical treatment and material conditions" but through the "medical discharge" of dying invalids, whom he concentrated in a separate room. The doctors obeyed Vostrikov's orders. In a single day in February 1945, they simultaneously "released" 135 emaciated prisoners. On one day in April of the same year, they concurrently declared another 104 sick invalids free. Dozens of them died almost instantaneously, but technically as free citizens.

From December 1944 to May 1945, local colony medics registered and reported to the central SANO only sixty-one deaths. In reality, as the procurators discovered, the actual death tally reached 116.[82] Almost 50 percent of the prisoners who died in Serovskaia Colony no. 17 during a six-month period—every second death—were dexterously omitted from the central registries (fig. 4.2). This is an extremely significant undercount for a substantial period.

To conclude, there was a clear-cut, iniquitous logic behind the statistical manipulations in both colonies. The first reason to distort and reduce the mortality statistics was fear of prosecution.[83] Tellingly, the procurator explicitly mentioned Beria's Order no. 0033 as an incentive for statistical fraud in the Sukholozhskaia colony. The failure to fulfill the order's demands (at least on paper) was risky for its expendable low-level officials. They could be sent to the Gulag as prisoners or even shot in rare cases. The second reason, in my view, was the unrealistic nature of central orders to lower mortality no matter what resources the localities had.

We should bear in mind that the two cases presented above concern "economically irrelevant" small labor colonies, traditional outliers in the Stalinist "hierarchy of redistribution," provisioned on a residual basis. This principle applied not only to material supplies but also to the workforce, as sick and depleted inmates were regularly taken off trains passing through Sverdlovsk oblast and headed to higher-priority camps and "dumped" in labor colonies, increasing the number of the sick and dying there by a high factor. Thus the UITLK procurator reported that "the mortality of prisoners in the second quarter of 1945 in comparison to the first is almost stable: if 367 prisoners died in the former, 366 died in the latter, but it is necessary to emphasize that a significant portion of the dead fell into transfer points and regional hospitals due to transit inmates taken off railroads."[84] This perpetual new arrival of gravely ill, moribund prisoners in conjunction with the inability to heal them due to meager resources and Moscow's unconditional demands for lower mortality landed colony administrators in a classic "Catch-22" quagmire. Trapped between the hammer and the anvil, the officials of small colonies "improved" their mortality returns by releasing dying prisoners.

But was medical release employed as a stratagem to lower death rates in bigger and more prominent forced-labor camps? These "advantaged" projects of "all-union importance" were entitled to the highest amount of supplies and the healthiest inmates, who could perform heavy labor. One such camp is analyzed below.

CASE STUDY: BEZYMIANLAG

The NKVD organized the Bezymianlag Camp in Kuibyshev oblast at the end of 1940 on the basis of Samarlag. It almost immediately received privileged status.[85] Its prioritized position in the supply chain predetermined its comparatively low registered mortality rates during the war, far below the system's average (table 4.4, fig. 4.3).

If we look at the worst years, the official Bezymianlag mortality rate hovered around 12 percent per annum in 1942, in contrast to the 22–24 percent per annum for the entire Gulag. Meanwhile, registered mortality in the harshest localities (forestry camps) could reach as high as 50 percent in Viatlag (Kirov oblast) or 54 percent in Unzhlag (Gor'kii oblast) in 1942.[86] In 1943–1944, the Bezymianlag death rate nose-dived to 1–2 percent per annum, being almost a tenth of the average for the system. If we take the data at face value, Bezymianlag can be characterized as comparatively lenient, or at least survivable.

Table 4.4. Official mortality in Bezymianlag, 1943–1944

YEAR/MONTH	AVERAGE POPULATION	DEATHS (ABSOLUTE)	MONTHLY DEATH RATE
1943			
January	27,592	291	1.06
February	23,167	257	1.11
March	20,809	269	1.3
April	18,181	232	1.3
May	13,232	162	1.22
June	8,966	73	0.9
July	8,077	52	0.6
August	7,135	35	0.5
September	6,416	31	0.5
October	6,064	22	0.36
November	6,129	11	0.18
December	6,055	—	0.08
1944			
January	5,867	9	0.16
February	6,165	2	0.03
March	6,859	7	0.1
April	7,298	11	0.15
May	7,407	11	0.14

Source: GASO f. R-2596, op. 1, d. 1999, l. 47.

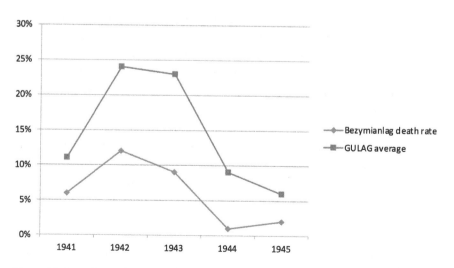

Figure 4.3. Annual mortality rate in the Gulag (average) and Bezymianlag (Kuibyshev oblast), 1941–1945. *Source:* Zakharchenko and Repinetskii, *Bezymianlag*, 256; GARF f. R-9414, op. 1a, d. 397, ll. 7–7 ob.; GARF f. R-9414, op. 1a, d. 412, ll. 11–11 ob.; GARF f. R-9414, op. 1, d. 2784, l. 10; GARF f. R-9414, op. 1, d. 2796, l. 102; GASO f. R-2596, op. 1, d. 1999, l. 47; Bezborodova and Kozlov, *Istoriia Stalinskogo GULAGa*, 4:55.

Local materials, however, reveal that, despite its preferential status and low registered mortality, Bezymianlag's prisoners nevertheless suffered from harsh conditions. According to Lieutenant of State Security Cherednichenko, the head of the Bezymianlag Secret Police Detachment (OCHO), officials' "soulless and, in some cases, outright disdainful attitude toward prisoners" catalyzed the meteoric rise of mortality in the camp.[87] Starvation, mass executions of shirkers, systematic beatings, and extreme overexploitation in 1941–1943 were near ubiquitous. The main causes of death, according to camp physicians, were "pellagra and emaciation."[88] Camp authorities had their priorities straight: meeting the production plan was paramount. Everything else was a second-order consideration—relevant only if it helped fulfill the ambitious industrial goal.

Medics, constrained by strict quotas, regularly denied genuinely sick inmates admittance to the overcrowded hospitals and sent ill convicts to die in the stone quarries.[89] But even more lenient physicians felt powerless to stop mass mortality. The feelings of acute despair and open bewilderment are noticeable in the words of a certain doctor, Medvedeva, during a conference of Bezymianlag medics. She stated that "we have a category of patients who will still perish, no matter how much effort we make. There is a certain category that is hopeless. . . . How many such hopeless patients—I cannot say for sure, but those in wards no. 4, no. 5, no. 6, are extremely emaciated and suffering from diarrhea. They are unable to properly digest the food that is given to them."[90] Another doctor somberly remarked that the systems of some prisoners had degraded so profoundly that they could not be "resurrected."[91]

The existence of this "hopeless subgroup" who "could not be resurrected" and all the other hardships raise a legitimate question. How did the camp physicians manage to report such a low mortality rate to Moscow for 1942–1943 when alternative sources reveal severely detrimental conditions? The answer lies in the large-scale calculated removal of the most emaciated prisoners from Bezymianlag's statistical registry through two parallel "streams": medical release (out of the system) and internal transfers (within the system). The camp released 9,100 certified invalids in 1941–1943 and transferred thousands more.[92] I present another recalculation case, based on a response of the Bezymianlag SANO to Colonel Loidin's Directive no. 42/233211. It contains the monthly distribution of released invalids' deaths from January to October 1943.

According to that handwritten document signed by Bernshtein, Bezymianlag's chief doctor, 355 ex-prisoners died in the camp from diseases they acquired while incarcerated. Other sources, however, indicate that Bernshtein

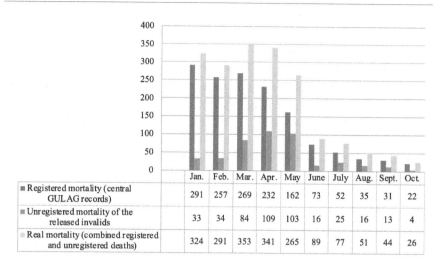

	Jan.	Feb.	Mar.	Apr.	May	June	July	Aug.	Sept.	Oct.
■ Registered mortality (central GULAG records)	291	257	269	232	162	73	52	35	31	22
■ Unregistered mortality of the released invalids	33	34	84	109	103	16	25	16	13	4
■ Real mortality (combined registered and unregistered deaths)	324	291	353	341	265	89	77	51	44	26

Figure 4.4. Mortality undercount in Bezymianlag (Kuibyshev oblast), January–October 1943 (absolute figures).

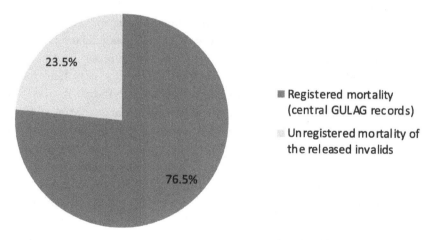

Figure 4.5. Relative mortality undercount in Bezymianlag (Kuibyshev oblast), January–October 1943. *Source:* GASO f. R-2064, op. 2s, d. 83, ll. 89, 123 (local data); GARF f. R-9414, op. 1A, d. 397, ll. 7–7 ob. (central data).

underreported these deaths as well (a remarkable "understatement within an understatement" phenomenon).[93]

In fact, at least 437 "hopeless" released invalids died in this timeframe. I compared the data to the registered mortality figures for the analogous months contained in the central URO summary reports for Bezymianlag located in the system's central archive in Moscow. This collation allowed me to determine the degree of undercount in the central records for this period (figs. 4.4–4.5).

That released invalids were dying in the camp every month under scrutiny is evident from the graphs. We can discern an entire demographic process spanning a significant period. The statistical undercount is practically and quantitatively significant (both in absolute and relative terms), especially for the spring months. As a case in point, according to central data 232 prisoners died in April 1943. In addition to that figure, 109 unregistered released invalids died in the camp during the same month.[94] That raises the actual number of the dead to 341 fatalities. All in all, 32 percent of deaths that occurred in April 1943 were never registered in the system's central medical records. Every third prisoner who died in Bezymianlag in that month was unaccounted for. In general, the understatement fluctuated from 5 percent in January to 20–30 percent in May or October 1943.

The oscillation of absolute mortality numbers, however, shows a puzzling, precipitous drop in both registered and unregistered deaths in May–June 1943. It seems implausible. Alternative evidence suggests that conditions in Bezymianlag in this period remained dire, reflecting the bleak situation in the country at large. Then how was this decline achieved on paper? The answer can be found in the following sequence of events. As early as January 1942, I. B. Ben', the head of Bezymianlag's OURZ, mentioned in his report to Aleksandr Pavlovich Lepilov, the camp commander, that it would be expedient to ask the central Gulag for permission to relocate up to six hundred invalids and old men to the Kuibyshev UITLK (regional labor colonies in the oblast where Bezymianlag was located).[95] The actual number of transferred inmates turned out to be much greater. During the 1941–1944 period, Bezymianlag initiated at least three massive conveyances of sick and invalids to labor colonies in the region.[96] The process especially intensified when Bezymianlag relocated to new production locations in 1943. On 29 May 1943, I. B. Ben' submitted a memo to the Gulag director Nasedkin, "On the Results of Certain Bezymianlag Subdivisions' Relocation to Kuibyshev UITLK."[97] According to the document, the camp moved its entire five divisions to the jurisdiction of the regional colonies, including the prisoners incarcerated there. Not long before the formal relocation, however, Bezymianlag officials carefully identified all the more or less healthy inmates and sent them instead to Bezymianlag production sites. Meanwhile, divisions designated for transfer to UITLK's jurisdiction were purposely staffed with the weakest prisoners, those who had lost their health in Bezymianlag's main works (fig. 4.6).[98]

Overall, the camp transferred 5,576 prisoners to the accounting records of the regional labor colonies of Kuibyshev oblast. Only 1,692 (30 percent) of them were officially classified as fit for medium or heavy labor, with 1,559 (28 percent) listed in the light labor category, 1,068 (19 percent) as full invalids,

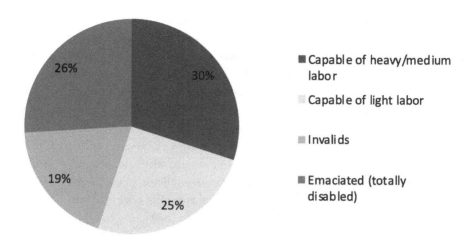

Figure 4.6. Physical profile of prisoners transferred from Bezymianlag to Kuibyshev UITLK, 5–16 May 1943. *Source:* Zakharchenko and Repinetskii, *Bezymianlag*, 257.

and 1,453 (26 percent) as emaciated/totally disabled. Among the invalids, 620 were already formally "liberated."[99] Bezymianlag admitted that it had trouble transporting this contingent out of the camp due to limited railroad capacity. Using its privileged status, the camp simply bullied the much less influential Kuibyshev UITLK into accepting these useless contingents, forcing it to deal with this logistical problem instead. The result of this data manipulation is evident in the graphs. As soon as the "certified" invalids and those in the light-labor category (who, taken together, accounted for the largest proportion of deaths) were sent to the regional colonies, the number of registered and unregistered fatalities in Bezymianlag artificially dropped. For instance, in May 1943, 162 centrally registered and 39 centrally unregistered prisoners or ex-inmates died; in September 1943, the numbers fell to 16 and 13, respectively.[100]

Concomitantly, this fake transfer apparently raised the mortality rate of regional UITLK colonies. But the colonies did not have either the political influence or the formal authority to resist Bezymianlag lobbying.[101] The regional colonies' administration resorted to mass releases of the terminally ill to rectify their own registered indicators of sickness and mortality. Thus invalids whose health had been ruined in Bezymianlag were set free from a different institution. Paradoxically, some of them had already been formally discharged even before their arrival in the colonies. In total, from the end of 1942 up to the beginning of 1944, the Kuibyshev UITLK released 5,358 prisoners suffering from "grave incurable illness" (some of whom were invalids received from Bezymianlag).[102] Their mortality is unknown.

To summarize, the official death figure for Bezymianlag in the central statistics for a ten-month period in 1943 is 1,424, but in reality at least 1,861 people passed away in this timeframe. This indicates a 23.5 percent undercount. Bezymianlag officials excluded every fourth death from Gulag's central accounting (fig. 4.5). It also artificially deflated the crude death rate by 23.5 percent. Certainly, the underreporting would be even more substantial if we take into account the massive removals of debilitated invalids to regional colonies and their deaths there or after release.

The case of Bezymianlag is peculiar in two aspects. First, it concerns a "prioritized camp" with a low officially registered mortality rate. Second, it offers an archetypal example of not a single deceptive scheme (medical release) but a pair of them, applied concurrently (removal from the system in conjunction with systematic transfers of sick prisoners within the system to other jurisdictions [colonies]). This certainly broadens our understanding of the types and variations of Gulag medicine's surreptitious strategies. It is no wonder that camp medics managed to achieve a sharp tenfold decline in mortality rates on paper by 1944.[103] The Bezymianlag case highlights and confirms the crucial importance of prisoner flows—both within the system and out of it—to adequately decipher Gulag morbidity, mortality, and release statistics.[104] If one were to ignore the internal movement of prisoners and, additionally, to take official mortality data at face value, such a cavalier attitude would make one susceptible to misconstruing the actual conditions in any camp. As mentioned above, Bezymianlag could be considered a "mild" camp during the war, based on its low registered death rates and high number of releases. This analysis helps us assess such judgments more critically. The whole concept of "positively characterized" camps during catastrophes may be misleading. Certainly one must be more cautious in declaring camps to be relatively "mild" (as, for example, Simon Ertz and Leonid Borodkin did in reference to Noril'lag) without taking into consideration the fate of their invalids.[105]

CASE STUDY: KARGOPOL'LAG

If Bezymianlag, one of the least deadly localities during the war years, had such a major undercount in its mortality data, what can be said about the infamously harsh Administration of Forestry Camps (ULLP)? Logging camps acquired a grim nickname among prisoners—"green execution."[106] Registered death indices alone peaked at 50 percent per annum during 1942–1943 in some of them. I have been able to discover data for one such camp (figs. 4.7–4.8). They allow me to address this inquiry.

One can discern an identical pattern in Kargopol'lag (located more than 1,400 miles to the north from Bezymianlag). There 451 registered inmates died in April 1943, and 150 additional fatalities occurred among discharged

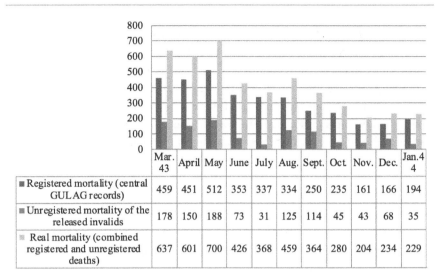

	Mar. 43	April	May	June	July	Aug.	Sept.	Oct.	Nov.	Dec.	Jan. 44
■ Registered mortality (central GULAG records)	459	451	512	353	337	334	250	235	161	166	194
■ Unregistered mortality of the released invalids	178	150	188	73	31	125	114	45	43	68	35
■ Real mortality (combined registered and unregistered deaths)	637	601	700	426	368	459	364	280	204	234	229

Figure 4.7. Mortality undercount in Kargopol'lag (Arkhangel'sk oblast), March 1943–January 1944 (absolute monthly figures).

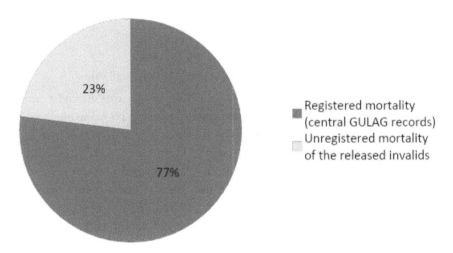

Figure 4.8. Relative mortality undercount in Kargopol'lag (Arkhangel'sk oblast), March 1943–January 1944. *Source:* GARF f. R-8131, op. 37, d. 2061, l. [52 (missing in original, deduced from nearest numbered pages)] (local data); GARF f. R-9414, op. 1A, d. 401, ll. 3–3 ob. (central data, 1943); GARF f. R-9414, op. 1, d. 2796, l. 101 (central data, 1944).

invalids.[107] This raises the real number of the dead to 601. Every fourth prisoner (25 percent) who died in Kargopol'lag in April 1943 was missing from the central summary reports. As in Bezymianlag, the mortality of the released was a systematic demographic process. Ex-inmates died during every month under scrutiny. In total, 1,050 ex-prisoners passed away in this temporal frame, in addition to the 3,452 "regularly" registered deaths. Twenty-three percent of the fatalities in Kargopol'lag for eleven months remained unrecorded by the Gulag statisticians in Moscow. Every fourth prisoner's death was obfuscated and concealed. This level of undercount again can be characterized as practically and quantitatively significant in both absolute and relative terms. Finally yet importantly, these statistics do not include those invalids whom officials transported to Iagrinlag or other locations via internal transfers or who died on their way to other destinations after release.[108]

CASE STUDY: IAGRINLAG

Exactly the same spurious application of medical release can be located in several other camps. One of these is Iagrinlag in Arkhangel'sk oblast. Here the data show that in addition to 496 registered deaths, 122 remained hidden (figs. 4.9–4.10).[109] All in all, 20 percent of the deaths in Iagrinlag during four months of 1943–1944 were consciously left unregistered in the regular summary accounting in Moscow. As in cases of Bezymianlag and Kargopol'lag, any statistician would qualify this level of underreporting as quantitatively and practically significant.

INCIDENTS OF EX-PRISONERS' MORTALITY IN THE CAMPS (1930–1955)

I have been able to gather data for many other penal locations and periods. These data illuminate the scale of the underreporting phenomenon and its persistence over time. The earliest archival evidence of released invalids' mortality in the camps dates to the famine of 1933. In April 1933, Abram Iakovlevich Belen'kii, the plenipotentiary of OGPU, informed Matvei Davydovich Berman, then the Gulag director, about the results of his inspection of Sazlag in Central Asia, which had an annual mortality rate of 25 percent in 1933. Belen'kii boasted that, after his intervention, the camp administration quickly released 2,333 invalids between 16 February and 27 March 1933. According to Belen'kii, "the relevance of unloading was confirmed by the fact of 480 fatalities" among the invalids eligible for release during this short timeframe.[110] These data denote that Sazlag's death rate would have been even higher than the registered 25 percent per annum if these thousands had continued to be recorded in the statistical registries of the camp.

Numerous analogous instances of invalids' deaths in the camps occurred between 1941 and 1945. Karpov, the procurator of the Khabarovsk UITLK, reported in February 1942 that eighteen ex-prisoners let go in the first mass release campaign of 1941 were still patients of the colony's central hospital, while twelve had died soon after discharge.[111] Procurator Mikhailov of Birlag

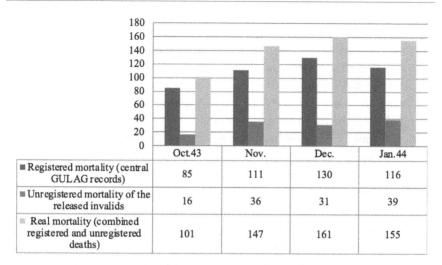

	Oct. 43	Nov.	Dec.	Jan. 44
■ Registered mortality (central GULAG records)	85	111	130	116
■ Unregistered mortality of the released invalids	16	36	31	39
▒ Real mortality (combined registered and unregistered deaths)	101	147	161	155

Figure 4.9. Mortality undercount in Iagrinlag (Arkhangel'sk oblast), October 1943–January 1944

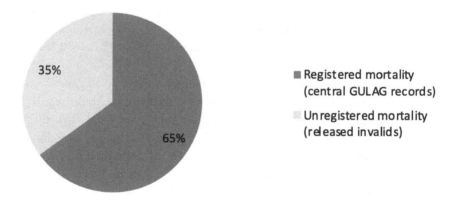

Figure 4.10. Overall mortality undercount in Iagrinlag (Arkhangel'sk oblast), October 1943–January 1944. *Source:* GAAO f. 5865, op. 2, d. 11, l. 74 (local data); GARF f. R-9414, op. 1A, d. 398, l. 3–3ob (central data, 1943); GARF f. R-9414, op. 1, d. 2796, l. 104 (central data, 1944).

in the Far East noted that "there were cases when the released received their documents but failed to leave the camp in time and died in the 'barracks for the freed.'"[112] According to the return signed by the head of URO in the small Shiroklag in Molotov oblast, twenty-one invalids passed away after their formal release following regional court decisions during the first four months of 1944.[113] In the spring of 1944, the deputy head of Ivdel'lag's OURZ (Sverdlovsk oblast) informed Moscow that in March and May 1944 eight invalids suffering from grave incurable illnesses and eligible for medical release died.[114] In addition to deaths at Iagrinlag and Kargopol'lag, 144 disabled inmates designated for release died in ten regional colonies of Arkhangel'sk oblast as of March

1943.[115] The procurator of Siblag in Western Siberia, a historic concentration point for "weakened contingents" (in dehumanizing Gulag-speak), in March 1943 reported that of 3,652 prisoners who were "eligible for medical release" from Siblag, 150 invalids died over the course of several months.[116] In some localities, the numbers of the dead reached substantial absolute values. In the spring of 1943, the regional labor colonies of Novosibirsk oblast marked 7,491 invalids for medical release but managed to set free only 2,917 inmates, while 875 invalids passed away during the process.[117]

The 1946–1947 period offers similar, although sporadic, data for various months, quarters, and half-years. The deaths of invalids eligible for release were recorded in the regional labor colonies of the Georgian SSR (71), Krasnoiarsk krai (13), the Bashkir SSR (22), Vladimir oblast (4 in July 1947 alone), and Gor'kii oblast (24 of 358 cases due for release from 27 October 1947 to 1 April 1948).[118] There were cases in Leningrad oblast (24 of 714 medical release cases in the second half of 1947), Vologda oblast (1 of 117 cases from 1 January 1946 to 1 February 1947), Orel oblast (3 of 307 cases from October 1946 to January 1947), and the Kirgiz SSR (5 of 95 cases in the first quarter of 1947).[119] The camp court for the Georgian SSR reported that of 405 cases 9 invalids died in March 1947.[120]

The same pattern reemerged in individual monthly reports generated by the camp court of the Gor'kii UITLK. Stefunin, its chairman, reported to the Ministry of Justice headquarters that of forty cases, two invalids died even before the court hearings in October 1947.[121] Polot'skii, an inspector for the Administration of Camp Courts, reported to S. A. Pashutina, his superior, that from 1 January 1947 to 1 June 1948 the camp court in Astrakhan oblast had processed 464 cases for medical release. Of that number, thirty-four invalids died.[122] Chichua, a camp judge for the Georgian UITLK, reported that "five prisoners died during the review of their cases for early release due to illness."[123] Frolov, a camp judge for the Azerbaijani UITLK, informed Moscow in 1947 that one invalid eligible for medical release died four days before court proceedings on his discharge, while another one passed away during the court session determining his fate.[124] Some camp judges did not furnish any statistics in their reports, providing only vague and nebulous mentions of invalids' mortality. Thus the camp court report on medical release provided by the Molotov UITLK for December 1947 noted that "a few prisoners died before court proceedings began."[125]

This kind of mortality occurred not only in colonies but also in larger forced-labor camps. During the first half of 1946 and the first quarter of 1947, of 133 medical release cases processed by the camp judiciary, ten invalids died during court proceedings in Vostokurallag (Sverdlovsk oblast).[126] A prisoner

Zhurukhambetov died from pulmonary tuberculosis in Astrakhanlag, one of ten cases for medical release during the first half of 1947 (Astrakhan oblast).[127] Similar cases emerged in Noril'lag (Krasnoiarsk krai) and Ivdel'lag (Sverdlovsk oblast).[128]

Invalids' mortality continued unabated in the second half of 1948. Of the forty-four cases for medical release in the third quarter of 1948 reviewed by the Sevzheldorlag camp court (Komi Republic), two candidates died.[129] In the third quarter of 1948, seven invalids among eighty-two cases presented to the Molotov UITLK judiciary died even before the court session began.[130] The Belarusian OITK camp court accepted ninety-four cases in the third quarter of 1948. Six invalids died during the formalization of their release.[131] For the entire USSR, 4,500 medical release cases in the third quarter of 1948 resulted in 4,002 people being set free (88.8 percent) and 498 denials, terminated cases, or deaths.[132]

All the recalculation cases in this chapter, as well as the general mortality statistics, are derived from times of famine and war. What about the other years? In fact, whereas the absolute number of those released on medical grounds dropped to marginal levels in the 1949–1955 period, the mortality of invalids designated for discharge can still be traced for nonfamine chronological periods. For example, according to the camp court materials, fatalities occurred in the Belarusian OITK in 1949 (February, March, May, and December), a nonfamine year.[133] In another case, the Belarusian OITK judiciary processed only twenty cases for medical release in May 1949. A certain K. A. Padagaiskii died before the court session dedicated to his release even convened.[134] In December 1949, another invalid designated for release died in the Azerbaijani labor colonies.[135] During the first quarter of 1949, the 104 cases for discharge processed by the UITLK court for the Georgian SSR included 4 invalids who died.[136] In the fourth quarter of the same year, two people passed away out of forty-two cases in the same locality.[137] Three deaths out of forty-four total medical release cases occurred in 1949 in the colonies of southern Kazakhstan.[138] Northern Kazakhstan officials recorded two fatalities in one month in 1949.[139]

Similar tantalizing evidence can be unearthed for the 1950s, the years of High Stalinism, when the officially registered mortality rate in the Gulag fell to a record low—below 1 percent per annum.[140] The following cases concern former prisoners of the Polianskii forced labor camp in Krasnoiarsk krai. Nikolai Il'ich Kaimakov received five years sentence for "theft of socialist property" in 1950. The Supreme Soviet of Ukraine granted him clemency on 13 August 1952. However, Kaimakov died two months before the pardon. Maksim Petrovich Berestenko, sentenced to fifteen years in March 1952, was freed by a decree of the Supreme Soviet of the USSR on 14 April 1953 but died from cancer of the stomach three days after release. Petr Akimovich Sarant'zev was sentenced in September 1951 to five years of deprivation of liberty and freed under amnesty, but he was so sick that he remained in the Polianskii camp hospital, where he died on 23 June 1953 as a "free citizen." The Supreme Soviet of the USSR granted clemency to Mikhail Ivanovich Lukonin, fifty-one years old and sentenced to ten years for theft of state funds, on 23 September 1954, but Lukonin did not live to see freedom, having died on 25 June 1954. Daniil Pavlovich Anufriev ended up behind bars in 1950, was released as an invalid on 11 October 1954, and passed away a month later, before he could leave the camp hospital. Mikhail Vsevolodovich Liubimov, a director of the Moscow Economic Institute, was sentenced to ten years of hard labor on 7 May 1952 for illegally printing movie tickets at the institute's printing house. The Supreme Court of the RSFSR granted him freedom on 15 May 1954, but Liubimov remained in the camp hospital and died two days after his formal discharge.[141] Shamarin, the deputy procurator of Kemerovo oblast, reported to party authorities that from May to 1 September 1954 Siblag contained more than six thousand certified invalids. Of this number, the procurator transferred 2,248 cases to the court for early release on medical grounds. But the court was slow and released only 375 disabled convicts. The delay caused thirty-seven deaths among the invalids designated for medical discharge.[142]

This evidence signifies that mortality of the *aktirovannye* continued to occur in nonfamine years as well, although probably on a considerably smaller scale than during famine years. There is still much research to be done to quantify this point more precisely.

The first goal of this chapter was to use statistics to empirically prove the reality of mortality among released invalids. A few scholars have claimed that such mortality is impossible to quantify (e.g., Tsepkalova). Therefore, one insight of the present piece is that all three bureaucratic superstructures involved (the Gulag, the Ministry of Justice, and the Procuracy) did, in fact, record these deaths. However, the record keeping was politicized, imprecise, and arbitrary.

Furthermore, I have endeavored to demonstrate the wide spatial and temporal dissemination of this kind of mortality. For the temporal dimension, I uncovered evidence of deaths among those eligible for medical release in the camps and colonies for the following years: 1933, 1935, 1941–1950, and 1952–1954.

In terms of the yet-uncharted spatial distribution, I discovered mortality among invalids designated for release in the following camps: Astrakhanlag,

Bezymianlag, Bodaibinskii Camp, Iagrinlag, Ivdel'lag, Kargopol'lag, Noril'lag, Polianskii Camp, Ponyshlag, Sazlag, Sevzheldorlag, Shiroklag, Siblag, Unzhlag, and Vostokurallag. Analogous fatalities were found in the corrective labor colonies (OITK and UITLK) of the following regions of the RSFSR: the Bash-kir and Tatar ASSRs; Khabarovsk and Krasnoiarsk krais; and Arkhangel'sk, Gor'kii, Kuibyshev, Leningrad, Molotov, Novosibirsk, Orel, Sverdlovsk, Tam-bov, Vladimir, and Vologda oblasts. Outside the RSFSR, instances of deaths have been identified for the Azerbaijan, Belarusian, Georgian, Ukrainian, Uzbek, and Kazakh republics. In several years, a consistent pattern can be detected in camps located thousands of miles apart, occurring with different intensities and magnitudes. The data range from one fatality (Vologda oblast) to more than a thousand (Kargopol'lag). More deaths occurred during cri-sis periods, fewer in nonfamine years. The main, if daunting, task for future research is to quantify this mortality more precisely. Nonetheless, this chapter has proved that ex-inmates' mortality was not a series of isolated incidents. It should not be discarded as a quantitatively negligible or irrelevant demo-graphic process. These deaths were not confined to one or two atypical camps but constituted a nationwide phenomenon.

The second goal of the present chapter was to elucidate how medical releases reduced death rates, using concrete examples to reveal the understate-ments in the central statistics. I have shown that during wartime the under-reporting was quantitatively and practically significant in several randomly picked localities, which were profoundly different from one another in terms of size, location, production profile, position in the supply chain, and offi-cially registered mortality. Central registries omitted 23.5 percent of deaths in "prioritized" Bezymianlag (Kuibyshev oblast), 50 percent in "nonprioritized" Serovskaia Colony (Sverdlovsk oblast), 35 percent in Sukholozhskaia Colony (Sverdlovsk oblast), 23 percent in Kargopol'lag (Arkhangel'sk oblast), and 20 percent in Iagrinlag (Arkhangel'sk oblast). Officials achieved these results via duplicitous application of medical release for substantive periods (ranging from four to eleven months).

This discovery confirms that the release-to-die argument—put forward by Alexopoulos, Berdinskikh, Ellman, Isupov, Khlevniuk, and others—can be supported with quantitative evidence. Conversely, central summary statistics on releases and deaths—considered to be sufficiently, if not perfectly, reliable by a significant number of historians (e.g., Getty, Rittersporn, Wheatcroft, and Zemskov) for more than twenty-five years—are seriously flawed, at least for some camps and periods. The data have turned out to be far from "exemplary" or "absolutely precise," as Zemskov claimed. Furthermore, the recalculations presented in this chapter clearly suggest that the "Mafioso internal records" analogy does not work in the case of classified Gulag mortality data. Secrecy did not safeguard the data from serious falsification due to an array of political incentives to suppress the mortality rate in the self-serving interests of the bureaucrats involved (e.g., fear of prosecution for high mortality, as shown by the Sukholozhskaia Colony's case). In contrast, Wheatcroft and Ertz were both right in arguing that the internal mortality data published in the early 1990s were "functional" or genuine in a technical sense and not entirely faked. The statistics reflected a part, but not the entire picture, of demographic reality. In essence, this chapter uses and expands on valid elements of both seemingly juxtaposed interpretations of data reliability—the release-to-die and "Mafioso internal records" arguments—to bridge the divide between them on behalf of a collaborative future effort to clarify Gulag mortality.

In this chapter, I have identified a new, previously overlooked substratum of the Gulag population: bedridden, extremely emaciated ex-inmates, stranded in the camp facilities in a legal limbo or gray zone between freedom and captivity. Crucially, some of these ex-inmates (in their thousands, at least) died in the camps and colonies, never leaving the premises. Their deaths provided an easy opportunity for officials to skew mortality figures. The mere existence of this liminal subgroup confounds and undermines entrenched historiographical notions of a 90 percent survival rate among Gulag inmates, derived from the system's central reports (quoted by many influential scholars as late as the 2010s). For instance, in his otherwise brilliant book on Nazi concentration camps, featuring a comparison of the Nazi and Soviet camps, Nikolaus Wachsmann maintained, "In all, some ninety per cent of inmates survived the Gulag."[143] As we have seen, however, the thousands of emaciated cadavers listed as released could hardly be categorized as survivors. These "half-freed" invalids may be considered the long-sought-after Rosetta Stone for a systematic revision of the Gulag central mortality data, at least for the war years. Another key insight of this chapter is that Moscow initiated an idiosyncratic parallel accounting of these "inconvenient" deaths (while excluding them from the regular record keeping), a truly remarkable Gulag bureaucratic phenomenon ipso facto.

To compensate for the arbitrariness of the record keeping, this chapter introduces a new methodological algorithm to recalculate death rates for the penal records (somewhat resembling Wheatcroft's approach to correcting the civilian mortality registration during the famine of 1932–1933). If a scholar needs to recalculate mortality for any camp now, there is a way to do it, starting in early 1943. The algorithm includes three steps. First, locate a response (statistical report) in the local camp archive to either Nasedkin's Directive no. 42/237546 or Loidin's Directive no. 42/233211 from 1943, sent to each of

112 local administrations under the auspices of the Gulag. Second, find the corresponding data for the same chronological period in the central statistics. Third, add concealed deaths of the released to the central data to arrive at the "actual" (although still somewhat understated) mortality.

Crucially, Loidin's and Nasedkin's central directives, viewed alongside Bezymianlag's and Kargopol'lag's answers to those directives, demonstrate the existence of a previously unknown (and apparently massive) corpus of sources containing "hidden" mortality data dating from the spring of 1943, at both the SANO and URO local levels. The majority of the pertinent accounting sheets remain in the internal archives of contemporary Russian security or state agencies (the Ministry of Internal Affairs and Federal Penitentiary Service). If they were to become available to the public one day, there would be a very real possibility of recalculating death rates for every single camp and colony that existed under the aegis of the Gulag from the spring of 1943. Now historians know where to look and what to look for.

On a final note, this chapter sheds new light on the deceitful strategies surrounding the registration of inmate mortality data on the ground, an aspect that has been so far quite poorly researched and understood. For years, scholars (myself included) have been writing histories of the Gulag through the tendentious prism of its central apparatus or have used local archives without the critical collation of local data with central figures. It has gradually become an analytical weakness of the field. Uncritical use of the Gulag central statistics can be dangerously misleading, tilt scholars toward false assumptions about its nature, and even present the system in a better light than it deserves. Thus the "revolving door" of Stalin's Gulag, often invoked in the literature without any caveats, was far from being entirely benign. At times, it covered up terminally ill, immobile, and even already dead people.

Essentially, we have neglected an entire plethora of contradictory factors that influenced lower-ranking bureaucrats during the collection, processing, and presentation of statistics to the central authority. The all-union regulations governing the system are well known, but we have a poor understanding of their implementation on the ground as well as of the interplay between the center and the periphery. Without factoring in the peripheral level of the system (at the archives of individual places of confinement), we overlook and possibly oversimplify numerous crucial aspects of mortality record keeping on the ground. The focus on local archives, if they become available one day, may lead to another full-blown "archival revolution" with discoveries that could be comparable in importance to the revelations of the 1990s, which were based on central all-union reports.

NOTES

1. For a fresh, excellent interpretation of the Gulag as a phenomenon, see Michael David-Fox, ed., *The Soviet Gulag: Evidence, Interpretation, and Comparison* (Pittsburgh: Pittsburgh University Press, 2016).
2. Steven Barnes, *Death and Redemption: The Gulag and the Shaping of Soviet Society* (Princeton, NJ: Princeton University Press, 2011), 10.
3. Robert Conquest, *The Great Terror: A Reassessment* (New York: Oxford University Press, 1990), 338–39.
4. Barnes, *Death and Redemption*, 10; Golfo Alexopoulos, "Amnesty 1945: The Revolving Door of Stalin's Gulag," *Slavic Review* 64, no. 2 (2005): 274–306.
5. J. Arch Getty, Gábor T. Rittersporn, and Viktor N. Zemskov, "Victims of the Soviet Penal System in the Pre-war Years: A First Approach on the Basis of Archival Evidence," *American Historical Review* 98, no. 4 (1993): 1017–49.
6. Getty et al., "Victims of the Soviet Penal System," 1041.
7. V. N. Zemskov, "O podlinnosti statisticheskoi otchetnosti GULAGa," *Sotsiologicheskie issledovaniia*, no. 6 (1992): 155–56; Zemskov, "Politicheskie repressii v SSSR (1917–1990)," *Rossiia XXI*, no. 1–2 (1994): 119.
8. J. Arch Getty and Oleg V. Naumov, *The Road to Terror: Stalin and the Self-destruction of the Bolsheviks, 1932–1939* (New Haven: Yale University Press, 1999), 593; Barnes, *Death and Redemption*, 289.
9. Stephen G. Wheatcroft, "Victims of Stalinism and the Soviet Secret Police: The Comparability and Reliability of the Archival Data—Not the Last Word," *Europe-Asia Studies* 51, no. 2 (1999): 324–25.
10. Stephen G. Wheatcroft, "On Comments by Keep and Conquest," *Europe-Asia Studies* 52, no. 6 (2000): 1150.
11. Stephen G. Wheatcroft, "The First 35 Years of Soviet Living Standards: Secular Growth and Conjunctural Crises in a Time of Famines," *Explorations in Economic History* 46, no. 1 (2009): 29.
12. John L. H. Keep, "Wheatcroft and Stalin's Victims: Comments," *Europe-Asia Studies* 51, no. 6 (1999): 1090; Wheatcroft, "On Comments by Keep and Conquest," 1143–59.
13. Simon Ertz, "Stroitel'stvo Noril'skogo gorno-metallurgicheskogo kombinata (1935–1938 gg.): Stanovlenie krupnogo ob"ekta ekonomicheskoi sistemy GULAGa," in *Ekonomicheskaia istoriia: Ezhegodnik 2003* (Moscow: ROSSPEN, 2004), 140–76; Ertz, *Zwangsarbeit im stalinistischen Lagersystem: Eine Untersuchung der Methoden, Strategien und Ziele ihrer Ausnutzung am Beispiel Norilsk, 1935–1953* (Berlin: Duncker & Humblot, 2006).
14. Wheatcroft, "Victims of Stalinism," 324.
15. Zemskov, "K voprosu o mashtabakh repressii v SSSR," *Sotsiologicheskie issledovaniia*, no. 9 (1995): 119.
16. The "release-to-die" phrase was coined by Michael Ellman, based on Vladimir Isupov's term. See Ellman, "Soviet Repression Statistics: Some Comments," *Europe-Asia Studies* 54, no. 7 (2002): 1152.
17. Viktor Berdinskikh, *Viatlag: Istoriia odnogo lageria* (Moscow: Agraf, 2001), 52; Ellman, "Soviet Repression Statistics," 1153; Oleg V. Khlevniuk, *The History of the Gulag: From Collectivization to the Great Terror* (New Haven: Yale University Press, 2004), 78; Anne Applebaum, *Gulag: A History* (New York: Anchor, 2004), 583; I. V. Bezborodova and V. P. Kozlov, eds., *Istoriia stalinskogo GULAGa* (Moscow: ROSSPEN, 2004), 4:28; Galina Ivanova, *Istoriia GULAGa, 1918–1958: Sotsial'no-ekonomicheskii i politiko-pravovoi aspekty* (Moscow: Nauka, 2006), 414–18; Khlevniuk, *Zakliuchennye na stroikakh kommunizma: GULAG i ob"ekty energetiki v SSSR. Sobranie dokumentov* (Moscow: ROSSPEN, 2008), 23; Nick Baron, "Conflict and Complicity: The Expansion of the Karelian Gulag, 1923–1933," *Cahiers du monde russe* 42, no. 2–4 (2001): 643; Wilson T. Bell, *Stalin's Gulag at War: Forced Labor, Mass Death, and Soviet Victory in the Second World War* (Toronto: University of Toronto Press, 2018), 61; Aleksei Tepliakov, "K voprosu o dostovernosti statistiki gosudarstvennykh repressii, 1918–1953 gg.," *Idei i idealy*, no. 4 (26) (2015): 64; Mikhail Nakonechnyi, "Factory of Invalids: Mortality, Disability, and Early Release on Medical Grounds in GULAG, 1930–1955" (PhD diss., University of Oxford, 2020).
18. Golfo Alexopoulos, *Illness and Inhumanity in Stalin's Gulag* (New Haven: Yale University Press, 2017), esp. chap. 6, "Releases," 133–59.

19. Alexopoulos, *Illness and Inhumanity*, 14.

20. Thus Alexopoulos's foundational work mainly builds on the central archive of the Gulag (Gosu-darstvennyi arkhiv Rossiiskoi Federatsii [GARF] f. R-9414) and does not use local camp archives or feature a multi-institutional overview of medical releases, using mostly NKVD records.

21. However, one should acknowledge the important if brief pioneering contributions by Galina Mikhailovna Ivanova and Marc Elie, who both employed central USSR Ministry of Justice mate-rials in their concise descriptions of medical releases (GARF f. R-9492): Ivanova, *Istoriia GULAGa, 1918–1958*, 414–18; Elie, "Les anciens détenus du Goulag: Libérations massives, réinsertion et réhabilitation dans l'URSS poststalinienne, 1953–1964" (PhD diss., EHESS, 2007), 74–76. Mean-while, the role of camp procurators in medical discharges constitutes a complete "blank spot." This chapter fills this gap by extensively using the newly discovered files of the camp procuracy (GARF f. R-8131).

22. This cogent point is raised by Steven Maddox in Alan Barenberg et al., "New Directions in Gulag Studies: A Roundtable Discussion," *Canadian Slavonic Papers* 59, no. 3–4 (2017): 376–95.

23. Alexopoulos, *Illness and Inhumanity*, 158, 244.

24. Anna Tsepkalova, "Dinamika dvizheniia kontingentov ITL BMK-ChMS i pokazateli smertnosti," in *Gedenkbuch: Kniga pamiati nemtsev-trudarmeitsev ITL Bakalstroi-Cheliabmetallurgstroi 1942—1946* (Nizhnii Tagil: Nizhne-Tagil'skaia gosudarstvennaia sotsio-pedagicheskaia akademiia [NTGSPA], 2014), 4:203.

25. Alexopoulos, *Illness and Inhumanity*, 15.

26. Khlevniuk, *History of the Gulag*, 327.

27. It is well known that penal locations varied dramatically in the conditions and health of their popu-lations over time. See Lynne Viola, "Historicizing the Gulag," in *Global Convict Labour*, ed. Christian G. de Vito and Alexander C. Lichtenstein (Leiden: Brill, 2015), 361–79; and Alexopoulos, *Illness and Inhumanity*, 15.

28. One needs to acknowledge the pioneers of the "central-local approach" to Gulag history generally. See Viola, *The Unknown Gulag: The Lost World of Stalin's Special Settlements* (New York: Oxford Uni-versity Press, 2007), 61–72; Alan Barenberg, *Gulag Town, Company Town: Forced Labor and Its Legacy in Vorkuta* (New Haven: Yale University Press, 2014); Jeffrey S. Hardy, *The Gulag after Stalin: Rede-fining Punishment in Khrushchev's Soviet Union* (Ithaca, NY: Cornell University Press, 2016); James R. Harris, *The Great Urals: Regionalism and the Evolution of the Soviet System* (Ithaca, NY: Cornell University Press, 1999); Barnes, *Death and Redemption*; and Bell, *Stalin's Gulag at War*.

29. Out of the 1.7 million prisoners who died in the Gulag from 1930 to 1955, approximately one million of them perished in the 1941–1945 period. See Zemskov, "Smertnost' zakliuchennikh v 1941–1945," in *Liudskie poteri v period Vtoroi mirovoi voiny: Sbornik statei* (St. Petersburg: Blitz, 1995), 174–77.

30. Regulations stipulated the transfer of the released invalids to the care of their families, civilian hospitals, invalid houses, or administrative exile. Overwhelming evidence indicates that in crisis periods relatives were often absent and hospitals habitually refused to accept the discharged. Some of the released died in the camps. There were additional thousands of deaths from starvation and exposure that happened in train stations and railcars during harrowing return journeys from the camps (Nakonechnyi, "Factory of Invalids," 55–189). However, the mass death of the released inva-lids outside camp premises is beyond the limited scope of this chapter, which concentrates on the mortality of the released in the camps themselves.

31. Directive no. 42/232546, according to the inventory list, was telegraphed to 112 local administra-tions (GARF f. R-9414, op. 1, d. 2785, ll. 43–43 ob.) This fact suggests that almost all local camps under the aegis of GULAG NKVD USSR had received the directive and had to provide a response. The ubiquitous dissemination of the directive and Nasedkin's personal interference may serve as a circumstantial indication of how pervasive deaths of the released were at the time.

32. The original central directive with Nasedkin's signature can be found in GARF f. R-9414, op. 1, d. 2785, l. 42. One of the regional copies was discovered by Vladimir Isupov in a local archive of

the Altaiskii Camp and quoted in Isupov and S. A. Papkov, *Glavnyi resurs pobedy: Liudskoi poten-tsial Zapadnoi Sibiri v gody Vtoroi mirovoi voiny (1939–1945)* (Novosibirsk: Sova, 2008), 169; V. A. Isupov, *Demograficheskie katastrofy i krizisy v Rossii v pervoi polovine XX veka: Istoriko-demograficheskie ocherki* (Novosibirsk: Sibirskii khronograf, 2000), 164. However, Isupov omitted any reference to the creation of a double accounting system, never traced any answers to this directive, and did not attempt to recalculate death rates.

33. GARF f. R-9414, op. 1, d. 2785, ll. 71–73.
34. GARF f. R-9401, op. 1A, d. 132, ll. 23–25, published in *Istoria Stalinskogo GULAGa*, 3:217–18.
35. See, e.g., GARF f. R-9414, op. 1, d. 2785, l. 65.
36. Alexopoulos, *Illness and Inhumanity*, 154.
37. Barnes, *Death and Redemption*, 117.
38. The supply of forestry camps was especially deficient. See GARF f. R-9414, op. 1, d. 1921, ll. 73–77. For comparison between prewar and war rations for the entire Gulag, see GARF f. R-9414, op. 1, d. 1921, l. 49.
39. GARF f. R-9414, op. 1, d. 1181, ll. 15–18.
40. The importance of the order is clearly reflected in the local camp materials. See Gosudarstvennyi arkhiv Cheliabinskoi oblasti (OGACHO) f. R-1075, op. 1, d. 227, l. 10.
41. See, e.g., B. A. Nakhapetov, *Ocherki istorii Sanitarnoi sluzhby GULAGa* (Moscow: ROSSPEN, 2009). In another example, Donald Filtzer attributed the sharp decline of Gulag mortality in 1944 exclusively to the improved supply. Whereas he is certainly partly correct in his assertion, he overlooks the medical release factor. The actual situation was apparently more complex. See Filtzer, "Starvation Mortality in Soviet Home-Front Industrial Regions during World War II," in *Hunger and War: Food Provision in the Soviet Union during World War II*, ed. Wendy Z. Goldman and Filtzer (Bloomington: Indiana University Press, 2015), 330.
42. For low-level self-congratulation, see the reports by the SANO of Tambov OITK in GATO f. R-3957, op. 2s, d. 61, ll. 46–47.
43. Alexopoulos, *Illness and Inhumanity*, 157.
44. GARF f. R-9414, op. 1, d. 2796, l. 214 ob.
45. The OURZ-URO or the Second Department (*uchetno-raspredelitel'nyi otdel*) was an internal statistical and "labor allocation" department within the Gulag. Its main responsibilities included prisoner registration and "labor utilization" (i.e., the assignment of prisoners to different types of work according to their health and "danger to the society"). The OURZ-URO, in addition to SANO, supervised mortality accounting and medical releases. See GARF f. R-9414, op. 1, d. 1143, l. 453.
46. Gosudarstvennyi arkhiv Arkhangel'skoi oblasti (GAAO) f. R-4994, op. 1, d. 280, l. 123.
47. GASO f. R-2064, op. 2, d. 47, l. 106.
48. GASO f. R-2064, op. 2, d. 47, l. 100.
49. I am grateful to Alexei Vladimirovich Zakharchenko for helping me find this source. The cumulative number "355" from this report was published in A. V. Zakharchenko and A. Repinetskii, eds., *Strogo sekretno: Bezymianlag, 1940–1946 (Dokumenty, fakty, suzhdeniia o Bezymianskikh lageriakh Osobogo stroitel'stva NKVD SSSR)* (Samara: Moskovskii gorodskii pedagogicheskii universitet, Samarskii filial, 2006), 256. However, Zakharchenko and Repinetskii, like Isupov before them, did not attempt to recalculate relative understatements of mortality data or double-check its completeness as well as the veracity of corresponding central records for Bezymianlag in Moscow.
50. A skeptic might still doubt that camp officials used medical release as an occasional statistical sleight of hand to deflate reported death rates, instead arguing for the "humanitarian" nature of such releases. In fact, this behavior does resemble a purely technical, innocuous bureaucratic practice discovered by Wheatcroft in the "civilian" registration of deaths during the famine of 1932–1933. See V. Kondrashin et al., eds., *Golod v SSSR, 1929–1934* (Moscow: Mezhdunarodnyi fond "Demokratiia," 2013), 3:719–71.To address this potential counterargument, I present the cases of the Sukholozhskaia and Serovskaia colonies. They contain explicit confirmation of the duplicitous

application of medical releases and explain the motives driving officials to artificial reduction of mortality rate.

51. *Tufta*—a slang word from the camp lexicon meaning false accounting to inflate one's successes (usually associated with production).

52. On the occasional tacit collusion between the camp procuracy and the NKVD in the manipulation of Gulag death rates, see Nakonechnyi, "Factory of Invalids," 181–223. On the term "pocket procurator," see Hardy, *Gulag after Stalin*, 104.

53. GARF f. R-8131, op. 37, d. 2046, l. 51.

54. GARF f. R-8131, op. 37, d. 2046, l. 52.

55. GASO f. R-2064, op. 2s, d. 83, l. 61.

56. GASO f. R-2064, op. 2s, d. 83, l. 123.

57. GASO f. R-2064, op. 2s, d. 83, l. 63 ob.

58. GARF f. R-8131, op. 37, d. 1266, l. 11.

59. GAAO Otdel dokumentov sotsial'no-politicheskoi istorii (ODSPI) f. 296, op. 1, d. 1172, ll. 14–15, quoted in *Arkhangel'skii Sever v dokumentakh istorii (s 1917 po 1945)* 1 (Arkhangel'sk: Severnyi [Arkticheskii] Federal'nyi Universitet, 2015), 1:319.

60. GARF f. R-8131, op. 37, d. 2061, ll. 52 (no. deduced from nearest numbered pages), 111.

61. For understatement in the procurator's report, see GARF f. R-8131, op. 37, d. 2046, l. 91. For SANO records, see GARF f. R-8131, op. 37, d. 2046, ll. 51–52.

62. GARF f. R-8131, op. 37, d. 1626, l. 52 ob.

63. GASO f. R-2064, op. 2s, d. 83, l. 89.

64. GARF f. R-8131, op. 37, d. 2061, l. 52 (no. deduced from nearest numbered pages).

65. GASO f. R-2064, op. 2, d. 83, l. 123.

66. GARF f. R-9492, op. 5, d. 66, l. 59.

67. GATO f. R-3957, op. 2s, d. 42, l. 22.

68. On the number of prisoners in the Tambov OITK, see GATO f. R-3957, op. 2s, d. 61, l. 25.

69. See, e.g., GARF f. R-9414, op. 1, d. 330, l. 1 ob.

70. GARF f. R-9414, op. 1, d. 1168, ll. 228–28 ob. It had an additional "only in person" stamp, signifying the highest level of possible secrecy used by the NKVD in this period.

71. GARF f. R-9414, op. 1, d. 1168, l. 228.

72. See Rebecca Manley, "Nutritional Dystrophy: The Science and Semantics of Starvation in World War II," in *Hunger and War*, 206–64. For more examples from the 1933 famine, see the diagnoses data for Dmitlag (GARF f. R-9489, op. 1A, d. 1, ll. 1–4). For 1943, see data on the Khabarovsk regional labor colonies (GARF f. R-8131, op. 37, d. 1267, l. 84); Bogoslovlag (GARF f. R-8131, op. 37, d. 2035, l. 108); Ivdel'lag (GARF f. R-8131, op. 37, d. 2059, l. 85); and the Moscow regional labor colonies Sevzheldorlag and Ryblag (GARF f. R-8131, op. 37, d. 1626, l. 95). For 1946, see data on the Arkhangel'sk regional labor colonies and Iargrinlag (GARF f. R-9492, op. 5, d. 30, l. 60). For 1947–1948, see data on the colonies of the Moscow region, Iaroslavskaia oblast, and Volgolag (GARF f. R-8131, op. 37, d. 3842, ll. 159–60, 172, 187).

73. GARF f. R-8131, op. 37, d. 2498, l. 148.

74. GARF f. R-8131, op. 37, d. 2498, l. 148.

75. GARF f. R-8131, op. 37, d. 2498, l. 148.

76. GARF f. R-8131, op. 37, d. 2498, l. 148.

77. GARF f. R-8131, op. 37, d. 2498, l. 214.

78. GARF f. R-8131, op. 37, d. 2060, l. 269; GARF f. R-9492, op. 5, d. 64, l. 13.

79. GARF f. R-8131, op. 37, d. 2498, l. 90.

80. GARF f. R-8131, op. 37, d. 2498, l. 223.

81. GARF f. R-8131, op. 37, d. 2498, l. 234.

82. GARF f. R-8131, op. 37, d. 2498, l. 122.

83. Alexopoulos, *Illness and Inhumanity*, 108, 154.

84. GARF f. R-8131, op. 37, d. 2498, l. 223.

85. One of the best document collections on Bezymianlag is Zakharchenko and Repinetskii, *Bezymianlag.*

86. The mortality rates for Viatlag and Unzhlag are calculated based on GARF f. R-9414, op. 1, d. 2784, ll. 18, 26.

87. Zakharchenko and Repinetskii, *Bezymianlag,* 288.

88. Zakharchenko and Repinetskii, *Bezymianlag,* 343.

89. Zakharchenko and Repinetskii, *Bezymianlag,* 332.

90. Zakharchenko and Repinetskii, *Bezymianlag,* 301.

91. Zakharchenko and Repinetskii, *Bezymianlag,* 303.

92. Zakharchenko and Repinetskii, *Bezymianlag,* 258.

93. GASO f. R-2064, op. 2s, d. 83, l. 89.

94. In this context, "unregistered" means not recorded in the central statistics.

95. GASO f. R-2064, op. 2s, d. 198, l. 96.

96. This is a trenchant illustration of Alexopoulos's discovery of the colonies' role as a "concentration spot" for sick and emaciated prisoners (corroborated by Bell using West Siberian material). See Alexopoulos, *Illness and Inhumanity,* 6, 184; and Bell, *Stalin's Gulag at War,* 50, 56.

97. Zakharchenko and Repinetskii, *Bezymianlag,* 54–55.

98. Zakharchenko and Repinetskii, *Bezymianlag,* 257–58.

99. Zakharchenko and Repinetskii, *Bezymianlag,* 54.

100. For deaths registered in the central statistics, see GARF f. R-9414, op. 1A, d. 397, ll. 7–7 ob. For invalids' deaths unregistered in the central records, see GASO f. R-2064, op. 2s, d. 83, l. 123.

101. We should remember that the Gulag had a quasi-military structure, and a colony commander usually held a rank no higher than army captain, while Bezymianlag commanders were colonels or major-generals.

102. GARF f. R-9414, op. 1, d. 1146, l. 24.

103. A 1.6 percent average monthly rate in January 1943 versus a 0.6 percent rate in January 1944.

104. See Alexopoulos, *Illness and Inhumanity,* 183.

105. On the relatively positive characterization of Noril'lag, see Leonid Borodkin and Simon Ertz, "Coercion versus Motivation, Forced Labor in Norilsk," in *The Economics of Forced Labor: The Soviet Gulag,* ed. Paul Gregory and Valery Lazarev (Stanford, CA: Hoover Institution Press, 2003), 78–80. I am not claiming that the authors are totally wrong. Noril'lag, indeed, was milder in comparison to the worst camps (e.g., forestry), but still one should determine the fate of its invalids to make a proper value judgment about its conditions. This inference is applicable to the whole Gulag as well.

106. Berdinskikh, *Viatlag,* 141.

107. GARF f. R-8131, op. 37, d. 2061, l. 52 (no. deduced from nearest numbered pages).

108. GARF f. R-8131, op. 37, d. 1266, l. 9.

109. GAAO f. 5865, op. 2, d. 11, l. 74. The procurator's report mentioning understatements of mortality (without monthly distributions) was first quoted in part in T. F. Mel'nik, "Iagrinskii ITL v Molotovske," in *Katorga i ssylka na Severe Rossii* (Arkhangel'sk: Kira, 2006), 216–44.

110. Tsentral'nyi arkhiv Federal'noi sluzhby bezopasnosti f. 2, op. 11, d. 548, ll. 70–113, published in *Istoriia Stalinskogo GULAGa,* 3:502. "Unloading" was a slang term used by the OGPU-NKVD, mostly in the early 1930s, to designate several procedures, including medical release.

111. GARF f. R-8131, op. 37, d. 799, l. 171.

112. GARF f. R-8131, op. 37, d. 799, l. 111.

113. GARF f. R-8131, op. 37, d. 2046, l. 76.

114. GARF f. R-8131, op. 37, d. 2059, l. 76.

115. GAAO f. R-4994, op. 1, d. 280, l. 129.

116. GARF f. R-8131, op. 37, d. 1265, l. 25. On Siblag's role, see Bell, *Stalin's Gulag at War,* 62.

117. Gosudarstvennyi arkhiv Novosibirskoi oblasti (GANO) f. P-4, op. 34, d. 171, ll. 280–84 ob.,

published in *Nasha malaia rodina: Khrestomatiia po istorii Novosibirskoi oblasti 1921–1991* (Novosibirsk: Ekor, 1997), 283, also quoted in Bell, *Stalin's Gulag at War*, 61.

118. GARF f. R-9492, op. 5, d. 42, l. 224; GARF f. R-9492, op. 5, d. 15, ll. 83–83 ob.; GARF f. R-9492, op. 5, d. 44, l. 290.
119. GARF f. R-9492, op. 5, d. 30, ll. 53–53 ob.; GARF f. R-9492, op. 5, d. 20, l. 16; GARF f. R-9492, op. 5, d. 22, l. 114; GARF f. R-9492, op. 5, d. 30, ll. 56–57.
120. GARF f. R-9492, op. 5, d. 18, l. 16.
121. GARF f. R-9492, op. 14, d. 138, l. 2.
122. GARF f. R-9492, op. 5, d. 44, l. 217.
123. GARF f. R-9492, op. 5, d. 30, l. 163.
124. GARF f. R-9492, op. 5, d. 58, l. 6.
125. GARF f. R-9492, op. 14, d. 144, l. 345.
126. GARF f. R-8131, op. 37, d. 3843, l. 30.
127. GARF f. R-8131, op. 37, d. 3841, l. 131.
128. GARF f. R-9492, op. 5, d. 44, l. 355; GARF f. R-9492, op. 5, d. 48, l. 30.
129. GARF f. R-9492, op. 5, d. 46, ll. 23–24.
130. GARF f. R-9492, op. 5, d. 46, l. 24.
131. GARF f. R-9492, op. 5, d. 59, l. 2.
132. GARF f. R-9492, op. 5, d. 42, l. 276.
133. GARF f. R-9492, op. 5, d. 59, ll. 18, 26.
134. GARF f. R-9492, op. 5, d. 59, l. 79.
135. GARF f. R-9492, op. 5, d. 58, l. 135.
136. GARF f. R-9492, op. 5, d. 60, l. 54.
137. GARF f. R-9492, op. 5, d. 60, l. 225.
138. GARF f. R-9492, op. 5, d. 61, l. 196.
139. GARF f. R-9492, op. 5, d. 63, l. 112.
140. Bezborodova and Kozlov, *Istoriia Stalinskogo GULAGa*, 4:55.
141. S. P. Kuchin, "Bratsy, pomiloserdstvuite! (amnistii i dosrochnye osvobozhdenia)," in *Polianskii ITL (GULAG-ugolovnyi)* (Zheleznogorsk, 1999), http://www.memorial.krsk.ru/Articles/1999Kuchin/17.htm.
142. Gosudarstvennyi arkhiv Kemerovskoi oblasti (GAKO) f. P-75, op. 7, d. 331, ll. 50–53, published in *Neizvestnyi Kuzbass: Sbornik arkhivnikh dokumentov*, no. 2: *Totalitarnaia sistema: Palachi i zhertvy* (Kemerovo: GAKO), 185.
143. Nikolaus Wachsmann, *KL: A History of the Nazi Concentration Camps* (New York: Farrar, Straus, and Giroux, 2015), 8–9; Timothy Snyder, *Bloodlands: Europe between Hitler and Stalin* (London: Bodley Head, 2010), xiii, 8–9; Richard Evans, "The Anatomy of Hell," *New York Review of Books* (9 July 2015).

Deciphering the Stalinist Perpetrators

The Case of Georgian NKVD Investigators Khazan, Savitskii, and Krimian

Timothy K. Blauvelt and David Jishkariani

THE SCALE OF STATE-SANCTIONED MASS VIOLENCE IN THE STALINIST SOVIET Union in 1937–1938, as with other cases in the twentieth century, provokes fundamental questions about human nature and about how and under what circumstances people can be induced to behave in seemingly inhuman ways. There has been a movement recently in the field of Soviet history to apply the insights taken from the historiography of Nazi Germany to investigations of similar mass state crimes in the USSR.[1] In part because of limited access to archival materials, much of the focus in studies of the Stalinist Great Terror during the Cold War centered on the role of Iosif Stalin himself and of the top leadership, viewing the mid-level implementers as either "cogs in the machine," at best obedient implementers devoid of agency, or as individual sadists and psychopaths whose natural criminal proclivities found a favorable context.[2] While orders from above clearly played a central role in the Terror, and without question there were sadists among the Soviet secret police investigators, the more interesting and troubling questions concern how "ordinary people" became perpetrators, and about the ways in which the secret police investigators fit into Stalinist society and themselves reflected that society.[3]

The extensive archival case files from the former Georgian KGB and documents that have become available from central Soviet and party archives about the trials of Georgian NKVD officials that took place in Tbilisi after 1953 provide an opportunity to examine the careers, motivations, and outlooks of individual officials, in effect "to change the perspective of research and create a differentiated image of the Soviet secret policeman."[4] Although not unproblematic as sources, the vast amount of testimony, commentary, appeals, and personal statements to be found in these files allows a fresh examination of the relationship of the individual to the state machine, the interplay of disposition and situation, of ideology and rationality, and the mutual influence and reinforcement of these factors.[5] Such materials permit a microlevel exploration of the "ecosystem of violence," the historical context in which individuals became perpetrators; the combination of context, culture, and ideology in the initiation and expansion of violence; and the way in which individual motivations shaped actions.

This chapter addresses these questions and attempts to "populate the macrohistorical," to paraphrase Lynne Viola, through an examination of a group of three mid-level investigators in the Georgian NKVD—Aleksandr Khazan, Konstantin Savitskii, and Nikita Krimian—whom a mass of reports, testimonies, and appeals place at the very epicenter of the machinery of the terror in Georgia in 1936–1938. The cases of these three investigators, put on trial in Tbilisi in 1955, provide an opportunity to seek a "balance between the micro- and macro-historical" and an understanding of how individuals working in the Stalinist secret police were capable of committing acts of oppression on such a scale against largely innocent victims.[6] This chapter introduces new and specific archival evidence on patronage politics and "Stalinism in practice" at the middle level of the Georgian NKVD and offers a multifactor interpretation concerning the motivations of the perpetrators that builds on the literature on this topic. Finally, employing the concepts of "subjectivity" and "imposture" to interrogate the interrelationship among discourse, action, and belief in the motivations of the perpetrators, it challenges that literature's criticisms of the applicability of the "ordinary man" concept to NKVD perpetrators by grounding it in the specifically Stalinist context.

KHAZAN, SAVITSKII, AND KRIMIAN

In the wake of Stalin's death in early March 1953, an intense struggle for succession ensued among his top lieutenants, Lavrentii Beria and Nikita Khrushchev, culminating later that year in the arrest and execution of Beria,

together with several of his closest associates.[7] One of the most effective culti-
vators of patronage in the Stalinist system, Beria rose through the ranks of the
secret police in the Transcaucasus during the 1920s, transitioning in the early
1930s to the leadership of the Party, becoming first secretary of the Georgian Party and then of the Transcaucasian party organizations. Beria brought
many of his clients with him into the party apparatus while retaining patronage control over the secret police in the Transcaucasus. In other regions of the
USSR, party leaders often had "their guy" in the NKVD; in the Transcaucasus
the party leadership essentially was the NKVD. The people's commissar of
internal affairs of the Georgian SSR during the period of the Great Terror
was Beria's appointee S. A. Goglidze, while another Beria client, B. Z. Kobulov, was deputy people's commissar as well as head of the Fourth Department
(Secret Political Division), responsible for investigating cases of "counterrevolution" (including "Trotskyism"), "anti-Soviet elements," and nationalist organizations, the department that in 1937 was at the very heart of the Terror in
Georgia.

Kobulov and Goglidze were among Beria's close confidants shot at the end
of 1953. The following year, prosecutions began of mid-level officials associated
with Beria's group. On 25 May 1954, USSR Procurator General R. A. Rudenko
sent a ten-thousand-word draft indictment (*obvinitel'noe zakliuchenie*) against
the former Georgian NKVD Investigators Khazan, Savitskii, and Krimian,
together with G. I. Paramonov, to the Communist Party of the Soviet Union
(CPSU) Central Committee. The indictment framed the accused as members
of "the treacherous group of plotters headed by the enemy of the people Beria"
who implemented the assignments of Beria, Goglidze, and Kobulov. The proposed charges—based on articles 58-1(b), 58-8, and 58-11 of the RSFSR Criminal Code—centered on conducting illegal arrests of innocent Soviet citizens;
falsifying evidence and criminal cases; baselessly accusing arrestees of preparing terrorist acts against Beria, Goglidze, and Kobulov and committing
serious state crimes; beating and torturing arrestees, personally or through
ordering subordinates, in order to extract made-up confessions "essential to
Beria, Goglidze, and Kobulov for terroristic reprisals with officials of party,
Soviet, scientific, and economic institutions who were inconvenient for them";
murdering arrestees during the course of interrogations; and engaging in a
number of other criminal acts directed toward arrestees and members of
their families.[8] The case against Khazan, Savitskii, Krimian, and Paramonov
was then incorporated into a broader indictment against former Beria clients
that included two Georgian SSR ministers of state security, A. N. Rapava and
N. M. Rukhadze, as well as two further former secret police officials, Sh. O.
Tsereteli and S. N. Nadaraia. The new 119-page draft indictment was prepared

by USSR Deputy Procurator General L. N. Smirnov and submitted to the CPSU Central Committee by KGB head Ivan Serov on 10 January 1955 with the proposal that an open, public trial be held in Tbilisi with the participation of the defendants and their official defense representation. It was included for discussion in the agenda of the Presidium of the CPSU Central Committee on 22 January 1955.

The trial took place over twelve days, on 7–19 September 1955, in the theater of the House of Culture of Railway Workers in Tbilisi in the presence of over six hundred spectators. It was heard by the Military Collegium of the USSR Supreme Court and chaired by General-Lieutenant of Justice A. A. Cheptsov. USSR Procurator General Rudenko prosecuted the case personally. The leadership viewed the trial as an opportunity to bring to public attention in the Georgian SSR the crimes of the Beria group against its political opponents, including the family of Sergo Orjonikidze and a number of highly placed former Transcaucasian and Georgian officials and intellectuals.[9] Taking place nearly a half-year before Khrushchev's "secret speech" at the Twentieth Party Congress in February 1956, the proceedings followed the model of Stalin-era show trials, with the accused denounced as enemies of the people and betrayers of the Motherland aiming to overthrow Soviet power and restore capitalism. Stalin remained beyond criticism, and when the defendant Rukhadze attempted to explain that Stalin knew about violations in the NKVD, he was cut off and reprimanded.[10] As typical for the Stalinist show trial model, the outcome was preordained: all the defendants were found guilty on 19 September and sentenced to execution, with the exception of Paramonov, who received twenty-five years' hard labor, and Nadaraia, who received ten years. Khazan, Savitskii, and Krimian were all shot on the same day, 15 November 1955.[11]

In addition to the materials from these specific indictments, held in the Russian State Archive for Socio-political History (RGASPI) in Moscow and much of it published, additional information relevant to these cases is contained in the case files of several former mid-level investigators of the Georgian NKVD tried later in the 1950s in Tbilisi and stored in the Georgian KGB archives there.[12] Much of the work examining the question of the Stalinist perpetrators has been based on case files from Ukrainian KGB archives relating to the trials of certain investigators for "violations of socialist legality" held by the NKVD itself in 1939–1941, the "purge of the purgers." Those trials followed the replacement of Nikolai Ezhov by Beria as head of the NKVD and were part of a process (the so-called Beria Thaw) that brought the Terror to an end, signaling that brutal and illegal measures against arrestees would no longer be tolerated and that the secret police would be conclusively subordinated to the state and the Party.[13] Overseen from the center under Beria's leadership and conducted throughout most of the USSR, no such trials of NKVD officials took place in the Georgian SSR in 1939–1941. While these trials were based on the "procedural" charge of misuse of power and exceeding authority (article 209, point 17, in the case of the Ukrainian SSR), in distinction from the "political" charge of Trotskyist counterrevolution (article 58 in most republics) most prevalent against arrestees during the 1937–1938 Terror, Beria's former associates in the 1950s were charged with counterrevolution, although this time not for complicity with Lev Trotsky but rather as part of Beria's alleged conspiracy to undermine the Party and restore capitalism.[14] Also in distinction from the 1939–1941 trials, those in Tbilisi in the 1950s were conducted by the USSR procurator general rather than by the secret police itself. While the trials in Georgia in the 1950s most likely shared with those of 1939–1941 a didactic goal of emphasizing to other secret police officials that the methods of 1937–1938 were no longer acceptable, arguably the broader goal of the 1950s trials was to demonstrate to party cadres and the public at large in the Georgian SSR that the Beria network no longer held sway there—a kind of local "de-Beria-fication" that preceded the union-wide de-Stalinization.[15]

Secret police archival materials—whether situation assessments (svodki), interrogation protocols, testimonies, or personal appeals and letters of individual investigators—are always inherently problematic as sources.[16] Those giving evidence in the 1950s trials in Tbilisi, both the accused and the witnesses (some of whom would later be accused themselves), were endeavoring to downplay their affiliation with Beria and their involvement in the machinations of which he was accused (or to show that the larger political accusations in general were groundless), and to present themselves in the most sympathetic light possible. At the time of the trials in the 1950s, in distinction from those in 1939–1941, Stalin was no longer alive and the Stalinist system was clearly undergoing significant changes. None of the testimony in the 1950s trials appears to have been obtained through torture, and in many cases the accused were provided with legal counsel. While the defendants in these trials occasionally denied a specific incident or using a particular method of violence, tried to show that others had committed worse infractions, and often endeavored to minimize their personal interactions with Beria and his top lieutenants in specific situations, in general they did not deny that they engaged in beating arrestees and in falsifying testimony and confessions. Furthermore, there is a noticeable consistency across the testimonies about who was considered to be the most enthusiastic and the most brutal, a consensus about how certain investigators took particular pride in expressing their initiative, enthusiasm, and brutality.

THE FOURTH DEPARTMENT OF THE GEORGIAN
NKVD DURING THE GREAT TERROR

In 1937, the Fourth Department (Secret Political Division) investigators A. S. Khazan, assistant to Kobulov and head of the department's First Section; K. S. Savitskii, Khazan's First Section deputy head; and N. A. Krimian, head of the Second Section (for "particularly important cases") of the Fourth Department, were mid-level implementers in the Georgian NKVD. All three of them were tied, via Kobulov, into Beria's party and secret police network. According to the testimony of the former NKVD official V. N. Gul'st in 1953: "In 1937–38, Kobulov played a nefarious role. He began to sweep all potential rivals out of his way. Together with this, and in the same way, Kobulov paralyzed anybody who, in his opinion or that of his chief Beria, could obstruct them in their careerist and scheming intentions. For this goal Kobulov grouped around himself trusted people who could take on any dirty task: Savitskii, Krimian, and Khazan."[17]

Aleksandr Samoilovich Khazan was born in Odessa in 1906 to a white-collar (*iz sluzhashchikh*) Jewish family and had a higher education in jurisprudence. He began his career in the GPU in Odessa in 1928 and was recruited into the Georgian GPU in 1933 by Goglidze after losing his position as a teacher at the OGPU Higher School in Moscow (where he taught "History of the West," among other things), and despite having apparent ties with known Trotsky allies from early in his career.[18] He later admitted that he had a number of close relatives living in the United States, as well as an uncle who was a professor in Shanghai and with whom he supposedly corresponded. In 1935, the Attestation Commission of the USSR NKVD issued a decree demanding Khazan's removal on the grounds that he was "absolutely unsuited" to police work, but apparently Goglidze refused to fulfill this decree and instead promoted Khazan to head of the First Section of the Fourth Department. This point was brought up in the 1954 draft indictment against Khazan, Savitskii, and Krimian as evidence of clear protection of Khazan by Goglidze.[19] In 1937, Khazan was given a simultaneous appointment as assistant to Kobulov, and he became a party member at the beginning of 1938. Also in early January 1938, at the very height of the Great Terror, Khazan was arrested for using "provocative measure of investigation" (see below), and held for several months. A case was not brought against him, but he was removed from the NKVD in April 1938. During the war, in 1942, Khazan was brought back into the central apparatus of the USSR NKVD on the initiative of Kobulov but then removed in 1945, apparently on the orders of V. N. Merkulov. Following this, he worked in the Georgian Industrial Institute, as an instructor in the NKVD interregional school, and then as a legal consultant at Giproenergoprom in Moscow. In 1948, he authored a book (under the pseudonym Aleksandr Samoilovich Aleksandrov) titled *On the Moral Profile of a Soviet Person*, advising party propagandists about proper gender relations, duty to the family, and the dangers of dissolute behavior (a book referenced by Sheila Fitzpatrick in her *Remove the Masks*, perhaps without knowing that the author was a former NKVD interrogator, a further layer of the eponymous "masking"!).[20] He was arrested after the fall of the Beria group, on 29 September 1953.[21]

Konstantin Sergeevich Savitskii, an ethnic Russian, was born in Tashkent in 1905 to a minor noble family, the son of a tsarist army officer who apparently served with the Whites in the Russian Civil War before emigrating to Persia. Like Khazan, he had a higher education, having studied at Tashkent State University and the Leningrad Agricultural Institute. He graduated from the Central Asian Agricultural Institute in Tashkent in 1928. He distributed literature for the Political Administration of the Red Army on the Turkestan Front in 1919–1921 and worked for the publisher Kommunist of the Uzbekistan Central Committee in Samarkand in 1924–1925, the Uzbekistan Commissariat of Finance in 1925, the Krasnaia Gazeta printing house in Leningrad in 1925–1927, as a worker at the Elektrosila Station in Leningrad in 1927, and as an inspector of the Uzbekistan Commissariat of Trade in 1928–1931 before arriving in Tiflis and beginning his secret police career in the Georgian GPU in June 1931.[22] Like Khazan, Savitskii rose through the ranks of the Georgian NKVD in the 1930s under the tutelage of Kobulov and became a party member in 1939. Also like Khazan, Savitskii found himself sacked from active service in the NKVD in July 1939. He was recalled from active military duty on the front in 1941 by Kobulov and appointed deputy head of the Fourth Department of the USSR NKVD in Moscow. When Kobulov became USSR deputy commissar for internal affairs in 1943, he made Savitskii his personal secretary, although Savitskii was removed from service again, based on unspecified "compromising materials," in June 1946. Savitskii went with Kobulov to Germany after the war with the lucrative Main Administration for Soviet Property Abroad (GUMIMZ) from 1947 until March 1953.[23] During Beria's bid for power after Stalin's death in the spring of 1953, Savitskii was brought back to the Ministry of Internal Affairs by order of Beria as assistant to Kobulov, who was by then USSR first deputy minister of internal affairs. As the indictment read: "Thus all of Savitskii's advancement in service was the result of his closeness to Kobulov, who unfailingly through his career brought Savitskii along with him as his particularly trusted and reliable accomplice."[24] Savitskii was arrested on 27 June 1953, a day after Beria's arrest, and on the same day as his boss Kobulov.[25]

Nikita Arkad'evich Krimian, an ethnic Armenian, was born in 1913 in Kars, a territory in Turkey which at that time was part of the Russian Empire, to the family of a machinist. He graduated from a nine-year school in Vladikavkaz in 1928, and much later he received a higher education at the Ul'ianovsk Pedagogical Institute in 1949. After finishing primary school, Krimian worked first as a carpenter and an electrician in Vladikavkaz in 1925–1928, a carpenter at the International Cooperative in Tiflis in 1928–1930, the head of a state farm (*sovkhoz*) in rural Armenia and Azerbaijan in 1931, and then as an administrator at Zakenergo in Tiflis from December 1931 until July 1932. He joined the Economic Department of the Georgian GPU in Tiflis in 1932–1933 as a trainee (*praktikant*).[26] He served as an officer in the Transcaucasian GPU-NKVD from 1933 to 1935, became an operational officer and later senior operational officer of the Georgian NKVD and deputy head of the Second Section of the Fourth Department (*po osobo vazhnym delam*) from 1935 to 1937, then the head of the Second Division in 1938. He was apparently a close friend of Savitskii, in an environment where friendship was clearly not encouraged, and similarly rose quickly through the ranks of the NKVD in the 1930s. In his memoirs, Suren Gazarian, who had previously been deputy head of the Fourth Department of the Georgian NKVD, wrote, "In a strange and incomprehensible way, Krimian, a very young employee, soon took the leading position in an investigating group, together with Savitskii," despite having been implicated in an earlier embezzlement incident while in the Economic Department of the Georgian NKVD, for which he "was for some reason never tried."[27] The Transcaucasian secret police official V. N. Gul'st described Krimian as "an unscrupulous person, a falsifier—his only authority came from Kobulov."[28] Krimian became a party member in 1939, and with the ascent of Beria's group to the leadership of the USSR NKVD, he was promoted from Georgia to take over as head of the NKVD in L'viv following the Soviet seizure of Western Ukraine from Poland in 1940. In 1945, he became the secret police chief in Armenia, although he soon antagonized local party officials in 1947 and was demoted and finally sacked for provoking local conflicts in 1951. He was elected as a delegate to the second session of the USSR Supreme Soviet that served from 1946 to 1950. Following his removal from the secret police and until his arrest in September 1953, he worked as head of the Personnel Department of the Armenian SSR Ministry of Justice.[29]

In addition to these more mundane aspects of their professional backgrounds, all three—Khazan, Savitskii, and Krimian—were members of the Tbilisi Dinamo Sports Society, and apparently Savitskii and Krimian played professional football for the Tbilisi Dinamo team.[30] As the former Fourth Department deputy head Gazarian testified in 1954:

How did Krimian, Savitskii, and Khazan make their way into the organs of OGPU-NKVD? After the decision was taken via the line of the Dinamo Sport Society that players on the Dinamo football team should be OGPU-NKVD officers, then the mercenary footballers Savitskii, Abashidze, Pachulia, and certain others were registered for work in the NKVD. Even then, when there was an order from the USSR NKVD that only party members should be retained in operational departments, an exception was made for nonparty footballers.[31]

Both Savitskii and Krimian were sent to Erevan and Baku in 1937 to instruct local NKVD investigators there how to "work effectively" during investigations. In his memoirs, Gazarian referred to Savitskii and Krimian as "future big shots [zapravily] of the lawlessness of 1937," calling them "the first violins in that horrible orgy of lawlessness and arbitrariness."[32]

PRACTICING STALINISM IN THE GEORGIAN NKVD

The activities of Khazan, Savitskii, and Krimian in this period illustrate the functioning of Beria's network at the middle level within the Georgian NKVD. During the trial, they tried to emphasize that as mid-level investigators they had little direct interaction with Beria personally. Khazan later testified that he had been in Beria's office only three times during his career. Yet as first secretary of the Georgian Central Committee, Beria was kept informed on ongoing cases and frequently gave orders (sometimes directly, but usually through Kobulov and Goglidze), reviewed interrogation protocols, and wrote resolutions on them ordering the arrest of individuals mentioned in the confessions therein. Beria often visited the NKVD headquarters and prison in person, sometimes at night, apparently taking part personally in interrogating and beating detainees in Kobulov's office or in one set up for his own use at the NKVD. Goglidze stated during an interrogation in October 1953 that he received instructions from Beria on whom to arrest, which he usually passed on to Kobulov: "Most often such orders were fulfilled by Kobulov's subordinates—Savitskii, Khazan, Krimian, Urushadze, and some others working in the SPO [Fourth Department] of the Georgian NKVD."[33] Thus Beria's network took on a hierarchical structure of protection and responsibility. According to the head of the Tbilisi prison V. N. Okroshidze, Khazan, Savitskii, and Krimian "were part of the group of Kobulov and were particularly distinguished by their ferocity."[34]

Khazan, Savitskii, and Krimian gained a particular reputation for enthusiasm, energy, and brutality: "The greatest number of cases on party leaders and Soviet officials were run by Khazan, Savitskii, and Krimian," testified

Investigator Babalov.[35] "Particularly immense vigor in beating arrestees was demonstrated by First Section head Khazan and investigators Krimian and Savitskii," said Investigator Kvirkadze.[36] Former NKVD guard S. G. Kovshov testified that "the investigators Khazan, Krimian, Savitskii, and Paramonov were distinguished by particular cruelty; from them we always brought the arrestees out heavily beaten."[37] Gul'st testified: "I would characterize Savitskii, Khazan, Krimian, and Paramonov as close associates of Goglidze and Kobulov in retributions against Soviet citizens; they firmly gained 'glory' as 'specialists' in fabricating cases, in torturing, maiming, and destroying innocent people . . . they served as 'teachers' for other [NKVD] personnel in this."[38] Nadaraia stated: "Working as the head of the internal [NKVD] prison over the course of almost three years, I was myself witness to the beating of arrestees, I am aware that arrestees were systematically beaten very brutally . . . the organizers of all these abuses of arrestees and harsh beatings were Bogdan Kobulov, Konstantin Savitskii, Nikita Krimian, and Khazan. It was no coincidence that NKVD staff members said that [these four] could execute any innocent person."[39] Investigator Barskii testified that "Krimian and Savitskii showed great enthusiasm for their work, staying till five or six in the morning; therefore they were visible and had privileges within the leadership."[40] I. I. Margiev, an internal prison guard for the NKVD, testified that "if other investigators tried to conceal that they beat arrestees, Khazan to the contrary did it openly, with no shame at all."[41] According to multiple testimonies, Khazan, Savitskii, and Krimian beat arrestees even after they had been sentenced to be shot. Okroshidze testified that Krimian pulled a former Interior Ministry driver named Dvali, who had just been sentenced to execution and was handcuffed, out of a car and beat and stomped on him with his feet. Gul'st testified: "Savitskii, Krimian, Khazan, and Paramonov also practiced beating individuals sentenced to shooting before the sentence could be carried out, and they encouraged other investigators to do this." Savitskii testified that he had been instructed to do this by Beria: "Before seeing them off to that other world, beat their faces in," Beria supposedly told him. The 1955 indictment, however, maintained that "in implementing the beating of those sentenced to the death penalty before the shooting could be carried out, the accused Savitskii, Paramonov, and Krimian acted not as simple implementers of criminal orders of the enemy of the people Beria but committed these crimes on their own initiative, demonstrating particular brutality and forethought; this is confirmed by the testimony of a number of witnesses."[42] Khazan apparently shocked even his NKVD colleagues by allowing the underaged children of an arrestee to be put out on the street for several days before a grandmother came from a different town to collect them, and in one incident he insinuated that a fellow investigator had "antiparty leanings" because he reminded the team that according to the NKVD instructions they were to make arrangements for the underaged children of a group of wives of convicted "enemies" whom they had just arrested. "We must crush counterrevolution," Khazan shouted, "it's not our job to deal with children!"[43]

A rivalry emerged among the investigators in the Georgian NKVD in making more arrests and obtaining greater and more elaborate confessions, creating an additional incentive to make or sanction arrests on the basis of minimal evidence and to use violent means to coerce arrestees into naming further potential victims. "In this period among the investigators there developed an unbelievable competition," Vasil'ev testified, "to see who could gather more denunciations of new people and arrest them."[44] Savitskii himself testified that Beria and the top NKVD leaders especially valued receiving reports of supposed plots directed against them personally, so investigators tried to include such admissions in the protocols as often as possible.[45] As the former NKVD official L. F. Tsanava testified in 1953, "terror plots against Beria became so fashionable that it was preferred to have admissions by arrestees in every case of preparing a terrorist act against Beria ... The arrestees said what Kobulov wanted them to, and he would summon his assistants—Krimian, Khazan, Savitskii, Paramonov, and others—and divide up among them which confessions each arrestee should give, and they set to work. They beat the arrestees until they gave the confessions that Kobulov needed."[46] In so doing, the investigators demonstrated their effectiveness and loyalty to their superiors and were rewarded in turn with protection and with formal recognition as heroes in the struggle with counterrevolution. Both Khazan and Krimian were given, by order of Goglidze, the apartments and property in an NKVD apartment building of former colleagues whom they had arrested and interrogated.[47] As Aleksei Tepliakov observed, "officials who delivered 'high operational indicators' (i.e., a large number of concluded investigatory cases, as well as people recruited, arrested, [and] shot) were reliably protected by the status of a good operative [operativnik]; they frequently could get away with serious misconduct, and in the case of criminal investigation they could count on the leniency of the institutional court—the OGPU Collegium or that of the military tribunal."[48]

Fourth Department Deputy Head Sergo Davlianidze testified that despite the situation in which most NKVD staff were suspicious of one another, "they held binges at each other's apartments, with Khazan, Savitskii, Krimian, and [Fourth Department Secretary Anna] Milova."[49] "There was such a situation in the NKVD then that colleagues were afraid of each other and therefore did not share with one another," testified the former NKVD investigator Barskii.[50]

Khazan, Savitskii, and Krimian, as heads of sections, were formally lower in rank than Davlianidze, who directly oversaw the department's fourth through seventh divisions. Yet their sections answered directly to Kobulov, bypassing Davlianidze, so the lines of subordination were not so clear. "Khazan, Krimian, and Savitskii in 1937 had greater authority than Davlianidze, and maybe he was afraid to speak with them and all the more so to protest, these were my observations," Davlianidze's former subordinate A. G. Galavanov testified.[51] "[They] should have been subordinates of Davlianidze, but in reality they were in a privileged position that no one understood, and I think Davlianidze himself was afraid of them," Galavanov also stated.[52] Investigator Babalov testified that "Savitskii, Krimian, [and] Khazan were close and trusted people of Kobulov, and Beria knew them; they were entrusted with handling the investigation of the most important cases. They were the physical implementers for dealing with those who were inconvenient for Beria . . . Savitskii and Krimian particularly excelled in using various methods of investigation on the arrestees."[53] According to Rudenko's 1954 draft indictment, "To protect [their fellow] conspirators from exposure, Beria, Goglidze, and Kobulov intentionally altered the usual practice of reviewing compromising materials received about NKVD officials in the apparatus of the Special Inspectorate [Upolnomochennyi], and instead they gave this assignment personally to Khazan." Krimian himself gave testimony about Khazan in which he stated:

> Khazan was Kobulov's right hand; he set the tone for the use of repression and was particularly trusted by Goglidze and Kobulov, and he even exerted a certain influence over them; all of the [NKVD] personnel thought of Khazan as a frightful falsifier [strashnyi lipach] and were afraid of him. He said about any investigator who was not able to get "usable" confessions or who didn't adequately use repression that "It seems that they sympathize with the Trotskyites and are linked with them." Khazan was apparently given the right to prepare criminal cases against NKVD personnel with the goal of accusing them of committing counterrevolutionary crimes.[54]

According to the 1954 draft indictment, Khazan allegedly made use of this authority to accuse any NKVD officials who refused to participate in falsifying cases and or beating arrestees of "liberalism and aiding the enemy," and he "declared as an enemy anybody who behaved disrespectfully toward him personally."[55] Khazan was thus tasked by Kobulov and Goglidze, together with Savitskii and Krimian, with collecting compromising materials on other NKVD personnel and investigating "counterrevolution" within the apparatus of the Georgian NKVD, an authority that Khazan began to press too far.[56] The former NKVD investigator Barskii later testified, "if anybody nodded to

Khazan or asked 'How are things?' he would conclude that they were interested in cases on rightists and Trotskyites and would immediately make a note in the observation file of that colleague."[57] Gul'st testified, "The [NKVD] officials and I personally were afraid to catch his eye, so as not to find ourselves considered members of anti-Soviet groups or plotters."[58] Another former colleague, G. A. Movsesov, testified that "I and other NKVD personnel saw in Khazan a dangerous person, able to arrest any coworker, enjoying colossal support from Goglidze and Kobulov."[59]

THE ARREST AND RELEASE OF KHAZAN, JANUARY–APRIL 1938

Apparently either as the result of pressure from colleagues because of this behavior or because arrestees in Khazan's charge were mentioning names of important officials, on 31 January 1938, a few days after a Central Committee plenum acknowledged that "mistakes" had been made in the investigations of party members, Goglidze ordered the arrest of Khazan.[60] Khazan was ultimately protected from criminal responsibility by Kobulov, with the support of Goglidze, released from arrest in April 1938, and only removed from operational NKVD work. During the war, in 1942, again with support from Goglidze and Kobulov, Beria brought Khazan into the central NKVD apparatus in Moscow, although in 1945, on the decision of V. N. Merkulov, he was sent to the reserves because of continuing rumors about his earlier association with Trotsky supporters.

The arrest of Khazan in early 1938, at the very height of the Terror, for using methods of investigation and interrogation that were entirely commonplace by that time among NKVD investigators, is arguably illustrative of the environment of mutual suspicion, competition, and also of patronage and protection in the organization, perhaps mirroring those in society as a whole. The arrest order, signed by Goglidze, specifies that "Senior Lieutenant Khazan undertook absolutely unacceptable methods of investigation, which as a result can lead to the discrediting of honest Soviet citizens . . . he continued to ignore orders, criminally making use of his position and opportunities . . . he in fact became a weapon in the hands of enemies and a megaphone for their provocations to discredit [the NKVD]." While personally conducting the investigations of cases on former NKVD officials, he "failed to draw the necessary conclusions for himself, and with false exhortations about Bolshevik vigilance he tried to insure himself." He was ordered to be removed from his position in the NKVD, and the operational personnel "should draw the essential practical conclusions from this."[61]

On 18 February, Khazan gave testimony about his relatives living abroad:

his sister Rozalia Isaakson, his father's brother Ralph Henry, his mother's brother David Morin, and two other relatives, L. and R. Henry, all living in the United States; his mother's sister in Romania, and his uncle in China, presumably the rumored professor in Shanghai. Some of his family members in the USSR continued to correspond with these relatives abroad and even received monetary support from them.[62] Khazan wrote several appeals to the leadership in which he emphasized his successes in important investigations and in uncovering Trotskyite and rightist plots and preventing assassination attempts on Soviet leaders. Khazan attributed his mistakes to overwork:

> It should not be forgotten that I was handling all these cases, together with ten or so more, over the course of 10–11 days in January [1938] . . . I won't conceal that the operational work was tense and the conditions harsh from 1935 until the beginning of 1937 . . . and the unyielding work during the course of 1937 seriously wore down my previous enthusiasm and my moderation in investigation. Impatience appeared, a straining to get results more quickly and easily; attention to detail and scrupulous adherence to proper conduct with the arrestees weakened. At the same time, because of our successes with the terrorist center, its terrorist organizations, the rightist and reserve centers, the counterrevolutionary plot in the NKVD and so forth, I experienced a certain "dizziness" [golovokruzhenie]. It began to seem to me that one could always achieve the complete destruction of counterrevolutionary organizations by being decisive and that I could always weed out the truth from slander. At the same time, an excessive suspiciousness developed in me. Any material coming in compelled me to seek out deeper roots.[63]

Goglidze's letter to Beria on 1 April 1938 explaining Khazan's release was mostly exculpatory:

> Khazan used provocative methods in the course of conducting investigations in the cases of arrested participants of counterrevolutionary formations, which allowed the arrestees to bring complaints against some of the leading officials. But his actions in investigatory cases did not bear an intentionally criminal character and were the resort of an unserious attitude toward the possible consequences of the use of provocative methods of work. Considering that Khazan understands the character of the mistakes that he made, and the two months that he spent under arrest, it is considered possible to limit the punishment and free him from incarceration, to remove him from the organs of the NKVD and use him for economic or Soviet work.[64]

Davlianidze stated that "it was characteristic that in searching Khazan's office after he was arrested, a special card index [kartoteka] and log books [*formuliary*] were found literally on all the personnel of the NKVD of Georgia, on some of the cards there were no notes, only some kind of incomprehensible marks."[65] Khazan's deputy D. Tvarchelidze similarly described Khazan's suspiciousness and eagerness to accuse his colleagues, especially if they dared to suggest criticism of him.[66] In the paranoid environment of the Georgian NKVD of late 1937 and early 1938, Khazan's vigorous insinuations about his NKVD colleagues and his perceived status as having a free rein to investigate and accuse them seems to have pushed Davlianidze—already hostile toward the team of Khazan, Savitskii, and Krimian and suspicious of their class backgrounds—to take advantage of Kobulov's temporary absence to strike first against Khazan by submitting a denunciation.[67] Davlianidze was most likely not alone in his hostility. As he stated: "after the arrest of Khazan all the officials expected that he would be tried for his provocative methods of investigation, but this did not happen. After some time, all the personnel were gathered and read the order of Goglidze on removing Khazan from his position from the organs; this decision of Goglidze caused indignation among all those present." He probably expressed the shared view of many of his colleagues in stating that "personally I think that this incorrect decision [to free Khazan] was because Goglidze and Kobulov were protecting him; it is known that Khazan worked under the direction of Kobulov and fulfilled his instructions and those of Goglidze, and that his full exposure through an investigation was not in their interests, so the case was covered up [*smazano*], and everything ended only with Khazan being removed from the organs."[68] Most likely Khazan's mistake was not the use of excessive and illegal methods, but rather that he had gone too far in extracting (and documenting) confessions on important figures close to Beria and his network. Khazan himself testified in June 1955 that "in 1937, I received testimony, statements in relation to the criminal actions of those close to Beria, Kobulov, Goglidze; I started cases on them. At the end of January 1938 I took the statement of [the NKVD official] S. I. Kugel' on the leadership of Merkulov, Rapava, and Stepanov in anti-Soviet work, for which I was immediately arrested and removed from the organs of the NKVD."[69] An excerpt from the September 1955 court hearing from the file on A. N. Rapava includes the following exchange:

Rudenko: Why were you arrested earlier?

Khazan: I was arrested on 31 January 1938 and accused of using incorrect methods of investigation to force innocent people to incriminate themselves.[70] I should say that at the time many other officials of the NKVD should have been arrested and tried and not only me for the falsification of files and illegal methods of investigation.

Rudenko: Were you beaten during the investigation?

Khazan: No.

Rudenko: Why not?

Khazan: I don't know. [NKVD Special Investigator Mirian] Kerkadze promised to use means of physical coercion on me, but he did not implement his threats. *Laughter in the hall.*

Rudenko: More concretely, what were you accused of?

Khazan: That I got testimony from Kugel' against Kobulov and Merkulov. *Laughter in the hall.*[71]

Kobulov, interrogated in August 1953, stated, "regarding Khazan, I was myself very cautious and took his proposals critically, because I had signals that, not knowing the concrete conditions in Georgia, he made mistakes in evaluating various political events and consequently the individuals taking part in them," implying that Kobulov also thought that Khazan had simply gone too far in the kind of testimony that he was soliciting.[72] The former NKVD and party official (and Beria client) Solomon Mil'shtein testified that "to create the impression of themselves as 'ceaseless fighters with enemies of the people,' Kobulov and Goglidze under the leadership of Beria fabricated cases of 'terrorists,' and to present themselves at the same time as devotees of legality, they made a show of arresting the 'falsifier' [*lipach*] Khazan, who a short time later quietly left his position."[73] The court officer and memoirist N. G. Smirnov commented that Khazan's arrest resulted from the fact that he had exceeded his brief and obtained confessions (directly or indirectly) incriminating the Beria loyalists Rapava, Merkulov, and Kobulov: "Naturally, these individuals could not make peace with the fact that there was incriminating testimony on them; real power was in their hands, and Khazan was arrested 'just in case.' But he was 'their guy,' and after only several months of being held in detention he was released."[74] Thus Khazan had to face some consequences as a signal to rival groupings among the NKVD staff, but at the same time he was too closely connected with Kobulov, Goglidze, and ultimately Beria to be unmasked as an "enemy of the people," as was taking place with so many others at the same time.[75]

A MULTILAYERED MOSAIC OF MOTIVATIONS

As Lynne Viola has pointed out, "more fully comprehending the perpetrator may ultimately increase our understanding of the nature of state violence. The question of why individuals . . . acted as they did in the implementation of state repression against officially labeled enemies, mainly innocent people, is a central question in ongoing efforts to fathom the mass violence of the Stalin era."[76] Understanding the NKVD investigators' actions requires considering a combination of factors and their complex interaction in the conditions of the highly fluid and volatile circumstances in the Georgian NKVD and the USSR in 1937–1938: the societal context, including the legacy of large-scale violence and trauma of war, revolution, and civil conflict over the preceding decades, as well as the societal positioning of the secret police investigators in relation to their victims; the specific institutional environment within the NKVD, such as the performance expectations, systems of reward and sanction, internal competition, peer pressure, and cohort cohesion, as well as the ways in which the institution conveyed the sanction of the state and society for the violence; and finally the attitudes and understanding of self among the investigators, how they individually understood the discourse behind the violence and internalized the ideology and exhortations of the regime in the name of which they acted.

SITUATION AND AGENCY

Khazan, Savitskii, and Krimian were formally charged with the political crime of counterrevolution (under article 58) in being accomplices in Beria's plots to undermine the Soviet state and economy, yet clearly the thrust of the prosecution's case was not counterrevolutionary intentions or involvement in conspiracy but willfully and knowingly engaging in a degree of violence that was compromising for the party and state. Ultimately the prosecutors sought to demonstrate not so much what the perpetrators did but the zeal with which they did it. There were almost always documented orders from superiors, so therefore the prosecution aimed to show that the accused were worse than lawbreakers; they were bad people and a harmful element, as demonstrated by their vigor, enthusiasm, and viciousness in carrying out those orders. The accused perpetrators could rightly argue that they were unaware of any conspiracies, and that their intentions had never been counterrevolutionary. One can sense the inevitable frustration with the paradox of the situation in which they were being tried and punished for those very actions that they had earlier been encouraged to commit by that very same authority. In testimony from 1955, Khazan expressed this paradox directly:

> [The order to use repressive methods] put me and all the NKVD personnel
> into a terrible position. In 1937, the NKVD leadership made it mandatory,
> as they told us, to beat arrestees on the orders of the higher organs. To refuse
> this was seen as enemy counterrevolutionary work, and now, after many

years, for the implementation of this very directive, you are accused of coun-terrevolutionary crime.[77]

Despite vociferously denying the official political charges to the end, Khazan, Savitskii, and Krimian freely admitted to being guilty of those things for which they were tacitly being prosecuted, of beating arrestees to extract false confessions, and of negligence in conducting cases and signing orders, leading to the baseless sentencing and execution of hundreds of innocent people. As with the stories of "ordinary men" among the perpetrators of other acts of mass violence in a variety of different historical settings, the case of Khazan, Savitskii, and Krimian hints at an unsettling aspect of human nature: in sit-uations such as those in which these investigators found themselves, where violence is enabled by contextual conditions, encouraged by the absence of accountability and a lowering of thresholds to violence, and justified by a pre-vailing ideology, a certain number of people will exercise their own agency to engage in such violence and unquestioningly do what they feel is expected of them. Yet the relationship between situation and agency in Stalinist society requires further unpacking.

ECOSYSTEM OF VIOLENCE

Viola has characterized early Soviet history as a continuation of the "unfin-ished" civil war that began in 1918, an ongoing ethos of conflict and violence that contributed to the context in which the state violence of 1937–1938 must be understood.[78] We have only sparse information about the early lives of Khazan, Savitskii, and Krimian, no evidence of traumatic experiences in their autobiographies during the earlier cataclysmic events of the period. All three were born between 1905 and 1913 and were too young to have been directly involved in World War I as combatants. Krimian was born in Kars in 1913, and while his biography as a deputy of the USSR Supreme Soviet in 1946 stated that both his parents "were killed while fleeing from Kars during the time of the mass killings of Armenians [in 1915]," his party documents attest that his mother died in 1934.[79] Savitskii was in the Red Army as a propagandist during the Civil War in Turkestan, though we know little further about his role or experiences there, or about the Civil War experiences of Khazan and Krimian (at which time all three were children or teenagers). All three became part of the secret police in Georgia in the early 1930s; there is no mention of involve-ment in the collectivization campaigns of the late 1920s and early 1930s or in suppressing insurrections; indeed, as discussed below, none of them seemed to have engaged in violent measures in their secret police careers prior to the

Terror (and in their appeals after their convictions they claimed that they committed no further violent acts after 1938).[80]

SOCIAL STATUS AND BEHAVIOR MODELING

Considerations of self-esteem and conformity within organizations and peer groups are common factors in other cases of mass violence: how perpetrators are held in the eyes of their comrades, considerations of toughness, doing one's share, acting as a good comrade; and conversely, the risks of isolation, rejection, and ostracism and the fear of the moral reproach of comrades make it easier to engage in violent acts than it might be to demur.[81] To such individual and group psychological factors may be added the relationship between the perpetrators and their victims and the unequal balances of power and status in the circumstances of 1937–1938. Like many of the Georgian NKVD personnel, Khazan, Krimian, and Savitskii were outsiders in Tbilisi—not ethnic Georgians, lacking family connections, prestige, or other forms of social capital in the very status-conscious environment of the Georgian capital of the late 1930s.[82] A most dangerous imbalance of authority and esteem may have obtained when the NKVD investigators found themselves in a position of unrestrained power over arrestees who until very recently had considered themselves to be the investigators' social betters. This, together with a perceived absence of accountability, most likely also contributed to the zeal with which the NKVD personnel dealt with the formerly high-ranking Transcaucasian and Georgian party officials and their spouses and the respected intellectuals and professionals who made up a significant proportion of the victims. Many of these belonged to the "Old Bolshevik" group that rivalled Beria's secret police cohort for control of the Caucasian party network.[83] Khazan and Savitskii were unusual among the NKVD personnel not only as nonlocals but also for having a higher education; most in the secret police had only a secondary or incomplete secondary education. Thus they may have additionally felt a sense of being undervalued by a Party and social elite that associated them with the stereotype of Beria's police group as unsophisticated and semiliterate toughs from the Transcaucasian provinces, tensions that clearly underlay the political conflict between the older party elites and Beria's upstart clients.[84] The involvement of Savitskii and Krimian as players on the NKVD-affiliated Tbilisi Dinamo football team may have contributed both to their sense of team camaraderie as chekists and to their sensitivity regarding their perceived prestige.

Furthermore, the situation in the Georgian NKVD over the course of the Terror was anything but static, instead shifting and evolving. In their testimony and memoirs, the perpetrators often described how they learned of the party directives obliging them to use violence and their first experiences of witnessing such violence being implemented in practice. A number of the Georgian NKVD officials were adamant in their testimony that they did not use beatings and torture prior to 1937.[85] During his interrogation in 1953, Krimian described hearing that Beria "gave the order to use measures of physical coercion" and recalled his shock at first seeing prisoners beaten in front of him in his superiors' offices:

> Partially opening the door [to Davlianidze's office], I was met by the following scene: an arrestee lay on the floor near Davlianidze's desk while the latter, leaning with his hands on the desk, was stomping on him with his feet. Several other investigators in the office were also taking part in the beating. This made such an impression on me that I was bewildered [ia rasterialsia]. Arrestees were also being beaten in other offices. The next day Kobulov explained Beria's instruction to me, Savitskii, and other officers who had been absent [during Beria's meeting]. Davlianidze beat arrestees particularly sadistically; he and Kobulov demonstrated the use of active measures of physical coercion on arrestees.[86]

Krimian may have been exaggerating his sensitivity, but what we see here is perhaps the need for this violent behavior to be "modeled" and thus normalized within the institutional context of the NKVD. In the same way that sociological theories about crowd violence suggest that riots may begin with the actions of a very small number of individuals, gradually through observation and imitation such behavior becomes normalized and thus more acceptable in the group. The thresholds to previously unacceptable behavior become reduced: to be the first person to throw a rock through a store window is a very different thing from being the thirty-first.[87] Mass state violence may resemble the dynamics of crowd violence in slow motion, with the majority taking cues and modeling their behavior on that minority with lower thresholds to violence; beating arrestees and falsifying confessions became normalized, routine, and an expected mode of behavior.[88]

PATRONAGE AND THE INSTITUTIONAL CULTURE OF THE GEORGIAN NKVD

Given the hypercompetitive atmosphere in the Georgian NKVD in 1937–1938, in which investigators were encouraged to produce grandiose results rapidly and in great quantity, the institutional environment within the organization created its own inertia. A climate of denunciations and paranoia had obtained in the Soviet secret police before the start of the Terror, since at least the early 1930s. As Aleksei Tepliakov has observed:

> Departments of cadres in the chekist structures and party organizations were
> flooded with an enormous quantity of denunciations from personnel. The
> denunciation, in essence, was one of the most important regulators of intra-
> institutional relations. The composing of "signals" was encouraged by the
> leadership. The mania for vigilance and the desire to curry favor through the
> demonstration of heightened vigilance, the wish to undermine a colleague, to
> frame and slander him stimulated the "composers" [of such denunciations]. . . .
> Both the bosses and the rank-and-file chekists felt themselves vulnerable cogs
> in the merciless machine, and they feared one another: the boss could easily
> arrest a regular chekist, but, on the other hand, he could find himself a target
> of some kind of clever denunciation.[89]

The protection of a patron in the leadership was critical, conveying a sense of
empowerment together with an absence of any further sense of transparency
or accountability.[90] The investigators' mutual rivalry and suspicion, combined
with the fact that violent behavior was the criteria on which they were evaluated, encouraged them to do everything possible to facilitate more and more
arrests, obtain dramatic confessions, and use any brutal methods and procedural shortcuts necessary. The investigators learned very quickly what behavior was rewarded and what was sanctioned in a situation of constant mutual
suspicion and paranoia. In the postwar trials of Einsatzgruppen members in
Germany, the perpetrators often argued that they had to commit violence lest
they become victims themselves, yet they were not able to demonstrate that
this would have been the case. In the Stalinist NKVD, however, operatives
seem to have legitimately feared that expressions of softness could be grounds
for suspicion and arrest. As N. M. Rukhadze, then the NKVD head in Gagra,
told his deputy Vasil'ev in July 1937, "he who doesn't beat is himself an enemy
of the people," and expressions of "mercifulness" (*miloserdie*) would be viewed
as aiding and abetting enemies of the people.[91] According to Savitskii's testimony, in early 1937 Beria gathered all the NKVD division and regional heads
for a meeting at the building of the Georgian Central Committee in Tbilisi to
berate them for their passivity in conducting arrests. Beria used the Ozurgeti
region as an example of poor work, and when the district head argued that
he had arrested twenty-eight Trotskyites, Beria shouted back, "You'll be the
twenty-ninth because you're arresting so few!"[92]

Moreover, acquiring a reputation within the Georgian NKVD as a particularly enthusiastic, "vigilant," and ruthless investigator could simultaneously
be useful in several regards: gaining and maintaining support from supervisors; winning peer acknowledgment and approval among fellow investigators;
and intimidating and discouraging potential rivals among NKVD peers who

might be tempted to bring accusations and denunciations against the officer in question. In the same way that a new inmate in a violent prison might try to enhance his own safety by encouraging an aura of somebody too crazy or dangerous to "mess with," so too the NKVD operatives' reputations may have served as a kind of branding intended to convey that taking advantage of them might be excessively costly.

SUBJECTIVITY AND IMPOSTURE

The role of ideology, belief, and attitudes toward authority must also be taken into consideration. As Christopher Browning has pointed out, there is an inevitable overlap of values with situations, and the relationship among authority, belief, and action is both complex and constantly changing.[93] Together with typical arguments of fulfilling orders from above, the perpetrators in their interrogations and appeals often referred to the mentality (or spirit) of the times within the NKVD and in Soviet society, an appeal to what has more recently been characterized as "Stalinist subjectivity."[94] This approach emphasizes intentions and motivations to action in the historical context of Stalinist society, the ways in which the regime incorporated the population through policies of social identification and mobilization, and in which the population "internalized" the discourse of the regime. Given the exigencies of the period, Sergo Davlianidze emphasized that he fundamentally believed in the urgency of the struggle with "class enemies" and their agents and that his orders were correct and morally justified: "As measures dictated by the spirit of the times and its demands, in connection with the critical situation for the USSR both domestically and internationally and the nearness of war of the capitalist country against the USSR, neither I nor others at that time had any basis at all not to believe in the leadership."[95] The authority of the Party and NKVD leadership, together with the constant and all-embracing campaigns against enemies and wreckers, created a situation in which an average person could not help but subject herself to the dominant narrative:

> Former People's Commissar Ezhov was second secretary of the Central Committee of the CPSU, and we believed in him. There were orders from Ezhov to use force, and I, like everybody else, was under an imaginary psychosis [*pod mnimym psikozom*]. Now, of course, I view everything through different eyes. But then all the instruction manuals, literature, newspapers, and articles screamed of counterrevolution, and through this they made us into obedient automatons.[96]

Khazan described being "swept up by a mania" that led him to see a not-yet-unmasked enemy in the face of every person, to believe that all his actions were "summoned by the necessity to destroy as quickly as possible the fifth column in the USSR."[97] Khazan denied using torture—which in this context seems to have meant "special measures" such as whips, boards, hot and cold isolation cells, means other than simply beating with fists—and claimed that because he lacked the physical strength of other NKVD colleagues he rarely did the actual beating himself, instead summoning local subordinates to do this. But he admitted to using regular beatings during interrogations "over the course of 6–7 months on the orders of Kobulov, and I used these beatings in the attempt to uncover a genuine enemy underground, in conjunction with that accursed directive [from the Party and Beria] that they declared to us." Beria was so exalted in 1937 "that I was obliged according to the orders and directives of the NKVD issued after the Decree of the Presidium of the Supreme Soviet of the USSR of 1 December 1934 to prevent by any means all the terroristic intentions directed against Beria . . . in 1937 I was inspired by the directives of the Party for struggle with enemies of the people."[98] The all-encompassing and ceaseless nature of the regime's discourse of threat and danger suggest that there is more to this for the investigators than simply an instrumental argument for self-justification: the discourse seems to have fundamentally shaped their categories of thinking and view of reality. This can only have been reinforced by the "discursive" element, the internalization of the unremittingly propagated ideology of class struggle and the fear and threat of counterrevolutionary enemy activity and wrecking. During the Terror, calls for vigilance and decisiveness echoed from all corners. As the "sword and shield" of the Party and state, the NKVD investigators saw themselves as the last line of defense against subhuman enemies of the people. The investigators seem to have deeply internalized this view and to have believed that the threats were genuine and the conspiracies and crimes to which their victims confessed were real, even as they themselves were fabricating these very confessions. As Savitskii and Khazan told Paramonov in 1937, "if an arrestee does not confess to terroristic activity, then he has simply not yet been fully unmasked."[99] Perhaps one of the most compelling pieces of evidence for the significance of worldview comes from an appeal written by one of the victims, the party member G. D. Dolidze, shortly before his execution. In his final words, Dolidze pointed out the absurdity of the system of using violence to compel testimony that was likely to be false. Yet he exculpated his torturers: "Our investigators are not guilty of anything; they are subordinated to this vicious system of investigation; they are firmly convinced ahead of time that the people they are interrogating are enemies of the people."[100]

There are clearly limitations to the "subjectivist" argument in its more extreme form: that the rhetoric of the party-state created an inescapable worldview encompassing all Stalinist subjects. Yet this approach may be particularly useful in understanding the NKVD perpetrators. Moreover, as we know from psychological theories of cognitive dissonance, people's values and worldviews are fluid and adaptive to situations, such that when their actions contradict their values and beliefs, they begin to change what they believe. The fact of perpetration of violence in itself perhaps thus adds additional impulse to the internalization of ideology and discourse: once one has begun committing previously unthinkable acts of violence in the name of a particular rhetoric, the greater one feels the need to internalize and to believe the rhetoric justifying the behavior.

An additional factor that is well illustrated in the cases of Khazan, Savitskii, and Krimian—and one that perhaps transcends and links together the environmental, psychological, and "subjectivity" explanations—is the phenomenon of "imposture." As Sheila Fitzpatrick has pointed out, a key aspect of revolutions is the need for individuals to reinvent themselves and find new modes of self-presentation. At the same time, the regime feared that its opponents could use such reinvention as a means of concealment. The drive for "vigilance" to expose such hidden enemies and other manipulative "careerists" became a particular motif during the Terror. As Fitzpatrick observed, "identifying and exposing such enemies became one of the cardinal virtues of a communist," and a core task of an NKVD investigator.[101] Yet Khazan and Savitskii clearly had highly compromising elements in their own biographies: Khazan's associations with active Trotsky supporters in the 1920s and his many relatives abroad; Savitskii's aristocratic background and his tsarist officer father, who apparently fought in the White Army and then went into emigration in Persia. These were things that in fact became at least temporary obstacles to the careers of both, as their boss Davlianidze, the deputy head of the Fourth Department, reported them to his superiors for this as soon as he was appointed in July 1937. These rumors and Davlianidze's reporting of them (other NKVD staff might have reported on them as well) seem to have played a role in Khazan's arrest in 1938 and his removal from the NKVD (until he was later reinstated by Kabulov). Davlianidze also claimed to be responsible for Savitskii's "unmasking" and removal from the NKVD in 1939, when he passed on a letter of denunciation that he claimed to have received from the head of the Intelligence Department of the Headquarters of the Transcaucasian Military District, Colonel Semenov, about Savitskii's father serving as an instructor in an Iranian military school.[102] It is undoubtedly a paradox that with such biographies, which in the context of 1937–1938 could easily be grounds for exposure and condemnation, Khazan and Savitskii were given the job of violently extracting or inventing exactly such "double-dealing" on the part of arrestees on a daily basis. Although perhaps not as extreme as in the cases of Khazan and Savitskii, Krimian was also concealing potentially damaging information from his past. Krimian wrote in a statement after the trial in September 1955 that as a young trainee in the Economic Department of the Georgian GPU in 1932–1933, he had served as assistant to the department head Mikhail Ivanovich Goriachev, during which time "over the course of almost two years I was like a foster child to him, as he had no children of his own." In 1937, while on official travel to Moscow, Goriachev was arrested by the USSR NKVD. Beria and Goglidze arranged for his transfer to Tbilisi to the authority of the Georgian NKVD, as well as for the arrest of Goriachev's wife. "This caused me alarm," Krimian wrote, not out of a sense of filial piety but rather because "I feared that given the system of interrogations that existed at that time, Goriachev and his wife might be subjected to beating and, considering my closeness with him in the past, they might identify me as one of their connections." Fortunately for Krimian, the case was assigned to Savitskii with orders to keep it very quiet, according to Savitskii because while in Moscow Goriachev had given testimony incriminating Beria.[103]

These cases perhaps represent simply a particularly acute variant of something experienced by the vast majority of Soviet subjects in the Stalin era. Most people manipulated their autobiographies in one way or another to emphasize the positive and downplay or conceal the potentially harmful. This was not necessarily merely an exercise in self-interested manipulation but rather a part of a desire to fit in, to be accepted as part of the larger revolutionary project, both by the bureaucracies that made the crucial decisions and (consciously or unconsciously) by the individuals themselves. The "unmasking" of enemies all around them perhaps chimed with people's inevitable sense of imposture buried deep within themselves and paralleled doubts that they may have felt about the problems that they encountered in daily life and the ways in which the real world failed to match the propagandized version: there was an enemy within all of us, waiting to be unmasked. As Malte Griesse has put it, a sense of doubt became pervasive throughout society from top to bottom as the "gap between discursive representation and material reality," a "subjective counterpart to the obscurity of taboo and the negation of many troubling aspects of reality."[104] One can imagine that NKVD investigators experienced a particularly large amount of such troubling aspects of reality, as well as few illusions about the consequences should either doubts or the "enemy within" be brought to the surface.

Clearly in the case of Khazan, Savitskii, and Krimian, as in the other recent studies of NKVD perpetrators during the Great Terror, the subjects' motivations are complex and must be understood through exploring the societal context, the institutional environment, and the individual's understanding of the discourse of the regime and their role within it. These particular examples shed light on the mechanisms of acculturation to the institutional environment within the NKVD and how the need for violence was modeled and conveyed at specific moments from 1937 in the Georgian NKVD; the role peer pressure, anxiety, and ambition in the competition to produce the results that brought reward, recognition, and protection from the bosses, together with the mutually reinforcing nature of clientalistic networks in providing both protection and further motivation; the gratification offered by the exercise of the power derived from position and a perceived absence of accountability; the belief that behavior was morally sanctioned, as well of the impossibility of imagining that they would one day be prosecuted for it by the same party and state that had ordered and encouraged them to undertake these very actions; an internalization of the transformational ideology of the regime and the rhetoric of the omnipresent existential threat of a fifth column; and last, the sense of imposture that both compelled the investigators to "excel" at the task before them and pushed down and reconstituted the inevitable doubts they must have experienced about themselves and their place in the discourse of the regime.

As with the findings of other studies of the Soviet secret police during this period, we find it difficult to isolate which of the factors in this mosaic of motivations are especially pivotal in the cases of Khazan, Savitskii, and Krimian or even to establish a clear hierarchy of causality among them. What we have hoped to accomplish with this case study is to add nuance to the understanding of the interaction of these factors in the Stalinist context. While in their recent works examining the trials of NKVD officials in Ukraine in 1939–1941, both Marc Junge and Lynne Viola emphasize the importance of understanding the Stalinist perpetrators in the context of their time and place in the larger society as well as the importance of situational factors, both have criticized the applicability of the "ordinary men" concept to Soviet cases. The NKVD was an elite organization in Stalinist society in positions of unusual power, an avant-garde, they point out, and its investigators viewed themselves as "the leading element" of Soviet society.[105] In the words of Viola: "[The NKVD officials] were trained in the ways of violence both historically through their participation in the Russian civil war or the collectivization campaigns and in the course of the mass operations." Those who did not have such training or experience were nonetheless "products of Soviet education."[106] Junge similarly argues that it cannot be demonstrated on the basis of the documentary evidence that ideology played a role in motivating the chekists, since in his view Marxist ideology is not inherently misanthropic in the way that Nazi ideology was.[107] Junge agrees that the "overheated atmosphere" resulting from the tumultuous Stalinist reconstruction of society and the economy and the sense of internal and external threat contained in the "psychology of civil war" were significant, but he nonetheless argues that "as a result of this there did not take place the systematic dehumanization of victims through their deindividualization and assignment to one or another category, as was characteristic of National Socialism."[108] Viola concludes that within the context of local conditions the investigators applied "a constrained or limited agency exercised within temporal and functional parameters that made them masters (as it were, little dictators) of their own domain and anything but ordinary men in the eyes of their victims."[109]

Part of this discussion seems to hinge on the definition of "ordinary" in the context of mass state violence. Surely in all such cases the perpetrators find themselves in a disproportionate position of power vis-à-vis their victims at the moment the crimes are being committed. The personal and career histories of Khazan, Savitskii, and Krimian seem to clearly show that none of them were at all predestined for work as investigators, nor did their previous experience or career trajectories endow them with any prestigious stature. All three held a variety of unrelated occupations before finding themselves in the secret police, and in the case of Khazan and Savitskii certain unfavorable elements of their biographies, as discussed above, made becoming a secret police investigator a somewhat unlikely outcome. Although the evidence is scant, none of them seem to have been directly involved in or trained for violence in their careers prior to 1937. They were doubtlessly "products of Soviet education," but so was the rest of the Soviet population by that time. This brings us to what we hope is the most significant conclusion of the present study, that the application of the "subjectivity" and "imposture" concepts from Soviet historiography can allow us to make use of the insights of the "ordinary men"—those concerning in-group dynamics, peer acknowledgment, and particularly the interrelationship between ideology and belief forged through action—in understanding the NKVD perpetrators by placing them in the particular context of Stalinist society. The most perceptive criticism of the "ordinary man" approach is that it can be "ahistorical" or "transhistorical," positing a psychological explanation devoid of time and place. The "subjectivity" approach helps us understand how the perpetrators internalized the rhetoric of the regime—ideology not in the sense of the textbook academic precepts of Marxism, but rather in the sense of a worldview that demanded extreme action in defense of the revolution—in ways that served both as motivation for action and as justification for it.[110] The "imposture" approach helps explain how the subjects reconciled the inconsistencies in their own backgrounds, including some that were potentially catastrophically dangerous, in ways that contributed to their extreme and violent personas as chekists, even while the mental categorization of arrestees as "enemies of the people" did in fact allow them to systematically dehumanize their victims. Both of these approaches situate the perpetrators as Stalinist subjects and part of Stalinist society, "ordinary" in the sense that they differed from other Soviet citizens, if fundamentally at all, then more in degree than in kind. The "ordinary men" approach, in turn, elucidates how committing violent acts compels the internalization of the rhetoric in the name of which the acts are committed, the mechanism through which action forms belief and vice versa. Moreover, this insight can perhaps suggest a means of intersection between "subjectivity" and "imposture," often posited as opposite and mutually incompatible approaches—the former characterized as positive, or "genuine," conformity, and the latter as negative, or "contrived," conformity.[111] The cases of these three NKVD investigators demonstrate the ways in which identities can be both tactically constructed and genuinely internalized through the act of engaging in unspeakable brutality at the behest of the regime and through the desire to survive and prosper in that system of extreme violence as it existed in Soviet society at that time, as well as the ways in which belief, ambition, and fear become mutually reinforcing in such an environment.

NOTES

The authors would like to thank the organizers of the "The Political Police and the Soviet System," particularly Michael David-Fox, as well as Marc Junge, Lynne Viola, Joshua Sanborn, and the anonymous peer reviewers for their suggestions and critiques on the draft manuscript.

1. Aleksandr Vatlin explored these questions using archival sources from the Kuntsevo district of Moscow oblast in *Terror raionnogo masshtaba: "Massovye operatsii" NKVD v Kuntevskom raione Moskovskoi oblasti 1937–1938 gg.* (Moscow, ROSSPEN, 2004), published in English as *Agents of Terror: Ordinary Men and Extraordinary Violence in Stalin's Secret Police* (Madison: University of Wisconsin Press, 2016). Lynne Viola issued a call to action in her article "The Question of the Perpetrator in Soviet History," *Slavic Review* 72, no. 1 (2013): 1–23; she subsequently published *Stalinist Perpetrators on Trial: Scenes from the Great Terror in Soviet Ukraine* (Oxford: Oxford University Press, 2017). Her call presaged a cross-regional project led by herself, Marc Junge, and Jeffrey Rossman, which included the present authors and resulted in the publication of a co-edited collection of articles, *Chekisty na skam'e podudimykh* (Moscow; Probel-2000, 2017), as well as three volumes of documents from Ukrainian, Georgian, and other archives: *Ekho bol'shogo terrora* (Moscow: Probel-2000, 2017–2018). Junge delved further into the topic through the prism of the Nikolaev region of the Ukrainian SSR in his *Chekisty Stalina: Mosh' i bessilie* (Moscow: AIRO XXI, 2017).

2. This was the view suggested by Nikita Khrushchev in his secret speech to the Twentieth Party Congress in 1956 denouncing Stalin and his henchman Lavrentii Beria. For a contemporary Russian view that holds that NKVD officials simply and honestly implemented orders from above, see

Oleg Mozokhin, *Pravo na repressii: Vnesudebnye polnomochiia organov gosudarstvennoi bezopasnosti, 1918–1953* (Moscow: Kuchkove pole, 2006); and the discussion in M. Iunge [Marc Junge], B. Bonvech [Bernd Bonwetsch], and R. [Rolf] Binner, "Sluchai i proizvol—tezisy issledovanii," in *Stalinizm v sovetskoi provintsii 1937–1938 gg.* (Moscow: ROSSPEN, 2009), 35–43.

3. Marc Junge, "Istoriografiia, metody i istochnikovaia baza," in *Chekisty na skam'e posudimykh*, 11.

4. The archive of the former Georgian KGB is now referred to as sakartvelos shinagan sakmeta saministro arkivi (sshssa), I [Section I of the Archive of the Ministry of Internal Affairs of Georgia], henceforth sshssa (I). Quotation from Junge, "Istoriografiia, metody i istochnikovaia baza," 29.

5. Junge, "Istoriografiia, metody i istochnikovaia baza," 11–41.

6. Quotation from Viola, "Question of the Perpetrator," 22.

7. Timothy Blauvelt, "March of the Chekists: Beria's Secret Police Patronage Network and Soviet Crypto-Politics," *Communist and Post-Communist Studies* 44, no. 1 (2011): 73–88. See also Blauvelt, "Patronage and Betrayal in the Post-Stalin Succession: The Case of Kruglov and Serov," *Communist and Post-Communist Studies* 41, no. 1 (2008): 105–20.

8. "Zapiska R. A. Rudenko v TsK KPSS," in *Delo Beriia: Prigovor obzhalovaniiu ne podlezhit*, ed. V. N. Khaustov (Moscow: Rossiia XXI vek, 2012), 461–85.

9. This was perhaps part of an effort to undermine support for Beria, which remained strong in the Transcaucasus. See Timothy Blauvelt, "Status Shift and Ethnic Mobilization in the March 1956 Events in Georgia," *Europe-Asia Studies* 61, no. 4 (2009): 651–68. Among the repressed figures mentioned in the indictment were the former Transcaucasian Party Regional Committee secretary Mamia Orakhelashvili; former Georgian Central Committee secretaries Mikheil Kakhiani, Samsom Mamulia, and Levan Gogoberidze; and members of the Georgian intelligentsia such as the poet Titsian Tabidze, the writer Mikhail Javakhishvili, and the former director of the Tbilisi Institute of Marx-Engels-Lenin Erik Bedia.

10. See the memoirs of N. G. Smirnov, himself present at the trial as a court secretary: *Rapava, Bagirov i drugie: Antistalinskie protsessy 1950-kh* (Moscow: AIRO, 2014), 19–23.

11. Gosudarstvennyi arkhiv Rossiiskoi Federatsii (GARF) f. 8131, op. 32, d. 4002, l. 236.

12. See, esp., Rossiiskii gosudarstvennyi arkhiv sotsio-politicheskoi istorii (RGASPI) f. 17, op. 171, dd. 474 and 476, published in *Delo Beriia*, ed. Khaustov, and *Politbiuro i delo Beriia: Sbornik dokumentov*, ed. O. B. Mozokhin (Moscow: Kuchkovo pole, 2012). For the information in Georgian archives, see esp. that on S. S. Davlianidze, discussed in Timothy Blauvelt, "'Kakova byla muzyka, takov byl i tanets,' Delo Sergo Semenovicha Davlianidze," in *Chekisty na skam'e posudimykh*, 631–61, and the files on Ashot Aslanov, Grigol Pachulia, Mikheil Shavgulidze, Kalistrat Aslanikashvili, and Giorgi Tavdishvili. Also valuable is the criminal case file on Khazan from 1938 following his arrest, described below.

13. Junge, *Chekisty Stalina*, 223–28.

14. Amy Knight, *Beria: Stalin's First Lieutenant* (Princeton, NJ: Princeton University Press, 1993), 217–24.

15. For a discussion of the unintended consequences of de-Stalinization in the Georgian SSR, see Blauvelt, "Status Shift and Ethnic Mobilization."

16. See Stephen Kotkin's review of Sarah Davies, *Popular Opinion in Stalin's Russia*, *Europe-Asia Studies* 50, no. 4 (1998): 739–42.

17. "Zapiska R. A. Rudenko v TsK KPSS," 464.

18. Khazan had supposedly given a copy of Marx's *Das Kapital* to a Trotsky supporter named Upshtein with an inscription criticizing Lenin. While under arrest in 1938, in his appeals Khazan described in detail his interpersonal conflicts with the leadership of the school, accusing them of being associated with the former secret police head Genrikh Iagoda. See sshssa (I) f. 6, d. 38-759, ll. 95–100.

19. "Zapiska R. A. Rudenko v TsK KPSS," 461.

20. A. S. Aleksandrov, *O moral'nom oblike sovetskogo cheloveka: Sbornik materialov v pomoshch' propagandistam i agitatoram* (Moscow: Moskovskii rabochii, 1948). Sheila Fitzpatrick discusses this book in

a section on "The Party and Private Life" in *Tear Off the Masks! Identity and Imposture in Twentieth-Century Russia* (Princeton, NJ: Princeton University Press, 2005), 244.

21. GARF f. 8131, op. 32, d. 4002, l. 247.

22. N. V. Petrov, *Kto rukovodil organami gosbesopasnosti, 1941–1954: Spravochnik* (Moscow: Memorial, 2010), 758–59.

23. Petrov, *Kto rukovodil organami gosbesopasnosti*, 759.

24. "Zapiska R. A. Rudenko v TsK KPSS," 466.

25. GARF f. 8131, l. 32, d. 4002, l. 247.

26. Petrov, in *Kto rukovodil organami gosbesopasnosti* (510), places Krimian's traineeship in 1932–1933 in the Economic Department of the Transcaucasian GPU, although other sources, including Krimian's own later appeals, make clear that this was in the Economic Department of the Georgian GPU. See sshssa (I) f. 6, d. 4643-58, t. 1, l. 45.

27. Suren Gazarian, *Eto ne dolzhno povtorit'sia: Dokumental'naia povest'* (Erevan: Khorurdain grokh, 1990), 22. Both Savitskii and Krimian were detained together with Davlianidze while working in the Economic Department of the Georgian GPU as the result of a conflict between the Beria group and the Lortkipanidze group in 1934 involving the arrests of a group of technical specialists in Georgia by the Georgian GPU, with minimal evidence and without the sanction of the Trancaucasian GPU. They were released with the victory of the former over the latter. The scheme also seems to have involved using the arrestees, while still under investigation, in a scheme to build a dairy combine. See Blauvelt, "Kakova byla muzyka," 635; Sergo Davlianidze's testimony in sshssa (I) f. 6, d. 38-759, ll. 103–4; and an earlier (never published) statement about the incident from 1954 by Gazarian in sshssa (I) f. 6, d. 37969, t. 3, ll. 97–102.

28. "Zapiska R. A. Rudenko v TsK KPSS," 465.

29. Petrov, *Kto rukovodil organami gosbesopasnosti*, 511–12.

30. The association between the Georgian NKVD and Tbilisi Dinamo is an especially curious one. Beria was an enthusiastic football fan and apparently played a central role in bringing Dinamo under the auspices of the NKVD and in developing the team, recruiting footballers as NKVD interrogators and vice versa. Often interrogators (including at least at some points, it seems, Savitskii and Krimian) would spend their days playing football and their nights beating arrestees. See David Jishkariani, "Georgia's Tbilisi Dinamo: Under Stalin, a Soccer Team for the Secret Police, *Eurasianet*, 20 May 2016, https://eurasianet.org/georgias-tbilisi-dinamo-under-stalin-a-soccer-team-for-the-secret-police; and Jishkariani, *butsebi da tqavis chekma: tbilisis "dinamo" kesistebis klebidan erovnul simbolomde (1925–1953)* (Tbilisi: Laterna, 2021).

31. sshssa (I) f. 6, d. 37969, t. 3, l. 103.

32. Gazarian, *Eto ne dolzhno povtorit'sia*, 21, 23.

33. Khaustov, *Delo Beriia*, 357.

34. Khaustov, *Delo Beriia*, 563.

35. "Zapiska R. A. Rudenko v TsK KPSS," 462.

36. "Zapiska R. A. Rudenko v TsK KPSS," 463.

37. "Proekt obvinitel'nogo zakliucheniia po delu Rapava, Rukhadze i dr.," in *Delo Beriia*, ed. Khaustov, 556.

38. "Proekt obvinitel'nogo zakliucheniia," 556.

39. "Zapiska R. A. Rudenko v TsK KPSS," 463.

40. sshssa (I) f. 6, d. 4643-58, t. 24/21 ("Protokol sudebnogo zasedaniia"), l. 62.

41. "Proekt obvinitel'nogo zakliucheniia," 557.

42. Khaustov, *Delo Beriia*, 563–64.

43. These things were included in a report by Khazan's deputy D. S. Tvalchrelidze following Khazan's arrest in early 1938, in sshssa (I) f. 6, d. 38-759, l. 161.

44. "Zapiska R. A. Rudenko v TsK KPSS," 463; see also Andrei Sukhomlinov, *Kto Vy, Lavrentii Beriia? Neizvestnye stranitsy ugolovnogo dela* (Moscow: Detektiv-Press, 2003): "Former investigators

Kvarikashvili, Krimian, and Khazan, sentenced in 1955 for such crimes, testified that the torture and humiliation of arrestees went on with the knowledge of Goglidze. There was a competition among officials over who could expose more enemies of the people. This was confirmed by investigative apparatus official Savitskii, also convicted in 1955" (167).

45. "Zapiska R. A. Rudenko v TsK KPSS," 463.

46. Testimony of Tsanava in "Zapiska R. A. Rudenko v TsK KPSS," 465.

47. sshssa (I) f. 6, d. 37-969, l. 57.

48. A. G. Tepliakov, *Mashina terrora: OGPU-NKVD Sibiri v 1929–1941 gg.* (Moscow: AIRO-XXI, 2008), 492. See also Vatlin, *Agents of Terror*, 13.

49. sshssa (I) f. 6, d. 4643-58, t. 24/21 ("Protokol sudebnogo zasedaniia"), l. 236.

50. sshssa (I) f. 6, d. 4643-58, t. 24/21 ("Protokol sudebnogo zasedaniia"), l. 62.

51. sshssa (I) f. 6, d. 4643-58, t. 24/21 ("Protokol sudebnogo zasedaniia"), l. 59.

52. sshssa (I) f. 6, d. 4643-58, t. 24/21 ("Protokol sudebnogo zasedaniia"), l. 21.

53. "Proekt obvinitel'nogo zakliucheniia," 556.

54. "Proekt obvinitel'nogo zakliucheniia," 557.

55. "Zapiska R. A. Rudenko v TsK KPSS," 468.

56. Khazan stated this directly in an appeal to Beria in March 1938. See sshssa (I) f. 6, 38-759, l. 100.

57. "Zapiska R. A. Rudenko v TsK KPSS," 467.

58. "Proekt obvinitel'nogo zakliucheniia," 556.

59. "Zapiska R. A. Rudenko v TsK KPSS," 467.

60. "Ob oshibkakh partorganizatsii pri iskliuchenii kommunistov iz partii, o formal'no-biurokraticheskom otnoshenii k apelliatsiiam iskliuchennykh iz VKP(b) i o merakh po ustraneniiu etikh nedostatkov," *Pravda*, 19 January 1938, 1. Kazan's arrest apparently took place under some haste: he was picked up on 31 January, the form for the arrest order was filled out on 1 February, but the actual order was signed by Goglidze only on 3 February. See sshssa (I) f. 6, d. 38-759, ll. 1–6.

61. sshssa (I) f. 6, d. 38-759, l. 5.

62. sshssa (I) f. 6, d. 38-759, l. 134.

63. sshssa (I) f. 6, d. 38-759, ll. 21–22. Perhaps the use of *golovokruzhenie* here is a reference to Stalin's famous "Dizziness from Success" headline in *Pravda* in 1930 to criticize "excesses" in the collectivization campaign.

64. sshssa (I) f. 6, d. 38-759, l. 19.

65. sshssa (I) f. 6, d. 4643-58, t. 1, l. 5.

66. sshssa (I) f. 6, d. 38-759, ll. 158–63.

67. It seems that Davlianidze reported on Khazan, Savitskii, and Krimian to his superiors almost as soon as he began working with them in the Fourth Department. See Blauvelt, "Kakova byla muzyka," 638; and sshssa (I) f. 6, d. 4643-58, t. 24/1, l. 73.

68. sshssa (I) f. 6, d. 4643-58, t. 1, l. 5.

69. V. N. Merkulov was head of the Department of the Central Committee of the Georgian Communist Party and then USSR deputy people's commissar for internal affairs, Beria's right-hand man in this period; A. N. Rapava served as deputy people's commissar and then people's commissar for internal affairs of the Georgian SSR; and M. A. Stepanov was deputy people's commissar of internal affairs of the Georgian SSR. Quotation from sshssa (I) f. 6, d. 4643-58, t. 3, p. 31. Khazan describes in detail how he overzealously solicited testimony from former Georgian SSR Sovnarkom Chairman G. A. Mgaloblishvili, who mentioned B. K. and S. G. (in the typed transcripts surnames of those not under suspicion are usually redacted to initials), almost certainly referring to Bogdan Kobulov and Sergo Goglidze, given that Koboluv was urgently summoned to the NKVD from a gala event at the opera theater. The former NKVD officials V. F. Maksimenko and S. I. Kugel' referred to the initials "M," "R," and "S," which from the 1955 file cited above we can see are Merkulov, Rapava, and Stepanov. In his appeals to Kobulov and Beria while under arrest, Khazan insisted that as trained spies, Maksimenko and Kugel' had been specifically tasked with entrapping him in

this way because the counterrevolutionary centers considered him, Khazan, to be such a danger to their plots. See sshssa (I) f. 6, d. 38-759, ll. 9–10, 68–71.

70. According to his file, Khazan was arrested on 2 February rather than 31 January. See sshssa (I) f. 6, d. 38-759, t. 1.

71. Khaustov, *Delo Beriia*, 225.

72. Khaustov, *Delo Beriia*, 281.

73. Here *lipach* may mean "patsy."'

74. Smirnov, *Rapava, Bagirov i drugie*, 28.

75. Khazan's arrest and removal from active service may have been associated with the January 1938 plenum of the Central Committee, where criticism was expressed toward excesses of the NKVD and which has been seen as a beginning of the turn toward reining in the Terror. See Oleg Khevniuk, "Party and NKVD: Power Relationships in the Years of the Great Terror," in *Stalin's Terror: High Politics and Mass Repression in the Soviet Union*, ed. Barry McLoughlin and Kevin McDermott (New York: Palgrave MacMillan, 2003), 27–28. Khazan may have been a convenient "fall guy" to nominally demonstrate adherence to the plenum's resolutions. Yet Khazan's arrest in late January seems very early to be associated with this turn in central policy, and in any case it does not necessarily exclude the possibility of additional reasons for why Khazan, in particular, may have been singled out in this way (considering how widespread "violations of Socialist legality" clearly were among NKVD personnel at the time). The role of the January 1938 plenum is perhaps a better explanation for the arrest and removal of the interrogators Odisharia and Grigoriadi many months later, in October 1938.

76. Viola, *Stalinist Perpetrators on Trial*, 9.

77. sshssa (I) f. 6, d. 4643-58, t. 24/3 ("Protokol doprosa A. S. Khazana"), l. 30. Marc Junge has highlighted a similar sense of abandonment and betrayal on the part of former secret police investigators who were accused and punished by the very institutions that they sought to protect during the trials of 1939–1941 (*Chekisty Stalina*, 243).

78. Viola, *Stalinist Perpetrators on Trial*, 179.

79. Petrov, *Kto rukovodil organami gosbezopasnosti*, 511.

80. GARF f. 8131, op. 32, d. 4002, l. 260.

81. See Christopher Browning, *Ordinary Men: Reserve Police Battalion 101 and the Final Solution in Poland*, repr. ed. (New York: Harper Perennial), 185.

82. Khazan's deputy D. S. Tvalchrelidze described how Khazan complained to him that Tbilisi residents greeted local officials warmly but "looked at him as someone sent from Moscow to crush counterrevolution, they feared him like thunder." See sshssa (I) f. 6, d. 38-759, l. 163.

83. Khazan, Savitskii, and Krimian were involved in the interrogations of the former top leaders of the Transcaucasian and Georgian Party institutions, Mamia Orakhelashvili and Mikheil Kakhiani, and the family members of the main patron of the Transcaucasian elite network, Sergo Orjonikidze, as well as in the cases of numerous representatives of the intelligentsia—for example, interrogating the poet Titsian Tabidze and repressing a group of students accused of forming a youth organization—as well as the director of the Tbilisi Medical Institute K. V. Tsomaia (who died during interrogation) and his subordinates; students and scientific personnel of the Georgian Industrial Institute; and a group of lawyers. See sshssa (I) f. 6, d. 4643-58, t. 24/18 ("Obvinitel'noe zakliuchenie"), ll. 75–82 (intellectuals), 85 (medical institute), 93–95 (industrialists); and sshssa (I) f. 6, d. 4643-58, t. 24/21 ("Protokol sudebnogo zasedaniia"), ll. 121–29 (lawyers).

84. For a discussion of the shared characteristics of the cohort of Beria's clients in the Georgian and Transcaucasian NKVD, see Blauvelt, "March of the Chekists," 3–4.

85. Davlianidze was insistent about this; see Blauvelt, "'Kakova byla muzyka,'" 646–47. In his appeals while under arrest in 1938, Khazan complained that his struggle against counterrevolution had been hindered in 1935–1937 because investigators were able only to "check party documents" and were restricted "to using only the 'kulak measures' imposed on us by the leadership of the traitor

Iagoda," implying that they were not yet able to use direct physical coercion. See sshssa (I) f. 6, d. 38-759, ll. 129–30.

86. sshssa (I) f. 6, d. 4643-58, t. 24/3, l. 157.

87. Mark Granovetter, "Threshold Models of Collective Behavior," *American Journal of Sociology* 83, no. 6 (1978): 1420–43. Christopher Browning refers to discussions of "brutalization" of soldiers in combat and the role that this may play in the commission of war crimes (*Ordinary Men*, 160–62); and Joshua Sanborn discusses the role of such brutalization in the training of soldiers to acclimate them to violence, which he compares to the acclimation to murder among violent criminals ("The Short Course for Murder: How Soldiers and Criminals Learn to Kill," in *Violent Acts and Violentization: Assessing, Applying, and Developing Lonnie Athen's Theories*, ed. Lonnie Athens and Jeffrey T. Ulmer [Amsterdam: JAI-Elsevier, 2003], 101–24). It seems to us, however, that the standard training of Soviet secret policemen, such as it was, was rather different from that of soldiers and did not in most cases involve preparation for the kind of violence that would be required of them in 1937–1938 and that the onset of the Stalinist Terror was so rapid and the situation in the NKVD so fluctuating as to preclude the kind of regularity or standardization of operating procedures that these approaches imply. Certainly, however, engaging in acts of brutality over the course of weeks and months caused a form of "brutalization" of the investigators, in the sense of normalizing violent behavior.

88. Malcolm Gladwell made a controversial attempt to use this approach to understand the spread of school shootings in the United States in "Thresholds of Violence: How School Shootings Catch On," *New Yorker*, 12 October 2015. In our opinion, the evolution of the mass state violence of the Great Terror arguably bears greater resemblance to the violence of a crowd than does the school shooting epidemic.

89. Tepliakov, *Mashina terror*, 488.

90. For a similar discussion of patronage and clientalism in the NKVD and Soviet society more generally, see Vatlin, *Agents of Terror*, 12–18.

91. Smirnov, *Rapava, Bagirov i drugie*, 29.

92. From the protocol of an interrogation of Merkulov in 1953, in *Politbiuro i delo Beriia*, 457.

93. Browning, *Ordinary Men*, 220.

94. Stephen Kotkin, *Magnetic Mountain: Stalinism as Civilization* (Berkeley: University of California Press, 1996), 22–23; Jochen Hellbeck, "Speaking Out: Languages of Affirmation and Dissent," in *The Resistance Debate in Russian and Soviet History*, ed. Michael David-Fox, Peter Holquist, and Marshall Poe (Bloomington, IN: Slavica Publishers, 2003), 103–37. For a critique of this approach, see Mark Edele, *Stalinist Society, 1928–1953* (Oxford: Oxford University Press, 2011), 237–38.

95. sshssa (I) f. 6, d. 4643-58, t. 24/21 ("Poslednee slovo"), ll. 254, 261.

96. sshssa (I) f. 6, d. 4643-58, t. 24/21 ("Protokol sudebnogo zasedaniia"), ll. 226–27. Davlianidze's colleague Khazan made a similar statement in early testimony used in Davlianidze's trial: "In 1937 I was inspired by the directives of the Party on struggle against enemies of the people." See sshssa (I) f. 6, d. 4643-58, t. 24/3 ("Protokol doprosa A. S. Khazana"), l. 32.

97. Smirnov, *Rapava, Bagirov i drugie*, 32.

98. Khazan refers to Decree (*postanovlenie*) no. 23 of the Central Executive Committee (TsIK) and Sovnarkom, which introduced changes to the criminal code for prosecuting "terrorist acts" following the assassination of Sergei Kirov in November 1934. Quoted passage from sshssa (I) f. 6, d. 4643-58, t. 24/3, l. 32.

99. Smirnov, *Rapava, Bagirov i drugie*, 32.

100. "Kopiia protokola doprosa obviniaemogo KhAZANA A.S. ot 6 noiabria 1953 goda," in *Delo Beriia*, 402.

101. Fitzpatrick, *Tear off the Masks!*, 5. See also her discussion of "imposture" (*Tear off the Masks!*, 18–21).

102. sshssa (I) f. 6, d. 4643-58, t. 24/1, l. 74.

103. sshssa (I) f. 6, d. 4643-58, t. 24/1, l. 45. According to Krimian, Savitskii informed him that Goriachev

was interrogated in secret and questioned personally by Goglidze and Kobulov, as they were trying to ascertain from him the name of the USSR NKVD official who had extracted the compromising confession regarding Beria. Goriachev was executed in November 1938.

104. Malte Griesse, "Soviet Subjectivities: Discourse, Self-Criticism, Imposture," *Kritika: Explorations in Russian and Eurasian History* 9, no. 3 (2008): 619.

105. Junge, *Chekisty Stalina*, 222.

106. Both quotations from Viola, *Stalinist Perpetrators on Trial*, 177.

107. Junge, *Chekisty Stalina*, 222.

108. Junge, *Chekisty Stalina*, 223.

109. Viola, *Stalinist Perpetrators on Trial*, 177.

110. Viola's conception of ideology in this context seems closer to this understanding of it as rhetoric than Junge's: "They were also 'ideologized,' but less in the sense of Marxist-Leninist-Stalinist dogma than in the sense of ideology in practice, or praxis" (*Stalinist Perpetrators on Trial*, 177).

111. See Andrei Savin, Aleksei Tepliakov, and Mark Iunge, *Ekho bol'shogo terrora*, vol. 3: *Chekisty Stalina v tiskakh "sotsialisticheskoi zakonnosti": Ego-dokumenty 1938–1941 gg.* (Moscow: Probel-2000, 2018), 12.

"Conflicts Are the Core of Social Life"

Fomenting Mistrust at the Tallinn State
Conservatory in the 1940s–1960s

Aigi Rahi-Tamm

"THE INFLUENCE OF BOURGEOIS SOCIETY IS TOO EVIDENT. WE FORGET THAT bourgeois intelligence spread bourgeois education and provided ideological support to the bourgeois government. . . . Even today it seems that Päts and Vettik have been 'caught'; let us see when and where the next ones are, at a certain point somebody has to be hit. In Leningrad [in the Soviet rear in 1944] we were too liberal—we made a big and deep mistake. Let us not repeat this mistake today! We have to raise the issue with the utmost rigor—despite friendly relationships." Such was the speech of Kaarel Ird, head of the Board of Arts of the Estonian SSR at the extraordinary general meeting of the Union of Composers (UC) of the ESSR on 3 October 1948. This meeting saw the condemnation of Tuudur Vettik (1898–1982) and Riho Päts (1899–1977), conductors honored and loved by the people. The UC had to admit that it had not exercised enough vigilance regarding the elimination of relics, and all members of the union now had to reevaluate their work in the light of the decisions of the Communist Party. Vigilance meant accusations of betrayal and hypocrisy leveled at colleagues, friends, and even oneself.[1]

By the autumn of 1948, Estonian cultural intellectuals had become the targets of a Soviet ideological offensive. This was a part of the postwar Zhdanovshchina, a movement that endorsed control over culture and set out to eliminate Western influences.[2] In 1947, the Sovietization of the Baltic countries had reached a new stage that included suppression of national developments and an active fight against "bourgeois nationalism." National feelings and attitudes had to be subordinated to Soviet norms, and this was accompanied by attacks against the values, everyday phenomena, mutual relations, and so on of the period of independence (1918–1940).[3] The contradictory position of the intelligentsia between official and unofficial values and practices makes them a difficult yet vitally important topic of investigation in the context of the era. The attitude of the Soviet authorities toward the intelligentsia was ambivalent, enabling diverse types of manipulation.[4]

The principles of control suggested by Lenin in his *State and Revolution* (1918) were developed and elaborated throughout the Soviet period. Consequently, the establishment of the ESSR implemented new "rules of the game," capitalizing on techniques ranging from severe punishments to skillful use of incentives. People's behavior could be most effectively controlled at the workplace, using moral exhortation and other tools. These techniques had devastating consequences on human relationships and mutual trust in the society as a whole. To this day people are ashamed of these practices.[5] As Geoffrey Hosking argues, the destruction of trust became a key element in governing the totalitarian state in the Soviet Union.[6] Even later, during the modernization of the Soviet state and normalization of life, trust and distrust continued to pose real problems, as did the effectiveness of control measures, and therefore should be assessed from a long-term perspective. This situation continued to the very end of the Soviet period.

To be effective, the manipulation of citizens through techniques of social control required the participation and collaboration of the people. For this, the authorities had to get to know the people and their cultural context. Andrei Zhdanov was sent to Estonia as special envoy during the coup of 1940. He learned quickly that Sovietization in the Baltic countries would clash with regional particularities. In Tallinn, Zhdanov reflected on the national problem at hand: "Mentality. Specific character. Imminent like the taste of an apple. Every nation is born with its own mentality, with its distinctive traits."[7] Estonian cultural distinctiveness as well as the national past remained an issue throughout the Soviet period, and the Baltic republics were always considered to be "different" from the rest of the Soviet Union.[8]

The song festival movement, which united society and involved the masses, became a particular feature of Estonian national culture in the late nineteenth century under the influence of German Romanticism. The festival needed to convey the right message. The song festival as a collective ritual characteristic of national identity is a kind of symbolic capital.[9] It unites the participants (singers, composers, conductors, families, relatives, friends) into a community of fellow-feeling united by common memories and experiences.[10] Thus what happened to popular conductors has a broader meaning in terms of defending Estonian national culture.

As an event that brought the masses together, the song festival with its choirs was a potential propaganda channel for the regime to further its interests.[11] While the 1947 song festival could still take place in the nationally minded spirit of "postindependence," the song festival of 1950 was the clearest expression of Soviet ideology of all the festivals held in Soviet Estonia. This chapter focuses on the developments between 1947 and 1950. Immediately before the 1950 song festival, the three general coordinators—Tuudur Vettik, Riho Päts, and Alfred Karindi (1901–1969)—were arrested. At the 1947 song festival each had been awarded the honorary title of ESSR Folk Artist, but in 1950 they fell into disgrace. They are the central figures in the story.

Such a dramatic change in social standing encourages an examination of the secret police files compiled on the three arrested conductors. The material in the files raised numerous questions and inspired me to undertake a more detailed investigation of events at the Tallinn State Conservatory (TSC), where they all worked. Hence the circle of persons to be studied on the microlevel began to widen, including their colleagues, friends, and pupils. The circle of issues that emerged—what measures were imposed by the authorities to control the world of culture; how different institutions and persons and information about them were involved in the process; which reactions and conflicts were caused by the new situation; what the consequences were, and so on—required the analysis of diverse sources.

Personal files reveal only some aspects of the phenomenon, like the tactics used by the secret police to manipulate people; usually further information must be obtained from other sources that are not as easy to find. I have sought answers to my questions in the minutes of meetings of the TSC, the Board of Arts of the ESSR, and the UC and in correspondence, various personal files, characterizations, memoirs, and other documents. The comparative analysis of diverse data reveals multiple mechanisms for mapping and controlling society, at the level of both institutions and people. This finding confirmed the principle used in Soviet society—conflicts are the core of social life; they enable control of the situation; hence the effectivity of control largely depends on interpersonal relations.[12]

This chapter does not offer a survey of all conflicts in the world of Estonian music but focuses on a specific group. Through this lens, I discuss processes at the TSC, including conflicts among the school administration, teaching, control of curriculum and forms of conformity or nonconformity. Several of these situations were deliberately obscured by administrative regulations (classified documents, etc.) but also by people's reluctance to document unpleasant situations or describe them openly since they were connected with personal life, families, or social factors.

The events that took place in the musical and cultural life of the USSR in the 1930s–1940s have been examined in numerous historical studies.[13] The same can be said of research on the new cultural policies of Zhdanov. Ideological attacks against different areas of culture were intertwined with the activities of the party structures and secret police as well as with Soviet nationalities policy.[14] Kiril Tomoff has argued that although many institutions and organizations were involved in the regulation and control of musical life, this system was profoundly inefficient.[15] Patrik Zuk's article about Nikolai Miaskovskii shows vividly how a composer who had never experienced any scandals was drawn into this maelstrom, probably as a result of the events of 1948.[16]

The musicians' relationships with the authorities and the destruction of connections between colleagues were some of the manipulations aimed at the strengthening of control. Jan Gross has described the paradigms of social control in terms of the totalitarian state enveloping individuals and monopolizing not only coercion but also the mechanisms for social conformity, playing people against each other and encouraging hatred or social submissiveness in an environment where the shame of submission became socially visible.[17] The politicization of social communication provokes uncomfortable emotions. Conforming to the rules of the authorities embarrassed many people, and this reaction has prevented them from openly discussing these topics both at the time and after the collapse of the Soviet Union. Thus more attention should be paid to the ways in which accusations were constructed and what happened to others involved in the process besides the authorities and the victims—their family members, friends, colleagues, acquaintances, and so on. Widening the net in this way also helps explain the long-lasting impact and significance of the repression.[18]

THE GRADUAL ACTUALIZATION OF CULTURAL ISSUES

The Sovietization of the Baltic states began in the summer of 1940. This meant dismantling the institutions of independent statehood and introducing Soviet power structures with social, economic, and cultural reforms imposed by Moscow. People quickly realized that the Soviets sought to reach everyone and everywhere. For many, the first encounter with Soviet power and its bureaucratic machinery was with the organs of surveillance and their effort to root out "enemies of the people," introducing the rules and struggles of Soviet reality to the Soviet Union's new Baltic frontier.[19] Sovietization was a set of processes and stages that had to transform life in Estonia to match that of the rest of the Soviet Union while retaining certain specific national and regional features and making compromises. Thus the establishment of the Soviet power was accompanied by violence and fear but also uncertainty as people sought and tested ways of adaptation and stuck to former values and attitudes. In the Soviet context, these retained traits were called relics, the "political past," or harmful influences of the bourgeois, capitalist, or Western world, among other things. Yet the fight between new and old ways of thinking lasted longer than the authorities expected, because the impact of the "old society" on culture was quite strong and kept its importance throughout the Soviet period.

While the restructuring of cultural life in Estonia in 1940–1941 appeared to take place quite quickly, internal reorganization took much longer because of fundamental differences from the Soviet Union. This lag increased dissatisfaction as well as uncertainty. Many people have stated that they seemed to live in two time zones simultaneously: in private life "Estonian time" continued, but in the public sphere "Soviet time" was gradually established.[20] Although cultural matters were not political priorities in the first Soviet year (1940–1941), deeper tensions and problems aggravated by the war emerged thereafter. They largely concerned human and professional relationships and had long-term consequences.

After the war, the pressure on the cultural landscape gradually increased. In 1946, the Committee on State Security started recruiting cadres from the local population, focusing on the intelligentsia because most of the spiritual leaders of anti-Soviet groups came from its ranks.[21] Sovietization became more aggressive in the Baltic countries after 1947, peaking in Estonia in 1949–1951.[22]

The first stage in the Sovietization of Estonian musical life was the dismantling of the institutional system, including the replacement of the director of the Conservatory. Johannes Semper, the new minister of education, offered the job to Riho Päts, who remained in his post for only three months. Päts, a leading figure in Estonian music and musical education in the 1930s, engaged in a broad range of activities—composer, conductor, music journalist, developer of children's musical education, and author of numerous songbooks. He wrote about five hundred articles, surveys, and reviews on both Estonian and foreign music; was familiar with the development of musical education in Germany, England, the United States, and Soviet Russia, especially innovations in children's music; and laid the foundation for the tradition of youth choirs and song festivals.

Why was Päts's term of office so short? According to one account, he was dismissed because he had the same family name as the former president of the Republic of Estonia (Konstantin Päts, 1874–1956). Another possible reason was his article in the paper *Muusikaleht*, published in 1937, in which he criticized Soviet reality after visiting Leningrad.[23] Päts himself blamed his dismissal on the ambitions of Nikolai Goldschmidt (conductor and composer, 1900–1964), the former head of the Tallinn Workers' Music Society, who desired to become director himself and spread rumors about anti-Päts protests at the school.[24] The confrontation between the two men had already emerged earlier. As an active music journalist, Päts had criticized Goldschmidt's choices of repertoire in a rather sharp tone and questioned his professional abilities.[25] Despite his efforts, Goldschmidt was in for a disappointment; he was not appointed as the new director. Personal conflicts fed into later intrigues and rivalries. When Päts was arrested in 1950, the secret police made use of Goldschmidt's statements as their primary justification for the prosecution of the three conductors (Päts, Vettik, and Karindi). It took some time for Estonians to realize how the authorities used facts from the past, largely from the pre-Soviet era, to manipulate them.

The gathering of data on Estonian citizens, mainly by employees of the Soviet embassy, had begun in the 1930s.[26] After the war, personal tensions and conflicts between people grew and multiplied. Although not all of these were publicly visible, the power structures skillfully mapped these situations, gathered information, and made use of it. The example of the Tallinn State Conservatory clearly illustrates the consequences of such activities.

At last, a suitable candidate appeared. With the appointment of the violinist Vladimir Alumäe (1917–1979) as director, the sharpest internal tensions of the first Soviet year at the TSC seemed to be resolved. Päts characterized Alumäe as a young and talented musician who was able to gain people's trust, adding that "he adapted quickly to needs and consulted with competent people."[27] It seems that in a situation of opportunism and rivalries, Päts gradually learned how to overcome difficulties and obtain support from more powerful people. The studies of Kiril Tomoff and many others have underlined the significance of official and unofficial networks in Soviet musical life.[28] Soviet measures of control were still unknown in Estonia, and many people hoped that appointing the right people to leading positions might help overcome the problems of the new era. However, the events that followed proved that these hopes were unfounded, and the position of political leaders might change overnight. Aleksander Perov, an education instructor for the Central Committee (CC) of the All-Union Communist Party (Bolshevik) (VKP[b]), started to monitor the behavior of Estonian educational workers and sent descriptions of them to Moscow.[29] The hope that Estonian intellectuals could maintain control over national cultural life proved to be naïve, yet the establishment of control in its different forms took some time.

The actual content of the changes became evident after the German occupation (1941–1944), when Soviet power was reestablished. In the autumn of 1944, teachers at the TSC were divided into three groups: those who had sought refuge in Russia and therefore earned the trust of the authorities; those who remained in Estonia during the German occupation and were therefore "marked"; and those who fled to the West and thus became "traitors to the homeland." The number of people compromised by their so-called political past increased drastically.

Other divisions used different principles. In early 1946, Nikolai Karotamm (1901–1969), the first secretary of the CC of the Estonian Communist Party (Bolshevik) (EC[b]P), divided Estonian intellectuals into three groups: those secretly hostile to Soviet power; those waiting for changes in the international situation (i.e., a Soviet war with England and the United States that might lead to the liberation of the Baltic states); and those sharing the Soviet worldview. Karotamm warned the first group about the harsh experiences of older republics: "the wheel of fate rolled over these intellectuals who did not learn to value the Soviet power."[30] Aware of earlier Soviet purges, the political leadership of the ESSR tried to set its own course in terms of personnel and preferred reeducation of the intelligentsia to violence. The criticisms of artistic creation made at that time were quite mild compared with later periods.

Director Alumäe tried to ignore political pasts and the Soviet worldview and chose lecturers based on professionalism and the need to maintain a serious and friendly atmosphere at the school. A key event was the Twelfth Estonian General Song Festival in June 1947, the first such event organized in the Soviet period considered a success by both organizers and foreign guests. The general coordinators of the song festival—Tuudur Vettik, Riho Päts, Alfred Karindi, and Gustav Ernesaks, who were also lecturers at the TSC—were awarded the honorary title of Folk Artist of the ESSR and a state prize. They were also guests of honor at the celebrations marking Moscow's eight-hundredth anniversary.

The festival opened with Muradeli's song "With Steely Will Stalin Has Led Us," which actually took the place of a hymn, and there were only three non-Estonian songs in the program.[31] Seventy-five percent of the repertoire represented Estonian national choir works, and several songs were genuinely patriotic. Thus the song festival was relatively Estonian-minded, but the ideological leaders realized this only much later. It was brought into sharp focus in the context of the 1950 song festival and the eighth plenum of the CC EC(b)P.

This period of stability did not last long, and soon conflicts arose in the TSC, resulting in accusations that Director Alumäe preferred those who had remained in Estonia in 1941–1944 and avoided Soviet people. His confrontation with Aleksander Arder (singer and singing teacher, 1894–1966) became especially tense. Arder, the party secretary of the school, accused Alumäe of obstructing his career advancement. Since Arder had seriously breached work discipline in 1944–1946 due to alcoholism, Alumäe refused to provide the Ministry of Higher Education with his application documents for a professorship, and this probably gave rise to the conflict. It was skillfully used in later intrigues, and Arder became one of the main accusers in Alumäe's expulsion from the Party.

An article published in the daily *Eesti Bolševik* (Estonian Bolshevik) in the summer of 1948 accused the TSC party organization of excessive tolerance and condemned the school administration's formal attitude toward party directives, declaring that a "principle of individualism characteristic of bourgeois schools" was still dominant.[32] Alumäe was accused of poor management because only four of the fourteen professors and eighteen associate professors belonged to the Communist Party and the Komsomol organization had been founded as late as February 1948. The chair of Marxism and Leninism was considered to be of marginal importance, since Alumäe had forbidden them to "ferment" (i.e., put ideological pressure on) the collective. The TSC was also accused of cultivating a heightened self-esteem, as if the level of musical education in Tallinn was higher than in other conservatories of the Soviet Union.

Dmitrii Kuzmin, personnel secretary of the CC EC(b)P, argued that an improvement in the situation would require radically strengthening the political education of lecturers and students by implementing systematic control.[33] The authorities started looking for a new director for the school. Several texts give the impression that Alumäe was allowed to withdraw quietly, by being sent to Leningrad for professional development in 1948–1951, yet secret police reports from 1951 confirm that he was dismissed from office.[34]

On 1 September 1948, Bruno Lukk (pianist, 1909–1991) took the position of acting director, and Jaak Ottender (1893–1972), who had studied at the Sverdlov Communist University and came from the USSR, became the chair of Marxism and Leninism. Ottender commented on the atmosphere at the school: "It felt as if I had entered some bourgeois institution. Even the outward appearance—no portraits, quotes, or slogans. The building was not Soviet in its culture."[35]

During the first years after the war, Estonian intellectuals acquired the skills necessary for survival in the new Soviet environment. These included forging contacts with "important" persons and learning acceptable ways of talking, pretense, compromises, and so on. At the same time, they maintained an ironic attitude toward the situation that offered a certain feeling of superiority and opportunity to defend their values and freedom of thought. Although society had already been divided into "us" and "aliens," earlier networks of friends and colleagues still mattered and shaped social relations. This irritated those who regarded such networks of trust as obstacles along their path to a career or smooth relationships with the authorities and started to undermine them by various means. The year 1948 marked a turning point.

TAKING THE ALL-UNION COURSE

Before people could be transferred from one cultural space to another and reeducated, information had to be gathered for analysis and corrective tactics developed.[36] By 1948, a considerable part of Estonian society had been mapped, using compromising data gathered by the secret police and other sources.[37] Denying "sensitive data" in personal forms became much more difficult. It would have been possible to dismiss about 80 percent of Estonian teachers based on "wrong" data in their personal files, yet such a step seemed too radical.[38] John Connelly has described similar measures used for purging the teaching staff in East Germany.[39]

The all-Union campaign of suppressing liberal intellectuals and their admiration for the West was adapted to the local context with key slogans like "Fight against Bourgeois Relics" and "Expose Nationalism." The causes of the 1948 antiformalism campaign were complex; as Ekaterina Vlasova has demonstrated, the purging of musical life had specific characteristics in Moscow, Leningrad, and on the periphery.[40]

The decision of the CC VKP(b) of 14 August 1946 on the journals *Zvezda* and *Leningrad* became the starting point of a new cultural policy implemented by Zhdanov.[41] In Estonia on 22 March 1948, the General Assembly of the Union of Composers discussed the decision of the CC plenum regarding Vano Muradeli's opera *The Great Friendship*.[42] There the ideological requirements for music and composers were formulated. Nikolai Goldschmidt expressed joy that "friendship-based" politics had finally collapsed: "It would be right to chase away all the old spirits and adopt the Soviet mentality."[43] These words, like numerous reports, confirm that people's relationships had withstood political pressure and adaptation to circumstances tended to be more apparent than real. But now *The Great Friendship* had to destroy any real networks of friends.

At first, musicians were involved in a dispute about the notion of formalism that was as incomprehensible as the mistakes of Muradeli's opera.[44] Deputy Director of the TSC Jüri Variste went to see the opera in Riga: "It was difficult for us to say anything: there were lots of things not in accordance with the content, but we could not understand what was wrong."[45] The situation was paradoxical: to hear what was bad about forbidden music, it had to be played.

Because Muradeli's opera was not known in Estonia and people needed to understand how formalist music sounded, the TSC organized performances of Arnold Schönberg's piano compositions for the purpose of collective reeducation.[46] Musical works with formalist tendencies were removed from the curriculum, and control was imposed on the repertoire. Still, the musicians took a "wait and see" attitude, since they could not define formalism and expected Moscow to send more detailed instructions. Most of them believed that there was no formalism in Estonian music![47] To follow the new requirements, Director Lukk asked the director of the Leningrad Conservatory to consult the TSC.[48] Finally, Chairman of the UC Eugen Kapp (1908–1996) concluded, "After all, music is like any other art; it is first of all ideology" that had to be in conformity with the directives of the Party.[49] Delay tactics no longer worked.

From then on, the UC USSR sent representatives to local organizations in a systematic manner to give creative support and solve organizational issues. Furthermore, pressure on members of the UC to join the Party increased.[50] Active party members were regarded as a resource for imposing more effective control. Audit committees of the Ministry of Higher Education of the USSR exercised special vigilance with regard to lecturers' personal histories.[51]

In Estonian society, which was small and tightly interwoven, the requirement for "criticism and self-criticism," which became a compulsory part of meetings, was one of the most iniquitous measures of the Zhdanovshchina. The cultivation of Soviet spirit meant totally absurd attacks on colleagues, friends, teachers, even oneself. The claims that were voiced led to increasing tensions; mutual accusations grew into direct insults and personal revenge. Aleksei Stepanov's comment conveys the atmosphere of arbitrary criticism: "I mentioned the name of Comrade Anna Klas once, and she mentioned my name nine times. This shows how sensitive we are. Goldschmidt referred to [Conductor] Prokhorov, who had no intention of speaking but then spoke anyway . . . I did not want to insult Comrade Klas."[52]

Practicing "criticism and self-criticism" was a regular means of purging aimed at testing relationships, opinions, and self-control in a collective.[53] These disciplinary campaigns were also woven into academic debates—or "discussions," as they were often called—and launched in philosophy, biology, physics, linguistics, physiology, and political economy. As Ethan Pollock has noted, these academic controversies often led to unpredictable results, and using such conflicts between scientists was Stalin's strategy.[54] What was said at meetings could be used as confessions at a suitable moment. They were not constructed by the secret police but formulated by colleagues. This undermined the intellectual climate of trust.

The accusations voiced at the General Assembly of the UC ESSR on 22 March 1948 continued at the sessions that followed. Like great figures of Russian music such as Dmitrii Shostakovich, Sergei Prokof'ev, Nikolai Miaskovskii, and Aram Khachaturian, many Estonian composers—Heino Eller, Eduard Oja, Lydia Auster, Eugen Kapp, Hugo Lepnurm, and others—"could not find a way to the people." Typically they were criticized for failure to compose in a popular style and lack of melody, among other things.[55] At the extraordinary UC General Assembly on 3 October 1948, Riho Päts and Tuudur Vettik were taught a lesson. In 1942, Päts had edited a music textbook for the fifth and sixth grades, *Favorite Songbook*, that included Vettik's "Song of the Forest Brothers." The song itself had been published earlier, but here the title became important, because it referred to men who fought against Soviet annexation in the woods. Although Vettik's song spoke about the fight for freedom in the thirteenth century, it was labeled a "hymn of bandits" in the accusations. Päts and Vettik were mainly accused of not mentioning the songbook before and omitting it from their resumes. The last point of the decision taken at the meeting included a severe order—all UC members had to reevaluate their creative past, demonstrate consistency at removing relics, and battle mercilessly against bourgeois nationalists. The opening quotation of this chapter comes from the same meeting: Kaarel Ird, the head of the Board of Arts, referred to a mistake made in Leningrad in 1944, by which he meant the principle that no punitive actions would be taken after the return to Estonia. This period of political neutrality was coming to an end. A friend could no longer be just a friend; he also had to be a political ally. Even the former director Alumäe, who had believed in the possibility of reeducating intellectuals and followed a liberal personnel policy, had to admit his mistakes.[56] Päts and Vettik were severely reprimanded and relieved of their positions at the UC. But the most humiliating demand was that each of them must compose a letter of atonement, confessing his mistakes and explaining his attitude toward Soviet power and its cultural policies. These letters were published in the press.[57]

Throughout 1949, attacks against the creative intelligentsia became more intensive and resulted in several waves of dismissals at the TSC. During the campaign against cosmopolitanism, the activity of music critics was thoroughly screened. At a meeting of the UC on 13 March, they were called "representatives of degenerating reactionaries, squirming in their agony." Those accused of bowing to the West were sharply criticized. Harri Kõrvits, the UC secretary, reminded everyone that Lenin's guideline—"to write about evil without hatred means to write in a boring manner" must be followed. The criticism had to be harsh, like Purgatory: "bowing to the sacred immunity of old authorities, specialists, and family relations . . . gives evidence of cowardice." Put aside any friendly feeling for your colleagues because it prevents you from seeing the shortcomings in their musical works; do not be afraid of insulting friends, older composers, professors—that is what the advice sounded like.[58] Negative emotions were empowered at all meetings. Operation Priboi (which deported twenty-one thousand people from Estonia to Siberia in March 1949) increased people's insecurity. Even cultural figures who had belonged to the governing elite of the ESSR—like Nigol Andresen (1899–1985), Johannes Semper, and Hans Kruus—fell into disgrace.[59]

The reeducation of musicians reached the next stage when belligerence replaced hesitancy. It became impossible to stop the offensive of heated aggression with window-dressing or silence. Most people tried to obey to avoid becoming the next target of repression, although the emphasis on highlighting facts of the past made this more difficult. To avoid conflict, the musicians had to compromise more. Quite a few people hoped that one person's conviction might cause others to be left alone. Such an attitude led to searches for culprits among colleagues, the criticisms bore fruit, and the minutes of meetings are full of accusations.

After the humiliation inflicted by their forced letters of repentance, Päts and Vettik were marked as "enemies," although they tried to improve their attitudes. Vettik composed a song about the Soviet army and exposed his faults at meetings; Päts thanked the Party for its vigilance. Over the next eighteen months, the situation for both seemed to stabilize, yet in early 1950 they were arrested and left to the mercy of the secret police. Investigators had gathered quite a lot of evidence against them. The party organization at the school tightened its grip on them; "signals" about their hostile influence on students were regularly sent to the district party committee.[60] The secret police also tried to tighten control. It seemed that the arrest of Päts and Vettik was just a matter of time, and the stranglehold on them tightened.

Here we need to look at the case of the third conductor, Alfred Karindi. He mainly composed choral and organ music as well as solo songs. For Karindi, events took an unexpected turn in November 1944, when his brother Eduard—who had been conscripted into the Red Army in 1941—returned home. The family quickly laid the table, but there was no milk, so Karindi went to fetch it from a neighboring farm—only to discover that he could not get back. While he was away, the seaside area had been declared a border zone without informing the inhabitants. Alfred Karindi was arrested for illegal border crossing and taken to Tallinn for interrogation. There it was made

clear to him that he would be released only if he agreed to collaborate with
the secret police. He received the agent name "Hope" and signed the papers
but renounced the deal five years later. At his last meeting in October 1949,
Karindi was instructed to inform on the activities of Päts and Vettik, but
he refused.[61] His arrest took place at midnight on 4 February 1950, when he
returned home with his wife from a friend's birthday party. At intervals of
two weeks, his colleagues Vettik and Päts were also arrested, leaving the song
festival without any of its general coordinators six months before it was due to
begin. The preparations for this event marked a decisive turning point in the
Sovietization of Estonian music.

"CONVERSATIONS" WITH THE INTERROGATOR

All three men were leading figures in their field, general coordinators of the
Twelfth Estonian Song Festival in 1947, and future general coordinators of
the song festival in 1950. In the independent Republic of Estonia, Vettik had
been an outstanding leader of the song festival movement. He had composed
songs for both choirs and solos and was active as a music theoretician. As a
lecturer on choral conducting and member of the Song Festival Commission,
he emphasized the importance of choir singing as a popular artistic medium
in the cultural service of the masses and the fight for the victory of communism.[62] In 1949, such calls could no longer help him.

In October 1949, at the same time as Karindi was excluded from the secret
police network, the song festival's Main Committee adjusted the repertoire
and added seven new names to the board. Thus the tasks assigned to Vettik,
Päts, and Karindi could be smoothly delegated to others. In April 1950, a
new Main Committee was appointed and the works of those arrested were
removed from the repertoire, replaced mostly by contributions from Russian
songwriters praising the Soviet Union. A short time before the festival, additional high-quality choir songs were removed from the program.[63]

It was clear that music had to give way to politics. All three conductors
were accused of bourgeois nationalism and anti-Soviet activities—manifested
in their views, songs, work and teaching methods, relationships with students,
and inability to overcome the past. From the investigator's viewpoint the cases
were not complicated. Most of the allegations had been previously voiced at
different meetings and documented in various protocols, reports, correspondence, and media. Before the arrests Nikolai Goldschmidt was asked to give
evidence. He fulfilled his task, reporting in detail on the anti-Soviet activities
of Päts, Vettik, and Karindi in the independent Republic of Estonia, during
the period of German occupation, and in the present. Goldschmidt's accusations were largely based on the fact that all three belonged to a group of

formalist composers in the Republic of Estonia and later, many of whom fled to the West. This authoritative group had broad support and a hostile attitude toward the workers' movement; their creative work called for bourgeois patriotism and a fight against realism. They also enjoyed support from leaders of the ESSR (Andresen, Semper, and others) who promoted their careers. The men were hostile to the Soviet Union and adopted an ironic view of life there.[64]

For Alfred Karindi, the interrogator's initial questions must have been familiar: What organizations have you belonged to? Have you been abroad? Why did you stay in Estonia after it was occupied by the Germans? How did you react to the establishment of Soviet power? Karindi's answers reveal his experience and "reeducation"; they are completely different from the uncensored answers he had given upon his first arrest in 1944. In addition, the ideological training people received taught them how to respond. To the secret police, Karindi was a supporter of Estonian independence who had connections with the underground National Committee during the German occupation. The committee aimed to organize resistance and prevent the reestablishment of Soviet power. When the interrogator asked "What is your attitude toward Soviet power?" during his earlier arrest, Karindi quite frankly admitted: "There was not much of the Soviet Union in Estonia at first, so I had no attitude at first. . . . Now I can say that I do not support the Soviet Union; I am a supporter of the bourgeois-democratic order . . . consequently, I believe I am against Soviet power."[65] Five years later, he gave the following answer to the same question: "I tried to work like a Soviet citizen! . . . Yes, I was a supporter of the bourgeois-democratic republic. But having examined Marxist-Leninist theory, I understood that there cannot be any other power, because for workers Soviet power is the fairest." When asked "Then do you think that music is separated from politics?" Karindi gave a politically correct answer: "Music is work on the ideological front—that is, part of politics." He attributed his change of mind to having strengthened his political orientation.[66] Despite these answers, the interrogator repeatedly told all three men the same thing: in Soviet society, music has to serve the political struggle above all. For this reason, he focused on reeducation. Toward this end, the suspects had to talk about their activities many times, reformulating their earlier misconceptions and including elements of class struggle and other ideologically appropriate motives to demonstrate their reeducation to the interrogator/educator and satisfy his demands.[67]

For the secret police, however, questions related to music were less important than contacts between people and the nature of relationships. They focused first on people who were actively involved in resistance and, second, on circles of friends united by music. A particular point of contention was the choir of the Tallinn Men's Singing Society—established in 1916, still active today, and conducted by Karindi in 1938–1950. In the Republic of Estonia it had been an elite choir, with members that included numerous intellectuals, state officials, clergymen, teachers, lawyers, military personnel, and entrepreneurs—all categories considered "dangerous" by the Soviets. The implications for the investigator were clear: such a "reactionary" choir was the equivalent of a nationalist anti-Soviet club. Consequently, Karindi repeatedly had to characterize the political views and activities of the choir members, many of whom had escaped to the West during the war. The interrogator tried to extract information about the attitude of these persons toward the Soviet authorities and descriptions of conflicts. For the purpose of prosecution, several examples of the anti-Soviet repertoire and performances of the choirs were gathered.[68] Like others, Karindi had to defend the content of his nationalist songs, which promoted the idea of a free Estonia. He refused to admit that his works were formalist: "I consider myself a realist in music. I tried to compose beautiful music that would sound nice, touch listeners' souls, and be understandable to them."[69]

Having extracted basic information from Karindi, Interrogator Klochko focused on the cases of Vettik and Päts. Because the same interrogator oversaw all three cases, we can compare and contrast his investigation practices. Vettik's interrogation started with the straightforward question, "Why were you arrested?" He could only answer, "Probably for my activities in the past." Next he was asked questions on issues already raised during meetings.[70] Thus a great part of the interrogator's job had been done.

The questions put to Päts were similar, although the interrogator took a harsher tone at the initial questioning. At first, Riho Päts continued with the strong self-criticism that had been forced on him since 1948. Perhaps, like many other convicts, he placed his hopes on a sincere confession, adding facts that seemed to endanger him. Later, when he was transferred to a general cell from solitary confinement, he accepted the suggestions of his prison mates, offering more combative answers and briefer descriptions.[71] He admitted that his creative mistake had been taking West European music psychology as his starting point.[72]

Yet, as noted above, issues of musical components and even formalism may be considered secondary, because the interrogator mainly focused on mapping the relationships between different groups and circles of friends. The statements were fixed as evidence that became the basis for conviction and was used to extort new confessions. Particularly effective in this effort were general, seemingly innocent questions such as what are the Estonian musical schools and who works at them; whose works have you performed; and what is the situation at the TSC. Answers to these questions yielded a larger number of names. Vettik was more talkative than Karindi and Päts and was asked more questions. He also had to characterize the political mindset of the singers in his mixed choir.[73] The opinions he let slip gave the investigators good reason to further examine the activities of those named and to take useful notes for the investigation. Clearly, the authorities wanted to impart a wider significance to the activities of the arrestees. Possible criminal groups were constructed around the academic schools of many acknowledged composers, such as Heino Eller and Eduard Tubin.

Relationships with students were also targeted. After the three lecturers had been arrested, some of their students were accused of ideological immaturity and expelled without being allowed to take their final exams.[74] After the war, many people of different ages and background had enrolled at the conservatory. Among them were those demobilized from the Red Army, for whom the authorities reserved special opportunities for studying and who were supposed to shape a Soviet mentality and attitude toward work at the schools.[75] Ernst Johanson, who had fought in the Red Army, began his studies at the TSC in 1946. He was more interested in politics than in music, and he made a habit of monitoring the behavior of lecturers. Several speeches at meetings, as well as his testimony to the secret police about how lectures were conducted, confirm his loyalty to the Party. According to him, Päts had publicly said in a lecture, "Do not expect education in the Marxist-Leninist spirit from me." Johanson interpreted his own underperformance at school as persecution—stating, for example, that Päts had ordered the piano teacher Veera Kansa to rate him as "unsatisfactory" because of his Red Army background.[76] At the trial, Päts asked for other students' testimony concerning his teaching to be taken into account, but this was regarded as unnecessary.[77]

Johanson also informed the school's party organization that those arrested had support groups at school and argued that it was wrong that their close relatives continued to work there.[78] That very evening, Associate Professor Made Päts, Riho Päts's wife, received a concise note from Director Lukk, saying "You can no longer work as teacher."[79] The sanctions hit the whole family. Made Päts's brother, the teacher Valfried Jakobson, was also fired. Päts's daughter Leelo was expelled from the school. Finally, she found a job in an orchard, because she could not be employed by any cultural institution. Her mother shared the same fate and became a worker at a knitting enterprise. Leelo's husband, Erich Kõlar, was arrested during a tour of the State Philharmonic's variety orchestra in the autumn of 1951. Leelo followed her husband to Kirov oblast with their daughter, who was born in 1951. Yet for the draft indictment, the interrogator also had to list the men's criminal musical works. The questions put by Interrogator Klochko reflect his confusion about the state of affairs in choral music—which songs were allowed or prohibited at the moment. Using musical terms and later works that reflected Soviet themes, the convicts could have rejected the allegations of formalism. Sometimes they formulated clever arguments in self-defense. For example, Vettik claimed that formalism could only occur in instrumental music and all those who later wrote vocal music had become realists.[80]

Here the interrogator got some help from colleagues of the composers whose testimonies downplayed the attempts to find compromises. The confession of Acting UC Director Harri Kõrvits (1915–2003) concerning Vettik's work was clear: although Vettik had written new, Soviet songs, they distorted Soviet reality. As an example, he cited the song "Immortality," using lyrics by Mart Raud, in which Lenin had been made faceless and listeners could not get a true picture of the immortality of the great leader and organizer of the Bolshevik Party.[81] As Vettik's pupil Linda Bachmann-Kallikorm remembered, "Immortality" ended with the phrase "let there be peace," which sounded like "rest in peace." As a result, it sounded like a speech at Lenin's funeral, instead of praise.[82] Kõrvits also informed the investigator about Karindi's distortions in his cantatas "Victory" and "A Song about Stalin," in which he had used common folk motives from the Bible.[83] When Bruno Lukk's turn came, he argued that the cantata "Victory" did not emphasize its main idea and therefore was not sincere.[84] Nikolai Goldschmidt, whose statements before the arrests had been the main basis for the investigator's accusations, had also taken notes at concerts. He was disturbed by a concert held in the Estonia Theater in 1948, where Vettik's songs "were greeted with strong ovations by nationalist circles," although he had previously been harshly criticized by the Union of Composers.[85] All these testimonies confirmed that the creative work of the three suspects contained anti-Soviet elements.

After almost a year of investigation, both Riho Päts and Tuudur Vettik were sentenced to twenty-five plus five years of imprisonment. The case of Alfred Karindi was to be sent to Moscow because it concerned an operative of the secret police.[86] He was convicted and sentenced to ten years in a forced labor camp with confiscation of all property. The same article was applied to all three. The charges were similar, although there were also a few differences. Karindi was accused of disclosing classified data (his connections with the network of agents), whereas Vettik supposedly tried to disseminate bourgeois-nationalist influences to the masses through his music and songs—evidence of his popularity among singers and those who participated in the song festivals.[87]

The report of ESSR Minister of Security Valentin Moskalenko to Secretary of the CC EC(b)P Johannes Käbin on 29 July 1950 describes the angry reactions of people provoked by cuts in the repertoire and the conductors' arrests.[88] The elimination of these popular conductors also sent a signal to the people to refrain from nostalgia for the past and stay within the limits of loyalty to the new regime. The continuity of the song festival tradition vividly reminded people of the past, boosting national self-consciousness and self-identity.[89] Although it was difficult to control the singers and the repertoire, the event as a whole was not cancelled because it was supposed to demonstrate the new authorities' friendly attitude toward Estonia's heritage, and the song festivals could be interpreted as examples of the positive influence of Russian culture.[90]

"PARTY MEMBERS HAVE STARTED TO PLAY A LEADING ROLE"

The conviction of the three conductors was a warning to all musicians.[91] Other lecturers at the TSC were also in danger of being arrested. Given the amount of information gathered by different institutions, it is actually surprising that no mass arrest of musicians occurred. For some, the past played a more crucial role than for others. Enhanced security measures were often imposed at the initiative of fellow citizens and due to detailed confessions as part of self-criticism: some shortcomings were admitted only under strong pressure. This unpredictability deepened the general feeling of insecurity in society, further amplified by the Eighth Plenum of the CC ECP in March 1950, where the ruling elite of the ESSR was replaced by figures more loyal to Moscow. Former leaders of the ESSR were accused of underestimating class struggle and personnel policy and excessive compromises; they were considered to be responsible for many mistakes. Riho Päts and Tuudur Vettik were also marked as persons related to the dismissal of Nigol Andresen (literary critic, people's commissar for education in 1940–1946, deputy chairman of the Presidium of the Supreme Soviet in 1946–1949, imprisoned in 1950–1955).[92] The interrogator, however, did not consider these relationships important, although Goldschmidt pointed to them and condemned them as "one group."[93]

By 1950, professional competence had been pushed aside in the TSC, and loyalty to party politics became decisive. All carriers of alien ideas had to be identified and all the personnel in every department had to be examined individually. To better understand the background of the employees, the party organization established a special commission that identified numerous falsehoods in resumes (wrong data about the past, social origin, family members who had escaped to the West, etc.). Many people were "caught." Also, many prohibited songs were still taught. The Estonian musical heritage as a whole had to be reassessed, and the former harmful examples had to be replaced by progressive Russian musical works. From the mid-1930s on, Russians came to be considered the most progressive Soviet nation, leading the way to the modernized socialist culture.[94] Composers faced a serious dilemma: how to create music that was simultaneously Estonian, Soviet (Russian), yet original. Using folk music was considered the only right approach in the fight against "formalism." This meant the restoration of national Romanticism in its original form, but in the 1950s this was not compatible with the style of most Estonian composers. Very few of the works written in 1945–1955 can be considered their best.[95]

Although everything revolved around criticism and self-criticism, there were still too many who remained "silent" or were not enthusiastic about the new campaigns. As mentioned at a special meeting of the State Philharmonic, "all criticism is welcome; even if it contains only 10 percent of the truth, it still helps us take corrective action."[96]

Auditors from the Ministry of Higher Education sent from Moscow to Tallinn shared guidelines for making the criticism even more effective—that is, they also participated in the students' music history exams.[97] The meetings of the party organization became a kind of courtroom where party members practiced trials on a personal level, thereby becoming direct instruments of the regime being enforced. At discussions of personnel issues, officials and colleagues actually behaved like interrogators. Political vigilance not only paralyzed teachers and had a depressing effect on the school's general atmosphere but also decreased the number of true followers of the new ideology. The number of party members remained extremely low; in 1951, only nine people at the TSC belonged to the party.[98] Bruno Lukk, the acting director of the TSC and a candidate party member as of June 1949, did not join the Party. Nor did Nikolai Goldschmidt, who declared that he would not become a member "so long as Andresen, Semper, and Karotamm remain there."[99]

Changes in personnel, direct repressions, exposure of "enemies," and conflicts fueled by extensive criticism led to the creation of a toxic workplace but did not strengthen the positions of party and Komsomol members as intended. Most people regarded Soviet loyalists as collaborators, careerists, even traitors. Endel Lippus, a student at the time, referred to such pressure as a battle for life. It was a time when "educated people tried to deny their principles, values, and knowledge—when friend climbed on friend, trying to keep his balance. Absurdity ruled and led. . . . Everyone who was not ready to prostrate himself before the authorities was attacked. . . . The Conservatory should be ashamed of this period."[100]

The Eighth Plenum of the CC ECP in March 1950 proved to be a culminating moment in the struggle between new and old modes of thought and values. The former director Vladimir Alumäe—who had employed Päts, Vettik, and Karindi and favored "cosmopolitans"—received most of the blame for the situation at the TSC. Eugen Kapp also held him responsible for the mistakes at the 1947 song festival, where the Soviet repertoire was pushed to the background.[101] The volatile antipathy between Alumäe and Arder resurfaced, as did old tensions. Arder accused Alumäe of being hypocritical, undervaluing the Soviet people, favoring un-Soviet elements and sect members, and with their support bowing to Western culture and "cultural traitors of the Estonian people" who had fled to the West.[102]

As was typical in such situations, the sinner had to begin by admitting his guilt. Alumäe did accept some responsibility, but he refused to take all the blame. According to him, the Union of Composers and the Party at both the republican and local levels had made the same mistakes: that is, he also saw Party Secretary Arder as responsible, since he had been complicit in covering up the un-Soviet phenomena. Thus Arder's accusations were turned against himself. In July 1951, the Bureau of the CC ECP made a decision that in the case of Alumäe a strict reprimand would be issued "for bluntness of political vigilance," although he would remain a party member so that he could correct his mistakes.[103] Perhaps Alumäe's skill in defending himself against the criticism was derived from his experience in Leningrad? It is known that he was under observation by the Fifth Section of the Committee on State Security. In April 1951, an agent code-named Bekaar was recruited to follow Alumäe.[104] Arder and several other creative people were also under the scrutiny of the secret police.[105]

Eighteen months later, in December 1953, Alumäe requested that his sentence be overturned, and this request was soon granted. Suddenly, his colleagues' statements became understanding and supportive. Arder even praised him in superlatives. He was described as an accomplished musician who loved teaching, had thoroughly corrected his mistakes, held authority among colleagues and students, and was a Communist with high moral standards and an exemplary family man.[106] The earlier hostility seems to have vanished. From 1964 to 1970, Alumäe again became rector of the TSC.

These are years of incredible twists in human relationships and abrupt changes. In this context, the activities and statements of Nikolai Goldschmidt deserve special attention because they reflect a strong need for recognition, a goal he had failed to attain for many years despite his efforts. In the 1930s, he contacted the Soviet embassy in Estonia, and in the Soviet rear he was recruited as an agent code-named Rex to keep an eye on cultural figures. Yet his efforts did not receive the approval he expected. In January 1951, Goldschmidt was arrested and excluded from the list of agents because his reports had been too general and of little value.[107] Before that, he was dismissed from his job as artistic director of the State Philharmonic due to the "formal" attitude he displayed toward his duties, leading to financial loss and scandals.

Paradoxically, Goldschmidt himself could not tolerate criticism. When complaints were voiced, he marched out of the party meeting, wrote numerous letters of complaint, and strongly objected to being "boiled in the same kettle as bourgeois nationalists like Vettik and Päts," against whom he had fought.[108] In lieu of the missing self-criticism, he launched attacks on several party members that resulted in accusations of defamation. When Moskalenko, minister of state security of the ESSR, sent a special message to Secretary Käbin on 3 April 1950 about the mood of the populace after the eighth plenum, he described Goldschmidt's joy over the dismissal of Karotamm and other leading figures. Goldschmidt compared them to migratory birds who had been caught, lessening his burden.[109]

He insulted Käbin, who had been appointed first secretary after Karotamm, by saying that "nothing has changed in the Central Committee since the plenum" and arguing that his own services and fight against bourgeois nationalists had not been valued enough. Although the security service had earlier noted his unsuitability as an agent, he could find facts in people's biographies that had remained unnoticed. One of the most remarkable examples was the case of Harri Kõrvits, who had served as acting secretary of the Estonian Union of Composers in 1944–1950 and himself inflicted harsh criticism, as mentioned above. Yet Kõrvits had omitted certain sensitive details of his career (membership in the Defense League, a job as a church organist) from his autobiography. After Goldschmidt lodged a complaint listing these compromising facts, First Secretary Käbin commented that clearly "nobody had taken a personal interest in Kõrvits," then proposed his dismissal. Even in the case of people whose background had been checked, signals about their "political past" could be decisive. The same happened to Goldschmidt with the disclosure of his participation in the War of Independence and fight against the Soviet army in 1919–1920, his Menshevik Party membership, and more. Although the list of his offenses was rather long, he was sentenced to five years of forced settlement in Kazakhstan as a socially dangerous element. He was granted amnesty in 1953 and cleared of the charges in 1962.[110]

After that, he worked as head of music and literature at the Estonia Theater. Kõrvits was dismissed from the post of secretary of the Union of Composers in 1952 due to his heavy workload and simultaneous studies at the TSC.[111] He was later director of a museum and worked at radio stations and journals.

Mass purges at Estonian universities stopped in 1952, when the Party adopted a more pragmatic attitude toward the "old intelligentsia" and punishment became more differentiated.[112] In 1952, Eugen Kapp, the director of the

TSC at the time, claimed that party members had acquired a leading role at the academy, but this opinion was rather subjective. At the UC board meeting discussing Kõrvits's dismissal, it was stated that endless intrigues and critical "takedowns" of composers had totally demotivated them. The terms "groups" or "gangs" were still used, but people were divided into those who could listen to others and tolerate criticism and those who could not. The fight to destroy friendships gave way to requests to organize meetings to get to know and help each other. Although there were still lots of critical speeches, Eugen Kapp expressed the hope that the tensions would be mitigated and consensus would soon be restored.[113] Yet many years passed before the situation was normalized, and the ignoble conflicts led to long-time complications. Mutual trust is easier to destroy than to restore.

VISIBLE AND INVISIBLE CONTOURS OF TRUST AND DISTRUST

Constant accusations and persecution made people more vulnerable. Many attacked each other instinctively through "criticism and self-criticism." Behind the excessive rhetoric of the authorities lay alienation, distrust, withdrawal, a decline in educational and creative work, and hypocrisy—heightened in an atmosphere of constant criticism and conflict. Analyzing these events more than a half-century later, we look for the consequences of destroying collegial and friendly relationships. What happened later between those complicit in the purging and those released from prison and excluded from the TSC? To what extent was reconciliation or mutual understanding possible? Such questions still meet with silence. It is difficult to find a suitable way to discuss these situations.

Alfred Karindi, whose imprisonment was shorter, was released in 1954. At first, he found a job as a piano tuner; many years later, he was invited to return to the TSC, where he worked until his illness in 1967. When Riho Päts was released from the prison camp in 1955, the TSC first made him a job offer, then withdrew it. He found work at the Tallinn Pedagogical Institute, which had opened its Department of Music Teaching. Tuudur Vettik was released in 1956 and returned to his professorship of conducting until 1962, when renewed conflict forced him to leave the school. A contradictory personality, Vettik expressed his frustration by sending anonymous letters to his colleagues, which led to the TSC demanding his resignation.[114] None of the three could restore his former social status or position.

Denis Kozlov and Eleonory Gilburd's *The Thaw* marks the period from Stalin's death to the end of the 1960s as a crucial time in Soviet history, one that produced significant shifts in policies, ideas, artistic practices, daily life, and so on.[115] One such shift concerned the reintegration of prisoners and forced settlers into society. Their reunions with those who remained at home were not easy. In fact, the attitudes and judgments of fellow citizens in the homeland were the most problematic. Adaptation and pragmatic collaboration with the Soviet system had become widespread in Estonian society.[116] The returnees often faced mistrust and discrimination in their new life.[117] Alan Barenberg and others have shown that reintegration is a multifaceted phenomenon.[118] As Amir Weiner has noted, regional variables and experiences must also be taken into account.[119]

Multiple entities were involved in both prosecution and exoneration. These included the Communist Party, the secret police, and local government but also fellow citizens (friends, colleagues, relatives, etc.). The deported experienced their return to the homeland as an emotionally long-awaited moment. Yet the ESSR authorities regarded them as problematic and therefore imposed restrictions on and intensified KGB surveillance of them. Rehabilitation of the repressed generally meant that the punishment they had been forced to endure was deemed excessive, if not misplaced, and regulatory limitations were usually removed. The removal, however, was a multistage process that differed according to categories and involved several court and governmental institutions and commissions, causing a lot of confusion.[120]

The authorities' tendency toward exclusion sent a message to the rest of society. Returnees were demoted to second-rate citizens whom others were advised to avoid. As a result, they became doubly marginalized people, who had been marked as enemies during the Stalinist period and retained a questionable status even after their return home. Various applications submitted to the authorities describe the unequal treatment meted out to former detainees. In examples of both compliance with the restrictions and the refusal to observe them we see evidence of maneuvering and manipulation that heightened tensions in society and individual relationships, indicating the authorities' desire to maintain an atmosphere of social distrust.[121] When we compare the views of Tallinn and Moscow on rehabilitation, it was the leaders of the Estonian Communist Party who were most hostile toward the repressed in the 1960s. In fact, in the 1950s–1960s only about 10 percent of the repressed were rehabilitated.[122]

All three of the conductors studied here applied for rehabilitation to get rid of the "stigma" and restore their reputations. Before approving rehabilitation, the secret police investigated these people again, reopening old personal files, gathering evidence, and, if necessary, interrogating the applicants and their acquaintances. Karindi was the first whose application for rehabilitation was successful. Vettik also began to fight for his rights as soon as possible. In 1954, an expert commission was formed at the TSC that had to give an assessment of him, but his activities were still characterized as bourgeois-nationalist. Only in 1968, after repeated petitions, did he secure a ruling annulling his sentence.[123]

In the same year, 1968, Päts was also rehabilitated. While waiting, he wrote his memoirs, where we can clearly see the emotional wounds that were torn open again at that time. For the new investigation, a secret expert commission of three was formed at the TSC to assess his creative work from a political standpoint. They reviewed the articles, textbooks, other writings, and songs produced by Päts in the 1930s about which questions had been asked during his interrogation in 1950. The experts tried to characterize the nature of this work in milder terms than in 1950, when they were labeled anti-Soviet and politically harmful. Yet they still mention problematic ideas in the written works and national motives in songs that "praise the fatherland that has become free"—that is, independent Estonia.[124] The questions about an individual's "political past" still remained relevant.

The UC's description of Päts portrays him as a many-sided musician who achieved remarkable results as a teacher and conductor. The union claimed not to know why Päts was unexpectedly arrested in 1950 and confirmed that after release he had taken an active part in musical life.[125] The lack of clarity about the details of Päts's and Vettik's cases, including their connection with the dismissal of Andresen, is also characteristic of other sources. Relying on diverse evidence, the ESSR Prosecutor's Office proposed to modify the conviction due to a lack of offenses. After that, the Supreme Court of the ESSR issued its ruling.

Reading both Päts's memoirs and his application for rehabilitation, which describes the accusations and the process of interrogation, reveals the most sensitive aspects of the events. Päts was particularly traumatized by what happened at the TSC, which set students against teachers and showed his colleagues to be hypocritical. The behavior of Bruno Lukk, a close family friend who served as director of the TSC in 1948–1951 and taught piano to Päts's daughter Leelo, was especially depressing. Leelo herself recalled how Lukk visited them often, how they sat with her father and talked until late at night. A short time before Päts's arrest, Lukk had praised him for his pedagogical work, but at the interrogation and in court, he said the opposite, speaking of the great damage that Päts's nationalist views and criminal activities had done to the education of Soviet youth.[126]

Bruno Lukk's personal files shed light on this situation. Although he appeared to be an obedient Soviet citizen, his story also has another side. In

April 1951, he asked to be relieved of his duties due to his deteriorating health. According to a report of the CC EC(b)P, however, he had been accused of serious shortcomings in his teaching and educational work. There was a "black spot" in Lukk's autobiography. His maternal grandmother was German, and his older sister and three brothers left Estonia during the resettlement (*Umsiedlung*), when Hitler invited the Germans to return to their fatherland. His second sister had already gone to live in Vienna in 1930. Between 1928 and 1938, Lukk studied and worked in Germany and traveled a lot in Europe with his ensemble. His political past was ruined, and he understood quite clearly how close relatives could influence his career, arguing with ever greater intensity in his statements about himself that he had had no contact with them since 1940. He even goes as far as to forswear them: "I consider it absolutely normal that I have nothing in common with them, and I cannot bear responsibility for their life and behavior."[127] His background, though, strongly influenced Lukk's behavior. Many years later, he repeatedly visited his relatives in West Germany and brought vinyl records from there. Colleagues and pupils recalled: "At Lukk's place we could enjoy records of world-famous performers—what was inaccessible to us at that time became accessible for him thanks to his sister, who lived in Germany."[128] Memoirs of Bruno Lukk published ten years ago speak of him as a man of great spiritual strength and uncompromising character, which made him the most beloved but also the most feared teacher. Being his pupil was considered to be a special privilege.[129]

As we can see, people were vulnerable to manipulation during campaigns of criticism and self-criticism. Some of them were able to hide behind double standards, but others were less successful. This second group obeyed orders to defend themselves because of their positions, ambitions, or personal rivalries. It is usually difficult to explain the reasons. In retrospect, it was embarrassing to acknowledge fears, contradictory emotions, the inability to find dignified solutions, ignorance, and guilt. The rejection of unpleasant, harmful, or immoral cases may later have been associated with various cover stories.

Päts and Lukk did not overcome their differences. Päts's return to the TSC would have increased the tensions within the university, and therefore he never got a job there. Leelo Päts-Kõlar has recollected that Lukk was very much afraid of her father; whenever he caught sight of Päts, he moved away to avoid a meeting. She characterized Lukk as a person who changed throughout his life.[130] The composer Veljo Tormis (1930–2017) recalled the case of the three conductors as follows: "All this was somehow alarming and incomprehensible. I have to admit that I did not actually dare to speak about such things with the others. . . . Even now, there are some things that people have agreed not to talk about, and at that time it was the ideological segregation and purging that one did not discuss. And even at home we did not dare, or rather, did not want to talk about it."[131] Even today, the painful consequences of these events have not been adequately acknowledged.

The Sovietization of the Baltic states meant importing Soviet models of life in all their multifarious details. This could not be a painless process because it implied the introduction of many levels of control, ranging from negative sanctions (the death penalty, arrest, deportation, dismissal, imprisonment, warning) to positive rewards (awards and privileges, promotion, recognition, respect, etc.).[132] The arrested conductors (Vettik, Päts, and Karindi) were subjected to all these measures of social control and discipline. After attempting to adapt to the new situation in 1940–1949 and making compromises, they were pushed out of the society and imprisoned. Such a horrifying turn of events had to make other musicians more compliant and clearly shows the political significance of music.

The slogan of "criticism and self-criticism"—which accompanied the all-union campaigns against "formalism" and "cosmopolitanism" and, in Estonia, were related to the fight against "bourgeois nationalism"—triggered a chain of mass accusations in cultural and educational institutions that nobody could evade. Even apolitical people who preferred to remain silent were forced to speak at the meetings. When the measures undertaken to reeducate intellectuals—giving them extra time, tolerating their mistakes, looking for a "special way," and so on—did not produce satisfactory results, the authorities increased the pressure. Their ideal was to extend social control to all spheres of life, so that it functioned as a "collective eye," combining the disparate forces and efforts of inspection agencies and activists.[133]

The conservatory was subjected to multiple levels of control, from all-union institutions to internal commissions. Furthermore, aggressive accusations affected interpersonal communication. People's resumes were damaged because of their "political past" in an environment polluted by old hostilities, personal ambitions, and initiatives. As a result, the number of good instructors declined until more unsuitable than suitable staff remained. Even those newly appointed to office might see their positions change quickly; there was also a lack of activists. The level of teaching fell, and the negative atmosphere hindered creative work. The UC party organization admitted that the air was so thick with accusations that work was impossible. By 1952, the Party's control of the TSC was firmly anchored, yet the "new rules of game" had created chaos in music and musical education.

The consequences of destroying old circles of friends and networks were most depressing and far-reaching. "Criticism and self-criticism" based on personal attacks, insults, humiliation, revenge, and disregard for authority turned the attackers into tools in the hands of the secret police and destroyed mutual respect and support among colleagues. Trust gave way to suspicion, a necessary component of control. Because the testimony of friends had a strong influence, they became part of the central reeducation battles and were sometimes more effective than fear. Under such pressure, people had to learn to defend themselves in a new way, to invent suitable arguments, use less harmful words, be as indirect as possible, and bear with criticism and manipulation. Personal files and minutes of meetings reflect the complicated process of acquiring experience. It is much more difficult to study trust in interpersonal relations, and as Yoram Gorlizki has recognized, systematic data for studying these processes can also be hard to find. While the notion of trust is not easy either to identify or to observe, it is widely used.[134]

Since the Soviet occupation (1940–1941 and 1944–1991) of Estonia lasted longer than the period of republican independence (1918–1940), the double standards of Soviet culture that were so violently attacked had the opportunity to grow roots and gain ground. According to the cultural historian and sociologist Aili Aarelaid-Tart (1947–2014), the time of cruel contradictions and social pretense gave rise to a new personality type—the so-called honest split person who behaved simultaneously in a Soviet and European manner yet did not recognize the contradiction and felt herself to be a coherent personality.[135] Yet for many people the internal censorship and double standards became problematic later when it would have been possible to speak honestly about past conflicts, and most of them avoided doing so. People preferred to remain silent about uncomfortable emotions, including the feeling of guilt. The writer Ene Mihkelson (1944–2017), whose novels shed light on the "dark spots" in Estonian history, has rightly pointed out: "How a person reacts at points of upheaval, how he interprets them later, shapes his further life and self-esteem."[136]

In the turmoil of purgings and campaigns, when almost all composers were threatened—not so much because of their work as due to other factors—the choirs suffered less. Without a doubt, the official repertoire of the choirs was controlled and filled with ideologically custom-made songs, but the mental atmosphere of the choirs remained intact, and they continued to sing national songs among themselves throughout the Soviet period. Although Soviet authorities hoped to "domesticate" the song festival for Soviet purposes, they were never able to make the song festival theirs.[137]

In the second half of the 1950s, the creative atmosphere began to recover, and modernist tendencies in art and music emerged.[138] Although Stalinism fell out of favor and gave way to the power strategies and dynamics of the Cold War, relationships within circles of friends, including the conscious fueling of conflicts, did not lose their relevance. For example, only after repeated petitions was Vladimir Alumäe—earlier accused of honoring the music of colleagues who had fled to the West, above all Eduard Tubin—commissioned to revive old contacts to get Tubin to attend the 1960 song festival in Tallinn, an initiative characteristic of the new policy of developing cultural relationships with the West. This is another story, yet it grows out of the distrust, conflicts, and relationships examined in this chapter.

NOTES

I am grateful to *Kritika*'s anonymous readers for their helpful commentary on this chapter and to David-Ilmar Beecher, Muriel Blaive, Michael David-Fox, Anu Kannike, Anu Kõlar, Laine Randjärv, Tõnu Tannberg, and Amir Weiner for their invaluable comments and suggestions. I also wish to thank the Fellowship at the Imre Kertész Kolleg, FSU Jena, and the Fulbright Visiting Scholar Program at Stanford University for funding my research and the archivists at the Estonian National Archives and my students, who provided invaluable practical help at various stages of the project. This research was supported by the project "War after War" (PHVAJ16908).

1. Eesti Rahvusarhiiv (RA) ERA R-1958/1/17/35–48.

2. Pauline Fairclough, *Classics for the Masses: Shaping Soviet Musical Identity under Lenin and Stalin* (New Haven: Yale University Press, 2016), 201–21; Ekaterina Vlasova, *1948 god v sovetskoi muzyke: Dokumentirovannoe issledovanie* (Moscow: Klassika-XXI, 2010).

3. David Brandenberger, *National Bolshevism: Stalinist Mass Culture and the Formation of Modern Russian National Identity, 1931–1956* (Cambridge, MA: Harvard University Press, 2002); Tiiu Kreegipuu, "Eesti kultuurielu sovetiseerimine: Nõukogude kultuuripoliitika eesmärgid ja institutsionaalne raamistik aastatel 1944–1954," in *Eesti NSV aastatel 1940–1953: Sovetiseerimise mehhanismid ja tagajärjed. Nõukogude Liidu ja Ida-Euroopa arengute kontekstis. Eesti Ajalooarhiivi toimetised*, ed. Tõnu Tannberg (Tartu: Eesti Ajalooarhiivi Kirjastus, 2007), 352–86.

4. Benjamin Tromly, *Making the Soviet Intelligentsia: Universities and Intellectual Life under Stalin and Khrushchev* (New York: Cambridge University Press, 2014); Michael David-Fox, *Crossing Borders: Modernity, Ideology, and Culture in Russia and the Soviet Union* (Pittsburgh: University of Pittsburgh Press, 2015); Vladislav Zubok, *Zhivago's Children: The Last Russian Intelligentsia* (Cambridge, MA: Harvard University Press, 2009); Toomas Karjahärm and Väino Sirk, *Kohanemine ja vastupanu: Eesti haritlaskond 1940–1987* (Tallinn: Argo, 2007); Violeta Davoliūtė, *The Making and Breaking of Soviet Lithuania: Memory and Modernity in the Wake of War* (New York: Routledge, 2013).

5. Sheila Fitzpatrick, "Politics as Practice: Thoughts on a New Soviet Political History," *Kritika: Explorations in Russian and Eurasian History* 5, no. 1 (2004): 43–51.

6. Geoffrey Hosking, *Trust: A History* (Oxford: Oxford University Press, 2014), 9–21; Hosking, "Trust and Distrust in the USSR: An Overview," *Slavonic and East European Review* 91, no. 1 (2013): 1–25.

7. Jelena Zubkova, *Baltimaad ja Kreml 1940–53* (Tallinn: Varrak, 2009), 93–94.

8. Anne E. Gorsuch, "From Iron Curtain to Silver Screen: Imagining the West in the Khrushchev Era," in *Imagining the West in Eastern Europe and the Soviet Union*, ed., György Péteri (Pittsburgh: University of Pittsburgh Press, 2010), 164–67; Simo Mikkonen and Pia Koivunen, *Beyond the Divide: Entangled Histories of Cold War Europe* (New York: Berghahn Books, 2018); Andres Kasekamp, *History of the Baltic States* (New York: Palgrave Macmillan, 2010), 124–71.

9. Pierre Bourdieu, *Outline of a Theory of Practice* (Cambridge: Cambridge University Press, 2005), 171–83.

10. Marju Lauristin and Peeter Vihalemm, *Minu laulu- ja tantsupidu: Sotsioloogilise uuringu aruanne* (Tartu: Eesti Laulu- ja Tantsupeo SA, 2013), 46; Kristin Kuutma, "Laulupeod rahvusliku identiteedi kandjana," *Mäetagused*, no. 1–2 (1996): 80–94; Kanni Labi, "Isamaalaulud ja okupatsioonirežiim—nostalgia, utoopia ja reaalsus," *Methis*, no. 7 (2011): 109–21; Emilia Pawłusz, "The Estonian Song Celebration (Laulupidu) as an Instrument of Language Policy," *Journal of Baltic Studies* 48, no. 2 (2017): 251–71.

11. David L. Hoffmann, *Cultivating the Masses: Modern State Practices and Soviet Socialism, 1914–1939* (Ithaca, NY: Cornell University Press, 2011), 224–37; Hoffmann, *Stalinist Values: The Cultural Norms of Soviet Modernity, 1917–1941* (Ithaca, NY: Cornell University Press, 2003), 166–75; Pauline Fairclough, *Classics for the Masses: Shaping Soviet Musical Identity under Lenin and Stalin* (New Haven: Yale University Press, 2016), 213–16; Gleb Tsipursky, *Socialist Fun: Youth, Consumption, and State-sponsored Popular Culture in the Soviet Union, 1945–1970* (Pittsburgh: University of Pittsburgh Press, 2016), 32–73.

12. Vladimir Shlapentokh, *A Normal Totalitarian Society: How the Soviet Union Functioned and How It Collapsed* (Armonk, NY: M. E. Sharpe, 2001), 75; Merle Fainsod, *How Russia Is Ruled* (Cambridge, MA: Harvard University Press, 1965); Sheila Fitzpatrick, *Everyday Stalinism: Ordinary Life in Extraordinary Times. Soviet Russia in the 1930s* (Oxford: Oxford University Press, 1999); Mark Harrison, *One Day We Will Live without Fear: Everyday Lives under the Soviet Police State* (Stanford, CA: Hoover Institution Press, 2016); A. V. Klimov, *Sotsial'nyi kontrol' v razvitom sotsialisticheskom obshchestve* (Saratov: Izdatel'stvo Saratovskogo universiteta, 1984), 62.

13. Richard Taruskin, *Defining Russia Musically: Historical and Hermeneutical Essays* (Princeton, NJ: Princeton University Press, 1997); Marina Frolova-Walker, *Russian Music and Nationalism: From Glinka to Stalin* (New Haven: Yale University Press, 2007); Frolova-Walker, *Stalin's Music Prize: Soviet Culture and Politics* (New Haven: Yale University Press, 2016); Meri E. Herrala, *The Struggle for Control of Soviet Music from 1932 to 1948: Socialist Realism vs. Western Formalism* (Lewiston, ME: Edwin Mellen, 2012); Simo Mikkonen and Pekka Suutari, eds., *Music, Art and Diplomacy: East-West Cultural Interactions and the Cold War* (Farnham: Ashgate, 2016).

14. J. Arch Getty and Roberta Thompson Manning, eds., *Stalinist Terror: New Perspectives* (Cambridge: Cambridge University Press, 1993); David L. Hoffmann, *Stalinism: The Essential Readings* (Malden, MA: Blackwell, 2003); Igal Halfin, *Stalinist Confessions: Messianism and Terror at the Leningrad Communist University* (Pittsburgh: University of Pittsburgh Press, 2009); Valentina Glajar, Alison Lewis, and Corina L. Petrescu, eds., *Secret Police Files from the Eastern Bloc: Between Surveillance and Life Writing* (Rochester: Camden House, 2016); Molly Pucci, *Security Empire: The Secret Police in Communist Eastern Europe* (New Haven: Yale University Press, 2020).

15. Kiril Tomoff, "'Most Respected Comrade . . .': Patrons, Clients, Brokers, and Unofficial Networks in the Stalinist Music World," *Contemporary European History* 11, no. 1 (2002): 65.

16. Patrick Zuk, "Nikolay Myaskovsky and the Events of 1948," *Music and Letters* 93, no. 1 (2012): 61–85.

17. Jan Gross, *Revolution from Abroad: The Soviet Conquest of Poland's Western Ukraine and Western Belorussia* (Princeton, NJ: Princeton University Press, 1989), 114–22.

18. Paul R. Gregory, *Terror by Quota: State Security from Lenin to Stalin* (New Haven: Yale University Press, 2009); J. Arch Getty, *Practicing Stalinism: Bolsheviks, Boyars, and the Persistence of Tradition* (New Haven: Yale University Press, 2013); Sheila Fitzpatrick and Robert Gellately, eds., *Accusatory Practices: Denunciation in Modern European History, 1789–1989* (Chicago: University of Chicago Press, 1997); Wendy Z. Goldman, *Inventing the Enemy: Denunciation and Terror in Stalin's Russia* (Cambridge: Cambridge University Press, 2011).

19. Amir Weiner and Aigi Rahi-Tamm, "Getting to Know You: The Soviet Surveillance System, 1939–1957," *Kritika: Explorations in Russian and Eurasian History* 13, no. 1 (2012): 44–45.

20. Aili Aarelaid, "Topeltmõtlemise kujunemine kahel esimesel nõukogulikul aastakümnel," *Akadeemia*, no. 4 (2000): 765.

21. Toomas Karjahärm and Helle-Mai Luts, *Kultuurigenotsiid Eestis: Kunstnikud ja muusikud 1940–1953* (Tallinn: Argo, 2005); Kreegipuu, "Eesti kultuurielu sovetiseerimine," 352-88.

22. Jelena Zubkova, *Baltimaad ja Kreml 1940–53* (Tallinn: Varrak, 2009), 217–31; Tynu [Tõnu] Tannberg, *Politika Moskvy v respublikakh Baltii v poslevoennye gody (1944–1956): Issledovaniia i dokumenty* (Moscow: ROSSPEN, 2010); Tannberg, ed., *Behind the Iron Curtain: Soviet Estonia in the Era of the Cold War* (Frankfurt am Main: Peter Lang, 2015); Olaf Mertelsmann, ed., *The Sovietization of the Baltic States, 1940–1956* (Tartu: Kleio Ajalookirjanduse Sihtasutus, 2003).

23. RA ERAF 130sm/1/6501/45–47p.

24. RA ERAF 130sm/1/6501/82–86; R. Päts, *Oh seda endista eluda. . .: Meenutusi möödunud aegadest*, ed. Leelo Kõlar and Airi Liimets (Tallinn: Tallinna Pedagoogikaülikooli kirjastus, 1999), 135.

25. Maret Tomson, "Riho Pätsi tegevus muusikaajakirjanikuna," *Teater. Muusika. Kino*, no. 2 (2000): 60.

26. Weiner and Rahi-Tamm, "Getting to Know You," 9–10.

27. Päts, *Oh seda endista eluda. . .*, 134–35.

28. Tomoff, "Most Respected Comrade," 33–65.

29. Erich Kaup, "Andrei Ždanovist ja tema missioonist Eestisse 1940. aasta suvel II," *Tuna*, no. 3 (2005): 80.

30. Nikolai Karotamm, *Uut elu ehitades: Kõnesid ja kirjutisi 1945./1946. aastal* (Tallinn, Poliitiline kirjandus, 1946), 340–41.

31. Urve Lippus, "Transformation of an Institution—the First Soviet Estonian Song Festival," in *Musik in Diktaturen des 20. Jahrhunderts: Internationales Symposon an der Bergischen Universität Wuppertal vom 28./29.2.2004*, ed. Michaela G. Grochulski, Oliver Kautny, and Helmke Jan Keden (Mainz: Are Musik, 2006).

32. F. Lätte, "Rohkem tähelepanu ideoloogilisele tööle Tallinna Konservatooriumis," *Eesti Bolševik*, 11 June 1948.

33. RA ERAF 1/83/11/23–32.

34. RA ERAF 131/1/219/22–23.

35. RA ERAF 1/7/246/9.

36. Klimov, *Sotsial'nyi kontrol'*; Lynne Viola, *Stalinist Perpetrators on Trial: Scenes from the Great Terror in Soviet Ukraine* (New York: Oxford University Press, 2017); Geoffrey A. Hosking, *Rulers and Victims: The Russians in the Soviet Union* (Cambridge, MA: Belknap, 2006).

37. Aigi Rahi-Tamm, "Arhiivid Nõukogude repressiivaparaadi teenistuses: 'Poliitvärvingute' kartoteek Eestis 1940–1956," *Ajalooline Ajakiri* (127/128), no. 1–2 (2009): 123–54; Rahi-Tamm, "Fulfilling 'Special Tasks' in the Soviet Rear: Activity of the Department of Archives in the Years of 1941–1944," in *Baltijas regiona vesture 20. gadsimta 40.–80. gados/History of the Baltic Region of the 1940s–1980s*, ed. Dzintars Erglis (Riga: Institute of the History of Latvia Publishers, 2009), 384–99.

38. Aigi Rahi-Tamm and Irena Saleniece, "Re-educating Teachers: Ways and Consequences of Sovietization in Estonia and Latvia (1940–1960) from the Biographical Perspective," *Journal of Baltic Studies* 47, no. 4 (2016): 457.

39. John Connelly, *Captive University: The Sovietization of East German, Czech, and Polish Higher Education, 1945–1956* (Chapel Hill: University of North Carolina Press, 2000).

40. Vlasova, *1948 god v sovetskoi muzyke*.

41. On the Zhdanovshchina, see Frolova-Walker, *Stalin's Music Prize*; Herrala, *Struggle for Control of Soviet Music*; and Leah Goldman, "Nationally Informed: The Politics of National Music during Late Stalinism," *Jahrbücher für Geschichte Osteuropas* 67, no. 3 (2019): 372–400.

42. Andrei Artizov and Oleg V. Naumov, eds., *Vlast' i khudozhestvennaia intelligentsiia: Dokumenty TsK RKP(b)-VKP(b)-VChK-OGPU-NKVD o kul'turnoi politike, 1917–1953 gg.* (Moscow, Mezhdunarodnyi fond "Demokratiia," 1999), 630–34.

43. RA ERA R-1958/1/19/96.

44. The reason for singling out "The Great Friendship" remains obscure (see Goldman, "Nationally Informed," 381). In the Moscow Conservatory Muradeli had studied under Miaskovskii, who had never been at the center of a scandal yet now found himself caught up in the antiformalist campaign as a dangerous corruptor of Soviet youth.

45. RA ERA R-1958/1/26/62.

46. Merike Vaitmaa, "Eesti muusika muutumises: Viis viimast aastakümmet," in Valgeid laike eesti muusikaloost, ed. Urve Lippus (Tallinn: Eesti Muusikaakadeemia, 2000), 147.

47. RA ERAF 1/83/11/42–49.

48. RA ERAF 1/83/11/85.

49. RA ERA R-1958/1/19/15–32.

50. Kiril Tomoff, Creative Union: The Professional Organization of Soviet Composers, 1939–1953 (Ithaca, NY: Cornell University Press, 2006), 190–95, 201–3.

51. Urve Lippus, ed., Muutuste kümnend: EV Tallinna Konservatooriumi lõpp ja TRK algus (Tallinn: Eesti Muusika- ja Teatriakadeemia, 2011), 40.

52. RA ERA R-1958/1/19/97.

53. Alexei Kojevnikov, "Games of Stalinist Democracy: Ideological Discussions in Soviet Sciences, 1947–52," in Stalinism: New Directions, ed. Sheila Fitzpatrick (New York: Routledge, 2000), 150–53.

54. Ethan Pollock, Stalin and the Soviet Science Wars (Princeton, NJ: Princeton University Press, 2006), 2–5.

55. On the background of the accusations and connections of music with mass culture and politics, see Patrick Zuk, "Boris Asafiev in 1948," Journal of the Royal Musical Association 144, no. 1 (2019): 123–56.

56. RA ERAF 1/7/246/10.

57. Public letters of T. Vettik and R. Päts, Sirp ja Vasar, no. 42 (16 October 1948). See about cases of tearing off the masks and practices of reassessing the past in Igal Halfin, Terror in My Soul: Communist Autobiographies on Trial (Cambridge, MA: Harvard University Press, 2003), 245–73.

58. RA ERA R-1958/1/26/1–94.

59. Olev Liivik, "Campaign against 'Bourgeois Nationalism' and Repressions in Estonia," in Estonia since 1944: Reports of the Estonian International Commission for the Investigation of Crimes against Humanity, ed. Toomas Hiio, Meelis Maripuu, and Indrek Paavle (Tallinn: Tallinna Raamatutrükikoda, 2009), 116–20.

60. RA ERAF 1/7/246/33.

61. RA ERAF 130sm/1/1423/38–41, 111–13.

62. RA ERA R-2018/1/2/35–37.

63. Laine Randjärv, Loovisiksuse roll Eesti laulupeoliikumises aastatel 1940–1980: Tuudur Vettiku ja Roland Laasmäe epistoloogilise pärandi põhjal (Tartu: Tartu Ülikooli Kirjastus, 2013), 58–60.

64. RA ERAF 130sm/1/6501/82–92.

65. RA ERAF 130sm/1/1423/23.

66. RA ERAF 130sm/1/1423/28–31.

67. On interrogation practices, see Aigi Rahi-Tamm and Meelis Saueauk, "Nõukogude julgeolekuasutuste Stalini-aegseist ülekuulamisprotokollidest: Allikakriitiline ülevaade," Eesti Ajalooarhiivi toimetised = Acta et commentationes Archivi Historici Estoniae 23, 30 (2015): 218–43; and Molly Pucci, "Constructing a Confession: The Language and Psychology of Interrogations in Stalinist Czechoslovakia," Revising Stalin and Stalinism: Complexities, Contradictions, and Controversies, ed. James Ryan and Susan Grant (New York: Bloomsbury Academic, 2020): 141–54.

68. RA ERAF 130sm/1/1423/28–31, 47–49, 81–84, 98–101; RA ERAF 130sm/1/6456/36–38.

69. RA ERAF 130sm/1/1423/81–82.

70. RA ERAF 130sm/1/6456/16–21.

71. Helju Tauk, Muusikast võlutud (Tartu: Ilmamaa, 2010), 365–67.

72. RA ERAF 130sm/1/6501/18–32.

73. RA ERAF 130sm/1/6456/81–82, 307.

74. RA ERAF 130sm/1/6501/56–58.

75. Olaf Mertelsmann, "Olla tudeng stalinismi ajal," in *Tartu Ülikooli ajaloo küsimusi XXXIII*, ed. Lea Leppik (Tartu: Tartu Ülikooli Kirjastus, 2004), 141.

76. RA ERAF 130sm/1/6501/107–9.

77. RA ERAF 130sm/1/6501/173–74.

78. RA ERAF 7068/1/136/13–25.

79. Tauk, *Muusikast võlutud*, 370.

80. RA ERAF 130sm/1/6456/225–30. In 1937, Riho Päts interpreted the phenomenon of formalism as follows: in Soviet Russia all art known in Estonia and contemporary art, but especially works regarded as distanced from Socialist Realism—that is, the masses—were labeled as formalist. Formalist art does not deal with the main issues of socialist life. It is argued that formalism is the inability to use one's skills, that formalism and naturalism reflect indifference to life ("Muljeid Nõukogude—Vene muusikaelust," *Muusikaleht*, no. 9 [1937]: 180). The first extensive campaign against formalists in the USSR was launched in 1936 (Oleg V. Naumov et al., eds., *Soviet Culture and Power: A History in Documents, 1917–1953* [New Haven: Yale University Press, 2007], 229–48).

81. RA ERAF 130sm/1/6456/118–20.

82. Randjärv, *Loovisiksuse roll Eesti laulupeoliikumises*, 144–47.

83. RA ERAF 130sm/1/1423/82–83, 106–8.

84. RA ERAF 130sm/1/1423/109–10.

85. RA ERAF 130sm/1/6456/82–86.

86. RA ERAF 130sm/1/1423/217.

87. RA ERAF 130sm/1/6456/218–19.

88. RA ERAF 131/1/201/162–78.

89. Marge Allandi, "Laulupidu kui rituaal: Eesti üldlaulupeod rahvusliku kultuurimälu ja identiteedi kujundajate ja kandjatena," MA thesis (Tallinn: Tallinna Ülikool, Eesti Humanitaarinstituut, 2009).

90. Labi, "Isamaalaulud ja okupatsioonirežiim," 114–15.

91. RA ERAF 130sm/1/6501/116.

92. Kaljo-Olev Veskimägi, *Kuidas valitseti Eesti NSVD-d: Eestimaa Kommunistliku Partei Keskkomitee büroo 162 etteastumist 1944–1956 vahemängude ja sissejuhatusega* (Tallinn: Varrak, 2005), 234–36. On the fights for power and position at the Union of Writers, see Sirje Olesk, "ENSV Kirjanike Liit ja EK(b)P KK kaheksas pleenum," in *Kohandumise märgid*, ed. Virve Sarapik, Maie Kalda, and Rein Veidemann (Tallinn: Underi ja Tuglase Kirjanduskeskus, 2002), 99–120. There were no such "purges" of the ruling elite in Latvia or Lithuania at that time. In Latvia the purge took place in 1959–1962; see Michael Loader, "The Death of 'Socialism with a Latvian Face': The Purge of the Latvian National Communists, July 1959–1962," *Journal of Baltic Studies* 48, no. 2 (2017): 161–81.

93. RA ERAF 130sm/1/6501/82–86.

94. Goldman, "Nationally Informed," 372–76; On Russian and Soviet musical nationalism, see Taruskin, *Defining Russia Musically*; and Frolova-Walker, *Russian Music and Nationalism*, esp. chap. 6.

95. Vaitmaa, "Eesti muusika muutumises," 145–47. The choral songs by Gustav Ernesaks and some pieces of music written by Lydia Auster and Eugen Kapp are considered to have enduring value. The beginning of a new stage in the development of Estonian music coincided with the arrival of a new generation of composers—Eino Tamberg, Veljo Tormis, Jaan Rääts, Arvo Pärt, and Kuldar Sink.

96. RA ERAF 130sm/1/4322 vol2/74.

97. RA ERAF 1/83/11/72–73.

98. RA ERAF 7068/1/137/16.

99. RA ERAF 130sm/1/4322/vol2/22.

100. Endel Lippus, "Õppimine sõja varjus ja veidi hiljem," in *Muutuste kümnend*, 127; Niina Murdvee, ed., *Vladimir Alumäe: Rektor, interpreet, pedagoog* (Tallinn: Eesti Muusika- ja Teatriakadeemia, 2017), 80.
101. RA ERAF 1/7/246/7–27.
102. RA ERAF 1/7/246/29–30.
103. RA ERAF 1/7/246/47, 72–73.
104. RA ERAF 131/1/219/22–23, 121–22.
105. RA ERAF 131/1/98/109–16.
106. RA ERAF 1/7/247/7–13, 18.
107. RA ERAF 130sm/1/4322 vol2/169–72.
108. RA ERAF 130sm/1/4322 vol2/23.
109. RA ERAF 131/1/201j/460.
110. RA ERAF 130sm/1/4322 vol 2/173–77, 187–94.
111. RA ERA R-1958/1/38/77–94.
112. Mertelsmann, "Olla tudeng stalinismi ajal," 143; Väino Sirk, "Haritlaskond osutus visaks vastaseks: Jooni stalinlikust intelligentsipoliitikast," *Tuna*, no. 1 (2004): 62.
113. RA ERA R-1958/1/38/77–94.
114. Laine Randjärv, *Sillad üle piiride* (Tallinn: Kirjastus SE&JS 2012), 174–75.
115. Denis Kozlov and Eleonory Gilburd, eds., *The Thaw: Soviet Society and Culture during the 1950s and 1960s* (Toronto: University of Toronto Press, 2013), 3–17.
116. Aigi Rahi-Tamm, "Homeless for Ever: The Contents of Home and Homelessness on the Example of Deportees from Estonia," in *Narratives of Exile and Identity in Soviet Deportation Memoirs from the Baltic States*, ed. Violeta Davoliūtė and Tomas Balkelis (Budapest: Central European University Press, 2018), 65–84.
117. Miriam Dobson, *Khrushchev's Cold Summer: Gulag Returnees, Crime, and the Fate of Reform after Stalin* (Ithaca, NY: Cornell University Press, 2009); Emilia Koustova, "(Un)Returned from the Gulag: Life Trajectories and Integration of Postwar Special Settlers," trans. Erina Megowan, *Kritika: Explorations in Russian and Eurasian History* 16, no. 3 (2015): 616–20; Polly Jones, ed., *The Dilemmas of De-Stalinization: Negotiating Cultural and Social Change in the Khrushchev Era* (London: Routledge, 2006).
118. Alan Barenberg, "From Prisoners to Citizens? Ex-Prisoners in Vorkuta during the Thaw," in *Thaw*, ed. Kozlov and Gilburd, 143–75.
119. Amir Weiner, "The Empires Pay a Visit: Gulag Returnees, East European Rebellions, and Soviet Frontier Poitics," in *Thaw*, ed. Kozlov and Gilburd, 308–61.
120. Aivar Niglas, "Release ahead of Time of Estonian Citizens and Residents Repressed for Political Reasons by the Soviet Authorities and Their Rehabilitation from 1953 to the 1960s," in *Estonia since 1944: Reports of the Estonian International Commission for the Investigation of Crimes against Humanity*, ed. Toomas Hiio, Meelis Maripuu, and Indrek Paavle (Tallinn: Inimsusevastaste Kuritegude Uurimise Eesti Sihtasutus, 2009).
121. Hosking,"Trust and Distrust in the USSR."
122. Aigi Rahi-Tamm, "Doubly Marginalized People: The Hidden Stories of Estonian Society (1940–1960)," in *War, Revolution, and Governance: The Baltic Countries in the Twentieth Century*, ed. Lazar Fleishman and Amir Weiner (Boston: Academic Studies Press, 2018), 256–57.
123. Randjärv, *Loovisiksuse roll Eesti laulupeoliikumises*, 94–96.
124. RA ERAF 130sm/1/650/238–44.
125. RA ERAF 130sm/1/650/214–18.
126. RA ERAF 130sm/1/6501/207–13; Tauk, *Muusikast võlutud*, 377–78.
127. RA ERAF 1/6/7076.
128. Maia Lilje, ed., *Meistri haare: Meenutusi Bruno Lukist* (Tallinn: Eesti Klaveriõpetajate Ühing, 2009), 73.
129. Lilje, *Meistri haare*, 3.
130. Leelo Kõlar, "Häid ja kehvemaid mälestusi," in *Muutuste kümnend*, 171–81.

131. Veljo Tormis, "Oreliklassist ja selle lõpust," in *Muutuste kümnend*, 147–48.

132. Beth B. Hess, Elizabeth W. Markson, and Peter J. Stein, eds., *Sociology* (Boston: Allyn and Bacon, 1996); David R. Shearer, *Policing Stalin's Socialism: Repression and Social Order in the Soviet Union, 1924–1953* (New Haven: Yale University Press, 2009).

133. Klimov, *Sotsial'nyi kontrol'*, 9–18.

134. Yoram Gorlizki, "Structures of Trust after Stalin," *Slavonic and East European Review* 91, no. 1 (2013): 119–46.

135. Aili Aarelaid, *Ikka kultuurile mõeldes* (Tallinn: Virgela, 1998), 126; Aili Aarelaid-Tart, "Double Mental Standards in the Baltic Countries—Three Generations," in *The Baltic Countries under Occupation: Soviet and Nazi Rule 1939–1991*, ed. Anu Mai Kõll (Stockholm: Dept. of History, University of Stockholm), 213–26.

136. Aigi Rahi-Tamm, "Ene Mihkelsoniga neetud ajastus," *Looming*, no. 12 (2020): 1723.

137. Karsten Brüggemann and Andres Kasekamp, "'Singing Oneself into a Nation'? Estonian Song Festivals as Rituals of Political Mobilisation," *Nations and Nationalism* 20, no. 2 (2014): 259–76.

138. Simo Mikkonen, "Winning Hearts and Minds? Soviet Music in the Cold War Struggle against the West," in *Twentieth-Century Music and Politics: Essays in Memory of Neil Edmunds*, ed. Pauline Fairclough (Farnham: Ashgate, 2013), 135–54.

Constructing Guilt and Tracking the Enemy

The Hunt for State Criminals in Soviet Lithuania, 1944–1953

Emilia Koustova

ON 19 MAY 1948, WHILE THE LITHUANIAN MGB WAS PREPARING THE FIRST large postwar deportation from Lithuania, Operation Vesna, a state security officer from Zarasaj District launched a police action of a completely different scale and nature:

ORDER ON THE OPENING OF A WANTED FILE

I, the undersigned, Lieutenant Popov, officer of the MGB Department of Zarasaj District, after having examined the materials concerning V. Antanas, son of Karolis, born in 1901 in Griva, Dvina District, Latvian SSR, Lithuanian, nonparty, illiterate, married, citizen of the USSR, formerly domiciled in the village of Ašvertiniškai, Imbradas Canton, Zarasaj District, Lithuanian SSR,

FOUND

That V. Antanas, son of Karolis, being hostile to the Soviet regime, joined the clandestine anti-Soviet organization Lithuanian Activist Front in 1941.[1] During the occupation of the Lithuanian SSR by the Germans, [he] was an active White [i.e., anticommunist] insurgent, participating in the arrests and shootings of Soviet citizens.

After the liberation of the Lithuanian SSR from the German occupiers, he began to live illegally. In November 1947, V. was identified by us and recruited as an agent, [but] not wanting to collaborate with the organs of the MGB, he disappeared after recruitment.

DECIDED

To open a wanted file, category "member of a Lithuanian bourgeois nationalist organization," targeting V. Antanas son of K., under covername ANTUCHKA, and to register it in the Department A [Archives] of the MGB of the Lithuanian SSR.

V. Antanas, son of Karolis, declared wanted.

Lieutenant POPOV, MGB Department of the Zarasaj District Officer

APPROVED, Lieutenant Colonel PIROGOV, Head of the MGB Department of Zarasaj District[2]

This document originated 1 of 1,773 investigations (*rozysk*) for "state criminals" launched by the Ministry of State Security of the Lithuanian Soviet Socialist Republic (LSSR MGB) in 1948, raising the number of wanted persons in this republic to 4,132 by the end of the year.[3]

The notion of "state crime," defined in the RSFSR Criminal Code of 1926 and supplemented in 1934, covered a broad spectrum of "counterrevolutionary crimes" and "particularly dangerous crimes against the state order," punished by articles 58 and 59 respectively.[4] These included high treason, espionage, sabotage, terrorist acts, anti-Soviet propaganda, and banditry. Most of the wanted files opened in Lithuania at the end of World War II targeted people with profiles similar to that of Antanas V. "Traitors to the fatherland," "accomplices of Germans," and "members of the nationalist underground" represented at that time about 70 percent of those under investigation. Composite profiles combining several offenses, like that of Antanas V., were also frequent—because of the distinctive features marking the history of World War II in Lithuania, the challenges posed by the country's Sovietization, and the reading of these events by the Soviet authorities. The fact of having been recruited as an MGB agent somewhat distinguishes this case (and probably explains the efforts made to find Antanas V., which led to his arrest in Latvia two years later), yet neither the recruitment of a person suspected of collaboration with the Nazis nor the rapid betrayal of that person were rare. Seeking to track down and infiltrate hostile milieus in Lithuania in the 1940s, the secret police (NKGB-MGB) recruited thousands of informers and agents whose loyalty and effectiveness were inversely proportional to their numbers.[5]

The hunt for state criminals is largely ignored by the historical literature, yet it deserves attention for several reasons, starting with the place it occupied at the heart of Soviet police activities after the war.[6] After long being a secondary activity, it changed in nature and scale at the end of World War II. With a rapid increase in the number of wanted persons, most suspected of collusion with the Nazi enemy, the hunt for state criminals became one of the main tasks of the secret police in the previously occupied territories.[7] No longer aimed primarily at fugitives who had fled from special settlements or camps (as had been true before 1941), it involved the formulation of suspicion and the designation of state criminals prior to any trial. This activity was thus intimately linked to the processes of constructing the enemy and defining guilt and loyalty, which figure among essential questions for the history of the Sovietization of the Baltic states as well as for the history of the postwar period on a pan-Soviet scale.

As scholars have shown, everywhere in the regions that experienced the occupation, the question of individual and collective behaviors during the war and how the actors of the reconquest and the population viewed this past were at the heart of the reconstruction of the Soviet regime. The purges were often violent, but they involved shifts, accommodations, and negotiations on the ground.[8] In the Baltic republics, especially Lithuania, these processes were particularly complex, because here war retribution was combined with coercive Sovietization.[9] This led the authorities to superimpose waves of repression, to define new targets, and to greatly expand the number of suspects. As the German-Soviet conflict receded and other challenges arose, especially in connection with an anti-Soviet insurgency, those in power increasingly had to choose between punishing past crimes and fighting present dangers. The hunt for state criminals offers a good point of observation for these choices, allowing us to study shifting political and policing priorities and redefinitions of the enemy as the construction of a Soviet Lithuania progressed. It also shows how pan-Soviet policies were transposed onto Baltic soil, leading to adaptations and sometimes provoking important discrepancies in their implementation at different levels. There were dynamics specific to the postwar retribution, and they did not always or completely follow changes in the "general line" decided at the top. These observations will let us revisit some of the conclusions drawn by studies of the coercive Sovietization of the Baltic countries—above all, the rapid replacement of targets inherited from the war by "enemies" whose threat potential came from their activities in the present.[10]

This hunt for state criminals sheds new light on another important aspect of the history of coercive Sovietization in the western territories and, more broadly, of the developments in repressive policies and methods during late

Stalinism. Even if this period remains understudied, some pioneering studies have revealed new trends in Soviet repressive practices since the end of the Great Terror. These included more systematic surveillance and regular information gathering as well as an emphasis on targeted individual repression by judicial conviction instead of mass operations against entire categories of the population.[11] In the territories annexed during World War II, this shift certainly took a while to express itself, as shown by the mass deportations carried out in 1940 and 1944–1951. With a few important exceptions, it is these deportations, together with the counterinsurgency activities, that have attracted most attention from historians.[12] The extent of the violence generated by these mass operations should not, however, obscure the existence of new trends manifested with particular force in the hunt for state criminals. The nature of this hunt made it highly dependent on police capacity to collect and process large amounts of information. During late Stalinism, these capacities were often lacking, but the situation was changing thanks both to improved police methods, especially in the field of information gathering, and to a Sovietization that was widening and deepening, through violence but also through compromise and accommodation. A more efficient surveillance registration system (*operativnyi uchet*), combined with better collection and processing of information coming from an extended network of informants or archives, made possible a wider and better informed surveillance apparatus. This increase in police skills and capabilities opened up new perspectives in the hunt for state criminals. At the same time, a more precise and targeted approach to potential threats, guilt, and evidence created conflict with the Stalinist "guilt factory," which continued to produce suspects by the thousands.[13] By revealing the signs of such tensions during the crucial years of late Stalinism, this chapter suggests ways to study the transition from Stalinism.

PEOPLE AND PROCEDURES USED IN THE HUNT FOR STATE CRIMINALS

Previously a secondary activity, the hunt for state criminals was scaled up and reorganized at the end of World War II. As a sign of its importance, this activity, initially carried out by the Second Directorate of the NKGB (counterintelligence), was given its own directorate: the Fourth Directorate of the NKGB-MGB USSR at the central level and the Fourth Department of the NKGB-MGB of Lithuania at the republic level. This change formed part of the reorganization of the secret police decided by the Politburo on 4 May 1946.[14]

The framework of this activity was defined a year earlier, on 29 May 1945, by Order no. 00252 of the USSR NKGB and its "Instructions on the Registration [*uchet*] and Hunt for Agents of Espionage, Counterespionage, Punitive, and Police Organs of the Countries That Made War against the USSR, as well as Traitors, Collaborators, and Creatures of the German Fascist Occupiers."[15]

Ordering the constitution of a centralized file of all state criminals wanted by the NKGB and SMERSH (Smert' shpionam, lit. Death to Spies), the document specified the modalities of this work, which combined monitoring from the center and hunting and surveillance in the field by local secret police offices. The launch of each new investigation led to the opening of a wanted file (*agenturno-rozysknoe delo*, called *rozysknoe delo* from 1954) in the district of the individual's last place of residence or work. This type of investigation (*mestnyi rozysk*) was carried out by the local NKGB-MGB office, which reported to the Fourth Department of the LSSR NKGB-MGB. The department had to give its approval and add the new suspect to the republic's alphabetical list, which was regularly distributed to local offices. If the wanted person had family elsewhere, a duplicate file (*dublikat*) was created. If the suspicions against the individual were deemed insufficient or if there was a lack of reliable identifying information (*ustanovochnye dannye*), a preliminary verification file (*delo predvaritel'noi agenturnoi razrabotki*) was opened for a maximum of six months, after which the verification had either to be closed and filed or converted into a wanted file.

If the local investigation was unsuccessful, the Fourth Directorate of the USSR NKGB/MGB was brought in to launch a hunt throughout the territory of the Soviet Union (*vsesoiuznyi rozysk*) by means of wanted notices (*orientirovki*) and alphabetical lists compiled and distributed by Moscow. The most dangerous criminals, spies, terrorists, and diversionists had to be tracked down throughout the Soviet Union without waiting for the results of a local search. The local MGB offices had to do everything possible to find "their" state criminals—those with local ties whose files they kept—and be on the lookout for persons wanted by other MGB branches.[16]

Once the person was found, he was either arrested and his file transferred to the MGB Investigation Department (Sledstvennaia chast', later Sledstvennyi otdel) in charge of pretrial investigation (*sledstvie*), or placed under surveillance while more information about his alleged crimes was gathered and preparations were made for his arrest. If, after this stage, the evidence necessary for a pretrial investigation was still lacking, the Fourth Department could either transfer his file to another MGB department that oversaw this type of profile (counterespionage, counterinsurgency, etc.)—which, in turn, would place the individual under surveillance (*operativnaia razrabotka*)—or close the case and possibly legalize the suspect if he had been living under a false name or hiding his past. Finally, in some cases, to which we will return below, the supposed state criminal found was recruited as an agent or informer by the

Fourth Department itself or by another MGB department. The work of the Fourth Department was thus judged by not only the number of state criminals found but also the number of arrests and pretrial investigations that resulted. These results were far from always considered satisfactory.

In the second half of the 1940s, the first instructions on hunting for state criminals were supplemented by others, particularly at the republic level, which provided ever more details and rules on the management of files, the organization of this activity, and its follow-up within the secret police. These rules and reminders reflected a gradual sophistication of police methods and a growing desire for control on the part of the MGB hierarchy but were at the same time implicit evidence of the many shortcomings of both the hunt for state criminals and police surveillance in general, before and after Stalin's death. For example, following the circulation of the USSR MGB instructions dated 1 February 1948, Lithuania's Deputy Minister of State Security Sergei Litkens deemed it necessary to reiterate to the heads of the district MGB offices (uezdnye otdely, which became raionnye otdely in 1950) the basic concepts used to pursue investigations and report on them. In particular, he repeated that decisions to close a case had to be justified, listed the elements to be contained in any wanted file, and stressed that only the individual whose place of residence had been identified and who was certain to correspond to the wanted state criminal could be considered found (razyskannyi).[17]

These repeated calls to order, as well as numerous critical reports at various levels, show how remote the practice of hunting for state criminals on the ground was from the police and bureaucratic utopia projected through Moscow's instructions. The shortcomings were particularly important in the district MGB offices. Studying the hunt for state criminals at this lowest level of the secret police pyramid raises awareness of the gap between Soviet ambitions for the information gathering and surveillance of populations and the logistical, technical, and human resources available to the secret police apparatus. Discipline and organization within the local offices were deficient, and the level of competence of their personnel was extremely low in view of the challenges posed by the hunt for state criminals, as defined by Moscow and Vilnius, and the accumulation of suspicion and multiplication of suspects.[18] In the early 1950s, a series of reorganizations and purges within the secret police aggravated these structural problems.[19] With the reorganization of work by territory in 1950–1951, the MGB offices in the districts no longer had personnel dedicated to hunting for criminals: the officers in charge simultaneously had other missions, such as counterintelligence and counterinsurgency, two fields that tended to dominate the others, not to mention the mass deportations that mobilized the entire MGB staff in 1948, 1949, and 1951.[20]

More generally, the Fourth Department of the LSSR MGB was struggling to assert its autonomy with respect to counterespionage. Although at
the republic level this department, which had twenty-four officers in 1951,
was directly subordinate to the Lithuanian minister of state security, in the
regions the hunt for state criminals continued to be associated with counterintelligence.[21] This created a certain amount of stress, as when the head of the
Fourth Department, Mikhail Starodubtsev, repeatedly requested in 1951–1952
that the sections (*otdeleniia*) in charge of hunting for state criminals in each
of the four regional directorates of the LSSR MGB (UMGBs of the oblasts
of Kaunas, Vilnius, Šiauliai, and Klaipėda) be separated from counterintelligence, with direct subordination to the head of each UMGB and adequate
staffing and resources.[22] In August 1952, the sections were finally turned into
departments (higher-level units), but these were severely understaffed and
undermanaged, while the MGB was hit by purges and dismissals following
the removal of Viktor Abakumov in July 1951.[23] Less than a year later, all the
activities and the entire organization of the Stalinist secret police were shaken
up after Stalin's death.

THE DEFINITION OF TARGETS

At all stages of the hunt, from the formulation of initial suspicions to the
decision whether or not to arrest the suspect in the event of his successful
identification, notions of the enemy, his threat potential, and guilt were at
the heart of this activity. As conceived on the eve of and at the end of the war,
the hunt for state criminals and, more broadly, surveillance registration were
based on procedures and targets of surveillance standardized throughout the
Soviet Union. The "Instructions on Registration of and Hunt for Agents" of 29
May 1945 listed some twenty target categories that applied throughout Soviet
territory. These categories reflected the priorities of the day—including, for
the most part, various types of "traitors," "collaborators," and "agents" of Germany and its allies.[24] Soon, however, the list for Lithuania grew and diversi-
fied, indicating a desire to develop a nomenclature of enemies that would take
into account the local situation while respecting the criteria identified for the
USSR as a whole. A tension between the global and the local, the universal and
the specific, emerged. Rather than being reduced by the rapid Sovietization of
annexed territories, it was amplified by the expansion of the purge to targets
other than those left by the war. In the field, adaptations and discrepancies
occurred, both between the pan-Soviet model and its Lithuanian version and
between what was advocated from above and what was carried out below.

A desire to clarify and adapt the categories used to identify and classify the enemies present on Baltic soil was visible even before the arrival of the Red Army in the summer of 1944. In preparing for its return, the directive of the USSR NKGB "On the Organization of Operational Work on the Liberated Territory of the Baltic Republics," of 3 March 1944 listed several dozen categories of individuals who could either be arrested immediately or placed under surveillance.[25] While sharing some of these categories with similar directives cited in its preamble, this document displayed a greater degree of detail and precision in identifying the institutions whose members were to be arrested. Dozens of names of different organizations operating in the Baltic territories revealed a major effort to gather information from across the front line. This directive also reflected a more flexible approach to guilt and compromise with the enemy: for many of the categories listed, only those in positions of responsibility were to be arrested immediately (sometimes with an indication of the precise rank at which the individual became a target). Reflecting a pragmatic turn in the pan-Soviet purge that had been underway since 1943, this directive thus attested to a desire to take into account the specific features of the Baltic terrain.[26] The goal was to better target those who, in the eyes of Moscow, were irreducible enemies, destined to be purged, and to outline a possible compromise with many categories of the population who, because of their professional activities or commitments during the occupation, corresponded to the very broad Soviet understanding of collaboration with the enemy.

While limiting, at least in theory, the spectrum of persons wanted for their activities during the occupation, the instructions and lists sent by the leadership of the republic's NKGB/MGB to local branches began at the same time to broaden them to include other enemy profiles, always set in the local context. Detailing the categories of persons to be included in the republic's list of wanted state criminals, the instructions issued by the LSSR MGB in January and April 1946 brought together, in a reactive logic, profiles linked to the war (Plechavičius army officers, members of insurrectional units who took part in the arrests and shootings of Soviet and communist militants in 1941, etc.) and those linked to a more distant past that had not ceased to haunt the Soviet present—that is, some of the key targets of the proactive purges carried out in 1940–1941 ("leaders and active members of former political parties" or "important officials of bourgeois Lithuania").[27] Finally, "members of the nationalist underground living in a clandestine manner [*na nelegal'nom polozhenii*]" also made their appearance, for the moment still to a limited degree.[28] The hunt for state criminals, an activity at first closely linked to the end of the war, expanded thus into a much broader repressive Sovietization of the western regions. The violent turn taken by this type of Sovietization quickly multiplied the challenges and targets; it required new adaptations of pan-Soviet categories and reading grids and, above all, raised the question of priorities.

PRIORITIES OF THE HUNT

Historians working on the Sovietization of the Baltic countries emphasize that the rise of a resistance movement led the Soviet authorities to give priority, as early as 1945, to the struggle against these opponents, called "bourgeois nationalists," "members of the anti-Soviet underground," or "bandits," instead of punishing German collaborators. In reference to Latvia, Juliette Denis considers that "the categories of 'traitors' gave way to that of 'bandits'" in May–June 1945.[29] The rapid shift in Soviet priorities resulted in relatively lenient purges in these areas, where former collaborators were prosecuted less often and punished less severely than elsewhere in the USSR.[30] As Elena Zubkova points out, it was accompanied by a reinterpretation of the phenomenon of Baltic resistance. After seeing the Baltic resistance as a consequence of the occupation and the subversive action of German intelligence, which was supposed to have formed armed groups before withdrawing, the Orgburo of the Communist Party's Central Committee proclaimed in October 1946 the end of its battle against "Lithuanian-German nationalists" and interpreted the continued armed resistance in Lithuania in terms of class struggle.[31]

An analysis of the MGB's hunt for state criminals makes it possible to round out and refine these findings, noting heterogeneous trends and highlighting a considerable gap between orders from the center and police practice in the field, which had its own dynamics and resisted the rapid changes in priorities and interpretations made in Moscow and Vilnius.

Certainly, here too key targets were redefined in response to internal and external political circumstances. It was the spy—first German, then Anglo-American—however, who soon came to the fore, displacing the "bourgeois nationalist" or the "bandit."

In May 1945, Ivan Veselov, the deputy people's commissar for state security of Lithuania, called for an intensification of the hunt for German agents and "parachutists" dropped over Soviet territory by the enemy.[32] With the onset of the Cold War, British and American spies took their place at the center of the Soviet police's imagination, created in Moscow and replicated through orders, instructions, and reports from the Lithuanian MGB.[33] A hierarchy of enemies emerged, dominated by parachutists—the most fantasized figure in the police imagination in these western territories, where the reality of conflict was mixed with phobias and suspicions forged in the pure Stalinist tradition. The obsession with an outside enemy, supported by locals in a territory that was insufficiently controlled and able to blend in with an unreliable population, reached its peak in the spring of 1952, when a massive raid of spies on the Baltic coast was expected. The LRSS MGB mobilized its services—especially the Fourth Department, which had to urgently go through its files, select the most dangerous state criminals among those who had been identified abroad, and place their relatives under heightened surveillance, in case they entered Soviet territory clandestinely.[34]

In view of the threat posed by the armed anti-Soviet movement in the western regions, the place occupied by its participants in the pan-Soviet pantheon of enemies seems rather modest. The new instructions on the hunt for state criminals issued by the USSR MGB in 1948 did not assign to them any of the six "colors" (*okraski*). These groups were dominated by outside enemies ("spies," "foreign counterespionage agents," and "agents and members of émigré organizations") but also reserved a place for people compromised during the war, as well as for the traditional targets of the hunt for state criminals (prisoners who had escaped from their place of confinement or people who eluded surveillance). To take into account the situation in Lithuania, the LSSR MGB had to send an explanatory note that recommended including "members of nationalist organizations and gangs" in the category of "traitors and active accomplices of the Germans."[35]

Beyond the dominance of a vision of the enemy ultimately determined more by the Cold War than by the situation in the margins of Stalin's empire, the nature of the hunt for state criminals undoubtedly explains the modest presence among its targets of those who presented the major challenge to the Sovietization of the western regions. The hunt concerned above all individuals living in society under a false identity or taking advantage of the state's failure to control the population. The anti-Soviet movement was the work of armed groups acting illegally, outside or on the margins of spaces controlled by the Soviets. Therefore, it was more likely to become the target of other types of repressive action: military operations, sweeps of forests, mass deportations to deprive the resistance of its support, and, increasingly, infiltration by Soviet agents. By the early 1950s, however, the intensification of the struggle against armed insurgency and changes in the methods used eventually placed the figure of the "member of the nationalist underground and of armed gangs" among the key targets of the hunt for state criminals.

THE REPRESSIVE BURDEN OF WAR

Did the priority given to profiles representing a danger in the present mean that the prosecution of those inherited from the war would be dropped? It is true that the officers in charge of hunting for state criminals gave spies and bandit chiefs a place of honor among the successful identifications and arrests touted in their reports. But behind the few, if any, cases at the forefront, year after year the statistics compiled in these reports showed a preponderance of war-related cases, whatever the category: criminals wanted, identified, arrested, and so on. For example, at the beginning of 1952, the 4,121 "traitors, German collaborators, and torturers" made up 58 percent of the 7,124 state criminals wanted by the MGB in Lithuania. This share was in fact even higher: 639 "agents and personnel of the German espionage services" (9 percent) and 725 "agents and personnel of foreign counterespionage and police services" (10 percent) should be added to that number, since they correspond to persons who served the Nazi authorities.[36] There were only 41 agents of foreign powers other than Nazi Germany, to which we may add most of the 101 "agents and members of anti-Soviet émigré organizations," since the diaspora was suspected of supplying agents to the imperialist espionage services. The 685 "gang and nationalist underground members" constituted less than 10 percent of wanted persons.[37]

On 10 January 1952, Order no. 0022 of the USSR MGB partially reorganized the surveillance registration system and ordered a review of existing surveillance and wanted files.[38] In Lithuania, the review was carried out with an instruction to give priority to enemies whose threat potential came from their current activities ("foreign intelligence agents, members of the nationalist underground, White émigrés, and other dangerous state criminals").[39] In Lithuania, the review was essentially completed by 1 October 1952; it led to the archiving of 1,931 files (25 percent of the initial number kept by the Fourth Department).[40] Not all target categories were affected to the same extent: "traitors, collaborators, and torturers" were more affected by the review (32 percent, or 1,338 fewer files at the end of the year) than "agents of foreign intelligence services" (11 percent, or 77 fewer files, bearing in mind that the reduction mainly concerned "German agents").[41] Yet given the quantitative importance of the first category, its share fell only slightly, from 58 to 52 percent at the end of the year. Individuals wanted for their wartime pasts were also prevalent among the identified state criminals: of the 506 people found in 1952, 250 were "traitors, German collaborators, and torturers."[42]

Even after several years when those at the top demanded spies, therefore, the hunt for state criminals at the grassroots level continued to be dominated by the figure of the "German accomplice." This inevitably led to criticism—for example, during inspections carried out at local MGB offices in early 1949. In the Vilkaviškis and Pasvalys districts, the inspectors complained about the concentration of investigations on "second-order criminals (former Nazi collaborators)." They considered only eleven files as "deserving attention": those concerned "one English intelligence agent, seven German intelligence agents, and three members of the nationalist underground."[43]

In 1952, Starodubtsev, head of the Fourth Department of the LSSR MGB, again denounced the tendency of local apparatuses to favor the easiest cases, neglecting "more serious files, which require more work"—namely, those on enemy intelligence and counterespionage agents. Indeed, the district MGB branches identified not a single foreign agent that year.[44]

As we shall see, the hunt for war criminals was anything but easy, and a considerable proportion of the files concerning them were "dead souls," who would never be found and who in some cases had never existed. But because the vast numbers of these files were opened at the end of the war, some of the suspects were demonstrably guilty, and the search was affected by local dynamics and inertia, the "German accomplice" continued to be a key figure, whose file clogged up the hunt yet who offered agents the chance of an arrest that could be reported to their superiors.

As a result, against all odds, individuals sought as spies were sometimes convicted for crimes committed during the war. In 1951, this metamorphosis, which diluted the rare and precious category of unmasked spies, exasperated Lithuanian MGB heads, who denounced the lack of seriousness shown by those officers of the Investigation Department who, rather than engaging in a demanding investigation to demonstrate espionage activities on behalf of the United States and Great Britain, chose the easy way out with an indictment for "torturers' activities."[45] Such recharacterizations were made possible by the blurring of police categories as well as by the tangle of real and imaginary guilt.

ENTANGLED TRAJECTORIES AND OVERLAPPING SUSPICIONS

The increasingly detailed instructions mentioned above not only reflect an approach that, over time, was becoming more rigorous, systematic, and better supervised at all levels. They also reflect the confusion in police practice when many of these labels were interchangeable and malleable.

This was particularly true during the first screenings (fil'tratsii) and arrests carried out by operational groups of the NKGB and the intelligence troops of the NKVD just after the arrival of the Red Army. In the documents they produced, which often served as the basis for future investigations of so-called state criminals, a few catch-all categories such as "Gestapo agents" or shaulisty were omnipresent.[46] While the former was portrayed as a universal enemy, the latter was a key figure in Soviet representations of the Baltic enemy. Especially for the first few months, they were applied in an approximate, even arbitrary, manner to anyone suspected of opposing Soviet power or of having collaborated with the Germans.[47]

Despite repeated instructions from Moscow and Vilnius, the loose application of culprit categories did not completely disappear over the years, especially when it came to the particularly vague labels the Soviet legislator had designed to punish collaboration with the enemy during the war. In individual cases, summarized in reports or the subject lines of investigation files, MGB personnel improvised composite descriptions: "district chief [under the Germans] bandit," "deputy chief of police [under the Germans] and member of the nationalist underground," "German accomplice and former mayor, member of the nationalist underground."[48]

Beyond the vagueness of the categories and their arbitrary use, these examples reveal a strong tendency to merge people's guilt and their backgrounds, their war or even prewar experiences, and their present. There are many cases where suspicions of collaboration and participation in Nazi crimes appear as a backdrop to accusations of anti-Soviet activities in the present. Once arrested, those wanted for their actions during the war were quite often surveilled or interrogated with the aim of uncovering their current anti-Soviet activities or contacts. Most of the individuals wanted as American or British spies had thick files referring to the occupation period, and so on.

This overlapping of charges was partly due to the active functioning of the Stalinist "guilt factory," in which a trifle was enough to give rise to and multiply suspicions. It also reveals how much violence these regions had undergone since 1939. Traces of it can be read in individual and collective experiences that combined commitments that constituted guilt in the eyes of the Soviets. Many people ticked more than one box, since they had been members of paramilitary organizations before 1940, taken part in the June Uprising (1941) with attacks against Soviet troops and activists and sometimes in the first murders of Jews, and served in police battalions during the German occupation before hiding in the forests and joining one of the many armed groups that operated there from 1944 onward.

Toward the end of the 1950s, these entangled trajectories and suspect backgrounds were woven into a standard profile of an "enemy of Soviet power." An official history of Soviet Lithuania conceptualized continuity between pre-1940 and post-1944 anti-Soviet engagements, including active collaboration and participation in Nazi war crimes.[49] Yet the foundations for this narrative were laid as early as 1944 in the wanted and investigation files, reports and summaries, where continuities between commitments before and after 1944 were almost systematic and the profiles of alleged German accomplices and bandits fitted together.[50] The MGB apparatus used this opportunity to widen its leeway in investigating cases and responding to changing orders from above, without disrupting its surveillance and investigation practices on the ground.

SOURCES OF SUSPICION

Whether sought for their alleged anti-Soviet activities in the present or suspected of having participated in Nazi crimes, most individuals dubbed state criminals under late Stalinism were in a very different situation from that of the fugitive prisoners and special deportees who had been at the core of this police activity before the war. Their cases also differed from the classic Stalinist pretrial investigation under article 58, which, when confronted with a real individual, set in motion a "guilt factory" to reinterpret his trajectory, relationships, acts, and words in order to indict him. In the cases under consideration here, the "guilt factory" generated suspicions and accusations in the absence—assumed to be temporary—of those targeted. Any hunt for an alleged state criminal was based on a police identity constructed from various elements (name, age, place of birth, profession, etc.), which had to be linked to a real individual as a target to be sought. Even though the instructions required a minimum of reliable information and serious grounds for suspicion before opening a wanted file, many of the police identities constructed at the end of the war existed only in police files.

The suspicions and information that formed the basis of a new wanted file might come from a variety of sources: accusations and leads from informers and the general public; archives produced by and seized from opponents of the Soviet regime (from the occupation, before 1940, or the anti-Soviet resistance); and statements and interrogations accumulated during previous investigations. In addition, there were analyses produced by the NKGB and the NKVD prior to the arrival of the Red Army in these territories, via intelligence missions or study of the occupation press.[51] The importance of these sources in opening up new investigations seems to have varied over time. At first, denunciations and pointing fingers played a crucial role. Later the NKGB-MGB accumulated compromising materials, produced in combination with a slow and uneven exploration of "trophy archives" (a term often used in the sources for documents left by the Germans).

The denunciations and pointing fingers were indeed essential after the Soviet authorities returned. Whether produced in response to police pressure or motivated by a thirst for justice and revenge, they were collected from the very first hours following the arrival of the Red Army or even beforehand, by intelligence departments of NKVD Troops for the Protection of the Rear (Voiska NKVD po okhrane tyla deistvuiushchei Krasnoi armii), SMERSH, and, soon, the NKGB, whose first measures in the reconquered regions were aimed in particular at rebuilding its network of informants.[52] Only some of these early accusations led to immediate arrests, while others fed into a lasting purge process fueled by the accumulation of compromising materials and additions to the list of suspects.

The number of wanted files also grew rapidly following the interrogations and statements taken during the first arrests and trials, which were particularly arbitrary and expeditious. Although the procedures for tracing state criminals presuppose at least some evidence to charge and identify an individual, in practice just a few leads were enough to open a wanted or surveillance file, especially at the end of the war.

This is shown by the content of summary accusations and statements and the number of investigations that subsequently led nowhere, as the secret police halfheartedly acknowledged a few years later. In 1952, for twenty-nine "British and American intelligence agents" wanted by the Lithuanian MGB (a priority category but also a particularly fragile one, since it was often based on the most fanciful suspicions), only twelve files had a minimum of "identifying information."[53] As for the remaining seventeen, only their names, sometimes their approximate age, and a few other bits of information were known (town of origin, place of work before 1940, etc.), which made it impossible to identify them even theoretically—that is, by linking them to individuals appearing in the civil register—to try to find them. Yet without having established a link between a police identity, constructed from police sources and suspicions, and a social identity—an individual whose existence was attested by administrative archives, the presence of relatives, or vague memories retained by classmates or former neighbors—there was little or no hope of finding the suspect. One Ilsa N., born in 1918, had been wanted for espionage ever since the detainee E. said during interrogation that she had worked as secretary in the Ministry of Foreign Affairs of independent Lithuania, then served in the Censorship Department of British intelligence in occupied Germany in 1946. For a long time, this "spy" existed only in the secret police world of interrogations and suspicions, with no trace of her existence in the real world. Neither interrogations of the former staff of the Ministry of Foreign Affairs nor research in the ministry archives confirmed her existence. Finally, the mobilization of several agents with contacts among the "old inhabitants of Kaunas" (*starozhily*) led to traces of a woman bearing this name who allegedly worked for American Oil in Kaunas. This time, the MGB thought it had the right information, especially since the detainee E. suddenly remembered that Ilsa N. had indeed mentioned her work for an American firm; a notation about a person bearing this name (but born ten years earlier) was also found in the municipal archives. Once the link was established between a culprit produced by the repressive universe and a real individual, the accusations against the former were transferred unaltered to the latter, without questioning their validity or coherence. The hunting machine was then set in motion, informants were recruited among former American Oil employees, and Ilsa N.'s family was sought in order to put them under surveillance.[54]

This is one example among many where the arrest of a person became the starting point for increasing suspicion and broadening repression. The network or "concentric circles" mode of operation of the Stalinist repressive machine is well known: confessions of complicity extracted under torture provoke new arrests within the same professional, friendship, and family environment. This mechanism was often present during the postwar purges in Lithuania, with one notable difference: although torture was commonplace, not all guilty complicities were products of the Stalinist repressive imagination.[55] Some referred to real engagements in anti-Soviet groups or military formations and participation in their acts, such as the insurgent units formed in June 1941 and the self-defense and police battalions created later, which took part—in some cases—in the Holocaust and other Nazi crimes.

For several years after the war, the same situation was repeated: the arrest and confession of a member of a particular group produced a domino effect, leading to a hunt for and often arrest of several of his former comrades, who in turn gave dozens of new names, sometimes with valuable information about their subsequent careers or even their current place of residence. Every inquiry file held by the Investigation Department also included a "list of persons compromised by the file materials." Without being systematically wanted, these lists, and the statements and interrogations to which they referred (known as "investigation archives," *sledstvennye arkhivy*) were potentially usable reserves of guilt that MGB personnel were supposed to explore in order to broaden and intensify the hunt for state criminals. This obligation seems often to have been ignored, judging by the recurrent criticisms aimed at the failure to use "case investigation archives" or the card index (*kartoteka*) even when it existed.[56]

The "trophy archives" were another essential source of suspicion and compromising materials (*kompromat*), especially with regard to official groups such as police battalions or administrative bodies that functioned during the German occupation. In the decades that followed, these archives were regularly mined to initiate or complete the construction of guilt, in particular for documents proving the wanted or accused individual's membership in a military, police, or administrative unit created by the Germans. But even though documents from institutions during the occupation were used right away—for example, to compile lists of persons enlisted in the Lithuanian police or find out how some of these bodies functioned—it took a long time before this practice became systematic and thorough.[57] This is hardly surprising in view of the huge size of these archives and the logistical and linguistic challenges involved in exploring them. That required a command of German and/or Lithuanian, while the staff of the Lithuanian MGB remained largely Russian-speaking before 1953.[58] The task appeared immense, especially in view of the broad and unclear criteria needed to place a person under suspicion.

As in the field of preliminary investigation, the situation was changing in the early 1950s.[59] In February 1951, the Fourth Department of the LSSR MGB listed, among its ongoing projects, a desire to study the interrogations of state criminals arrested since 1944, transmitted by the Investigation Department, and to examine archival materials concerning members of self-defense battalions. These two bodies of documents, "investigation archives" and "trophy archives," were being mobilized with the explicit aim of opening new investigations of state criminals.[60]

A year later, this work was already bearing fruit, according to the report on the activities of the Fourth Department between 1 August 1951 and 1 May 1952, which devoted several paragraphs to the prospects offered by the extensive use of archives:

> The State Archive of the Ministry of Internal Affairs of the Lithuanian SSR contains materials related to punitive organizations and institutions established by the Germans in Lithuania, a significant part of which has not yet been studied. The results of the work devoted to the Second Self-Defense Battalion demonstrate the importance of their study. Thanks to the use of archival materials related to this battalion, in the past nine months, twenty-six state criminals who took part in the mass shootings of Soviet citizens, served as guards in the Maidanek Death Camp, and conducted operations against Belarussian partisans have been arrested; seventeen others are currently under surveillance. The Fourth Department started processing the archival material related to the 1st, 3rd, and 252nd Battalions.[61]

This work was, however, hampered by a lack of personnel, since the proposal to set up special groups to explore the archives, made in February 1951, was not followed up. In January 1953, referring to the results of this work, in particular the arrest of thirty-four former members of the Third Auxiliary Battalion and the identification of sixteen others, Starodubtsev again emphasized the inability of his services to continue examining the documents properly, due to lack of resources.[62] Yet the project involved not just the battalions: all police, prison, court, and procuratorial personnel who had served from 1941 to 1944 in occupied Lithuania had to be scrutinized. This process was far from complete, as the example of Saugumas shows: while this branch of the secret police, according to MGB information, had employed no fewer than 306 people in 1941–1944, only 170 of them were wanted persons in 1953.[63]

The accumulation of knowledge about the history of the Nazi occupation, as well as the attempts to explore the archives more systematically and to understand the functioning of the various institutions and military and police units so as to better reconstruct their crimes and the responsibilities of their members, seem to herald better-founded suspicions and a more effective hunt for state criminals. This trend, which began in the early 1950s, was nevertheless permanently undermined both by the change of priority targets and by the pattern of Stalinist purges, which coincided in Lithuania with violent Sovietization and mass repression. The Fourth Department was overwhelmed by a flood of suspicions, files and archives, traces of real and imaginary crimes, slanderous accusations and confessions extracted under torture, guilt based solely on membership in an incriminated body, and evidence of participation in real violence. These archives and files concerned a mixture of executioners, victims, bystanders, and accomplices with responsibilities of a complexity unsuited to the overly rigid and broad framework of Stalinist state crime.

TRACKING TRICKS AND TACTICS

Between the end of the 1940s and the beginning of the following decade, with the gradual consolidation of Soviet control over the western territories, the number and effectiveness of the technical, police, and administrative tools available to those hunting state criminals increased. "Passportization," conducted since 1945 even in rural areas, and the deployment of a network of "address offices" facilitated this work, despite the large number of people living without papers or under false identities.[64] Although more sophisticated listening and recording equipment was introduced only in the mid-1950s, the use of photography was extended earlier—for example, to create and distribute albums picturing wanted persons.[65] Stricter postal controls made it possible to better monitor the families of wanted state criminals. The consolidation of local militia bodies facilitated "open operations" (glasnye meropriiatiia), designed to conceal the MGB sources used to find a wanted individual.[66]

In parallel with this technical and logistical increase in power, MGB informants and agents remained crucial at all stages of the hunt for state criminals, from the formulation of suspicions to the collection of information to identify individuals and enable surveillance of their families. Such networks, which had been deficient for a long time, improved during the years of late Stalinism, as evidenced by the reports on state criminals identified after long hunting.[67]

COMPROMISED AND RECALCITRANT AGENTS

The Fourth Department and its local branches had their own network of informants who specialized in tracking down criminals, and their numbers grew steadily, reaching 1,600–1,800 in 1950–1951. To be useful, these informants had to be recruited among former contacts—family, friends, colleagues—of the wanted individuals. As with counterinsurgency, the informants were often members of the same networks and bodies considered criminal by the Soviet regime: various anti-Soviet formations, police battalions, Saugumas, pre-1940 political and paramilitary organizations.[68] Often a member of such an organization, himself wanted as a state criminal, would first be arrested secretly (*neglasno*) for interrogation and sometimes recruited as an informant. Although not explicitly defined, the criteria for recruitment are sometimes mentioned in the reports: social origin; vulnerability to the MGB (for example, a person's strong attachment to his family); a wide network of knowledge or special skills, such as a good memory. But the most important criterion was a prior confession that named accomplices.[69]

What about the guilt of a potential agent who had belonged to self-defense battalions or police units wanted for mass murder? Some cases reveal a "ceiling of guilt" above which recruitment became problematic: one informant, initially hired on the basis of his participation in transporting "Soviet citizens" (probably Jews) to forced labor camps, was later arrested after it was discovered that he had informed on members of the Komsomol. Another suffered the same fate after the discovery of his activities as a "torturer," aggravated by his lies.[70] To avoid these surprises, one solution was to recruit mainly former technical personnel, such as drivers, who knew the environment well but had not participated in the massacres themselves.[71] But tolerance appeared to be the general rule, especially with regard to people with a promising network of knowledge.[72] One case involved a teacher who, after actively participating in the June 1941 uprising, had various responsibilities in the Lithuanian nationalist movement. Although approached as a potential informer during the hunt for leaders of the Lithuanian Freedom Army (Lietuvos laisvės armija, LLA), he was later arrested after refusing to collaborate during a secret interrogation.[73] An informer known as Kolia, recruited in 1946 by another MGB department based on his pro-Soviet positions, turned out to be a former deputy chief of police (a discovery made thanks to archival research). When interrogated, he confessed he had voluntarily enlisted in the police and taken part in arrests and investigations during the occupation; in view of his confessions and his good knowledge of the milieu of former collaborators, the decision was taken to re-recruit him (*pereverbovat'*) for use in the hunt for state criminals.[74]

The use of threat and blackmail made these informants unreliable collaborators, whose past and present might be a can of worms. MGB reports regularly referred to double agents who were unmasked, informers who fled after being recruited or supplied no information.[75] Reviews of the agents' network were intended to remedy this—for example, in 1946, 1949, and especially following Order no. 0015 of the USSR MGB, signed on 10 January 1952.[76] This directive reorganized the agents' network, creating two categories (*agent* and *spetsial'nyi* [special] *agent*) instead of three, drastically reduced their numbers, and cut back on further recruitment. Although initial reports on the reform's implementation in Lithuania mention positive effects, since the reduced number of agents made it possible not to disperse their forces, less than a year later Starodubtsev criticized the errors and excesses committed, which reduced the number of informers used to hunt for state criminals from 1,600 to 600.[77]

AGENTS IN ACTION

Yet these agents' work was essential: they were the main, if not the only, gateway to largely hostile milieus. They were among the few who could recognize wanted persons, whose photographs were not always available, and they often benefited from the trust of the accused's relatives.

Informants specializing in the hunt for state criminals were used in various ways. "Reconnaissance agents" (*agenty-opoznavateli*), themselves often members of targeted bodies (battalions, nationalist organizations), were sent to places such as markets, stations, or churches in the hope of meeting former comrades who were wanted.[78] In a paradoxical sign of Sovietization, in 1953 the May Day parade was used to organize such an operation, with agents dispatched to identify state criminals among the attendees.[79] Although this method required a lot of time and men, it did produce results during the early postwar years, judging by the reports—which, admittedly, detail only successful operations. For example, Stasys K., a former chief guard at the Vilnius Prison and participant in the Paneriai (Ponary) massacres, was arrested after giving his new address to another guard, an MGB informant whom he passed in the street.[80]

Much depended on the odds, which the MGB did its best to improve, and on contacts and trust that had endured despite the ongoing repression. The MGB made extensive use of such tactics to approach and trap people—for example, when it sent routing agents (*marshrutnye agenty*) into towns or neighborhoods likely to be frequented by relatives of a wanted state criminal. Family was essential to the survival of those in hiding or seeking a new identity; but it was also their weak point, the focus of all surveillance, pressure, and trickery by the police. In the rural Lithuania of that time, where the countryside and its forests were the center of anti-Soviet resistance, many farms and individual homes had hiding places to house one of their own who felt targeted for refusing to serve in the Red Army or taking up arms in the service of the Germans or the national cause. Intrafamily solidarity was crucial—and the Soviet regime made the family a prime target with mass deportations—but it was not infallible, especially when life in hiding was prolonged or police pressure increased. Repression, especially mass deportations, made everyone vulnerable and gave the MGB more opportunities for pressure and blackmail. In 1949, while Napoleonas B. was wanted for participation in the arrests and murders of the summer of 1941, his father was hiding from deportation in X.'s house. The MGB used this fact to threaten X. and recruited him to look for Napoleonas B. By helping the father, X. gained his trust and obtained the address of the house where Napoleonas was hiding.[81]

What is most striking in these stories is the trust that seems to have survived the violence and conflicts of the 1940s. Stories abound of brothers, sisters, wives, and parents who risk everything to help their relatives yet invite old acquaintances from the street into their homes, give them news of relatives wanted by the police, or even show them the hiding place they have set up in the house.[82] So numerous are these cases, often forming whole chains of betrayed trust, that it is difficult to attribute the phenomenon solely to individual thoughtlessness. Bronislavas P., wanted for his participation in Nazi crimes, was found in 1949 after a long hunt involving several agents who knew various members of his circle. Leads from two informants first enabled the police to approach his former girlfriend, who gave information about Bronislavas P.'s life before the war. From there, the officers could find his relatives, living in another city. A new agent contacted them and obtained the name of the factory where Bronislavas P. worked in 1947. After some additional steps, such as obtaining a photo of Bronislavas P. from his family, he was identified.[83]

These often surprising incidences of trust partly grew out of the experience of anti-Soviet commitment and struggle—not only shared opinions but also shared responsibilities, which erroneously seemed to guarantee silence. By recruiting as informants individuals who were just as compromised as the alleged state criminals they were helping to find, the MGB managed to trap quite a few.

The case of Aloizas K. illustrates these patterns of trust, based on past complicity and (wrongly assumed) solidarity in the present. Since 1949, incriminating information had been accumulating about Aloizas K., who was suspected of having led a group of insurgents and then the police in Kuršenai in the summer of 1941.[84] In 1951, several agents reported his presence first in Šiauliai, then in Panevėžys, and the MGB intensified its efforts to find him and document his current and past activities. This work was based mainly on two informants, a man and a woman, who had known the target and his family since before the war and, as neighbors, were familiar with his wartime activities. They were sent to Panevėžys, where they "happened" to meet Aloizas K.'s wife and started seeing the couple. The two informants seem to have had more in common with him than simply being neighbors, judging by the advice Aloizas K. and his wife gave them: move as often as possible, do not get involved in big enterprises where you have to fill in a lot of forms, and avoid meetings with X. and Y., who were unreliable because they were pro-Soviet.[85] In spite of the great caution shown by the K. couple, who were very suspicious of their current circle, they showed many signs of trusting the two informants: talking about common acquaintances who were hiding from the authorities, sharing an underground newspaper brought by their daughter, and praising her anti-Soviet convictions.[86] One may well wonder whether these conversations are not products of the imagination of the informant and/or MGB officer, eager to supplement Aloizas K.'s past guilt with "anti-Soviet activities in the present" or even to fabricate an "anti-Soviet youth organization." The content and degree of detail nevertheless argue for the statements' veracity: it is hard to imagine an investigator dictating to an informer an account of a conversation during which Aloizas K.'s wife mentioned Soviet attempts to make the Germans bear responsibility for the massacre of Polish officers in 1940.[87] In parallel with the surveillance of Aloizas K., the MGB was collecting the testimonies of several Soviet activists who were arrested or persecuted by the police and Kuršenai insurgents in 1941. Arrested on 18 November 1952, Aloizas K. was tried by the Military Tribunal on 18 March 1953 and sentenced to twenty-five years' imprisonment under article 58-1a.

ON THE EVE OF 1953, SIGNS OF CRISIS?

The stories cited above are success stories of officers hunting for state criminals. These are the tales that dominate the reports and lead to arrests, investigations, and trials. However, they are only the tip of the iceberg, as shown by the statistics in the same reports, as well as the contents of many wanted files. On 1 January 1952, this iceberg comprised 6,634 wanted files, a mountain that had grown since 1944 through purges of collaborators, repression of anti-Soviet resistance, and the mass deportations that accompanied the forced Sovietization of Lithuania. Interactions between priorities defined at the Union level and republican specifics, between pan-Soviet models and their Lithuanian adaptations, and between instructions from above and practices on the ground constantly accompanied this growth. But whatever the adaptations and deviations produced, each new turn in this policy, each tightening of the screws or new priority target, produced new wanted files.

For several years, the scale of this repression and the ease with which suspicions were formulated meant that the number of cases increased continuously, despite successful identifications. In 1949–1951, the secret police found 700–800 wanted people per year, a success rate of 15–20 percent of cases registered at the beginning of each year. At that time, the identification of state criminals led to arrest in 30–45 percent of cases; the rest were placed under temporary surveillance (razrabotka) or identified as dead, abroad, or already in a camp. Many files, however, remained open for years without any progress being made or even without specific agents, who offered almost the only chance of tracing a wanted person (25–35 percent of files were in this category in 1949).

These results were due to a lack of resources as much as the repressive logic on which the hunt was based. The MGB clearly did not have the means to achieve its ambitions: in 1951–1952, the nine officers of the Fourth Department of the Kaunas region were expected to hunt down 2,082 state criminals.[88] The theoretical quality of this work matched the equally theoretical existence of some of those wanted, many of whom had fled with the Germans, been killed during the early postwar years, or never existed outside the world of Soviet suspicions, which produced "police identities" disconnected from any social reality.

The impossibility of efficiently handling a multitude of investigations, many with shaky foundations, led to a review of surveillance and wanted files in January 1952. The review sought to relieve the bottleneck by reducing the number of open files and to further prioritize the targets. In line with the Moscow and Vilnius directives issued several years earlier, profiles of people who might be dangerous in the present, especially spies, were given priority over those left over from the war. Even so, as with similar measures in the past, the effects of these changes had limited results. Although more files of "traitors, collaborators, and torturers" were archived than those of "agents of foreign intelligence services," the first group continued to constitute more than half of the wanted files. Above all, the review did not boost high-priority investigations. Judging by reports made in late 1952 and early 1953 by the head of the Fourth Department of the LSSR MGB and the very critical response from Moscow, foreign intelligence and counterintelligence agents were still not being tracked, because local MGB branches preferred to deal with cases that were easier to find. One parameter in particular was stressed: the rate of arrests among state criminals once found. In 1952, this number fell to 20 percent, whereas it had been 30–45 percent in 1947–1951; the low rate was seen as evidence that only minor state criminals were being sought and found, people who had committed no offenses serious enough to merit indictment.[89]

The absolute number of arrests fell gradually from 1947 to 1951, from 465 to just over 300, before dropping to 101 in 1952. As there was also a significant drop in the number of new files opened (134 in 1952, compared to 700–800 per year previously), we can deduce a slowdown in hunting activities in 1952.

How can we explain this decline? We can, of course, echo the reasons put forward by Starodubtsev to justify his department's poor results. Above all, its already insufficient staff was strongly affected by purges within the MGB (which he does not mention) and by the restructuring of the repressive apparatus (which he does mention). The number of officers tasked with hunting for state criminals in Vilnius fell from twenty-four to seventeen between August 1951 and May 1952.[90] The local sectors found themselves without management for several months, while more than half of their staff were replaced at the same time. These men spent a lot of time reviewing files when they were not mobilized by other missions.

But we can also ask whether the hunt for state criminals declined around 1952 because the Stalinist pattern of postwar purges and repressions had reached its limits. The Fourth Department was not able to keep up with the unbridled production of suspicion and guilt, which had already generated thousands of files, interrogations, and wanted notices. As a result, it could not translate these accusations into prosecutions. As each new wave of repression added a layer of wanted files, the department was required to deal with both past and present; it was therefore overwhelmed by work, which was at the same time becoming more sophisticated, methodical, and demanding in terms of time and knowhow. The decline in the number of new investigations and the attempts to archive less serious cases and examine more thoroughly the groups involved in Nazi crimes reflect a tension between the traditional model of mass Stalinist repression and the new trend toward more targeted, individual, judicialized repression based on more sophisticated surveillance and information management, as well on "the aspiration to professional pride and ethos" of MGB officers noted by Amir Weiner and Aigi Rahi-Tamm.[91] This shift foreshadows the priorities that would develop under de-Stalinization. In the context of the hunt for state criminals, this would mean, first, no new investigations, and then, from 1954 on, an extensive review of files that would declare many suspicions and supposed cases of guilt null and void, even though purges linked to the war were never completely halted.[92]

NOTES

I am grateful to the Lithuanian Special Archives for their welcome and accessibility, which were crucial in conducting this research supported by the Groupe d'études orientales, slaves et néo-helléniques (University of Strasbourg) and Agence nationale de la recherche (Project "Nazi War Crimes in the

Courtroom—Central and Eastern Europe, 1943–1991/WW2CRIMESONTRIAL1943–1991," led by Vanessa Voisin). I would also like to thank Alain Blum, Juliette Cadiot, Catherine Gousseff, Vanessa Voisin, and *Kritika*'s anonymous reviewers for their comments on earlier drafts of this chapter.

1. Hereafter the last names of suspects and informants mentioned in the sources are reduced to their initials. And although after the first instance, the term "state criminal" does not appear in quotation marks, it should be understood that those assigned this status by the secret police were often innocent of any crime.

2. Lietuvos ypatingasis archyvas (LYA) f. K-30, ap. 1, b. 1757, wanted file of Antanas Karolio V. (1948–1950).

3. The *rozysk* studied in this chapter corresponds only to the hunt for suspects. I translate it as "investigation," "hunt," or "tracking." It should be distinguished from *ugolovnyi rozysk*, another type of police activity that corresponds to a criminal investigation.

4. More precisely, the term "state crime" was introduced into the Criminal Code a posteriori by the Statute on State Crimes (Polozhenie o prestupleniiakh gosudarstvennykh [kontrrevoliutsionnykh i osobo dlia Soiuza SSR opasnykh prestupleniiakh protiv poriadka upravleniia]"), adopted by the Central Executive Committee of the Soviet Union on 25 February 1927. See A. I. Chuchaev, T. K. Aguzarov, and Iu. V. Gracheva, *Gosudarstvennye prestupleniia v ugolovnom prave Rossii v XX veke: Istoriko-pravovye ocherki* (Moscow: Prospekt, 2015), 67–68. The Russian Criminal Code of 1926 was applied in the Baltic republics from their annexation until the adoption of their own codes in 1961.

5. On 1 January 1951, after evicting more than 9,000 agents and informants in 1950, LSSR MGB had a network of 21,655 informants, 3,770 agents, 599 residents, and 615 occupants of "safe houses" (LYA f. K-41, ap. 1, b. 416, l. 3).

6. Among the very few publications on this subject is Vladimir Makarov, "Rozysk voennykh prestupnikov, izmennikov Rodiny i posobnikov okkupantov na osvobozhdennoi territorii SSSR v 1941–1943 gg.," *Voenno-istoricheskii zhurnal*, no. 6 (2017): 46–52.

7. Viktor Chebrikov et al., *Istoriia sovetskikh organov bezopasnosti* (Moscow: KGB, 1977), 476.

8. Franziska Exeler, "What Did You Do during the War? Personal Responses to the Aftermath of Nazi Occupation," *Kritika: Explorations in Russian and Eurasian History* 17, no. 4 (2016): 805–35; Exeler, "The Ambivalent State: Determining Guilt in the Post-World War II Soviet Union," *Slavic Review* 75, no. 3 (2016): 606–29; Tanja Penter, "Local Collaborators on Trial," *Cahiers du monde russe* 49, no. 2 (2009): 341–64; Vanessa Voisin, *L'URSS contre ses traîtres: L'épuration soviétique (1941–1955)* (Paris: Publications de la Sorbonne, 2015); Amir Weiner, *Making Sense of War: The Second World War and the Fate of the Bolshevik Revolution* (Princeton, NJ: Princeton University Press, 2002).

9. Olaf Mertelsmann, ed., *The Baltic States under Stalinist Rule* (Cologne: Böhlau, 2016); Juliette Denis, "La fabrique de la Lettonie soviétique, 1939–1949: Une soviétisation de temps de guerre" (PhD diss., Université Paris X Nanterre, 2015); Kevin McDermott and Matthew Stibbe, eds., *Stalinist Terror in Eastern Europe: Elite Purges and Mass Repression* (Manchester: Manchester University Press, 2010), 19–38; Toomas Hiio and Meelis Saueauk, eds., *Sovietisation and Violence: The Case of Estonia* (Tartu: University of Tartu Press, 2018); Mertelsmann, ed., *The Sovietization of the Baltic States, 1940–1956* (Tartu: KLEIO Ajalookirjanduse Sihtasutus, 2003); Tynu [Tõnu] Tannberg, *Politika Moskvy v respublikakh Baltii v poslevoennye gody (1944–1956): Issledovaniia i dokumenty* (Moscow: ROSSPEN, 2010); Elena Zubkova, *Pribaltika i Kreml', 1940–1953* (Moscow: ROSSPEN, 2008).

10. Juliette Denis, "Identifier les 'éléments ennemis' en Lettonie," *Cahiers du monde russe* 49, no. 2–3 (2008): 297–318; Olaf Mertelsmann and Aigi Rahi-Tamm, "Cleansing and Compromise: The Estonian SSR in 1944–1945," *Cahiers du monde russe* 49, no. 2–3 (2008): 319–40; Zubkova, *Pribaltika i Kreml'*.

11. The trend toward increased surveillance and information gathering is visible in the very detailed Order no. 001223 of the USSR NKVD, dated 11 October 1939, "On the Introduction of a Unified

System of Surveillance Registration [*operativnyi uchet*] of Anti-Soviet Elements Detected by Agent Surveillance [*agenturnaia razrabotka*]," published in *Nakanune Kholokosta: Front litovskikh aktivistov i sovetskie repressii v Litve, 1940–1941 gg. Sbornik dokumentov*, ed. Aleksandr Diukov (Moscow: Istorich-eskaia pamiat', 2012), 469–85. This system was reformed in part by Order no. 0065 of the USSR NKGB, dated 18 February 1944, "On the Reorganization of Surveillance Registration of Anti-Soviet Elements" (HDA MVSU [Haluzevyi derzhavnyi arkhiv Ministerstva vnutrishnikh sprav Ukraïni], f. 45, op. 1, spr. 123). On the shift from mass to individual operations, see James Heinzen, "Informers and the State under Late Stalinism: Informant Networks and Crimes against 'Socialist Property,' 1940–53," *Kritika: Explorations in Russian and Eurasian History* 8, no. 4 (2007): 789–815; David R. Shearer, *Policing Stalin's Socialism: Repression and Social Order in the Soviet Union, 1924–1953* (New Haven: Yale University Press, 2009); and Amir Weiner and Aigi Rahi-Tamm, "Getting to Know You: The Soviet Surveillance System, 1939–1957," *Kritika: Explorations in Russian and Eurasian History* 13, no. 1 (2012): 5–45.

12. Exceptions are discussed in Jeffrey Burds, "The Early Cold War in Soviet West Ukraine, 1944–1948," *Carl Beck Papers in Russian and East European Studies*, no. 1505 (Pittsburgh: University of Pittsburgh, 2001); Burds, *Sovetskaia agentura: Ocherki istorii SSSR v poslevoennye gody (1944–1948)* (Moscow: Sovremennaia istoriia, 2006); and Weiner and Rahi-Tamm, "Getting to Know You." On counter-insurgency activities, see Arvydas Anušauskas, "La composition et les méthodes secrètes des organes de sécurité soviétiques en Lituanie, 1940–1953," *Cahiers du monde russe* 42, no. 2–4 (2001): 321–56; George Reklaitis, "Cold War Lithuania: National Armed Resistance and Soviet Counter-insurgency," *Carl Beck Papers in Russian and East European Studies*, no. 1806 (Pittsburgh: University of Pittsburgh, 2007); and Alexander Statiev, *The Soviet Counterinsurgency in the Western Borderlands* (Cambridge: Cambridge University Press, 2010).

13. The term "guilt factory" was coined by Pavel Chinsky to describe the production of charges and evidence of guilt in an individual case (*Micro-histoire de la Grande Terreur: La fabrique de culpabilité à l'ère stalinienne* [Paris: Denoël, 2005]). I use it here to refer to the whole range of activities of the secret police related to the formulation of suspicions and the designation of suspects.

14. A. I. Kokurin and N. V. Petrov, eds., *Lubianka: Organy VChK-OGPU-NKVD-NKGB-MGB-MVD-KGB, 1917–1991. Spravochnik* (Moscow: Mezhdunarodnyi fond "Demokratiia," 2003), 139.

15. Chebrikov, *Istoriia sovetskikh organov bezopasnosti*, 477.

16. LYA f. K-20, ap. 1, b. 134, ll. 28–29 (1949); LYA f. K-20, ap. 1, b. 153, l. 266 (1951).

17. LYA f. K-19, ap. 1, b. 402, ll. 41–44 (1948).

18. On the failures of the NKGB-MGB personnel in Ukraine, see Burds, *Sovetskaia agentura*, 76.

19. Oleg Khlevniuk, "Stalin i organy gosudarstvennoi bezopasnosti v poslevoennyi period," *Cahiers du monde russe* 42, no. 2–4 (2001): 535–48; Nikita Petrov, "Repressii v apparate MGB v poslednie gody zhizni Stalina, 1951–1953," *Cahiers du monde russe* 44, no. 2–3 (2003): 403–36.

20. LYA f. K-19, ap. 1, b. 402, ll. 80–86 (1950); LYA f. K-20, ap. 1, b. 153, l. 94 (1953).

21. LYA f. K-20, ap. 1, b. 153, ll. 71–80 (1951).

22. LYA f. K-20, ap. 1, b. 153, l. 76 (1951); LYA f. K-20, ap. 1, b. 152, l. 201 (1952).

23. LYA f. K-20, ap. 1, b. 152, ll. 93–94 (1953).

24. Chebrikov, *Istoriia sovetskikh organov bezopasnosti*, 477.

25. Vasilii S. Khristoforov, ed., *Organy gosudarstvennoi bezopasnosti SSSR v Velikoi Otechestvennoi voine* (Moscow: Kuchkovo pole, 2007), 5, pt. 1:220–23.

26. Voisin, *L'URSS contre ses traîtres*.

27. On the approaches taken toward Soviet purges in the Baltic States, proactive and reactive, see Aldis Purs, "Soviet in Form, Local in Content: Elite Repression and Mass Terror in the Baltic States, 1940–53," in *Stalinist Terror in Eastern Europe*, 19–38.

28. LYA f. K-19, ap. 1, b. 402, l. 11 (15 January 1946) and p. 12 (3 April 1946).

29. Denis, "Identifier les 'éléments ennemis' en Lettonie"; Denis, "'Les traîtres, les bandits et les autres':

Représentations de l'ennemi dans la Lettonie soviétique de sortie de guerre (1944–1947)," in *Pour une histoire connectée et transnationale des épurations en Europe après 1945*, ed. Marc Bergère et al. (Brussels: Peter Lang, 2019), 215.

30. Mertelsmann and Rahi-Tamm, "Cleansing and Compromise," 332, 339.

31. Zubkova, *Pribaltika i Kreml'*, 239–40.

32. LYA f. K-19, ap. 1, b. 402, l. 6 (1945).

33. Notably with the decree of the Central Committee (20 August 1946), followed on 2 February 1947 by Order no. 0048 of the USSR MGB "On Strengthening Counterintelligence Work against American and British Intelligence Agents" (Chebrikov, *Istoriia sovetskikh organov bezopasnosti*, 460, 465). On the importance of counterespionage activities, see David R. Shearer and Vladimir Khaustov, *Stalin and the Lubianka: A Documentary History of the Political Police and Security Organs in the Soviet Union, 1922–1953* (New Haven: Yale University Press, 2015), chap. 8. On the reflection of this development in Lithuania, see LYA, f. K-19, ap. 1, b. 402, ll. 80, 83 (1950); and LYA f. K-20, ap. 1, b. 152, ll. 85, 112 (1951).

34. An early report on so-called state criminals identified abroad is in LYA f. K-20, ap. 1, b. 152, ll. 62–64 (16 April 1952). On the surveillance, see LYA f. K-19, ap. 1, b. 402, ll. 122–23 (March 1952), l. 137 (April 1952); and LYA f. K-19, ap. 1, b. 30, ll. 204–7 (November 1952).

35. LYA f. K-19, ap. 1, b. 402, ll. 41–44 (1948).

36. This category included Lithuanian personnel of the Sicherheitsdienst (SD) and Sicherheitspolizei (SiPo), as well as agents who had worked for the counterespionage service Abwehrstelle Östland.

37. LYA f. K-20, ap. 1, b. 152, l. 83 (1952).

38. Chebrikov, *Istoriia sovetskikh organov bezopasnosti*, 460; LYA f. K-20, ap. 1, b. 152, l. 100 (1952).

39. LYA f. K-20, ap. 1, b. 152, l. 201 (1952).

40. LYA f. K-20, ap. 1, b. 152, ll. 93, 134 (1953).

41. LYA f. K-20, ap. 1, b. 152, ll. 101–28, 134 (1953); LYA f. K-20, ap. 1, b. 184, l. 46 (1953).

42. LYA f. K-20, ap. 1, b. 184, ll. 15, 31; LYA f. K-20, ap. 1, b. 152, ll. 90, 131 (1953).

43. LYA f. K-51, ap. 1, b. 67, ll. 77, 85 (1949).

44. LYA f. K-20, ap. 1, b. 152, l. 95 (1953); LYA f. K-20, ap. 1, b. 168, ll. 83–84 (1953).

45. LYA f. K-51, ap. 1, b. 123, l. 83 (1951).

46. From the Lithuanian *šauliai* (riflemen), members of the paramilitary organization Lietuvos Šaulių Sąjunga, created in 1919 to defend Lithuania against the Poles and Bolshevik Russia. It was indeed perceived—accurately, to some extent—as an irreconcilable adversary, a purveyor of tightly knit and organized opponents. On the important role played by members of this organization during the June 1941 uprising and the first period of the Holocaust in Lithuania, see Hektoras Vitkus, "Lietuvos šauliai, Latvijos aizsargai ir Estijos kaitseliitai Holokausto akistatoje: Lyginamoji analizė," *Lituanistica*, no. 3 (2015): 196–220.

47. LYA f. K-41, ap. 1, b. 23 (1944); LYA f. K-18, ap. 1, b. 27 (1944).

48. LYA f. K-20, ap. 1, b. 88, l. 281 (1949); LYA f. K-20, ap. 1, b. 41, ll. 106, 111 (1947).

49. LYA f. K-41, ap. 1, b. 530, ll. 23–36 (1957).

50. LYA f. K-41, ap. 1, b. 23, ll. 512–24 (1944).

51. LYA f. K-15, ap. 1, b. 10 (1944). On advance information gathering, see Denis, "Identifier les 'éléments ennemis'"; Weiner and Rahi-Tamm, "Getting to Know You"; and Makarov, "Rozysk voennykh prestupnikov."

52. LYA f. K-41, ap. 1, b. 23, ll. 66, 205, 209, 520 (1944); LYA f. K-51, ap. 1, b. 16 (1944); LYA f. K-30, ap. 1, b. 1869, surveillance file (*agenturnoe delo*) "Karateli" (1945). Compare with Khristoforov, *Organy gosudarstvennoi bezopasnosti SSSR*, vols. 5–6; and A. B. Opalev et al., eds., *Velikaia Otechestvennaia voina 1941–1945 godov*, vol. 6: *Tainaia voina: Razvedka i kontrrazvedka v gody Velikoi Otechestvennoi voiny* (Moscow: Kuchkovo pole, 2013).

53. LYA f. K-20, ap. 1, b. 152, l. 137 (1953).

54. LYA f. K-20, ap. 1, b. 152, ll. 137–38.

55. LYA f. K-40, ap. 1, b. 28 (1946). See Lynne Viola, *Stalinist Perpetrators on Trial: Scenes from the Great Terror in Soviet Ukraine* (New York: Oxford University Press, 2017).

56. LYA f. K-19, ap. 1, b. 402, ll. 14–15 (1946); LYA f. K-19, ap. 1, b. 402, l. 104 (1951); LYA f. K-51, ap. 1, b. 123, l. 14 (1951).

57. See esp. the report on the archives seized by the NKGB operational group in Kaunas in early August 1944 and their first uses (LYA f. K-18, ap. 1, b. 26, l. 3 [1944]).

58. Anušauskas, "Composition et les méthodes," 327, 331; Rasa Baločkaitė, "The Hidden Violence of Totalitarianism: Policing Soviet Society in Lithuania," *European History Quarterly* 45, no. 2 (2015): 215–35.

59. I propose a more precise chronology of the enlargement of a circle of suspects and the use of German and Soviet archives through a series of investigations that targeted, between 1944 and 1957, about fifteen people accused of having participated in the crimes committed during the Nazi occupation of Pabradė, a small town on the Lithuanian-Polish border, in Emilia Koustova, "Instruire, juger et négocier le passé de guerre dans la Lituanie soviétique (Pabradė, 1944–1957)," *Revue d'histoire de la Shoah*, no. 214 (2021): 149–83.

60. LYA f. K-20, ap. 1, b. 153, l. 266a–70 (1951).

61. LYA f. K-20, ap. 1, b. 152, ll. 203–4 (1952).

62. LYA f. K-20, ap. 1, b. 152, l. 97 (1953).

63. LYA f. K-20, ap. 1, b. 152, l. 158 (1953).

64. Zubkova, *Pribaltika i Kreml'*, 238; Weiner and Rahi-Tamm, "Getting to Know You," 16; Vitalija Stravinskienė, "Soviet Passports and Their Implementation in East and Southeast Lithuania (1944–1989)," *Lithuanian Historical Studies* 23, no. 1 (2019): 117–43.

65. On more sophisticated equipment, see LYA f. K-41, ap. 1, b. 575, l. 92 (1957). On the use of photography, see LYA f. K-19, ap. 1, b. 402, l. 155 (1952).

66. Chebrikov, *Istoriia sovetskikh organov bezopasnosti*, 462, 479.

67. Shearer, *Policing Stalin's Socialism*. On the frequent criticisms aimed at the informants' networks, despite the advantages that these presented, see Heinzen, "Informers and the State." On the increasing use of informants under late Stalinism, see Burds, *Sovetskaia agentura*; Statiev, *Soviet Counterinsurgency in the Western Borderlands*, 233–38; and Jeffrey S. Hardy, "'A Very Important Yet Complicated Matter': Informant Networks in the Estonian Gulag, 1952–1964," *Russian History* 44, no. 2–3 (2017): 411–48.

68. On counterinsurgency, see Burds, *Sovetskaia agentura*; and Reklaitis, *Cold War Lithuania*.

69. On attachment to family, see LYA f. K-20, ap. 1, b. 134, l. 78 (1950). On special skills and other factors, see LYA f. K-20, ap. 1, b. 88, l. 129 (1949); and LYA f. K-20, ap. 1, b. 134, ll. 76, 78 (1950). On the importance of prior confession, see Chebrikov, *Istoriia sovetskikh organov bezopasnosti*, 479.

70. LYA f. K-51, ap. 1, b. 129; LYA f. K-20, ap. 1, b. 88, l. 350 (1950).

71. LYA f. K-20, ap. 1, b. 10, l. 164 (1947); LYA f. K-51, ap. 1, b. 68, l. 173.

72. Compare with Weiner and Rahi-Tamm, "Getting to Know You," 26–30.

73. LYA f. K-20, ap. 1, b. 88, ll. 277–79 (1949).

74. LYA f. K-20, ap. 1, b. 134, l. 41 (1950).

75. LYA f. K-30, ap. 1, b. 1757, wanted file of Antanas Karolio V. (1948–1950).

76. LYA f. K-20, ap. 1, b. 88, l. 347 (1949); Chebrikov, *Istoriia sovetskikh organov bezopasnosti*, 460; Weiner and Rahi-Tamm, "Getting to Know You," 34–35.

77. LYA f. K-20, ap. 1, b. 152, l. 94 (1953).

78. LYA f. K-20, ap. 1, b. 88, l. 227 (1949).

79. LYA f. K-20, ap. 1, b. 184, l. 55 (1953).

80. LYA f. K-20, ap. 1, b. 134, l. 53 (1950).

81. LYA f. K-20, ap. 1, b. 88, l. 188 (1949).

82. LYA f. K-20, ap. 1, b. 88, ll. 1, 77, 78 (1949).

83. LYA f. K-20, ap. 1, b. 88, l. 268 (1949).

84. LYA f. K-30, ap. 1, b. 756, surveillance file (*dos'e-formuliar*) of Aloizas K. (1952).

85. LYA f. K-30, ap. 1, b. 756, ll. 32, 35.

86. LYA f. K-30, ap. 1, b. 756, ll. 34, 39.

87. LYA f. K-30, ap. 1, b. 756, l. 37.

88. LYA f. K-20, ap. 1, b. 153, ll. 71–80 (1951); LYA f. K-20, ap. 1, b. 152, l. 200 (1952).

89. LYA f. K-20, ap. 1, b. 168, ll. 83–84 (1953). The study of the prosecution of participants in war crimes in Pabradė provides two examples of such investigations, which ended in 1951–1952 with the release of the found state criminals for lack of evidence to justify their indictment (Koustova, "Instruire, juger et négocier le passé").

90. LYA f. K-20, ap. 1, b. 152, l. 190 (1952); LYA f. K-20, ap. 1, b. 153, l. 71 (1951).

91. Weiner and Rahi-Tamm, "Getting to Know You," 6.

92. Emilia Koustova, "Les héritages de la guerre dans la Lituanie soviétique des années 1950: Les épurations, la soviétisation et la transformation des pratiques répressives," in *Pour une histoire connectée et transnationale des épurations en Europe après 1945*, 309–26.

The Mug Shot and the Close-Up

Identification and Visual Pedagogy in Secret Police Film

Cristina Vatulescu

AMONG THE NEW DIRECTIONS IN THE STUDY OF SECRET POLICE ARCHIVES in Russia and Eastern Europe, we notice an emerging preoccupation with the visual. This chapter is part of a research effort to grapple with the long-overlooked visual aspects of secret police archives, with particular attention to film. It investigates the entanglement of policing and cinema in their uses of visual identification strategies, with a focus on the relationship between the mug shot and the close-up. I argue that in grappling with the visual aspects of the secret police archives, we are missing the point if we just look at the images themselves. These images were embedded in particular ways of seeing, deciphering, and interpreting, which they were further tasked to teach their viewers through what I designate as their *visual pedagogy*. The main concern of this visual pedagogy was to teach citizens how to look at and, I will argue, *through* each other to see "the hostile elements" hiding behind apparently innocent faces. The litmus test of this visual pedagogy was the face, and cinema and policing collaborated in teaching citizens to distrust visual appearances and see through the internal enemies hiding in their midst. Without identifying and understanding this visual pedagogy, we run the risk of seeing only the tip of the iceberg of these visual collections.

The bibliography on the visual aspects of secret police archives is still limited, but it is growing. Some highlights are the online *Hidden Galleries* created by a team of researchers headed by James Kapaló, as well as the related exhibits and exhibit catalogue; the online exhibit *Beauty in Hell: Culture in the Gulag*, organized by Andrea Gullotta and The Hunterian; Tatiana Vagramenko's work on the visual records produced by the secret police during surveillance and investigation of religious groups; Aglaya Glebova's short but provocative article "A Visual History of the Gulag in Ten Theses"; and Olga Shevchenko and Oksana Sarkisova's work on the amateur photo album.[1] My first book, *Police Aesthetics* (2010), investigated the ways in which visual arts and technologies were implicated in policing.[2] My argument here builds on and extends an earlier argument I made then about "the look of high Stalinism," which was not an image but a way of looking: *bditel'nost'*.

Translated as "watchfulness" or "vigilance," *bditel'nost'* was first a suspicion directed toward vision and the visible, doubled by the urge to peer through the surface of reality in expectation of the worst. Alan Sekula has documented the emergence of "a crisis of faith in optical empiricism" in the late nineteenth century, and writers such as Martin Jay, Michael Leja, and Malcolm Turvey have documented its pervasive spread in modernity and modernist image making.[3] *Bditelnost'* partakes in this widespread skepticism toward vision and the visible, but it also constituted a distinctive Soviet way of looking, a key element of an evolving yet strongly codified visual pedagogy. *Bditel'nost'* was strongly connected to the prevalent visual rhetoric of masking and unmasking, famously analyzed by Sheila Fitzpatrick in *Take off the Masks*.[4] While in the 1920s images of criminals could appear glamorous or exotic, by the 1930s even mug shots became highly suspect and unsatisfactory, since enemies could hide behind the most politically correct-looking faces. The solution was to shift the focus from the image itself to policing the way of reading the image—thus the growing importance of a visual pedagogy that would teach citizens how to decipher reality visually.

This chapter follows the development of this visual pedagogy after Stalin's death, tracing its reach across the Eastern bloc. The main focus is on Romania, a country whose infamous secret police closely followed its Soviet model.[5] I start by closely analyzing the infamous 1960 *Reconstituirea* (Reenactment, 1960), a film that was carefully constructed as a secret police *ars cinematica*, deliberately laying out and putting into practice cinema's potential uses for policing.[6] Chief among them was the exposition of a visual pedagogy targeted at teaching viewers strictly codified ways in which they were to participate in the visual drama on, and eventually off, screen. Furthermore, I argue that *Reenactment* was not a freak of post-Stalinist cinematic history but rather one particularly elaborate and cinematically self-conscious expression of this visual pedagogy. The chapter goes on to show that key hallmarks of this visual pedagogy were present in other productions of the Romanian State Documentary Film studio, Sahia, as well as in other contemporary collaborations between the secret police cinema and cinema across Soviet space, from Moscow to Saratov, from Ukraine to Belarus.

Declared the most important of all arts, and able to transcend the linguistic differences across Soviet space, cinema was tasked with educating the public in Soviet ways of looking. Tasked but not entrusted, for suspicion—not trust—ruled the day. Thus the various "collaborations" of cinema with the police, often the secret police. Most obviously, secret police agents depicted on screen provided models of vigilant looking and deciphering. More often and more insidiously, their control over the evolving visual pedagogy was wielded by commissioning, censoring, scripting, and overlooking visual representations of criminals and the correct ways of looking at and through them. Ultimately, what most clearly distinguishes the Soviet suspicion of vision within a more generalized modernist ocular skepticism is that the unreliability of vision and treacherous nature of the visible is presented as a dangerous ideological threat—a threat that is unfailingly neutralized by the state's policing apparatus. In the films, the problem is always followed by the solution, to the point that one wonders if the problem (the crime, the criminals, but also the whole suspicion toward the visible) was not fabricated in order to justify the need for the solution (the police and its quest for identification). Cinema's task was to present this visual drama to the public, heightening both the threat and the ingenuity of the solution, while also giving visual instruction for the identification of criminals. The films analyzed below offered their viewers master lessons in navigating the ideologically treacherous visual realities of their days.

INTRODUCING *REENACTMENT*

I first, and most extensively, focus on an infamous 1959 film collaboration between the Romanian secret police and the State Documentary Film Studio, Sahia. The resulting film, *Reenactment*, is a feature-length reenactment of a bank heist against the Romanian national bank, where the six apprehended suspects played themselves, alongside the secret police extras and agents working on the case. Not long after the movie was completed, all five male suspects were shot, and the sole female defendant, Monica Sevianu, was sent to a women's prison. The objective of the movie, as explained in an introductory speech before a fall 1960 screening, "was to demonstrate the power of the Militia and the vigilance of the Party, which knows how to unmask enemies of the people even among its own members."[7] This off-screen message was reinforced almost *ad literam* at the end of the movie, where the voice-over encouraged the audience "to be vigilant and ready to unmask all enemies of the people, even when they are found in the bosom of the Party."[8]

The significance of the case and of the 1960 film *Reenactment* is also visible in the cinematic chain reaction it generated after 1989, with three full-length movies taking up the subject again. The first, Irene Lusztig's *Reenactment* (2001), is a sophisticated first-person documentary animated by the filmmaker's search for her grandmother, Monica Sevianu. Lusztig's film takes on the 1960 secret police movie directly: she starts her documentary with a clip of the earlier film's opening sequence, then deconstructs its main narrative and replaces it with her own self-reflexive reenactment of her grandmother's story. A more traditional documentary, Alexandru Solomon's *Marele jaf al băncii naționale* (The great communist bank robbery, 2004), shares Lusztig's preoccupation with the original 1960 film and introduces its own markers of documentary self-reflexivity. For instance, the ending shows the movie's "talking heads" watching and debating the movie they have just seen, in a cinematic homage to the iconic ending of the first cinema verité documentary, *Chronique d'un été* (Chronicle of a summer, 1963). *Mai aproape de lună* (Closer to the moon, 2013), one of the most expensive productions in Romanian cinema, left the documentary genre behind and went mainstream. Directed by Nae Caranfil, the Romanian-American drama featured Vera Farmiga in the role of Monica Sevianu.

This attention given to *Reenactment* in post-1989 cinematic productions is probably due to the film's peculiar involvement in the sensational story of the bank heist and its subsequent trial, and to the disturbing use of secret police agents, witnesses, and especially defendants to play themselves. Alongside the film's extensive blending of reenactment with footage from the actual trial, the film's active showcasing of cinema's own apparatus and role in the drama also proved particularly intriguing to the filmmakers engaging with it. With self-conscious references to Soviet and Western cinematic traditions and new directions, *Reenactment* is, to my knowledge, the most elaborate and confounding example of a secret police film declassified to date.

The focus of this chapter is resolutely on the cinematic aspects of secret police archives, often ignored or treated as subsidiary to their textual collections. Thus the close analysis of the film opens backward and forward in time to the cinematic traditions it enters into dialogue with and laterally to the contemporary films that were its shaping context, a context that is often illegible from our historical distance. My cinematic focus mostly excludes other aspects of the actual case, including the twenty-seven volumes of case files that I mine at length in a separate book chapter.[9] However, inasmuch as volume 18 of this file contains a plethora of written documents pertaining directly to the movie—such as versions of the scripts and shooting directions—a brief discussion of it can contribute to the cinematic focus of this chapter. These documents throw some light on the meaning of the "collaboration" between the filmmaking studio and the Ministry of Internal Affairs. It appears that the film originated in a "plan of action" drawn up by the latter.[10] The document starts by asking for one director and two cameramen and then provides a rough draft of the script. A second plan of action revises the initial script, which had asked for the participation of the actual agents and the witnesses connected to the case, and introduces the prisoners together with the genre of reenactment.[11] The four actual scripts, which reveal a process of careful revision, give no credit to any author, except for the last, which credits the Ministry of Internal Affairs.[12] The name of the director does not appear in any of these documents; instead, each of them bears the seal of approval of the Ministry of Internal Affairs. The last such note laconically states: "The recording of the film can begin."[13] It was thus the Ministry of Internal Affairs that had the first and last word on the script.

The ministry's choice of film studio, director, and cameraman was wholly unsurprising. Sahia opened in 1950 and was operating at full speed by 1959–1960 when *Reenactment* was filmed.[14] Over the course of its first decade, Sahia built its filmmaking credentials by hiring graduates of Moscow's famous All-Union State Institute of Cinematography (VGIK), and later those of the Romanian Institute of Theatrical and Cinematographic Arts I. L. Caragiale (founded in 1954).[15] For *Reenactment*, the Ministry of Internal Affairs chose Sahia's two best-known names in political films, the director Virgil Calotescu and the cameraman Pantelie Tuțuleasa.[16] The latter was the main cameraman charged with shooting Romania's heads of state from the 1940s through the 1990s, including Ceausescu's infamous last speech. Virgil Calotescu, Sahia's most powerful political director, had a similarly long-lived career. After *Reenactment* he took his interest in using the camera to penetrate the surface of reality with the first Romanian underwater film.[17] While he continued making propaganda documentary films to the end of his career, he also ventured into fiction film, including one of the most popular comedies of the 1980s, *Buletin de Bucuresti* (Bucharest ID, 1982). Among the constants of his long and prolific career was a conviction that filmmakers "should not be afraid of the audience," because the audience will accept and "consume" any film genre, documentary and fiction, short and full-length films, if "the film expresses the audience's legitimate demands (such as *unmasking* vices, conformist or anti-social attitudes)."[18] Calotescu's belief in unmasking as a powerful audience hook across film genres is related to his lasting collaboration with the secret police, which he continued to eulogize for unmasking foreign spies and becoming themselves master of disguises in films, such as *Acţiunea Autobuzul* (The bus, 1978) and *Reţeaua "S"* (The "S" network, 1980).

BEGINNINGS AND VISUAL PEDAGOGY: SEATING THE AUDIENCE IN ITS PROPER PLACE

If we aim to understand a film's visual pedagogy, a good place to start is the opening sequence. The beginning orients the spectator in the world of the movie, most obviously with establishing shots and less obviously, but often more powerfully, by setting some parameters for their position as spectator. *Reenactment* opens on an extensive commentary about the new role of the camera and of the spectator in socialist society. The first shots of the film reveal a collection of open history books. The determined voice-over tells us that these chronicles record some of our past, while some is forever lost in the darkness of history. A shot of an open book gradually covered in darkness illustrates this meditation. We are cheerfully informed that today, for the first time, history is written by a chronicler—the film camera—that offers a perfect record. As the book disappears in darkness, a film camera literally turns to the audience and looks it up and down. Following a shot-reverse-shot order, this unusual, unsettling image would normally be followed by a shot revealing what the camera is looking at; however here, adding to the uneasy suspense, a seemingly blank screen follows the image of the camera. As the camera pans down, we come upon a panorama of crowded apartment buildings. The audience is probably relieved to find out that it is today's Bucharest, rather than itself, that the camera is recording. Our job, the voice-over informs us, is simply to read the cinematic chronicle of the ongoing construction of socialism.

Just as we start relaxing into the blasé seats of a propaganda movie audience, the camera reveals the precarity of our viewing position. As the camera zooms out, what appeared to have been a fixed, privileged observation point offering an unobstructed view of the city is revealed as dizzying scaffolding. The scaffolding supports the camera while cutting straight across its field of vision. Coming down from the scaffolding, the camera gets into a car and starts following another camera mounted in another car. This sequence is a close reenactment of one of the most famous sequences in film history: the sequence in *Chelovek s kino-apparatom* (Man with a movie camera, 1928), which features the cinematographer Mikhail Kaufman setting his camera atop a moving car while his brother, Dziga Vertov—the most influential Soviet documentary filmmaker—films Kaufman filming the city.[19] Vertov's *Man with a*

Movie Camera has been hailed as the summa of documentary theories and practices of its times, a movie whose immense influence is deeply felt to this day.[20] Calotescu's reenactment of one of the signature metacinematic moments of *Man with a Movie Camera* introduces a host of other references to Vertov's documentary. The playful camera movements designed to trick and unsettle the viewer while making her aware of the often precarious position of the camera also harken back to the hallmark of Vertov's style. In *Man with a Movie Camera,* the cameraman famously filmed from scaffoldings, cars, and from under running trains. As opposed to mainstream feature film cameras that erase their traces, attempting to make the audience as unaware as possible of their presence, the camera movements in *Man with a Movie Camera* and *Reenactment* constantly draw attention to the camera's mobility and speed in contrast to the spectator's fixed point of view.

Reenactment's references to signature sequences of Vertov's movie and the subtler references to camera movement point to the ideological kinship of the two projects. Vertov made his film in 1928, a decade after the beginning of socialist construction in the Soviet Union. Calotescu's film was made in 1959, a decade after the beginning of socialism in Romania. Both movies emphasize the film camera's role in recording as well as participating in the construction of socialism.

But despite these multileveled parallels, a close look at these cameras reveals key differences. Their very appearance marks them as products of different times, and they are certainly put to different uses. For example, over the close-up of Vertov's camera climbs, in an amusing special effect, another full-length camera and its operator. In a related sequence later in the film, the full-length camera faces the audience and does a little dance. Vertov's camera is playful, flaunting its animated moves as special effects designed to entertain the audience. The camera in *Reenactment* turns slowly and motions to the viewers in a highly controlled and potentially threatening way. It is not a self-conscious trick that animates this camera but rather a hand that becomes invisible in the zoomed-in shot.

Images of cameras and filmmaking, as well as the gaze addressed directly to the audience, are programmatically avoided in mainstream cinema; they have come to be almost automatically associated with an alternative, reflexive cinema. But just in case we might be inclined to interpret the image of the camera as a reminder that what we see are mediated images rather than "a mirror carried on the highways of reality," the voice-over that accompanies the first image of the camera in *Reenactment* informs us that this new eye offers us "images that are alive and identical with reality." Vertov's conception of the relationship between images and reality was certainly more sophisticated. He did not believe that his images were identical to the reality seen by the human eye. Instead, he thought that the images created by his camera's eye (*kino-glaz*) were much better.[21] They could reveal aspects of reality that the fallible human eye had not been able to see before. Yet what connects these two sequences is their affirmation of the superiority of the film camera over other means of representation, such as print, and over the fallible human eye.

The end of the framing sequences in *Man with a Movie Camera* and *Reenactment* further articulate the differences in the ways these two films participate in their respective ideological battles. Both framing sequences end in an empty room. After the first sequence when the camera as well as its object—the city—is introduced, Vertov takes us into an empty film theater. Vertov reminds us of our position as spectators watching a film, thus inviting our self-reflexivity to match the self-reflexivity of the camera. As we have seen, *Reenactment* also starts with a sequence that introduces the camera and its objective—the city. The last shot of this framing sequence also shows an empty seat, an empty school bench in an elementary school classroom. Just as the audience might heed the invitation and sit down, however, a matching shot of a different bench is superimposed, replacing the shot of the school bench. The voice-over turns suddenly threatening, admonishing us that in order for today's children to appreciate socialism they must know about our enemies. The word "enemies" is synchronized with an extremely close shot of a bench. The camera pulls up and away from this bench and reveals its wooden enclosure. The bench that we were about to sit on is in the defender's dock, and the room is a courtroom. As we inspect the ominously empty seats, we are told that "those who are brought into this room have not deserved the title of human beings."

Both Vertov and Calotescu use their opening sequences to frame their films self-referentially. Both films tell us that what we are seeing is a movie, thus correcting the conventional illusionistic pact between films and their audiences. Once this correction is in place, the actual film can begin. Vertov's film begins on its own turf, in the cinema, and presents itself to the viewers as entertainment. In *Reenactment*, the empty room is not a cinema but a courtroom. The initial position assigned to the audience by the voice-over is that of children about to learn the hard facts about "the struggle with socialism's enemies." The audience might find its place—a school bench—rather confining, but there is not much room to maneuver and the alternatives that the camera alludes to are threatening. From the very beginning, the camera makes it clear that this is a slippery position. The school bench can easily dissolve into a defender's bench. The visual and verbal lesson of the film is forcefully clear, and whatever ambiguities there are do not leave room for interpretation but rather work as veiled threats to the audience.

As a result, despite the striking parallels with Vertov's film, we might well believe the voice-over as it boasts that this way of writing history with the movie camera is, if not unprecedented, then at least of its time. This is a self-fulfilling prophecy if there ever was one. The very existence of a voice-over, no less an unrelenting, authoritative commentary, completely breaks with Vertov's tradition and announces a new way of approaching history. The ever-present voice-over completely overpowers and structures the editing of the images, which are fully subordinate to its rhetoric. The power dynamic in Vertov was completely different, with images ruling over words to the point of ruling them out. Indeed, one of the main criticisms against Vertov was his refusal to work based on a scenario. *Reenactment*, however, represents a different moment, one when documentary was a fully scripted genre that at the same time claimed to offer images that were "alive, and identical with reality." Any spectator doubting this new documentary concoction was threatened by annihilation by the forceful rhetoric, since "the facts registered by this automatic scribe [the film camera] can be doubted by *nobody*."

THE SEARCH FOR CLOSE-UPS

Tasked with reenacting the drama of a bank heist, the film does so while augmenting it with a carefully choreographed *visual* drama. In parallel with the police's quest for the criminals, the camera engages in a quest for visibility. The trajectory of this quest spans the whole film, which starts with long shots of city crowds and ends with extreme close-ups of isolated human faces. The first views of the country under socialist construction are taken from so high up on the scaffoldings as to make people either invisible or at least unidentifiable. When the voice-over invites us "to look at the constructors of this new world," the camera incongruously shows the backs of people in a crowd. While we try to follow the invitation of the camera, the backs hurriedly recede in the distance. This elusiveness of the crowd becomes explicitly suspicious only a couple of minutes later. Once we are informed about the bank heist, the camera roams the city in the shoes of a security investigator who muses: "I wonder if in the midst of these people going about their usual business hide the terrorists?" The constructors of socialism have all been turned into criminal suspects, and the camera has openly adopted the searching look of the investigator. We are told that "hundreds of such investigators have been searching the whole city" for the criminals. Hectic long shots of people crowding stores, sidewalks, restaurants, and dance floors suggest that finding the criminals in the city crowds is no easier than finding the proverbial needle in the haystack.

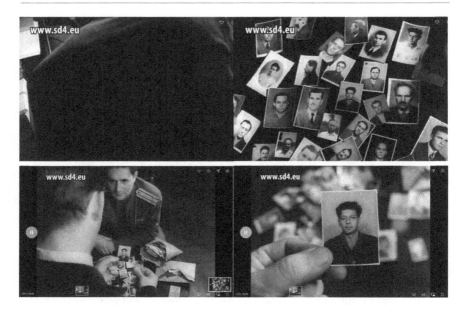

Figure 8.1a–d. Progression of a witness's identification of Igor Sevianu. *Reenactment*, 1960

The end of the film comes full circle to the scaffolding where the camera began shooting. The construction of socialism continues unimpeded now that the criminals have been punished. However, instead of the large panoramas of the city, we are now presented with close-ups of those formerly elusive constructors of socialism. In an all-inclusive gesture, the camera shows individual shots of workers, artists, doctors, writers—all enthusiastically contributing to the construction of socialism. As the criminals have been forever isolated, the crowd's threatening anonymity has been replaced by unambiguous close-ups of its members. Similarly, the position of the audience has changed. If the film started with a searching look toward the audience, wondering if among us, as among those walking the streets of the city, hide any of the criminals, now that the crime is solved, the audience, along with the rest of the community, is cleared of the initial suspicion.

This quest for visibility that ends in the film by replacing long shots with extreme close-ups is closely connected to the police practice of identification. Indeed, Walter Benjamin described identification precisely as the task of isolating the individual criminal out of the anonymous crowd.[22] In the film, the whole quest for visibility is dramatically summarized by its representation in a scene of identification, where the puzzle of the criminals' identities is solved by a witness. As the witness approaches the table full of suspect photographs, his back, the leitmotif of obstructed vision throughout the film, completely covers our view of the table (fig. 8.1a). The next shot shows the confounding mass of photographs—a crowd of faces completely unknown to the audience (fig. 8.1b). The witness, visibly confused, picks one photograph, then hesitates and reaches for Igor Sevianu's mug shot, conveniently placed in the very center of the table (fig 8.1c). The camera signals the correctness of his choice by an extreme close-up of Sevianu's photograph (fig. 8.1d). The climactic moment of identification coincides with not just any close-up but the close-up of an identity picture. Upon close examination, the files reveal—often unwittingly—the dirty investigation practices of wiretapping and torture that were actually used in identifying and prosecuting the suspects.[23] The film, on the contrary, sweeps out any such unpalatable material and unremittingly glamorizes the investigation process. The quest for visibility is itself a cinematic mask that covers up the unsavory forensic practices actually used in the case.

Dramatically summarized in this scene, the camera's quest for visibility goes beyond the limited scope of the police identification. The dichotomy between long shots and close-ups frames the whole film; it also runs deep throughout its embedded reenactment narrative. The reenactment starts with an image of obstructed vision. As the voice-over tells us about a similar attack by an armed gang composed of four men and a woman using a stolen taxicab, we are shown the first reenactment. The image divulges nothing more than the voice-over narration. It shows four men and a woman furtively getting into a taxi. The audience is purposefully denied the chance to see their faces or otherwise identify them. Shot from a high angle and with carefully limited lighting, this sequence could be easily taken from a film noir. This foreign aesthetic of obstructed vision is not cited accidentally. As both the film and the files repeatedly mention, "the criminals have robbed using the methods of American gangsters," learned from where else but American film noirs. The police and the camera share a common goal to bring the criminals to light—a forensic as well as an aesthetic challenge. It means replacing elusive suspects with captured criminals and the noir aesthetic of obstructed vision with a police state aesthetic of unimpeded visibility.

The next reconstructed scene comes immediately after the turning point of the witness's identification of Igor Sevianu. By contrast with the previous mystifying night shot of the five unidentified suspects, this time the camera focuses on the faces of suspects Igor and Monica Sevianu as they emerge from their shaded house into the broad daylight of the police-surveilled street. The other suspects are identified one by one as informers or policemen enter their homes. The penetration of the camera inside the house is an integral part of the film's quest for visibility. In the first images of the film, as the camera surveys a long row of windows mostly covered in heavy blinds, the voice-over warns that we cannot come to know the constructors of socialism from this

Figure 8.2a–d. Review of Sevianu's visual identification narrative, from a masked suspect filmed
in long and medium shot to the exposing close-ups shot at the trial. *Reenactment*, 1960

perspective. Instead, we have to penetrate under the roofs of their homes. The
only homes that we enter, however, are those of the six suspects. As the camera
hungrily takes in the chic apartments of the suspected Ioanid brothers—full
of "decadent" art nouveau, books, and jazz records—the voice-over asserts that
"within the walls of these apartments the evil character of the criminals is
made manifest."

Once all the suspects are identified, the reenactment of the bank heist
begins. The camera follows them as they traverse the city on the way to the
bank; clearly recognizable, they walk in a crowd that is no longer a mass of
suspicious backs but rather a succession of smiling faces, most likely secret
police extras. During the reenactment entire streets were closed to traffic
while one hundred undercover secret police agents were deployed throughout
the area. If the first shots of the city show a crowd of criminal suspects, the
reenactment shows a city populated exclusively by secret police agents. Totalitarian paranoia is replaced by totalitarian fantasy, and suspects reenact their
crimes for the edification of the police and their public. The bank heist reveals
a glaring gap in police surveillance, in Romanian literally "an escape/skip from
vision" (*o scăpare din vedere*). The reenactment of the crime under hundreds of
secret police agents' eyes, backed by the "unfailing eye of the camera," excessively compensates for this deficiency.

Interspersed with actual trial footage, a summary of highlights of this reenactment were once more presented to the film audience as the prosecutor characterizes each suspect in his/her turn at the end of the movie. The summary foregrounds the visual narrative of identification, rehearsing the initial images of obscured identity, through long then medium shots, to close-ups. Indeed, the climax of the forensic drama corresponds to the climax of the visual drama: as the prosecutor delivers his request for the death sentence, the camera closes up on each of the accused (fig. 8.2a–d). The quest for the criminals and the quest for visibility (bl)end triumphantly in the capture of the criminals in inescapable close-up and in a convergence of police and cinematic practices.

REENACTMENT IN THE CONTEXT OF ITS FILM STUDIO

While *Reenactment* does stand out as one of the most infamous productions of the political wing of the Sahia Film Studio, it did not exist in a void. Indeed, *Reenactment* shares a visual language and many defining elements with the studio's other contemporary productions. To start with, the studio's collaboration with the Ministry of Internal Affairs was the catalyst for a number of Sahia films.[24] Ranging in topic from traffic violations to juvenile theft and prostitution, these films cluster around an emerging Sahia genre, the investigation film (*film anchetă*), whereby the cinematic investigation was modeled on a police investigation and often overlapped with it. Filmmakers were present during the police interrogation of juvenile delinquents, their interviews seamlessly picking up where the interrogator or prosecutor left off (*A cui e vina?* [Whose fault is it?], *Să treacă vara* [Let summer pass]). The use of the actual suspects, juvenile or adult, as well as of the police agents, also appears across many of these films (*Whose Fault Is It?, Let Summer Pass*). The police were always a phone call or short visit away for the filmmaker. All-knowing agents were ready to assist with identification of subjects/suspects, their addresses, histories, and access to their archives (*Cazul D* [Case D], 1966).

This collaboration as well as the organizing theme of unmasking through an identification narrative is most saliently at work in one of the most famous Sahia creations, *Case D*, a film that Calotescu admired so much that he publicly spoke against its censorship.[25] This investigation film starts out by attempting to help a seemingly helpless old man, Ilie Dobrotă, find the daughter who abandoned him in an elderly home. The cinematic investigation "uncovers the fictional biography Dobrotă created to hide a very different past from the one he projects," a past of domestic abuse that the filmmaking team brings to light with the help of the police.[26] In a scene that closely echoes *Reenactment's* photo identification scene, the filmmakers are welcomed into the police archives; the camera follows the police agent browsing through files until he stops on the identity photograph of Dobrotă's daughter. It is the job of the camera to zoom onto the identity photograph taken, archived, and retrieved by the police and offer it, thus magnified on the cinema screen, for the audience's scrutiny as a potential mug shot, for at this moment in the film the daughter is the prime suspect.[27]

This preoccupation with the identifying image and the camera's potential to use its cinematic powers to assist in this identification was present throughout these collaborations, sometimes leading to experiments. In *Let Summer Pass*, some suspects were filmed in silhouette (*contrejour*), thus preserving their anonymity, while others were filmed in unforgiving close-ups. The 1963 film titled *Uzina* (The plant) presented a most original and experimental treatment of this leitmotif of the identifying image.[28] The cameraman joined the quality control process that checked on each tool produced by the workers. In a striking sequence preceded by a title image with the name of the inventor of the X-ray, Rontgen, progressive close-ups of the tools reach a graininess that metamorphosizes into black and white profile sketches of the workers, then profile photographs, then their photo negatives (fig. 8.3a–d). The voice-over explains the camera's ambition to identify from each product the imprinted image and "life story" of its maker. The eulogizing voice-over is overshadowed, however, by the gravity of the profile portraits and by the context—this is a quality control investigation that attempts to identify defects in the tools and so in workmanship, and thus the workers themselves.

The last key element that *Reenactment* shares with other contemporary Sahia productions is its didactic tone and overall commitment to visual pedagogy. The authoritative voice-over that directly interpolates the audience of the film is a standard of this time, and the camera often supports this interpellation with abundant images of everyday people whom it frames as the audience of the film.[29] Another peculiarly telling 1960 Sahia production is the promotion film of the Cinema Village Festival.[30] This festival brought contemporary movies, from documentaries about Soviet space achievements to landmarks such as *Letiat zhuravli* (The cranes are flying, 1957) to villages across the country. The promotional film imaginatively casts a talkative farmer introducing the idea of cinema to his villagers and reassuring them that the films will be followed by folk dances and live explanation sessions. Often screened before a foreign feature, Sahia documentaries took seriously their role of connecting with local audiences, carefully molding their viewing position before the main feature even began.

Children were an important tool in this visual pedagogy, whose didactic tone is often set in addressing a partial audience of children. In another 1960 production, *Cei mici despre lumea mare* (Little ones about the big world),

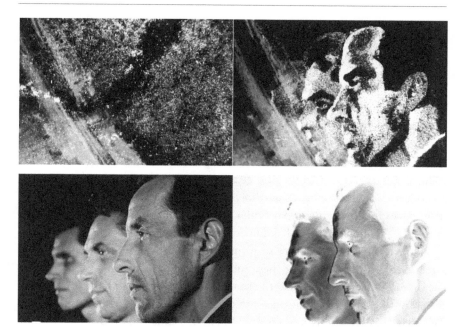

Figure 8.3a–d. The camera makes magically visible the profile of the workers in an extreme close-up of the tool they created. *The Plant*, 1963

the film presents a father and daughter viewing the work of a young painter: "peasants correctly inscribed in the symbolic economy of the new regime— indentured peasants and kulaks," as well as an unemployed Italian.[31] The bewildered father points out that the painter had never seen a kulak or an unemployed person, to which his daughter replies that "while he did not see any, he imagined, because he has imagination!" Cinema played a key role in providing the images shaping that imagination. The daughter is here a model viewer, both because she gets the new art and reality and because she models this politically correct viewing for her father. Indeed, not only are children omnipresent among the imagined audience of these movies, the adults too are asked to model themselves on the children, ready to learn new ways of viewing and imagining that go beyond what can be seen in their immediate reality.[32]

POST-STALINIST SECRET POLICE AND CINEMATIC COLLABORATIONS ACROSS THE EASTERN BLOC

Post-Stalinist collaborations between documentary film studios and the secret police were not a local Romanian phenomenon. While bank heist trials were not the order of the day in the Soviet Bloc around 1959, this period had its share of show trials orchestrated by the secret police, often related to Khrushchev's antireligious campaign (1958–1964). A significant number of these trials triggered collaborations between documentary film studios and the secret police. While the regular militia appears at times in these films, at a closer look its actions prove to be either subservient or a rather transparent front for the actions of the secret police.[33] Aiming to sketch *Reenactment*'s cinematic context in the Soviet Bloc, as I researched this section I found a significant body of films sharing striking commonalities with *Reenactment*, to the point of constituting a largely forgotten documentary film genre. While a full review of such collaborations goes beyond the scope of this chapter, the following paragraphs form a first attempt to identify some of the common characteristics of this corpus of films. These commonalities reach beyond the differences in the profile of particular criminals or crimes, clustering instead around a common visual code and pedagogy.

Indeed, the similarities are so pronounced that I have often had to make a real effort to keep some of these movies separate in my mind. Sometimes, the directors seem to have had the same problem, as particular shots recur in different films. For example, one of the most infamous of these trials, the 1960 Trial of the Pentecostals, was covered in two documentary movies and a slide film (*diafil'm*), all of which use some of the same images.[34] Whether the events, the filming, and the trials took place in Brest or Minsk (Belarus), Saratov, or in the vicinity of Moscow (Russia), all these films share the same overall narrative told through a very particular combination of documentary film genres.[35]

The antireligious films each start with a city symphony-like presentation of a bright and dynamic site of socialist construction, which often includes shots of citizens of all stripes at work and leisure. Shots of happy children are a must. The camera work is dynamic: aerial shots from cranes, airplanes, high buildings and moving shots from cars and trains alternate with street scenes and portraits of the constructors of socialism. This short eulogy of socialism is interrupted as the voice-over reminds the viewers that even today there are still enemies (*vragi*) hiding in their midst. The city symphony makes room for reenactment and hidden camera sequences, often involving religious rituals such as baptism, washing of the feet, sermons, and communal prayer. The boundary between reenactment and the hidden camera is blurred, as reenactment sequences are often passed off as hidden camera sequences involving the suspects themselves, the victims, or stand-ins for the victims (photographs or actors), law enforcers and other community members. The position and movements of the camera, the lighting, and the attitudes of those filmed often give away the illusion of a hidden camera through well-composed shots, including close-ups of which suspects could not have been unaware. At times, suspects attempt to hide their faces from the camera, and this willed obstruction of the camera's power is included among other shots of obstructed vision (such as back shots and poorly lit long shots) and is contrasted with the power of the camera to capture close-ups (fig. 8.4a–c).[36] The camera, following the footsteps of the police and prosecutors, gradually identifies and indicts the suspects. There is usually then highly edited footage of the trial (and sometimes popular mock trials such as workers' collective meetings). The trials are often, just like in *Reenactment*, a chance to recap the narrative presented so far, including a passage from the initial occluded shots of the suspects through the reenactments to close-ups taken during their depositions or the reading of their sentences. Shots of the audience modeling the film audience's reactions to the case at hand are plentiful. They often include close-ups of a limited range of facial expressions—tense attention, indignation, and laughter. The latter is a particular telltale identification sign of a politically correct face (enemies don't laugh in these films). The trial footage sometimes ends the film, but there is often a short return to the city symphony shots of a socialist life temporarily freed of its enemies.

Alongside the particular combination of documentary film genres discussed above, the key element that these films share with *Reenactment* is the narrative of unmasking and visual identification, with its arc leading from occluded vision (crowds and back shots, masks) to full exposure (close-ups of the face coded to work as cinematic versions of the photographic mug shot). In *This Concerns Us All*, one of the suspects is followed into the house of prayer at dusk in a poorly lit shot despite his attempt to hide his face and identity from the camera (fig. 8.5a) He keeps up his attempt: he gives his testimony with the back to the camera, then tries to put his coat over his head to maintain his anonymity (fig 8.5b–c). This series of shots of obscured vision are followed by his capture both through arrest and through the image. He is now presented in a frontal medium shot, and as the voice-over talks about his condemnation, the cover of his file frames his face on both sides (fig. 8.5d–e).

In a film based on another Pentecostal trial, *Pust' torzhestvuet zhizn'—sud nad sektantami v Saratove* (Let life triumph—trial of the sect members in Saratov, 1961), after standard shots of the new Saratov and its happily strolling citizens, the voice-over reminds us that there are still enemies even in a village close to Saratov. The music and the following shots suddenly turn ominous and highly disorienting. Mysterious shot after shot presents challenges to vision and interpretation. We approach a village house at dusk. The camera gets closer and closer to the windows, until all we can see are branches blocking our view (fig. 8.6a). Traveling from pane to pane, the camera finally enters the room. The next shot, the first interior shot, shows women's bare feet hanging a little distance from the floor (fig. 8.6b). At first it appears that the women are perhaps dead and hanging from the ceiling. A slow tilt up

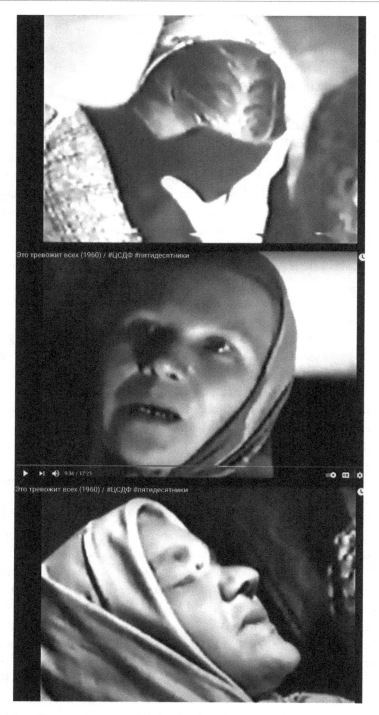

Figure 8.4a–c. Woman attempting to hide her face from the camera, followed by the camera's capture of frontal/profile close-ups. *This Concerns Us All*, 1960

Figure 8.5a–e. Suspect who repeatedly attempts to hide from the camera is finally shown in frontal close-up framed by his police files. *This Concerns Us All*, 1960

shows them on a bench, praying. What follows are close-ups of their praying hands, then intense close-ups of different members of the congregation,
largely edited in pairs of front-facing and profile shots (fig. 8.6c–f). After a
long series of these close-ups, a dark night shot shows the members of the congregation escorted out of their clandestine house of prayer. The following shot
sees them in the bright daylight of the courtroom—they have been brought
to judgment, and to light. (The title of another antireligious film from 1961,

Figure 8.6a–f. Mostly illegible shots of obscured vision, such as a branch blocking a window, are gradually replaced by identifying images largely edited in pairs of front-facing and profile shots. *Let Life Triumph*, 1961

Ot t'my k svetu [From darkness to light], underscores the overall narrative of visibility organizing these films.) Just like in *Reenactment*, in *Let Life Triumph* the trial footage is carefully edited and juxtaposed with the reenactment/ hidden camera sequences, in a way that recaps and foregrounds the overall identification narrative advancing from occluded vision to unmasking and unimpeded visibility.

As we have briefly seen in the account of these antireligious films, not even the peculiar use of reenactment is an aberration. Rather, it is part of a larger secret police practice shared across the Soviet Bloc. Reenactment photographs were more widespread because of the relative accessibility of the medium, but the secret police in the region made other reenactment films, some of which were preserved and declassified. For instance, Tatiana Vagramenko has discovered and analyzed a Ukrainian file from the same year, 1959, which contains a reenactment film (*Konets pauka/Kinets' pavuka* [The end of Spider]) and production stills (*fotos"emki*).[37] While the film scenes and production stills pass themselves off as hidden camera work, Vagramenko convincingly argues that based on their lighting, camera position, and quality of the photographs, they are in fact reenactment images. This passing of reenactment images for hidden camera images is a common secret police strategy in the region. Commenting on a 1955 reenactment photograph labeled as hidden camera evidence in a Romanian file on Jehovah's Witnesses, Agnes Hesz writes: "The photos follow the common standards of crime scene photography of Eastern European secret services. These photos were often 're-enactments,' a common method to illustrate the crime and incriminate its perpetrator."[38] Vagramenko also notes the choreographed overlaps and collusion among the file, the film, and the trial: the file uses stills from the film as evidence; the film, just like *Reenactment*, shows the file itself; and the trial's depositions for witnesses and defendants are culled from mixed-up interrogation records and written by the police agents.[39] Based on her research in Romanian secret police files on the Calendarist community, Anca Șincan also notes, "It was common practice for the secret police to bring suspects back to the (crime) scene in order to produce staged photographs as incriminating evidence."[40]

VIEWING *REENACTMENT* THEN AND NOW

This brief overview of kindred cinematic projects within Sahia and across the region around the turn of the 1960s shows that *Reenactment* was part of a larger visual and political project. Rather than an outlier, *Reenactment* was rather the more elaborate and ambitious *ars cinematica* of a significant number of films poised at the intersection of investigation, reenactment, and trial movie, all of which were structured around a strikingly similar visual identification plot and presented to an infantilized public through a common visual pedagogy. And yet, unlike many of these kindred projects, *Reenactment* was never released for public viewing. After several showings in front of a handpicked audience of secret police agents, journalists, and party members, the film was shelved and did not resurface until after the 1989 revolution, when Monica Sevianu's granddaughter, the filmmaker Irene Lusztig, battled the reluctant Romanian Film Archives to unearth it. There is no explanation for this perplexing decision to bury the film in the twenty-seven volumes of files connected to the case, or anywhere else in the Securitate archives I have searched. Instead, in my most serendipitous archival find, I found a possible reason for this decision in the Open Society Archives in Hungary. A short secret report prepared by an unnamed source for Radio Free Europe suggests that the reason was the carefully monitored audience reaction.[41] Knowing smiles were registered at the exit doors after the movie, and the emaciation of the prisoners/film protagonists was repeatedly noted.[42] Even this handpicked audience misbehaved, miswatched, and misinterpreted. The secret police did not take any chances with the general audience. Instead they promptly censored themselves. The record of the wry smiles of the handpicked audience, buried in a forgotten archive file, suggests that the encounter of words, images, minds, and bodies, even if emaciated or saddled to a cinema seat, can collude to seal off what actually happened but can also exceed that carefully choreographed suture. That encounter can put a dent here or there, or even crack the suture open for the length of a smile, or it can make it close onto itself, like the rolls of *Reenactment*, sulkily coiled in the archive can in which they had been shelved for half a century.

But I am afraid I cannot quite end on this happy ending of audience resistance. At first sight it may seem that those smiles signify the audience's transformation from "ignoramuses invited to see people suffering," as Jacques Rancière describes the Platonic view of the spectator, into "emancipated" spectators, spectators who resist the places assigned to them and instead question the old dichotomy between acting and passive viewing by engaging in viewing as an action.[43] Such an emancipated spectator "observes, selects, compares, and interprets. She links what she sees to a host of other things that she has seen on other stages, in other places. She participates in the performance by refashioning it in her own way—by drawing back, for example. . . . They are thus both distant spectators and active interpreters of the spectacle offered to them."[44] While it is true that the smiles of *Reenactment*'s audience suggest a certain distance from the spectacle and a refusal of the place assigned to the spectator from the very opening scene of the movie, and while those smiles may have been responsible for the film's censorship, I do not think that they qualify as a sign of emancipated spectatorship. Nor do I think we should reenact them. The smiles did take note of the accused in ways that the secret police did not mean the audience to take note, but the audience reaction to the emaciation of the protagonists is, to say the least, strange. The Radio Free Europe source explains that "the audience left the cinema looking at each other smilingly, because they knew the reality of the facts, which were different from those exposed in the film."[45] While looking at each other smilingly may show a certain measure of resistance to the official narrative and solidarity among the audience, the smiles are strange in response to the starved bodies of the prisoners—and to the death sentences that end the movie. The audience "looked smilingly at each other" but also *looked through* the emaciated, soon to be killed bodies of the prisoners. The Romanian word for "emaciated" used in the report is *very slăbiți* (very thin/weak); a more fitting synonym would have been *strãvezii*, which literally means "see-through." While looking *at* and even looking *with* other members of the audience, the smiling audience also show a worrisome appropriation of the Stalinist way of looking—*bditel'nost'*, looking *through* the prisoners. As such, they also prove the extent to which the visual pedagogy lessons of the state shaped even the look of dissent.

They also continue to haunt contemporary cinema. In the beginning of the chapter, I mention three post-1989 films—*Reconstruction*, *The Great Communist Bank Robbery*, and *Closer to the Moon*. While these three films cite the bank heist case and the original 1960 film directly, the cinematic afterlife of the 1960 *Reenactment* goes far beyond these direct quotations. Indeed, the most famous Romanian art film of all times, Lucian Pintilie's *Reenactment* (Reconstituirea, 1968), released eight years after Calotescu's *Reenactment*, in addition to sharing the earlier film's title, depicts another police reenactment. If the death of the protagonists is left off-screen by Calotescu, Pintilie brings it, unforgettably, onscreen. In his movie, the presence of a cameramen and his desire to impress his police boss with the perfect shot ends up killing the boy coerced into reenacting a fight with a friend. Pintilie's *Reenactment* was an unforgettable critique of the complicity between cinema and policing, a complicity epitomized by the genre of the filmed police reenactment. In 2012, when I asked Pintilie about Calotescu's movie, he confirmed having seen it before working on his *Reenactment*.[46] His angry invectives toward the movie confirmed not just that he still remembered it well but that he retained a powerful affect toward it.[47] Pintilie's *Reenactment* has been hailed as the real origin of the Romanian New Wave.[48] As it often happens with origins, a little digging uncovers uncomfortable, often repressed precedents. Looming large behind Pintilie's *Reenactment* is the secret police reenactment. A repressed primal scene of complicity between cinema and policing, its legacy haunts more recent landmarks of Romanian film such as *Polițist, adjectiv* (Police, adjective, 2009) and *Visul lui Alambert* (Adalbert's dream, 2011), just as it haunted Pintilie's masterpiece.

THE CREATION OF THE CINEMATIC MUG SHOT

This chapter argues that at the core of the visual pedagogy of these post-Stalinist secret police films is a quest for identification that ends in the close-up of the suspect's initially obscured face. This fixation on the close-up is by no means accidental. In her comprehensive review and reevaluation of the most influential cinematic theories on the close-up, Mary Anne Doane starts by reminding us of the "pivotal role of the close-up in film history and theory."[49] To begin with "the close-up . . . seems to mark the moment of the very emergence of film as a discourse, as an art"; the close-up was "the guarantee of the cinema's status as a universal language, one of, if not *the* most recognizable units of cinematic discourse." She partly explains this fascination through Walter Benjamin's theory that the close-up was "one of the significant entrance points to the optical unconscious, making visible what in daily life went unseen."[50] This is particularly true for the most famous type of close-up, the close-up of the face:

> Almost all theories of the face come to terms in some way with this opposition between surface and depth, exteriority and interiority. There is always something *beyond*. . . . It is barely possible to see a close-up of a face without asking: what is he/she thinking, feeling, suffering? What is happening beyond what I can see? Or, in Balázs's terms, the close-up of the face allows us to understand that "we can see that there is something there that we cannot see" (76). Hence are born all the metaphors of textuality, of the face as book, of reading and legibility. The face is the intensification of a locus of signification.[51]

This passage explains the fascination in these secret police films with the face, which becomes—in the paranoid visual logic of the time—the last mask, the degree zero of the mask, both tempting and eluding a deciphering impulse working in overdrive. However, as Balázs observes, the close-up of the face can also invite empathy, and equally dangerous in the context of a secret police film, it can invite curiosity about the other, as in the question: "What is he thinking, feeling, suffering?"

How could these films ward off the typical audience reactions to a close-up of a face—empathy and curiosity, together with the other host of emotions that the close-up has elicited both in its audience and in its theorists, and instead control its interpretation? A pathway had been already charted by Eisenstein. According to Doane, his theory of the close-up marks a singular departure from previous theories and uses of the close-up. Eisenstein defined his understanding of the close-up in opposition to what he called the American approach to the close-up. "Eisenstein argued for the disengagement of the close-up from reality, criticizing Griffith for his inability to abstract, to get beyond the 'narrowly representational' (Film 243). The function of the close-up in Soviet cinema was 'not so much to *show* or to *present* as to *signify*, to *give meaning*, to *designate*' (238). . . . Tearing the object from the real, the close-up introduced 'absolute changes in the dimensions of bodies and objects on the screen' (Eisenstein, *Au-delà* 229)."[52] The trajectory of the visual identification performed by these secret police movies can be charted as a move away from a close-up that shows or presents a face in a way that could raise questions about its feelings, thoughts, or suffering toward a mug shot, or a face that is designated as a criminal face.

This designation of the cinematic close-up as a cinematic mug shot may have been the most ambitious aim of the collaboration between cinema and the post-Stalinist secret police. These films employ a rich variety of designation strategies, from the most obvious, the incriminating voice-over that identifies the suspects by their names and teaches us that they do not deserve to be called human beings, to editing that baldly juxtaposes the face and the profile in a cinematic mug shot and frames the close-up as the culmination of a visual identification narrative that takes over the whole film. In the process, post-Stalinist collaborations between cinema and policing prove to have fully assimilated the defining visual knowhow that led to the creation of the mug shot. In his groundbreaking work on the emergence of the mug shot in the nineteenth century through the intersection of visual technologies and policing, Christian Pheline sees photography as one key step in the mediation that transforms the messy, moving, and moved image of the body in a crowd into a stilled mug shot of the face.[53] This first step opened the path for further reductions of the body to numbers and words, through standardized measurements and descriptions that further cut it from its original reality and inserted it into the police archive. The mug shot's function was to reduce the three-dimensional body to two dimensions and separate the face from the body. It forcefully stilled the moving body long enough for the first cameras to capture an "unmoved," well-focused photograph. The secret police films under consideration here have all assimilated this lesson: they excel at "cutting, fragmenting," and separating the face from the vulnerable body, introducing it into new chains of signification that can change anyone (a random passerby, a relative, a priest) into a criminal suspect. Yet to the extent that the mug shot attempted to freeze the moving body and the chain of empathy and signification, these films' project of creating a *cinematic mug shot* was challenged by the essence of their very medium, film, which is defined by movement and the succession of moving images. To meet this challenge, these films mustered a rich repertoire of cinematic techniques into a visual identification narrative. The final close-up image becomes a cinematic mug shot as a result of this identification narrative and its accompanying visual pedagogy. It takes all their cinematic groundwork to turn the close-up into a mug shot. The mug shot does not stand on its own, and it can always threaten to turn back into an ambiguous, or even celebratory, image when lifted out of that narrative, as various recuperations of these police images for personal, historical, or artistic projects have shown.

If the viewer was lured into the film with the hope of one day being able to assimilate the lesson to the point of being able to solve the ultimate visual riddle of the face on their own, the more films they watched and the more adept they became in this visual pedagogy, the more they were disabused of such foolish hopes. The ultimate lesson of this visual pedagogy turned out to be that reality is treacherous and the spectator's vision and judgment are fallible, unlike the state's. Film after film proved that the state was always a few good steps ahead in identifying criminals, thanks to its police officers and their mastery over both treacherous visual reality and edifying visual technologies, cinema included.

NOTES

I am grateful to Irene Lusztig, Monica Sevianu's granddaughter and the director of *Reconstruction*, for sharing her copy of the film and file excerpts with me long before they were declassified. I am grateful to CNSAS for granting me full access to the files and photo albums, and to the Arhiva Naționala de Filme, Jilava, for allowing me to view the original version of *Reenactment* in their projection room. I am also grateful to Michael David-Fox, Andrew Jenks, Carolyn Pouncy, and the editorial board for their support during the review and revision process and to the two anonymous *Kritika* reviewers for their singularly thought-provoking, thorough, and engaged readings. Finally, I am grateful to my research assistants, Leila al Dzheref and Rebekah Smith, for precious help during the revision of this article.

1. *Digital Archive of the Hidden Galleries Project*, http://hiddengalleries.eu/digitalarchive; James Kapaló and Tatiana Vagramenko, eds., *Hidden Galleries: Material Religion in the Secret Police Archives in Central and Eastern Europe* (Zurich: Lit, 2020); Andrea Gullotta, *Beauty in Hell: Culture in the Gulag* (Glasgow: The Hunterian, 2017); Tatiana Vagramenko, "KGB 'Evangelism': Agents and Jehovah's Witnesses in Soviet Ukraine," *Kritika: Explorations in Russian and Eurasian History* 22, no. 4 (2021): 757–86; Aglaya Glebova, "A Visual History of the Gulag: Nine Theses," in *The Soviet Gulag: Evidence, Interpretation, and Comparison*, ed. Michael David-Fox (Pittsburgh: University of Pittsburgh Press, 2016), 162–69; Olga Shevchenko and Oksana Sarkisova, "The Album as Performance: Notes on the Limits of the Visible," in *Russian Performances: Word, Object, Action*, ed. Julie Cassiday, Julie A. Buckler, and Boris Wolfson (Madison: University of Wisconsin Press, 2018), 42–53.

2. Cristina Vatulescu, *Police Aesthetics: Literature, Film, and the Secret Police in Soviet Times* (Stanford, CA: Stanford University Press, 2010).

3. Allan Sekula, "The Body and the Archive," *October* 39, no. 4 (1986): 3–64; Martin Jay, *Downcast Eyes: The Denigration of Vision in Twentieth-Century French Thought* (Berkeley: University of California Press, 1993); Malcolm Turvey, *Doubting Vision: Film and the Revelationist Tradition* (Oxford: Oxford University Press, 2008); Michael Leja, *Looking Askance: Skepticism and American Art from Eakins to Duchamp* (Berkeley: University of California Press, 2004).

4. Sheila Fitzpatrick, *Tear off the Masks! Identity and Imposture in Twentieth-Century Russia* (Princeton, NJ: Princeton University Press, 2005).

5. Dennis Deletant, *Ceaușescu and the Securitate: Coercion and Dissent in Romania, 1965–1989* (London: Hurst and Co., 1995); Deletant, *Communist Terror in Romania: Gheorghiu-Dej and the Police State, 1948–1965* (London: Hurst and Co., 1999).

6. *Reconstituirea*, directed by Virgil Calotescu and Pantelie Tuțuleasa (Bucharest: Arhiva Natională de Filme Jilava, Ministerul de Interne, Studioul Documentar Sahia, 1959).

7. Anonymous, Item no. 2869/61, "Filmarea furtului de la banca RPR/Movie of a Bank Robbery," 1960,

box 103, file 803, HU OSA 300-60-1, Radio Free Europe/Radio Liberty Research Institute: Information Resources Department: East European Archives: Romanian Unit, Budapest, 3.

8. "Filmarea furtului de la banca RPR."

9. P 181 (40038) (1959), Fond Penal, Arhiva Consiliului Național pentru Studierea Arhivelor Securității (ACNSAS), vols. 1–27. While this article on identification and visual pedagogy focuses on a close reading of the film itself, I dedicate a long chapter of my forthcoming second book, *Reading the Archival Revolution: Declassified Stories and Their Challenges*, to the bank heist case and its accompanying files, paying attention to its contexts, multimedia character, and afterlives.

10. Ministerul Afacerilor Interne, "Plan de măsuri I" (Plan of action 1) (1959), P 181 (40038), vol. 18, Fond Documentar, ACNSAS, Bucharest, 9–15.

11. "Plan de măsuri privind filmările" (Plan of action regarding the filming), undated, P 181 (40038), vol. 18, Fond Penal, ACNSAS, Bucharest, 127–30.

12. "Titlurile filmului" (The titles of the film), 1960, P 181 (40038), vol. XVIII, Fond Penal, ACNSAS, Bucharest, 81–86.

13. This last seal of approval concerned the script in its entirety, including its credits, the particular selection and order of archival and reconstructed material. This untitled script, written on Ministry of Internal Affairs letterhead, is dated 5 March 1960, weeks after the four defendants were executed ("Titles of the Film," 82).

14. "Deceniul cinci in studioul Sahia," Sahia Vintage, https://sahiavintage.ro/timeline/.

15. "Deceniul cinci in studioul Sahia."

16. "Comandă politică," https://sahiavintage.ro/keywords/.

17. *Scoicile n-au vorbit niciodată* (Shells never spoke), directed by Virgil Calotescu (1962). His other work in underwater filming, *Subteranul* (The subterranean, 1967), also made the Fifth Moscow International Film Festival.

18. Virgil Calotescu and Redacția "Cinema," "Ce părere ai, Virgil Calotescu? Față în față," *Cinema* (August 1968), http://aarc.ro/en/articol/fata-in-fata-ce-parere-ai-virgil-calotescu.

19. *Man with a Movie Camera*, directed by Dziga Vertov (Image Entertainment, 2002), DVD.

20. Lev Manovich, *The Language of New Media* (Cambridge, MA: MIT Press, 2001), xiv–xxvi.

21. Dziga Vertov, *Kino-Eye: The Writings of Dziga Vertov*, ed. Annette Michelson, trans. Kevin O'Brien (Berkeley: University of California Press, 1984); "Kino-Eye," in *Lines of Resistance: Dziga Vertov and the Twenties*, ed. Yuri Tsivian (Gemona: Le Giornate del cinema muto, 2004); "The Artistic Drama and Kino-Eye," in *Lines of Resistance*.

22. Walter Benjamin, *Charles Baudelaire: A Lyric Poet in the Era of High Capitalism* (London: Verso, 1983), 43.

23. The Sevianus' summer residence was wiretapped, and the file contains long transcripts of private conversations. As I show at length in my book in progress, Monica Sevianu's cell-mate informer inadvertently provided proof of the torture Sevianu underwent.

24. *Cum circulăm?* (How do we travel?), directed by Slavomir Popovici (Bucharest: Sahia, 1963); *A cui e vina?*, directed by Florica Holban (Bucharest: Sahia, 1965); *Cazul D*, directed by Alexandru Boiangiu (Bucharest: Sahia, 1966); *Martorii* (Witnesses), directed by Adrian Sârbu (Bucharest: Sahia, 1983); *Să treacă vara*, directed by Holban (Bucharest: Sahia, 1972).

25. Calotescu and "Cinema," "Ce părere ai."

26. "Filmele după an," Sahia Vintage, https://sahiavintage.ro/timeline/.

27. Interestingly, the camera's subsequent search will find the actual daughter, whose frozen identity photograph thaws under our eyes into moving pictures whereby she delivers a moving testimony. While many of the films at the time work toward the creation of a cinematic mug shot, the preoccupation with the power of the mug shot more rarely also leads to its critique when it comes to the wrongly accused. A most intriguing contemporary example is Binka Zhelyazkova's *A byahme mladi* (We Were Young, Bulgaria, 1961). The film starts with the archived mug shots of young Communists killed in the Resistance and animates them and their stories through a feature film. In *Case D*,

while the daughter's cinematic representation turns from an identity photo bordering on mug shot into a complex moving filmic portrait, the father's representation travels in the opposite direction, culminating into an unmasking of the abuser.

28. *Uzina*, directed by Slavomir Popovici (Bucharest: Sahia, 1963).

29. "The partisan, abrupt-didactic voice-over that recalls Reenactment's voice-over" is already in place in the Sahia documentary *Evenimentele din Ungaria* (The events in Hungary, 1957); "Filmele după an."

30. *Village Film Festival* (Festival de film la sate) (Bucharest: Sahia, 1960).

31. *Cei mici despre lumea mare*, directed by Gabriel Barta (Bucharest: Sahia, 1960); "Filmele după an."

32. Besides this infantilization of the audience, the presence of children is also used as a sentimental hook: whether portrayed as hapless victims or as juvenile delinquents, children are overrepresented in these films to show the vulnerability of the new society to lingering criminality. See *Whose Fault Is It?* and *Să zâmbească toți copiii* (Let all children smile), directed by Marta Meszaros (Bucharest: Sahia, 1957).

33. In his account of the Trial of the Pentecostals, the first main investigator in the trail, Fridriks Nezhanskii, testifies that Bishop Ivan Fedotov's file was composed "not by the militia or prosecutor's office but by the KGB" (Elena Minushkina, "Opium dlia naroda: Kak SSSR borolsia s piatidesiatnikami," *Diletant* [2019], https://diletant.media/articles/45275728/). Fedotov's lawyer, Semen Aria, also testifies to the involvement of the KGB in the trial in *Sud nad veruiushchimi i oproverzhenie dokumental'nogo fil'ma "Eto trevozhit vsekh"* (The trial of the believers and the refutation of the documentary film *This Concerns Us All* [2011]). In a rare account of the shooting of his antireligious film *The End of Spider*, the director Rafail Nakhmanovich documents this use of the local militiamen by the two plain clothes secret police agents de facto overseeing the arrests and the filming. See Rafail Nakhmanovich, *Vozvrashchenie v sistemu koordinat, ili, Martirolog meteka* (Kiev: Feniks, 2013), 47.

34. *Eto trevozhit vsekh* (This concerns us all), directed by V. Musatova (Moscow: Tsentral'naia ordena Krasnogo Znameni studiia dokumental'nykh fil'mov, 1960); V. Troshkin, *Pered litsom suda* (Before the court), directed by V. Troshkin (Moscow: Tsentral'naia ordena Krasnogo Znameni studiia dokumental'nykh fil'mov, 1960); *Izuvery* (The fanatics), directed by Musatova, L. Likhodeev, and E. Baisburg (Moscow: Diafil'm, 1961).

35. The two films and the slide film about the 1960 Trial of the Pentecostals were filmed on location in Brest, Belorussia, where the believers were based. The trial started there but was soon moved to Drezna, near Moscow, where the trial scenes were filmed. Pentecostals had already been victims of another trial in Minsk, Belorussia, a case taken up by the documentary film *Pravda o sektantakhpiatidesiatnikakh* (The truth about Pentecostal sectants), directed by V. Pushevich and V. Tsesliuk (Minsk: Belorus'fil'm, 1959). Below I also explore *Pust' torzhestvuet zhizn'—sud nad sektantami v Saratove*, directed by Ia. Volovik, N. Surovtsev, and D. Ibragimov, *Povolzh'e*, no. 26 (Saratov, 1961). A recent compilation of films from the antireligious campaign brings together many striking images of other largely forgotten movies, such as *From Darkness to Light* or *Stolen Childhood*. These two present strikingly similar narratives and include some highly disturbing shots of children giving testimony in the trials. See *O lzhi religii i mrakobesii* (About the lies of religion and obscurantism) (RetroTV, 2019).

36. For fascinating research, including stunning visuals, into the resistance to mug shots, see Tatiana Vagramenko and Gabriela Nicolescu, "The Hand at Work or How the KGB File Leaks in the Exhibition," *Martor* 26 (Fall 2021): 24–46.

37. Tatiana Vagramenko, "Filming the Ioannites," in *Hidden Galleries*, 51.

38. Ágnes Hesz, "Crime Scene Photographs from a File on Jehovah's Witnesses in Romania," in *Digital Archives of the Hidden Galleries Project* (2019).

39. Vagramenko, "Filming the Ioannites."

40. Anca Șincan, "Incriminating Photographs on Old Calendarist Underground Community Bucharest," in *Digital Archives of the Hidden Galleries Project* (2018).

41. "Filmarea furtului de la banca RPR."

42. "Filmarea furtului de la banca RPR," 3, 2.

43. Jacques Rancière, *The Emancipated Spectator* (London: Verso, 2011), 3.

44. Rancière, *Emancipated Spectator*, 13.

45. "Filmarea furtului de la banca RPR," 3.

46. Lucian Pintilie, e-mail communication with the author, 30 March 2012. Lucian Pintilie's answer was typed on email by his assistant Andreas Belgun, to whom I am grateful.

47. Lucian Pintilie, personal e-mail communication with the author, 29 March 2012. Interestingly, the Romanian film critic Tudor Caranfil notes that Calotescu's "*The Bus* also anticipates, in a minor register, the bus scene in *The Oak*, shot fifteen years later by Lucian Pintilie." See "The Bus (Acți-unea Autobuzul)," Cinemagia, https://m.cinemagia.ro/filme/actiunea-autobuzul-392/sinopsis/.

48. Mihai Chirilov, "Închid ochii şi văd—interviu cu Lucian Pintilie," *Dilema veche*, 8–14 March 2012.

49. Mary Ann Doane, "The Close-Up: Scale and Detail in the Cinema," *differences* 14, no. 3 (2003): 91.

50. Doane, "Close-Up," 91.

51. Doane, "Close-Up," 96.

52. Doane, "Close-Up," 92.

53. Christian Phéline, "L'image accusatrice," *Les cahiers de la photographie*, no. 17 (1985): 134.

The Soviets Abroad

The NKVD, Intelligence, and State Building
in East-Central Europe after World War II

Molly Pucci

By the time Nikolai Kovalchuk was removed from service in 1954, he had worked in the Soviet secret police for over twenty years. He had served not only in Soviet Russia and Ukraine but also in the Baltic states soon after they were annexed to the Soviet Union and the NKVD adviser apparatus in Poland and Germany after World War II. Born in Kiev in 1902, Kovalchuk had completed only two years of high school before joining a local militia. He served in the Red Army between November 1926 and April 1932. While in the Red Army, he joined the Communist Party of the Soviet Union in November 1927 at the age of twenty-five, after the defeat of Lev Trotsky had cemented Iosif Stalin as sole dictator of the Soviet Union. He was one of the hundreds of thousands of new, young recruits who entered the party between 1924 and 1928, when it expanded from 472,000 to 1,304,471 members.[1] He was recruited to the NKVD from the Red Army in April 1932; there, from 1936, he was promoted rapidly in the ranks during the campaigns of mass violence known as the Great Terror. During World War II, he served in military intelligence on the Fourth Ukrainian Front and attained the rank of lieutenant general.

From 1945, he was moved from country to country to oversee security operations in territories newly annexed to, or increasingly under the influence of, the Soviet Union. He served as a chief NKVD adviser in Soviet-occupied Germany (August 1946–August 1949) and Poland (June 1953–July 1953) and was stationed in Ukraine (August 1949–September 1952) and Latvia (February 1953–May 1953) before ending his career in the Russian city of Iaroslavl' (September 1953–May 1954).[2]

As a study of the careers of NKVD security officers serving as advisers in Europe from 1945 shows, Kovalchuk's career path was not unusual. He was part of a generation of Soviet security officers trained and promoted in the continuum of war and revolution that shook the Soviet Union to its core between the Russian Civil War and World War II. Most NKVD advisers serving in East-Central Europe after World War II were, similar to Kovalchuk, of high rank (the majority held the title of colonel or general) and had been promoted during the years of the Great Terror and World War II because of their willingness to prove their dedication to Stalin by pushing forward domestic terror, arrests, and violence. As Kovalchuk's career shows, two eras commonly separated in scholarship, the Great Terror and World War II, in fact represented a continuous period for those living through them.

The shadow of the Great Terror was long, not only in the Soviet Union but on a global scale and into the 1950s and beyond. The Soviet security advisers who arrived in East-Central Europe to help build secret police forces in the new communist states of East Germany, Czechoslovakia, Poland, Romania, Bulgaria, Hungary, and Albania brought with them a conspiratorial worldview, a certain operational and political language, strongly held convictions about social and political enemies, and assumptions about policing methods, law, and evidence first honed in domestic terror in the Soviet Union. They came to postwar Europe with the conviction, forged in the Terror and the victory in World War II, that their version of communism was the best fit for all countries. They deeply mistrusted outsiders—particularly Germans, Poles, and Jews, groups that they had targeted as enemies of the Soviet state during the Terror. They were certain that a true revolution required violence against class enemies and the recruitment of workers into the highest state and party positions, since that was the revolution they had carried out at home.[3] Yet the same qualities and practices Soviet security officers and advisers had internalized in war and terror in many ways undermined Soviet influence, flexibility, and understanding of Communists abroad.

The lives of the men who brought the "Soviet model" to Eastern Europe and the Baltic states shed light on the *version* of communism—forged in war, revolution, and terror—that the Soviet Union exported globally after World War

II. As Michael David-Fox has pointed out, ideology had many meanings in the Soviet context.[4] This issue was all the more pressing when the Soviet system was exported abroad for the first time. How was such an all-encompassing concept to be codified, explained, translated, and shipped to new parts of the world? As the careers of the NKVD advisers in Europe show, this was more than a process of translating Marxist-Leninist doctrine. It involved exporting a worldview that integrated these texts with other influences, including officials' class background, military discipline, institutional culture, and political language, which had been internalized in a time, place, and institution of immense political violence. To understand the "Soviet model" that was exported to East-Central Europe, it is necessary to conceive of ideology in a broad way, as encompassing communist ideas, institutional culture, and campaigns in which officials had been trained, promoted, and selected.

NKVD security advisers, moreover, were not only important in establishing communism in East-Central Europe and the Baltic states after 1945. Soviet security advisers with backgrounds similar to Kovalchuk's advised and trained security forces in China, Mongolia, and North Korea at the same time.[5] In all cases, "security" was a broad concept that included, to take an example from China in 1950, issues such as jamming foreign radio frequencies, guarding borders, building militias, and developing surveillance technologies.[6] To cite a document from Czechoslovakia from the same year, it involved creating counterintelligence departments to prevent foreign infiltration of state institutions, carrying out the "struggle against espionage, subversion, and sabotage in industry," and organizing a card catalogue system to store and access information over time.[7] In cases such as East Germany, Soviet security advisers selected, trained, and promoted virtually all the officials in the postwar security elite, decisions that affected the personnel of the institution until 1989.[8] Since many of these measures were directed against the West—whether through the blocking of Western radio, the militarization of the border with the West, or the selection of security officials with no ties to the West—these processes entrenched the Cold War over time. Officials trained by the Soviets helped bring socialism, and its model of security, to countries in Latin America, Africa, and Asia during the latter half of the Cold War.

After World War II, Soviet advisers consulted countries in Europe and Asia not only on matters of security, although this was a central priority, but also on the economy, military, culture, communist party, and fields such as engineering, technology, and infrastructure. As Norman Naimark has explored in Soviet-occupied Germany, the fact that Soviet advisers had been trained in key domestic campaigns such as the New Economic Policy, First Five-Year

Plan, Socialist Realism, and collectivization shaped their approach to state building in Germany.[9] Elena Zubkova and Jan Gross have pointed to similarities between the "Sovietization" of countries in Eastern Europe and the Baltic states and domestic campaigns against elites and socially harmful elements in the Soviet Union.[10] Recent studies of Soviet advisers in the fields of the economy and technology have shown that Soviet and local interests aligned in countries such as Albania and China that perceived of themselves as economically backward, suggesting that Soviet crash-economic campaigns such as the First Five-Year Plan and the military victory in World War II in fact appealed to many countries at the time.[11]

While these studies point to convergences between Soviet politics and the systems they exported abroad, none has delved into the backgrounds of the advisers, who often remain (as they appear in European documents) shadowy, behind-the-scenes figures. Yet as Kovalchuk's itinerant path from Russia to Ukraine, the Baltic states, East-Central Europe, and back again shows, the territories under Soviet influence were linked through personnel, who brought worldviews, practices, and assumptions about policing from one to the next. Soviet domestic politics and terror were connected in this way to the systems they built in the global socialist empire.

THE CIVIL WAR, COLLECTIVIZATION, AND GREAT TERROR AS FORMATIVE EXPERIENCES

In the lifetimes of the men who served as NKVD advisers in East-Central Europe, Russia had gone from autocracy to civil war to dictatorship. Political pluralism in Russia had been destroyed in 1918, when the Bolsheviks banned and persecuted their rival political parties, the Mensheviks and Social Revolutionaries. For many advisers, the first free elections they witnessed (and helped influence from behind the scenes) were in postwar Germany.[12] Most frequently, these men had begun their careers, as Kovalchuk had, in the Red Army. As Sheila Fitzpatrick has pointed out, the formative experience for young men who rose in the Stalinist period was not the revolution but the Civil War and its lessons of violence, enemies, and military discipline. In this way the "behavior, language, and appearance of the communists" in the Civil War set the foundations of the majority of the officials and employees of the Soviet state.[13] Nikolai Selivanovskii, chief Soviet security adviser in Warsaw between April 1945 and April 1946, had joined the Red Army in the early Civil War period and fought between 1920 and 1922.[14] Stepan Filatov, deputy head of the NKGB in the German state of Brandenburg, was born into a family of peasants and joined the secret police after a career in the Red Army.[15]

A similar trajectory was followed by Dmitrii Nikitin, NKVD adviser to the German regional state of Mecklenburg-West Pomerania. Nikitin was born in 1899 and joined the Red Army in 1918, where he served until 1926.[16]

Many had joined the secret police (from 1922 the OGPU and from 1934 the NKVD) when the force expanded its ranks and powers in the collectivization drives of the First Five-Year Plan. The force had many tasks at this time, but chief among them were waging class war against the peasantry, conducting mass arrests, and enforcing collectivization.[17] Since many of these men in fact came from peasant backgrounds, their participation in class warfare would in a sense have created these divisions, rather than merely reflecting them. Widely propagated campaigns—such as the Shakhty trial, held in May and June 1928—spread a message of class justice and anti-intellectualism on a mass scale and shaped the practices of institutions like the secret police enforcing these principles.[18] Although many were recruited to the NKVD first through the Red Army and participated in campaigns of violence associated with the industrialization and collectivization campaigns of the First Five-Year Plan, the professional rise of many coincided with the years of the Great Terror (1936–1939), a period when an estimated 800,000 Soviet citizens were executed.[19] It was common for young NKVD officials to be promoted rapidly in the force from 1937 as the language of spies, enemies, and conspiratorial plots overtook newspapers, party congresses, and popular culture alongside the exponentially growing NKVD files. As the memoirist Evgeniia Ginzburg recalled: "Those were the days of the Zinoviev-Kamenev trial, the Kemerovo affair, the trial of Bukharin and Radek. The newspapers were red hot, the news clawed and stung. After each trial the screw was turned tighter. The dreadful term 'enemies of the people' came into use."[20] An average of 2,200 arrests and 1,000 executions took place every single day between 1937 and 1938.[21]

Unsurprisingly, the powers and jurisdiction of the secret police grew tremendously at this time. A July 1936 decree lifted the requirement for party members to sanction and review the appointments of local investigators. As David Shearer has put it, "by the end of 1936, the political police force was nearing its zenith of power as an institution answerable to no one but Stalin."[22] The decision to join or rise in the NKVD in the late 1930s meant, as Lynne Viola has pointed out, adopting "apocalyptic thinking and a conspiratorial view of the world that grew out of war, revolution, militaristic language, and civil war."[23] Participation in violence was compensated with state awards, promotions, and pay increases.[24] Although the NKVD was subject to mass arrests toward the end of the terror, the institution as a whole grew at this time, reaching an estimated one million officials in the spring of 1938. This included an increase in the central and regional forces, which doubled in size, particularly as the civil police, railroad police, and Gulag employees were incorporated into the force.[25]

This period instilled a deep institutionalized paranoia into the NKVD. While some "internal enemies" were demarcated by class background or nationality, the rhetoric of the time claimed others were hiding in the very institutions that were fighting them (the NKVD itself, as well as the Communist Party, judiciary, and procuracy). In a March 1937 speech, Stalin blamed the recently discredited NKVD chief Genrikh Iagoda and those working under him for failing "to discern the real countenance of wreckers, diversionists, spies, and murderers" and proving "so unconcerned, complacent, and naïve that they assisted in promoting the agents of foreign states to one or another responsible post."[26] As Iagoda and thousands who worked under him were arrested or executed, the officials who rose in the force to take their place doubled their efforts to prove *their* loyalty and vigilance.

The arrest of the NKVD chief Nikolai Ezhov in 1938 sparked a veritable generational revolution in the institution as 7,372 officers (22 percent of all operative agents at the time) were removed from service, arrested, or executed, and 14,506 new recruits took their place.[27] This campaign changed the social profile of the institution, since most new recruits were young, of Russian nationality, and of working-class or peasant backgrounds. Jews and Poles, both prominent groups in the revolutionary Cheka, were expelled from the service almost entirely.[28] It is unsurprising that most of the men serving in the NKVD after 1945 shared this foundational experience. One example was General Ivan Serov. Serov, similar to others, had served in the Red Army between 1928 and 1934. He joined the NKVD in 1939 as thousands of his predecessors were being removed from the service.[29] Serov was more than willing to unmask the enemy activities of the former security elite.[30] During World War II, he oversaw the deportation of Tatars from Crimea in 1944.[31] He also served in the Baltic states and Eastern Poland between 1939 and 1941. After the war, he was appointed chief NKVD adviser in Poland (6 March 1945–27 April 1945) and in Soviet-occupied Germany (4 July 1945–24 February 1947). He continued his career in the secret police even under Nikita Khrushchev, playing a central role in shaping the information received by Moscow during the Hungarian Revolution in 1956. As Serov's career shows, this dramatic overhaul in personnel had consequences for the subsequent two decades of the institution's history both at home and abroad.

The revolution in NKVD personnel did not necessarily mean a revolution in institutional methods, since the officials who joined or rose in the force took over the card catalogues, offices, and training materials left behind by their executed predecessors. Turnover was also not total, which meant that

there were still men in the force to train the newcomers in established practices. But it did mean that those who joined had witnessed and taken part
in the arrests, torture, and execution of their superiors and predecessors for
"insufficient vigilance," an experience that would have made them less willing
to make the same "mistakes." It also meant that they fiercely internalized the
political language of the age, language that was a vehicle for both a certain
political culture and reading of communist ideology, and its prejudices against
certain national groups, intellectuals, classes, and social strata. In some cases,
such as the anti-intellectual bias in many of the materials from the time, this
language would have both spoken to the class backgrounds of officials and
reinforced previous campaigns such as the Shakhty trial. Other terms, such
as the phrase "socially harmful element," first came into use at this time, as in
the infamous Order no. 00447 of 16 July 1947. The NKVD tried 767,397 Soviet
citizens and executed 386,798 of them in accordance with this order and the
central quotas it set on the number of arrests, deportations, and executions
of certain categories of the population.[32] Given the initiative that almost all
NKVD offices showed from below during the campaign, as many lower-level
offices requested raising quotas, officials were at pains to prove their loyalty
and vigilance against particular groups and categories of enemies. In this and
countless other ways, the Great Terror was imprinted on the force.

It shaped NKVD officials' perceptions of foreign Communists and national
groups in particular, an issue with important implications for how the institution would interact with these same groups in Europe after 1945. From 1936,
a deep xenophobia began to characterize the NKVD's reports, discussions,
and internal correspondence. The USSR, such reports claimed, had been
penetrated by spies and saboteurs "disguised as political emigres and members of the fraternal parties," information that culminated in the arrests and
executions of foreign nationals and the decimation of the Communist International.[33] These reports were not written as speculations that needed to be
proved ("it is possible that the USSR has been penetrated by enemies") but as
facts ("the USSR has been penetrated by enemies"), an important distinction
that defined the task of the NKVD: to *find* these enemies. And almost all of
the information they received at the time from all institutions in the USSR,
from the Party to the Comintern to the judiciary, seemed to substantiate this
base assumption. To take one example, the Cadres Department of the Comintern provided information to the NKVD on three thousand foreign Communists living on the territory of the USSR, claiming that they were unreliable
and their ranks likely to be penetrated by spies, provocateurs, and wreckers.[34] Around 40 percent of those arrested in the campaigns against national
minorities between August 1937 and November 1938 were Poles.[35] The force

arrested 144,000 ethnic Poles and executed 110,000. In the eyes of NKVD agents, Poland was an enemy nation, a fact that could not but influence the institution's interactions with Poland during and after the war. As Ivan Serov explained in a note to Lavrentii Beria, he was suspicious even of Polish agents on their own side since he believed the institution had been infiltrated by Home Army (AK) agents seeking to "wreck general operations."[36] There was little reason for Polish Communist Party members, for their part, to trust the NKVD, because the institution had, within living memory, decimated its predecessor.[37] Hundreds of Polish Communist Party activists had been arrested during the Terror, including every member of the Politburo.[38] Józef Światło, later a leading Ministry of Public Security (MBP) official, related years later in a series of interviews with Radio Free Europe that he initially hid his Communist Party membership from the NKVD because the institution had executed so many Polish Communists.[39] Ethnic Germans were also a prominent NKVD target, particularly under NKVD Order no. 00439. Around 55,000 Germans were arrested and 42,000 executed during the Terror.[40] Forty-one of the sixty-eight German Communists who had taken refuge from Hitler in the USSR were executed, including seven members of the pre-1933 German Politburo.[41]

The NKVD advisers carried the language of spies, confessions, and enemies of the people they internalized in the late 1930s to East-Central Europe. The language of plots, conspiracies, hidden enemies, or "taking root in the enemy milieu" (vnedriatsia vo vrazheskuiu sredu) described the NKVD's operational methods. The latter term signaled methods of operative work, long-term operations in which agents infiltrated suspects' private lives and social milieus, methods taught to the security forces they trained in Eastern Europe. The Soviets introduced a legal terminology to the region internalized in the Stalinist 1930s. Seventy-two percent of cases held by Soviet military tribunals in eastern Germany charged defendants with article 58 of the Soviet Penal Code. Crimes such as "diversion," "agitation," and "counterrevolution" were introduced to eastern Germany.[42] Similar legal formulations were introduced to the Baltic states of Estonia, Latvia, and Lithuania, which were forcibly annexed to the Soviet Union in 1940 and 1941. In these territories, the NKVD was also told to reveal "counterrevolutionary elements" in the first months of the Soviet occupation.[43] Since their experiences in violence and civil war were a base line to assess new communist states, their reports to Moscow claimed that East Europeans had not gone far enough in arresting enemies.

NKVD officials' reports on the elections they observed in postwar Europe suggest that they viewed them in terms of enemies and underground conspiracies rather than as a peaceful contest between political parties. Such a view is evident in a report written by Dmitrii Nikitin, a chief NKVD adviser in Germany. Nikitin had joined the secret police (OGPU) in 1926 and been rapidly promoted in the force from 1939. In 1946, he described a pre-election campaign in Soviet-occupied Germany, using a language more suitable to civil war than electoral politics.[44] Since he considered the policies of the Communist Party of Germany (KPD) and the Soviet occupation authorities correct, he referred to criticism of them as antistate activity. Elections were a battle between right and wrong, between the correct side and the enemy side, and between progressive and reactionary forces. The Christian Democratic Union (CDU), he asserted, was "openly conducting propaganda against the Socialist Unity Party to deceive the population and achieve superiority in the elections." His agents (who, it was evident from the report, had infiltrated these parties) had uncovered a group of former Social Democrats (SPD) who were holding secret meetings to wage a battle against the Socialist Unity Party (SED).[45] He interpreted a meeting held in an SPD candidate's apartment as a plot. Attempts by noncommunist political parties to organize electoral strategies were depicted as a conspiracy. Criticisms of state policies by the CDU and the Liberal Democratic Party were deemed "enemy comments" that compromised the SED or expressed reactionary points of view.

Perceptions of enemies, loyalty, and political culture shaped NKVD advisers' selection of local informers. Although in the period immediately following World War II the prerogative seemed to be to collect as much information as possible and to encourage local citizens to bring information to the Soviet occupiers, it became clear over time that the Soviets favored the information brought by some over others and developed working relationships with certain Communists whom they felt could be trusted over others. In Czechoslovakia in the 1950s, for example, they worked closely with and eventually sought to actively promote men in the Party, judiciary, and security forces who generally fit a profile matching their own: young, Czech officials who joined the State Security (StB) in or after 1945. Non-Czech nationals, and Jews in particular, were mistrusted or actively expelled from the force. Their informers tended to fit a similar profile in terms of class background, be nonintellectual, or express hatred of target groups such as Jews, intellectuals, or "cosmopolitan" Spanish Civil War veterans. Such qualities—not "loyalty to the Communist Party," as it is so often seen in the literature—came to define how the Soviets marked loyalty in the 1950s.

From the perspective of East Europeans, the willingness to provide information to the Soviets changed as the euphoria of postwar liberation, which had granted the Soviets considerable authority in the region, turned by 1949 into an atmosphere of fear, anxiety, and uncertainty. After arrests broke out in the Czechoslovak Party and state from 1950, the act of providing information to the Soviets became less about building states or spreading communism than about saving oneself, shielding others, exposing others, or proving loyalty. The nature of the information people provided changed accordingly, as reports began to focus increasingly on personal minutiae about individuals' connections, beliefs, and previous political affiliation than their countries' economic policies or progress toward socialism. A discussion between a Soviet representative in Bratislava and a Slovak politician in late 1949 showed how locals reproduced the language of internal enemies and plots in conversations with Soviet representatives. With reference to the trial of László Rajk in Hungary, the Slovak politician noted that there were doubtless links between the Slovaks and the "Hungarian traitors on trial in Budapest." He had undertaken investigations to "determine these connections and purge these elements."[46] The local informer agreed that Slovak institutions were filled with people with suspicious backgrounds who should be removed from the service. It is worth asking how useful such information was and in which ways terror shaped the information the Soviets were receiving and the general perception of the Soviet system in Europe. In some cases, there is evidence that Soviet connections became a liability for local Communists as fear spread of the Soviet advisers and their intentions. Communists in Poland were stigmatized in local parties for being "too" Soviet. As a report from July 1949 noted, a Pole whom local Communists deemed to be a Soviet informer was "kept at a distance" and "compelled to hide his links with the Soviet embassy."[47] In the midst of the search for enemies in the Party in Poland, Polish Communists threatened violence against those perceived as "pro-Soviet" members of the Communist Party.[48]

The Soviet advisers promoted not only informers but also local security officials with trusted characteristics in the force, a tendency with implications for the forces' social composition. Such was the case in Czechoslovakia, where NKVD advisers Mikhail Likhachev and Nikolai Makarov arrived in the fall of 1949. Likhachev had been born in 1913 into a family of poor peasants and joined the NKVD at the end of 1935. He rose in the force between 1938 and 1945. He was on "official business" in Poland between August 1944 and May 1945 and in Soviet-occupied Germany between November 1945 and February 1946 before being sent to Czechoslovakia.[49] Makarov was born into a family of carpenters in 1905. After years of odd jobs and unemployment, he joined the OGPU in October 1929 and the NKVD in 1935.[50] After serving in Czechoslovakia, he was sent to East Germany between 25 December 1951 and 22 June 1954. These advisers' impressions of Czechoslovakia were evident in a report sent to their superior, Viktor Abakumov, in March 1950. They described their duties in Prague as providing "practical help" with investigations and uncovering "evidence of enemy activity among high-ranking members of the Czechoslovak government."[51] While there, they "confirmed" that former Foreign Minister and Slovak national Vladimír Clementis was engaging in subversive activities as part of a bourgeois nationalist conspiracy. Although the Communist Party of Czechoslovakia (KSČ) leader Klement Gottwald objected to the arrests, this had no bearing on the advisers' decision to push the terror forward. They believed that the case against Clementis proved that local security forces could not be trusted, since they had failed to uncover it. Likhachev and Makarov also raised concerns about the military, which was "clogged" with "reactionary elements" with connections to Britain and the United States. This is also unsurprising, given the role of the NKVD in carrying out arrests and executions in the Red Army both during the Great Terror and World War II. As this report suggests, Soviet advisers in Czechoslovakia saw their task as uncovering those they perceived as preventing the Soviet model from being implemented and determining who was willing to push forward arrests of other party members. Locals' reluctance to carry out the terror or divert or stop investigations from high-ranking officials was interpreted as evidence of subversive activity.

The idea that enemies or "undesirable elements" were hiding inside foreign communist parties, militaries, and state institutions was treated as self-evident. They were in Europe precisely to uncover "subversive activity" (*podryvnaia deiatel'nost'*) and "enemy plots" (*raskryvat' zamysly vraga*). Little wonder, given their role in uncovering such plots in communist party, military, and state institutions in the Soviet Union. Their documents describe institutions in Europe as clogged (*zasorennyi*) with enemies. They were clogged with former Nazis in Germany and with noncommunist political parties in Czechoslovakia. This situation could be remedied only by expelling thousands of employees from them, a conviction that fit the general drive of postwar de-Nazification campaigns but was also taken farther in the internal party purges they pushed forward in the region from 1949. NKVD reports were peopled with "unreliable elements" (*nenadezhnye elementy*), a term used to describe local officials who had joined communist parties but who—in the Soviets' opinion—had not fully dedicated themselves to the cause. The presence of such people necessitated verification campaigns and purges. Of course, the practice in Eastern Europe in 1945 had been to open up the ranks of communist parties to mass recruitment, so complete dedication to the service had indeed been far from a requirement, something that the NKVD eyed with suspicion.

The embeddedness of such language in Soviet experience, both the NKVD's professional terminology and the language of enemies and plots that dominated popular discourse at the time, made the transfer of "Bolshevik" to new countries a bumpy process. It was not always comprehensible in countries that did not have the same experiences.[52] The term "Trotskyite" was raised by the Soviet advisers regardless of its applicability or relevance to local conditions. When East European secret police forces were told to create units to uncover Trotskyites, the order was sometimes met with confusion, because Trotsky had long since ceased to be a political influence in communist movements.[53] Since there were rarely local equivalents for terms that had arisen in the social and political context of the Great Terror, a flood of what even at the time were identified as "Russianisms" entered the official and institutional language of European communism. Sometimes Russianisms displaced local terms for concepts like informers. Sometimes they coexisted with them. And sometimes they were adopted to describe a concept that was completely new. Whatever the situation, language—official and unofficial—continued to perpetuate difference among Soviets, local officials, and population in a way that would never disappear.[54] It was also an important, and still underappreciated, vehicle for the Sovietization of East European political culture and institutions in a way that helped establish these regimes in the short term, while undermining them in the long term. The stilted, often incomprehensible language of officialdom played a central role in the Czechoslovak criticism of the Party during and after the Prague Spring.[55] In the Baltic states, conflicts over language had political overtones and perpetuated difference between locals and Russian-speakers that appeared in protests, resistance movements, and official discourse that persisted until (and after) the breakup of the Soviet Union.[56]

If the Soviet language, both Russian and the language of enemies particular to Stalinism, continued to be a marker of its foreignness, so was the historical narrative imported by the Soviets at the time, which was as influenced by the Terror as the Soviets' institutions and personnel. As David Brandenberger and Mikhail Zelenov have pointed out, the Terror shaped Stalin's "master narrative" about the Soviet Union and world communism. The same narrative internalized by NKVD officials during the terror—a Russo-centric communism in which the Party was threatened by enemy infiltration, spies, and internal and external enemies—was the regime's official narrative from 1938. *The History of the Communist Party of the Soviet Union (Bolsheviks): Short Course* cemented the interpretation of history the Soviets exported to the rest of the world. Since it was written during the Great Terror and in part to explain and justify it, it placed the struggle with enemies at the center of the communist worldview.[57] The story was entirely a Russian one. Somewhat awkwardly from the perspective of Europe, it wrote world communism and the Comintern out of the history of the socialist revolution. It is difficult to believe that European Communists failed to notice the total absence of references to key European

Marxists who had helped build world communism in the 1920s and 1930s. Stalin himself had personally erased references to the Comintern from the *Short Course*, probably in part because of the large number of Comintern agents being executed as spies and wreckers at the time. In wiping out the Comintern, the *Short Course*, and even Stalin himself, pulled Marxism from its roots in European societies, cultures, and national movements and depicted it as a Russian import.

Even though the Soviet advisers were mired in the language, worldview, and narrative of the Terror, the violence carried out in the Soviet Union in 1937–1938 was never reproduced in Europe. In part, this was because of hedging, foot-dragging, and passive resistance on the part of local communist officials. In part, it was because the period of "Stalinism" in Europe did not last nearly as long as in the Soviet Union. Generally, it is understood in Eastern Europe to be the period between 1949 and 1954. Even give or take a few years depending on the country, it lasted approximately six years, as opposed to three decades in the Soviet Union. It also does not seem that the Soviets aimed to reproduce the extent of the mass arrests they had perpetuated in their own country. The memory of the Terror also remained complex. Stalin himself, after all, had condemned its excesses, blamed local NKVD leaders for taking it "too far," and erased its main figure, Nikolai Ezhov, from history and public memory. The *Short Course* "resolved" the issue by not mentioning officials by name and speaking in broad, sweeping statements about communism as a system.[58] When speaking with East European leaders about state security in 1949, Stalin made no mention of Nikolai Ezhov.[59] Official Soviet memory therefore had two interpretations of the Terror. While it demonstrated the strength and triumph of the Stalinist regime, it also represented a period of violence run amok in the hands of power-hungry NKVD officers. Locals could, and did, reference the Soviet model as an example of what *not* to do as well as what to emulate. The Polish Politburo member Hilary Minc warned the Polish United Workers' Party (PZPR) in late 1949 not to start another "Ezhovshina," a negative term for the Terror in Soviet discourse.[60] Such issues were one example of the room for interpretation, or even gaping holes, at the heart of the Soviet "model."

THE NKVD AND WORLD WAR II

The Terror was not the only formative experience for the Soviet advisers. All, without exception, were promoted in the service while fighting on fronts in Stalingrad, Ukraine, Belarus, Germany, and elsewhere during World War II. Some observed the Nuremberg Trial firsthand or took part in de-Nazification investigations in postwar Germany after the surrender of the Nazis. These experiences explained their obsession with securing the country's borders from foreign attack. It was also the lens through which they would have understood the Soviet Union's increased influence in Europe, which was viewed as compensation for the tremendous civilian and military sacrifices, devastation, and mass death suffered on the path to Berlin.[61] Victory in the war had also granted the Stalinist regime unprecedented prestige on the domestic stage and seemed to many to have justified the sacrifices of the violence, Terror, and civil conflict of the 1930s.[62] For the NKVD, the militant conviction that the Soviet system had proven itself during the war contributed to the conviction that East Europeans should replicate it in every detail.

The NKVD also had a particular role in the war, one that combined fighting on the front with the battle against perceived enemies in the conquered territories, Red Army, and territories annexed to the Soviet Union after the war (Western Ukraine and Belarus and the Baltic states). By 1945, these men had spent their entire professional careers in military-style institutions, whether the Red Army, NKVD, or SMERSH (the military intelligence service). The experience of uninterrupted war instilled, as Elena Zubkova described of Red Army soldiers in general, "the custom of command and submission, strong discipline, unquestioned authority of a command" and the conviction that it was necessary to destroy enemies, traitors, and deserters.[63] A singular obsession with military-style discipline was evident in NKVD reports abroad. M. S. Bezborodov, the chief NKVD adviser in Poland between March 1950 and June 1953, had joined the Red Army at the age of seventeen and fought in it until 1923. He entered the OGPU in 1924 and rose in the force between late 1936 and the end of World War II, reaching the rank of colonel in 1943. In a report from Poland in July 1951, he criticized the Polish secret police for its lack of discipline.[64] He asserted the "low quality" of the Polish service's operative work and "inability of the vast majority of agents to root themselves in the enemy milieu and uncover the plans of the enemy." Polish agents in lower-level offices in particular, who had often been recruited to the force in an ad hoc manner in the last months of the war, frequently showed up late to work, lied in their reports to the central office, and drank on the job. The answer was more discipline: "Employees of the security service lack discipline. The struggle against violators of discipline is waged only weakly." It was necessary to "declare war on violators of discipline, drunkards, and loafers, not only through administrative means but by strengthening political and educational work." He demanded total dedication, to the point of subordinating one's private life, to the force. Hundreds of lower-level security officials were arrested in Poland for disciplinary infractions in the late 1940s and early 1950s, doubtless in part because of Soviet intervention on the matter.[65]

NKVD operations during the war in many ways continued campaigns begun during the Great Terror. Soon after the Nazis invaded the Soviet Union, the NKVD took up national operations once again. Hundreds of thousands of Volga Germans were exiled to Siberia and Kazakhstan.[66] Such operations were expanded to new territories. When the Soviets annexed the Baltic states of Estonia, Latvia, and Lithuania, the NKVD deported an estimated 118,599 Lithuanians, 52,541 Latvians, and 32,540 Estonians to Siberia, Central Asia, and the Far North.[67] Poles once again became a target. An estimated 300,000 Poles were deported from territories annexed to the Soviet Union.[68] In April and May 1940, the NKVD executed 21,857 Polish officers who had been taken as prisoners of war (POWs), a war crime long denied by the Soviet state that came to be known as the Katyń Massacres.[69] After the war, campaigns against non-Russian nationalities were accompanied by a campaign to promote Russian nationalism inside the Soviet Union.

Soon after the war, and in the years 1948–1949 in particular, Stalin initiated a series of antisemitic campaigns against prominent Jewish doctors and intellectuals. New categories of enemies included "rootless cosmopolitans" and "Zionists."[70] These campaigns influenced Soviet advisers in Eastern Europe, whose intelligence reports from the time reflect the resonance of this campaign among those working abroad as well as in the USSR. In 1949, the Soviets suggested that they expected the Czechoslovaks to adopt the term "rootless cosmopolitanism" to a "Czechoslovak reality," a term that took on significance in the internal party terror in Czechoslovakia and the trial of former General Secretary Rudolf Slánský in late 1952 in particular.[71] The Soviets reported on the number of Jews serving in the highest ranks of East European communist parties and states. The Soviet ambassador informed Moscow in 1949 that an unusually large number of Jews were serving in the Polish Ministry of Internal Affairs. There was evidence, he believed, of "Jewish nationalism" in the Polish Communist Party and security force.[72] Influence did not work only one way. The trial of Rudolf Slánský that the NKVD advisers helped stage in Czechoslovakia was perceived as a forerunner for a trial of Jewish doctors in Moscow that was never staged.[73] Antisemitic rhetoric was so powerful in part because locals were prepared to act on and enforce it. The ferocity of these trends can only be explained by the changes in the social composition of Soviet institutions at the end of the 1930s. The generational revolution in the NKVD, for example, had explicitly removed Jews from the force. The number of Jews in the NKVD went from 38.54 percent in 1934 to 3.92 percent in 1939, a shift that reinforced the Russian identity of the institution.[74]

The war, for all the sense of solidarity it created in the Soviet Union against the common enemy, seemed to have little bearing on the NKVD's conviction that there were enemies hiding inside Soviet institutions. If anything, the rhetoric at the time strongly emphasized the link between war and enemy infiltration. War scares in the Soviet Union had previously been exploited to escalate domestic terror and did so in this case as well.[75] During the Great Terror, the NKVD had decimated the ranks of the Red Army and expelled, arrested, or executed leading officers from the Civil War period. During World War II, the NKVD similarly policed the Red Army. They arrested officers and soldiers deemed potentially disloyal, a category that included those who fell captive to the Germans.[76] As Kovalchuk's experience shows, agents were sometimes moved from the NKVD to SMERSH, the counterespionage institution created in 1943 to monitor anti-Soviet activity in the military.[77] The founding document of SMERSH made clear its role in the "struggle against anti-Soviet elements who have infiltrated units and offices of the Red Army" and the "struggle against treachery and betrayal of the Motherland in units and offices of the Red Army (deserting to the enemy's side, concealment of spies, and in general, assistance to the latter); verification of military personnel and other persons who have been in captivity and encircled by the enemy."[78] The NKVD carried out summary executions of Red Army soldiers labeled as deserters, sometimes in front of their units in order to deter others from similar actions.[79]

One of the few documents revealing the tensions—or more accurately, resentments—between the NKVD and the Red Army is from Soviet-occupied Germany in October 1945. A report by a Soviet military commander related the disorderly behavior of two NKVD operatives taken into custody after starting drunken fights outside a workers' club.[80] The NKVD agents attacked and threatened the military officers who had detained them, saying, "I have had more than one military commander fired," and calling everyone present a "suspicious individual." One operative repeatedly yelled the name of Ivan Serov, who, he threatened, would "teach them" not to detain members of the NKVD. This interaction said a great deal about how NKVD officials perceived their power over the Red Army and the fear inspired by the names of their superiors. The report described this as "one of a number of incidences" in which NKVD operatives were engaging in raucous behavior in occupied Germany, whether carrying out unjustified arrests, confiscating property from German citizens, or using their positions for personal gain or racketeering. After the war, the NKVD continued to closely inspect Soviet citizens and POWs who returned to the country from Europe, a screening process explicitly to catch "spies" and "traitors" in their ranks and in which hundreds of thousands of returning soldiers and citizens were arrested.[81]

While these advisers' origins were in many ways similar, their trajectories from 1953 were not. The Khrushchev period proved a time of great uncertainty.[82]

Some officials, such as Viktor Abakumov and Mikhail Likhachev, were executed alongside Beria in 1954. Ivan Serov continued his career as head of the KGB between 1954 and 1958, spearheading the purge of 18,000 of his fellow officers from the institution. Those expelled from service, particularly after 1956, were charged with "violations of socialist legality."[83] Others were purged under Serov's successor.[84] Some continued to serve in the KGB in the Soviet Union, Eastern Europe, or even in Third World countries such as Cuba in a new wave of Soviet global influence after 1953.

CASE STUDY: SOVIET INTELLIGENCE AND THE CZECHOSLOVAK REVOLUTION

Moscow received intelligence not only from the NKVD but also from Soviet diplomats, press correspondents, and representatives of the Pan-Slavic movement sent to the region on official business. The NKVD, far from being a world of its own, was only one Soviet institution deeply shaped by the terror, fear, purges, arrests, and denunciations in which Soviet officialdom had been created in the late 1930s. This section examines the materials other observers sent to Moscow with a focus on the communist takeover of power in Czechoslovakia in 1948. At the time, Stalin received intelligence from TASS press correspondents, journalists for *Pravda* or *Izvestiia*; officials from the Pan-Slavic organization; and Soviet diplomats working in the embassy in Prague.[85] The reports we have from the time show that the mentalities instilled by the Terror affected all Soviet institutions collecting information abroad after World War II. After all, Soviet embassies, just to take one example, had also been decimated during the Terror. As Stephen Kotkin has written of the late 1930s, "Soviet embassies were emptied of personnel. To the extent that dispatches were still being sent to Moscow, the paperwork often went unanswered from lack of personnel."[86] The new officials who replaced those arrested at the time were monolingual, untrained in diplomacy, and closely linked with Soviet intelligence agencies.[87] Because of the impact of the Terror on Soviet institutions such as the diplomatic corps, security forces, agents, and others serving abroad, their documents reveal a lack of understanding—even a culture clash—between European and Soviet conceptions of communism. Soviet reports evoked panic, alleged enemy or Western infiltration, and even claimed that the bourgeois order was being reinstated.

Soviet reports on events in Czechoslovakia during and after the communist takeover of power in February 1948 were far from celebratory about Czechoslovak communism.[88] Soviet observers watched the takeover of power in February 1948, when grassroots action committees representing the Czechoslovak Communist Party seized control of state institutions, public life, civil organizations, and lower levels of the administration. While publicly claiming victory, Soviet intelligence from Prague told a different story. An early report on the situation was written by a representative of the Pan-Slavic movement on 29 March 1948. After speaking to local Communists and activists in the Czech lands, Moravia, and Slovakia, he characterized the KSČ's revolutionary councils as chaotic and claimed that there was an "absence of clarity" on what the role of these councils would be after February.[89] Action committees had indeed been the product of improvisation, local laws, and extensive grassroots mobilization. They had grown out of the Czechoslovaks' own organizational practices rather than deriving from the "Soviet model," however broadly defined. Although the call for the creation of action committees came from Prague, the Czechoslovak system in 1948 was not driven by the political "center" in the same way as the Soviet system, consisting instead of a number of different power bases in regional governments, local administration, personal networks, and civic organizations, a system the Soviet observer (and many outside observers) would have understood as "chaotic."

The following year, a Soviet observer working for TASS reported that KSČ leaders were being lenient on enemies of socialism and that they failed to carry out a true revolution. They achieved victory "without serious struggle or bloodshed, a victory of meetings and demonstrations."[90] Rather than transforming the country, the KSČ had, in his view, revived the symbols and rituals of the former liberal state and its seat at the Prague Castle. While for the Czechoslovaks, building a communist state had involved expanding the ranks of the Party, drawing on the symbols of the previous regime, and allowing former political rivals to enter the KSČ, representatives of Moscow looked on these decisions with suspicion. Of particular concern was the KSČ's decision to allow former members of noncommunist political parties ("dubious political elements") to join the Communist Party, a policy General Secretary Rudolf Slánský had celebrated as "opening the doors of the Party" to all who would join. From the perspective of the KSČ, the strategy was based on the Party's long history in parliamentary politics and fixation on increasing mass membership to achieve success in elections. In the words of the Soviet observer, "KSČ leaders, although recognizing the danger that hostile elements and defectors from other parties would enter the Party, firmly believe there is a need for mass admission into the Party, citing the elections as the reason for such a policy." Indeed, the strategy expanded the Communists' ranks by millions of members. But in the view of the Soviet observer, forgiving former non-Communists was a mistake, since it would bring enemies into the Party's ranks.

Allowing members of non-communist political parties to join the KSČ also meant that locals could retain their position in the state service or administration by doing so. This was a source of agitation for the Soviet representative. He described February as a political rather than a class struggle and made clear that the real struggle was far from over. KSČ leaders were faulted for being "conceited" in considering the revolution at an end. In a sense, he was correct in pointing to February 1948 as more of a political than a social or economic revolution. It targeted the country's political pluralism rather than its distribution of wealth, social composition, or economic structures. Only the "Stalinist" revolution the advisers helped push forward from the end of 1949 redistributed property and promoted women, minorities, and workers in the political establishment.[91] But the Soviet observer underestimated the significance of 1948 in the Czechoslovak context. Whereas political pluralism had shallow roots and little meaning in the Soviet Union, it had always been an integral part of Czechoslovak politics and culture.

Such issues reflected misunderstandings over the meaning of the communist revolution. A similar clash in understandings between the two sides was over the role of intellectuals under communism. The Soviet observer, doubtless influenced by the anti-intellectual campaign underway in the Soviet Union, criticized the role of intellectuals in Czechoslovakia in 1948: "Intellectuals lack an understanding of internal events and suffer from a shocking amount of ideological confusion in assessing the subversive activities of right-wing parties and their leaders." His term for "ideological confusion" was *razbrod*, a Russian word with a root meaning "to wander in different directions." There could be no more accurate way to describe the difference between Soviet and Czechoslovak conceptions of ideology. For Soviet officials who had risen in the Stalinist system, ideology had a single meaning provided by the center. For the Czechoslovaks, it was a jumping-off point for discussion, disagreement, or even jealously fought-over schools of thought. The "Czechoslovak model" of socialism presupposed a significant role for intellectuals as participants in, or discussers, of policy and its implementation.[92] The Soviet criticism of Czechoslovak intellectuals became harsher over time, noting their unwillingness to accept Andrei Zhdanov's 1946 attacks on Soviet literature, theater, and the cultural figures Anna Akhmatova and Mikhail Zoshchenko. After praising Zhdanov in vague terms, *Rudé právo* had apparently stated that Czechoslovakia would not go "as far" in its approach to cultural issues. "It appears from the article in *Rudé právo* that Zhdanov's party and ideological questions about the role of literature and art in educating the masses do not have the slightest meaning in Czechoslovakia," noted one Soviet report acerbically.[93]

Soviet reports on Czechoslovakia became more hostile as the Cold War progressed. A note by a TASS correspondent in Prague in May 1949 railed against the country's relationship with the West. He attributed the influence of the West to the failure of Czechoslovaks to carry out a true revolution. The KSČ was condemned for its lack of decisiveness in repressing political enemies, which had spread US influence in the country in two ways. First, political enemies had gone into exile and continued their activities abroad rather than being killed. "After suffering defeat, the leaders of the reactionary parties left unhindered for London, New York, or Paris." Second, Czechoslovak institutions were filled with people with wealth and connections to the West: "Entrepreneurs, merchants, and millionaires who had accumulated wealth in the new Republic remained. Reactionary officials remained (true, many were dismissed from service, but allowed to retire). Reactionary generals and officers remained in the military and National Security Service. In short, the Americans maintained a broad, essentially old, but illegal base to continue subversive activities against the People's Democracies and the Soviet Union." In the mind of this observer, there was an indelible connection between foreign and domestic enemies. He created a wildly exaggerated picture of domestic discord in Czechoslovakia, claiming that there was resistance to February in form of antigovernment fliers (which was true). He quickly leaped from this to the "likely" possibility of a larger conspiracy: "facts show that reactionary powers go from propaganda and agitation to more aggressive forms of struggle." He was convinced that it was necessary to crush even small acts of resistance before they became larger ones, adding that the Czechs had a "traditional spirit of resistance" that these fliers would apparently evoke.[94]

A point of discord between the Soviets and Czechoslovaks was the attitude toward the West. Even after the takeover of power, Czechoslovak Communists saw no contradiction in adopting practices from the Soviet Union and the West to shape their socialist system. For them, it was a matter of choosing the best forms from all systems, while favoring the experiences of the Soviets. The Soviets, deeply ingrained with anti-Western convictions, had little patience for this approach. The Czechs were depicted as "sitting between two chairs": "the intensification of the struggle between the imperialist and the democratic camps raises the desire among the Czechs to sit out the conflict."[95] Prague was pushed in late 1949 to implement an "isolation campaign" to cut cultural and foreign ties with the West. But many lower-level security offices did not implement it, and it had little success outside of Prague.[96] The Czechoslovak revolution was deemed not only a failure but even a reinstatement of bourgeois power. The communist ministers, the Soviet observer wrote, lived in mansions, villas, and aristocratic quarters in Prague. He described the Czechoslovak "national road to socialism" in the following way:

The supporters of the "Czechoslovak path to socialism" are trying to squeeze new socialist content into old bourgeois democratic forms. The old is not destroyed but preserved and modernized. . . . As before, celebratory trumpets are played when the president makes a public appearance. In addition to his residence in the castle, the president has a castle in the countryside. His wife performs the same rites (such as patronizing the society of the Red Cross and charitable causes) as before. The new ministers live as the old ones did in villas with servants and drive not in locally made vehicles (which, by the way, are not bad) but in foreign cars. They allow themselves to be photographed endlessly at public gatherings. Outwardly, they act like the old ministers. A Czech citizen (and Czechs are prone to philistinism) or average person looking at all this might begin to ask himself: What has actually changed?

American influence would seep into the vacuum of this failed revolution. While the 1948 report had admitted that the workers had played an important part in the revolution, the 1949 one asserted that they were "hostile and unfriendly" toward the new leaders: "the number of workers and Communist Party members who are indifferent or resentful of the situation is widespread."

After reading these reports and the fear, anxiety, and panic they evoked, it is not surprising that the Soviets insisted on sending advisers to Czechoslovakia who would push forward the repression inside the Communist Party and state. The Soviet critiques of the Czechoslovaks, particularly the country's links with the West and the unfinished or merely "political" nature of the February Revolution, were not necessarily wrong. But they were based on a highly selective reading of the evidence and a strong tendency, conscious and unconscious, to collect evidence that supported their particular worldview and to ignore evidence that did not.

The NKVD advisers saw plots, conspiracies, resistance, and disorder everywhere they looked. It was a reason they decided to push forward the arrests of local officials in East-Central Europe (to the bafflement of these officials, who believed that they had followed Moscow's orders precisely). Yet it was precisely the internal party terror that would deeply undermine the influence of the Soviet Union, spread fear and mistrust, damage the authority the Soviets had earned through their tremendous sacrifices in World War II, and cripple their information networks in the region. The Soviets distorted their own information base by compelling locals to hide information and become "bilingual" in the language of spies and enemies to save themselves from suspicion. From the internal party terror of the late 1940s, local informers began to think of Soviet representatives not only as advisers, diplomats, or teachers of a "model" but as connections to Moscow to prove credentials, loyalty, and hatred of the enemy, a tendency that skewed the information they provided. Disagreements between Soviet and local conceptions of communism were evident in clashes of values and assumptions never fully expressed or even understood, since the Czechoslovaks were not privy to the Soviets' internal reports. Differences arose not over broad goals such as "achieving socialism" but over countless small issues of interpretation, methods, and organization, with implications for global communism. As powerful as the Soviet advisers were, it was precisely their insistence on replicating the Soviet model in the most minute detail that made many aspects of it incomprehensible to Communists abroad who had often joined communist movements *before* the onset of high Stalinism and—whether they would have admitted it or not—strategized and reasoned in their own domestic contexts.

INFORMATION AND TERROR

Soviet security advisers arrived in Europe in 1945 with a particular *version* of the "Soviet model" deeply influenced by their experiences, training, and personal backgrounds in the Russian Civil War, Great Terror, and World War II. The Great Terror, given its far-reaching influence in every single state and party institution in the Soviet Union, had in this way a "second life" in Europe, since it was embedded in advisers' worldviews, institutional practices, language, the official historical narrative of the Stalinist regime, and the institutional memory of agents trained and promoted in it. Images of enemies from the Soviet Union in the late 1930s—whether intellectuals, Jews, bourgeois nationalists, or supporters of the West—were "found" again in Eastern Europe. Within the Soviet Union, these advisers played a central role in annexing the Baltic states and eastern borderlands of Poland in 1940 and 1941, territories that underwent a process of Sovietization similar to Eastern Europe in part because it was carried out by the same officials.[97] The backgrounds of these men helps explain why the spread of communism was so closely linked to terror and genocide, a fact generally attributed to communist doctrine.[98] What was learned by the rest of the world was an interpretation of ideology learned during the most violent period of Soviet history. While this chapter has focused on the impact of these years on the security forces, similar studies of Soviet economic or military advisers would suggest further links between Soviet domestic experiences and the version of communism taught, learned, and adopted after 1945. By the time communism was exported abroad, after all, it was more than a doctrine. It was a dictatorship in which Marxism—or more specifically, Marxism-Leninism-Stalinism—was embedded in the worldviews of those who had been created by it and in its law, historical narrative, conspiratorial mindset, military-style discipline, and other institutional practices internalized as much in common campaigns of violence as formal training. The Soviet advisers brought with them a brutal form of rule that, while powerful in the short term, proved in many ways shortsighted in the long term. After all, the territories they incorporated into the Soviet empire at this time, whether the Baltic states or Eastern Europe, were the first territories that brought down Soviet power in 1989 and 1991.

NOTES

I would like to thank the anonymous reviewers and my colleague, Katja Bruisch, for their thoughtful and helpful comments on early drafts of this chapter. Thanks to Daniela Richterova and Christopher Andrews for the opportunity to present part of it at the Cambridge Intelligence Seminar, and to Michael David-Fox for organizing the conference on the Soviet political police at Georgetown University that got the chapter off the ground.

1. Leonard Shapiro, *The Communist Party of the Soviet Union* (London: Eyre and Spottiswoode, 1960), 309.

2. Nikita Petrov, *Kto rukovodil organami gosbezopasnosti, 1942–1954* (Moscow: Zven'ia, 2010), 431–32.

3. Sheila Fitzpatrick, "Stalin and the Making of a New Elite, 1928–1939," *Slavic Review* 38, no. 3 (1979): 377–402.

4. The discussion of the ideology as a worldview is raised by Michael David-Fox, *Crossing Borders: Modernity, Ideology, and Culture in Russia and the Soviet Union* (Pittsburgh: University of Pittsburgh Press, 2015), 150–55.

5. Petrov, *Kto rukovodil organami gosbezopasnosti*, 39–40.

6. "Decision of the Politburo of the TsK VKP(b): On Assistance to Organs of State Security of the People's Republic of China," 6 November 1950, as cited in David Shearer and Vladimir Khaustov, *Stalin and the Lubianka: A Documentary History of the Political Police and Security Organs in the Soviet Union, 1922–1953* (New Haven: Yale University Press, 2015), 163.

7. "Decision of the Politburo of TsK VKP(b) on sending MGB Advisers to Czechoslovakia, 21 December 1950," as cited in Shearer and Khaustov, *Stalin and the Lubianka*, 283.

8. Jens Gieseke, *Die hauptamtlichen Mitarbeiter der Staatssicherheit: Personalstruktur und Lebenswelt* (Berlin: Ch. Links, 2010).

9. Norman Naimark, *The Russians in Germany: A History of the Soviet Zone of Occupation, 1945–1959* (Cambridge, MA: Belknap, 1995), 467.

10. Elena Zubkova, *Pribaltika i Kreml', 1940–1953* (Moscow: ROSSPEN, 2008); Jan Gross, *Revolution from Abroad: The Soviet Conquest of Poland's Western Ukraine and Western Belorussia* (Princeton, NJ: Princeton University Press, 2002).

11. Austin Jersild, *The Sino-Soviet Alliance: An International History* (Chapel Hill: University of North Carolina Press, 2014); Elidor Mehilli, *From Stalin to Mao: Albania and the Socialist World* (Ithaca, NY: Cornell University Press, 2017), 132.

12. Marc Jansen, *A Show Trial under Lenin: The Trial of the Socialist Revolutionaries* (The Hague: Kluwer, 1982), 3.

13. Sheila Fitzpatrick, "The Civil War as a Formative Experience" (Kennan Institute for Advanced Russian Studies, 1981), 2.

14. Petrov, *Kto rukovodil organami gosbezopasnosti*, 777. He was promoted in 1935, 1938, 1941, and 1943.

15. "Zakliuchenie upravleniia kadrov MGB SSSR ob utverzhdeniii v TsK VKP(b) S. I. Filatova v dolzhnosti nachal'nika operativnogo sektora MGB zemli Brandenburg," 19 January 1949, in *Apparat NKVD-MGB v Germanii, 1945–1953: Dokumenty*, ed. Nikita Petrov (Moscow: Mezhdunarodnyi fond "Demokratiia," 2009), 419.

16. Petrov, *Kto rukovodil organami gosbezopasnosti, 1942–1954*, 639.

17. Shearer and Khaustov, *Stalin and the Lubianka*, 4.

18. The message of class justice was explicit in the materials published on the trial at home and abroad. See the detailed transcripts of the trial published in the Czech communist press at the time: "Proces proti kontrarevolučním sabotážníkům z donské pánve: Třída proti třídě," *Rudé právo*, 20 May 1928, čís. 120, st. 2.

19. Norman Naimark, *Stalin's Genocides* (Princeton, NJ: Princeton University Press, 2010), 111.

20. Evgenia Ginzburg, *Journey into the Whirlwind* (New York: Harcourt Brace Jovanovich, 1967), 26.

21. Stephen Kotkin, *Stalin: Waiting for Hitler, 1929–1941* (New York: Penguin, 2017), 649.

22. Shearer and Khaustov, *Stalin and the Lubianka*, 9.

23. Lynne Viola, *Stalinist Perpetrators on Trial* (Oxford: Oxford University Press, 2019), 173.

24. Kotkin, *Stalin*, 668.

25. Kotkin, *Stalin*, 736.

26. Kotkin, *Stalin*, 580.

27. Viola, *Stalinist Perpetrators on Trial*, 69. She writes that 3,830—or 62 percent of the leading operative officials—were replaced, including half of the heads of NKVD district offices in Moscow.

28. Naimark, *Stalin's Genocides*, 86.

29. Nikita Petrov, *Pervyi predsedatel' KGB: Ivan Serov* (Moscow: Materik, 2005), 15–17.

30. Petrov, *Pervyi predsedatel' KGB*, 19; Ivan Serov, *Zapiski iz chemodana: Tainye dnevniki pervogo predsedatelia KGB* (Moscow: Prosveshchenie, 2016), 20.

31. Anne Applebaum, *Iron Curtain: The Crushing of Eastern Europe, 1944–1956* (New York: Allen Lane, 2012), 215.

32. Naimark, *Stalin's Genocides*, 67.

33. William Chase, *Enemies within the Gates? The Comintern and the Stalinist Repression, 1934–1939* (New Haven: Yale University Press, 2001), 105.

34. Chase, *Enemies within the Gates?*, 162.

35. Andrzej Paczkowski, "Poland, the 'Enemy Nation,'" in *The Black Book of Communism: Crimes, Terror, Repression*, ed. Stéphane Courtois, Jonathan Murphy, and Mark Kramer (Cambridge, MA: Harvard University Press, 1999), 363–67.

36. "Soobshchenie narodnogo komissara vnutrennikh del SSSR L. P. Berii narodnomy komissary inostrannykh del V. M. Molotovu o khode osvobozhdeniia pol'skikh grazhdan iz mest zakliucheniia, ssylki i spetsposelenii NKVD," in *NKVD i pol'skoe podpol'e, 1944–1945: Po 'osobym papkam' I. V. Stalina*, ed. T. V. Volokitina et al. (Moscow: Rossiiskaia akademiia nauk, 1994), 40.

37. Marci Shore, *Caviar and Ashes: A Warsaw Generation's Life and Death in Marxism, 1918–1968* (New Haven: Yale University Press, 2006).

38. Jan de Weydenthal, *The Communists of Poland* (Stanford, CA: Hoover Institution Press, 1978), 31.

39. Zbigniew Błażyński, ed., *Mówi Józef Światło: Za kulisami bezpieki i partii 1940–1955* (Londyn: Polska Fundacja Kulturalna, 1985), 11–13.

40. Kotkin, *Stalin*, 672.

41. Kotkin, *Stalin*, 662.

42. Ulrich Weissgerber, *Giftige Worte der SED-Diktatur: Sprache als Instrument von Machtausübung und Ausgrenzung in der SBZ und der DDR* (Berlin: Lit, 2010), 94–284.

43. Amir Weiner and Aigi Rahi-Tamm, "Getting to Know You: The Soviet Surveillance System, 1939–57," *Kritika: Explorations in Russian and Eurasian History* 13, no. 1 (2012): 18.

44. "Pis'mo nachal'nika Opersektora MVD SSSR po provintsii Meklenburg i Zapadnaia Pomeraniia D. M. Nikitina nachal'niku provintsii M. A. Skosyrevu ob itogakh vyborov v nemetskie organy samoupravleniia provintsii," 24 September 1946, in *SVAG i nemetskie organy samoupravleniia, 1945–1949: Sbornik dokumentov*, ed. V. V. Zakharov (Moscow: Rossiiskaia politicheskaia entsiklopediia, 2006), 190–91.

45. The election took place soon after the unification of the Communist (KPD) and Social Democratic

(SPD) parties into the Socialist Unity Party (SED) in April 1946. The Soviets had helped orchestrate this merger and continued to favor the influence of the KPD within it.

46. "Iz dnevnika general'nogo konsula v Bratislave N. G. Novikova: Zapis' besedy s predsedatelem Slovatskogo natsional'nogo soveta K. Shmidke o neobkhodimosti vyiavleniia sviazei L. Raika i ego gruppy v KPCh o nekhvatke politicheskii podgotovlennykh kadrov i dr.," 4 October 1949, in *Vostochnaia Evropa v dokumentakh rossiiskikh arkhivov, 1944–1953*, ed. T. V. Volokitina et al., 2 vols. (Moscow: Sibirskii khronograf, 1997), 2:244–45.

47. "Pis'mo V. Lebedeva A. Ia. Vyshinskomu o polozhenii v rukovodstve PORP," 10 July 1949, in *Vostochnaia Evropa v dokumentakh rossiiskikh arkhivov*, 2:173.

48. "Iz pis'ma vitse-konsula SSSR s g. Shchetsine M. L. Dzhibladze poslu SSSR v Pol'she A. A. Sobolevu u zaveduiushchemu IV EO G. P. Arkad'evu o situatsii v organisatsiiakh PORP," 28 June 1951, in *Vostochnaia Evropa v dokumentakh rossiiskikh arkhivov*, 2:553–56.

49. Petrov, *Kto rukovodil organami gosbezopasnosti*, 548.

50. Petrov, *Kto rukovodil organami gosbezopasnosti*, 568–69.

51. "Soprovoditel'noe pis'mo V. S. Abakumova V. M. Molotovu s prilozheniem soobshcheniia sotrudnikov MGB SSSR M. T. Likhacheva i N. I. Makarova o rabote chekhoslovatskikh organov bezopasnosti," 16 March 1950, in *Vostochnaia Evropa v dokumentakh rossiiskikh arkhivov*, 2:285–87.

52. Stephen Kotkin, *Magnetic Mountain: Stalinism as a Civilization* (Berkeley: University of California Press, 1997).

53. "Spravka o nedostatkakh agenturno-operativnoi raboty organov obshchestvennoi bezopasnosti," 8 July 1951, Instytut Pamięci Narodowej (IPN), Warsaw, IPN BU 01988-1.

54. One of many examples was an exam for officers in the Internal Security Corps in Poland in 1947 that contained, noted one critical report, "too many Russianisms." It was difficult to avoid this, came the response, since "our lecturers have been trained in Russian regulations." See untitled letter to the head of the KBW, 24 March 1947, IPN BU 578/513.

55. There are many instances of this, but see, for example, Václav Havel, "On Evasive Thinking," speech given to the Union of Writers, 1965, https://www.vhlf.org/havel-quotes/speech-at-union-of-writers-1965.

56. Zubkova, *Pribaltika i Kreml'*, 158.

57. Zubkova, *Pribaltika i Kreml'*, 6.

58. David Brandenberger and Mikhail Zelenov, eds., *Stalin's Master Narrative: A Critical Edition of the History of the Communist Party of the Soviet Union (Bolsheviks). Short Course* (New Haven: Yale University Press, 2019).

59. Marc Jansen and Nikita Petrov, *Stalin's Loyal Executioner: People's Commissar Nikolai Ezhov, 1895–1940* (Stanford, CA: Hoover Institution Press, 2002), x.

60. "Pis'mo B. Z. Lebedeva I. V. Stalinu ob otsenke K. K. Rokossovskim situatsii v rukovodstve PORP, noiabr'skogo plenuma TsK PORP, nastroenii pol'skikh rabochikh i krest'ian I dr.," 26 February 1950, in *Vostochnaia Evropa v dokumentakh rossiiskikh arkhivov*, 2:311.

61. Vladislav Zubok, *A Failed Empire: The Soviet Union in the Cold War from Stalin to Gorbachev* (Chapel Hill: University of North Carolina Press, 2009), 8.

62. Elena Zubkova, *Russia after the War: Hopes, Illusions, and Disappointments*, trans. and ed. Hugh Ragsdale (Armonk, NY: M. E. Sharpe, 1998), 32.

63. Zubkova, *Russia after the War*, 19.

64. "Spravka o nedostatkakh agenturno-operativnoi raboty organov obshchestvennoi bezopasnosti," 8 July 1951, nonpaginated, IPN Warsaw, IPN BU 01988-1.

65. I describe this campaign at length in the chapter "Conquering the Polish Secret Police," in my *Security Empire: The Secret Police in Communist Eastern Europe* (New Haven: Yale University Press, 2020).

66. Amy Knight, *Beria: Stalin's First Lieutenant* (Princeton, NJ: Princeton University Press, 1993), 126.

67. Naimark, *Stalin's Genocides*, 89.

68. Jan Gross, *Revolution from Abroad: The Soviet Conquest of Poland's Western Ukraine and Western Belorussia* (Princeton, NJ: Princeton University Press, 2002).

69. Piotr Kosicki, "The Katyń Massacres of 1940," 8 September 2008, http://www.sciencespo.fr/mass
-violence-war-massacre-resistance/en/document/katyn-massacres-1940.

70. Zubkova, *Russia after the War*, 136.

71. Volokitina et al., *Vostochnaia Evropa v dokumentakh rossiiskikh arkhivov*, 2:87n2.

72. "Pis'mo V Lebedeva A Ya. Vyshinskomu o polozhenii v rukovodstve PORP," 10 July 1949, *Vostochnaia
Evropa v dokumentakh rossiiskikh arkhivov*, 2:177–78.

73. Amy Knight, *Beria: Stalin's First Lieutenant* (Princeton, NJ: Princeton University Press, 1993), 169.

74. Viola, *Perpetrators on Trial*, 21.

75. Naimark, *Stalin's Genocides*.

76. Knight, *Beria: Stalin's First Lieutenant*, 113.

77. David R. Shearer, *Policing Stalin's Socialism: Repression and Social Order in the Soviet Union, 1924–1953*
(New Haven: Yale University Press, 2009), 255.

78. Shearer, *Policing Stalin's Socialism*, 256.

79. Shearer, *Policing Stalin's Socialism*, 257.

80. "O nepravil'noi rabote mestnoi opergruppy organov NKVD: Raport voennogo komendanta g.
Kosvitz V. Kh. Gordienko nachal'niku komendantskoi sluzhby SVA provintsii Saksonii G. D.
Mukhinu o protivozakonnykh deistviiakh rabotnikov mestnoi opergruppy NKVD v otnoshenii
rabotnikov voennoi komendatury u apparata burgomistra," 31 October 1945, in *SVAG i nemetskie
organy samoupravleniia, 1945–1949: Sbornik dokumentov*, ed. N. V. Petrov, O. V. Lavinskaia, and D. N.
Nokhotovich (Moscow: ROSSPEN, 2006), 290–95.

81. Geoffrey Roberts, *Stalin's Wars: From World War to Cold War, 1939–1953* (New Haven: Yale University
Press, 2015), 332.

82. Julie Fedor, *Russia and the Cult of State Security: The Chekist Tradition from Lenin to Putin* (London:
Routledge, 2011), 30.

83. The term, of course, was *narusheniia sotsialisticheskoi zakonnosti*.

84. Fedor, *Russia and the Cult of State Security*, 30.

85. On *Izvestiia*, see "Pis'mo predstavitelia Sovinformbiuro V. Sokolovskogo i korrespondenta gazety
'Izvestiia' v Pol'she M. Iarovogo V. G. Grigor'ianu o nedostatkakh v propagande pol'skoi storo-
noi peredovogo opyta sovetskikh rabochikh i deiatel'nosti sovetov s SSSR," 3 November 1950, in
Sovetskii faktor v vostochnoi Evrope 1944–1953, ed. T. V. Volokitina et al. (Moscow: ROSSPEN, 2002),
2:395. The Soviet advisers taught the Czechs that 70–80 percent of embassy employees should also
be intelligence agents. See Karel Kaplan, *Sovětští poradci v Československu, 1949–1956* (Malá Strana:
Ústav pro soudobé dějiny AV ČR, 1993), 39–40; *Vostochnaia Evropa v dokumentakh rossiiskikh arkhivov*; and Volokitina et al., *Sovetskii faktor v vostochnoi Evrope*, vol. 2.

86. Kotkin, *Stalin*, 664.

87. Kotkin, *Stalin*, 852.

88. The best account of February 1948 in Czechoslovakia is Karel Kaplan, *Pět kapitol o únoru* (Brno:
Doplněk, 1997).

89. "Informatsionnaia zapiska otvetstvennogo sekretaria Obshcheslavianskogo komiteta I. N. Medvedeva v TsK VKP(b) o vnutripoliticheskom polozhenii v Chekhoslovakii posle fevral'skogo krizisa
1948," 29 March 1948, in *Vostochnaia Evropa v dokumentakh rossiiskikh arkhivov*, 1:806–11.

90. "Zapiska korrespondenta TASS v Prage V. S. Medova o vnutripoliticheskoi situatsii v Chekhoslovakii," 17 May 1949, in *Vostochnaia Evropa v dokumentakh rossiiskikh arkhivov*, 2:114.

91. Molly Pucci, "A Revolution in a Revolution: The Secret Police and the Origins of Stalinism in
Czechoslovakia," *East European Politics and Societies* 32, no. 1 (2020): 3–22.

92. Bradley Abrams, *The Struggle for the Soul of the Nation: Czech Culture and the Rise of Communism*
(Lanham, MD: Rowman and Littlefield, 2004), 51–52; Jiří Kocian and Markéta Devátá, *Únor 1948
v Československu nástup komunistické totality a proměny společnosti* (Prague: USD AV ČR, 2011).

93. "Zapiska korrespondenta TASS v Prage V. S. Medova," 111–12.

94. The Russian is *traditsionnyi dukh soprotivleniia*. It is unclear where this impression came from since

classic works in Czech culture such as *The Good Soldier Svejk* satirize precisely the opposite national trait. The purpose of the statement seems to be to build an otherwise questionable case for Soviet intervention.

95. "Zapiska korrespondenta TASS v Prage V. S. Medova," 115.

96. Volokitina et al., *Vostochnaia Evropa v dokumentakh rossiiskikh arkhivov*, 2:44.

97. Zubkova, *Pribaltika i Kreml'*, 6.

98. This issue is best explored in Stephane Courtois et al., eds., *The Black Book of Communism: Crimes, Terror, Repression* (Cambridge, MA: Harvard University Press, 1999).

The Black Sea Coast as a Landscape of Cold War Intelligence

Erik R. Scott

IN THE MIDST OF THE COLD WAR, IF VISITORS TO KOBULETI, A POPULAR resort town on Soviet Georgia's Black Sea coast, wandered south, they would follow a seaside road lined with palm trees or walk along the shores of its pebble beach, passing high-rise vacation complexes. On the outskirts of Batumi, they would be greeted by a lush botanical garden reaching up into the hills and showcasing the region's subtropical abundance with citrus groves and areas devoted to the exotic plants of the Mediterranean, South America, East Asia, and even distant Australia. In Batumi itself, they would find a bustling international port, visited by container ships and tankers from across the world; they would pass sailors strolling the streets, conversing in foreign languages. The Black Sea coast was a showcase for Soviet achievements and, especially in the post-Stalinist era, an opening to the world beyond Soviet borders.

If our travelers continued to head south from Batumi, however, they would soon enter a "forbidden border zone" (*zapretnaia pogranichnaia zona*) open only to carefully screened local residents and Soviet border troops, a restricted stretch of land whose topography was not detailed in public maps but instead considered classified information. The forbidden zone served as a buffer between the heavily trafficked port to the north and the nearby border with Turkey, a country described in a training manual for the Soviet border troops as a US-funded "base for the organization of subversive activity directed against the USSR."[1] If our imaginary travelers were not seized by the border troops, who patrolled the restricted area with guard dogs, or turned over by one of the local residents, who earned money for apprehending unauthorized outsiders, they would soon encounter the physical realities of the border itself: high-voltage fences, watchtowers, alarm systems, and search lights trained along the coast to catch those who sought to cross by sea.

Recent scholarship has depicted the Black Sea region as a "bridge" for international flows within and beyond the socialist camp, a welcome correction to an older historiographical tradition that rendered the Soviet Union as an isolated state behind a restrictive Iron Curtain.[2] Yet historians do not necessarily need to choose between bridges and borders. Along the Black Sea, resort complexes and border checkpoints operated in close proximity and were part of an interlocking system for governing mobility through positive inducements as well as disciplinary coercion; extending far beyond the border strip, this system was designed to channel the authorized movement of people, goods, and culture while restraining unauthorized exit.[3] The same mobility regime that transported ideologically reliable workers from deep in the Soviet interior to vacation along the Black Sea coast, fostered travel within the socialist camp, and permitted the entry of vetted foreign ships, sailors, and goods also enforced the immobility of those who sought to move beyond Soviet borders without state sanction.[4]

Most historians of Soviet borders have focused on their creation in the 1920s and 1930s and argued for their hardening over time.[5] Andrea Chandler has claimed that Soviet border controls as "institutions of isolation" took shape in this period and became "more elaborate, more convoluted, and more prohibitive," remaining in place until the collapse of the USSR.[6] Terry Martin, Nathalie Moine, and David Shearer have detailed the toolkit Stalinist authorities developed to govern movement in the borderlands: restricted zones, passport and registration controls, secret police surveillance, and, when these measures were deemed insufficient, full-scale ethnic cleansing.[7] Andrei Shlyakhter has argued for an "interwar Iron Curtain" that arose out of efforts to combat contraband trade.[8] While Sabine Dullin has traced a number of Soviet border enforcement practices back to the late tsarist period, her book focuses on the border's role in constructing the Stalinist "fortress" state and its dual nature as a line of defense but also a front for ideological and military expansion.[9] Scholarly understanding of how Soviet border enforcement evolved after Stalin, by comparison, remains tentative and largely confined to small sections of the state's western border.[10]

Despite the solidity suggested by the Iron Curtain paradigm, Soviet border enforcement continued to evolve over the course of the Cold War, responding in sophisticated ways to the global outreach policies of the post-Stalinist state as well as the external pressures of economic and cultural globalization.[11] To be sure, the repertoire of those tasked with defending the border drew on some long-standing practices: gathering statistics, running informants, employing undercover operatives, and collaborating with local residents. Yet these practices grew more refined, infused with new technologies, benefiting from increased capacity for "prophylactic" policing, and integrated into the expansion of sanctioned mobility within and beyond the Soviet state. Although most scholarship chronicles the closing—or opening—of Soviet borders over time, the post-Stalinist mobility regime consisted of regulated and surveilled openings as well as enforced closures.

The borderlands along the Black Sea arguably offer the best view of the Soviet state's governance of external and internal mobility in a Cold War context.[12] The Black Sea was home to the Soviet Union's busiest port, Odesa, which was open to foreign ships and sailors even as port cities elsewhere, such as Vladivostok, remained closed. It offered a limited point of entry for capitalist commerce, and it was a key node where economic and social linkages forged among Warsaw Pact states came together. The region featured the longest boundary between the socialist superpower and the North Atlantic Treaty Organization (NATO), a critical fault line for Cold War mobility; after the construction of the Berlin Wall, neighboring Turkey was the primary destination for Soviet citizens seeking to defect abroad.[13] Even more than the area surrounding the Baltic, the Black Sea littoral was ethnically diverse, home to dozens of nationalities and dotted with ethnically defined autonomous regions, including the one where Batumi was located: the Adjar Autonomous Soviet Socialist Republic, a region of Georgia with a historically Muslim population. In more practical terms, the recent declassification of KGB archives in Ukraine and Georgia offers scholars an unprecedented view into the state's southern maritime border and its development until the very end of the Soviet period. Despite the region's diversity, the KGB, which oversaw border enforcement, conceived of the entire region—its resorts and ports as well as its restricted areas and military installations—as a single border district and a unified landscape to be cultivated and monitored in the interests of Cold War intelligence. Not only did this landscape of intelligence bear the physical imprint of border fences, guard posts, and radar stations, but its cultural and economic infrastructure was also sown with agents and informants.

If we consider the region's entry points, leisure areas, trade facilities, and exit controls as constituting a single landscape, then secret police officials sought to be that landscape's primary architects: they sculpted the region's demographics, first by "weeding" and culling unwanted nationalities in the Stalinist era, and later by the more selective pruning of undesirable individuals and unwanted visitors in its restricted areas; they sought to guide its channels for movement as they might control a landscape's watercourses, allowing for the flow of authorized trade and travelers to build up the Soviet Union's international economic linkages, but shoring up against the flow of contraband trade and unauthorized migrants; finally, in the most literal sense of shaping the landscape, they supervised their own construction projects—building fences, digging trenches, and pouring concrete in ways that transformed the physical environment in a manner no less profound than the massive, centrally planned resorts that lined the Black Sea coast.[14]

Landscape also provides a useful metaphor for analyzing KGB records as historical sources. It directs our attention to the circumstances of their production and their modes of representation, skirting the temptation of treating documents authored by the secret police as authoritative accounts of the past because of the naturalistic detail with which they recorded events, actions, and even the habits of everyday life.[15] The art historian W. J. T. Mitchell argues that landscapes in painting are an "instrument of cultural power" that "naturalizes a cultural and social construction, representing an artificial world as if it were simply given and inevitable." Although it is often perceived as stemming from a "quest for pure painting, freed of literary concerns and representation," Mitchell makes the case that landscape painting was in fact an instrument of European imperialism.[16] The KGB's rendering of the Black Sea coast can similarly be described as an exercise in seemingly objective representation that rendered the region as a zone of secret police control and shored up the multiethnic Soviet empire. Because KGB reports, like the maps that detailed the border region's geographic terrain, were classified, it can be assumed that the KGB's authors conjured this representation of the region's landscape to suit their own purposes.

The imagined landscape detailed in KGB documents was perhaps a self-serving exaggeration to impress supervisors in Moscow, and its hold on the human actors who inhabited the landscape was never complete. Yet it did shape the way people moved through the territory, and it was constituted through real systems of screening and surveillance. In these ways, it overlaid the entire Black Sea coast: thriving ports were also places of information gathering; the internationally celebrated resort destination of Yalta was just down the coast from the tightly secured Sevastopol Naval Base, and facilities in both locales were closely monitored by agents of the KGB. Soviet officials envisioned cultivating the region as an orderly and governable border space while keeping it sufficiently open to the outside world to meet state aims. As will be seen, however, their policies inadvertently destabilized this vision, and various forms of disorder crept into the picture.

This chapter draws primarily on the files of the Red Banner Western Border District (Krasnoznamennyi Zapadnyi pogranichnyi okrug, KZPO) of the Soviet Border Troops, which operated under the auspices of the KGB. Based in Kyiv but tasked with patrolling most of the Black Sea littoral, it had a "special department" responsible for monitoring "special government objects" and engaging in counterintelligence along the coast. The chapter also incorporates criminal cases from the Georgian KGB to examine the operation of the "forbidden border zone" with Turkey, and it uses *Pogranichnik*, the closed-circulation Soviet Border Troop journal, to look at how the border was understood by those tasked with defending it. Whenever possible, these sources are complemented by KGB materials deposited in Moscow's state and party archives. The chapter begins by considering how the Black Sea's intelligence landscape took shape after World War II, continues by examining how this landscape was monitored to allow for selective openings and closings, and concludes by looking at how state-led efforts to maintain the landscape along the border paradoxically produced further illegality, even as other elements of the Soviet mobility regime proved more enduring.

DESIGNING THE LANDSCAPE

Although its strategic importance increased with the advent of the Cold War and the entry of Turkey into NATO, the Black Sea region had long been seen as a troublesome and poorly defended borderland.[17] A profoundly multiethnic space, many of its local inhabitants shared ethnic, religious, cultural, and economic connections with populations outside the Soviet Union. These ties were sometimes viewed positively as a beachhead for the expansion of Soviet influence into neighboring countries, as they were in the 1920s and even in more briefly after World War II.[18] More often, they were seen as a source of vulnerability. The sense of ideological danger was heightened by the state's limited capacity to patrol the maritime expanses of the Black Sea, the thriving market in illicit foreign goods that could be found in its port cities even after licit trade was curtailed, and the ease with which foreign media broadcasts could be picked up in the region.[19] These perceived security challenges were addressed by transforming the region's demographic landscape, augmenting the border's physical presence on the ground, enforcing a restricted border zone, and building the network of spies and informants in its ports and resorts.

Sorting the region's population and shaping its demographic contours were the top priority: as Soviet ideology had it, "the people defend the border," and the boundary was only as strong as the population's ideological loyalty.[20] The most drastic efforts to design the landscape in demographic terms built on previous mass deportations pursued by the Stalinist state: in 1944, Meskhetian Turks and Kurds were deported away from the Turkish border; from 1945 to 1951, deportations of nearby ethnic groups, including Laz and Pontian Greeks, continued on a smaller scale, sometimes targeting particular families.[21] Ideological loyalty was defined by nationality, and groups with historic cross-border ties were deemed unreliable and moved to the interior. At the same time, the Black Sea's western borderlands, which had been invaded and occupied by the German army during the war, were a primary site for the repatriation and filtration of Soviet citizens. Even as Meskhetian Turks, Kurds, Laz, and Pontian Greeks were removed, Ukrainians were returned, sometimes by force, and screened for wartime collaboration or participation in anti-Soviet organizations, such as the Organization of Ukrainian Nationalists.[22] Those found guilty were typically barred from living in the border zone, while the families of those who refused to return home were monitored for contact with their sons, daughters, brothers, and sisters abroad.[23]

The local residents who remained were depicted as a reliable feature of the landscape in the Soviet Border Troop journal *Pogranichnik*. One article from a 1962 issue recounted the story of a simple Georgian woman working on the rising hills of a tea plantation near the border; unexpectedly confronted by an unknown man who emerged from the bushes nearby, she bravely eluded him and ran to the border guard base to report the intruder.[24] Transplanted onto this landscape of lush vegetation and trusty locals was a border troop leadership that was overwhelmingly Slavic—rather than Georgian, Armenian, or Azerbaijani—in composition and, among its rank-and-file, included border guards drafted from the landlocked Soviet interior who were away from home for the first time in their lives.[25] *Pogranichnik* portrayed the hierarchically oriented but interdependent relationship between border troops and locals as a voluntary expression of Soviet unity, signaling the ways that the locals, with their knowledge of the terrain, could prove useful by signing up for voluntary people's guards (*druzhiny*), patrolling roads and population centers, and informing border troop units of the appearance of any suspicious persons in the border zone.

Internal reports from the Western Border District reveal a more uneasy relationship with the local population. Border guards rotated in and out, while local residents remained; the latter were not always inclined to cooperate. For example, a pair from Georgia seeking to flee across the Soviet-Turkish border reported that local shepherds gave them bread and advice on how to proceed.[26] Instead of counting on the "fraternal brotherhood" of Soviet nationalities, KZPO officials established material incentives for locals to assist Soviet intelligence. On the one hand, *druzhinniki* (members of *druzhiny*) might be rewarded for their efforts: the 1966 work plan for the KZPO noted that locals could be paid up to 400 rubles for apprehending illegal border crossers, an enormous sum of money.[27] On the other hand, failing to report a potential case of defection could lead to prosecution. At the very least, KZPO officials counted on the fact that many of those seeking to flee to Turkey were not even from the region and thus struck local villagers as suspicious outsiders in any case.

Even as KZPO officials surveilled the local population, the KGB in Moscow kept a close eye on the effectiveness of KZPO border measures as well as the readiness of regional authorities to prevent exit. A report submitted by KGB Chief Aleksandr Shelepin to the Party's Central Committee in August 1959 reported on the illegal crossing of a twenty-eight-year-old Georgian man, Valiko Sepiashvili, to Turkey. In part, Shelepin was worried that Sepiashvili had managed to elude the relatively new motion-sensitive alarm and flood-light system set up in the "forbidden border zone" by fleeing in the middle of the night during a loud thunderstorm. An even greater concern, however, was that Sepiashvili, a person without a fixed occupation who did odd jobs as a carpenter, had been cleared to reside in the border town of Sarpi by the Batumi police. Shelepin's report hinted at corruption by pointing out that the carpenter had ties with prominent local officials, whose houses he worked on. Tasked with addressing the case, Georgia's Communist Party found that local authorities and the local branch of the KGB in the Adjara region had failed to enforce the rules that would have kept Sepiashvili away from the "forbidden border zone." Responding to the Central Committee, Georgia's Communist Party leaders called for stricter enforcement and a "strengthening of political-educational work" among the local population.[28]

Establishing a system of surveillance to monitor nearby Batumi and other Black Sea port cities was more difficult: these cities had to remain open for trade, while remaining impervious to contraband goods, "harmful" foreign influences, and the designs of hostile Western intelligence agencies. In 1963, the KGB in Moscow launched a comprehensive plan to improve and expand counterintelligence operations in Soviet ports and on Soviet ships traveling abroad. Officers were tasked with investigating foreign sailors for ties to the "intelligence services of the opponent" and identifying Soviet citizens in ports inclined to "treasonous" behavior, such as making plans to defect to Turkey.[29]

Despite such efforts to strengthen central control over the Black Sea landscape, however, enforcing its physical, economic, and ideological borders proved difficult. In 1968, a report submitted by Georgia's leadership to the Central Committee noted 219 cases of border violations in the prior five years; of these, 180 occurred in the vicinity of Batumi. The "mass influx of citizens" into Batumi and the "possibility for their unlimited and uncontrolled stay there" meant that the port city was "turning into a base for violators of the border and the border regime," especially for those "preparing to flee abroad." The port city needed to remain open for trade and travel, but such openness meant that from 1963 to 1968 a staggering fifty thousand Soviet citizens were stopped by the police in the region for either not carrying the correct identification documents or not having the right to be in the "forbidden border zone." To address the issue, the Soviet Council of Ministers approved a tactic that had first been employed along sections of the western border in the 1930s: the complete "passportization" of the rural population outside of Batumi and in other Georgian border regions, with documents to be carried by every adult and regular passport checks sealing the port of Batumi off from the sensitive border zone to its south.[30] While rural residents elsewhere in the Soviet Union remained ineligible to obtain passports—the result of a long-standing policy bent on binding them to local collective farms—the state's desire to render the population living in border regions legible overrode concerns about the internal mobility of rural Soviets.[31] Yet despite the use of established Stalinist methods, the extension of oversight from Moscow, the expansion of material incentives, and the deployment of new technologies like the motion-sensitive alarm, the tension between the port, a place of international opening, and the border area, a place of enforced enclosure, remained.[32]

PATROLLING THE LANDSCAPE

This tension meant that the intelligence landscape so carefully rendered in KGB reports required constant tending. Yet the KZPO's leadership worried that those responsible for monitoring and defending the Soviet border might be lulled into a false sense of security by the region's charms as a seaside destination. These concerns surfaced on the pages of *Pogranichnik*, sometimes couched in humor: a 1968 issue included a cartoon depicting Soviet vacationers relaxing and going on romantic strolls along the seaside, while in the background a snorkel appeared (presumably belonging to a foreign agent) and, coming out of it, a text bubble reading, "Jack, over here!"[33] The call for constant vigilance in the region's ports and resorts was no joke: a KZPO work plan from the same year alerted Border Troop units that Western states not only sought to infiltrate the Soviet Union by sending undercover agents posing as foreign sailors and tourists, but that the Soviet Union's opponents were also poised to use robotic "ducks" to spy on military installations along the Black Sea coastline.[34]

Part of the issue was that the waters surrounding port cities were notoriously difficult to patrol: border guards posted to the Black Sea region not only had to guard land crossings, but they also had to surveil coastal waters, relying on speedboats to monitor unauthorized movement within two miles of the coast as best they could.[35] On the water, there could be no fences, no stable guard posts, and no mobilization of local villagers to aid in surveillance efforts. As a feature in *Pogranichnik* noted, the Soviet state's maritime boundaries had "neither distinguishable markings nor striped columns," but they made up the world's longest "anchor chain": at over 47,000 miles, they exceeded the length of the equator.[36] The fact that these relatively porous maritime boundaries were proximate to bustling cities where Western spies could easily blend in with tourists and sailors from around the world made defending the border even more complicated.

The global connections of Soviet port cities such as Batumi and Odesa, however, also made them zones of opportunity for Soviet intelligence gathering. The KZPO's leadership urged intelligence officers to keep a particularly close watch on foreign sailors; some were cultivated as assets and informants who could collect information and alert Soviet officials to the activities of Western intelligence, while others were investigated for participating in contraband trade or offering to smuggle Soviet citizens out of the country.[37] Even before foreign visitors arrived, Soviet border troops carefully screened the passenger manifests of incoming ships, scrutinizing any foreign sailors with Russian-language skills or relatives in the USSR as foreign spies or potential recruits. In port, the facilities opened for sailors from abroad, billed as places of international maritime friendship, were consistently surveilled to identify sailors of "operational interest." Odesa's Interklub, the crown jewel in a state-sponsored network ostensibly designed to provide sailors of all nationalities— "the Englishman and the Italian, the resident from sultry Africa and the one from chilly Norway, the German and the Pole, the Greek and the Russian"— the opportunity to socialize together was in fact a frequent site of intelligence operations.[38]

The number of foreigners in Soviet ports to be monitored was by no means negligible: by 1978, thirty-two Soviet ports were visited annually by over five thousand ships from capitalist countries carrying over 120,000 people.[39] KGB reports give a sense of those who were seen as targets of opportunity: a Greek sailor who had befriended a young Soviet woman working in the processing area of the port of Odesa was said to have a "loyal attitude . . . toward the Soviet people" and a "dislike of Americans," recruited under the codename

"Olimp" (Olympus), and used to gather information on the operation of foreign shipping lines; an Italian sailor working on an Israeli ship who hoped to marry a Soviet woman he met in port was recruited to spy on his shipmates; and still more foreign sailors were recruited by the gathering of "compromising materials" on them, usually related to participation in contraband trade (which typically broke the rules of foreign ships as well as Soviet laws) or sexual misbehavior on shore.[40]

In addition to surveilling the activities of foreign crews, authorities scrutinized Soviet citizens who engaged in improper "contact with foreign sailors."[41] In the late fall and winter of 1969, an undercover agent, code-named "Birch Tree," reported that a nineteen-year-old woman who worked as a secretary in the town of Izmail, located near Odesa, maintained connections with visiting Austrian sailors in the town port. Some simply gave her presents, Birch Tree reported, while others reportedly engaged in "intimate relationships" with the young woman. In the eyes of the KGB, these sexual transgressions were inextricable from ideological transgressions, since she also praised living standards in Austria and spoke of her desire to live there. She was flagged by the KZPO's intelligence division in Odesa for further investigation; her fate is unclear, but it is possible that she was subsequently recruited as an agent, which would have allowed her to avoid criminal prosecution.[42]

Along with the risk of unauthorized sexual relations, contraband trade was seen as an ideologically dangerous violation of Soviet borders by harmful goods, linked to the presence of foreign sailors and tourists.[43] The phenomenon was particularly pronounced in Odesa, the Soviet Union's busiest port for both licit and illicit trade: in 1960 alone, 603,979 rubles of contraband goods were seized in the Black Sea city.[44] These goods consisted of prosaic consumer items—such as clothing, scarves and jewelry—but also included foreign books and magazines deemed counter to Soviet ideology. By the 1970s, KZPO officials were particularly concerned about the circulation of *tamizdat*, samizdat, and "nationalist" publications in port cities that might foster anti-Soviet sentiment among the region's Ukrainian and Jewish populations.[45]

Black Sea port cities not only were a place of foreign infiltration but also functioned as a point of unauthorized exit for Soviet citizens who might sneak aboard a foreign ship in secret or as a result of a deal arranged with foreign crewmembers. In this regard, even sailors from other socialist countries were viewed warily. In 1966, the KGB arrested Gennadii Zakharov, an eighteen-year-old from Krasnoiarsk, who, facing "family difficulties" and reportedly falling under the influence of Voice of America broadcasts, had left his home in the Russian interior and made his way toward the Black Sea in the hope of fleeing abroad. In the port of Zhdanov, he befriended the captain of a Bulgarian ship.

After a night spent drinking together, the captain promised the young man that he would bring him to Bulgaria, introduce him to his daughter, and sign him up for English-language classes. From Bulgaria, Zakharov hoped to make his way to the capitalist West. Through its network of informants, the KGB learned of the conversation and sentenced Zakharov to death for "betrayal of the Motherland in the form of flight abroad." However, in a telling sign of its shift to subtler tactics in the post-Stalinist period, Soviet intelligence ultimately chose to take a "prophylactic" approach and instead turned Zakharov into an agent to identify other potential escapees in the port.[46]

Soviet officials sought to prevent unauthorized exit by targeting foreign crews: foreign ships could be penalized for harboring fugitives from Soviet justice, and the Soviet criminal code had a special provision allowing Soviet authorities to board ships and seize people in Soviet territorial waters if a crime was committed, including the crime of "illegal exit or illegal entry into the USSR."[47] Accordingly, ships from capitalist as well as socialist states frequently turned stowaways over to Soviet law enforcement.[48] Defectors sometimes had better luck bribing foreign crewmembers to look the other way. KGB records suggest that this method of smuggling oneself out of the Soviet Union was not arranged through specialized middlemen but instead organized on an ad hoc basis, with deals reached between Soviets wishing to emigrate and foreign sailors willing to assist them. The money involved was substantial: in 1979, one Soviet citizen offered ten thousand US dollars and three thousand Soviet rubles to a Greek captain to spirit him out of the country after he was denied an exit visa.[49] The KGB sought to prevent the formation of more permanent smuggling networks by recruiting agents among foreign sailors and domestic dock workers, whose duty it was to report any suspicious activity and whose presence raised the possibility that the person a would-be defector approached was cooperating with Soviet authorities.

Those desperate to leave sometimes pursued extreme measures. A number of people sought to swim across the Black Sea to gain asylum. In 1962, Petr Patrushev, a professional Soviet swimmer, managed to successfully swim from Batumi to Turkey, a distance of several miles. Abroad, he was celebrated as "The Man Who Swam from Russia."[50] Others followed his example but were not so fortunate. In August 1963, Iurii Vetokhin, a young man from Leningrad and a Communist Party member, sought to swim the same route. Arrested by the authorities, he was sent to a psychiatric hospital for treatment. In December 1967, expelled from the Communist Party, he sought to flee again, this time from Crimea. Entering the waters of the Black Sea, he began to swim in the direction of Turkey but was detained by a Soviet military ship five miles from the Crimean coast. Once again, he was hospitalized, this time with an alleged "paranoid personality disorder." Although his treatment showcased the harsh measures the Soviet state took against unauthorized border cross-ers, his final journey evidenced the difficulty of fully controlling maritime boundaries: freed from psychiatric imprisonment, in 1979 Vetokhin booked a ticket on a Soviet cruise ship that traveled across the Pacific but made no stops in foreign ports; diving off the ship, he managed to swim to Indonesia, where he successfully claimed asylum.[51] Efforts to evade the border by swimming continued into the late Soviet period: in 1985, Oleg Sofianik, a dissident who had refused to serve in the Soviet army, sought to swim from a cruise vessel sailing from Sukhumi to Batumi. After three days in the water, he was appre-hended by a border patrol ship, accused of "illegal border crossing," and sent to a psychiatric clinic after stating that he would rather die at sea than live in the Soviet Union.[52]

Soviet officials strove to shore up the border in the wake of such crossings. At a closed meeting of the KGB's Counterintelligence Directorate in March 1978, KGB Chief Iurii Andropov warned of the continued problem of "weakly defended spots on maritime and waterway borders."[53] A subsequent directive from the KGB's headquarters in Moscow called on the KZPO's counterin-telligence branch to report all "politically immature and morally unstable" Soviet citizens involved in construction, sporting ventures, and fishing along the coastline for potential transfer to the interior.[54] Concerns grew that Soviet border troops themselves were unreliable to guard port cities, and numerous disciplinary cases were initiated against border guards accused of participat-ing in contraband trade, carousing with domestic and foreign sailors, consort-ing with prostitutes, and carelessly handling classified information.[55]

In a few prominent cases, Soviet border troops themselves harbored plans to flee abroad. In 1977, Sergei Savchenko, a nineteen-year-old who served with the border troops along the Black Sea, was called in for questioning. Agents had heard him speaking to a fellow recruit about the possibility of using underwater breathing equipment to flee across the border by sea. Perhaps because his plan was so poorly developed, he was not dismissed or imprisoned but instead reassigned to a construction unit of the border guards near Sverd-lovsk, far from the border. In response, he wrote, "I am thankful to the organs of the KGB that they caught me before I committed the gravest of crimes—treason—stopping me before I took the fateful step down this criminal path." While such a statement was clearly made under pressure, KGB officials relayed it to their superiors and claimed success for reeducating an impressionable young man who had fallen "under the influence of foreign anti-Soviet radio programs" near the border.[56]

In reality, dramatic waterborne escapes were a rare occurrence, punctuating an existence for border troops that was more often characterized by the distractions of a seaside setting or the tedium of standing guard at a border post for hours at a time. In his novel *nu geshinia, deda!* (Don't Be Afraid, Mama!), published in 1971, the Georgian author Nodar Dumbadze portrayed the subtle yet crucial nature of the boundary that ran between the Georgian SSR and Turkey and divided the Black Sea coast. For the novel's protagonist, a young Georgian man assigned to guard this sensitive section of the border, the geographic limits of the Soviet Union at first seem like a dull rather than a dangerous place. Dumbadze's prose lulls the reader into a sense of complacency, until a dramatic incident occurs: a Russian man attempts to illegally cross into Turkey and the troops are suddenly called into action, arresting the violator of the Soviet Union's border regime.[57] Dumbadze's description had official support and was based on several months the author spent with the Batumi border troop detachment while conducting research for the novel. A subsequent feature in *Pogranichnik* praised Dumbadze for depicting the border not simply as a "line on the map," but as a "border of social and moral values, a border between good and evil."[58] In addition to supporting publications like Dumbadze's novel, the KGB organized frequent exercises in which "educational 'border violators'" tested the readiness of border troops, with undercover Soviet agents appearing at checkpoints with forged documents to see if guards noticed them, asking about border defenses in sensitive areas to see if local inhabitants reported them, and wandering along rail lines to see if they would be apprehended.[59] Such exercises meant that those on the ground, whether local residents or border guards themselves, could never be sure when they were being surveilled by Soviet intelligence.

WANDERERS IN THE LANDSCAPE

The effort to establish a meticulously monitored Black Sea coast turned the landscape into one of permanent suspicion. In effect, Soviet laws and KGB methods produced illegality by criminalizing any unauthorized movement, especially in the "forbidden border zone" outside Batumi. KZPO reports generally did not indicate whether those apprehended near the border were sneaking into the Soviet Union or seeking to defect; instead, they referred to any unsanctioned human presence in the border zone as a "violator" (*narushitel'*), regardless of whether the person seized was a duplicitous Western agent or simply a hapless Soviet citizen. KZPO policies that established incentives for border troops to seize as many "violators" as possible fueled a sense of rampant criminality.[60] Each KZPO border unit tabulated instances of illegal border crossing, defection, and contraband trade in quarterly and annual reports. These reports were bundled by the KZPO's leadership in Kyiv and sent to the headquarters of the Soviet Border Troops in Moscow. The leadership of the Soviet Border Troops responded by issuing instructions and guidelines for improvement, such as the 14 March 1964 directive "On Measures for the Improvement of Counterintelligence Work by the KGB Border Troops."[61] The directive used percentages of people and goods seized at various areas of the Soviet border to indicate the relative effectiveness of different border units. Such directives were issued each year and adhered to a similar format; the value of contraband goods seized and the number of border crossers apprehended compared to the previous year were considered key performance indicators.[62] While quotas were not set from on high, central directives identified favorably performing border divisions, such as the troops of the Transcaucasian District, and criticized border divisions whose numbers had slipped, including the KZPO.[63] As a result, there was constant pressure from above to criminalize and prosecute any potentially suspicious activity along the border.

An examination of case files from the Georgian KGB shows how marginal border "wanderers"—nearly always young men—were criminalized as dangerous violators and prosecuted, even though their motives were often murky and not explicitly political.[64] For some, flight into the border zone was precipitated by legal difficulties. One such case was that of Vladimir Kuziakin, a young man from Krasnoiarsk Krai who had worked on a steamship in Odesa. After stealing a box of fur hats from the ship, he feared getting caught and journeyed south into the Soviet-Turkish border zone, where he was apprehended in January 1956.[65] Others sought to escape personal problems or family troubles. Nikolai Sergeev, a nineteen-year-old painter, fled a Moscow worksite where his mother had helped secure employment for him and departed for Batumi, traveling southward into the restricted border zone, where he was seized by local residents.[66] Others apprehended in the border zone had a falling-out with a spouse, a history of drinking, or a previously documented mental illness.

Some, such as the twenty-one-year-old Valentin Pozhilov, seemed to be perpetual itinerants rather than rooted members of Soviet society. Pozhilov had the proper proletarian credentials—he had been trained as a plumber—but rather than finding a fixed place of employment, he moved from his home in the northwestern city of Petrozavodsk to Sverdlovsk in Siberia, and then to Krasnoiarsk. He turned up twice in the restricted border zone outside Batumi: once in 1958, and again in 1960, when he was seized in a local village and found to be without documents. Investigators noted that it had been several years since he had last worked and reported that following his stay in Krasnoiarsk he had "taken up wandering" (*stal brodniazhnichat*).[67] Another "wanderer" was Viktor Rochniak, a twenty-eight-year-old from the Russian Far East who did odd jobs in Siberia, Uzbekistan, and Turkmenistan before traveling to Sochi and then Batumi. Reportedly inspired by a Voice of America broadcast he heard in Turkmenistan, he acquired a basic map of the European portion of the USSR and walked into the border zone, where he was seized in October 1960 on the banks of the Chorokhi River.[68] Blaming an ideologically inimical foreign radio program for the unauthorized mobility of a person who had already crisscrossed the Soviet Union may have been an effort to rationalize Rochniak's seemingly aimless peregrinations. In cases where KGB investigators failed to establish a clear motive for unlawful migration, they were prepared to consider the very "attempt to infiltrate the forbidden border zone as evidence of intent" to commit treason.[69]

The level of scrutiny was only slightly less outside of the restricted border zone. The KGB's prosecution of suspicious individuals seized in Yalta and Batumi cast the broader Black Sea coast as a dangerous place of contact between problematic Soviet citizens and foreigners. In 1961, the Ukrainian KGB arrested twenty-three-year-old Valerii Balakirev in Yalta. The young man, who had earlier been charged with theft, reportedly moved to the resort area by using a false passport. There he repeatedly approached foreign tourists, seeking to buy things from them, including "anti-Soviet" books and magazines; he even reportedly "praised Fascist Germany and its former leaders" in a conversation with tourists from West Germany. His alleged engagement in contraband trade, pro-Nazi sympathies, and confessed desire to flee abroad were, in the KGB's view, symptomatic of an ideological orientation antithetical to socialism; he was immediately removed from the border region and sentenced to five years of hard labor.[70] The meticulous detail with which his crimes were reported suggests that the agent and informant networks the KGB operated in Yalta and other resort destinations had tracked him long before his arrest. The following year, the KGB arrested two young men found clinging to a Yugoslav ship docked in Batumi's harbor. A subsequent investigation found that their attempted exit in the sensitive border region was linked to harmful foreign influences that had lured them to the border city: one, surveilled for years by the KGB, had maintained ties with a US journalist he had met at the American Exhibition in Moscow in 1959, and both were part of a circle of young people in Tbilisi drawn, in the words of investigators, to "new and repulsive forms of entertainment," including dancing to "rock-and-roll and boogie-woogie" and mixing with "unknown girls of easy virtue and youths without a determined occupation."[71] Among the crimes they were charged with was possession of a stolen map detailing the Soviet-Turkish border zone. Even as shades of lawlessness crept into its margins, it was the KGB's privilege alone to know the contours of the Black Sea's intelligence landscape.

THE STRUGGLE AGAINST FORMALISM AND
THE FATE OF THE SOVIET LANDSCAPE

If landscape is a suitable metaphor for describing the KGB's rendering of the Black Sea borderlands, then it is fitting that another term with artistic connotations, "formalism," consistently appeared in KZPO reports and in the pages of the Soviet border troop journal, beginning in the early 1960s and continuing through the late 1980s.[72] In the words of one article in *Pogranichnik*, "the defense of the border is an art"; formalism, however, entailed the loss of the creative impulse. It meant going through the motions of a job that largely consisted of watching and waiting, patrolling the same routes each day, relying on the same circle of agents and informants, asking them the same questions, mindlessly filling out forms, and failing to notice the covert movements of ideologically suspect individuals.[73] Border troops were urged to be more vigilant in patrolling the landscape, to develop new networks of informants rather than relying on existing contacts, and to take the initiative if they observed suspicious behavior rather than waiting for orders from above.[74] Yet this rendering of the Black Sea coast as a landscape meriting constant vigilance verged on paranoia and led to bizarre conspiracy theories. With the advent of Gorbachev's policies of glasnost and perestroika, *Pogranichnik* published several articles addressing—and attempting to dismiss—the UFO sightings frequently reported by troops posted along the Soviet border.[75] It is not unreasonable to assume that such sightings may have been stoked by official publications that warned border guards to be alert to unusual sounds, light signals, and even robotic ducks.

Of course, not all suspicions were paranoid, and this landscape of Cold War intelligence was to some extent mutually constituted by Western as well as Soviet policies. A glimpse at the records of the intelligence agency of the Soviet Union's "main opponent" reveals no evidence of robotic ducks but does establish that Soviet concerns that Western civilian vessels were being used to carry out visual and radio surveillance of Soviet naval installations on the Black Sea were not unfounded.[76] Soviet border troops who defected to Turkey were questioned at length about border defenses by US intelligence, and Soviet sailors who jumped ship were asked about the layout of Soviet ports and the working conditions on board Soviet vessels.[77] While more aggressive efforts by the Central Intelligence Agency (CIA) to sneak agents into the Soviet Union, launched in coordination with anti-Soviet émigré organizations, fizzled by the late 1950s, they contributed to the sense of insecurity in the socialist state's borderlands and remained a residual concern in the KZPO's reports decades later.[78]

Although these foreign threats were real, the KGB's securitization of the entire region to counter them raises the question of whether the secret police's methods were effective in achieving its goals. A fine-grained examination of the border zone reveals a far more haphazard intelligence operation than that suggested by the scholarly literature describing the KGB as a tightly disciplined and nearly omnipotent institution.[79] Relations with local residents were strained and characterized by mutual distrust, alarm systems malfunctioned, falsified documents were overlooked, and border troops grew complacent or dreamed of taking flight even as their supervisors exaggerated the apprehension of "violators" to impress superiors in Moscow. Where KGB policies were strictly implemented, they criminalized a wide swath of behavior, causing cases of unauthorized movement to rise steeply. Granted, widespread suspicion, to the extent that it undermined undesirable solidarities between Soviets and foreigners, may have been an intended byproduct of the KGB's web of surveillance, and boosted figures may have served the KGB's institutional interests in justifying the need for further policing. However, if we assume that the ultimate goal of KGB policies was the maintenance of order, it is striking that they effectively generated a constant state of unrest along the border.

While the KGB used increasingly sophisticated means to surveil the region and regulate its openings to the outside world, a 1987 report depicted a border buckling under the weight of global flows across Soviet-enforced boundaries as well as tensions within them. According to the report's authors, the trade in Western contraband goods in the Black Sea region was booming, and border guards were taking part in it. In a telling sign of the times, one guard was even caught with videocassettes of two of the decade's leading anticommunist blockbusters, *Rambo* and *Red Dawn*. The same report warned that recruits entering the border guards were unreliable, with several having a history of narcotics use. Even among those already enlisted there was a risk of a breakdown in discipline, with instances of hazing, rising nationalist sentiment, and a growing religious fervor reported among Muslim recruits.[80] In the broader socialist camp, even graver problems loomed: while Romania had gone from a fraternal socialist ally to a hostile Black Sea neighbor that spied on Soviet border guard posts following Nicolae Ceaușescu's ascent two decades earlier, the KZPO's resources in the 1980s also had to be devoted to shoring up the Soviet-Polish border and keeping a close watch on its Polish counterparts to suppress the Solidarity movement.[81] Within two years of the dire warnings expressed in the 1987 report, the socialist bloc that had helped insulate the borderlands of the Black Sea from foreign intervention would dissolve; within four years, the Soviet state's collapse would deprive Moscow of the ability to constrain mobility on the Black Sea coast, and the region's unified landscape would fracture into a set of loosely connected pieces divided by new state borders.

Reading reports like this one, it is tempting to conclude that the Soviet border regime was doomed and the demise of the Soviet state presaged by faltering border controls. Yet it is worth remembering the limitations of the picture of the borderlands painted in KGB documents. Although the secret police organization was a key instrument of centralized political control, its emphasis on finding, chronicling, and tabulating suspicious activity of any kind tended to render the USSR as a perpetually vulnerable state beset by dangerous internal and external forces. The KGB's detailed reports on border "wanderers," for example, obscured the fact that defections were rare among Soviet citizens. Far more moved along authorized pathways of mobility, circulating through the Black Sea region to take advantage of state-sponsored opportunities for rest and leisure before returning home, or traveling abroad to allied states in the socialist camp or even capitalist countries under the careful supervision of state-run tour groups and delegations. The Soviet border may have been a rather ramshackle Iron Curtain when viewed up close, but it can be argued that the actual border line that enclosed the Soviet state mattered less over time. While exit controls and other coercive elements of the Soviet mobility regime never disappeared, positive incentives grew more important and produced patterns of movement that became habitual for Soviet citizens. By the late Soviet period, even the borderland populations that had once been viewed as disloyal or subjected to forced removal tended to naturalize Soviet borders, subscribe to a sense of Soviet patriotism, and view co-ethnics abroad at a remove.[82]

Soviet border policies, though costly and cumbersome, were not a complete failure. When viewed from a comparative perspective, the Soviet Union was perhaps more successful than its contemporaries in "regularizing" internal and external migration.[83] While the control of contraband trade proved elusive, coordinated human smuggling operations of the kind commonplace across the US-Mexico border were relatively rare.[84] In some ways, Soviet tactics anticipated those pursued by post–Cold War capitalist states striving to facilitate the movement of global capital while restraining the global movement of people. The current practice of gathering and sharing massive sets of data on migrants, now aided by technological advances, was preceded by the Soviet habit of stockpiling dossiers and agent reports; the filtering of migrants based on perceived risk was foreshadowed by the application of prophylactic policing to those deemed likely to violate the border regime; and the linking of border security to internal systems of surveillance was commonplace in the Soviet Union before it became widespread in the United States after

11 September 2001.[85] Perhaps most tellingly, regional migration patterns still mark the former Soviet Union as a distinct "space" decades after the lifting of exit controls and the splintering of the Soviet state that once enforced them.[86]

NOTES

Research for this chapter was supported by fellowships from the National Endowment for the Humanities and the American Council of Learned Societies. I would also like to express my appreciation to Michael David-Fox, Gregory Afinogenov, Diane Koenker, Joshua Sanborn, Carolyn Pouncy, and the anonymous referees for their insightful and helpful comments and suggestions on earlier drafts of this chapter.

1. P. I. Zyrianov, ed., *Uchebnik pogranichnika* (Moscow: Voennoe izdatel'stvo Ministerstva oborony SSSR, 1967), 35–36.

2. For an overview, see the introduction to "The Black Sea and the Question of Boundaries," *Kritika: Explorations in Russian and Eurasian History* 19, no. 2 (2018): 237–42, as well as the cluster's component articles: Diane P. Koenker, "The Taste of Others: Soviet Adventures in Cosmopolitan Cuisines," *Kritika: Explorations in Russian and Eurasian History* 19, no. 2 (2018): 243–72; Stephen V. Bittner, "A Problem of Taste: An American Connoisseur's Travels through the Soviet Union's Black Sea Vineyards," *Kritika: Explorations in Russian and Eurasian History* 19, no. 2 (2018): 305–25; and Johanna Conterio, "'Our Black Sea Coast': The Sovietization of the Black Sea Littoral under Khrushchev and the Problem of Overdevelopment," *Kritika: Explorations in Russian and Eurasian History* 19, no. 2 (2018): 327–61.

3. On "channeling" movement, see Valeska Huber, *Channelling Mobilities: Migration and Globalization in the Suez Canal Region and Beyond, 1869–1914* (Cambridge: Cambridge University Press, 2013); on exchanges within the socialist camp, see Anne E. Gorsuch and Diane P. Koenker, eds., *The Socialist Sixties: Crossing Borders in the Second World* (Bloomington: Indiana University Press, 2013); and Elidor Mëhilli, *From Stalin to Mao: Albania and the Socialist World* (Ithaca, NY: Cornell University Press, 2018).

4. On "regimes" of migration and mobility, see Lewis Siegelbaum and Leslie Paige Moch, *Broad Is My Native Land: Repertoires and Regimes of Migration in Russia's Twentieth Century* (Ithaca, NY: Cornell University Press, 2014); and Ronen Shamir, "Without Borders? Notes on Globalization as a Mobility Regime," *Sociological Theory* 23, no. 2 (2005): 197–217.

5. Peter Sahlins's influential *Boundaries: The Making of France and Spain in the Pyrenees* (Berkeley: University of California Press, 1991) argues that borders, far from being an issue confined to the periphery, are intimately bound up with the history of the state itself.

6. Andrea Chandler, *Institutions of Isolation: Border Controls in the Soviet Union and Its Successor States, 1917–1993* (Montreal: McGill-Queen's University Press, 1998), 5.

7. Terry Martin, "The Origins of Soviet Ethnic Cleansing," *Journal of Modern History* 70, no. 4 (1998): 813–61; Nathalie Moine, "Passeportisation, statistique des migrations et contrôle de l'identité sociale," *Cahiers du monde russe* 38, no. 4 (1997): 587–99; David R. Shearer, *Policing Stalin's Socialism: Repression and Social Order in the Soviet Union, 1924–1953* (New Haven: Yale University Press, 2009).

8. Andrei Shlyakhter, "Smuggler States: Poland, Latvia, Estonia, and Contraband Trade Across the Soviet Frontier, 1919–1924" (PhD diss., University of Chicago, 2020).

9. Sabine Dullin, *La frontière épaisse: Aux origines des politiques soviétiques* (Paris: EHESS, 2014). In *The Great Departure: Mass Migration from Eastern Europe and the Making of the Free World* (New York: W. W. Norton, 2017), Tara Zahra emphasizes the legacies of emigration restrictions in East Central Europe that predated the Cold War.

10. Two significant initial works in this regard are György Péteri, "Nylon Curtain: Transnational and Transsystemic Tendencies in the Cultural Life of State-Socialist Russia and East-Central Europe,"

Slavonica 10, no. 2 (2004): 113–23; and Sabine Dullin, "Des frontieres s'ouvrent et se ferment: La mise en place d'un espace socialiste derrière le rideau de fer, 1953–1970," *Relations internationales*, no. 147 (2011): 35–48. Péteri, however, does not address how the border allowed goods and culture to move but restrained human mobility, while Dullin looks primarily at the border between Soviet Ukraine and socialist Czechoslovakia and concludes her analysis in 1970. A crucial study that examines borders along the Black Sea, though centered on their contemporary significance, is Mathijs Pelkmans, *Defending the Border: Identity, Religion, and Modernity in the Republic of Georgia* (Ithaca, NY: Cornell University Press, 2006).

11. On the Soviet Union's relationship to globalization, see Oscar Sanchez-Sibony, *Red Globalization: The Political Economy of the Soviet Cold War from Stalin to Khrushchev* (New York: Cambridge University Press, 2014); and James Mark, Artemy M. Kalinovsky, and Steffi Marung, eds., *Alternative Globalizations: Eastern Europe and the Postcolonial World* (Bloomington: Indiana University Press, 2020).

12. On governmentality and population management, see Michel Foucault, *Security, Territory, Population: Lectures at the College de France, 1977–1978*, trans. G. Burchell, ed. M. Senellart (New York: Picador, 2007).

13. Vladislav Krasnov, *Soviet Defectors: The KGB Wanted List* (Stanford, CA: Hoover Institution Press, 1986), 109–11.

14. For a discussion of transforming the landscape through violent "weeding," see Amir Weiner, ed., *Landscaping the Human Garden: Twentieth-Century Population Management in a Comparative Framework* (Stanford, CA: Stanford University Press, 2003); for a comparative view of the Soviet police's role in constructing other landscapes, see Kate Brown, "Gridded Lives: Why Kazakhstan and Montana Are Nearly the Same Place," *American Historical Review* 106, no. 1 (2001): 17–48; on the impact of resorts on the Black Sea's landscape, see Conterio, "'Our Black Sea Coast.'"

15. My understanding of the aesthetic sensibilities of KGB files is influenced by Cristina Vatulescu, *Police Aesthetics: Literature, Film, and the Secret Police in Soviet Times* (Stanford, CA: Stanford University Press, 2010).

16. W. J. T. Mitchell, *Landscape and Power* (Chicago: University of Chicago Press, 2002), 2, 13.

17. On Soviet-Turkish relations before the Cold War, see Samuel Hirst, "Anti-Westernism on the European Periphery: The Meaning of Soviet-Turkish Convergence in the 1930s," *Slavic Review* 72, no. 1 (2013): 32–53; and Onur Işçi, "Yardstick of Friendship: Soviet-Turkish Relations and the Montreux Convention of 1936," *Kritika: Explorations in Russian and Eurasian History* 21, no. 4 (2020): 733–62.

18. A tendency that Terry Martin describes as the "Piedmont Principle" in "Origins of Soviet Ethnic Cleansing" and *The Affirmative Action Empire: Nations and Nationalism in the Soviet Union, 1923–1939* (Ithaca, NY: Cornell University Press), 2001. For the period after World War II, see Jamil Hasanli, *Stalin and the Turkish Crisis of the Cold War, 1945–1953* (Lanham, MD: Lexington Books, 2011).

19. Ross A. Johnson and Eugene R. Parta, eds., *Cold War Broadcasting: Impact on the Soviet Union and Eastern Europe* (Budapest: Central European University Press, 2012).

20. P. Elistratov, "Narod okhraniaet granitsu," *Pogranichnik*, no. 7 (1963): 37–40.

21. Pelkmans, *Defending the Border*, 33–35.

22. On the legacies of collaboration and Sovietization in Ukraine, see Tarik Cyril Amar, *The Paradox of Ukrainian Lviv: A Borderland City between Nazis, Stalinists, and Nationalists* (Ithaca, NY: Cornell University Press, 2015).

23. Based on a reading of Haluzevyi derzhavnyi arkhiv Sluzhby bezpeky Ukraïni (HDASBU) f. 1 (Second Directorate of the Ukrainian KGB), op. 11 (1959), d. 7, t. 7 ("UKGB Drogobychsoi obl. Nevozvrashchentsy," 1952–1957). Presumably, similar files were compiled for other regions of Ukraine.

24. M. Kadzhaia and O. Gumberidze, "Komsomol'skie kordony deistvuiut," *Pogranichnik*, no. 19 (1962): 49–50.

25. By contrast, Ukrainians—at least those with no record of family involvement in World War II–era nationalist movements and no relatives in the diaspora—appear to have been seen as more loyal;

the KZPO itself was headquartered in Kyiv, and Ukrainians rose to the top ranks of the border troops at the all-Union level.

26. sakartvelos shinagan sakmeta saministro arkivi (sshssa) f. 6 (Criminal Cases of the Georgian KGB), d. 19647–60 ("Riza, Safar Ogly").

27. HDASBU f. 24, op. 2 (1968), d. 2 ("Plany raboty," 1966).

28. Rossiiskii gosudarstvennyi arkhiv noveishei istorii (RGANI) f. 5 (Central Committee of the Communist Party of the Soviet Union, 1949–1991), op. 47, d. 305, ll. 144 (Letter from KGB chief Shelepin to Central Committee, 10 August 1959), 170–73 ("O narushenii Gosudarstvennoi granitsy SSSR v raione s. Sarpi, Batumskogo raiona, Adzharskoi ASSR," 5 October 1959).

29. HDASBU f. 1, op. 17 (1965), d. 12 ("Materialy . . . po ulushcheniiu raboty na sudakh zagranplavaniia i v portakh," 1963), ll. 1–2.

30. RGANI f. 5, op. 60, d. 250, ll. 11–13 (Letter to Central Committee and Council of Ministers of the USSR from the leadership of the Georgian Communist Party and the Georgian Council of Ministers, 26 March 1968).

31. For an overview of the passport system of the Soviet Union and other states, see John C. Torpey, *The Invention of the Passport: Surveillance, Citizenship, and the State* (Cambridge: Cambridge University Press, 2000); on "legibility," see James C. Scott, *Seeing Like a State: How Certain Schemes to Improve the Human Condition Have Failed* (New Haven: Yale University Press, 1998).

32. RGANI f. 5, op. 60, d. 250, ll. 11–13 (Letter to Central Committee and Council of Ministers of the USSR from the leadership of the Georgian Communist Party and the Georgian Council of Ministers, 26 March 1968).

33. A. Iakovlev, "Likvidatsiia vooruzhennoi bandy narushitelei granitsy," *Pogranichnik*, no. 5 (1944): 26–27; *Pogranichnik*, no. 14 (1968).

34. HDASBU f. 24, op. 1 (1970), d. 1.

35. M. Sokolov and M. Gorzhei, "Pogranichnyi rezhim na morskom poberezh'e," *Pogranichnik*, no. 8 (1967): 22–24. The Soviet Union, like other states, consistently struggled to enforce maritime borders. For a comparative perspective, see Renaud Morieux, *The Channel: England, France, and the Construction of a Maritime Border in the Eighteenth Century* (Cambridge: Cambridge University Press, 2016).

36. "Govorit morskaia granitsa," *Pogranichnik*, no. 13 (1968): 14–19.

37. See, e.g., HDASBU f. 24, op. 4 (1965), d. 2 ("Rukovodiashchie ukazaniia," 1961).

38. A. Belousov, "Zamorskie gosti v Igarke," *Za vozvrashchenie na Rodinu* (December 1959): 2; HDASBU f. 24, op. 15 (1988), d. 1 ("Rukovodiashchie ukazaniia," 1979–1980), ll. 173–77.

39. HDASBU f. 24, op. 15 (1988), d. 1, l. 167.

40. HDASBU f. 24, op. 2 (1968), d. 3 ("Plany raboty otdela," 1966), ll. 329–33; l. 363.

41. HDASBU f. 24, op. 2 (1968), d. 3, l. 340; op. 2 (1972), d. 4 ("Plany raboty otdela," 1969), l. 58.

42. HDASBU f. 24, op. 2 (1972), d. 4, l. 87. Although there is no overt discussion of this young woman's recruitment in the given document, many people became agents after a brush with the law, and her connections would have lent her "operational value."

43. For a comparative view of contraband trade in the Baltic Sea, see Tomasz Blusiewicz, "Kaliningrad, Pribaltika, Leningrad: Trade and the Cold War in Soviet Port Cities, 1956–1991," unpublished paper, https://scholar.harvard.edu/tomaszblusiewicz/publications/kaliningrad-pribaltika-leningrad-trade-and-cold-war-soviet-port-cities.

44. HDASBU f. 24, op. 4 (1965), d. 1 ("Rukovodiashchie ukazaniia," 1961).

45. HDASBU f. 24, op. 5 (1972), d. 1 ("Rukovodiashchie ukazaniia," 1970).

46. HDASBU f. 24, op. 2 (1968), d. 3, ll. 190–92; on "prophylaxis," see Edward Cohn, "A Soviet Theory of Broken Windows: Prophylactic Policing and the KGB's Struggle with Political Unrest in the Baltic Republics," *Kritika: Explorations in Russian and Eurasian History* 19, no. 4 (2018): 769–92.

47. William Eliot Butler, *The Soviet Union and the Law of the Sea* (London: Oceana, 1987), 72.

48. See, e.g., HDASBU f. 24, op. 9 (1965), d. 1 ("Otchety po agenturno-operativnoi rabote," 1963), l. 7.

49. HDASBU f. 24, op. 15 (1988), d. 1, l. 164.

50. Peter King, "The Extraordinary Life of Interpreter Pyotr Patrushev," *Sydney Morning Herald*, 29 April 2016, https://www.smh.com.au/national/the-extraordinary-life-of-interpreter-pyotr-patrushev-20160429-goi425.html.

51. Vetokhin's experience is detailed in his memoir, *Sklonen k pobegu*, published in 1983 and available on the website of the Sakharov Center, https://www.sakharov-center.ru/asfcd/auth/?t=page&num=5611.

52. "V Turtsiiu na naduvnoi lodke i v FRG s avtomatom: Kak krymchane sbegali iz SSSR," *V gorode*, 16 March 2012, https://crimea.vgorode.ua/news/luidy_horoda/104815.

53. HDASBU f. 24, op. 15 (1988), d. 1, l. 89.

54. HDASBU f. 24, op. 15 (1988), d. 1, l. 156.

55. HDASBU f. 27 (Osobyi otdel KGB SSSR po Zapadnomu pogranichnomu okrugu), op. 23 (1982), d. 3 ("Materialy informatsii komandovaniia i politorganov," 1978).

56. HDASBU f. 27, op. 23 (1982), d. 2 ("Otchety, dokladnye zapiski i spetssoobshcheniia," 1978), l. 31.

57. Nodar Dumbadze, *nu geshinia, deda!* (Tbilisi: nodar dumbadzis tsignebi, 2013), originally published in 1971.

58. V. Goland, "Net nichego iarche solntsa: Shtrikhi k portretu Nodara Dumbadze," *Pogranichnik*, no. 2 (1976): 81–83.

59. HDASBU f. 24, op. 7 (1969), d. 1 ("Rukovodiashchie ukazaniia," 1967), ll. 33–37.

60. For a comparative look at crime statistics, see Peter Andreas and Kelly M. Greenhill, eds., *Sex, Drugs, and Body Counts: The Politics of Numbers in Global Crime and Conflict* (Ithaca, NY: Cornell University Press, 2011).

61. HDASBU f. 24, op. 3 (1967), d. 1 ("Rukovodiashchie ukazaniia," 1964).

62. HDASBU f. 24, op. 4 (1972), d. 1 ("Ukazaniia v chasti okruga," 1969).

63. HDASBU f. 24, op. 4 (1972), d. 1.

64. The phenomenon of "wanderers" calls to mind the discussion of "itinerants" in Siegelbaum and Moch, *Broad Is My Native Land*, 334–86.

65. sshssa f. 6, d. 297–56 ("Kuziakin, Vladimir Ivanovich").

66. sshssa f. 6, d. 903–57 ("Sergeev, Nikolai Nikolaevich").

67. sshssa f. 6, d. 22125–61 ("Pozhilov, Valentin Aleksandrovich")

68. sshssa f. 6, d. 22126–61 ("Rochniak, Viktor Valer'evich")

69. Gosudarstvennyi arkhiv Rossiiskoi Federatsii (GARF) f. 8131 (Prokuratura SSSR), op. 31, d. 82148 ("Fomichev, N. I."), l. 10.

70. GARF f. 8131, op. 31, d. 91518 ("Balakirev, V. G.").

71. sshssa f. 6, d. 28496–63 ("Mkheidze, Revaz Vissarionovich; Orekhov, Iurii Petrovich"), t. 5, l. 133.

72. The quote is from Mitchell, *Landscape and Power*, 2. I found the first mention of "formalism" in a 1964 issue of *Pogranichnik* and the last in a 1987 issue of *Sovetskii pogranichnik*, KZPO's newspaper. The term had negative connotations in the Soviet context given the campaign against formalism in music under the Zhdanovshchina in the late 1940s and the critiques of formalism in art and cinema in the 1930s. For background, see Maria Belodubrovskaya, "Abram Room, *A Strict Young Man*, and the 1936 Campaign against Formalism in Soviet Cinema," *Slavic Review* 74, no. 2 (2015): 311–33.

73. "Okhrana granitsy—iskusstvo," *Pogranichnik*, no. 16 (1966): 1.

74. HDASBU f. 24, op. 4 (1972), d. 1, ll. 21–30.

75. Discussed in multiple issues of *Pogranichnik* in 1989.

76. HDASBU, f. 24, op. 9 (1965), d. 1. The term "main opponent" was often used in KGB files to refer to the United States.

77. For an example of the interrogation of a Soviet sailor, see National Archives College Park (NACP), RG 59, Political Refugees, Soviet Union, 1960–1963, Box 1856 ("Duties and Qualifications of the Crew of the Soviet Freighter S. S. *Povolzh'ye*: Based on Interrogation of Former Seaman," 15 January 1960).

78. For details, see Benjamin Tromly, *Cold War Exiles and the CIA: Plotting to Free Russia* (New York: Oxford University Press, 2019).

79. To cite a few representative examples in a vast literature, much of it based on "insider" accounts, emphasizing the effectiveness of the KGB's most insidious operations, see Christopher Andrew and V. N. Mitrokhin, *The Sword and the Shield: The Mitrokhin Archive and the Secret History of the KGB* (New York: Basic Books, 2001); Oleg Kalugin, *Spymaster: My Thirty-Two Years in Intelligence and Espionage against the West* (New York: Basic Books, 2009); and Boris Volodarsky, *The KGB's Poison Factory: From Lenin to Litvinenko* (Minneapolis: Zenith, 2010).

80. HDASBU f. 27, op. 109 (1990), d. 7 ("Perepiski s osobym otdelom KGB SSSR," 1987).

81. HDASBU f. 24 (Razvedotdely KGB SSSR Zapadnogo pogranichnogo okruga), op. 1 (1970), d. 1 ("Plany raboty otdela," 1968); HDASBU f. 24, op. 1 (1973), d. 1 ("Rukovodiashchie ukazaniia GUPV KGB SSSR," 1971).

82. A process described in Zbigniew Wojnowski, *The Near Abroad: Socialist Eastern Europe and Soviet Patriotism in Ukraine, 1956–1985* (Toronto: University of Toronto Press, 2017); and Pelkmans, *Defending the Border.*

83. Matthew A. Light, "What Does It Meant to Control Migration? Soviet Mobility Policies in Comparative Perspective," *Law and Social Inquiry* 37, no. 2 (2012): 395–429.

84. Peter Andreas, *Border Games: Policing the U.S.-Mexico Divide* (Ithaca, NY: Cornell University Press, 2000); Kelly Lytle Hernández, *Migra! A History of the U.S. Border Patrol* (Berkeley: University of California Press, 2010).

85. In *The Politics of Borders: Sovereignty, Security, and the Citizen after 9/11* (Cambridge: Cambridge University Press, 2018), Matthew Longo, a political theorist, argues that these are distinctly twenty-first-century practices. All, however, have Soviet antecedents.

86. See Mikhail Denisenko, Salvatore Strozza, and Matthew Light, eds., *Migration from the Newly Independent States: 25 Years after the Collapse of the USSR* (Cham: Springer, 2020), for a look at enduring regional migration trends.

Recidivism, Prophylaxis, and the KGB

Edward Cohn

IN DECEMBER 1969, THE KGB OFFICE IN ŠIAULIAI, LITHUANIA, SUMMONED a thirty-three-year-old physician named Vincas Filipavičius to a collective meeting of the city's doctors. At the assembly, a KGB officer accused Filipavičius of "distributing ideologically harmful literature" and making anti-Soviet comments among the city's intelligentsia; the doctor's peers then criticized him for his actions and urged him to change his ways. This was in many ways a typical example of the KGB tactic known as *profilaktika* (prophylaxis), in which KGB officers did not arrest relatively minor political offenders but summoned them to an intervention designed to change their behavior.[1] In a majority of cases, profilaktika victims were "invited" to a "prophylactic chat" (*profilakticheskaia beseda*), where a KGB officer grilled them on their behavior for several hours, instructed them about the importance of regime values, and then let them go home, warning that they would be prosecuted if they broke the law again. In other cases, like Filipavičius's, the target was subjected to "profilaktika with the public's help" (*profilaktika s pomoshchiu obshchestvennosti*), in which the officer led a discussion of the offender's behavior before a collective organization like the Komsomol or a trade union. KGB documents consistently portray profilaktika as a powerful crime-fighting tool that prevented minor offenders from turning into more dangerous critics of the Soviet system. In this case, the Šiauliai KGB even declared that "Profilaktika went successfully, compromising Filipavičius before the collective" and helping him reform.[2]

Filipavičius's case stands out in one key respect: it directly challenges the widespread assumption that profilaktika was an effective tool for changing the behavior of its targets. After announcing that Filipavičius's "prophylaxis" had gone "successfully," the KGB later quoted surveillance reports showing that the doctor "did not fully renounce his hostile anti-Soviet views and intentions, became more withdrawn, suspected everyone of ties to the KGB," and began to associate mostly with other KGB victims. The KGB noted its plans to do further explanatory work with him.[3] Its efforts apparently failed, however: a 1973 report stated that he had written "anti-Soviet compositions" and had refused to abandon his views even after two KGB interventions.[4] That remark referred to an even more striking fact (absent from the KGB's 1969 records): Filipavičius had been called to a chat once before, in 1964, when he tried to send anti-Soviet literature abroad.[5] Filipavičius, in short, had been through profilaktika twice without a major long-term change in his behavior or beliefs.

This chapter uses evidence from the Baltic republics to argue that Filipavičius's story was more typical than historians have assumed and that prophylactic chats and similar interventions were less effective than KGB sources and Western historians have asserted. Since the 1990s, KGB archives in the Baltic republics and other regions on the Soviet periphery have allowed historians to begin analyzing the tactics and ideology of the KGB at a time when Russian security archives remain closed. Some of their conclusions are most applicable to the Baltic region, where anti-Soviet feelings ran high and profilaktika was used somewhat more often than elsewhere in the USSR.[6] But Baltic archives also include their share of directives and publications from the Lubianka—demonstrating that the Soviet security police was in many ways highly centralized, that KGB tactics on the periphery closely resembled models proposed by Moscow, and that discussions of police methods in local sources were in line with the KGB's larger theoretical literature. KGB operational files from the Baltic region and theoretical writings from Moscow consistently argue that the tactic was effective in changing its targets' behavior and beliefs; historians of the USSR have yet to challenge or complicate this idea, and several scholars who have written insightful accounts of profilaktika have accepted it. Robert Hornsby, for instance, notes that "these individual prophylactic sessions seem to have been highly effective in stifling dissent" and concludes that "had prophylaxis not been effective in keeping dissent at manageable levels around the country the authorities would more than likely have reverted to far more aggressive means of maintaining domestic stability."[7] Mark Harrison has described profilaktika as "astonishingly effective" and notes (referring to one set of profilaktika statistics): "One per thousand is a reoffending rate that Western justice systems can only dream about."[8] Given the biases and gaps within KGB records, archival sources do not provide definitive evidence about profilaktika's impact, but evidence from Baltic KGB archives strongly suggests that the tactic had fewer long-term effects on its targets' outlook and behavior than KGB officers claimed. Some types of profilaktika victim (including dissidents and women who associated with foreign sailors) appear to have had a high recidivism rate. Other KGB targets were unlikely to become recidivists (including sailors who behaved badly abroad), but not necessarily because of the KGB's use of prophylactic chats. More broadly, there are serious flaws with the main piece of evidence for profilaktika's effectiveness—surveillance reports about the victim's behavior. This chapter therefore argues that profilaktika most likely had a short-term impact on its targets' behavior, but that it was less successful in changing their beliefs and actions in the long run. Although past studies have noted that profilaktika could be a useful tool in crisis management, it does not appear to have lived up to its champions' rhetoric about the power of prophylactic interventions to reshape the lives of "immature" or "deluded" citizens.[9]

That conclusion, in turn, has important consequences for understanding the Soviet surveillance state in the Baltic republics and beyond. There was sometimes a mismatch between KGB rhetoric and theory, on the one hand, and KGB practice, on the other—a mismatch evident both in all-Union records (which strongly assert the effectiveness of profilaktika while raising questions about its implementation) and in local case files. While KGB rhetoric was consistent with the idea that the USSR was a police state seeking the transformation of its citizens and the elimination of dissent, KGB practice focused less closely on profilaktika's long-term redemptive power and more directly on its tactic's short-term impact.[10] In fact, the strongest conclusion that can be drawn from this chapter is not that profilaktika failed. (After all, the exact impact of the tactic can be hard to discern, the precise goals of the KGB can be debated, and KGB theorists may not always have seen eye-to-eye with officers on the ground about what the tactic was meant to do.) Instead, this chapter shows that the KGB's surveillance system did not consistently provide the regime with the information needed to determine whether the tactic was a success. The story of profilaktika, in short, is the story of a surveillance state whose ambitions were not always matched by its capacities, and whose on-the-ground personnel were more concerned with the day-to-day politics of personal control than with transforming the lives of their targets.

KGB SOURCES ON THE EFFECTIVENESS OF PROFILAKTIKA

From the Khrushchev years until the 1980s, KGB sources painted a consistent picture of how profilaktika worked. The tactic was to be used, operational reports and theoretical writings noted, when everyday citizens committed misconduct because of "errors" and "delusions" (*zabluzhdeniia*) due to their inexperience and "immaturity" (*nezrelost'*); prophylactic interventions were meant to set those citizens on the right path and to change their lives for the better. KGB sources frequently state that profilaktika achieved this ambitious goal, highlighting the tactic's redemptive power and low recidivism rate. Nevertheless, KGB records at both the Baltic and the all-Union levels hint that reality did not always match the regime's rhetoric, sometimes criticizing KGB officers for their shortcomings in implementing the tactic. KGB writings, in short, strongly endorse the tactic's efficacy while suggesting—at a minimum— that some officers could have been more dedicated and conscientious in their use of profilaktika.

From the 1950s onward, KGB theoretical writings and memoirs universally emphasize the tactic's effectiveness as an "educational" measure that could redeem its victims and place them back on the "correct path." N. F. Chistiakov, the head of the KGB's investigative department, declared in a 1979 memoir that the KGB often used "prophylactic, educational measures" against people who had fallen under the influence of bourgeois ideology, "helping them to realize and correct their mistakes and to become full members of socialist society. The organ's workers consider it their duty not to wait until a person, having fallen under the influence of a hostile ideology, aggravates his political mistakes but to strive to protect him from committing antisocial actions at the initial stage, to warn him, to help him understand his delusions and become a full-fledged builder of communism."[11]

N. R. Mironov, a KGB official sometimes described as the "father of profilaktika" for his work with the tactic in Leningrad, went even further in emphasizing the tactic's redemptive power. "Invitations of a person to the organs of state security," he wrote, "with the goal of explaining to him the anti-social character of his actions and warning him that he stands on a dangerous path, have a large educational effect. Experience shows that in a majority of cases, people summoned to such conversations, recognizing that the organs of state security are sincerely interested in their fate and want to help them, reform themselves and enter into a healthy working and public life."[12]

In this case, Mironov merely noted profilaktika's success in a majority of cases, but he mirrored other KGB sources in emphasizing the tactic's educational efficacy.[13] In 1959, he argued more categorically that there were "no recidivists in anti-Soviet activity" among Leningrad's recent profilaktika victims, a fact that—he believed—demonstrated the tactic's "effective character" and provided the "best confirmation of the utility and correctness of applying measures of a preventative-educational character."[14]

By the same token, KGB officers frequently praised profilaktika's effectiveness in operational reports from Lithuania using stark, unambiguous language, beginning in the 1950s and extending until the perestroika years. A 1975 report on the Lithuanian KGB's use of prophylactic measures hailed the tactic's "great effectiveness," noting that only 6 of 404 profilaktika targets that year were repeat offenders. The report concluded that the tactic "has become one of the main and most effective measures of positive influence" on wrongdoers and added that interventions involving public organizations, "as a rule, positively influenced not only those subjected to profilaktika themselves, but their milieu."[15] A 1965 report declared that the republican KGB's prophylactic work had prevented defections, blocked the creation of nationalist groups, and slowed the spread of anti-Soviet leaflets, noting that the "overwhelming majority" of people who underwent profilaktika "deeply recognized their previous mistakes and errors and are now actively involved in socially useful activities."[16] The Lithuanian KGB's 1959 annual report called attention to the tactic's "positive results" and announced, "The effectiveness and propriety of prophylactic measures were confirmed by a whole host of examples, when KGB organs gave timely warnings to individual Soviet citizens about serious mistakes and crimes (especially from among the youth) and helped them escape from ideological delusions and set out on the right path."[17] KGB reports were rarely this explicit in endorsing the "positive results" of other KGB methods or in noting that victims of tactics other than profilaktika went on to do "socially useful" labor and become productive citizens.

Nevertheless, even reports and theoretical writings that hailed profilaktika's effectiveness sometimes hinted that the tactic's implementation could be improved. A 1959 article in *Sbornik*, the all-Union KGB's theoretical journal, sang the praises of profilaktika but noted several pitfalls that sometimes faced KGB officers. "Operative workers cannot consider their mission finished after the conversation," the article noted, urging KGB officers to monitor profilaktika targets in the days that followed, to help them find jobs, and to increase their use of the more intensive forms of profilaktika that involved "the public."[18] At a republic-level conference of Lithuanian KGB leaders in 1961, one officer began by noting that a majority of profilaktika targets went on to help the KGB fight "hostile elements" after their intervention but argued that some

KGB officers did not get to know profilaktika targets well enough to pick the proper form of the tactic and did not pay sufficient attention to the fate of the wrongdoer after the chat.[19] KGB reports from the Baltics regularly echo these themes, calling for increased use of "profilaktika with the public's help" (supposedly the most effective form of the tactic) while reminding officers not to neglect their post-profilaktika surveillance of offenders. A 1983 KGB publication from Moscow on the dangers of foreign exchange students, finally, concluded by noting several flaws in the KGB's "large and very successful prophylactic work." Some KGB officers failed to select the right form of profilaktika for young people, the leaflet noted, "and therefore the chosen form of profilaktika does not give the desired results"; some prophylactic measures took place too late to influence the accused; and, most damningly, "agent-operational work is not always organized for the observation of the behavior of one or another young person after profilaktika" and sometimes involved merely "formal control, which does not allow an objective conclusion about the effectiveness of the measures taken."[20] From the 1950s onward, in short, KGB sources agreed that profilaktika was very effective—but regularly noted potentially troublesome ways in which its implementation could be improved.

The same ambiguity can be seen in KGB statistical reports, which suggest that the tactic was effective without giving the evidence needed to test this assertion. One of the KGB's few available sets of all-Union statistics notes that there were 121,406 profilaktika cases between 1966 and 1974 and only 150 instances in which a profilaktika victim was subsequently prosecuted—a rate of 1 in 809.[21] Republic-level statistical reports show that of the 3,282 people subjected to profilaktika by the KGB in Lithuania between 1966 and 1974, 56 (or 1 in 59) had been summoned to a prophylactic chat before, with slightly higher (but still low) recidivism rates in later periods.[22] For instance, 1 in 33 Lithuanian profilaktika victims were repeat cases between 1979 and 1987, at a time when the KGB began to use the tactic less frequently.[23]

But there are reasons to doubt the accuracy and meaningfulness of these statistics. Research for this chapter involved the analysis of 2,779 Lithuanian profilaktika cases, at least 4 percent of which involved repeat offenders by one definition or another (i.e., two-time profilaktika victims, people who were arrested or punished in some other way by the KGB after profilaktika, or people who were reported to have committed later crimes).[24] This is undoubtedly a low estimate. Many KGB reports on repeat offenders (including Filipavičius) do not list earlier prophylactic chats and KGB interventions involving the alleged wrongdoer, obscuring the offender's status as a recidivist; other cases in the sample were almost certainly first offenders who later committed a second offense that was not discussed in records used for this chapter. Certain types of repeat offenders (say, past profilaktika targets who were later fired from their jobs or placed under surveillance rather than being arrested) were not tracked in Lithuanian KGB files. Finally, official KGB statistical reports can be seriously flawed. It is not obvious how to best measure recidivism (official statistics cover either prosecutions or repeat profilaktika cases, but never both, and never cover subsequent firings or cases in which a profilaktika victim was surveilled and interrogated but not arrested). Some KGB statistics even include serious errors, listing fewer profilaktika cases in a given year than appear in the archives, most likely because KGB officers wanted to minimize the number of anti-Soviet offenses.[25]

Evidence from Latvia supports the conclusion that recidivism was higher than KGB statistics suggest. This chapter also analyzes 858 Latvian profilaktika targets from the Delta-Latvija database—a reconstructed KGB computer database with information on a wide range of Latvians who ran into trouble with the secret police.[26] Of those 858 people, at least 55 ran into trouble with the KGB after going through profilaktika—a total of 6.8 percent. This included people who were subjected to profilaktika more than once, as well as people who continued to have illicit contact with foreigners who were mentioned in reports by informers as being anti-Soviet, or who appeared at anti-Soviet demonstrations during the perestroika era. Given the incompleteness of the records and apparent randomness of who appeared in the database, the odds are high that fuller records would show that at least 10 percent of profilaktika targets continued to run into trouble with the KGB. When KGB officers raised questions about the implementation of profilaktika, they were expressing very legitimate concerns.

KGB SURVEILLANCE AND THE RESULTS OF PROFILAKTIKA

The KGB's assessment of profilaktika was based on two factors, one more important than the other. Each profilaktika file featured a summary of the moment of confession, when the profilaktika target typically admitted guilt, pleaded that he or she had acted "thoughtlessly" and out of "immaturity," and promised to behave better in the future. More importantly, each file also used surveillance records to describe the offender's post-profilaktika behavior, generally noting that wrongdoers had changed their ways and become better citizens. Although in principle these files served as a powerful argument for profilaktika's effectiveness, in practice the situation was often more complicated. KGB reports were full of formulaic language and were often based on only a short period's worth of surveillance reports. Although these records were almost certainly effective in identifying wrongdoers who immediately reverted to their old ways, they are short on depth and say very little about profilaktika's longer-term impact. Profilaktika undoubtedly had an impact on many of its targets, but the KGB did not provide the evidence needed to justify the confident tone with which it proclaimed the tactic's effectiveness.

Prophylactic chats were intended to elicit not only a confession of guilt but an admission that the offender's actions had resulted from a lack of understanding and an acknowledgment of the harm inflicted on others—— which meant, unsurprisingly, that many arguments for the effectiveness of profilaktika focus on the moment of confession. Most cases resemble a 1984 prophylactic chat involving a Latvian medical student accused of making anti-Soviet comments. The student at first denied the charges but, when presented with evidence, admitted that he "repeatedly made nationalist comments that exerted a politically negative influence on his connections"; he explained that these "ideologically immature comments . . . were the result of his not under-standing" party policy, admitted the harmfulness of his actions, and prom-ised not to repeat them (both orally and in a written explanation).[27] Other profilaktika victims thanked KGB officers for their help, cried, pleaded inex-perience, or explained that their misdeeds resulted from one or another char-acter flaw, but—after some level of mild "denial" (zapiratel'stvo)——nearly all profilaktika targets both admitted guilt to the KGB officer and wrote up an explanation of what they had done.[28] These descriptions can be difficult to interpret, however. Some confessions sound powerful and meaningful, if the KGB's account can be relied upon. But many sound formulaic and by the book and are too brief for historians to develop a clear sense of their "sincerity." Still other confessions are confidently described as evidence for the tactic's effec-tiveness but read as obstreperous and challenging. What are we to make, for instance, of a Lithuanian factory worker who vigorously denied an accusation of making anti-Soviet comments, demanded that the KGB provide evidence and witnesses, admitted to "thoughtless" actions only when he saw how "well informed" the KGB was, and "categorically refused" to provide a written con-fession? The KGB concluded that the chat had played a "positive role" and called for only three months of surveillance—a shorter-than-usual term—but its confidence feels jarring in context.[29]

In principle, profilaktika's most important test came after the prophy-lactic chat, when the KGB conducted surveillance on profilaktika targets to determine whether they had changed their ways; in practice, post-profilaktika surveillance was spottier and less systematic than KGB theoretical writings might lead readers to believe. A small number of alleged wrongdoers were des-ignated as the targets of particularly intensive investigations and subjected to high levels of surveillance, as "cases of operative surveillance" (DON) or "cases of operative verification" (DOP).[30] In most instances, however, the KGB merely assigned an informer or two—either "trusted people" (*doverennye litsa*) who provided oral reports or "agents" who submitted written reports—to observe the profilaktika victim for a period of time after the chat.[31] In a set of 501 Lithuanian cases examined for this chapter that specified whether the victim was subjected to post-profilaktika surveillance, 19 were observed for three months, 75 for six months, 26 for a year, 12 for another period (such as "until the end of the school year"), and 161 for an unspecified length of time, while 208 (41.5 percent) went without further surveillance.

Decisions not to conduct surveillance on profilaktika victims were typically based on the alleged offender's background and the prophylactic chat's outcome. Many case files ascribe the decision not to conduct surveillance to an offender's references at work, to his or her age, to his or her background as a worker or poor peasant, or to the lack of "compromising materials" on an offender or his family. (The KGB was suspicious of wrongdoers who had connections to anti-Soviet "bandits" or whose relatives had been exiled in the 1940s, for instance.) A few profilaktika victims were not surveilled because they were deemed unlikely to commit offenses again for very particular reasons: the KGB criticized a hard-drinking sailor for his "insincere" response to accusations of smuggling, for example, but chose not to surveil him because he had been denied further access to foreign ports.[32] Most cases, however, involved profilaktika targets who "sincerely" (*iskrenno*) and "frankly" (*chistoserdechno*) repented and announced that their actions had been based on "immaturity." When it heard the case of a mechanic who drunkenly praised life in pre-Soviet Lithuania and told an anti-Soviet joke, the KGB announced that he had "listened with great attention, said he fully agreed with these arguments, and thanked the KGB for saying this to him openly."[33] The KGB had even more dramatic results in a 1976 case involving a married couple who wrote illicit letters to foreign relatives and made anti-Soviet comments. The husband recognized the harmfulness of his actions and asked the KGB to recognize that he was poorly educated, often did not understand Soviet policy, and would do better in the future; he noted that he had suffered a lot from his ordeal and would remember his encounter with the KGB "for a long time." His wife confessed to being nervous, controlling, and impetuous, saying that she had been angry at a communist co-worker and therefore stupidly announced that all Communists were bad workers. She "repeatedly cried" at the chat and asked the KGB to "understand her correctly" and not interpret her "immature comments" as deep beliefs. The KGB announced that there was no need for further surveillance, since the pair had "conducted themselves with an understanding of the correctness of what was presented to them, recognized that they said politically harmful things, but repented and assured in writing and orally that they won't do it again."[34]

When the KGB did conduct post-profilaktika surveillance, it typically included a short addendum to the case file noting that an offender's behavior had changed; in some cases, these addenda were *very* short. One report stated simply that the offender in question "behaved himself well after profilaktika," while another said that its subject "behaved properly" after the chat, and a third wrote that "other compromising materials were not received."[35] Another report noted, "Further surveillance shows that he made positive conclusions from the prophylactic chat and now does not present himself from a hostile direction."[36] Still another declared: "no anti-Soviet actions on her part were observed. On the contrary, after profilaktika, she became more active, happier, and more cheerful."[37] One report noted passively that "information about the renewal of [the profilaktika target's] hostile activity was not received."[38] More helpful reports quoted the KGB's target: referring to profilaktika, several members of an anti-Soviet youth group reportedly told an agent, "This will be for us a lesson for our whole lives," while a Lithuanian priest told an informer, "Earlier I had a totally different opinion about the security organs, but now I'm personally convinced that very smart people who can give good advice work there."[39]

More concrete surveillance reports referred to the subject's changed behavior. Many profilaktika targets, unsurprisingly, were teenaged students—and reports by agents and trusted people sometimes noted that students' grades improved after they went through profilaktika.[40] (This makes sense, of course: alleged offenders sometimes felt a need to show their seriousness to the authorities, they sometimes benefited from closer parental supervision if their parents were also "invited" to the chat, and the schools attended by profilaktika victims sometimes felt pressure to show results.) Other surveillance reports note an offender's improved work discipline, often providing specific details—describing a collective farmer promoted to brigadier, a sailor who began to write patriotic poems and "actively speak against insufficiencies on the ship," and a barber who began working more conscientiously and told the KGB about criminal activity by kolkhoz workers. The KGB considered recruiting the third man as a collaborator.[41] Summaries of post-profilaktika surveillance can be broken down into three categories. A small minority describe failures of profilaktika, such as a teenager who asked an informer how to acquire an illegal gun or an older man who told an agent that he could not carry out a threat against a Communist due to KGB interference, but that his son would finish the job.[42] A larger number—but still a minority—provide concrete examples of an offender's changed behavior, suggesting that profilaktika had at least some impact. A majority, however, are vague, formulaic, and short—often a sentence or two in length. They note a lack of further offenses, state simply that the offender "drew the correct conclusions" from profilaktika, or briefly mention that his or her behavior improved. In short, these summaries leave much to the imagination. Surveillance was effective enough to catch a small number of unredeemed offenders who failed to change their behavior, such as a Lithuanian teenager who began developing plans to flee the country soon after going through profilaktika for involvement in an anti-Soviet youth group.[43] But most reports indicate a lack of immediate evidence of criminal activity, rather than concrete evidence that an offender had changed in a more fundamental way. The vagueness and brevity of many surveillance summaries may even suggest a lack of clear evidence for an offender's redemption, and they certainly suggest that KGB officers lacked a strong incentive to provide detailed evidence that offenders had changed their ways. These reports indicate that the KGB trusted its officers to know if wrongdoers had altered their views—a decision whose merits are impossible to judge from the written evidence.

KGB reports on profilaktika victims suffer from one final problem: a large majority cover only a short period of time after profilaktika. A December 1959 report praised the "good behavior" of a man accused of drunkenly threatening two activists and praising life in pre-Soviet Lithuania, for example, but this meant very little—since he had only gone through profilaktika the previous month.[44] By contrast, most of the profilaktika victims who got into trouble again did so more than a year later. The priest who noted in 1959 that "very smart people who can give good advice" work at the KGB frequently appeared in the samizdat *Chronicle of the Lithuanian Catholic Church* for his religious activities during the 1980s.[45] An eighteen-year-old woman accused of "amoral ties" to foreign sailors in the port of Klaipėda in 1965 went through profilaktika three more times, even though a KGB officer had singled her out at a party cell meeting as an example of how profilaktika led to "positive results."[46] A Latvian television producer was summoned to profilaktika in 1979 for complaining about the Soviet economy and the position of journalists; the KGB chose not to surveil him after he said that these comments were "thoughtless" complaints about temporary problems, but he was summoned to profilaktika again in 1984 for repeatedly making "harmful" comments among his co-workers, including the claim that the Soviet economy "was a mistake at its very roots."[47] Cases like these are not hard to find.

Common sense says that profilaktika victims would act cautiously in the months after a prophylactic chat, and several have noted in oral history interviews that they acted "more carefully" in its aftermath.[48] The evidence suggests that the KGB's most extravagant claims—that profilaktika transformed deluded wrongdoers into productive citizens—were exaggerated, and that KGB surveillance summaries are more effective in highlighting a short-term lack of criminality than in showing that an offender's attitude, beliefs, and behavior had changed in the long run. The KGB could potentially claim some successes: the number of profilaktika targets who were later prosecuted for major state crimes does seem to have been low (although it is unclear how many profilaktika victims fit the profile of a major state criminal), and in some instances, merely stopping a citizen's antisocial behavior for a year could be considered a success. Nevertheless, although the ability to change citizen's short-term behavior is a very valuable tool for the secret police, profilaktika's track record suggests that KGB sources were right to warn against "formalistic" or superficial surveillance reports that did not allow the KGB to draw an "objective conclusion" about the tactic's long-term impact.[49]

THE OBSTACLES TO PROFILAKTIKA'S EFFECTIVENESS

In short, both the gaps in the archival record and the biases within KGB documents make it difficult to draw a definitive overall conclusion about profilaktika's impact. Nevertheless, one conclusion is clear: the tactic appears to have had a fairly small effect on the behavior of certain classes of offender. In particular, people whose behavior was based on strong ideological or religious beliefs were unlikely to change their ways because of profilaktika, as were those whose livelihood had gotten them into trouble with the security police. The cases of dissidents and people with ties to foreigners, then, highlight both the tactic's limitations and its potential usefulness in short-term behavioral management.

When the KGB compiled a list of people who had attended Vilnius's 23 August 1987 protest against the Molotov-Ribbentrop Pact, it reached a surprising conclusion: that eighteen of the eighty-eight people there—roughly 20 percent—had been subjected to profilaktika in the past.[50] This fact can be difficult to square with the KGB's rhetoric about prophylaxis. KGB theorists would be disappointed to learn that people who had been through profilaktika were willing to participate in the first unsanctioned political protest in the republic in decades. And, given that the list doubled as a who's who of Lithuania's perestroika-era dissident movement, the episode also complicates our understanding of the typical profilaktika target. In principle, organized foes of the regime were among the least promising targets of profilaktika, a tactic best suited for the "politically immature" and "illiterate," for youth, and for other redeemable offenders. Nevertheless, many high-profile members of the dissident movement were subjected to profilaktika at one point or another, as evidenced by the list mentioned above, by cases in the Delta-Latvija database involving past profilaktika targets who were subjected to profilaktika again after participating in protests at Riga's Freedom Monument in 1987, and by a wide variety of KGB criminal files.[51]

Some prominent dissidents were first subjected to profilaktika as youth, as part of a failed attempt to prevent them from becoming more organized antiregime activists. For example, Vytautas Bogušis, a teenager from Lithuania's Varėna region, began to associate with the dissidents Viktoras Petkus and Antanas Terleckas in 1976. Over the next four years, he wrote several anti-Soviet letters, left flowers on the grave of a Lithuanian nationalist, and became more involved with the dissident movement; when he was summoned to a prophylactic chat in 1980, he answered questions defiantly and demanded a written summary of the accusations against him.[52] Unsurprisingly, he and several friends ended up becoming active anti-Soviet nationalists during the perestroika era. Robertas Grigas, meanwhile, grew up in a religious family, joined the Eucharistic movement as a teenager, and began to associate with the dissident priests Sigitas Tamkevičius and Juozas Zdebskis; he was summoned to profilaktika in 1981 (at age twenty-one) for distributing anti-Soviet literature, was called to the KGB again for an "official warning" in 1982, and became a high-profile dissident after being drafted into the army.[53] Rimantas Matulis, a student summoned to profilaktika in 1962, later noted that he did not originally consider himself a nationalist but was radicalized by his encounters with the KGB.[54] The poet Tomas Venclova—a founder of the Lithuanian Helsinki Group exiled in 1977—was subjected to profilaktika as a student in 1961.[55] Of course, using profilaktika against youth may have been more effective than doing nothing and less expensive than arresting every anti-Soviet teenager, so it was not necessarily a failure. (Other high-profile dissidents—like Estonia's Enn Tarto, Latvia's Ints Calitis, and Lithuania's Petras Plumpa—were arrested as youth, after all.) But at a minimum, the tactic could not prevent several young profilaktika targets from becoming high-profile dissidents.

In fact, a majority of the Baltic region's dissident leaders were summoned to profilaktika as a result of their dissident activities. In March 1980, Tarto underwent profilaktika for signing the Baltic Appeal and joining the dissident Mart Niklus in a meeting with a recently released "bandit."[56] (Tarto had been imprisoned from 1956 to 1960 and from 1962 to 1967 and was sent to the Gulag again in 1984, when he was declared a "very dangerous recidivist.")[57] Calitis was subjected to a prophylactic chat at roughly the same time, accused not only of signing the Baltic Appeal but of trying to form a pan-Baltic nationalist group.[58] Like Tarto, Calitis had been convicted of anti-Soviet activity twice (in 1947 and 1958), and was imprisoned a third time in 1983—making it unlikely that a mere prophylactic chat would change his behavior. Plumpa was summoned to a chat in the 1980s for holding illicit lectures with youth concerning Catholic teachings and life in the Gulag, after serving two terms in labor camps.[59] These prophylactic interventions did not make sense by the KGB's official standards—since they did not target the redeemable, the "illiterate," and the "immature"—suggesting that the KGB had another objective in mind. Several anti-Soviet activists—including Tarto, Plumpa, and Rünno Vissak—have noted that profilaktika inspired them to become more careful in the short run, which was probably the KGB's goal.[60] Prophylactic chats against the dissident movement sometimes came in waves, with a number of chats following the announcement of the Baltic Appeal in 1979 and then again in 1983 and 1984 (when Tarto and Calitis were arrested and other leaders received KGB warnings), highlighting their role in political crisis management.[61]

Profilaktika was similarly ineffective against a second—sometimes overlapping—group: religious believers. Many Catholic priests, including Karolis Garuckas and Vincas Jalinskas, ran into KGB trouble for their preaching after going through a prophylactic chat.[62] In 1986, the KGB recommended firing a teacher who did not learn her lesson after a prophylactic chat for her religious activism two years before.[63] But the KGB also used profilaktika multiple times against non-Catholics and nondissidents. These included Jehovah's Witnesses who continued to meet for worship but were not involved in political activity, such as a sixty-seven-year-old man summoned to chats in 1979 and 1983, as well as Latvian Baptists and members of the Hare Krishna sect.[64]

Another category of profilaktika target was likely to run into repeated trouble: residents of port cities who associated with foreign sailors, in locales such as Klaipėda, Lithuania; Tallinn, Estonia; and Riga and Ventspils, Latvia. These people included men involved in "speculative" sales of foreign consumer goods and women who met with sailors in restaurants and cafés and took them home to their apartments.[65] KGB reports from the 1950s onward emphasize the dangers of foreign sailors, pointing to the risks of international espionage, increased speculation in contraband, defection to the West, and the spread of drunkenness, hooliganism, and membership in deviant subcultures such as the stiliagi.[66] By the 1960s, KGB activity followed a clear pattern, pursuing a steady stream of prophylactic chats with low-level offenders while occasionally pursuing high-profile trials of speculators and more tightly organized campaigns against youth who "shamed our city." This pattern extended into the 1980s.

Cases involving women were especially common in Klaipėda. On average, these women were twenty-three years old, though they could be as young as fifteen and as old as forty; more than a quarter were ethnically Russian or

Belorussian (a higher percentage than in Baltic profilaktika cases overall), while others were Tatar or Kazakh.[67] Many are listed as having jobs, though others were supposedly unemployed (and pursuing a "parasitic lifestyle"). These cases followed several patterns. Profilaktika targets were accused of being both greedy and sexually promiscuous. Some allegedly hung around the city's port looking for foreign sailors, while others spent time in restaurants and cafés frequented by visiting sailors. (No women got into KGB trouble for consorting with sailors from the USSR and its satellites.) Some case files are vague about exactly what the accused women had done, charging them with "base motives," but others are more specific. Some women drank and socialized with sailors; some invited sailors back to their apartments; many accepted small gifts, in the form of Soviet money, foreign currency, and portable consumer goods. Some women were charged with keeping foreign sailors in their apartment for days at a time, even making them miss their ships home. A few were even accused of trying to get foreign men to marry them (and help them emigrate). Many were treated like prostitutes even when they were not involved in sex work, but whatever the details of the case, women who consorted with foreign sailors were treated the same way. They were summoned to the KGB for a chat in order to achieve three goals: to prevent their "descent into the commission of a crime," to "alienate" them from "undesired contact with foreigners," and to "exert positive influence" on them.[68]

The KGB often seems to have failed in these goals. A December 1973 report from Klaipėda, concerning the cases of thirteen women, noted that although some profilaktika targets ceased their ties with foreigners, many did not. A December 1974 report from Klaipėda noted that seven of the sixteen women it discussed had already been summoned to at least one prophylactic chat and that three had earlier had their photos publicly displayed at a Komsomol photo stand under the title "They Shamed Our City."[69] To be sure, most profilaktika victims said that they had learned a lesson from their encounter with the police, and KGB informers often reported that the offender had changed her ways. (One informer noted that a profilaktika victim explained that it was time for her to settle down, while another was reported to have gotten married to a Soviet citizen and moved to Tbilisi.)[70] But they often returned to the same behavior. One woman—a worker in a hosiery factory—was summoned to profilaktika at least four times for associating with foreign sailors.[71]

Profilaktika also had a poor record in changing the behavior of young Klaipėda men allegedly corrupted by foreign sailors into a life of hooliganism, smuggling, and petty speculation. A profilaktika target named Rimantas Petrauskas told the local newspaper: "About four years ago I met on the street a sailor arriving from abroad, who gave me chewing gum. That's how it all began."[72] He added that his goal was an "easy life," and he and his friends engaged in drunkenness, hooliganism, and the wearing of bright, colorful socks.[73] One offender told a KGB informer that profilaktika had corrected his behavior "in time" and that he would not make a deal with a foreign sailor even if he was offered a nylon slicker for one ruble.[74] But he appears to have been the exception: several defendants in high-profile trials of speculators had been subjected to profilaktika "repeatedly," including the defendants in trials in both 1963 and 1973.[75] Klaipėda men appear to have been less likely than women to become recidivists, but several male recidivists nevertheless became the subject of high-profile prosecutions for black-market activity. Profilaktika was not enough to overcome the appeal of an "easy life."

By contrast, one common type of offender was unlikely to commit a subsequent crime after undergoing profilaktika: men accused of "violating the rules of conduct for a Soviet sailor abroad," typically by slipping away from the group while visiting a foreign country or engaging in illegal contraband. In a typical 1978 case, the KGB interrogated a twenty-eight-year-old man who slipped away from his group in Freetown, Sierra Leone; got drunk at a dive; spent the night with a "woman of easy behavior"; and narrowly escaped the police.[76] Similarly, a 1960 case from Klaipėda involved a sailor accused of "treacherous intentions" when he told fellow sailors about his desire to flee the country in a foreign port.[77] A 1980 case concerned two Latvian sailors who left their group in Salaverry, Peru; traveled to a nearby city with local women while drunk; and got back to their ship thirteen hours late.[78] Still other cases involved sailors who violated Soviet rules on contraband by picking up consumer goods or illegal items abroad, ranging from chewing gum and nylons to the works of Aleksandr Solzhenitsyn.[79] Many sailors were accused of trading vodka for goods like chewing gum and perfume.[80]

Recidivism appears to have been almost nonexistent among Lithuanian sailors accused of engaging in contraband speculation and drunkenness in foreign ports. This might be partially explained by the fact that ships were an environment unusually well-suited for surveillance, but another explanation is more likely: most sailors summoned to profilaktika were not only warned by the KGB and placed under surveillance but denied the right to a passport allowing foreign travel. These sailors therefore never had the chance to misbehave abroad again—and this may have shaped their actions more than a KGB chat. Evidence from the Delta-Latvija database supports this conclusion, featuring a higher number of sailors who were *not* denied a foreign passport (some of whom went on to become recidivists), as well as several cases involving foreign sailors who committed other types of misconduct after a chat.[81] A 1981 case from Riga, for example, involved a former sailor who had been given an official warning—an especially serious form of profilaktika—five years before for seeking not to return to his ship while abroad. He got into trouble a second time for telling informers that he wanted to flee to Finland, that he hoped to go by sea and owned a motor boat, and that he had been invited to visit by several Finnish tourists he befriended.[82]

To be sure, dissidents, religious believers, women who consorted with foreigners, and sailors were not a representative sample of profilaktika victims. But their stories cast doubt on the idea that profilaktika could change the attitudes and worldview of KGB targets whose actions were driven by strong beliefs—a category that also included thousands of Lithuanians, Latvians, and Estonians called to prophylactic chats for participation in anti-Soviet youth groups, among others. Moreover, other profilaktika victims—beyond those described in this section—were driven by a desire to acquire Western consumer goods or to escape economic hardship, and they too may not have been inclined to change their ways because of a KGB chat. In all likelihood, both the KGB's officers and its targets were diverse in their attitudes toward profilaktika. Some officers on the ground (and theorists in Moscow) presumably believed in the tactic's redemptive power, while others were more interested in intimidating regime critics or carefully managing the level of anti-Soviet activity. Some profilaktika victims were presumably terrified into better behavior, while others returned to their old ways when it became safe to do so. The stories told in this section show that profilaktika was unlikely to transform the attitudes and the long-term behavior of many of its targets, and that—despite KGB rhetoric—the security police may have been as interested in shaping its victims' short-term behavior as in transforming their lives.

The story of profilaktika, then, is the story of a secret police force whose rhetoric and official theory exceeded its capacities and perhaps even the goals of its officers on the ground. It would be a serious mistake to write off the KGB's desire to transform the behavior of profilaktika victims: internal documents in the 1970s and 1980s still show the didactic tone taken by many officers, who appear intent on lecturing, cajoling, or berating their victims into admitting wrongdoing, pleading ignorance, admitting the effects of their actions on others, and endorsing the principles of Soviet rule. (Although they were certainly coercive, these chats played a didactic function that went beyond mere intimidation.) But whether because of a lack of resources or a lack of desire, KGB officers did not conduct surveillance that was intensive enough to determine whether profilaktika had achieved its stated objectives. The goals of profilaktika were sweeping and ambitious, but the practices of the KGB were often narrower in scope.

NOTES

This chapter was first presented at the April 2020 ASEEES webinar on "The Political Police and the Soviet System: Insights from Newly Opened KGB Archives in the Former Soviet States," whose participants provided useful comments. Particular thanks to David Brandenberger, the discussant on the panel where the chapter was presented, and to the two anonymous reviewers of the chapter. Research for this chapter was completed with the support of grants from Grinnell College, the Association for the Advancement of Baltic Studies, the American Philosophical Society, and the National Endowment for the Humanities. Any views, findings, conclusions, or recommendations expressed in this chapter do not necessarily represent those of the National Endowment for the Humanities.

1. For more on profilaktika, see Julie Fedor, *Russia and the Cult of State Security: The Chekist Tradition, from Lenin to Putin* (London: Routledge, 2011), 51–56; Robert Hornsby, *Protest, Reform, and Repression in Khrushchev's Soviet Union* (New York: Cambridge University Press, 2013), 211–12, 218–21; Vladimir Kozlov et al., eds., *Sedition: Everyday Resistance in the Soviet Union under Khrushchev and Brezhnev* (New Haven: Yale University Press, 2011), 43–44, 56; Mark Harrison, *One Day We Will Live without Fear: Everyday Lives under the Soviet Police State* (Stanford, CA: Hoover Institution Press, 2016), chap. 5; Harrison, *If You Do Not Change Your Behaviour: Managing Threats to State Security in Lithuania under Soviet Rule* (CAGE Working Paper 247, University of Warwick, 2015); Edward Cohn, "Coercion, Reeducation, and the Prophylactic Chat: *Profilaktika* and the KGB's Struggle with Political Unrest in Lithuania, 1953–64," *Russian Review* 76, no. 2 (2017), 272–93; and Cohn, "A Soviet Theory of Broken Windows: Prophylactic Policing and the KGB's Struggle with Political Unrest in the Baltic Republics," *Kritika: Explorations in Russian and Eurasian History* 19, no. 4 (2018): 769–92.

2. Lietuvos ypatingasis archyvas (LYA) f. K-18, ap. 1, b. 505, ll. 49–50.

3. LYA f. K-18, ap. 1, b. 505, ll. 49–50.

4. LYA f. K-41, ap. 1, b. 799, l. 143.

5. LYA f. K-18, ap. 1, b. 511, ll. 22–23.

6. Romuald Misiunas and Rein Taagepera cover Soviet-era Baltic history in *The Baltic States: Years of Dependence, 1940–1990* (Berkeley: University of California Press, 1993), while Alexander Statiev, *The Soviet Counterinsurgency in the Western Borderlands* (New York: Cambridge University Press, 2010), and Elena Zubkova, *Pribaltika i Kreml', 1940–1953* (Moscow: ROSSPEN, 2008), cover early Soviet rule. Cohn, "Coercion, Reeducation, and the Prophylactic Chat" (275), briefly compares the use of profilaktika in Lithuania to the larger Soviet trend.

7. Hornsby, *Protest, Reform, and Repression*, 221.

8. Harrison, *One Day We Will Live Without Fear*, 136.

9. For such prior arguments, see Cohn, "Soviet Theory of Broken Windows"; and Harrison, *One Day We Will Live Without Fear*, chap. 5.

10. For an argument that Soviet surveillance was the "guiding hand" of a "totalitarian enterprise," see Amir Weiner and Aigi Rahi-Tamm, "Getting to Know You: The Soviet Surveillance System, 1939–57," *Kritika: Explorations in Russian and Eurasian History* 13, no. 1 (2012): 45.

11. N. F. Chistiakov, *Po zakonu i povesti* (Moscow: Voenizdat, 1979), chap. 10, http://militera.lib.ru/memo/russian/chistyakov_nf/10.html.

12. N. R. Mironov, *Ukreplenie zakonnosti i pravoporiadka v obshchenarodnom gosudarstve—programmnaia zadacha partii* (Moscow: Iuridicheskaia literatura, 1969), 141.

13. For more on profilaktika as a form of *vospitanie*, see Edward Cohn, "Coercion, Reeducation, and the Prophylactic Chat."

14. N. R. Mironov, "Za smeloe primenenie profilakticheskikh, predupreditel'nykh mer i usilenie sviazi s narodom," *Sbornik*, no. 1 (1959): 59.

15. LYA f. K-51, ap. 1, b. 439, ll. 128–29, 132.

16. LYA f. K-51, ap. 1, b. 323, ll. 12–13.

17. LYA f. K-51, ap. 1, b. 250, l. 18.

18. S. Marfunin, A. Zubov, and G. Ermolenko, "O praktike raboty po provedeniiu profilakticheskoi meropriatii," *Sbornik*, no. 1 (1959): 48, 50–51.

19. LYA f. K-51, ap. 1, b. 301, ll. 82–84.

20. V. S. Prasolov and V. A. Zolototrubov, *Nekotorye voprosy ideologicheskoi diversii protivnika protiv SSSR na kanale mezhdunarodnogo studencheskogo obmena i bor'by s nei organov gosudarstvennoi bezopasnosti* (Moscow: Vysshaia ordena oktiabr'skoi revoliutsii Krasnoznamennaia shkola KGB SSSR imeni F. E. Dzerzhinskogo, 1983), 79–80.

21. Volkogonov Papers, Library of Congress microfilm, Box 28, reel 18 (pages unnumbered).

22. LYA f. K-15, ap. 1, b. 307.

23. LYA f. K-15, ap. 1, b. 356, 360, 366, 379, 390, 397, 427, 467, and 527.

24. This set represents roughly 25 percent of Lithuanian profilaktika cases between 1959 and 1991, with relatively few cases from after 1982. Some of these cases were discussed in detailed KGB documents, while others were covered more briefly in longer reports on KGB activities. The recidivism rate was determined not just by looking at profilaktika case reports but by comparing these records to other KGB documents, some of which list repeat cases by profilaktika targets.

25. Lithuanian KGB records for 1974 understate the number of profilaktika victims given an official warning (*predosterezhenie*), for example.

26. The Delta-Latvija database has been available to researchers since 2018 and can be accessed by computer in a special reading room of the Latvian State Archives (Latvijas Valsts arhīvs, LVA); KGB officers attempted to destroy the database in 1991, but researchers have partially reconstructed it, resulting in a searchable database of over nine thousand cases resulting from KGB agent reports and other operational activities. (The sample of 858 used in this chapter came from running keyword searches for terms related to *profilaktika* and appear to include a large majority of the profilaktika cases in the database.) For more on Latvia's recent opening of KGB materials, see Eva-Clarita Pettai, "Delayed Truth: Latvia's Struggles with the Legacies of the KGB," *Cultures of History Forum*, https://www.cultures-of-history.uni-jena.de/debates/latvia/delayed-truth-latvias-struggles-with-the-legacies-of-the-kgb. See Joshua Sanborn's contribution to this volume for more on the Delta computer systems in different Soviet republics.

27. LVA Delta-Latvija database, entry 301294.

28. For more on the typical course of a prophylactic chat, see Harrison, *One Day We Will Live Without Fear*, 126–27; and Cohn, "Coercion, Reeducation, and the Prophylactic Chat," 278–80.

29. LYA f. K-41, ap. 1, b. 682, l. 39.

30. See LVA Delta-Latvija database, entry 62913, for a man named as the subject of a two-year operative surveillance case (DON), a high level of surveillance; in both Lithuania and Latvia, people given an official warning (*ofitsial'noe predosterezhenie*)—an especially intense form of profilaktika—sometimes became the subjects of DON or DOP cases after profilaktika, as did a handful of other offenders.

31. For more on the KGB's system of informers, see Weiner and Rahi-Tamm, "Getting to Know You"; and Fedor, *Russia and the Cult of State Security*, chap. 2.

32. LYA f. K-41, ap. 1, b. 682, l. 48.

33. LYA f. K-41, ap. 1, b. 682, l. 51.

34. LYA f. K-41, ap. 1, b. 744, ll. 1–5.

35. LYA f. K-18, ap. 1, b. 345, ll. 29–30; LYA f. K-11, ap. 2, b. 283, ll. 86–87; Eesti Riigiarhiivi Filiaal (ERAF) f. 131SM, n. 1, s. 393, ll. 82–83.

36. LYA f. K-18, ap. 1, b. 511, l. 207.

37. LYA f. K-11, ap. 1, b. 143, ll. 19–21.

38. ERAF f. SM131, n. 1, s. 393, ll. 27–28.

39. LYA f. K-18, ap. 1, b. 144, ll. 20–24; b. 122, ll. 154–55.

40. See, e.g., LYA f. K41, ap. 557, l. 21; f. K-1, ap. 10, b. 257, ll. 287–88; f. K-18, ap. 1, b. 494, ll. 12–14; f. K-11, ap. 1, b. 990, ll. 1–2; and f. K-18, ap. 1, b. 479, l. 15.

41. For these cases, see LYA f. K-1, ap. 10, b, 324, ll. 34–36.

42. LYA f. K-41, ap. 1, b. 556, ll. 87–89; f. K-1, ap. 10, b. 257, ll. 305–6.

43. LYA f. K-51, ap. 1, b. 274, ll. 17–18.

44. LYA f. K-51, ap. 1, b. 257, ll. 62–63.

45. See, e.g., *Chronicle of the Catholic Church in Lithuania*, vols. 73, 75, and 76.

46. LYA f. 17377, ap. 1, b. 42, ll. 43–44.

47. LVA Delta-Latvija database, entry 63860.

48. See, e.g., oral history interviews with Petras Plumpa (19 July 2015, Vilnius, Lithuania), Enn Tarto (29 March 2018, Tartu), and Rünno Vissak (13 October 2016, Tartu).

49. Prasolov and Zolototrubov, *Nekotorye voprosy*, 80.

50. LYA f. 1771, ap. 270, b. 182, ll. 1–10.

51. For the 1987 cases, see LVA Delta-Latvija database, entries 310092 and 308337.

52. LYA f. K-6, ap. 2, b. 193, ll. 77–79.

53. LYA f. K-1, ap. 46, b. 1375, ll. 149–69.

54. See LYA f. K-18, ap. 1, b. 134, ll. 55–65 for Matulis's 1962 case and f. K-6, ap. 2, b. 159, l. 61, for his 1974 case; he described his radicalization by the KGB in a 21 July 2016 oral history interview in Vilnius.

55. LYA f. K-41, ap. 1, b. 627, ll. 15–16.

56. ERAF f. 129SM, n. 1, s. 29155, l. 62.

57. "Christmas in the Gulag, as told by Enn Tarto," *Estonian World Review*, 16 December 2011, http://www.eesti.ca/christmas-in-the-gulag-as-told-by-enn-tarto/print34404.

58. LVA f. 1986, op. 2, d. P-9274, ll. 39–40.

59. Oral history interview with Plumpa on 19 July 2015.

60. See, e.g., the oral history interviews with Plumpa, Tarto, and Vissak cited above.

61. "Lagle Parek, Heiki Ahonen, Arvo Pesti (Soviet Estonia)," *Index on Censorship* 13, no. 2 (1984): 42.

62. LYA f. K-11, ap. 1, b. 660, ll. 8–9, 24–25, 39, 53; f. K-18, ap. 1, b. 122, ll. 154–55.

63. LYA f. K-18, ap. 1, b. 315, ll. 5–6.

64. For the Jehovah's Witness, see LYA f. K-6, ap. 2, b. 211, ll. 35–37. See LVA Delta-Latvija database, entry 303726, for a recidivist Baptist; and LYA f. K-18, ap. 1, b. 206, ll. 102–3, for a Hare Krishna.

65. See Erik Scott's contribution to this volume for a similar case from Odessa.

66. See, e.g., LYA f. K-41, ap. 1, b. 633, ll. 55–60.

67. These calculations are based on a set of fifty-eight cases from Klaipėda between 1963 and 1984. See LYA f. K-41, ap. 1, b. 682, 697, 713, 744, and 753; f. K-18, ap. 1, b. 360, 374; and f. K-6, ap. 2, b. 198 and 299.

68. Many profilaktika files involving supposedly loose women use this exact terminology; see, e.g., LYA f. K–41, ap. 1, b. 744, l. 33.

69. LYA f. K-41, ap. 1, b. 713, ll. 73–77, 78–81.

70. LYA f. K-41, ap. 1, b. 753, ll. 34–35, and b. 744, ll. 27–28.

71. LYA f. 17337, ap. 1, b. 42, ll. 43–44; f. K-41, ap. 1, b. 697, ll. 15–20; and f. K-41, ap. 1, b. 713, ll. 11–17, 73–78.

72. Rimantas Petrauskas, "Ia ponial, kak nado zhit'," *Sovetskaia Klaipeda*, 19 November 1964, found in K-41, ap. 1, b. 633, l. 61-1.

73. Petrauskas, "Ia ponial, kak nado zhit'."

74. LYA f. K-41, ap. 1, b. 633, l. 58.

75. LYA f. K-51, ap. 1, b. 314, ll. 24–25.

76. LYA f. K-41, ap. 1, b. 753, ll. 29–30.

77. LYA f. K-41, ap. 1, b. 1163, l. 325.

78. LVA Delta-Latvija database, entry 62461.

79. For a sailor accused of smuggling *The Gulag Archipelago,* see LYA f. K-41, ap. 1, b. 744, ll. 102–3.

80. LVA Delta-Latvija database, entry 62477.

81. See, e.g., LVA Delta-Latvija database, entry 301257.

82. LVA Delta-Latvija database, entry 304361.

Human Rights Activism as International Conspiracy

Iurii Andropov, Soviet Dissidents, and "Ideological Sabotage," 1967–1980

Douglas Selvage

IURII ANDROPOV, APPOINTED CHAIRMAN OF THE KGB IN MAY 1967, made the combatting of dissidence within the Soviet Union a top priority. Confronted with a new wave of dissidence in the form of civil and human rights activism, he reacted with a time-tested tactic of the Soviet regime and its secret police. Under his leadership, the security organs moved to discredit domestic critics of the regime—in this case, Soviet civil- and human-rights activists—by accusing them of conspiracy with foreign enemies of the Soviet Union. The KGB, just like its chekist forebears, played an active role in gathering, constructing, and—when necessary—falsifying the necessary evidence to "prove" the allegations of conspiracy with foreign powers.[1] This manufactured proof then served to justify the repression of the alleged conspirators—in this case, civil and human rights activists—not only in court proceedings (real or would-be show trials) but also in domestic and international propaganda.

This chapter analyzes two phases of KGB repression against Soviet civil and human rights activism and the corresponding conspiracy narratives authored and promoted by the KGB to justify such repression. In the first, during Andropov's early years as KGB chairman, 1967–1975, the Soviet chekists focused on dissidents' contacts to the West German–based anti-Soviet and anticommunist Russian émigré organization, the National Alliance of Russian Solidarists (Narodno-trudovoi soiuz rossiiskikh solidaristov, NTS). The minimal contact of some dissidents with NTS couriers, as well as the NTS's publication of some dissidents' texts at its Posev Press in Frankfurt, served for the KGB, Soviet propaganda, and Soviet prosecutors as proof of the dissidents' collaboration with an external enemy allegedly bent on destroying the Soviet Union. The KGB campaign reached its zenith with the trial of the dissidents Petr Iakir and Viktor Krasin in 1973, at which they confessed their cooperation with the NTS after having revealed the identities and alleged roles of other dissenters. The ensuing wave of repression, along with the expatriation of the leading regime critic Aleksandr Solzhenitsyn in 1974, silenced most civil and human rights activism. In early 1975, Andropov proclaimed victory for the KGB in its battle against the dissidents.

The proclamation of victory, it turned out, was premature. The revival of human rights activism in the wake of Moscow's signing of the Final Act of the Conference on Security and Cooperation in Europe (CSCE) at Helsinki in August 1975 surprised and angered Andropov and his minions. This new wave of "Helsinki" activism presented them with a dilemma: how could they suppress this new wave of dissent, based in part on the ongoing relationships between dissidents and Western journalists, in a way that would not endanger East-West détente? More specifically, how could they suppress this new wave of human rights activism in a way that would allow the Soviet government to plausibly deny that it was violating the provisions on human rights, human contacts, and improved working conditions for journalists in the Helsinki Final Act?

In the second phase of Andropov's repression of human-rights activists, 1976–1980, the KGB constructed a new conspiracy narrative to justify the repression of Soviet human-rights activists. According to this narrative, certain US correspondents known for their reporting on dissidence, the Jewish national movement, and other topics of concern to Soviet authorities were, in fact, spies for the CIA, and thus—in a textbook example of guilt through association—the Soviet human-rights activists in contact with them were spies as well. KGB counterintelligence laid the groundwork for this conspiracy narrative with a campaign of active measures, its Operation Wedge. In the initial stage of the campaign, based on revelations in the US Congress in 1975–1976 regarding the CIA's recruitment and use of US journalists for intelligence activities, the KGB targeted several US journalists with close ties to the dissidents for enhanced surveillance, manipulation, and entrapment through its secret agents. The KGB then exploited the results of these efforts to "unmask" the journalists in Soviet propaganda as alleged spies for the United States.

In the second stage of Operation Wedge, the KGB built on the alleged proof that the journalists were spies to suggest that the dissidents in contact with them were organizing the "anti-Soviet" campaign regarding human rights upon the orders of the CIA and were likely spying for the United States as well. The KGB exploited these accusations of anti-Soviet conspiracy not only in domestic and international propaganda but also in the trials of leading dissidents from the Moscow Helsinki Group, established in 1976 to monitor the Soviet government's compliance with the human-rights provisions of the Helsinki Final Act. A wave of arrests and imprisonments, culminating in the exile of the leading dissidents Andrei Sakharov and his wife, Elena Bonner, to Gor'kii in 1980, served to curtail this latest wave of human rights activism within the Soviet Union. However, despite the KGB's best efforts—indeed, even owing to its success at domestic repression—human rights and the fate of the dissidents remained a point of contention that undermined Moscow's relations with the West.

The major primary sources for the chapter come from the archives of the former KGB in Ukraine—namely, the Sectoral State Archive of the Security Service of Ukraine (Haluzevyi derzhavnyi arkhiv Sluzhby bezpeki Ukraïni, HDASBU). These sources include issues of the top secret internal journal by and for KGB officers, *Sbornik statei ob agenturno-operativnoi i sledstvennoi rabote Komiteta gosudarstvennoi bezopasnosti SSSR* (henceforth *Sbornik KGB*), published on a quarterly to bimonthly basis by the Higher School of the KGB since 1959, along with secret, internal volumes of key speeches by the KGB's leaders, also published by the Higher School.[2] Further, valuable primary sources for the chapter include records of speeches, discussions, and negotiations of the KGB's leaders with its "fraternal organs" in the Soviet bloc—in this case, from the archives of Bulgarian State Security and the East German Ministry of State Security (MfS or Stasi)—and published KGB documents in various collections of declassified documents since 1991. The chapter thus seeks to make use of the best primary sources available on the KGB's offensives against Soviet civil- and human-rights activists until such time as the Russian government opens the central archives of the former KGB to external researchers.

The chapter builds on, benefits from, expands upon, critiques, and revises several bodies of current scholarship. First, a relatively large body of scholarship in recent years has focused on the Soviet and Russian leaders' fear of conspiracies in which real or perceived domestic opponents or critics of the regime—perceived as a potential fifth column—might plot with a foreign enemy—usually a so-called imperialist power—to overthrow it. To prevent such a possibility, the ruler(s) in Moscow preemptively arrested perceived dissenters and frequently accused them of plotting with a foreign enemy to justify their public denunciation, imprisonment, or—in the Stalin era—execution. This research into perceived conspiracies, conspiracy narratives, or even official "conspiracy theories" has focused largely on the era of Iosif Stalin's rule or similar practices under the Russian leader Vladimir Putin today.[3] This chapter provides the first case study of the Soviet rulers' construction of such a conspiracy narrative during the years 1953–1991—that is, without the scripted, public confessions, generally extracted through torture by the secret police, during the widely publicized show trials in the Stalin era.

Second, there have been many recent publications on Soviet-Bloc "active measures"—that is, clandestine propaganda and especially disinformation—against foreign states and actors, especially against the US government.[4] In contrast, scholars have generally ignored the KGB's exploitation of such active measures to attack, neutralize, and destabilize individuals, such as US correspondents or Soviet human-rights activists.[5] As this chapter shows, such active measures inside the USSR could also feed into KGB and Soviet propaganda abroad. Third, a vast body of scholarship has been published regarding the CSCE process, including the Soviet Union and its role not only in the diplomatic deliberations leading up to the Helsinki Final Act and in the CSCE follow-up meetings through 1991, but also how the Soviet government sought to curtail and suppress unwanted domestic consequences from this "Helsinki process," including human rights activism.[6] Many of these studies discuss only in very general terms the KGB's role in this regard and have not analyzed the mechanisms by which it sought to repress post-Helsinki activism domestically. This chapter provides a case study of such largely neglected KGB activity. Fourth, a number of recent studies have examined the role of US and Western correspondents in Moscow, their role in the US-Soviet ideological and political struggle during the Cold War, and—most importantly for this study—their relationship to Soviet dissidents.[7] Based largely on the remembrances of the journalists and dissidents themselves, these studies discuss in general terms the activities and roles of the KGB in seeking to curtail journalists' reporting on the dissidents and the repression of the dissidents themselves. This chapter reveals and makes explicit at least some of the otherwise hidden activities of the KGB as it sought to sabotage and repress the dissidents' and journalists' activities.

THE KGB, SOVIET DISSIDENTS, AND
WESTERN CORRESPONDENTS, 1965–1976

In a speech to senior staff on 17 May 1975, KGB Chairman Iurii Andropov proclaimed victory in his organization's struggle against Soviet dissidents—a "wretched army," he called them. Speaking of the activists in the past tense, he underlined the role of Western journalists and the Western press in popularizing their activities: "It is also undeniable that the 'dissidents' could remain above ground only with the help of the Western press and foreign anti-Soviet centers, which not only published their materials but also provided them with material support. It was the Western press and radio that tried to portray a miserable bunch of renegades as a critically thinking part of Soviet society, which should be ensured freedom of action."[8]

Despite Andropov's apparent and factually incorrect attempt to blame the West for the existence of civil- and human-rights activists—that is, "dissidents"—in the USSR, he was correct in citing the close ties between dissidents and Western journalists and especially US correspondents. This relationship originated, along with the modern dissident movement itself, in the arrest and trial of the Soviet writers Andrei Siniavskii and Iulii Daniel', who had published satirical literary works critical of the Soviet system under pseudonyms abroad. Their trial in February 1966 marked not only the end of de-Stalinization and the Khrushchev-era thaw in Soviet literature but also a turning point in the history of Soviet dissent.[9] Many dissidents moved beyond their traditional criticism of such repression, based on the perceived historical role of the writer as critic in Russian society, to a new form of opposition based on civil rights, in accordance with the ideas of the Russian poet and mathematician Aleksandr Esenin-Vol'pin.[10] During the trial, dissident supporters of the defendants and Western correspondents discovered each other as the police forced both groups to wait for news outside in the cold.[11] In the wake of the trial, a symbiotic relationship developed between the dissidents and especially certain US correspondents.[12] The dissidents, as Andropov noted, could reach a Soviet and the international public through the journalists; some journalists even proved willing to smuggle dissidents' manuscripts to the West. Contacts with Western journalists could also help dissidents avoid potential arrest because the Soviet authorities, hoping to establish and build on the contemporary détente with the West, sought to avoid negative publicity. The journalists also helped the dissidents obtain products in short supply in the USSR, including food, various consumer products, and even vital medications. The journalists, for their part, had had difficulties before 1966 in making contact with "ordinary Russians" beyond official Soviet sources; now the dissidents provided them not only with personal stories of government abuse and repression but also with further insight into Soviet life and society. Due to such contacts and exchanges, many US correspondents and Soviet dissidents began to view each other as "kindred spirits" and "fellow truth-seekers" in a common struggle against the Soviet authorities. Many US correspondents stationed in Moscow, having already challenged the US government with their investigative reporting on the Vietnam War and various US government abuses, sought to apply the same ethos to their journalistic activities in the USSR. A number of dissidents came to view the Western journalists with whom they regularly had contact as "insiders" within their circles.[13]

The KGB, quite naturally, struck back. Western journalists in contact with the dissidents received anonymous warnings and threats, had their tires slashed, and fell victim to attacks by "random" street thugs. At demonstrations and dissident gatherings, journalists were subject to police beatings and potential arrest, if only for a few hours. The KGB increased surveillance against correspondents with undesired contacts and sought, along with the regular police, to block their entry into dissidents' apartment buildings or, conversely, visits by dissidents to their apartments. The Soviet press often vilified correspondents with frequent contacts to dissidents by name. The journalists, for their part, learned to speak practically in code with their dissident contacts in arranging meetings and undertook their own efforts, with varying success, to evade KGB surveillance and police controls. Such evasive tactics contributed to the traditional—and instrumentalized—belief of the KGB and other Soviet officials that all foreign correspondents were spies.[14] At the KGB's urging, Soviet authorities expelled a number of Western and especially US correspondents beginning in 1968. After Washington began to retaliate by expelling Soviet correspondents in the United States, Moscow curtailed the practice in 1971 until its expulsion of George Krimsky from the Associated Press in 1977, discussed below.[15]

Of course, the KGB focused its repressive measures against the dissidents themselves because they, as Soviet citizens, could not easily escape its grasp. Nevertheless, the dissidents' demands that the Soviet regime fulfill the civil rights embodied in the Soviet Constitution and—beginning in the 1970s— the universal human rights in the conventions of the United Nations, confronted the KGB with new and unprecedented difficulties. Internally, the KGB's leaders admitted that the dissidents' activities did not violate—or at least seem to violate—Soviet law, and their use of "outwardly positive slogans," such as "universal humanism and abstract freedom," made it difficult to justify their repression.[16] The trial of Siniavskii and Daniel' had demonstrated the KGB's difficulties. Whereas the dissidents had decried the judicial proceedings as a return to the show trials of the Stalin era, the officers of the KGB's investigations division voiced regret that this, in fact, had not been the case. Although Siniavskii and Daniel' had admitted to the authorship of various publications under pseudonyms in the West, they had refused to confess their alleged anti-Soviet intentions.[17] Such confessions, usually coerced with torture, had played a key role in the Stalin-era show trials.[18] The apparent failure to prove the defendants' anti-Soviet intentions had created a legal and thus a public relations problem for the Soviet regime. The prosecution had charged Siniavskii and Daniel' under article 70 of the Russian Criminal Code, "anti-Soviet agitation and propaganda," which required proof of such intentions. A belated admission of the prosecution's—and the KGB's—failure to do so came on 15 September 1966, with the adoption of a new article (190-1) to the Russian Criminal Code, "dissemination of fabrications known to be false, which defame the Soviet political and social system," which—in contrast to article 70—did not require proof of anti-Soviet intentions.[19] Although the court, all legal considerations aside, did convict and sentence the two authors under article 70, both the KGB and the Soviet legal system, based since Stalin on the principle of "socialist legality," had suffered a blow to their respective reputations.

Andropov, appointed chairman of the KGB in May 1967, sought to avoid such mistakes, even as he made the vilification, humiliation, and repression of the dissidents—along with other dissenters, such as nationalists and religious activists—a top priority. Only two months after his appointment, Andropov obtained the Soviet Politburo's approval for the creation of a new Fifth Directorate within the KGB, tasked with fighting the "ideological sabotage" (*ideologicheskaia diversiia*) of the "enemy" from abroad. In fact, the new directorate focused on repressing dissidents, along with other domestic dissenters, who—from the perspective of the KGB and in keeping with Soviet ideological precepts—had to originate in such foreign "sabotage."[20] Not surprisingly, Andropov's KGB thus sought to prove the existence of concrete connections between leading dissidents and the "imperialist" enemies of the Soviet Union, usually in the form of foreign intelligence agencies or individuals and organizations accused of collaborating with them. On this basis, the KGB could then claim that the dissidents in fact took orders from—or, at the very least, were manipulated by—these foreign enemies. This echoed, of course, the accusations of conspiracy with foreign enemies typical of the show trials of the Stalin era.[21]

In the various political trials during the early years (1967–1973) of Andropov's chairmanship, as well as in the ensuing propaganda generated by the trials, the KGB focused on "proving" the existence of ties between the dissidents and the NTS.[22] The NTS had cooperated with Nazi Germany for most of World War II in seeking the overthrow of the Soviet government, and during the 1950s, it had assisted the CIA in its policy of "rollback."[23] In the first political trial of the Andropov era, against Aleksandr Ginzburg and Iurii Galanskov in 1967, the prosecution and Soviet propaganda focused, in keeping with Andropov's wishes, on the defendants' alleged ties to the NTS.[24] The KGB also came closer to orchestrating the show trial that it had sought and failed to achieve against Siniavskii and Daniel', thanks to the confession of a third defendant, Aleksei Dobrovol'skii, regarding Ginzburg's and Galanskov's alleged ties to the NTS.[25] In 1973, the KGB and the procuracy successfully organized a trial against Petr Iakir and Viktor Krasin from the Initiative Committee for Civil Rights in the Soviet Union; in keeping with the rituals of Stalin-era show trials, both confessed in a press conference after their sentencing to having served as foreign agents of the NTS.[26]

The KGB's ongoing accusations of conspiracy against the dissidents raises the question: why did the KGB focus on the dissidents' alleged or real ties to the NTS, as opposed to other groups in the West, in justifying their repression? Certainly, Soviet authorities could exploit such alleged ties propagandistically to portray the dissidents as individuals who did not seek to fulfill the Soviet Constitution or promote human rights; instead, they sought, along with the NTS, an organization formerly allied with Nazi Germany, to overthrow the Soviet government.[27] Still, beyond such propagandistic exaggerations, Andropov's KGB did have real concerns about the NTS; it had begun to revive its activities in the Soviet Union in 1966–1967 after Andropov's predecessor, Vladimir Semichastnyi, had basically proclaimed the KGB's final victory over the allegedly defunct organization.[28] More importantly, NTS couriers had indeed been visiting Soviet dissidents to collect manuscripts for publication in the West, to provide them with *tamizdat* from Posev, or to interview them for various publications.[29] NTS couriers, for example, had likely been in contact with Galanskov, although the Soviet prosecutors had not provided any compelling proof in the case of Ginzburg.[30] Long before the arrest of Iakir and Krasin, a split had developed in their Initiative Committee between them and most other members over whether to maintain contact with the NTS in pursuing their goals or to accept funds from the organization to assist political prisoners' families.[31]

Still, with the possible exceptions of Iakir and Krasin, the KGB and Soviet propaganda clearly exaggerated the extent and nature of the dissidents' contacts with the NTS in a bid to discredit them and their cause. Often, Posev's publication of a declaration or samizdat from individual authors—even without their knowledge—served as proof for the KGB of collaboration with the

NTS in pursuit of anti-Soviet goals. For example, on Andropov's initiative, the deputy procurator general of the Soviet Union summoned the most prominent dissident and "father" of the Soviet hydrogen bomb, Andrei Sakharov, to his office in August 1973 for a "prophylactic" conversation. He warned Sakharov that he was engaging in anti-Soviet activities, punishable under Soviet law; among other things, he cited Posev's publication of several essays by Sakharov. To the anger of the procuracy and Andropov's KGB, Sakharov, having denied any personal contacts to the NTS or even knowledge of its political program, refused to denounce—and indeed voiced gratitude for—Posev's publication of his various essays critical of the Soviet regime.[32] To the extent that certain Soviet civil- and human-rights activists maintained contacts with the NTS or did not turn away its couriers, who often arrived unannounced, they shared Sakharov's pragmatic view of the organization's role, especially with regard to the publication and circulation of tamizdat.[33] There is no reason to conclude—as Soviet propaganda insinuated—that all dissidents, let alone the dissidents on trial in 1966–1973, shared the NTS's long-term goal of toppling the Soviet regime. Indeed, the NTS itself, following the example of its key financial patron, the CIA, had modified its activities—if not necessarily its ultimate convictions—in the early 1960s. The CIA had begun to focus at this point on "stimulating and sustaining pressures for liberalization and evolutionary change" inside the USSR. Although the CIA doubted that the dissidents' activities could "significantly influence Soviet society in the short term," it hoped to inspire long-term change by popularizing the dissidents' views through its covert financing of tamizdat and its broadcasting of their publications and appeals back to the USSR through Radio Liberty (RL). In keeping with these goals, the NTS continued to receive funding from the CIA for the "procurement, publication and distribution of Soviet dissident literature and socio-political commentary."[34]

Exploiting the list of persons whose names Iakir and Krasin had revealed during their interrogations, the KGB launched an unprecedented wave of prophylactic conversations with dissidents implicated in the pair's civil and human rights work, if only as recipients or distributors of samizdat.[35] The wave of repression following the arrests of Iakir and Krasin, followed by the forced expatriation of Aleksandr Solzhenitsyn at Andropov's urging in February 1974, led to a marked decline in dissident activity.[36] In November 1974, Andropov told his "comrades" in Bulgarian state security:

as soon as he [Solzhenitsyn] left the Soviet Union, anti-Soviet activity diminished. It is good that we got rid of Solzhenitsyn and did not send him to prison. Now the enemy is left with Sakharov and several Jews whom we cannot allow to emigrate because they have worked in missile units. The enemy now relies on Sakharov to come out with various protests. However, we have adopted the tactic of deliberately not reacting to Sakharov. If he protests, we will be silent.[37]

THE HELSINKI FINAL ACT, SOVIET DISSIDENTS, AND US JOURNALISTS

Andropov's epitaph for the dissidents' political activities, along with their contacts to Western journalists, turned out to be premature. On 1 August 1975, the Soviet Union joined thirty-four other states from Europe and North America in signing the Helsinki Final Act. The Soviet leader Leonid Brezhnev considered the Final Act to be a victory for the East, given the West's acceptance of the inviolability of the existing borders in Europe, along with its agreement to increased trade and scientific and technical cooperation with the East in part 2 of the document.[38] Many Soviet human-rights activists focused, however, on other parts of the Final Act. Brezhnev's signing of the Final Act helped resurrect the cause of human rights, given the document's reaffirmation of "human rights and fundamental freedoms" (principle 7) and the call in part 3—known as "Basket 3"—for greater human and cultural contacts and the freer flow of information between East and West, including improved working conditions for journalists. Exploiting the international nature of the agreement, Soviet human-rights activists now appealed directly to Western and neutral governments, nongovernmental organizations (NGOs) outside the USSR, and international public opinion to pressure the Soviet government to comply with these provisions.[39] The foremost pioneer in this regard was Sakharov. Andropov's strategy of ignoring him, it turned out, had not worked. The physicist threatened to publicly renounce his Hero of Socialist Labor medals on the opening day of the CSCE summit conference in Helsinki if the Soviet authorities did not finally relent and permit Bonner to travel to Italy for an eye operation. Andropov gave in, and the Politburo approved Bonner's trip. During her visit to Italy, Sakharov dictated to her over the telephone the introduction to his new book, *My Country and the World*. In the introduction, he called on the West to exploit Moscow's signature on the Helsinki Final Act to actively pressure it to fulfill the provisions for human rights and human contacts in the agreement. Bonner repeated this demand, contained in Sakharov's acceptance speech, when she traveled to Oslo in October 1975 to accept the Nobel Peace Prize on his behalf.[40]

A few months later, in May 1976, other Soviet dissidents—including Iurii Orlov, Aleksandr Ginzburg, Liudmila Alekseeva, and Anatolii Shcharanskii— went a step further and established the Moscow Helsinki Group. They undertook the task of monitoring the Soviet government's compliance with the human-rights and human-contacts provisions of the Helsinki Final Act and publicizing any potential violations both inside and outside the Soviet Union. Dissidents in other Soviet republics founded their own Helsinki groups, and by 1977, a transnational Helsinki network had arisen between human-rights groups in the Soviet Union and the Soviet bloc in general, Western and especially US journalists and NGOs, and certain Western politicians and governments.[41]

The dissidents naturally built on their existing relationships with Western correspondents in constructing this transnational Helsinki network. In this new wave of human rights activism, US and other Western correspondents played a central role, just as they had during the 1960s and early 1970s. They served as a channel for Soviet human-rights activists to Western and international public opinion, including the dissidents' supporters in the CSCE member-states, often organized in human-rights and other NGOs. Individuals and groups advocating for human rights, having heard about developments in the USSR through the journalists' reports in the Western media, could then lobby their own governments to pressure Moscow bilaterally and at CSCE follow-up conferences to implement the human-rights and humanitarian aspects of the Final Act.[42]

Western and US journalists also benefited from Moscow's signature under Basket 3 of the Final Act, in which the CSCE signatories committed themselves to the "improvement of working conditions for journalists" from their respective states.[43] In response, the Soviet Foreign Ministry announced in January 1976 an easing of travel restrictions for foreign journalists. They would no longer need to request permission from its Press Department to leave Moscow; they could simply advise it of their destination and the route they planned to take, as long as they avoided certain restricted zones. Travel within the Moscow region was now unrestricted with the exception of military zones. In June, a further decree permitted foreign journalists to speak with Soviet officials without first obtaining permission from the Press Department—a step that potentially opened up new stories and new sources. The Soviet authorities also agreed to make multiple-entry visas available to Western correspondents—a practice that would make it more difficult to expel correspondents by simply not letting them return to the Soviet Union after a foreign vacation. At least on paper, the Helsinki Final Act would make the expulsion of foreign journalists more difficult in general. The signatory states reaffirmed that journalists' "legitimate pursuit of their professional activity" would not render them "liable to expulsion" or other penalties. Moreover, the Final Act provided: "If an accredited journalist is expelled, he will be informed of the reasons for this act and may submit an application for re-examination of his case."[44] The US and Western correspondents in general exploited the easing of restrictions not only to expand the topics on which they reported from the Soviet Union but also to report more intensively on the dissidents and their human rights activism, which—at least from the West's perspective—had received sanction, if only indirectly, from the Helsinki Final Act.[45]

OPERATION WEDGE (1976): THE KGB STRIKES BACK

At a meeting with his colleagues in the East German Ministry of State Security (Stasi) in East Berlin in April 1976, Deputy KGB Chairman Viktor Chebrikov voiced frustration with the new wave of human rights activism based on the Helsinki Final Act. The "enemy," he complained, was attaching itself to Sakharov and other dissidents, and its mass media was "artificially and propagandistically blowing up every matter." "Western journalists," he said, "are playing a major role in this regard."[46] Although the KGB continued to harass Western journalists and threaten Soviet dissidents with imprisonment, a swift or massive crackdown on either group could undermine Moscow's détente with the West—an option that could bring the KGB difficulties with the leadership of the Communist Party of the Soviet Union (CPSU) and Brezhnev personally. The KGB would need to lay the groundwork and build up a case to justify a crackdown. The repressive measures should not conflict with Moscow's interpretation of the Helsinki Final Act or, even better, the KGB should be in a position to argue that the West's attempted "abuse" of Helsinki had compelled it to act.

The KGB saw an opening in 1975–1976 as a heated debate arose in the United States over the relationship of US journalists to the CIA. In 1975, a committee of the US House of Representatives, investigating illegal activities by the CIA, had publicly revealed that the agency had been employing US journalists and using US media organizations as a cover for some of its agents.[47] This revelation, along with the decision of the US Senate's Church Committee to further investigate the CIA's relations with journalists, led the new CIA director, George H. W. Bush, to issue a directive in February 1976 forbidding the CIA from entering into "any paid or contractual relationship" with any part- or full-time correspondent accredited to any newspaper or media outlet.[48] This did not end the ongoing disputes between journalists and the US Congress, on the one hand, and the CIA and the executive branch, on the other. The directive left open such possibilities as voluntary cooperation with the CIA by correspondents or the CIA's paid use of nonaccredited journalists and freelancers for spying.[49]

This dispute in the United States provided the KGB with the opportunity that it was seeking. It could gather or, if necessary, concoct evidence to claim that certain US journalists with close ties to Soviet dissidents were in fact CIA agents. This could serve not only to exacerbate the ongoing dispute between the US press and the CIA but also to denounce certain US correspondents in Moscow and the dissidents in contact with them as alleged "spies," as it had previously done with regard to dissidents and the NTS. This, in turn, would help justify a wave of repression against both US journalists and dissidents, who were allegedly "abusing" the Helsinki Final Act to nefarious ends. These were the goals that KGB counterintelligence set for itself as it launched Operation Wedge in early 1976.[50]

A group of KGB counterintelligence officers, apparently involved in this campaign of active measures, published an article about it in *Sbornik KGB* in 1981. Among the major immediate goals of the operation, they wrote, had been "to expose and document the espionage and other subversive activities of US journalists and their connections with [foreign] intelligence" and "to portray the CIA as the chief organizer of subversive activities against the USSR and as the inspirer of the anti-Soviet campaign [regarding human rights] in the Western press."[51] Based on the operation, the KGB apparently came to—the arguably foregone—conclusion in 1978 that the US embassy in Moscow directed the US journalists stationed in Moscow to engage in "subversive and espionage activities . . . aimed at inspiring and creating so-called Soviet dissidents out of volatile, misguided and negatively inclined citizens of the Soviet Union."[52] After creating these "so-called dissidents," the US correspondents, the KGB claimed, would then hand them over to the CIA's station chief ("resident") at the embassy.[53]

KGB counterintelligence initially focused on three journalists in its Operation Wedge: the US correspondents George Krimsky from the Associated Press (AP), Christopher Wren from the *New York Times*, and Alfred Friendly, Jr., from *Newsweek*.[54] Krimsky was a known quantity to the KGB. He had covered the dissident scene for the AP since 1967; maintained contacts to Ginzburg, Orlov, and Shcharanskii from the Moscow Helsinki Group; and was a friend of the Sakharov/Bonner family.[55] Wren had also attracted the attention of Soviet authorities. During an unofficial exhibition of nonconformist art in 1974 on the outskirts of Moscow—the "bulldozer exhibition," nicknamed after the Soviet authorities' use of heavy machinery to disburse the gathering—Wren had suffered a chipped tooth after police had shoved his camera into his face.[56] Wren had also become known for accompanying US politicians visiting Moscow to meetings with Soviet dissidents; he served as a guide, even when US embassy officials sought to avoid such duties.[57] Friendly, for his part, was in contact with Sakharov, Shcharanskii, and other dissidents and had smuggled various samizdat works out of the Soviet Union for publication in the West.[58] The three correspondents, the KGB officers alleged in 1981, had inspired "anti-Soviet" attitudes among a number of Soviet citizens; had provoked "politically unstable persons" to carry out "anti-social demonstrations"; had been "fomenting a desire to emigrate among persons of Jewish nationality," and had allegedly exploited their Soviet contacts "for the collection of intelligence and defamatory information" about the USSR.[59] The KGB thus blamed the correspondents for provoking the dissidents' activities, when in fact, the dissidents generally sought out the correspondents and asked that they cover a given story.[60]

All three correspondents, the KGB officers claimed in 1981, had also been "actively engaged in the collection of political and other—including classified—information."[61] That is, based on the journalists' collection of political and other information for their reporting that the Soviet government considered secret, the KGB could portray them as spies, or at least as contractors, for the CIA. To obtain the necessary details to accuse the journalists of espionage, the KGB engaged in intensive surveillance of the journalists' visits and contacts with US diplomats, along with their activities during travel within the USSR. The Soviet chekists also gathered details about the journalists' efforts to arrange secret meetings with their sources, away from the prying eyes and potential repressions of the KGB; this served as alleged evidence of their training in the tradecraft of espionage. The KGB also strove to find out whether the US journalists' Soviet contacts—including human-rights activists—had access to secret documents through their work or maintained ties with other individuals having such access.[62] This information would later serve to portray the journalists, along with the human-rights activists interacting with them, as spies for the US government.

To help matters along, the KGB also sought to replace the journalists' existing Soviet contacts with its own recruited agents. To this end, the KGB utilized "prophylactic measures." Many of the journalists' known Soviet contacts were summoned to local KGB headquarters, warned about the journalists' alleged espionage activities, and threatened with arrest and prosecution if they did not break off contact.[63] While the journalists' real Soviet sources thus dwindled, the KGB sent its own agents to the reporters with various types of "information." These KGB recruits sought to win the given journalist's confidence. If they succeeded, they could then spy on the latter and help set them up, if necessary, for subsequent accusations of espionage by offering them "secret" information.[64]

After this initial phase of Operation Wedge, consisting of surveillance, espionage, and manipulation of the three journalists, KGB counterintelligence launched the second phase on 26 May 1976: a campaign of active measures to discredit them, along with the Soviet dissidents with whom they had had contact, the CIA, and the US government in general. On this date, *Literaturnaia gazeta* published an article titled, "The CIA's Amendment . . . to the USA's Constitution."[65] The choice of newspaper was not accidental; although *Literaturnaia gazeta* enjoyed recognition as the most important journal of the intelligentsia during and after the Thaw, it also often served as a front for launching KGB disinformation.[66]

The KGB-inspired article argued that the CIA had undermined the US press's independence from the government, guaranteed by the First Amendment, by recruiting US and foreign journalists for espionage activities abroad. Reflecting the KGB's knowledge of the "great importance" that US citizens attached to the First Amendment, the article cited statements by representatives of the US press opposing the CIA's use of journalists.[67] The article, in keeping with the KGB's plans, succeeded in exacerbating the existing tensions in the United States between the press and the CIA.[68] For example, in an official denial of the Soviet accusations against Wren, the *New York Times*'s publisher, Arthur Ochs Sulzberger, renewed his earlier call that the CIA release a list of all journalists in its employ.[69] Sulzberger's statement unwittingly played into the KGB's efforts. In a follow-up article in June 1976, *Literaturnaia gazeta* commented that Sulzberger apparently did not know whether Wren or his other employees worked for the CIA. *Literaturnaia gazeta* also referred positively to a commentary by the *Washington Post*'s ombudsman, Charles Seib.[70] Although Seib had also rejected Moscow's allegations against the US correspondents, he had suggested that "the CIA's unwillingness to cut its ties to American journalism" could feed "the suspicions that lead to such charges" and make it more difficult to refute them.[71]

Owing to such public pressure from the US media, the CIA was compelled to strictly limit its use of journalists. On 30 November 1977, Admiral Stansfield Turner, Bush's successor under President James "Jimmy" Carter, issued a directive further restricting the CIA's contacts to journalists, including now "stringers" and technical staff.[72] Many US publishers, for their part, forbade their staff and journalists to enter into contractual or other paid relationships with US intelligence under penalty of dismissal. Although the revelations by the US Congress had arguably proved decisive, the KGB's attacks in *Literaturnaia gazeta* against US correspondents had contributed to the ongoing controversy.[73] Thanks to the new regulations in the United States, the KGB won an advantage in the world of espionage and covert warfare; in contrast to the CIA, its agents continued to work around the globe under the cover of Soviet press agencies and publications.[74]

The article also served the KGB's more immediate goal of discrediting US correspondents with contacts to Soviet dissidents.[75] It asserted that Friendly, Krimsky, and Wren were engaged in espionage activities inside the USSR, but in keeping with the KGB's guidelines, the article did not provide any specifics in this regard.[76] It simply referred to letters that the newspaper's editors had received from Moscow, Tbilisi, and Tallinn that spoke "convincingly" of the "hostile subversive activities of these 'correspondents in civilian clothes,'" who were allegedly interested in "certain materials and facilities clearly beyond the scope of the journalistic profession."[77] The letters to the editor, the KGB officers revealed in 1981, had actually been written by local and regional KGB officers, who had surveilled the correspondents' activities with the explicit goal of uncovering real or alleged espionage.[78]

As was often the case with KGB active measures, denials from the other side helped fuel the ongoing disinformation campaign.[79] After fourteen accredited US journalists in Moscow submitted a protest to *Literaturnaia gazeta* denying its accusations—an action that, the KGB officers claimed, had been inspired by US intelligence agencies—the Soviet newspaper responded with yet another article, "That's It, Gentlemen!" The June 1976 article included details about the three correspondents' alleged activities, taken from the aforementioned letters to the editor from "Soviet citizens"—actually, the KGB.[80] Their activities, it claimed, were "closer to the 'exploits' of the prolific heroes of Ian Fleming's novels than to the work of journalists."[81] For example, the newspaper reprinted accusations against Krimsky from a Soviet soldier's letter regarding the journalist's alleged attempt to obtain intelligence about the Red Army.[82] In 1981, the KGB officers revealed the identity of the soldier and letter writer: the agent code-named Arkhipov from the KGB's Third Chief Directorate, responsible for military counterintelligence. With the assistance of another agent, Javier, from the KGB's regional office in Moscow, Arkhipov had won Krimsky's trust as part of the KGB's efforts to unmask him as a spy.[83]

The decision by Friendly to sue *Literaturnaia gazeta* for defamation in a Soviet court in response to the article in June 1976 provided yet another opportunity for *Literaturnaia gazeta*—and the KGB—to amplify its claims about the alleged intelligence connections of the US correspondents. *Literaturnaia gazeta* responded with an article, "Ha Ha! Involuntary Spies," mocking Friendly's alleged claim that the Soviet press's silence on military affairs had compelled him to gather his own information on the topic for his reporting. The article warned Friendly, who had decided himself to go to court, that *Literaturnaia gazeta* had enough information about his activities not only for "public condemnation" but also for his criminal punishment.[84] Friendly, who concluded his scheduled term with *Newsweek* in Moscow shortly thereafter, obtained an indefinite postponement of his lawsuit in Moscow.[85] After his return to the United States, Friendly joined the staff of the US Congress's bicameral Commission on Security and Cooperation in Europe, which investigated Soviet and Soviet-Bloc violations of the human-rights and human-contact provisions of the Helsinki Final Act, including those regarding foreign journalists. He would remain a thorn in the side of the Soviets for years to come.[86]

The KGB and other Soviet officials hoped that the articles in *Literaturnaia gazeta* would also compel Wren and Krimsky to leave Moscow or convince their employers to withdraw them. However, both sought to remain. Wren, the KGB officers claimed, began to tone down his reporting, to avoid contact with "anti-social elements," and to curtail his trips within the Soviet Union.[87] He remained in Moscow until the completion of his assigned term with the *New York Times* in late September 1977.[88]

KRIMSKY, SAKHAROV, AND THE KGB

Krimsky, in contrast, remained defiant. On 13 January 1977, he met with Sakharov regarding a bomb attack on the Moscow subway the week before. Sakharov had sought the interview in response to an article published by the Soviet journalist and KGB agent Viktor Louis in the London *Evening News*, which claimed on the basis of "official" Soviet sources that a dissident group had been responsible for the attack.[89] The group, Louis had also written, had perhaps been encouraged by information from the West, which was flowing more freely into the USSR owing to Basket 3 of the Helsinki Final Act.[90] Sakharov, who feared that the article foreshadowed a crackdown by the Soviet regime on the dissident movement, countered Louis's claim by stressing Soviet human-rights activists' commitment to legality and nonviolence. He also voiced suspicion that the KGB might have organized the bomb attack itself in a bid to discredit Soviet dissidents.[91]

Andropov exploited Sakharov's latter statement in a joint proposal with Soviet Procurator General Roman Rudenko and Soviet Foreign Minister Andrei Gromyko to his colleagues on the Soviet Politburo on 18 January 1977. Andropov recommended that Sakharov be called in to the procurator's office once more and warned that his statement slandered the government (i.e., the KGB) and was thus punishable under Soviet law. Subsequent statements, he should be warned, would not be tolerated. The Politburo accepted the joint proposal, and Sakharov received his official warning on 25 January.[92]

Andropov also exploited the occasion to tie up the KGB's loose ends with regard to Krimsky. The joint proposal, approved by the Politburo, declared: "it is imperative to prepare and implement measures that, once we expose the fact of his [Krimsky's] connections with the CIA and his violation of customs regulations, would force the American side to recall him from the Soviet Union. If the Americans decline, he is to be expelled from the country."[93]

After the Politburo approved the measures against Krimsky, a Moscow police officer just happened to detain a "Soviet citizen" at a Moscow food store for foreign diplomats on 21 January 1977. In violation of Soviet law, the "citizen" was using coupons provided by Krimsky to purchase foodstuffs otherwise unavailable in normal Soviet stores.[94] Whoever the "citizen" might have been, Krimsky subsequently claimed that he had given coupons only to his maid. At the time, providing servants with such coupons was a common practice among foreign correspondents in Moscow, and the Soviet authorities generally tolerated it, despite its illegality.[95] Nevertheless, the stage had been set for Krimsky's departure. After the AP rejected Moscow's request to voluntarily recall Krimsky on 24 January, *Literaturnaia gazeta* published a new article on 2 February, repeating its allegations about Krimsky's alleged spying for the CIA, along with the new accusations regarding his illegal "foreign currency operations."[96] The article also included his business and private phone numbers in Moscow; a flood of threatening, anonymous phone calls followed to his apartment, condemning his espionage activities.[97] The AP's refusal to recall Krimsky, it suggested, had forced Moscow's hand. The article preemptively rejected any appeal to Basket 3 of the Helsinki Final Act, which stated "that the legitimate pursuit of their professional activity will neither render journalists liable to expulsion nor otherwise penalize them." Spying and illegal "currency operations," *Literaturnaia gazeta* noted, were not legitimate activity.[98] On 4 February, the Soviet Foreign Ministry summoned Krimsky and officially expelled him from the Soviet Union.[99]

THE KGB, US CORRESPONDENTS, AND THE SUPPRESSION OF THE MOSCOW HELSINKI GROUP

A growing wave of repression against Soviet human-rights activists built on and quickly became intertwined with the KGB's activities against US correspondents under Operation Wedge. Two days after the Soviet Politburo approved Andropov's proposal regarding Sakharov and Krimsky, the KGB chairman followed up with a resolution, co-signed by Rudenko, to the Central Committee's (CC's) Secretariat regarding "measures for stopping the criminal activities" of leading members of the Soviet Helsinki groups. The "security services and ideological centers of the enemy," the resolution claimed, "are making serious efforts to revive and expand the hostile activities of anti-Soviet elements on the territory of the USSR." The resolution singled out in this regard not only US diplomats assisting Soviet human-rights activists but also the "accredited Moscow correspondents from the United States" and other

Western countries, who "are persistently encouraging the leaders of the anti-Soviet movement to use such methods as 'addresses' to the governments of various countries, containing vile slanders of Soviet life, 'press conferences,' and open protests against the projects of the Soviet Union in their anti-Soviet activities."[100] The resolution thus built on the propagandistic groundwork that the KGB had laid with its "revelations" regarding Friendly, Wren, and Krimsky in *Literaturnaia gazeta*.

The resolution from Andropov and Rudenko, citing the failure of pro-phylactic measures, called for various repressive measures. These included the arrest of Orlov, the head of the Moscow Helsinki Group, for "dissemination of knowingly false fabrications that defame the Soviet state," as well as the arrest—and conviction—of the group's founding member Aleksandr Ginzburg for the more serious political offense of "anti-Soviet agitation and propaganda."[101] For several years, Ginzburg had been distributing assistance from Solzhenitsyn's fund for Soviet political prisoners, financed by the worldwide proceeds from *Gulag Archipelago*.

The resolution from Andropov and Rudenko, subsequently approved by the CC's Secretariat, also stated: "In connection with the propaganda requirements of the suggested measures, the KGB will prepare and present to the Central Committee . . . the necessary proposals."[102] Perhaps not surprisingly, on 2 February 1977, the same day that the article on Krimsky and Sakharov appeared, *Literaturnaia gazeta* also published a harsh attack against Orlov and especially Ginzburg. It took the form of an open letter from Aleksandr Petrov-Agatov titled, "Liars and Pharisees." The author, who had once shared a prison cell with Ginzburg because of his "anti-Soviet" writings, had received assistance from the latter after his release. In the letter, he denied that Ginzburg and the other members of the Moscow Helsinki Group truly believed in human rights; he portrayed them as mere speculators, paid by the West, seeking to make a profit. Ginzburg, he alleged, distributed assistance only in return for (implicitly fabricated) accounts of Soviet human rights abuses, which then appeared in the famous dissident publication, *A Chronicle of Current Events*. Petrov-Agatov denounced the dissidents as "embittered, morally unstable persons" and "criminal elements" dealing in matters that "run contrary to the interests of the Fatherland, its culture and its spiritual mode, and contrary to the interests of our fellow-countrymen."[103]

Although Petrov-Agatov's letter was not part of Operation Wedge, Deputy KGB Chairman Chebrikov revealed that his agency had stood behind the article in a speech to a gathering of the Soviet-bloc security services at the end of May 1977. The article, he said, served as an example of the necessary "validation of chekist measures" in domestic propaganda and the successful exploitation of individuals who "have given up their criminal activities and now condemn them," as was the case with "our [the KGB's] agent" Petrov-Agatov.[104]

OPERATIONAL GAME "COLLEAGUES":
THE KGB AND ANATOLII SHCHARANSKII

The KGB adopted the same tactic to discredit and to justify its arrest of another leading member of the Moscow Helsinki Group, Anatolii Shcharanskii. (Shcharanskii changed his first name to the Hebrew "Natan" after his release from Soviet prison and immigration to Israel in 1986.) In the early 1970s, he had joined the Jewish national movement in the USSR and applied for a visa to leave for Israel. After the rejection of his application, he joined other Jews who had been refused such visas in demonstrating for the right to emigrate to Israel—the so-called refuseniks. However, in contrast to the other refuseniks, who rejected any dissipation of their energies to help reform a society that they sought to leave, Shcharanskii had decided to join the broader human-rights movement in the USSR to compel Moscow's observance of the right to emigrate. By the end of 1976, Shcharanskii had become a leading figure in the Moscow Helsinki Group.

On 4 March 1977, *Izvestiia* published an open letter from Doctor Sania Lipavskii. He had attached himself to the Jewish national movement in 1972, subsequently won the trust of leading figures from its various factions, and come to serve as an unofficial "archivist" for some of its leaders. Lipavskii claimed in *Izvestiia* that he had become disillusioned with the movement owing to its leaders' self-serving use of funds from abroad and their alleged contacts to the CIA through the US embassy and US correspondents in Moscow. Lipavskii claimed that he himself had been recruited for the CIA in 1975 by a diplomat from the US embassy assisting the Jewish national movement. He had subsequently tasked Lipavskii with gathering information regarding sonar technology on Soviet submarines.[105] An article accompanying Lipavskii's open letter renewed the previous attacks against Friendly, Krimsky, and US correspondents in Moscow in general. The journalists, along with several named US embassy employees in contact with the human-rights and Jewish activists, the article suggested, were working for US intelligence.[106]

Lipavskii's open letter also insinuated a connection between the CIA and the Jewish national movement, including Shcharanskii. Some leading activists, he claimed, had gathered information about Jews who had been refused exit visas due to their work at research facilities allegedly tasked with secret work. The goal was to compare this list of scientific facilities with those making use of imported Western technology; such facilities, the Jewish activists could then argue, were apparently violating Western licensing agreements limiting the use of the imported technology to civilian purposes. Based on this information, supporters of the refuseniks in the United States could then lobby the US Congress to ban such technology transfers and thus further restrict trade with the USSR. However, the actual goal of this information gathering, Lipavskii insinuated, had been to provide the CIA with intelligence about such secret facilities, along with a list of disgruntled employees for potential recruitment as spies.[107]

In his open letter, Lipavskii alleged that Shcharanskii, with whom he had shared an apartment, was engaged in collecting this allegedly secret information for transmittal to the United States The subtext was clear—namely, that Shcharanskii, just like Lipavskii, had been recruited by the CIA.[108] Soviet prosecutors subsequently used Lipavskii's "evidence" to justify Shcharanskii's arrest on 15 March and his planned prosecution not only for anti-Soviet agitation but also for treason, a crime that carried a potential death sentence.[109] Based on the available evidence, Shcharanskii had apparently contributed to compiling such a list, whether on his own initiative; at the request of the Moscow correspondent of the *Los Angeles Times*, Robert Toth, who subsequently published an article on the issue; or at the request of other representatives from the Jewish national movement in the United States and Moscow, but there is no evidence that the CIA ever recruited Shcharanskii or tasked him with preparing such a list.[110]

As had been the case with the earlier polemics in *Literaturnaia gazeta* against US journalists, the KGB stood behind this latest propaganda. Indeed, the counterintelligence division of KGB's Moscow administration dubbed the preparation and publication of the article its own "operational game," code-named "Colleagues."[111] It had allegedly recruited Lipavskii in 1972 as its agent "Ervin" and tasked him with infiltrating and spying on Jewish nationalist circles in Moscow.[112] After a CIA officer from the US embassy in Moscow had sought to recruit Ervin in 1975, the KGB decided to employ him as a double agent against the CIA.[113] That the KGB was willing to "burn" Lipavskii as its agent for the sake of the *Izvestiia* article demonstrated the importance that it attached to discrediting Shcharanskii, along with the Jewish nationalist and human-rights movements, as paid spies for the United States.

The decision to sacrifice Ervin to discredit Shcharanskii apparently came straight from Andropov, who had obtained the approval of the other Soviet leaders for the *Izvestiia* articles. Andropov trumpeted their success in a subsequent memorandum to the Politburo. The articles, he wrote, had "played a positive role in discrediting the anti-Soviet campaign about 'human rights' . . . in the USA," "caused confusion among the accredited American diplomats and correspondents in the USSR," "had a moderating influence upon their contacts with 'dissidents,'" and created a "certain confusion . . . among pro-Zionist individuals and 'dissidents' who are in active contact with American representatives in the USSR." Andropov, citing the alleged opinion of "the overwhelming majority of Soviet citizens," concluded that the articles, "revealing the role of the USA's secret services in the anti-Soviet campaign regarding 'human rights' and showing the true face of the 'dissidents' . . . will have a sobering effect upon 'dissidents' who are in contact with foreigners and on emigration-minded people."[114] The KGB chairman proposed further propaganda measures to build on this apparent success, including publication of a subsequent interview with Lipavskii in *Izvestiia* to continue the campaign; increased pressure against US correspondents and diplomats on the basis of the accusations; and the exploitation of the articles in Moscow's international propaganda to discredit the dissidents' activities and the Carter administration's human-rights campaign as a mere front for CIA subversion against the USSR. The Politburo approved Andropov's proposals.[115]

The KGB's new offensive against Shcharanskii and the US correspondents helped resurrect Operation Wedge. The new target was Robert Toth of the *Los Angeles Times*, who had frequently used Shcharanskii as a source for his articles and employed him as a translator.[116] An apparent factor in the KGB's decision to lean on Toth was a telegram that he had sent to his editors in the United States; a "janitor"—or the KGB itself—had found a draft in a wastebasket at the *Los Angeles Times*'s Moscow bureau in mid-March 1977. The telegram consisted of Toth's draft article about Shcharanskii's arrest and a short note at the end from Toth to his editors.[117] Andropov personally summarized the purloined document in a memorandum to his colleagues on the Politburo:

> The correspondent of the *Los Angeles Times*, Toth, in an official report from Moscow, warned his newspaper's editors that he might be in difficult straits because of Shcharanskii's arrest, since the latter helped him to prepare articles with information on Soviet secret facilities that use American equipment. In addition, this information was obtained from people who had earlier worked at these installations and who had been provisionally denied permission to emigrate from the USSR.[118]

The KGB had apparently also purloined a letter from Toth's trash from a family acquaintance working for the Defense Intelligence Agency (DIA). It provided the necessary "evidence" that the KGB needed to connect Toth with a US intelligence agency.[119] The materials collected from Toth's trash presented the KGB with the necessary opportunity—and the worldwide condemnations of Shcharanskii's arrest, with the necessary motivation—to move against Toth.[120]

In a bid to provide more "evidence" of Toth's espionage, the KGB officers from Operation Wedge set a trap. Specifically, they arranged for their agent "Anisimov" to present Toth with allegedly secret documents, at which point the journalist would be arrested.[121] On Saturday, 11 June 1977, Valerii Petiukhov from the Institute of Biomedical Problems, in keeping with a prior arrangement with Toth, handed the journalist a paper on parapsychology while walking down a Moscow street. Immediately thereafter, five plainclothesmen seized Toth and Petiukhov. The US journalist was arrested on charges of espionage. Petiukhov's paper on extrasensory perception, an affidavit from the Soviet Academy of Sciences claimed, constituted secret research. Both Toth and Petiukhov were subsequently released. While Toth, forbidden to leave the country, awaited further interrogation by the KGB, Petiukhov returned to work without any further consequences. He had helped the KGB, Soviet authorities explained, to "expose an arch-intelligence agent from one of the imperialist countries."[122]

Toth went to KGB headquarters for several hours of interrogation on 14–15 June. On the first day, the interrogations focused on his research for articles on Soviet science, for which he had interviewed various scientists with Shcharanskii sometimes serving as translator. On the second day, the questioning focused exclusively on Shcharanskii.[123] Unbeknownst to Toth, the same KGB interrogators were also questioning the imprisoned dissident, who was being held in solitary confinement with limited sleep, food, and water.[124]

The KGB interrogators were particularly interested in the article to which Toth had referred in the draft telegram found in his trash.[125] For the article, Shcharanskii had arranged Toth's receipt of the aforementioned list of refuseniks denied exit visas due to their alleged employment in facilities engaged in secret work, which—despite their apparent research for the Soviet military—were using imported technology from US firms. To Shcharanskii's chagrin, the *Los Angeles Times*'s editors had published the article in November 1976 under a title claiming that the visa denials "indirectly" revealed Soviet "state secrets."[126]

During the interrogations, Toth confirmed his research topics, as well as Shcharanskii's general contributions to the aforementioned article—that is, information already in the public domain. On 17 June 1977, Toth received permission to leave the USSR.[127] The KGB reached its own preconceived conclusions from its interrogation of Toth, whom they proclaimed to be a spy for the DIA: "During his questioning by the investigatory organs, Toth admitted that he had been engaged in collecting political and scientific-technical information, especially in the field of gene technology. Although he denied any contacts to [US] intelligence by ascribing it to his professional (journalistic)

activity, he divulged out of necessity concrete proof of his contacts to Shcharanskii, which [thus] unmasked the illegal connection of the latter to the secret
services of the enemy."[128]

The KGB exploited the materials collected in its investigation, entrapment,
and interrogation of Toth for Operation Wedge in its own tendentious way.
It used them not only for the prosecution and eventual conviction of Shcharanskii but also to discredit Shcharanskii and other dissidents as spies and
renegades operating under orders from US intelligence officers under cover
as journalists and diplomats in Moscow.[129] On 31 August 1977, *Literaturnaia
gazeta* published an article titled, "This Is Strange Parapsychology—Several
Small, but Significant Additions to the Misadventures of Mr. Toth in the
USSR." The article portrayed Toth as a DIA agent and renewed its attacks
against the US correspondents Friendly and Krimsky—already long departed
from Moscow—as spies for US intelligence.[130]

Iurii Andropov, during his years as KGB chairman (1967–1982), made the
repression of dissidents a top priority. To this end, his secret police accused
dissidents of joining or falling into a conspiracy based on the West's—and
especially the United States'—efforts at "ideological sabotage" against the
Soviet Union. During the early years of his chairmanship, 1967–1975, the KGB
focused on proving the human-rights activists' conspiracy with the anti-Soviet
NTS, whose activities with regard to the smuggling and publication of dissidents' manuscripts was subsidized by the CIA. In 1975–1980, the KGB gathered and fabricated evidence in its Operation Wedge that US correspondents
in Moscow were working as spies for the CIA. In this way, it could claim
to prove once again the dissidents' conspiracy with US intelligence against
the USSR, with US correspondents assuming the place previously held by the
NTS.

As the KGB was wont to do, both in its internal assessments and in its
reports to the Soviet leadership, it proclaimed Operation Wedge, along with
its general active measures to discredit Soviet dissidents, to have been a success.[131] Was this in fact the case?

The KGB arguably achieved its initial goal in Operation Wedge—namely,
driving a wedge between US media organizations and the CIA. The KGB's
efforts to discredit the United States' Moscow correspondents in the Soviet
press arguably strengthened the ultimately successful demands of the US press
that the CIA strictly curtail its use of US journalists. At the international
level, despite the claims of the KGB officers involved in Wedge, it did little
to enhance the pressure on the Carter administration from other Western

governments to tone down its human rights policy toward Moscow. Based on the propaganda output from Wedge, the official Soviet Novosti Press Agency published a "white book," *The CIA and Human Rights*, which it distributed internationally, along with translations of the *Literaturnaia gazeta* article about Toth ("Strange Parapsychology"). Through such publications, the KGB sought to discredit the Carter administration's campaign for human rights in the Soviet Bloc by exposing the involvement of US intelligence agencies in the person of US correspondents.[132] However, such Novosti brochures probably had little or no influence in contrast to the larger issues that motivated US allies such as France and West Germany to criticize Carter's human rights policy. Carter, they worried, was endangering the achievements of détente in terms of East-West contacts, the ongoing emigration of ethnic Germans from Eastern Europe to the Federal Republic, East-West trade, and the potential for arms control agreements. Even without the KGB's propaganda brochures, Moscow could openly play on these divisions in the West, especially in the CSCE process.[133]

If anything, the attempted slander of the human-rights activists and their subsequent repression and imprisonment arguably backfired and compelled Western governments that were otherwise reluctant to raise the human rights issue to do so. The mainstream Western media continued its positive reporting about the dissidents as heroes struggling for human rights against a repressive regime. The sentencing of such leading dissidents as Orlov, Ginzburg, and Shcharanskii to long terms in prison or labor camps and the eventual banishment of Sakharov and Bonner to Gor'kii made them into martyrs for much of the Western press. This, in turn, helped spur an even greater wave of human rights activism in the West, along with even more vocal criticism of the Soviet government.[134] Arguably, Soviet counterpropaganda focusing on human rights abuses in and by the West and especially the United States proved to be more effective in discrediting the United States' human rights policy than Moscow's failing efforts to portray the dissidents as mere tools of US intelligence agencies.[135] Even the Carter administration's very vocal, public denials that Shcharanskii had worked for the CIA—accompanied by a high-level leaked admission that Lipavskii had, in fact, done so—did not alter this dynamic, despite the public embarrassment of the Carter administration.[136] In her memoirs, Avital Shcharanskii documents, for example, the ongoing, international support for her husband and his release from prison.[137]

Perhaps the greater—and for KGB counterintelligence, the more important—impact of Operation Wedge was domestic. One of the major successes of Operation Wedge, at least in the KGB's internal assessment, had been to sow mistrust between Western and especially US journalists and their current and potential sources in the Soviet Union, including individuals within the dissident community. The well-publicized experiences of Krimsky and Toth with Arkhipov and Petiukhov, respectively, did make Western journalists more suspicious of Soviet citizens who approached them with potential stories. At the same time, the denunciations of US journalists in the Soviet press as spies—a topic also covered in the Party's routine propaganda lectures—helped "increase the vigilance" of Soviet citizens regarding contacts with Western journalists in general. To hammer the point home, the KGB oversaw the production of a film for Soviet television, broadcast in April 1978. Titled *The Free Press in the Service of the CIA*, it included surveillance footage—accompanied by sinister music—of Friendly, Krimsky, Wren, and Toth. The program also referred to ongoing disputes in the United States about the CIA's use of journalists. The message to Soviet viewers, the US embassy reported, was clear: "Stay away from correspondents. You have been warned." The decline in dissident-journalist contacts, the KGB officers from Wedge implied, helped contribute to a decline in Western reporting about human rights violations.[138]

Wedge and the KGB's other active measures succeeded in undermining the dissidents' reputation domestically and contributing to their isolation within Soviet society. The portrayal of the dissidents' relations to US and other Western journalists as that of paid spies to Western intelligence agencies contributed to the Soviet government's larger propaganda efforts to discredit them at home. It conformed to their portrayal in a *Pravda* article, approved by the CPSU's leadership, as an "insignificant group of people, who do not represent anyone or anything, distant from the Soviet nation, and who exist only because they are supported, paid, and extolled by the West."[139] Soviet readers, the KGB undoubtedly knew, would interpret the reports regarding the human-rights activists' receipt of goods and favors from US correspondents, as well as payments for political prisoners from the Solzhenitsyn fund, in terms of the Soviet Union's second economy, "in which every 'gift' had its price." The KGB propaganda thus undermined the human-rights activists' larger legitimacy within Soviet society based on their identity as individuals sacrificing themselves for the good of their country.[140] A number of (post-)Soviet intellectuals still refer to them today as "opportunists."[141]

NOTES

1. Hiroaki Kuromiya, "Stalin's Great Terror and International Espionage," *Journal of Slavic Military Studies* 24, no. 2 (2011): 238–52; James Harris, "Intelligence and Threat Perception: Defending the Revolution, 1917–1937," in *The Anatomy of Terror: Political Violence under Stalin*, ed. Harris (Oxford:

Oxford University Press, 2013), 29–43; Iain Lauchlan, "Chekist Mentalité and the Origins of the Great Terror," in *Anatomy of Terror*, 24–27.

2. On order of the Supreme Soviet, the Higher School was renamed in 1962 in honor of the founder of the Soviet Cheka as the F. E. Dzerzhinskii Higher Red Banner School of the Committee of State Security of the USSR (Vysshaia krasnoznamennaia shkola Komiteta gosudarstvennoi bezopasnosti SSSR imeni F. E. Dzerzhinskogo; henceforth VKSh KGB).

3. For the Stalin era, see, e.g., Kuromiya, "Stalin's Great Terror"; Harris, "Intelligence and Threat Perception"; and Lauchlan, "Chekist Mentalité." For the Putin era, see Ilya Yablokov, *Fortress Russia: Conspiracy Theories in Post-Soviet Russia* (Cambridge: Polity, 2018).

4. See, e.g., Thomas Rid, *Active Measures: The Secret History of Disinformation and Political Warfare* (New York: Farrar, Straus, and Giroux, 2020); and Douglas Selvage, "Operation 'Denver': The East German Ministry of State Security and the KGB's AIDS Disinformation Campaign, 1985–1986," *Journal of Cold War Studies* 21, no. 4 (2019): 71–123. For two official KGB definitions of active measures, see Vasili Mitrokhin, *KGB Lexicon: The Soviet Intelligence Officer's Handbook* (London: Frank Cass, 2002), 13; and VKSh KGB, *Kontrrazveditel'nyi slovar'* (Moscow: Scientific Publications Division, 1972), 161–62.

5. For two exceptions, see Olga Bertelsen, "The KGB Operation 'Retribution' and John Demjanjuk," in *Russian Active Measures: Yesterday, Today, Tomorrow*, ed. Bertelsen (Stuttgart: ibidem, 2021), 93–136; and Douglas Selvage, "KGB, MfS und Andrej Sacharow, 1975 bis 1980," in *Der "große Bruder": Studien zum Verhältnis von KGB und MfS 1958 bis 1989*, ed. Selvage and Georg Herbstritt (Göttingen: Vandenhoeck & Ruprecht, 2021), 235–78.

6. Yuliya von Saal, *KSZE—Prozess und Perestroika in der Sowjetunion: Demokratisierung, Werteumbruch und Auflösung 1985–1991* (Munich: Oldenbourg, 2014); Svetlana Savranskaya, "Human Rights Movement in the USSR after the Signing of the Helsinki Final Act and the Reaction of Soviet Authorities," in *The Crisis of Détente in Europe: From Helsinki to Gorbachev, 1975–1985*, ed. Leopoldo Nuti (Abingdon: Routledge, 2009), 26–40.

7. Barbara Walker, "Moscow Human Rights Defenders Look West: Attitudes toward US Journalists in the 1960s and 1970s," *Kritika: Explorations in Russian and Eurasian History* 9, no. 4 (2008): 905–27; Walker, "The Moscow Correspondents, Soviet Human Rights Activists, and the Problem of the Western Gift," in *Americans Experience Russia: Encountering the Enigma, 1917 to the Present*, ed. Choi Chatterjee and Beth Holmgren (London: Taylor & Francis, 2012); Julia Metger, *Studio Moskau: Westdeutsche Korrespondenten im Kalten Krieg* (Paderborn: Schöningh, 2006); Dina Fainberg, *Cold War Correspondents: Soviet and American Reporters on the Ideological Frontlines* (Baltimore: Johns Hopkins University Press, 2020).

8. The speech is reprinted in the top secret internal KGB publication *Deiatel'nost' organov gosudarstvennoi bezopasnosti SSSR na sovremennom etape: Sbornik dokumentov i materialov*, pt. 1 (Moscow: Redaktsionno-izdatel'skii otdel VKSh KGB, 1980), 82, in HDASBU f. 13, op. 1, spr. 671.

9. Vladislav Zubok, *Zhivago's Children: The Last Russian Intelligentsia* (Cambridge, MA: Belknap, 2009), 259–61.

10. Zubok, *Zhivago's Children*, 263–64; Benjamin Nathans, "The Dictatorship of Reason: Aleksandr Vol'pin and the Idea of Rights under 'Developed Socialism,'" *Slavic Review* 66, no. 4 (2007): 630–63, esp. 655, 658.

11. Walker, "Moscow Human Rights Defenders," 913–14. See also Metger, *Studio Moskau*, 146–47.

12. Whitman Bassow, *The Moscow Correspondents: Reporting on Russia from the Revolution to Glasnost* (New York: William Morrow, 1988), 244–45; Peter Osnos, "Soviet Dissidents and the American Press," *Columbia Journalism Review* 16, no. 4 (1977): 34. Osnos had served as correspondent for the *Washington Post* in Moscow from 1974 to 1977.

13. Walker, "Moscow Human Rights Defenders," 914–20; Fainberg, *Cold War Correspondents*, 206–8, 218–19; Metger, *Studio Moskau*, 165; Bassow, *Moscow Correspondents*, 257–58; Osnos, "Soviet Dissidents and the American Press," 34.

14. Metger, *Studio Moskau*, 145, 155; Bassow, *Moscow Correspondents*, 239–43, 267; Hedrick Smith, *The Russians* (New York: Times Books, 1976), 15, 21, 418–19.

15. Bassow, *Moscow Correspondents*, 245; Walker, "Moscow Correspondents," 148.

16. S. K. Tsvigun, "Ob usilenii bor'by organov gosudarstvennoi bezopasnosti s ideologicheskoi diversiei protivnika," *Sbornik KGB*, 3, no. 39 (1968): 21. See also Vladimir A. Kozlov, "Introduction to the Russian Edition: The Meaning of Sedition," in *Sedition: Everyday Resistance in the Soviet Union under Khrushchev and Brezhnev,* ed. Kozlov, Sheila Fitzpatrick, and Sergei V. Mironenko (New Haven: Yale University Press, 2011), 54–55.

17. "Bericht über die Dienstreise einer Arbeitsgruppe der Hauptabteilung IX zum Untersuchungsorgan des KGB in Moskau," 4 June 1968, Hauptabteilung (HA, Main Division) IX, Bundesbeauftragten für die Unterlagen des Staatssicherheitsdienstes der ehemaligen DDR (BStU), Ministerium für Staatssicherheit (MfS), Sekretariat des Ministers (SdM), no. 1432, pp. 129–30.

18. William Chase, "Stalin as Producer: The Moscow Show Trials and the Construction of Mortal Threats," in *Stalin: A New History,* ed. Sarah Davies and James Harris (Cambridge: Cambridge University Press, 2005), 228–30.

19. F. J. M. Feldbrugge, "Law and Political Dissent in the Soviet Union," *Current Legal Problems* 26, no. 1 (1973): 244–45.

20. N. V. Petrov, "Spetsial'nye struktury KGB po bor'be s inakomysliem v SSSR, 1954–1989 gg.," *Trudy Obshchestva izucheniia istorii otechestvennykh spetssluzhb* (Moscow: Kuchkovo Pole, 2007), 3:306–17.

21. Chase, "Stalin as Producer," 234–48.

22. "Dokladnaia zapiska predsedatelia KGB pri SM SSSR i General'nogo prokurora SSSR v TsK KPSS o podgotovke sudebnogo protsessa nad Ginzburgom A. I., Galanskovim Iu. T., Dobrovol'skim A. A., i Lashkovoi V. I.," 22 November 1967, in *Kramola: Inakomyslie v SSSR pri Khrushcheve i Brezhneve 1953–1982 gg.,* ed. V. A. Kozlov and S. V. Mironenko (Moscow: Materik, 2005), 384–85.

23. Pavel Litvinov, ed., *The Trial of the Four: A Collection of Materials on the Case of Galanskov, Ginzburg, Dobrovolsky and Lashkova, 1967–68* (London: Longman, 1972), 171. On the NTS more generally, see Benjamin Tromly, "The Making of a Myth: The National Labor Alliance, Russian Émigrés, and Cold War Intelligence Activities," *Journal of Cold War Studies* 18, no. 1 (2016): 80–111. It should be noted that Nazi Germany imprisoned many leaders of the NTS after it became clear that they were recruiting Russian prisoners of war for their own national goals.

24. "Memorandum from the Chairman of the KGB and the Prosecutor General of the USSR to the CC of the CPSU," 22 November 1967.

25. Litvinov, *Trial of the Four*, 11–14; Andrej Amalrik, *Aufzeichnungen eine Revolutionärs* (Berlin: Ullstein, 1983), 52–53.

26. Robert Horvath, "Breaking the Totalitarian Ice: The Initiative Group for the Defense of Human Rights in the USSR," *Human Rights Quarterly* 36, no. 1 (2014), 156–57; A. Yakobson, P. Yakir, et al., "An Appeal to the UN Committee for Human Rights," *New York Review of Books,* 21 August 1969, https://www.nybooks.com/articles/1969/08/21/an-appeal-to-the-un-committee-for-human-rights/; "TASS Report of Yakir, Krasin Press Conference," 5 September 1973, in Foreign Broadcast Information Service (FBIS), *Daily Report: White Book* (FBIS-FRB-73-173), 6 September 1973, R1. "TASS Report of Yakir, Krasin Press Conference," 5 September 1973, in Foreign Broadcast Information Service (FBIS), *Daily Report: White Book* (FBIS-FRB-73-173), 6 September 1973, R1.

27. See, e.g., the article by F. Ovcharenko, "Lackeys," originally published in *Komsomol'skaia pravda* on 18 January 1968 in *Trial of the Four*, 288–95.

28. "Notiz über ein Gespräch mit den sowjetischen Genossen am 13.11.1969 von 13.00 bis 15.30 Uhr in Moskau," 17 November 1969, HA BStU MfS SdM, no. 577, pp. 91–92.

29. Amalrik, *Aufzeichnungen*, 53–56.

30. Amalrik, *Aufzeichnungen*, 53; Litvinov, *Trial of the Four*, 13.

31. Horvath, "Breaking the Totalitarian Ice," 167–68. On Krasin's and Iakir's contacts with the NTS, see also Viktor Krasin, *Poedinok: Zapiski antikomunista* (Surbiton: Hodgson, 2012), 220–21.

32. Andrei Sakharov, "The Deputy Prosecutor-General and I," *Index on Censorship* 2, no. 4 (1973): 19–20; Joshua Rubinstein and Aleksandr Gribanov, eds., *The KGB File of Andrei Sakharov* (New Haven: Yale University, 2005), 168–69.

33. See, e.g., Amalrik, *Aufzeichnungen*, 53–56.

34. Central Intelligence Agency, "Tensions in the Soviet Union and Eastern Europe: Challenge and Opportunity," n. d. (ca. April 1970), in US Department of State, *Foreign Relations of the United States, 1969–1976*, vol. 12: *Soviet Union, January 1969–October 1970*, ed. Erin R. Mahan (Washington, DC: US Government Printing Office, 2006), 457; CIA Memorandum for the 303 Committee, "United States Government Support of Covert Action Directed at the Soviet Union," n.d., CIA, Freedom of Information Act Electronic Reading Room (FOIA Reading Room), https://www.cia.gov/readingroom/document/519a2b75993294098d50f0f3.

35. Colonel Iu. Denisov, "Iz opyta profilakticheskoi raboty," *Sbornik KGB* 63, no. 4 (1974): 27–30, HDASBU f. 13, op. 1, spr. 763.

36. On Iakir and Krasin, see Ludmilla Alexeyeva, *Soviet Dissent: Contemporary Movements for National, Religious, and Human Rights* (Middletown, CT: Wesleyan University Press, 1987), 313–16.

37. "Stenografskii zapis' na informatsiiata na drugaria Andropov—Predsedatel' na KGB pri saveta na Ministrite na SSSR, naproven na Plenarnoto zasedanie na dvete delegatsii na 14 noembri 1974 g.," in *KGB i DS—Br'zki i zavisimosti*, DVD Version, ed. Tatiana Kiriakova and Nadezhda Angelova (Sofia: Committee for Disclosing the Documents and Announcing Affiliation of Bulgarian Citizens to the State Security and the Intelligence Services of the Bulgarian National Army, 2010), 621.

38. On this point, see, e.g., von Saal, *KSZE—Prozess und Perestroika*, 40. "Inviolability of Frontiers" constituted principle 3 in part 1 of the CSCE Final Act (Organization for Security and Cooperation in Europe [OSCE], "Helsinki Final Act," 1 August 1975, 5, https://www.osce.org/files/f/documents/5/c/39501.pdf). Despite Brezhnev's unilateral interpretation, the Final Act provided only for the "inviolability" of borders—not their "immutability," as Moscow had originally demanded. To the USSR's chagrin, it also had to accept a clause in the Final Act permitting the peaceful change of borders—something that West Germany, with the support of its NATO allies, had successfully insisted on. This left open the possibility of a future, peaceful unification of Germany (Stephan Kieninger, *Dynamic Détente: The United States and Europe, 1964–1975* [Lanham, MD: Lexington Books, 2016], 86, 237).

39. Savranskaya, "Human Rights Movement in the USSR," 30–33.

40. Selvage, "KGB, MfS und Andrej Sacharow," 237–39.

41. Sarah B. Snyder, *Human Rights Activism and the End of the Cold War: A Transnational History of the Helsinki Network* (New York: Cambridge University Press, 2011), 57–60. Regarding the term "transnational Helsinki network," see Snyder, *Human Rights Activism*, 18.

42. Snyder, *Human Rights Activism*, 64–65.

43. OSCE, "Helsinki Final Act," 44–45.

44. Bassow, *Moscow Correspondents*, 262–66. The quotations are from OSCE, "Helsinki Final Act," 45.

45. Metger, *Studio Moskau*, 158.

46. "Consultations with the Soviet Chekists from 19–24 April 1976 in the Guest House of the MfS in Oberseestrasse in the Capital of the GDR, Berlin," 29 April 1976, in BStU MfS, HA XX/AKG, no. 779, p. 145.

47. "The CIA Report the President Doesn't Want You to Read," *Village Voice*, 16 February 1976, 88–89.

48. David E. Rosenbaum, "C.I.A. Will Keep More Than 25 Journalist-Agents," *New York Times*, 27 April 1976, 26.

49. Loch Johnson, *America's Secret Power: The CIA in a Democratic Society* (New York: Oxford University Press, 1991), 196–97.

50. V. Kevorkov, S. Lekarev, V. Ponomarev, and I. Iashechkin, "Operatsiia 'Klin,'" *Sbornik KGB*, no. 88 (1981): 7–17, in HDASBU f. 13, op. 1, spr. 788. The author thanks Mark Kramer of Harvard University for bringing this article to his attention.

51. Kevorkov et al., "Operatsiia 'Klin,'" 8.

52. Lieutenant-Colonel Schenk, Division 13 of Main Division (*Hauptabteilung*) II of the MfS (HA II/13), "Report from the Official Trip (Short Version) regarding the Exchange of Views with Division 7 of the Second Chief Directorate of the KGB in Moscow on 23–24 May 1978," 30 May 1978, in BStU MfS, ZAIG, no. 5160, p. 25. The KGB officers singled out not only the US embassy and US journalists in their remarks, but also their West German counterparts.

53. Schenk, "Report from the Official Trip."

54. The KGB officers also mentioned James Jackson from the *Chicago Tribune*. However, Jackson remained only for a brief period of time in Moscow (Kevorkov et al., "Operatsiia 'Klin,'" 12).

55. Bassow, *Moscow Correspondents*, 268–69; Natan Sharansky, *Fear No Evil: The Classic Memoir of One Man's Triumph over a Police State*, trans. Stefani Hoffmann (New York: Public Affairs, 1998), 117, 163. Regarding Ginzburg and Krimsky, see Cambridge University, Churchill College, Churchill Archives Centre, Vasilii Mitrokhin Papers, MITN 2/25, p. 186; and Andrei Sakharov, *Memoirs*, trans. Richard Lourie (New York: Vintage, 1992), 459–60.

56. Christopher S. Wren, "Russians Disrupt Modern Art Show with Bulldozers," *New York Times*, 16 September 1974, 1.

57. Amy Schapiro, *Millicent Fenwick: Her Way* (New Brunswick, NJ: Rutgers University Press, 2003), 168–69.

58. Sharansky, *Fear No Evil*, 162; Andrei Sakharov and Elena Bonner, *Dnevniki [1]: Roman-dokument* (Moscow: Vremia, 2006), 282; Peter Reddaway, *The Dissidents: A Memoir of Working with the Resistance in Russia, 1960–1990* (Washington, DC: Brookings Institution Press, 2020), 126.

59. Kevorkov et al., "Operatsiia 'Klin,'" 8.

60. In fact, US correspondents often complained that the dissidents tried to push stories on them that, in their opinion, were not newsworthy (Bassow, *Moscow Correspondents*, 248–52; Metger, *Studio Moskau*, 154–57; Osnos, "Soviet Dissidents and the American Press," 32).

61. Kevorkov et al., "Operatsiia 'Klin,'" 8.

62. Kevorkov et al., "Operatsiia 'Klin,'" 9–11.

63. Kevorkov et al., "Operatsiia 'Klin,'" 10. The journalists apparently became aware of the efforts to isolate them from potential Soviet sources. See, e.g., David K. Shipler, "Reporters Find Hospitality in Soviet but Little News," *New York Times*, 11 June 1976, 8.

64. Kevorkov et al., "Operatsiia 'Klin,'" 10.

65. Kevorkov et al., "Operatsiia 'Klin,'" 12; V. Valentinov, "Popravka TsRU k . . . konstitutsii SShA," *Literaturnaia gazeta*, 26 May 1976, 9.

66. Oleg Kalugin, *The First Directorate: My Thirty-two Years in Intelligence and Espionage against the West* (New York: St. Martin's, 1994), 158; Cambridge University, Churchill College, Churchill Archives Centre, Vasilii Mitrokhin Papers, MITN 2/4, Entry 122.

67. Valentinov, "Popravka TsRU," 9; Kevorkov et al., "Operatsiia 'Klin,'" 8.

68. Johnson, *America's Secret Power*, 196–98. See also "CIA Report the President Doesn't Want You to Read," 88–89.

69. "Paper in Moscow Links 3 U.S. Correspondents to the C.I.A.," *New York Times*, 26 May 1976, 2.

70. "Vot tak-to, dzhentel'meny!," 9.

71. Charles B. Seib, "CIA Taint on the Press," *Washington Post*, 11 June 1976, A27.

72. Johnson, *America's Secret Power*, 198–99.

73. Kevorkov et al., "Operatsiia 'Klin,'" 13.

74. US Congress, House of Representatives, Permanent Select Committee on Intelligence, *Soviet Active Measures: Hearings before the Permanent Select Committee on Intelligence*, 97th Cong., 2nd sess., 1982, 10, 35, 173.

75. Kevorkov et al., "Operatsiia 'Klin,'" 13.

76. Kevorkov et al., "Operatsiia 'Klin,'" 12.

77. Valentinov, "Popravka TsRU," 9.

78. Kevorkov et al., "Operatsiia 'Klin,'" 11–12.

79. On this point, see Douglas Selvage, "Operation Synonym: Soviet-Bloc Active Measures and the Helsinki Process, 1976–1983," in *Need to Know: Eastern and Western Perspectives*, ed. Władysław Bułhak and Thomas Wegener Friis (Odense: University Press of Southern Denmark, 2014), 92–93.

80. Selvage, "Operation Synonym," 13; "Vot tak-to, dzhentel'meny!," 9.

81. "Vot tak-to, dzhentel'meny!," 9.

82. "Vot tak-to, dzhentel'meny!," 9; Kevorkov et al., "Operatsiia 'Klin,'" 9.

83. "Vot tak-to, dzhentel'meny!," 9.

84. "Kha kha! 'Shpiony nepovole,'" *Literaturnaia gazeta*, 7 July 1976, 9; Kevorkov et al., "Operatsiia 'Klin,'" 12. See also Peter Osnos, "U.S. Journalist Sues Russian Magazine," *Washington Post*, 26 June 1976, A2.

85. "U.S. Newsman's Suit Awaits Soviet Move," *New York Times*, 24 July 1976, 2; David K. Shipler, "Soviet Expels AP Reporter, Harasses Other Newsmen," *New York Times*, 5 February 1977, 3.

86. Snyder, *Human Rights Activism*, 44, 50, 52, 103.

87. Kevorkov et al., "Operatsiia 'Klin,'" 12.

88. See "Telegram 1801 from the US Embassy in Moscow," 15 August 1977, National Archives and Records Administration (NARA), General Records of the Department of State, Record Group (RG) 59, Central Foreign Policy Files (CFPF), 1973–1979 (hereafter CFPF 1973–1979); downloaded from Access to Archival Databases at http://www.archives.gov.

89. Sakharov, *Memoirs*, 463; "Memorandum from Andropov, Gromyko, and Rudenko to the CC," 18 January 1977, in *KGB File of Andrei Sakharov*, 221. On Louis's work as a KGB agent, see the interview with his former KGB control officer, Viacheslav Kevorkov: Andrei Vandenko, "Poslednii romantik," *Itogi*, no. 49 (756), 6 December 2010, https://web.archive.org/web/20170614093401/http://www.itogi.ru/kultura/2010/49/159665.html.

90. "Telegram 399 from the US Embassy in London," 10 January 1977, CFPF 1973–1979.

91. Sakharov, *Memoirs*, 463; "Sakharov Suspects Police in Moscow Subway Blast," *New York Times*, 15 January 1977, 7; "Memorandum from Andropov, Gromyko, and Rudenko to the CC," 18 January 1977, 221.

92. For the details, see "Concerning the Explosions in Moscow," *A Chronicle of Current Events*, no. 44, 16 March 1977, 128–29.

93. "Memorandum from Andropov, Gromyko, and Rudenko to the CC," 18 January 1977, 222.

94. "Telegram 1555 from the US Embassy in Moscow," 2 February 1977, CFPF 1973–1979.

95. "Telegram 17060 from the Department of State to the US Embassy in Moscow," 25 January 1977, CFPF 1973–1979.

96. "Telegram 1551 from the US Embassy in Moscow," 2 February 1977; V. Valentinov, "Vremeni vopreki: 'Pod flagom' informatsionnogo agentstva," *Literaturnaia gazeta*, 2 February 1977, 9.

97. "Telegram 1555 from the US Embassy in Moscow," 2 February 1977, in CFPF 1973–1979.

98. Valentinov, "Vremeni vopreki," 9. For the relevant passage, see CSCE, "Final Act," Helsinki 1975, 45, https://www.osce.org/helsinki-final-act.

99. Shipler, "Soviet Expels AP Reporter," 3.

100. Resolution of the Secretariat of the CC CPSU, "On Measures for Stopping the Criminal Activities of Orlov, Ginzburg, Rudenko, and Venclova," trans. Svetlana Savranskaya, in "The Moscow Helsinki Group 30th Anniversary: From the Secret Files," *National Security Archive Electronic Briefing Book* (NSAEBB), no. 191, http://www.gwu.edu/~nsarchiv/NSAEBB/NSAEBB191/index.htm.

101. Resolution of the Secretariat of the CC CPSU, "On Measures for Stopping."

102. Resolution of the Secretariat of the CC CPSU, "On Measures for Stopping."

103. Aleksandr Petrov, "Letter to *Literaturnaia Gazeta*: Liars and Pharisees," *Current Digest of the Soviet Press* 29, no. 4 (1977): 3–5.

104. Viktor Chebrikov, "The Struggle of the Organs of the KGB against the Ideological Subversion of the Imperialist States under Current Conditions," BStU MfS, ZAIG, no. 5106, 248–49.

105. "Otkrytoe pis'mo grazhdanina SSSR, kandidata meditsinskikh nauk S. L. Lipavskii," *Izvestiia*, 4 March 1977, 3.

106. L. Morev and K. Iarilov, "Poslelovie k otkrytomu pis'mu S. Lipavskogo: TsRU, shpioni i 'prava cheloveka,'" *Izvestiia*, 4 March 1977, 6.

107. "Otkrytoe pis'mo," 3.

108. "Otkrytoe pis'mo," 3.

109. "Telegram 04362 from the US Embassy in Moscow," 31 March 1977, CFPF 1973–1979.

110. For the idea that Shcharanskii acted on his own initiative, see "Telegram 07266 from the US Embassy in Moscow," 24 May 1977, CFPF 1973–1979. Shcharanskii himself claimed that the list for Toth was based on the "same old list" that he and other Jewish activists had been providing to US legislators and synagogues since 1975 (*Fear No Evil*, 101, 109). For Toth's article, see Robert C. Toth, "Clues in Denials of Jewish Visas: Russ [sic, USSR] Indirectly Reveal 'State Secrets,'" *Los Angeles Times*, 22 November 1976, 1. For the possible involvement of the Jewish national movement, see V. Novitskii and S. Kuznetsov, "Agent 'Ervin' v operativnoi igre 'Kollegi,'" *Sbornik KGB*, no. 101 (1984), 31, in HDASBU f. 13, op. 1, spr. 801.

111. The KGB defined an "operational game" as follows: "Agent-operational measures using dangles, and hostile agents who have been turned, as well as technical-operational means, to identify and disrupt the adversary's subversive activities" (Mitrokhin, *KGB Lexicon*, 81).

112. Novitskii and Kuznetov, "Agent 'Ervin,'" 23–25.

113. Novitskii and Kuznetov, "Agent 'Ervin,'" 28.

114. Yuri Andropov, "On Further Measures to Discredit the Role of US Intelligence in the Anti-Soviet Campaign for 'Human Rights,'" no. 575, 21 March 1977, in *NSAEBB*, no. 191.

115. Andropov, "On Further Measures." For Lipavskii's subsequent interview, see "Kak menia verbovalo TsRU: Rasskazyvaet S. Lipavskii na vstreche, provedennoi 'Izvestiiami,'" *Izvestiia*, 7 May 1977, 4.

116. Kevorkov et al., "Operatsiia 'Klin,'" 13.

117. Sharansky, *Fear No Evil*, 143–46.

118. "Memorandum from Andropov to the CC," 29 March 1977, in *KGB File of Andrei Sakharov*, 225.

119. "Telegram 12628 from the US Embassy in Moscow," 31 August 1977, and "Telegram 214447 from the Department of State to the US Embassy in Moscow," 8 September 1977, CFPF 1973–1979.

120. Kevorkov et al., "Operatsiia 'Klin,'" 13.

121. Kevorkov et al., "Operatsiia 'Klin,'" 13–14.

122. Christopher Wren, "K.G.B. Questions U.S. Reporter about Shcharansky," *New York Times*, 16 June 1977, 8.

123. Wren, "K.G.B. Questions U.S. Reporter about Shcharansky."

124. The KGB officers had the surnames Chernysh and Volodin. See Robert C. Toth, "Toth's Story: From the Chilling to the Ridiculous," *Los Angeles Times*, 19 June 1977, 23; and Sharansky, *Fear No Evil*, 108–10.

125. Toth, "Toth's Story," 24.

126. Sharansky, *Fear No Evil*, 101. The article in question was Toth, "Clues in Denials of Jewish Visas."

127. Toth, "Toth's Story," 23–24.

128. Kevorkov et al., "Operatsiia 'Klin,'" 14.

129. Kevorkov et al., "Operatsiia 'Klin,'" 13.

130. V. Valentinov and B. Roshchin, "Eta strannaia parapsikhologiia ... Neskol'ko nebol'shikh, no sushchestvennykh dopolnenii k 'zlokliucheniiam' m-ra TOTA v SSSR," *Literaturnaia gazeta*, 31 August 1977, 14.

131. On the KGB's exaggeration of the success of its active measures, see Christopher Andrew and Vasili Mitrokhin, *The Sword and the Shield: The Mitrokhin Archive and the Secret History of the KGB* (New York: Basic Books, 2001), 224; and Andrew and Oleg Gordievsky, eds., *More 'Instructions from the Centre': Top Secret Files on KGB Global Operations, 1975–1985* (London: Frank Cass, 1992), 34.

132. Kevorkov et al., "Operatsiia 'Klin,'" 15.

133. Douglas Selvage, "The Superpowers and the Conference on Security and Cooperation in Europe, 1977–1983: Human Rights, Nuclear Weapons, and Western Europe," in *Die KSZE im Ost-West-Konflikt: Internationale Politik und gesellschaftliche Transformation, 1975–1990*, ed. Matthias Peter and Hermann Wentker (Munich: Oldenbourg, 2012), 22–24.

134. Snyder, *Human Rights Activism*, 115, 131.

135. Regarding active measures attacking US and Western human rights violations, which also had only limited success, see Selvage, "Operation Synonym"; and Douglas Selvage and Walter Süß, *Staatssicherheit und KSZE-Prozess: MfS zwischen SED und KGB (1972–1989)* (Göttingen: Vandenhoeck & Ruprecht, 2019), 149–53.

136. Murrey Marder, "Soviets May Dispute Carter Credibility," *Washington Post*, 7 March 1978, A1; Rowland Evans and Robert Novak, "High-Level Bungling on the Scharansky Case," *Washington Post*, 10 March 1978, A1.

137. Avital Shcharansky and Ilana Ben-Josef, *Next Year in Jerusalem* (New York: William Morrow, 1979).

138. Kevorkov et al., "Operatsiia 'Klin,'" 10, 15–17. For the quotation, see "Telegram 06537 from the US Embassy in Moscow," 3 April 1978, CFPF 1973–1979.

139. "Chto skryvaetsia za shumikhoi o 'pravakh cheloveka,'" *Pravda*, 12 February 1977, 4. Regarding the article's approval by the Soviet leadership, see the speech by the CPSU's international secretary, Boris Ponomarev, at the multilateral meeting of the international and ideological secretaries of the Soviet Bloc's communist parties in Sofia, 2–3 March 1977, BStU MfS, SED-Kreisleitung, no. 831, p. 89.

140. Walker, "Moscow Correspondents," 152.

141. Walker, "Moscow Correspondents," 139–40.

Cybernetics and Surveillance

The Secret Police Enter the Computer Age

Joshua Sanborn

IN LATE 2020, NEWSPAPERS ACROSS AMERICA PUBLISHED WORRYING reports about ongoing Russian attacks on the United States.[1] The narrative was confusing. No soldier fired a gun. No missile was launched. No spy was dragged away in handcuffs. Some of the forces involved did not even bear national markings. Instead, American citizens were informed that "Cozy Bear" slipped around the defenses of Solar Winds and compromised FireEye. Most of the relevant details were closely guarded national security secrets, but even the publicly available details were too complex for most to understand. Nevertheless, reporters and government officials had a language with which to communicate these events to readers. This was hacking, or a cyberattack, or a "violation of cybersecurity," or an instance of "information warfare."[2] The notion of cyberthreats seems new, but in fact it has a long history. The term "cybernetics" was coined more than seventy years ago, the CIA formed its first cybernetics threat assessment team about sixty years ago, and it was more than twenty-five years ago that defense intellectuals from the RAND

Corporation began publicly shrieking that "Cyberwar Is Coming!"[3] So you can't say we weren't warned.

If few heeded the warning in the early 1990s, the same cannot be said today. Governments and businesses around the world are very alert to cyberthreats. With good reason, they are particularly concerned about the capacities of Russian intelligence services to launch offensive operations. In 2007, Russia launched a crippling malware attack on Estonia to protest the removal of Soviet World War II memorials in Tallinn. In 2008, Russia combined cyberattacks with more traditional assaults in its conflict with Georgia. Beginning in 2014, Russian operatives launched multiple cyberattacks on Ukraine, targeting its election systems, its power grid, and its economy. One of those attacks, the NotPetya worm, had significant global effects, devastating the computerized systems of Maersk, a Danish shipping company critical to international trade, to the tune of hundreds of millions of dollars in losses.[4] Finally, Russia conducted special cybernetic operations to influence elections in the United Kingdom and the United States in 2014 and 2016, not only undermining specific candidates and policies deemed unfavorable to Russia but sapping the legitimacy of the political systems in those countries to a significant degree.[5] It would seem self-evident that examining the history of cybernetics within the context of Russian intelligence services would have some relevance.

Still, we should be cautious. Language changes at least as quickly as technology. What Norbert Wiener meant by "cyber" when he wrote the first text on the subject in 1948 is not what newspaper reporters mean by the term when they use it in headlines today.[6] Above all, the current sense that "cyber" means "computer-based" would have been vigorously rejected by the early leaders of the cybernetic movement, who were primarily interested in studying feedback processes in human-machine systems. In the late 1940s and early 1950s, cybernetics got its start at a series of interdisciplinary conferences (the Macy Conferences) that included scholars from many different fields, including not only mathematics and electrical engineering but also biology, psychology, and anthropology. While each participant pursued different projects (and defined cybernetics slightly differently), the collective promoted the field as a productive new way to look at complex systems that incorporated several key insights: (1) the homologies between organic and mechanical systems and the resulting possible interchangeability/interoperability between them, (2) the centrality of "information" as the key packet that circulates through these systems, (3) the importance of "feedback" loops to "learning" in these systems, and (4) the recognition that stability is not natural, but rather that "homeostasis" must be actively maintained in the face of entropy. Cyberneticists were thus fundamentally concerned with information, the ways in which it is communicated and distributed throughout a system, and the ways in which it can be controlled. Norbert Wiener, seeking a broad definition, coined the term "cybernetics" from the Greek word for "steersman" to describe "the entire field of control and communication theory, whether in the machine or in the animal."[7]

Though cybernetics took root most quickly in the United States and Great Britain, Soviet thinkers were rapidly attracted to the concept. The movement was partially and briefly suppressed by a typical Stalinist science war, but by the late 1950s it was back on track and exceedingly popular. As Slava Gerovitch, Benjamin Peters, and Eglė Rindzevičiūtė have shown, cybernetics became something of a craze among Soviet scholars, not least because it promised to have some answers to the problems facing the planned economy.[8] For Viktor Glushkov, the director of the Institute of Cybernetics in Kyiv and the primary proponent of reforming the Soviet economy through cybernetics, computerization would be a key aspect of the transformation, as indeed it was in the Soviet military.[9] The same was also true in the Soviet intelligence services. At the present time, however, there is very little written on the subject of the KGB, cybernetics, and computers.[10] There are three basic reasons for this gap in the scholarship, I think, one obvious and two slightly less so. The obvious reason is the lack of archival documentation. In the early 2000s, Vilnius was the only place where relevant KGB records were available; by 2015 it was possible to do research in Latvia, Estonia, and Ukraine as well. The second reason is one I discuss in more detail below. Most KGB officers were less than thrilled with computer technology and did not think it merited discussion in their memoirs. Third, cyberneticians and computer scientists were prohibited from talking about their work prior to 1991 and were not eager to open up about their association with the KGB even after the end of the Soviet regime.

Finally, it is worth noting that each separate directorate within the KGB had functionally different tasks, and this created a variety of contexts for the adoption of computers and cybernetic strategies. Even though the work of the KGB's First Directorate, which dealt with espionage abroad, is by far the most popular topic related to the work of the KGB in the Cold War, it seems likely that the promises and perils for cybernetic approaches were most acute for the Second Directorate, which dealt with domestic counterintelligence. In any case, these are the files to which we have the most extensive access. It is not currently possible for scholars to conduct detailed research in Moscow on central intelligence services, so I have little to say about the Union-level KGB or the First Directorate, much less about the activities of Soviet military intelligence (GRU).[11] Instead, the sources for this chapter come from Ukrainian

KGB records, which detail the adoption and adaptation of computer systems by intelligence agents in one of the most vital and active counterintelligence services in the Soviet Union and shed some light on the processes taking place more broadly within the KGB as a whole.

The particularities of the source base condition the structure of this chapter to a significant degree. I argue below that the intelligence services in the Soviet Union (and later in Russia) engaged with the promise of cybernetic operations in three basic phases, each of which was dependent on, and limited by, the technology available to them and their targets. The first period, which began in the late 1960s, is the "database" phase. This was when the KGB first turned to mechanized systems not only to store data but also to analyze it, first in the form of punch card databases and then in electronic storage on newly purchased mainframe computers. The ambitious cybernetic hopes of those in KGB leadership roles (including Iurii Andropov) were not (yet) met, but the groundwork was laid for the better integration of intelligence work with computing technology in the future. The "hacking" phase began in the mid-1980s and relied not only on Soviet technological capabilities but also on technological developments (especially in the field of networking) on the other side of the Iron Curtain. As with the first phase, this second phase was only partially, and imperfectly, "cybernetic." Instead, it was conceived of as a new variation on an old theme: using existing technologies to steal information from one's enemies. The culminating phase, when we see the maturation of a true cybernetic potential, is the "control" phase, which began bearing fruit in the first decade of the twenty-first century.[12] A complete history of these three phases would be very desirable. Unfortunately, as I have already noted, the sources for the second two phases remain classified. We can judge them only by studying the patterns of activity by Soviet and Russian intelligence services, not by getting an inside view of the process. This chapter, as a result, focuses intensively on the "database" phase, for which we do now have accessible (if still incomplete) archival sources. I will take the opportunity to explore this phase more deeply, paying attention as much to the organizational dynamics of the process as the technological ones. I hope to shed some new light on the nature of the late Soviet KGB as a result.

CYBERNETICS IN THE COLD WAR

Cybernetics was one of the three charter Cold War "Big Science" enterprises. Like the nuclear and space programs, it was anticipated by theorists before it could be realized in practice, developed secretly in the World War II period, announced its arrival at the very start of the Cold War, and developed in a competitive fashion from the 1950s onward.[13] Two secret wartime programs were especially important. The huge computer developed by Alan Turing and his associates at Bletchley Park in England during the war would prove important in the long run, but the more important project was the one that consumed Norbert Wiener and several other early cyberneticians: developing analog automated feedback machines to improve the targeting of anti-aircraft systems. Both of these projects confirm Jon Agar's observation that World War II was in part an information war: "Not only did the concept of information crystallize in the practical context of warfare, but also a string of new organizations emerged to collect, process, and distribute it."[14] This experience of designing a symbiotic system involving human beings, targeting mechanisms, and guns set the parameters for the postwar development of the field. Cybernetics jumped beyond the disciplines of military engineering when its early proponents, most notably Wiener, suggested that the concepts and mathematical models they were developing had applications in a wide variety of other fields. That interdisciplinarity (or, in Andrew Pickering's framing, that "anti-disciplinarity") gave cybernetics its early cachet, but it would ultimately play a role in the decline in the usefulness of the label.[15] In the United States, the most promising features of the concept were domesticated by the contributing scientific disciplines, and the term (and interdisciplinary engagement) fell into disuse.[16] In the Soviet Union, the interdisciplinary enthusiasm surrounding the label led to its transformation and dilution. "Cyberspeak," observed Slava Gerovitch, "began closely to resemble newspeak. Cybernetics laboratories and institutes mushroomed throughout the Soviet Union, and many career-minded scientists began using cybernetics as a buzzword. It was now trendy to call oneself a cybernetician, and suddenly the cybernetics movement became very crowded."[17]

Nevertheless, even in this modified form the cybernetic competition was fundamental to the future economies, societies, and political structures of the two superpowers. The most visible form of this competition was in the field of computer science, which was deeply immersed in (and implicated by) the field of cybernetics from the very start. The computer race was short-lived, with an American victory even more evident than those achieved in nuclear and space technologies. American superiority in computers became so pronounced that Soviet leaders threw in the towel, copying IBM technology as the basis for its future computer systems in the early 1970s to howls of protest from its own computer scientists, who believed (not wholly without reason) that they had the expertise to sustain a domestic computer sector.[18]

It was also not lost on Cold War observers that rapid advances in the manipulation of information and the improvement of control of complex systems might be of particular use for intelligence agencies. George Orwell's

1984, written at the dawn of the cybernetic era, gave Western observers plenty of pause regarding the dangers of an ever-perfecting (if still, in this novel, analog) information regime.[19] Every hint that a socialist state might be pursuing cybernetic goals led statesmen and observers to fear the worst. True to form, the CIA raised the alarm to the White House in the 1960s about a cybernetics gap. These fears were only eased after the debriefing of US computer scientists who had actually visited computer labs in the Soviet Union.[20] Even so, the efforts of cyberneticists in Salvador Allende's Chile in the early 1970s to create Project Cybersyn, an economic management system, so alarmed editorialists in the West that they warned of the onset of totalitarian social control. These accusations strained credulity. At the time, Chile had just 50 computers (compared to 48,000 in the United States). Only one aging IBM 360 was devoted to Cybersyn, and that for only part of the time.[21]

The Chilean example is a perfect example of the late Cold War frictions related to cybernetics. On one end of the spectrum, most active users of computers treated them as "giant, expensive calculators."[22] On the other, there were both optimistic and pessimistic visionaries who saw the potential for artificial intelligence, comprehensive economic planning, and extensive social control. In between lay the reality of computing in the 1970s, with its massive mainframes, its buggy and limited software, input systems that still often relied on punch cards, and the need for nearly constant professional attention from information technologists and engineers for successful operation. Again, cybernetics, computer science, and computer engineering are not the same thing. Early cyberneticists (including Stafford Beer, the eventual leader of Project Cybersyn) could and did articulate their ideas about information, feedback loops, and homeostasis with little to no reference to computers.[23] But those data-rich feedback loops, many of them designed for high-speed operation, depended on high-speed data processing. As a result, computing power was virtually always a limiting factor for cybernetic plans. In principle, computer scientists and electrical engineers might have done without cybernetics, but in practice the confluence between the rapid development of computer science and the explosive popularity of cybernetic ideas meant that the two were joined virtually at birth, and computer scientists are still trained using cybernetic concepts (regardless of whether they call them "cybernetic" today or not).

In these early days (and beyond) eager cyberneticists oversold the scale of initial transformations that computers could produce within societies and institutions. This led, of course, to inevitable frustrations with undelivered promises. But despite all the missteps and frustrations one sees when one looks in a granular way at these developments, there is no doubt that the overall trendline has been remarkably, and sharply, upward. If the young Vladimir Putin was like most of his contemporaries in the KGB in the 1970s, he was both annoyed by and dismissive of the use of computers in his office. Nevertheless, his own power now rests, if a bit precariously, on cybernetic capacities only dreamed of at that time.

THE COMPUTERIZATION OF THE KGB

Computers were first promoted by the analysis wing of the KGB. This branch of service, which originated in 1943, did what intelligence analysis branches do around the world: make use of the information gathered either from open or clandestine sources to provide insight to policy makers. Still, the analytical department was a poor stepsister to the field agents who dominated the self-image of the organization. That situation began to change, if only slowly, as a result of Iurii Andropov's leadership upon taking up the position of head of the KGB in 1967. According to Nikolai Leonov, the head of the analytical department in the First Main Directorate throughout the 1970s, Andropov modeled a more "intellectual and intelligent" approach in the agency, one that was apparently more forward-looking than those of his predecessors.[24] Two years after Andropov assumed his post, in October 1969, he issued Order no. 0395, which established informational-analytical subdivisions (IAP) in KGB offices throughout the Soviet Union.[25] This order not only expanded the reach of analytical departments to branch offices (mainly to serve the Second and Fifth Directorates) but tasked them with adopting computer technology. These analytical bureaus would expand further (into foreign residencies) during the 1970s as well.[26] Throughout his tenure, Andropov would continue to press local KGB chiefs on issues related to computerization, "repeatedly stressing" this work as a "task of primary importance."[27]

The IAPs had significant work in front of them. They had to conceptualize a new paradigm for dealing with information, devise systems that could control that information and make it productive, and acquire the hardware necessary for the job. Short-staffed from the start (each branch devoted only a handful of officers to these tasks, and many had only two individuals working in the entire analytical subdivision), they nevertheless got down to work. In 1971, the KGB USSR piloted the regularization of information production by insisting that reports by agents and trusted individuals who traveled abroad be done on a standardized report template. This template was coded by assigning numbers to human characteristics whenever possible. This regularization was necessary for creating useful databases, and it would spread to other forms in the following years.[28]

The first information system used by KGB counterintelligence was Fregat. Introduced in 1973, it used the newly coded data prescribed by the 1971 order to create a database of the information collected by agents abroad. Officers were instructed to collect data on the members of foreign anti-Soviet organizations, on indications of subversive activities carried out against Soviet citizens abroad, on suspicious activities that foreigners conducted in relation to Soviet citizens, and so forth. These reports were then encoded and stored on superpositional punch cards, a data storage technology that had existed since the late nineteenth century.[29] Punch card readers could be then used to analyze the data, though in limited ways.[30]

More ambitious attempts to create usable databases soon followed. Later in 1973, the first database placed on an electronic computer was rolled out. Fort-67 was a catalogue of all contacts made between foreigners and Soviet citizens on Soviet territory. These were separated into three categories: (1) contacts with regular Soviet citizens; (2) contacts with Soviet citizens who were suspect in one way or another (having a criminal record, belonging to a religious group, etc.); and (3) contacts with active agents or "trusted individuals" of the KGB in cases where those contacts were "personal" and not part of an assignment from their superiors. The use of a computer expanded possibilities considerably. This database was significantly larger than Fregat. As of the autumn of 1980, Fort-67 included data on 30,618 incidents of contact in Ukraine, while Fregat had punched cards for 6,366 reports.[31] The options for creating a usable product were also expanded, as the IAP produced regular statistical reports and syntheses of the data.[32]

Apparently, the successful launch of Fort-67 gave the agency confidence that it could successfully use computer databases. In the next year, three new databases would be created (Ftor-74, Slavutich, and Fakel-Skif). The largest by far was Ftor-74, which attempted to catalogue every piece of correspondence between foreigners and Soviet citizens in Ukraine. By 1980, the agents had already gathered data on 114,000 pairs of correspondents, despite the fact that complete data were only available for a few regions within the republic (Vinnitsia, Dnipropetrovsk, Mykolaiv, Odesa, Donetsk, and Crimea). Data from some of the other regions (most notably Kyiv) was present but incomplete. Slavutich was a database of foreigners suspected of espionage or hostile actions on the territory of the republic (with 22,000 foreigners in the database by 1980). Fakel-Skif was yet another database of foreigners committing suspicious acts, but these (roughly four thousand) files were limited to those who were under surveillance by the KGB. One more significant punch-card database was created in the 1970s, the aptly named Rubikon, which held materials on more than 25,000 Soviet citizens who had established permanent residence outside the Soviet Union in Israel, West Germany, the United States, Canada, and "other countries." Two other, smaller punch-card databases (Antei and Mars) kept track of operational and agent "possibilities" in Ukraine.[33]

The machine used for the four databases kept on a computer was the venerable Minsk-32, which was adopted as the standard machine by the KGB in 1976.[34] Unfortunately, the Minsk-32, a mainframe in use since the 1960s, was already obsolete, with the last unit rolling out of a Belarusian factory in 1975. It would take much of the next ten years for the KGB to plan for, and eventually develop, a new computer system that could combine the operations of the databases and connect, when necessary, to the systems of other socialist states. This was the ESIOK (*Edinaia sistema informatsionnogo obespecheniia kontrrazvedki*) system. It had been envisaged as early as 1971 in an order by the Union-level KGB to establish Del'ta systems. Each republic was to have its own Del'ta system (Del'ta-Litva in Lithuania, Del'ta-U in Ukraine).[35] These systems were run on newer model computers. By the early 1980s, the KGB was upgrading from the Minsk-32 to the ES-1022, a more modern mainframe.[36]

The ES series was designed and implemented in part by reverse-engineering the very popular IBM 360 mainframes (and the software they ran). It was the response to the significant variation in computer hardware present in the Soviet Union at the end of the 1960s, by which time there were roughly twenty different kinds of mainframes.[37] The differing architectures meant that there was a great deal of time spent programming for each specific model. As a result, the ES, in its various "lines'" (*riady*) was meant to be the third generation of digital computing, which would allow for the more rational and less expensive expansion of computing in offices across the Soviet Union.[38] In terms of this expansion, it is notable that the period in which the ES-1022 was adopted by the KGB was also the period in which this model became the bestselling model of the series, despite its more limited usefulness in other enterprises.[39] One would not be surprised to learn that the KGB made a mass purchase of ES-1022s in the last years of the 1970s and first years of the 1980s in an effort to extend and standardize computer access throughout its regional branches. This move toward a unified system was happening in similar ways in firms across the Soviet Union over the 1970s and early 1980s. In the KGB, it was hoped that the new computers would allow them to break down the existing structure, which stored information based on particular operational goals (such as monitoring contacts between Soviet citizens and foreigners) and particular KGB republican branches. It also proposed to bring all of the punch-card databases online and make them usable on the computer system.

HARANGUING AND FOOTDRAGGING: THE PAINFUL TRANSFORMATION OF AN INFORMATION ARCHITECTURE

As this summary suggests, the KGB leadership saw potential in transferring at least some of its data from paper to electrical storage over the course of the 1970s.[40] That potential was exactly what worried the commentators on the computerization of intelligence services and science fiction writers from Orwell onward—the increasing perfection of the surveillance state, able to connect the data of a human's existence across space and time. Indeed, the KGB did want to improve its collection and manipulation of data in these ways. Counterintelligence officials repeatedly argued that the country was under constant assault from the West, and they complained about "floods" of foreigners coming into Ukraine. These rivers of data were pushing the paper-based system to its limits. One of the databases developed later in the 1970s for ESIOK was named Del'ta-Potok (torrent or flood), and it kept data on "individuals present in the torrent of foreigners entering the republic." In 1981, they had 180,000 cards in the file.[41] The KGB (Ukraine) IAP soberly reported in 1980 that it had data on "64,000 foreigners belonging to or sus-pected with a basis for belonging to special services, OUN abroad, Zionist, and other anti-Soviet organizations, who undertook spying or other action on the territory of Ukraine between 1957 and 1974," in addition to the thousands they had catalogued since then. These numbers would have left foreign spy services slack-jawed (the CIA certainly did not think it had access to 64,000 friendly agents in Ukraine alone in this period), but they represent the scale of the problem the Second Directorate thought it was facing.[42] That alarm inten-sified exponentially in the Reagan years, when KGB reports were filled with dark warnings of looming nuclear war.[43] Dealing with this "flood" of enemy agents called for ever-increasing competence with databases and computers, and the KGB invested in those systems accordingly.

Nevertheless, the initial fruits of these efforts, while real, were modest. They began mostly by using the databases in conjunction with one another to identify targets of interest. In 1980, they used Fort-67 to determine that they had logged 1,500 contacts between foreigners and Soviet citizens in Kyiv. Those citizens lived on 432 different streets in the capital. The agents then used this data together with their maps of particularly sensitive installations and infor-mation from censored letters to identify particularly suspicious individuals.[44] By the following year, more data showed them that in fact there were 2,600 contacts made with citizens living on seven hundred different streets. Fur-ther analysis allowed the agents to identify eight sensitive locations that they believed were being regularly targeted by foreign agents. Cross-referencing this data once more with censored letter data took only two hours and allowed them to take "concrete operational measures."[45] Increased success led to an increasing use of databases by agents. Between 1980 and 1983, KGB staff increased the number of queries made into the system from 1,209 annually to 3,507, including more than 170 regularly scheduled searches.[46]

Despite this improvement in efficiency, information-analytical agents were mostly frustrated in their jobs. Database management will do that to you. Unsurprisingly, organizing the complete entry of data eluded most bureaus of the KGB, with some regions falling well behind. Of the 66,150 foreigners who entered Crimea in 1980, only 80 connections were entered into the system. L'viv was little better, registering 117 links of 5,888 foreign visitors. Even those who entered data normally did it with significant delay. Almost every office violated the time limits the KGB USSR had established for data entry.[47] The issue was not getting better, with fewer contacts registered in 1980 than in 1979.[48] As the exasperated chief of the Ukrainian KGB IAP (Colonel P. F. Fedorov) commented, "a certain segment of the leadership cadre and operational workforce still does not use the system; several of them hold a mistaken notion about the uselessness of the systems, and others simply fear them [the systems], since they have a weak understanding of them."[49] The regional leadership was little help, since those officers "still undervalue the importance of analysis as a method of operational agent work and do not enforce the relevant commands with their subordinates."[50] Part of this resistance was due to the fact that database technologies had not advanced far enough to show agents truly earth-shattering potential. These early databases did not, of course, link to full documents, so officers had to go through the process of retrieving paper files from the archive in most cases. Further, the information systems preserved on punch cards held only "limited possibilities" for analysis. These "limited" gains are typical for the early years of any form of data innovation, especially in fields (such as intelligence) which have already developed systematic approaches to data and data management. In those institutions, new technologies (including computer technologies) rarely create a "wholly new data culture."[51] It therefore took continuous pressure from above to try to force a cultural shift. In 1979 Andropov approved the final technical configuration for the Del'ta program, and in 1980 special orders of the Central Committee and the Council of Ministers set out a timetable to finish creating ESIOK and Del'ta by 1983.[52]

All big organizations struggle to a greater or lesser degree when they overhaul their information systems, as anyone who has worked in such an organization in the past half-century knows. What may appear to be a simple technological upgrade actually represents a new way of conceptualizing, ordering, saving, and using information. This friction is also a constant feature of organizational change.[53] The KGB was, of course, not immune to this set of complicating factors. But the problem was compounded by issues that, if not unique to intelligence services, are especially prominent within them.[54] The first issue has to do with the low status assigned to what could easily be seen as nerd work in an organization that prided itself on its combative manliness. The second issue has to do with structures of secrecy and compartmentalization in an organ that was allergic to sharing information and understood the power that came with having exclusive access to particular sources or documents.

The low status was only too clear. Nikolai Leonov remembered that the "overwhelming majority of the leadership looked on informational work with contempt. . . . No one entered this work of their free will, more frequently people fell into it either as a result of disciplinary action or because they couldn't cut it as 'useful' spies." It was also suspect as a feminine enterprise, not only because it involved working with keyboards and typing, but also because a "high percentage" of the workers were women.[55] In sum, being transferred from an operational unit to the information service was the "equivalent of a guards officer from the capital being transferred to a provincial, backwater garrison."[56] Finally, as Fedorov's comments above suggest, the most common mode of agents' interaction with these systems was not through realizing some new operational advantage but through assigning field officers additional, deeply unpopular paperwork tasks.

Trial and error showed the KGB leadership that the best way to encourage compliance and a more complete database was to relieve agents from the job of data entry by giving that work to the information-analytical teams. In 1980, there was still hope among some that requiring an after-hours seminar on the "collection, analysis, and valuing of incoming information"[57] might have an effect, but this naïve hope was misplaced. A year later, IAP leaders were still grousing that there was insufficient attention paid to their work during the training periods and schooling of KGB recruits.[58] By 1984, Fedorov had come closer to the truth: "As study has shown, the operational staff, which is occupied with completing its core functions, *unwillingly completes the complicated technical work of completing formalized documents for registering the gathered material into information systems.*" Instead, the "*most reliable way* to guarantee the regular entry of operationally significant information is *using the IAP for . . . entry into active information systems,* freeing the operational staff from this work, which requires a level of expertise and knowledge." This resolution was not simply a clever plea for more staffing from Fedorov and other IAP leaders, though it was that too.[59] It was the result of the variety of haphazard

attempts made in various districts. In Kyiv and other districts where agents
were expected to do their own paperwork, the databases were incomplete, and
data entry was hopelessly behind schedule. In Dnipropetrovsk, L'viv, and districts that had recently decided to turn over data entry to their informational
units, records were up to date.[60] The reason was clear enough: "*Practice shows
the necessity of the complete freeing of operational staff from composing formalized
system documents.* . . . We have to *interest the operational agent* in presenting
the information received by him to the IAP for concentration and the fastest
possible entry."[61]

This observation hints at the second, but less stated, reason for agent resistance to the databases. Intelligence officers are accustomed to keeping their
information closely held. The larger the distribution, the more likely the leak
and the more likely that some other agent would receive credit for one's own
work. Paper archives had done a better job of ensuring limited distribution.
The process by which an agent could get access to a report in the archive was
formalized and ensured that, if not the agent, at least his boss could keep an
eye on who was searching for information produced in his shop. Handing
this information (even if only the easily coded parts of it) over to a system
that could potentially be used by anyone in the agency was off-putting, and
it hardly provided an incentive to do one's paperwork on time and properly.
Even the public shaming of officers who failed to ensure compliance on the
part of their subordinates appeared to have little effect.[62] It took a combination of all these efforts to improve data entry, but this improvement was
finally becoming noticeable by 1985.

All of this highlights how difficult the creation of systematic databases
for counterintelligence work was. We may look, by way of comparison, to
the computerization of the FBI. J. Edgar Hoover had a keen appreciation for
subject databases well before electronic computers were invented. He kept
files on prominent figures for moments when he needed political leverage,
but much larger card files were also constructed. As part of his promotion of
the Lavender Scare against gays and lesbians in the federal government, he
ordered the creation of a huge Sex Deviate File in 1942 that would remain a
key tool of FBI repression until the late 1970s.[63] The Sex Deviate File was just
a part of a larger collection of files against "subversives" that guided the FBI's
actions as a political police in the twentieth century.

Hoover, too, had to deal with the tension between making files usable by
a wide spectrum of law enforcement agencies and the desire to keep information compartmentalized. Early in the Cold War, he stumbled some. Threatened, ironically, by the proliferation of antisubversion investigations by
state and local level commissions created in the McCarthy era, he created a

Responsibilities Program that he used to warn the military, state governors, and even private organizations like the March of Dimes of particularly suspect individuals in their employ. Many of these files related to teachers at all levels of the public education system. In sum, Hoover tried to negotiate this tension by placing himself at the hinge between secrecy and distribution. When word of what two historians generously call this "extralegal" program eventually leaked, Hoover turned to greater secrecy, eliminating the Responsibilities Program and creating COINTELPRO.[64] At the same time, recognizing the need to reassure the public that the FBI was not turning into the KGB, Hoover promised that the FBI would respect jurisdictional lines and leave the bulk of policing information in the hands of local and state authorities, using its federal status only to coordinate necessary information sharing between those smaller police departments. This was a dubious promise, and in 1967 Congress refused to approve Hoover's request to build a national criminal database. In 1970, however, in the wake of social unrest and spreading war protests, Congress quietly authorized the step. These developments led critics on the left to throw accusations that computers might lead to totalitarianism back in the government's face.[65]

As with the KGB, the FBI struggled mightily in practice to make the shift from paper card files to computerized ones. Darren Tromblay suggests that "as technology has advanced, the FBI has failed to keep pace in leveraging cutting-edge breakthroughs in adapting information technology to its benefit. The failure is not one of bits and bytes but of the culture that pervades the organization and its people."[66] In the 1970s, the bureau used ADP (Automated Data Processing), which was already seen to be obsolete by internal auditors in 1977 and was critiqued by Congress in 1979 for poor data management and insufficient security. The lengthy process to replace the system resulted in a new ACS (Automated Case Support) system being unveiled in 1995. At a time when even college students could afford a Macintosh in their dorm rooms, the new system was still stuck with green-screen technology and lacked point-and-click capabilities, relying extensively on function keys. The system was also not integrated with those of other intelligence agencies, though this was by design. It was not only hardware that was the issue. The agency proved unable to systematically standardize the data it was entering into its systems, and it was not putting a high priority on doing so. In 1983, the Government Accounting Office noted this deficiency but had no one to alert, as at the time the FBI's position for ensuring data standardization was vacant. Twenty-five years later, the FBI had still not effectively achieved this goal.[67] To the government's regret, even though the benefits of improved data processing and dissemination were absent, the costs of decompartmentalization nevertheless had to be paid. The great fear of counterintelligence agents regarding the danger of oversharing information throughout the organization was realized. The deadliest mole in FBI history, Robert Hanssen, obtained most of the information that he turned over to the Soviet Union (and, later, the Russian Federation) from the agency's computer system.[68]

All of this suggests that the stumbles of the Second Main Directorate were not the result of backwardness in terms of national computer technologies but derived from the special challenges of creating a counterintelligence computer database. The desire for both comprehensiveness and compartmentalization in these systems meant that large bureaucracies with ingrained habits and strong organizational cultures that ran contrary to the new demands of data standardization and data entry were unlikely to succeed in this endeavor, at least in the short run. All the managers and a significant majority of agents had to buy into the new system for it to succeed.

Nevertheless, even the imperfect computerization of counterintelligence files had significant outcomes. Both the FBI and the KGB had compiled massive paper databases over the course of the twentieth century, but by the end of that century, the potential for an even greater quantity of data collection was made possible by the simultaneous processes of institutional computerization and the improvement of computing and electronic storage systems. Computerization also contributed to the rapidly changing "political economy of personal data." As Dan Bouk has recently noted, starting in the 1970s, the "data doubles" that bureaucracies used to stand in for real individuals were no longer simply treated as units in a mass or as representatives of statistical categories but were increasingly individuated within the context of these statistical matrices.[69] This has allowed for new forms of counterintelligence, most notably in the form of the problematic algorithms devised to identify potential terrorists in the wake of the attacks on the United States of 11 September 2001.[70]

The system of incentives was somewhat different for foreign intelligence and (especially) technical intelligence. By the mid-1980s, the KGB's foreign intelligence service, the First Main Directorate, had also begun the process of computerization. Agents had long followed a practice by which an operational agent produced an index of names mentioned in a bound file headed for storage as part of the normal archival process. In the 1980s, these name indexes were also entered into a computer database. By the middle of the decade, this huge card index had been completely transferred to computers. Files, however, were still kept in paper form, not just in one place but in two. All files were duplicated, with one copy sent for protective reasons to a secret bunker deep inside the country. As a result, in a process not unfamiliar to those using

Russian archives today, an agent had to go to the archives, order a file, and wait several days for the order to be filled. A search for computerized records was not much faster, no doubt because the delays in the process were less about data retrieval than with establishing whether the agent ordering the file was to be allowed to see the compartmentalized information. When First Directorate agents needed records produced by other directorates, the process was longer still, since the bulk of the KGB archives was still held at the Lubianka, far from the First Directorate's headquarters, which had moved to Iasenevo in 1972. Agents had to travel to the Lubianka reading room to access any of these files. Still, this cumbersome process was not unwelcome, as it allowed them to spend their working day in the city center.[71] Most foreign intelligence agents appear to have been only slightly touched by computerization by the time that Mikhail Gorbachev came to power.[72]

The situation is far murkier when it comes to technical intelligence. There are hints in the files that signal intelligence was of growing interest to the IAPs, and they certainly tried to include data from telephone surveillance in their databases, especially when providing support for the Fifth Main Directorate (censorship and internal security against political dissent). Electronic intelligence was also being established as a separate agency within the KGB, forming the Sixteenth Main Directorate. Again, these operations can be glimpsed only dimly through the IAP documents, which pledged to broaden cooperation with the Sixteenth Main Directorate but provided little detail about the nature of this cooperation.[73]

Nevertheless, it was probably in these realms that the KGB was beginning to make its first real strides in computer-based espionage. It would have been far less administratively taxing to deploy technical expertise in limited offensive operations run by a handful of savvy experts than to overhaul a nationwide system of counterintelligence. Within most KGB foreign residencies, there were line "X" agents, who were tasked with securing scientific and technological intelligence. These agents had been critical throughout the 1960s and 1970s in acquiring developing computer technology abroad. One Russian-born French citizen code-named ALVAR had worked in IBM's Paris office for years and apparently was responsible for revealing not only secrets regarding particular machines but also details of the emerging computer networks and network security in place in the West.[74] The KGB was therefore aware of the growing network of machines storing highly classified documents abroad and sought ways to infiltrate those systems to access that data. Still, their first success was not accomplished by their own computer experts but by a loose group of hackers calling themselves the German Chaos Computer Club. In 1986, this club made contact with the KGB in Berlin, which provided the chaotic savants with a list of items the Soviets would pay well to acquire, especially those surrounding the US Strategic Defense Initiative program.[75] The hackers succeeded in breaking into military computer networks. They were undone not due to military security systems or FBI agents but because a Berkeley scientist named Cliff Stoll noticed their traces on his system and insisted to skeptical agents that they had a problem on their hands.[76] The hackers were arrested before much information was gathered, but intelligence services on both sides of the Iron Curtain were made aware of this rich new arena of action.

Finally, when Andropov reached the pinnacle of power by becoming the general secretary in November 1982, he presided over an even more ambitious effort to coordinate computers, intelligence, and national security. Andropov had not only been a persistent supporter of computerization throughout his term as head of the KGB; he had also been responsible during that time for stressing the KGB's role in detecting signs of a surprise attack by the enemies of the USSR. He combined these two initiatives by launching the (now) well-known Project RYaN.[77] Project RYaN promised to systematize data collection on a variety of military and civil defense metrics in enemy countries and feed those data into computers that would warn the Soviet leadership if the United States and its allies were about to launch a nuclear strike. The KGB began sending lists of desired data points to its agents abroad in February 1983, and the proposal took on added relevance as the downing of KAL 007 and NATO's Able Archer exercises raised superpower tensions to a high degree later in the year. But Project RYaN was not an apocalyptic emergency measure. It was, instead, a long-term study of how computers, signals intelligence, and human intelligence might best be coordinated. Tellingly, it was housed not in one of the KGB's main directorates but in the KGB's Institute for Research on Operative Problems, an institute staffed by scientists rather than field agents. As Simon Miles observes, up until 1985, RYaN remained a problem to be solved, not an operation to be executed. Indeed, in the midst of the political crises of 1983, the project was only in rudimentary form. The security services in the USSR and other Warsaw Pact countries were skeptical about the reliability of the system, and the full list of data points necessary for the system to run was not even developed until 1986.[78] Project RyaN appears to be both a sign of Andropov's cybernetic ambition and evidence that those ambitions were years away from fruition. Although scientists worked on the project until 1991, it never became operational.

GLIMPSES OF A CYBERNETIC FUTURE

This chapter ends in the mid-1980s, a point at which we can clearly see the transition between one era of intelligence agency computerization and the next. This first "database" phase was largely directed toward using computers to do tasks that these agencies had done before, just (ideally) more quickly and efficiently. Maintaining files on individuals and events while trying to establish meaningful connections between them had long been part of intelligence practices. Creating computer rather than paper databases did not change this. The second, "hacking" era, which added practices that relied on system networking to conduct computer-based espionage, gained steam in the mid-1980s, not just through the Soviet-German plot described above but also in other agencies. In the United States, "computer exploitation and network activities began at NSA [the National Security Agency] in 1985" and operations began soon afterwards.[79] These were definitely possibilities that had not existed before, but they were quickly understandable to intelligence professionals and policy makers alike. Stealing information using new technology had also been part of the secret world's arsenal, in particular in the realm of signals intelligence, and it required little imagination to see this as yet another form of that practice.

But cybernetics had always promised something different. It suggested that a paradigm shift in conceptualizing the relationship between information and power and humans and machines was possible, not just improved efficiencies in carrying out the old paradigm. It was one thing to command a computer to conduct a search that cross-referenced foreign contacts and the residences of suspiciously open-minded citizens. It would be another if the computer were to indicate dangers that no one had thought to query. It would be yet another thing if humans were to start carrying out computer directions in addition to the other way round. Utopians, dystopians, science fiction writers, and indeed anyone who grasped the cybernetic principle could see this possibility. It is important to note that the Soviet intelligence community was attuned to this point in the Soviet Union in the 1960s and 1970s. Despite the underwhelming results that computerization was bringing in the short term, the dream of cybernetic potentials led the leadership to press forward on these very expensive undertakings in the face of significant internal resistance. Fedorov explicitly used cybernetic language in his explanation of the future he was trying to bring about. He urged IAP chiefs to "explain the relationship and value to operational units of information given by Information Analytical Systems in the realm of signals notification, differential distribution, and periodic synthesis—that is, to guarantee *feedback*. This will help the Service to improve the quality of the information it provides."[80] As we have seen, that future of cybernetic secret policing had not arrived by 1985.

This feared and desired third phase, which extended beyond databases and hacking to cybernetic "control," developed over the course of the 1990s and the first decade of the twenty-first century, and it is maturing before our eyes. This is not only evident in the human-machine warfighting capabilities demonstrated by military drones but in a wide variety of new and emerging systems as well. To take just one recent example, the US Defense Intelligence Agency (DIA) is currently developing a system called the Machine-Assisted Analytic Rapid-Repository System or MARS system, which involves rapid and dynamic integration of human and machine intelligence with the aim of providing them to the human-machine units that carry out American warfare. In one recent discussion of the system, the former acting head of the CIA and the current head of the DIA talked about this information being provided not to the pilot of an F-35, but to the cockpit, which is an accurate description of the mixed human/machine cybernetic reality of contemporary warfare.[81]

In the realm of intelligence, the best example of the new cybernetic era is what is often called "Russian interference in the 2016 American elections." I put this in quotation marks not because I disagree that this interference occurred, but that this description of events reveals the fact that those responsible for creating and maintaining public discourse have still not fully grasped the nature of cybernetic operations. It presumes that there are discrete and identifiable perpetrators and victims of the process by which political opinion was shaped over the course of 2016. In fact, the genius of the plan apparently hatched in the GRU is that it did not represent a simple assault with an attacker and a victim but was instead the contouring of a set of information systems created by transnational profit-making behemoths, using algorithms written in Silicon Valley in "new" media and relying on the cybernetic loop of ratings and news content developed indigenously by the "old" media. Leaders of the political campaigns locked in the 2016 contests were participants in this process too. Prosecutors, journalists, and citizens spent an enormous amount of time and energy trying to discover whether President Donald Trump was a conscious perpetrator of this scheme, but the beauty of the operation was that in the end it mattered very little for the outcome of the election whether he was or was not. The GRU perpetrated this scheme, but it was not the only perpetrator. It was joined not only by the president but also by everyone who shared political posts on Facebook or boosted ratings for news organizations by assiduously following the scandalous path of the election campaign. The effectiveness of the operation—and the shared complicity it produced—has disoriented many regular citizens, but for intelligence agents it represents a long-expected new phase of state action that will make cybernetic strategy and high-speed computing the operational center, rather than the nerdy periphery, of the secret police for the foreseeable future.

NOTES

My thanks go to David M. and Linda Roth, whose support of endowed chairs at Lafayette made the research on this chapter possible. I would also like to thank Ben Cohen, DC Jackson, Steve Norris, the participants in the Political Police and the Soviet System Workshop, and the anonymous reviewers for *Kritika* for helpful comments on earlier drafts of this piece.

1. David E. Sanger and Nicole Perlroth, "FireEye, a Top Cybersecurity Firm, Says It Was Hacked by a Nation-State," *New York Times*, 8 December 2020, https://nyti.ms/3oDEvF5; Ellen Nakashima and Craig Timberg, "Russian Government Hackers Are Behind a Broad Espionage Campaign That Has Compromised U. S. Agencies, Including Treasury and Commerce," *Washington Post*, 14 December 2020, https://www.washingtonpost.com/national-security/russian-government-spies-are-behind-a -broad-hacking-campaign-that-has-breached-us-agencies-and-a-top-cyber-firm/2020/12/13/d5 a53b88-3d7d-11eb-9453-fc36ba051781_story.html; Kevin Johnson and Nathan Bomey, "US under Cyber Attack Believed to Be Tied to Russia: Private Sector, Infrastructure, All Levels of Government at Risk," *USA Today*, 17 December 2020, https://www.usatoday.com/story/news/politics /2020/12/17/ongoing-cyberattack-poses-grave-risk-government-private-sector/3946658001/.

2. The Russian government officially denied involvement in a statement that made reference to all these terms. It claimed no role in the "hacker attacks" (*khakerskie ataki*), argued that "attacks in the information space" (*napadeniia v informatsionnom prostranstve*) were contrary to its national interest, and urged further cooperation in "cybersecurity" (*kiberbezopasnost'*) (Embassy of Russia in the USA, "Embassy Comment," Facebook, 13 December 2020, 8:32 PM). These denials carried little weight on the global stage, as multiple intelligence agencies and investigative reporters were able to connect attacks of this nature to Russian military intelligence and to the operations of Russia's foreign intelligence service, the SVR (Sluzhba vneshnei razvedki). For a detailed treatment of the most recent era of cyber-conflict, see Andy Greenberg, *Sandworm: A New Era of Cyberwar and the Hunt for the Kremlin's Most Dangerous Hackers* (New York: Doubleday, 2019).

3. John Arquilla and David Ronfeldt, "Cyberwar Is Coming!," *Comparative Strategy* 12, no. 2 (1993): 141–65.

4. Greenberg, *Sandworm*.

5. Department of Justice, *Report on the Investigation into Russian Interference in the 2016 Presidential Election*, by Robert S. Mueller (Washington, DC: US Department of Justice, 2019).

6. Norbert Wiener, *Cybernetics, or, Control and Communication in the Animal and the Machine*, 2nd ed. (Cambridge, MA: MIT Press, 1961 [1948]).

7. Wiener, *Cybernetics*, 11.

8. Slava Gerovitch, *From Newspeak to Cyberspeak: A History of Soviet Cybernetics* (Cambridge, MA: MIT Press, 2002); Benjamin Peters, *How Not to Network a Nation: The Uneasy History of the Soviet Internet* (Cambridge, MA: MIT Press, 2016); Eglė Rindzevičiūtė, *The Power of Systems: How Policy Sciences Opened Up the Cold War World* (Ithaca, NY: Cornell University Press, 2016).

9. Peters, *How Not to Network a Nation*.

10. The sole scholar to have found answers regarding the early history of Soviet computing in the KGB, as far as I am aware, is Rindzevičiūtė. In her dissertation, she uncovered some of the ways that the KGB used computers in the 1970s and 1980s (Eglė Rindzevičiūtė, "Constructing Soviet Cultural Policy: Cybernetics and Governance in Lithuania after World War II" [Ph.D. diss., Linköping University, 2008], 224–27). This chapter adds a new dimension to her study, as the sources made available to me in the Ukrainian KGB archive in Kyiv are more extensive than those made available to her. There is now information on the nature of KGB computer databases in the late Cold War period and the struggles the KGB encountered trying to implement the new technology. These files are held in Haluzevyi derzhavnyi arkhiv Sluzhby bezpeki Ukraïni (HDASBU) *fond* 32.

11. This absence of GRU materials is regrettable not only because of the significant role that the GRU played in intelligence collection during the Cold War, but also because its successor military

intelligence organizations have (apparently) led the way in contemporary Russian cyberwarfare as well. For an overview of the relationship between the KGB and the GRU, see Jonathan Haslam, *Near and Distant Neighbors: A New History of Soviet Intelligence*, 1st ed. (New York: Farrar, Straus, and Giroux, 2015).

12. The term "control" is somewhat enigmatic in studies of cybernetics. Although it derives from Wiener's background in electrical engineering, in some ways it certainly can be understood in the traditional sense of political control, especially in the "closed-world" systems described by Paul Edwards (*The Closed World: Computers and the Politics of Discourse in Cold War America* [Cambridge, MA: MIT Press, 1996]). But Pickering usefully reminds us that there was another strand of cybernetic thinking that proposed much more open-ended processes and outcomes and stressed guidance and observation more than domination. In his words, the "entire task of cybernetics was to figure out how to get along in a world that was not enframable, that could not be subjugated to human designs—how to build machines and construct systems that could adapt performatively to whatever happened to come their way. A key aspect of many of the examples we will examine was that of open-ended search—of systems that would explore their world to see what it had to offer, good and bad" (*The Cybernetic Brain: Sketches of Another Future* [Chicago: University of Chicago Press, 2010], 32).

13. There is now an extensive literature on the history of cybernetics, much of it focusing on the critical moment of its emergence as a term and a metadiscipline among "Western" scientists in the late 1940s. Special attention is paid to the interdisciplinary Macy Conferences (1946–1953) and the publication of Norbert Wiener's *Cybernetics* in 1948. For the most recent and comprehensive survey, see Ronald R. Kline, *The Cybernetics Moment: Or Why We Call Our Age the Information Age* (Baltimore: Johns Hopkins University Press, 2015). For a study of British cybernetics, see also Pickering, *Cybernetic Brain*. Regarding the early theoretical bases of cybernetics prior to World War II, most works rightly give pride of place to the English mathematician Alan Turing, though Benjamin Peters has also noted important "prehistories" of cybernetic concepts in Russia and Eastern Europe as well. For Turing, see Edwards, *Closed World*, 186; and Peters, *How Not to Network a Nation*, 28. Cybernetics was also critical to the development of Cold War social science in the United States. Edwards is an important source for this, but for the impact on Cold War thought and epistemology more generally see also Philip Mirowski, "A History Best Served Cold," in *Uncertain Empire: American History and the Idea of the Cold War*, ed. Joel Isaac and Duncan Bell (New York: Oxford University Press, 2012), 70; and Nicolas Guilhot, "Cyborg Pantocrator: International Relations Theory from Decisionism to Rational Choice," *Journal of the History of Behavioral Sciences* 47, no. 3 (2011): 279–301. For similar observations regarding the Soviet Union, see Rindzevičiūtė, *Power of Systems*, 6, 43.

14. Jon Agar, *The Government Machine: A Revolutionary History of the Computer* (Cambridge, MA: MIT Press, 2003), 201.

15. Pickering, *Cybernetic Brain*, 9.

16. See Kline, *Cybernetics Moment*, chap. 7, "Cybernetics in Crisis."

17. Gerovitch, *From Newspeak to Cyberspeak*, 261.

18. Stanislav V. Klimenko, "Computer Science in Russia: A Personal View," *IEEE Annals of the History of Computing* 21, no. 3 (1999): 24. The USSR was not alone in this regard, as American computers established a position of global dominance over the course of the 1960s. The British case is instructive. Building on the experience of Bletchley Park, Great Britain was an early leader in computer development. Nearly all computer hardware in the 1950s in the United Kingdom was domestically produced. By the end of the 1960s, most computers in use in Britain were North American (Edwards, *Closed World*, 62).

19. George Orwell, *Nineteen Eighty-Four* (London: Secker and Warburg, 1949).

20. Slava Gerovitch, "The Cybernetics Scare and the Origins of the Internet," *Baltic Worlds* 2, no. 1 (2009): 35, http://balticworlds.com/the-cybernetics-scare-and-the-origins-of-the-internet/; Nicholas Lewis, "Peering through the Curtain: Soviet Computing through the Eyes of Western Experts,"

IEEE Annals of the History of Computing 38, no. 1 (2016): 36; Eden Medina, *Cybernetic Revolutionaries: Technology and Politics in Allende's Chile* (Cambridge, MA: MIT Press, 2011), 183.

21. Medina, *Cybernetic Revolutionaries*.

22. Medina, *Cybernetic Revolutionaries*, 62.

23. Medina, *Cybernetic Revolutionaries*.

24. N. S. Leonov, *Likholet'e* (Moscow: Mezhndunarodnye otnosheniia, 1995), 122.

25. I. I. Necheporenko, "Perechen' osnovnykh deistvuiushchikh normativnykh aktov KGB SSSR i KGB UkrSSR po voprosam organizatsii i vedeniia informatsionno-analiticheskoi raboty v organakh gos-bezopasnosti," 18 June 1981, HDASBU f. 32, op. 1, d. 3, l. 143.

26. Leonov, *Likholet'e*, 129.

27. P. F. Fedorov, "Analiz i otsenka postupaiushchei i nakoplennoi informatsii v deistvuiushchikh IPS KGB respubliki—vazhnoe sredstvo podgotovki iskhodnykh dannykh dlia prognozirovaniia ten-dentsii razvitiia operativnoi obstanovki, planirovaniia i povysheniia effektivnosti kontrrazvedy-vatel'noi deiatel'nosti (Lektsiia dlia rukovodiashchego sostava KGB UkrSSR. Vremia 1 chas)," 30 January 1981, HDASBU f. 32, op. 1, d. 3, l. 90.

28. Necheporenko, "Perechen' osnovnykh deistvuiushchikh normativnykh aktov," ll. 143–44.

29. For more on punch-card technology, the broad history of its usage in government institutions, and some of the cultural impact, see Agar, *Government Machine*. See also Christine von Oertzen, "Machineries of Data Power: Manual versus Mechanical Census Compilation in Nineteenth-Century Europe," *Osiris* 32, no. 1 (2017): 129–50; and Steven Lubar, "'Do Not Fold, Spindle or Muti-late': A Cultural History of the Punch Card," *Journal of American Culture* 15, no. 4 (1992): 43–45.

30. "Pamiatka o naznachenii, kharaktere uchityvaemykh operativnykh dannykh, vidakh reshaemykh zadach i poriadke obrashcheniia s zaprosami v deistvuiushchie informatsionnye sistemy KGB Ukrainskoi SSR," 8 July 1981, HDASBU f. 32, op. 1, d. 3, l. 175.

31. P. F. Fedorov, "Spravka o provedennoi rabote IAS KGB UkrSSR (v sentiabre 1980 goda)," HDASBU f. 32, op. 1, d. 2, l. 24.

32. "Pamiatka o naznachenii," 171.

33. P. F. Fedorov, "Operativnye vozmozhnosti zadeistvovannykh v organakh KGB respubliki informatsionno-poiskovykh sistem i praktika ikh ispol'zovaniia dlia opredeleniia sredy kontrraz-vedyvatel'nogo poiska i v khode ee operativnogo izucheniia," 23 August 1980, HDASBU f. 32, op. 1, d. 3, ll. 23–24; Fedorov, "Spravka o provedennoi rabote," l. 21. Punch cards could, of course, also be processed using computers. I have been unable to determine why certain databases were not computerized.

34. "Spravka po AIS 'Fort-67,'" 29 October 1981, HDASBU f. 32, op. 1, d. 3, l. 233.

35. Rindzevičiūtė, "Constructing Soviet Cultural Policy," 225.

36. P. F. Fedorov and K. Kh. Akhmideev, "Nekotorye aspekty prakticheskogo ispol'zovaniia AIS v kon-trrazvedyvatel'noi rabote KGB UkrSSR (Tezisy k vystupleniiu na nauchno-tekhnicheskoi konfer-entsii 13 maia 1981 goda)," 8 May 1981, HDASBU f. 32, op. 1, d. 3, l. 157.

37. This was a large project that included participation from countries across the Soviet Bloc and relied heavily on difficult industrial espionage. For a description of East Germany's participation in this process, including the observation that as much as a third of all foreign espionage conducted by East Germany was focused on acquiring computer technology, see Kristie Macrakis, *Seduced by Secrets: Inside the Stasi's Spy-Tech World* (Cambridge: Cambridge University Press, 2008), chap. 6.

38. Sergei P. Prokhorov, "Computers in Russia: Science, Education, and Industry," *IEEE Annals of the History of Computing* 21, no. 3 (1999): 10.

39. V. V. Przhiialkovskii, "Istoricheskii obzor semeistva ES EVM," http://computer-museum.ru/hist ussr/es_hist.htm.

40. Punch cards are also a digital, though not always electronic, technology, since they operate as a binary system: each hole location is either punched (0) or not (1).

41. Fedorov and Akhmideev, "Nekotorye aspekty," l. 157.

42. Fedorov, "Operativnye vozmozhnosti," l. 24.

43. "O merakh po dal'neishemu sovershenstvovaniiu raboty s agenturnym apparatom v sootvetstvii s trebovaniiami prikaza KGB SSSR no 00140-1983g. i povysheniiu organizuiushchei roli rukovodiashchego sostava v etom protsesse (Doklad na seminare rukovodiashchego sostava operativnykh podrazdelenii KGB UkrSSR) (indecipherable signature)," 15 March 1985, HDASBU f. 32, op. 1, d. 17, l. 137.

44. Fedorov, "Operativnye vozmozhnosti," l. 26.

45. Fedorov, "Analiz," ll. 92–95.

46. P. F. Fedorov, "Spravka o merakh po dal'neishemu sovershenstvovaniiu otbora operativnoi informatsii v podrazdeleniiakh KGB-UKGB UkrSSR dlia ee polnogo ucheta, obrabotki i analiza v informatsionnykh sistemakh," 7 March 1984, HDASBU f. 32, op. 1, d. 17, l. 4.

47. Fedorov, "Analiz," l. 104.

48. Fedorov, "Analiz," l. 105.

49. Fedorov, "Analiz," l. 106.

50. G. P. Grebeniuk and P. F. Fedorov, "Predsedateliu Komiteta gosbezopasnosti Ukrainskoi SSR general-polkovniku tovarishchu Fedorchuku, V. V.," 17 July 1980, HDASBU f. 32, op. 1, d. 3, l. 19.

51. David Sepkoski, "The Database before the Computer," *Osiris* 32, no. 1 (2017): 178. See also Jon Agar, "What Difference Did Computers Make?," *Social Studies of Science* 36, no. 6 (2006): 869–907.

52. Fedorov, "Analiz," l. 107.

53. Sepkoski, "Database before the Computer," 178.

54. Because the history of data has largely been conducted within the field of the history of science, many of the detailed histories of "data" study scientific organizations. There are also notable studies of the history of data and data processing in government organizations, most notably Agar, *Government Machine*. Many of these studies understandably focus on the census as a location for (and driver of) new data technologies. See here von Oertzen, "Machineries of Data Power." But even in excellent and extensive studies such as Agar's, only glancing attention is paid to intelligence services.

55. For an important comparison regarding modes of feminization and masculinization in the development of computers in the United States, see Jennifer S. Light, "When Computers Were Women," *Technology and Culture* 40, no. 3 (1999): 455–83.

56. Leonov, *Likholet'e*, 121–22.

57. Grebeniuk and Fedorov, "Predsedateliu Komiteta gosbezopasnosti," l. 20.

58. Fedorov and Akhmideev, "Nekotorye aspekty," l. 163.

59. Fedorov, "Spravka o merakh," ll. 8–9. Emphasis in original.

60. Fedorov, "Spravka o merakh," l. 9.

61. P. F. Fedorov, "O sostoianii i merakh uluchshcheniia raboty informatsionno-analiticheskikh podrazdelenii KGB i UkrKGB obl. po sozdaniiu respublikanskogo zvena ESIOK 'Del'ta-U', dal'neishego sovershenstvovaniia informatsionnogo obespecheniia operativnykh podrazdelenii (doklad na soveshchanii-seminare nachal'nikov IAP KGB-UkrKGB UkrSSR 28 marta 1984 g.)," HDASBU f. 32, op. 1, d. 17, l. 34. Emphasis in original.

62. P. F. Fedorov, "Protokol ofitserskogo sobraniia sotrudnikov IAS KGB UkrSSR i 3 laboratorii filiala NIIAI OTU KGB SSSR v g. Kieve na temu: 'Chekist—politicheskii boets partii,'" 17 March 1985, HDASBU f. 32, op. 1, d. 17, l. 180.

63. Douglas M. Charles, *Hoover's War on Gays: Exposing the FBI's "Sex Deviates" Program* (Lawrence: University Press of Kansas, 2015), 33.

64. Cathleen Thom and Patrick Jung, "The Responsibilities Program of the FBI, 1951–1955," *The Historian* 59, no. 2 (1997): 347–70.

65. Michael Sorkin, "The FBI's Big Brother Computer," *Washington Monthly* 4, no. 7 (1972): 24–31.

66. Darren E. Tromblay, "Information Technology (IT) Woes and Intelligence Agency Failures: The

Federal Bureau of Investigations Troubled IT Evolution as a Microcosm of a Dysfunctional Corporate Culture," *Intelligence and National Security* 32, no. 6 (2017): 817.

67. Tromblay, "Information Technology (IT) Woes," 819.

68. Tromblay, "Information Technology (IT) Woes," 824.

69. Dan Bouk, "The History and Political Economy of Personal Data over the Last Two Centuries in Three Acts," *Osiris* 32, no. 1 (2017): 85–106.

70. Bouk cites here Louise Amoore, "Data Derivatives: On the Emergence of a Security Risk Calculus for Our Times," *Theory, Culture, and Society* 28, no. 6 (2011): 24–43.

71. Oleg Gordievsky, "The KGB Archives," *Intelligence and National Security* 6, no. 1 (1991): 10–11.

72. Agents assigned to foreign embassies also apparently worked without the help of computers prior to the mid-1980s. Vladimir Kuzichkin, who worked for the KGB in Tehran between 1977 and 1982, recalled that central headquarters in Moscow employed "no computers: reports are kept on microfiches," and that all of his work was document-based (*Inside the KGB: My Life in Soviet Espionage* [New York: Pantheon, 1991], 187).

73. Fedorov and Akhmideev, "Nekotorye aspekty," l. 166.

74. Gordon Corera, *Cyberspies: The Secret History of Surveillance, Hacking, and Digital Espionage* (New York: Pegasus, 2015), 150.

75. On the intersection (and collision) between "bureaucrats" and "hackers," see more broadly Fred Turner, *From Counterculture to Cyberculture: Stewart Brand, the Whole Earth Network, and the Rise of Digital Utopianism* (Chicago: University of Chicago Press, 2010).

76. Clifford Stoll, *The Cuckoo's Egg: Tracking a Spy through the Maze of Computer Espionage* (New York: Doubleday, 1989).

77. RYaN stands for *raketno-iadernoe napadenie*, nuclear missile attack.

78. Simon Miles, "The War Scare That Wasn't: Able Archer 83 and the Myths of the Second Cold War," *Journal of Cold War Studies*, 22, no. 3 (2020): 104–6.

79. Steven Loleski, "From Cold to Cyber Warriors: The Origins and Expansion of NSA's Tailored Access Operations (TAO) to Shadow Brokers," *Intelligence and National Security* 34, no. 1 (2019): 119.

80. Fedorov, "O sostoianii," l. 41. Emphasis in original.

81. Michael Morell, "Defense Intelligence Agency Director Lt. Gen. Robert Ashley on DIA's Core Mission," 15 January 2020, in *Intelligence Matters with Michael Morell, Former Acting Director of the CIA*, 37 minutes, https://rss.art19.com/intelligence-matters. For a press release on the MARS system, see DIA Public Affairs, "DIA's Vision of MARS: Decision Advantage for the 21st Century," last modified 23 May 2019, https://www.dia.mil/News/Articles/Article-View/Article/1855910/dias-vision-of-mars-decision-advantage-for-the-21st-century/. The "cockpit" has long been a favored example of the cyborg "man-machine" system described by theorists and practitioners alike.

Contributors

TIMOTHY K. BLAUVELT is professor of Soviet and Post-Soviet Studies at Ilia State University in Tbilisi, Georgia, and regional director for the South Caucasus for American Councils for International Education. He has published several dozen peer-reviewed articles and book chapters. He has co-edited *Georgia after Stalin: Nationalism and Soviet Power* (with Jeremy Smith, 2016); and *The Transcaucasian Democratic Federative Republic of 1918: Federal Aspirations, Geopolitics, and National Projects* (with Adrian Brisku, 2021). His *Clientelism and Nationality in an Early Soviet Fiefdom: The Trials of Nestor Lakoba* was also published in 2021.

EDWARD COHN is professor of Russian and Soviet history at Grinnell College. His first book, *The High Title of a Communist: Postwar Party Discipline and the Values of the Soviet Regime* (2015), examined the Communist Party's system of expulsion and censure in the postwar USSR, and his articles on the KGB in the Baltic republics have been published in *The Russian Review* and *Kritika: Explorations in Russian and Eurasian History*. He is now completing his second book, *The Admonitory State: KGB Surveillance and Political Control in the Late USSR*.

MICHAEL DAVID-FOX is director of the Center for Eurasian, Russian, and East European Studies at Georgetown University, where he is professor in the School of Foreign Service and Department of History. He is a founding and executive editor of *Kritika: Explorations in Russian and Eurasian History* and author or editor of thirteen books on Russian, Soviet, and modern history. He is currently completing *Crucibles of Power: Smolensk under Nazi and Soviet Rule*.

DAVID JISHKARIANI is an invited lecturer at Ilia State University in Tbilisi, Georgia. In 2021 he published a book about the Tbilisi Dinamo football club and Georgian football under Stalin. Now he is working on projects about the German ethnic minority in the Georgian SSR in 1921–1941 and about Georgia in transition from Stalin to Khrushchev in 1953–1957.

MARC JUNGE—research assistant in the Department of History, Section on Eastern European History, University of Erlangen, Germany—is the author of *Stalin's Mass Repression and the Cold War Paradigm* (2016); and *Stalinistische Modernisierung: Die Strafverfolgung von Akteuren des Staatsterrors in der Ukraine 1939–1941* (Stalinist modernization: The purge of state terror agents in Ukraine, 1939–1941 [2020]). His current research project examines extrajudicial boards in the Soviet Union from 1917 to 1953.

EMILIA KOUSTOVA is associate professor of Russian studies and director of the Department of Slavonic Studies at Université de Strasbourg. Her current research deals with the history of Stalinist deportations from the western regions of the USSR, as well as the history of World War II and its legacy in Russia and Eastern Europe. She recently edited *Combattre, survivre, témoigner: Expériences soviétiques de la Seconde guerre mondiale* (Fight, survive, bear witness: Soviet experiences during World War II [2020]) and has authored articles on this topic in French, Russian, and English, including "Survivors, Collaborators, and Partisans? Bringing Jewish Ghetto Policemen before Soviet Justice in Lithuania," *Jahrbücher für Geschichte Osteuropas* 68, no. 2 (2020): 222–55 (with Alain Blum and Thomas Chopard); and "(Un)Returned from the Gulag: Life Trajectories and Integration of Postwar Special Settlers," *Kritika: Explorations in Russian and Eurasian History* 16, no. 3 (2015): 589–620.

ANGELINA LUCENTO is assistant professor of history and art history at the National Research University Higher School of Economics. Her article "Painting against Empire: Béla Uitz and the Birth and Fate of International Socialist Realism" was recently published in *The Russian Review*. She is completing her first book, *The Socialist Surface: Painting as the Source of Soviet Media Culture, 1918–1941*.

MIKHAIL NAKONECHNYI received his PhD from the University of Oxford in 2020 and is now a postdoctoral researcher at the Aleksanteri Institute, Finnish Centre of Russian and Eastern European Studies, University of Helsinki. Currently he is working on the five-year project GULAGECHOES, funded by the European Research Council (ERC), about the construction of ethnic identities in the Soviet Gulag and post-Soviet prison systems. His work has been published in *Kritika: Explorations in Russian and Eurasian History*, *Cahiers du monde russe*, and the edited volume *Rethinking the Gulag: Identities, Sources, Legacies* (2022). His principal research interest is the comparative history of prison health care and medicine.

MOLLY PUCCI is assistant professor of twentieth-century European history at Trinity College Dublin. Her first book, *Security Empire: The Secret Police in Communist Eastern Europe*, came out in 2020. It won the Kulczycki Book Prize in Polish Studies from the Association for Slavic, East European, and Eurasian Studies and the Oskar Halecki Prize in Polish and Central European History from the Polish Institute of Arts and Sciences of America. She has written several articles on the history of the communist secret police in Poland, Czechoslovakia, East Germany, and the Soviet Union. Her current book project focuses on the history of communism in Czechoslovakia in the 1920s, from the Comintern to the artistic avant-garde.

AIGI RAHI-TAMM is professor of archival studies at the University of Tartu, Estonia. Her field of research involves the study of society's control mechanisms in the period of Sovietization, emphasizing the relationship between people and the state, the influence of politics and political decisions, and historical experience. Her publications include *In Siberia: Imprisoned and Exiled* (2021), a photo book; and an article, cowritten with Liisi Esse, "'In Spite of Everything, Life Is Still Beautiful!' War and Postwar Experiences in Estonia through the Example of Oskar Nõmmela's Life Story (1893–1969)," *Journal of Baltic Studies*, no. 2 (published online, March 2022). Her current project is "War after War: Individual and Societal Experience of War in Twentieth-Century Estonia."

JOSHUA SANBORN is the David M. '70 and Linda Roth Chair of History at Lafayette College. He is the author of three books: *Drafting the Russian Nation: Military Conscription, Total War, and Mass Politics, 1905–1925* (2003); *Imperial Apocalypse: The Great War and the Destruction of the Russian Empire* (2014); and, with Annette Timm, *Gender, Sex, and the Shaping of Modern Europe: A History from the French Revolution to the Present Day*, 3rd ed. (2022). He is currently working on a project on spies, scientists, and the politics of adventure in the Soviet Union and the United States in the period of the Cold War. He is also a co-founding contributor to the *Russian History Blog*.

ANDREI SAVIN—senior researcher at the Institute of History of the Siberian Branch of the Russian Academy of Sciences, Novosibirsk, Russia—is the author, with Marc Junge and Aleksei Tepliakov, of *Ekho Bol'shogo terrora: Chekisty Stalina v tiskakh "sotsialisticheskoi zakonnosti." Ego-dokumenty 1938–1941 gg.* (Echo of the Great Terror: Stalin's chekists in the vise of "socialist legality." Ego-documents, 1938–1941), vol. 3 (2018); and, with Victor Dönninghaus, *Unter dem wachsamen Auge des Staates: Religiöser Dissens der Russlanddeutschen* *in der Breschnew-Ära* (Under the watchful eye of the state: Religious dissent among Russian Germans in the Brezhnev Era [2019]).

ERIK R. SCOTT is associate professor of history at the University of Kansas, the director of KU's Center for Russian, East European, and Eurasian Studies, and the editor of *The Russian Review*. His first book, *Familiar Strangers: The Georgian Diaspora and the Evolution of Soviet Empire*, a study of migration and diaspora within the USSR, was published in 2016 and translated into Russian in 2019. His forthcoming book follows the global journeys of Soviet defectors through the contested borderlands of the Cold War, including refugee camps, restricted border zones, diplomatic missions, international waters, and airspaces.

DOUGLAS SELVAGE is a senior research associate (*wissenschaftlicher Mitarbeiter*) at the Institute for History at the Humboldt University in Berlin. He has published a co-edited volume with Georg Herbstritt, *Der "große Bruder": Studien zum Verhältnis von KGB und MfS 1958 bis 1989* ("Big Brother": Studies regarding the relationship between the KGB and the Stasi, 1958–1989 [2022]) and a monograph with Walter Süß, *Staatssicherheit und KSZE-Prozess: MfS zwischen SED und KGB (1972–1989)* (State security and the CSCE process: The [East German] Ministry of State Security and the KGB, 1972–1989 [2019]). He is currently writing *Active Measures and Propaganda, 1966–1989: The Stasi, the KGB, and Their European Allies*.

ALEKSEI TEPLIAKOV is senior researcher at the Novosibirsk State University of Economics and Management, Department of Philosophy and Humanities, Russian Federation. His publications include *Mashina terrora: OGPU-NKVD Sibiri v 1929–1941 gg.* (Machine of terror: The Siberian OGPU-NKVD in 1929–1941 [2008]); and *Deiatel'nost' organov VTsK-OGPU-NKVD, 1917–1941: Istoriograficheskie aspekty* (Activities of the Cheka-GPU-OGPU-NKVD, 1917–1941: Historical and source study aspects [2018]).

TATIANA VAGRAMENKO is a senior postdoctoral researcher at the Study of Religions Department, University College Cork, and principal investigator of the SFI-IRC Pathway–funded project "History Declassified: The KGB and the Religious Underground in Soviet Ukraine." Her publications include "KGB 'Evangelism': Agents and Jehovah's Witnesses in Soviet Ukraine," *Kritika: Explorations in Russian and Eurasian History* 22, no. 4 (2021): 757–86; and *Hidden Galleries: Material Religion in the Secret Police Archives in Central and Eastern Europe*, co-edited with James Kapaló (2021).

CRISTINA VATULESCU is associate professor of comparative literature at New York University. Her *Police Aesthetics: Literature, Film and the Secret Police* (2010), a study of the relationships between cultural and policing practices in twentieth-century Eastern Europe, won the 2011 Heldt Prize and the 2011 Outstanding Academic Title Award, sponsored by Choice. She also co-edited *The Svetlana Boym Reader* (2018) with five other scholars and a *Perspectives on Europe* special issue on "Secrecy" (2014) with Neringa Klumbytė. Her articles have appeared in *Law and Literature, Diacritics, Comparative Literature, Poetics Today*, and the *Brooklyn Rail*. She is currently working on a project titled *Illegible Archives? The Challenges of Reading an Archival Revolution*.

Index

Note: References in *italics* refer to figures and tables.